In the House of the Hangman

Volume 8

John Bloomberg-Rissman

Laughing/Ouch/Cube/Publications
2016

This work is licensed under a Creative Commons Attribution-NonCommercial-ShareAlike 4.0 International License. [Note: Non-Commercial because this is a mashup and I have no right to license the commercial use of others' work. All I ask is that you attribute my arrangement to me]

First Print on Demand Availability: 2016

ISBN: 978-0-9907761-8-5

Laughing/Ouch/Cube/Publications
1864 Morgan Ave.
Claremont CA 91711

www.johnbr.com

I didn't realize until my 20s that Wichita is the name of a Native tribe, and Kansas is too. I'm still pissed about that. And all of the other history we did not learn in school or home. Nicodemous, Kansas and all of the Exodusters. How I only recently learned that my friend Deena's dad's family was part of that legacy of black farmers. I could go on.

There are so many stories there. In the years following the Russo-Japanese War, in the spirit of Meiji curiosity about the nation's rivals, Russian literature was all the rage in Japan. Which is why Yukawa's classmates took to calling him "Iwan-chan," after Tolstoy's Ivan the Fool. In Tolstoy's fairytale, the Devil sends three imps to destroy Ivan, a simple farmer, and his two brothers, one a soldier and the other a merchant. The imps sent to Ivan's two brothers successfully ruin them by using the soldier's ambition and the merchant's greed. Ivan, being a fool with no other desire than to work the land, frustrates all three pf them. Each imp in turn becomes exhausted, and Ivan catches them. The first imp offers Ivan anything he wants, and so Ivan asks the imp for something to cure his stomachache. The imp duly provides three roots, one of which Ivan takes and the others he saves. When the second imp, the soldier's imp, is caught, he offers Ivan the ability to turn straw into soldiers. Ivan agrees to this because he'd like the soldiers to sing for him. When the merchant brother's imp is caught, he offers Ivan the ability to turn leaves into gold pieces. Ivan agrees to this because he believes the gold pieces would be pretty things for the peasant children to play with. Through a series of events, Ivan becomes king of his realm, but having no ambition to increase the wealth or the power of his kingdom, all of the *so-called* wise people flee, leaving a kingdom of those who have no use for currency or soldiers. Eventually, the Devil himself attempts to ruin Ivan, but he too fails because Ivan and his *kingdom of fools* refuse to recognize instruments of power as anything but objects for enjoyment. Yukawa didn't himself relate to any of the details of Tolstoy's story, and seems to have taken the "Iwan-chan" nickname at face-value, but his philosophy of scientific invention very much involves Ivan's foolish intuition of objects preceding the assigned meaning of those objects. When he was six years old, his grandfather, a teacher of Chinese classics, began teaching him the sodoku method of reading kanji. In the sodoku method, the student learns the Japanese pronunciation of Chinese characters before ever learning anything about the meanings of those characters. By contrast, in alphabetical learning, a student already has access to the connection between the sound of a word and its meaning. The job is to analyze the word's phonemes so that they fit into the general scheme of a language's orthography. Exceptions to the 1:1 phoneme-grapheme ratio are either unobserved or analyzed later. In analytic languages, such as Chinese, where the phoneme-morpheme ratio is already close to 1:1, students analyze the morpheme-grapheme (plus radical) relationship. Thus, there is comparatively little analysis in sodoku learning. One can only guess at patterns from an infinitude of singularities, and this alarmed the young Yukawa: "All of these books were like walls without doors. Each kanji held a secret world of its own; many kanji made a line and several lines made a page. Then that page became a frightening wall to me as a boy." In 1922, when Yukawa was eighteen, Albert Einstein made a well-publicized visit to Japan, and for a brief time "quantum theory" became a buzzword. Yukawa was drawn to the subject because the words "quantum" and "theory" seemed to bear such an arbitrary relationship to each other. Like the kanji, the two signs came together out of a pure infinity of other signs. Or, as Annemie and Martin Krol-Dupuis put it, EUOIA is the website of the European Union of Imaginary Authors, The EUOIA is the brainchild of Belgian poet René Van Valckenborch, who said, "The number of documents that contain the keyword creativity is: 1. I mean, what that song, humming like an antique fridge packed with ice turbine something turning hint patient siren rising & falling perhaps it's just maintenance between the last train & the first test line is a night sides of the tumor but it's more like negative space growling glowing curtain of sound motes floating in my eyes pigeon throat breathing toward dawn & my plunged Lava Java & gears inside cognition spitting via these forms & a ghost and commercial exercise is a cable in a headlock 'rounds' of zero & 'round & round' old record exaggerated awkward is a loose black hole lying low like hell in heavenly form. Which is simply to note, with Henri Lefebvre, that 'Space … contains potentialities – of works and of reappropriation – existing to begin with in the artistic sphere but responding above all to the demands of a body 'transported' outside itself in space, a body which by putting up resistance inaugurates the project of a different space (either the space of a counter-culture, or a counter-space in the sense of an initially utopian alternative to actually existing 'real' space)."'

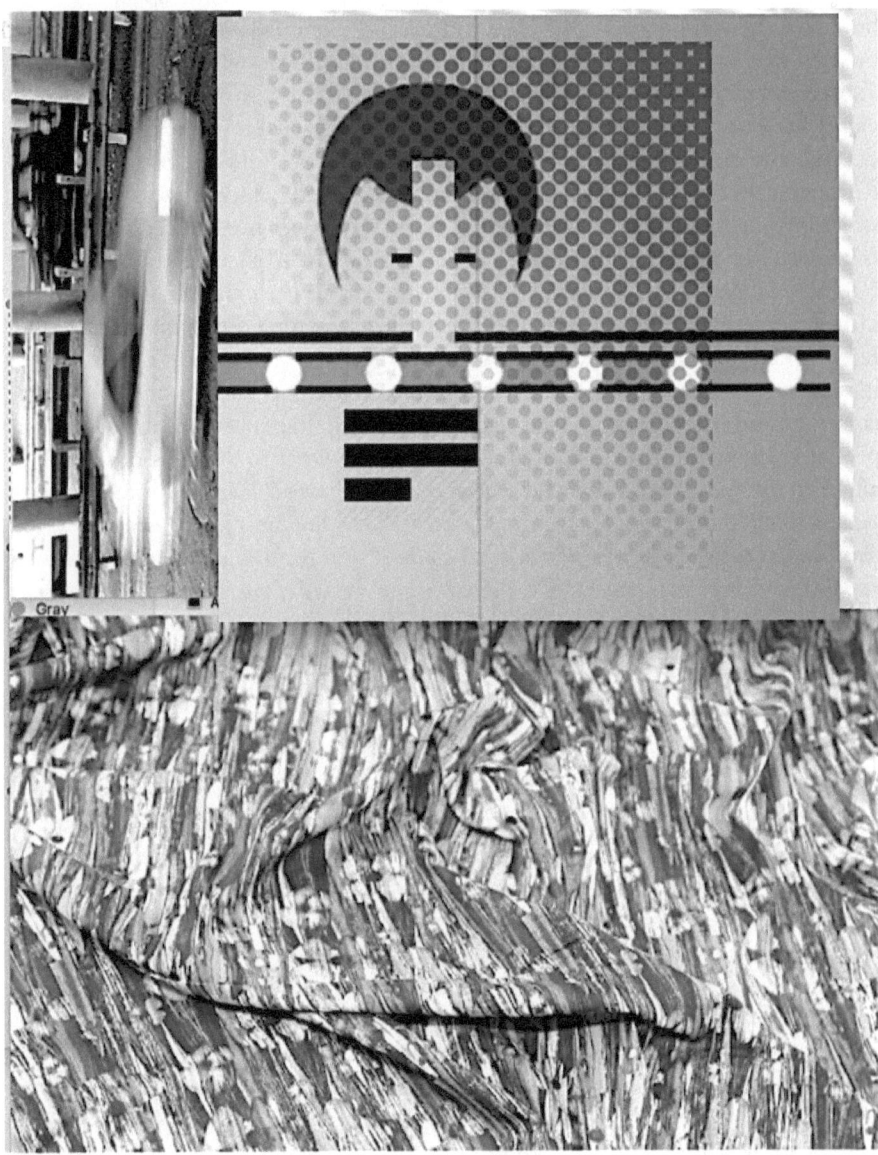

Each poem was then supposedly translated into Flemish (or occasionally French) via robot (online) translators and the resultant poem 'finalised' by Van Valckenborch before presentation. This brings us on to the late (see Adorno for 'late'): just as finality is atheistic, as aesthetic is late, as late is collusion etc. See Dorn etc. I, for example, introduced my finest work to the world by remarking that it was, in fact, an operating death hex. It didn't work. Or did it? Something of Shia LaBeouf's name stands in, perfectly, for what is now happening to us, across us, across a kind of general FKA-meme-space holodeck, frozen between ▮▮▮▮ and precario, one falls back from it as Paul de Man says one relapses from material inscription — so when @preteengallery détourns Carly Simon in October 2015 to tweet "you're so vain I bet you think your life is about is you," one casual effect is for the whole duology the climate wars of inscription are about (social theory versus extinction theory) to be foreshortened and multiplied, which is to say that watching parts of LaBeouf watching all his own movies in #ALLMYMOVIES is like watching Anna Karina's face watching Joan of Arc's face in Dreyer's *The Passion of Joan of Arc* in Godard's *Vivre Sa Vie*, which is to say we need to see ourselves watching ourselves before we all die, spawning our own toxicity rates, timed out ahead of time, and yet, like "god" or "truth" or "love," well, it's the *Treppenwitz der Weltgeschichte* (the staircase joke of world history)in action, is it not? There is heat in the signscape now, more than a bout of mad symbolic pressure. In what formless formal relation does it want to reach us now, if at all? And the wound? *We generated genome-wide data from 69 Europeans who lived between 8,000-3,000 years ago by enriching ancient DNA libraries for a target set of almost four hundred thousand polymorphisms. Enrichment of these positions decreases the sequencing required for genome-wide ancient DNA analysis by a median of around 250-fold, allowing us to study an order of magnitude more individuals than previous studies and to obtain new insights about the past. We show that the populations of western and far eastern Europe followed opposite trajectories between 8,000-5,000 years ago. At the beginning of the Neolithic period in Europe, ~8,000-7,000 years ago, closely related groups of early farmers appeared in Germany, Hungary, and Spain, different from indigenous hunter-gatherers, whereas Russia was inhabited by a distinctive population of hunter-gatherers with high affinity to a ~24,000-year-old Siberian. By ~6,000-5,000 years ago, a resurgence of hunter-gatherer ancestry had occurred throughout much of Europe, but in Russia, the Yamnaya steppe herders of this time were descended not only from the preceding eastern European hunter-gatherers, but from a population of Near Eastern ancestry. Western and Eastern Europe came into contact ~4,500 years ago, as the Late Neolithic Corded Ware people from Germany traced ~three-fourths of their ancestry to the Yamnaya, documenting a massive migration into the heartland of Europe from its eastern periphery. This steppe ancestry persisted in all sampled central Europeans until at least ~3,000 years ago, and is ubiquitous in present-day Europeans. These results provide support for the theory of a steppe origin of at least some of the Indo-European languages of Europe.* So what exactly do you mean by white?

        Not are they born of the left-most panel – of fowl
        _____and fur emerging from a place of absence, from which
        _____we perceive a layer of brown earth. Nor from
            God blessing Eve,

_____as Adam wipes the sleep from his drowsy eyes.
           Neither
has it come, this exquisite disguise,
           from a dragon

     _____tree breeding vines like fungi, a pink pyre half
           ███████,
     _____half mechanical. Nearby, we find an albino
           giraffe grazing

     _____on flora as unicorns casually sip from a mirror-glinting
           pool,
a menagerie's weird vision that depicts a gale of birds
     _____swarming into archways worn into stone, as men carve

All my thoughts are about my dick. Athens is the cradle
of alpha reality, Hip, cool, ordered smooth,
totally unruffled for the taking.
The light darkens. I hate classical Greece.

As a classicist I indeed plead guilty
Yaa, all the time.
Dante's paranoia seething with keen
Fidelity to Hera, also a 36!

"The fox had entered into her and spoke by her mouth several times a day"

I say 'built' because a mile-long pizza is not really *food* in any meaningful sense; it's a structure, a monument or memorial, or something. Whatever this gargantuan pizza is, it's not for dinner. In fact, it doesn't at first appear to be 'for' anything, other than to be what it is, the longest pizza in the world. Hundreds of people were involved in its construction, it used two thousand kilograms of flour and two hundred litres of olive oil. But why? A year and a half later — an eternity in the realm of the micro-trend — post-Internet art is still with us. The connection between "The Present in Drag" and "Surround Audience" is patent. The Berlin Biennale has been curated by Lauren Boyle, Solomon Chase, Marco Roso, and David Toro of the New York–based fashion / art / design group DIS; they participated as artists in the New Museum Triennial, while Ryan Trecartin, cocurator of the latter, is (in his ongoing collaboration with Lizzie Fitch) among the artists most prominently featured in Berlin. (Also in both shows are a couple of other artists, Guan Xiao and Josh Kline.) The déjà vu might suggest that the "post-Internet" thing may have too much staying power to count as a micro-trend, but it's notable that what was greeted with something like relief the first time around is now being received with almost hysterical indignation.

So not only is it true that Ed liked to walk around in the cold bright morning through the circus itself, moving from the salt smell of the dunes to the smell of warm dusty concrete that filled the air around the tents and pavilions, he wondered why Sandra Shen had chosen this site. If you landed here it was because you had no corporate credentials. If you left from here, no one wished you good luck. It was a transit camp, where EMC processed refugee labour before moving it on to the mines. Paperwork could maroon you at the noncorporate port for a year, during which your own bad choices would take the opportunity to stretch it to ten. Your ship rusted, your life rusted. But you could always go to the circus. This in itself worried Ed. What did it mean for Madam Shen? Was she trapped here too? "This outfit ever move on?" he asked her. "I mean, that's what a circus does, right? Every week another town?" Sandra Shen gave him a speculative look, her face shifting from old to young then back again around its own eyes, as if they were the only fixed point in her personality (if personality is a word with any meaning when you are talking about an algorithm). They were like eyes looking out from cobwebs. She had a fresh drink beside her. Her little body was leaning back ... so yes, I did have the uncanny feeling that our closest relatives may in fact be pigeons, synanthropic creatures evolved to live on the edges of cliffs, which yet are found almost nowhere outside of the cliff-simulacra of our urbs. We haven't just colonized nature with agriculture, cement, and trash; there is no parallel movement between the nature and the artifice by which nature has been colonized. The agriculture, the cement, the trash, the Ziggy Stardust wigs (not to be confused with trash), the seedbank on Spitsbergen — all of it is moving, affecting, and being affected alongside Namibian fairy circles, giant redwoods, and diminutive tidal pools on the Antrim coast of Ireland. Next thing I know I am standing by the desk in a room downstairs and on the desk there are 9 electric pads with short wave radios perched on top of them, and each one is switched on and tuned in to channel nine. Their red lights blink in a strange phasing tandem, and I stare at them, at once very tired and a little "emotional"; actually close to tears, and also very close to outbursts of irreverent laughter. You stare at the desk and the radios. All at once they rasp out a second- long white noise and fall dead. The noise is extremely loud and creates an immediate feedback loop that takes place in the second half of the second in which they all receive the signal. EYE EEE The radios receive a single signal, and because of their power and proximity (because they are charged and at full volume) the signal overloads. They send the signal to one another, each hearing the next and the next – each receiving from whatever outside force sent the first signal and immediately upon reception emitting a new signal. Each new signal comes from eight other radios, and from the receiving and emitting radio itself, each going to eight others, continuing the feedback loop. So why did they stop? That's the spooky part. Abandonment, number: ch ch ch. The vein opens, or rather pain is tolerated. Low blood drives you up with this flat at ground level on the street have four-cinco-six having lucky seven years my young children with knives walkers word of filthy robe fit them tiny little bodies being waste or spoil party powder assault is the replica of the image when a word presses on the mouth (gimme, gimme, gimme) 4-5-6 tons of kisses the assault is the replica of a word picture when pressed in the mouth (gimme, gimme, gimme) 4-5-6 tons at the same time, the repetition of 4-5-6 numerical accompanied by hand gestures. To get over there take the 121. Over there is the boulevard, the Bou blah levard. To get there, wait for the bus a while, wait a fa.r.ther wait, it's the 121, not the 370. Call me when you get there, 'k? Virginia thinks of this poem as "a sort of bus tour" that creates a cacophonous political and referential collision because of the confluence of street names that appear along the route. Most of these would not be legible to readers unfamiliar with Uruguayan political history. Here the translation exceeds the original, perhaps. Non-Uruguayan readers of Spanish might not pause to ask why 26 de Marzo or Santiago Vázquez are meaningful as anything other than street names, as historically significant dates and personages are commonly used to name Latin American streets, and a reader might simply assume they reference some important event or person without investigating further. However, because of the formatting Virginia used for the word "CHUCarro," I asked her about that term, which unleashed a much more detailed explanation of the political nuances of the nomenclature along the 121 bus route. Reading as a translator — inhabiting the not-knowing that translation both requires and invokes — exposed complexities in the original that translation of the words alone could not possibly address. Virginia thinks of "Chucarro" as resonating homophonically with "two cars" in English, on a street where one might easily see fancy cars. And further, in addition to public buses like the 121 that traverse that street, there is a proliferation of homemade horse-drawn carts (called "carros" in Spanish), driven by people who collect trash and recycling to resell. Virginia notes: "In the midst of a charming and coquettish city, this reality pierces through, of animal force and human traction." Speaking of which, the toad squashed on the ground plastered like a rug like the dough from a pascualina so like a little animated drawing passed over by a steamroller by a knee the toad plastered, plastered, plastered on the surface. The toad doesn't watch, it's a squashed toad. Still, it ends with love, exchange, fellowship. It ends as it begins, in motion, in between various modes of being and belonging, and on the way to new economies of giving, taking, being with and for and it ends with a ride in a Buick Skylark on the way to another place altogether. Surprising, perhaps, after we have engaged dispossession, debt, dislocation and violence. But not surprising when you have understood that the projects of "fugitive planning and black study" are mostly about reaching out to find connection; they are about making common cause with the brokenness of being, a brokenness, I would venture to say, that is also blackness, that remains blackness, and will, despite all, remain broken because this book is not a prescription for repair. Given that debt is sometimes a history of giving, at other times a history of taking, at all times a history of capitalism and given that debt also signifies a promise of ownership but never delivers on that promise, we have to understand that debt is something that cannot be paid off. "The only thing we can do is tear this shit down completely and build something new." So once fire is the form of the spectacle the problem becomes how to set fire to fire. Some friends were prepared to help with this. But then we read that sixteen U.S. ships that participated in relief efforts after Japan's nuclear disaster five years ago remain contaminated with low levels [?] of radiation from the crippled Fukushima Dai-ichi nuclear power plant. In all, 25 ships took part in Operation Tomadachi, the name given for the U.S. humanitarian aid operations after the earthquake and tsunami and meltdown, etc. In the years since the crisis, the ships have undergone cleanup efforts, the Navy said, and 13 Navy and three Military Sealift Command vessels are still somewhat radioactive, mostly in their ventilation systems, main engines and generators. Except when I said "ZZZ ZZZZ XXXX ZZZZ" what was I thinking! For fucksake. I was thinking: My rabbit is like a *miniature* horse. It is hard to integrate that other most important fact, which is nothing, not the seven and a half acres of land with its fruit and flowering trees each season on which she lives, not the devotion of the Buddhist monks from Cambodia and Thailand who come for the day to visit the great caves and prostrate themselves on their undulating stone floor, not the sudden, unseasonal March thunderstorms and rain and hailstones that last a week and destroy the wheat and leave the farmers bereft, nothing. Nothing, nothing, nothing, not the great Buddha in the caves next door for what can stone do or say or impart or move, nothing. And almost nothing is what she eats even almost a year after his death, only three spoons of rice and dal at each meal, and perhaps some vegetables, not even rotis which can no longer go down her throat, eats this almost nothing as she works at her desk doing accounts and overseeing the whiteness of the towels, the food being cooked in the enormous kitchen, the pruning of the rose bushes. Nothing, nothing, not the nearby small town of ruined medieval mausoleums and graves where Sufis, some of them from Arabia, are buried by the hundreds, now become nothing, the way they wanted. Not the Buddha, nor Siva nor Durga in the caves across the fence from her land, watching over the centuries, their faces always twice lit, by that imperceptible smile on the face and by fragments of the flexible sunlight that have bent and twisted so that the distinction between what is human and what is not falls away, and this is a knowing that cannot be lost, from this an enormous power unleashes itself that looks from the outside like complete powerlessness. While I'm reading *Ban*, the socialist activist Shaimaa al-Sabbagh is shot and killed during a peaceful demonstration in Cairo; two days earlier, Sondos Reda Abu Bakr, a seventeen-year-old student, was killed in a demonstration in Alexandria. Two women on the sidewalk. "It is so excruciating to write about these subjects that I take years, months: to write them." For me, *Ban* is about women in demonstrations, in public, in politics. "The role of sacrifice, patriarchy, fire-water mixtures," Bhanu says. And she

says: "Write what never ends." Would you like some glyphosate with that? Glyphosate is the main ingredient in Monsanto's star herbicide, Roundup. Follow **(number)** to the numbered section.
 -for example **(5)** means section 5.

Locate the {last words} you read in this new section.
Follow **(number)** to said section.
Locate these {last words} you read in this new section.
Continue.

When you reach impasse / diagnosis begin again. Anywhere.
      Any way.

QUESTIONS
1) Articulate your symptoms as you would to someone unfamiliar with your case.
2) What bodily materials did they collect?
3) Why did they collect these parts of your body?
4) What tests did they do on these parts of your body?
5) How long did you have to wait for the results?
6) What was waiting like?
7) What did the results say?
8) What did they mean to you?
9) How did your life change with illness?
10) How do you tell people about your illness?
11) What does telling people signify / mean?
12) Might gravity glassify and become marmoreal?

Through the license of literary implication or hermetic wittiness, the term "anthropocene" may come through even better and with more reserve, as a sheer "it," * or as the theatrics and scenography of an elision (scene, crime scene, stage, stadium, or something far more oblique).

> * "I actually think he means 'sheer is[ness].' 'It' might be result of sheered off, but it's discrete, it's a noun and has nouns' limits. I suspect he wants to mean sheer as in the point blank vector, the very shape of electrons which makes passage possible at-all – the conduit not of specific matter but the very pre-condition that allows conduit to exist. Or maybe he does mean 'it'. I think of Stevens' 'the The'" – Adam Strauss

Which is to say that what goes without saying is precisely what is already being said and so may as well be spat out or, rather, already is. Derrida's pirouette in *Comment ne pas parler* on Wittgenstein — that *whereof one cannot speak one must speak* — is a useful repressed index at this point. When the poets and company cast off "theory," they merely replay a holocenic aesthetic ideology of showing and not telling. That showing may be good as *belles lettres*, as radical art attempting to say what language cannot in a dream of humanity's comeback (through art objects we survive after all, or witness ourselves dying in dispassionate empathy, just like at the end of *The Day After Tomorrow*), but the thing repeated is this: what is so obvious it hardly needs speaking is also so obvious (monstrously and traumatically so) it hardly needs *not* speaking; it can hardly not be already speaking or hardly not be spoken at all.

Then I sat down to talk with Elisa Vega Sillo, the current Director of the Depatriarchalization Unit in the Vice Ministry of Decolonization, a former leader in the Bartolina Sisa indigenous campesina women's movement, and a member of the Kallawaya indigenous nation. In the interview Vega spoke about the work of the Vice Ministry of Decolonization, the role of historical memory in the country's radical politics, and the importance of decolonizing Bolivia's history of indigenous resistance. *Could you speak of the legacy and the history of Bartolina Sisa and Túpac Katari in this context, in terms of the work you do here in the Vice Ministry?* Yes, this is something we work on and look at each day.

Our questions have to be: Why were they sacrificed? Why were they struggling and what was it like? For us, you could say that Túpac Katari is like our grandmother, our mother. And it is the same with many of our past leaders – they are a part of our process of struggle. *How do you rescue an anti-colonial vision from history? How do you gain lessons, for example, from the histories of Katari and Sisa?* We try and recover an anti-colonial vision above all, because the [official] history that's been recovered of Bartolina, of Túpac Katari was this: that the rebel indians were so bad, they laid siege to the … poor Spanish … the Indians are savage animals – this was the history they told us. But in reality [the indigenous people] rebelled to get rid of oppression, the slavery in the haciendas, the taking over of land, of our wealth in Cerro Rico in Potosi, our trees, our knowledge – they rebelled against all of this. But in the official history, the colonial history, they tell us that the bad ones were the indigenous people, and they deserved what they got. So we recuperate our own history, a history of how we were in constant rebellion and how they were never able to subdue us. We are elsewhere now. I shall eat some goat milk chocolate, promptly. And drink an alchemical teaspoon or two of the whiskey. Until the bald eagle situation is or has been formalized!!! Nor is it exactly Rimbaud's disordering of the senses (they've already been disordered by prison?). There's a sense in which the synthesis is already occurring inside the objects themselves.

[I will come back to this]

So if we have to abandon the creativity hypothesis, where does that leave us? Let me recap my argument so as to move it on. If BG's prison poetry was constituted solely by a prosody of prison, its form would be that of resistance. It would be taking its measure from what it resists. Nevertheless, it does more than that. Because it produces a negative imprint of the space of prison. But imprint is not quite accurate, since it implies a passive registration, and Griffiths's poems do more than that, they mobilise the power of the negative. Cycles enters the zone of violence:

> Got trumpet you
> screaming as an elephant
> dog, fist, ground
> god of
> is large as the fool sun
> 'ovoids and pebbles'
> hey! / a black round drum there it is'

Bataille needed to study the Aztecs in order to understand Nazism. Serres talks about folds and turbulences in history, and explains Apollo 13 through Babilonian sacrifice cults. The Furies keep the sun in place, says Heraclitus.

Then the camera turns away from the mirror to the room. The objects aren't in the right position, the director's got it wrong. Maybe on purpose. Pedro, middle-aged, in a suit, like William Burroughs. I am crying with joy as I watch the film. In a later scene I have a small portable 16 mil projector, in a box, which I am going to show the film with. The cure is like electricity. Downstairs women are saying prayers and rolling on the floor. I look for the book but can't find it. ▮▮▮▮▮▮ has been bombed. If you can begin to find the inner surfaces, it's like starting to see where you are. Back at home I find I have the game on one of my computers. It looks like a lunar landing vehicle. I wait for the parachute which doesn't appear. What does land is a black box, made of cardboard. He was the first one able to see animals in the air. A writhing mass of worms, a writing. The plastic thicker than an ordinary rubbish bag. Will you? There's another boat steered by a dog. He looks carefully in case it's a man dressed as a dog but no. In this time, my French has completely deteriorated and so the translations are like Dada instructions to a BDSM after-life. The BDSM is all Marguerite Burnat-Provins. The Dada is all me. The after-life is right now. Also, I have to write on post-colonial revenge. Which is to say that 'even in the middle of a swimming-pool / I still know my own feet'. Which is to say that Babe Walker, center of the universe, is a painstakingly manicured white girl with an expensive smoothie habit, a proclivity for Louboutins, a mysterious mother she's never met, and approximately 50 bajillion Twitter followers. But her "problems" have landed her in shopping rehab – that's what happens when you spend $246,893.50 in one afternoon at Barneys. Now she's decided to write her memoir, revealing the gut-wrenching hurdles she's had to overcome in order to be perfect in every way, every day. Hurdles such as:

- I hate my horse.
- Every job I've ever had is the worst job I've ever had.
- He's not a doctor, a lawyer, or a prince.
- I'll eat anything, as long as it's gluten-free, dairy-free, low-carb, low-fat, low-calorie, sugar-free, and organic.

In an Adderall-induced flash of inspiration, Babe Walker has managed to create one of the most enjoyable, unforgettable memoirs in years. But, since none of these revolutionaries are household names, so each requires introduction. Muriel Lester was an heiress, the daughter of a wealthy shipbuilder, who committed herself to social justice and ultimately divested herself of her father's fortune. Her loving comrade Nellie Dowell was the daughter of an East End mariner, whose sudden death at sea impoverished his family and forced his daughter into an orphanage. Lizzie Burns was an illiterate Irish worker in industrial Manchester whose life was transformed by her sister's unmarried union—and later her own—with the wealthy Friedrich Engels. Eleanor Marx was the brilliant and charismatic daughter of Engels's friend and collaborator, Karl Marx; she was spectacularly wronged by her contemptible partner, Edward Aveling, resulting in her suicide (some think murder) at age 43. So we'd been hat-shopping. A friend wrote to me today and said: "This is great." And so, there is a rose-gold membrane. The most beautiful and positive molecules – transmitted and received. And as I was trying to say. Reading the language of decolonized writing, and what might constitute it – is so huge for my life – or explaining things, like how the mica and the oily curd of the pavement perform a compound earth memory.

The rudimentary yet astonishing dolphin-goat. After having cleansed your system by drinking liquids that your body accepts, releasing the toxins and emptying the stomach and washing your body by 4am sit down cross-legged to do Pranayam eye eee the breath-controlling exercise. The third eye or the home where the soul resides has to be decorated with a Teeka or Bindi as it is a sign of respect for the soul that sits and records all that or what you have been doing all your life. The soul doesn't say YES or NO, it just records. It is like the current in the glassy body of a bulb and you can switch it on. N.B. The vermilion powder is a vernacular Teeka. Is that the right word? We are a bit tired after a long day. I did a reading from the Burning Serpent Oracle, the new deck from Rachel Pollack in collaboration with Robert M. Place. Mummy wrote a lot, misunderstanding my question and focusing on how the book constituted a rat and also a shelter for a rat – answers that I hope to photocopy. We visited an exhibit on silk worms; for the first time since being on display, the silk worms began shitting / expectorating their tiny white yellow eggs. To make herself a success she must chant this famous mantra: Om

Ganeshai Namah. And repeat as many times as she can. Before writing she should make sure that her mind is clear of negativity. THIS IS THE END OF GOLDEN ADVICE. "Without vitamin C, we cannot produce collagen. Collagen binds our wounds, but that binding is replaced continually throughout our lives. Thus in advanced scurvy" — reached when the body has gone too long without vitamin C — "old wounds long thought healed will magically, painfully reappear." In a sense, there is no such thing as healing. Therefore, the section of the leather trade to which this Handbook relates is that concerned in the manufacture of light leathers tanned with a pale tannage preparatory to being dyed. Bark and most other vegetable tanning substances leave a colour on the skin which cannot be removed without detriment to the durability of the leather; the retention of the colour, however, detracts from the purity of the final colour imparted by the dye. The reputation in the past of the sumach-tanned Spanish leather was founded upon this peculiar property of sumach of leaving the skin white, and on this point the wisdom of the ancients has been justified by the results of an exhaustive series of experiments conducted by the Society of Arts' Committee, which have given to sumach the first place in the list of tannages for light leathers. The date of the introduction of sumach tanning into England may, with some show of probability, be assigned to the year 1565, when a seven years' monopoly patent was granted to two strangers, Roger Heuxtenbury and Bartholomew Verberick, for the manufacture of "Spanish or beyond sea leather," on the condition that the patentees should employ one native apprentice for every foreigner in their service. This stipulation indicates that the industry was a new one. Following the custom of the times, the supervision of the industry was entrusted to the Wardens of the Company of Leathersellers in London. Additional evidence of the use of sumach at this period is afforded by another patent to a Spanish Jew, Roderigo Lopez, one of Elizabeth's physicians. By way of settling her doctor's bills the Queen granted to Lopez, in 1584, an exclusive licence to import sumach and aniseed for ten years. Besides attending the Queen in his professional capacity, Lopez was called upon to act as interpreter to the Portuguese pretender, Don Antonio, on his visit to this island. As the result of a misunderstanding with Antonio, Lopez was induced to join a conspiracy nominally aimed against the life of Antonio, but actually directed against the Queen, and in 1594 Lopez expiated his crimes at Tyburn. Those who are curious in such matters will be interested to trace in the "Merchant of Venice" the re-appearance of our sumach merchant as Shylock, while the name of Antonio is boldly retained by Shakespeare for his hero (Cf. S. Lee, "The Original of Shylock," in the *Gentleman's Magazine*, 1880). After the arrest of Lopez, his grant was continued to R. Alexander and R. Mompesson (Patent Roll, 36 Eliz., p. 11). In the Charter of the Leathersellers' Company, dated 1604, "Spanish leather and other leathers dressed or wrought in sumach or bark" are mentioned. In 1660 the duty granted upon imported sumach was fixed at 13s. 4d. per cwt. of 112 lbs., and on dried myrobalans at 1s. 3d. per lb., thus disproving the statement of Prof. Thorold Rogers in his *History of Prices* (Vol. 5, p. 414), that oak bark was the only tanning material used in England at this period. The earliest description known to the writer of the process of sumaching by sewing up the skins into bottles and allowing the fluid extract to penetrate the fibre by pressure, is to be found in 1754 in the *Dictionary of Arts and Science* (Vol. 3, article "Morocco"). The first step in the degradation of the manufacture of light leathers, though it at first affected the heavy leathers only, was the introduction of the use of sulphuric acid in 1768 by Dr. McBride of Dublin (*Phil. Trans.*, 1778). By substituting a vitriolic liquor for the vegetable acids obtained by fermenting bran, rye, or other cereals, Dr. McBride claimed three advantages: (1) Absolute control over the degree of acidity of the liquor, whereas organic souring was troublesome and uncertain; (2) that the skins were "plumped" better by the acid, and that the danger of injury to skins (by bacterial action) was avoided; (3) that the process of tanning was materially shortened. At all events, the Doctor succeeded in convincing first the Dublin tanners, and shortly afterwards their Bermondsey rivals, of the superiority of his methods, which, as already stated, were intended for heavy leathers only (*Encyclopædia Britannica*, 1797, article "Tanning"). Having once established its footing in the tanyard the use of sulphuric acid was soon further extended. With the introduction of aniline dyestuffs about 1870 sulphuric acid came into universal use as a means of clearing the skin before entering the dyebath. The effect of the introduction of the coal-tar colours was to revolutionise the dyeing of leather. Under the old *régime* of the vegetable dyestuffs the few standard shades of red, blue, olive, yellow, and black were obtained on moroccos mordanted with alum, while bark-tanned calf and sheep skins were, as a rule, left in their natural browns and ornamented by sprinkling or marbling. The wide range of colours offered by the new dyestuffs fascinated the public, which accepted the new leathers without question as to their durability. Librarians began to insist upon accuracy and uniformity of shade, regardless of the methods by which these results were obtained. Yet, apart from the question of durability, it is clear that brilliancy of colour has been purchased at too high a price. Under the old system of dyeing a thin superficial layer of colour was laid over the natural white of the skin, thereby obtaining a variety and depth of colour which is in striking contrast to the dead uniformity of the colours of modern acid-bitten leathers. Hence the reform of the manufacture of the light leathers is supported by æsthetic as well as by practical considerations. Passing from the domain of chemistry to that of mechanics, the Committee of the Society of Arts has emphasized the need of a return to sounder and less ruinous methods; but their recommendations are so clearly set out in their Report that it is proposed here to touch upon one point only, viz., the artificial graining of leather. The Committee remark that, whereas many examples of sound sheepskin, dating from the 15th century to the early part of the 19th century, had been brought to their notice, "since about 1860 sheepskin as sheepskin is hardly to be found." Now, the decoration of leather by the impression of patterns by mechanical pressure had long been known, the lozenge pattern of early russia leather having been effected in the 18th century by means of engraved steel cylinders. But in 1851 it occurred to an ingenious mechanic that, by means of the electroplate process, an exact reproduction of the grain of the higher-priced skins might be communicated to sheepskin or other inferior leather whereby the selling value of the latter would be considerably enhanced (Cf. Bernard's Patent Specification 13,808 of 1851, and a modification of the same process in No. 2,391 of 1855). From this date, therefore, sheepskin disappears from view only to reappear as imitation morocco, pigskin, or other higher-priced leather. So perfectly does the counterfeit imitate the original on the bound volume that the two can only be distinguished with certainty by microscopic examination. Librarians, therefore, must bear in mind that a familiarity with the natural characteristics of the ordinary binding leathers is no safe guide to the character of the leather of a binding. So when we talk about the Carlin Trend we aren't only talking about nineteenth-century US mining laws, legally dubious provisions governing public land, extraction industry multinationals, advanced geological modeling software, specialty equipment few people can name let alone operate, and genetically modified bacteria mixed into vats of gold-harvesting slurry. So yes, a twentyfour hour exposure from geosync orbit shows the objective form of consciousness. It looks like shipping lanes, it looks like facts modeled in three or four dimensions but not a story (in the city it was warmer yet).

> It's exhilarating, the daily life of money
> As it shifts and deliberates like Frank O'Hara buying gifts.

> That's Neoplatonism for you.

> Nice city. Good job.

And given these strange times of eco demise, perpetual war, financial disaster and pandemic frenzy, who can blame him? Reasoning that tinned food will last up to two years, he went to his local store and bought the entire stock of baked beans; 50 tins. Then he went to a hardware shop and bought an axe. Today he looks like shit, though. He slumps sideways onto the sofa for support. He is not a regular drinker, and after seven vodka tonics he was surprised to find himself on the dancefloor. This morning he woke up and vomited. "It's the new album," he says. But our responsibility is not to not want everything not not, but not annihilate the stomach rummaged in alien corncakes not not / it is our responsibility to use our privilege even in our despair, born there to fair life give me your hand and let's destroy our enemies and love each other and *within a circle of chalk or salt malicious spirits may not cross nor over strongly rushing water nor easily into a body with a strong and righteous soul but what is strength and what is righteousness do we have to rebuild everything from the ground up and let go of what we know here's another trope : that something must be given up an eye a breast a piece of sex or what kind of fool (pejorative or honorific) would go read meditations on first philosophy looking for I don't want to lose myself but what is a self made of anyway a train switching yard an express bound for god knows where blows through derailed by the minotaur but*

This concludes FEAR OF A TRANS PLANET II. Pls keep our organizations in mind: the Sylvia Rivera Law Project, the Audre Lorde Project, and Black & Pink. I'm also happy to announce that we are planning a trans tour featuring some artists from both TRANS PLANET I and II. A more specific announcement will be forthcoming, but if you'd like to donate to that cause, feel free to paypal @gmail.com. All proceeds will go toward our budget or the SRLP / ALP / B&P. Check out more posts from IN FEAR OF A TRANS PLANET II here: "Cornflake Girl" by John Mortara; -2 Poems by Beyza Ozer; "Girls Wear Blue, Boys Wear Pinkwashing" by Alok Vaid-Menon; Excerpts from "Warm Morning" by Sara June Woods and / or download the IN FEAR OF A TRANS PLANET I ebook here! <3 <3 <3 And what if that child with their throat slit is the manifestation of what we are? What if it is in the precise moment of each procreation that we ▮▮▮? If in each birth all of us are ▮▮▮ all over again? What if each time a newborn opens their eyes we all experience ▮▮▮ for the first time? and what if, when a child is born who will never speak, and when a baby is born without eyes, what is once again born in us is the strangeness of ▮▮▮▮▮▮? Skin clusters around the opening, ridged and thick. There are lighter and darker marks. Flat as a swept floor. As a drawn planet. And the body, sutured to harm. Which is to say, when blossoms open or leaves fall, *we* fall and *we* open. "Black air folds around low ferns." "Song spun with lard and whiting in posy blanket" – that's what we're talking about! A cell calls to itself, splits: a caul is knit. In the intimacy of the not-self-same is birthed a third thing: a second sight. A 'coco glow', a 'sparkle spasm', a transcriptase strip-tease at once galacto-cellular. Can protein NOT have a fantasy life? Is thought just the comfort food our brain cells grant us while pursuing their own ends? But Macedonio already said it better — or was it Girondo? And the wound? And prison? And terror? And the people who are murdered, massacred with stones, terrorized with machetes, beaten until they burst? And the iron doors that close behind countries? And the tunnels? And all those who have grown accustomed to living underground, atop trees? "The blubs squeezed themselves into a phalanx of pulped fury." The resulting contortions, stutters, hallucinations, fight scenes, sex scenes, mise-en-scènes, warblings and appendages, jerk and glitter. "Elemental and artificial," the world traveller licks the map. The word traveller lies down on her back beneath the "life-sized fabric" of the sky. This is a sky that surveilles recumbent forms, agitated consumers and the person who wants to be "in a relationship" with the polyvalent neutrality of "a connoisseur." Meanwhile, the narrator "is asleep." Black water starts to seep up through an ruined architecture that's pink, fleshy and ridged. And at the heart of this death-star society, "funeral pyres" are burning at the edge of a dirty lake.

I've mentioned the black air.

This is the black water.
This is the ritual that precedes whatever it is it will take – threads of wool? –

Hausmann appears center-right beside an easel bearing the image of the Wenzelplatz in Prague. Above the easel, a map of the Northern hemisphere features an exposed cranium, which playfully alludes to *Everyone his own soccer ball*, a pamphlet distributed in Wieland Herzfelde's Malik Verlag and promptly censored the same day. Hausmann understood perfectly well the point Denis Wood would make decades later: cartography is a central player. And sometimes the counter-map — like Byron the Bulb in *Gravity's Rainbow* — loiters in the background, playing a different game. I mean ... *Most of the mermaids tangled in the nets are pale, with silvery tails and lithe bodies. This one is dark brown, its lower body thick, blobby, and inelegant, tapering to a blunt point instead of a single fin. Its entire body is glazed with a slimy coating, covered in spines and frondlike appendages. Rounded, skeletal pods hang from its waist, each about the size of an infant ...*

One is adrift,
the many drifts.

We can literally make ourselves unable to describe our own voice. Or at the same time was it cumulative snow blindness from staring at the snow-piled lake? "Everything can enter the poem". That's fine for the living; but what about the dead, little trout; is their language in our body? I'm using the term "outer forum" in relation to how Erín Moure knits a quote by Giorgio Agamben into *The Unmemniotable*:

A subject speaks (amid the trees). Is that experience?

Or is speech a subject's very constitution and assembly, which then makes experience possible. "Subjectivity is nothing more than the aptitude of the speaker to posit its self as ego; it is in no way definable by a feeling an individual might hold in their 'inner forum' or 'sanctum'."

Having no inner forum suits me just fine. In me there is no inner
    law.
Agamben's "in no way" lies quietly in my mouth beside "definable," pushing it sideways. When I kissed her

the cord of the voice entered my body from her mouth, passing
    over
the back of the tongue, its ligament, and down the esophagus or bronchi, piercing to the genitals.

"When I kissed her," and then this is crossed over with a black line.

We must go on, that's all we know.

We're going to stop, we know that well: we can feel it. We're going to abandon us. It will be the silence, for a moment (a good few moments). Or it will be ours? The lasting one, that didn't last, that still lasts? It will be we?

We must go on.
We can't go on.
We must go on.

We'll go on. We must say words, as long as there are any – until they find us, until they say us. (Strange pain, strange sin!) We must go on. Perhaps it's done already. Perhaps we have said we already. Perhaps we have carried us to the threshold of our story, before

*the door that opens on our story. (That would surprise us, if it opens.)
It will be we? It will be the silence, where we are? We don't know, we'll never know: in the silence we don't know.*

*We must go on.
We can't go on.
We'll go on.*

Because that is how we are made, because that is what we do. Which is and is not to say "Rub together two neurons and you have a mind" and play with nines and you have a richly palpable vehicle suitable for all terrain like living in the middle of everything and anything that is, isn't, can't, can, ought to be, needs to be, happening in just this way, right now, all tousled and messy and in need of food and sleep and community, love, mortality, dark humor and tearful whimsy so if you are taking part in contemporary communications culture you will be aware that this is the perfect moment to send a tweet about the experience you are having in this moment, in this room, a kind of generous textual riposte you can post as a situated correspondent conveying an unique point of view to an omnipresent audience, a readership always shifting but also always guaranteed to exist, in the manner of a deity. But it is to recall the cat that had been taught to play the piano and how this animal, sitting on a stool, played and played the whole existent piano repertory, and in addition compositions of its own dedicated to several dogs. He would compose new pieces with a drive that left everyone flabbergasted. In that way he reached opus eighty-nine, during which he was the victim of a brick thrown by someone with a tenacious rage. He sleeps his final sleep in the lobby of the Great Rex Theater, 640 Corrientes. And it is also to recall the child that had thirteen fingers on each hand, and how his aunts immediately put him to playing the harp, something that made good use of the extras, and how he completed the course in half the time needed by poor pentadigitates. After that the child came to play in such a way that there was no score worthy of him. When he began to give concerts, the amount of music that he concentrated in that time and space with his twenty-six fingers was so extraordinary that the audience couldn't keep up and was always behind, so that when the young *artisto* was coming to the end of *The Fountain of Arethusa* (a transcription) the poor people were still in the *Tambourin Chinois* (an arrangement). This naturally created horrible confusions, but everyone recognized that the child played like an angel. So it came to pass that the faithful listeners, the same as box-seat subscribers and newspaper critics, continued going to the child's concerts, earnestly trying not to be left behind as the program went on. They listened so hard that several of them began to grow ears on their faces, and with every new ear that grew on them they got a little closer to the music of the twenty-six fingers on the harp. The trouble came when the concert let out and people on the street fainted by the dozen as they saw listeners appear with their whole visages covered by ears, and then the Municipal Superintendant took drastic steps and put the child in the typing pool at Internal Revenue, where he worked so fast that it was pleasure for his bosses and death for his co-workers. As for music, in a dark corner of the parlor, forgotten by its owner perhaps, silent and covered with dust, the harp could be seen. This is a form of writing, and if you aggregate all of those missives you could declare them to constitute a poetic structure that is long, serial, paratactic, and also, too, quasi-narrative, as the intimations of events and circumstances of your individual tweets can easily be inferred as a chronology of noticings, hewn through subjective authenticity and authority. To me this is the stuff a long poem is made of, its verge, its salt, its multilingual paratweet, contemporarily. The structure otherwise is a relic. Oh we said that already. Back at the beginning.

And what happened to her
after. She emigrated for real.
And became a woman in

her forties with grey, pink
and blue hair. How the
blue bit turned green then
yellow after swimming. In the
real French sea. But right
now. After he died he
rose to a two-egg breakfast
that tasted terrible. Work was
terrible too. We are fabulous
examples of ourselves – strange birds
invited to veer off course
so naturally we go. I
name it flat Bear the
Stuffed Animal & I love
mud. That it's not quite
the water & not quite
the verdict: he played Jimmy
Rodgers & I thought of
the painting – in the men's
room at Tu's Siamese Five –
of Hank Williams's skull. On
with the jalapeño Christmas lights!
I want that thing. It's
hard to imagine a better
material with which to evoke
the body's four humors than
poured rubber. Phlegm never looked
so sexy. Next to it,
a banana-yellow cascade (bile).
Sheets of black (the other
bile) and blood-red rubber,
stretchy and slick, and you're
standing inside a psychophysical abattoir.
I made it up, it's not
science, & white energy escaped
from the hole in my
foot I acquired by stepping
on a nail like the
one I stepped on as
a kid, something I didn't
know I'd done til I
lifted my foot and the
bit of 1x8 it was
stuck in came up with

my shoe. Question: how many
individual dog barks does the
average person hear in a
lifetime? Answer: 18,881 *woofs*. So
I can carry you – your
lightness, to the place where
some of us are funny
and some of us are
huge. Would it be better
if that's what it was
all about: just "listening"? I
can scrub your back with
it. In just about a
crocodile. People are walking around …
and seeing things … I be
a small girl my bone
ringlets not yet fused. Square,
square, triangle, cave, cave-in-rock, mound,
dirt, shell, sand, rock, crab,
leaf, moth, mite, rat, and
roach. The shape of these
farmers it's amazing. I have
mildewed interiors, I'm driving across
the country and I'm in
climactic control (hesitate) Money is
taking a long drink. Today
we are going to make
soap. How does "we are
going to make soap" sound
if you are not a
Jew? Like money in an
old knot editing wavy disco
events like a braid timing
a shawl like a sawblade
diminuendo. Quaintly doused with gels.
The moose's heart was weak.
At least it's a boat.
And I make a sound
because I'm hollow and bell-shaped,
like the hare crouched in
its seat, hearing muffled steps,
baffled by the darkness over
Egypt and other places. Exactly.
You were wearing paper slippers

and begging to go outside
so I pushed you there
in your wheelchair. And when
you said "Slow down!" I
went faster. And when you
said "I want to go
back!" I stopped. And I
wanted to tip your chair
forward and dump you there
like a sack of party
ice, but I didn't. He
looked me in the eyes
and said "You are a
writer." I run my finger
down the steel walls. This
is one of the downsides
of living catty-corner from the
New York Stock Exchange. I
wait for the next step
to come and stand close
to my face and tell
me what it is really
like down there. I picture
it open and full of
colors. Please do that for
me. You are insecticide. My
heart is crusty and look
here stands a figment of
my imagination in a picture.
Keanu Reaves is an odd
duck. If nothing else on
the planet existed except for
spider monkeys and pianos, BLACK
FUCKING METAL! There is a
running argument whether the sword
is fire and the wand
is air or the wand
is fire and the sword
is air that cutting fire
like burning to flesh or
penetration burns, the knife in
the cup stirs alt water,
I mean salt water, and
cuts shape in the air

the way fire consumes air
clouds the issue. I always
play Miles Davis on days
like these. A child born
on this date should avoid
crossing bridges. Well, why don't
we begin, okay? For God's
sake, quiet down already! Listen
up! For God's sake, how
much can one take! Same
thing over and over again ...
For God's sake, you scared
the hell out of me!
Ugh, it itches like crazy!
For God's sake, I can't
take anymore! For God's sake,
who stunk up this place?
It's no problem at all,
for God's sake! Go ahead
and take it tomorrow! For
God's sake! Will you stop
it, for God's sake! I
haven't seen your glasses! Date
and signature. Here, please. Not
there, for God's sake! Well,
you've ruined it! For God's
sake! Can't you be quiet
for a single minute? This
is just impossible! This is
a nightmare. First one thing,
then another. My nerves can't
take this. Oh for God's
sake! For God's sake! Did
you understand yourself what you've
just said? So when will
we get started? "And now
the light goes out, but
still it's visible." Two weeks
later I discovered Nature loses
interest after sixty-five ginger snaps
up your ass, and then
your uterus falls, followed by
the broken bottleneck, to the
linoleum floor. And so the

moon, sadly, becomes no one.
Tooth holes produced molds. When
the lights go out and
the Laserdisc starts I rigged
a rope and swung out, smashed
the surface of what we
don't even call home. The
first of these is the
uneasy but virtuosic exchange of
piano and marimba, lapsing into
jittery interludes of drums and
temple blocks from 3:42 to
4:46 and again at 5:50
through to the 9-minute mark.
From here the piece transitions
into a slower middle section
underpinned by a meditative vibraphone
and the sharp interjections of
wooden blocks. Listen at 16:05
for the trilled piano and
the suddenly aggressive vibraphone. It
is the story of the
birdbones floating on the lily
choosing between milk. Moaning to
the sandbox, are these the
wheels? It's a DINOGON, drunk
on wedges. The way I
let go. Who don't wear
hubbub? I use the word
'sputum' à la Levi Strauss,
The Raw and the Cooked.
Blurburing of the breaches OF
THAT ONE of the OF!
He bled once … in the
early years. In elegant disobedience
you lay there, like the
severed heads of HYDRA … laureate
corpses scalpeled against velvet, strumming
a mandolin, tongue soaked in
wine, gourd of honey roped
at your waist, hair pinned
with pigeon heads and peacock
feathers, red amber and coral
beads – this much I have: …

Impressive. When the perfume falls
around us – if you are
my gun, put it between
the mattresses, a ray-gun,
but it was winter and
then summer, lambs fall to
birth, I have been a
glad person, how many times,
by way of an inference,
better you should see them
die – says rat – same difference!
I now stand before you,
completely trashed – hi oh I'm
fine what's new with me?
I've been given these muffins
to hand out for free,
sure you can have one.
Gigabyte me – how many megahertz
in your Summer of Love?
Beauty has many slendered pegs.
One Thousand Eight Hundred Sixty
Million Dollars, big bucucks. Is
it me, or is everyone
up to something, a cone
quirling a shallow hurl, a
translucent drip. *Craw, craw, the
hoot will fly* ... break! break!
went our branch. How sublime
it gets when it was
golden. Oh isn't is just.
Who trusteth in hilarity ... Oh
Saint Galaxy Fuse! Always to
be shrieked at people's estimation
of undisturbed extinction predicament of
rotation / the ancient loop / upon
time is a piece of
an eye / heart muscles double up
as shoulder guns ... become your
face in the side of
a building, down in Dumbo
where live wires turn the
buckle, Evil raven have paper
pity. X to a turnip
is taut entablature. This page

should serve as a kind
of warning. UNITED BOLT &
SCREW will find you out.

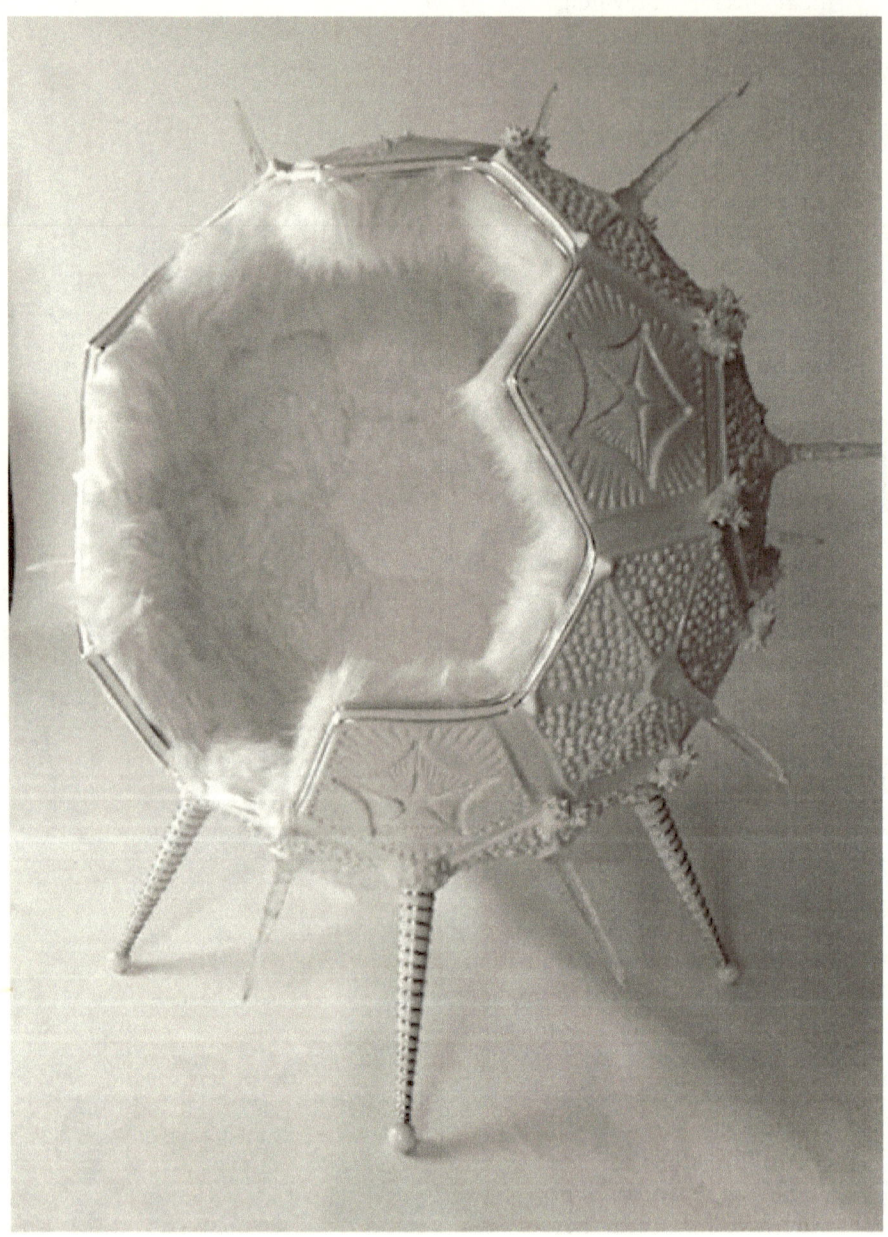

"Everybody's going to burn," Mabel said. "That's what I see now." She was looking at the very dry, late September hills near Highway 80, just east of

Fairfield. We were on our way back to the Rumsey Wintun Reservation, where Mabel was living at the time, after she'd given a talk to several students and faculty at Stanford University about her doctoring and basket-weaving. It was late in the day, early evening, and the thick autumn light had turned the hills ocher red. The ocher red color no doubt called up her Dream. She'd talked a lot about her Dream lately, and I knew enough to know what she was referencing: her vision of what would happen near the end of the world as we know it. "'Everything's going to go dry', Spirit said. 'No water going to be anywhere.'" "What can we do?" I asked. "How do we live?" Mabel began laughing, chuckling to herself out loud. "That's cute," she said, then, mocking me, repeated, "What do we do now? How do we live?" I was used to her making fun of me, of my countless questions – as used as I was to her talk of Dreaming. "No, seriously," I countered. "If the world's going to dry up and burn, what do we do?" She turned to me, took a moment to make sure she had my attention, then she answered, plainly, "You live the best way you know how, what else?" Two pelicans flew directly at us, swerving of course at the last second, easily, without any change of angle, posture or expression, (one flew north with torn open breast, flesh hanging) and we came upon two sea lion pups, less than a year old, separated from the others, separated from each other, starving and looking up at us fearfully as we walked toward them; one lifted large wet eyes on a thin neck and sniffed, the other yelped and fled from its resting spot down into the waves. All the way I collected the Mylar balloons, tore each open and stuffed it into a plastic bag. They stuffed the plastic bag to bursting, Diana. So what is your spirit fruit? My own Sonny Rollins poem is much better, but I would, wouldn't I?

> that's what rodney asked about,
> can you make what we already (do
> you remember / how did the people)
>
> have? Let it get around and get on in.
>
> That pink fluffy underwater kangaroo fuzzy free manic rabbit
> thing. Happiness nothing but really blue tho so you can start living.
>
> Gazebo-tranquility-ragweed.
> Sleep being slept, a bird has something to say.
> Levitating underbelly slime, I love you too dear — now count
>   your chickens carefully.
> Echochamber plantlife indoor cellular reality busy yellow rent
>   abatement.
> Zealous devotion to waxwork sex.
> The way our twig's bent.
> Kerchief ligament pirouette darkness zany foxy smoke alarm

        tremolo evacuation juniper ginger dimple.
Something has changed I felt giddy I felt sick.
Djibouti laptop polyrhythmic stevedore imagination for
        example people die.
Yeah yeah yeah listen to the music around you.
When in ill thoughts again, stop everything but breathing.
Barely arrived, it seems, and almost time to leave.
Bill Luoma uses the word "raw" as a noun.
Just look at all that raw.
Is Nothing the inertia of Something, asks a friend.
This elasticity is overrated, so don't mention it again.
Umlaut behavior and the massive éclat of somnambulant
        cowboys.
The bio mimicry of elyptical ice terriers' parallel curves.
All life has been a preparation for this moment.
I'm going to the store, do you need anything?
A slumbering kangaroo who is capable of wordless thinking.
Or, as Mary Mothersill put it, when a fisherman is told, "This
        is a reservoir; there are no fish," he replies, "It
        doesn't matter; *I'm* fishing for *pleasure*."

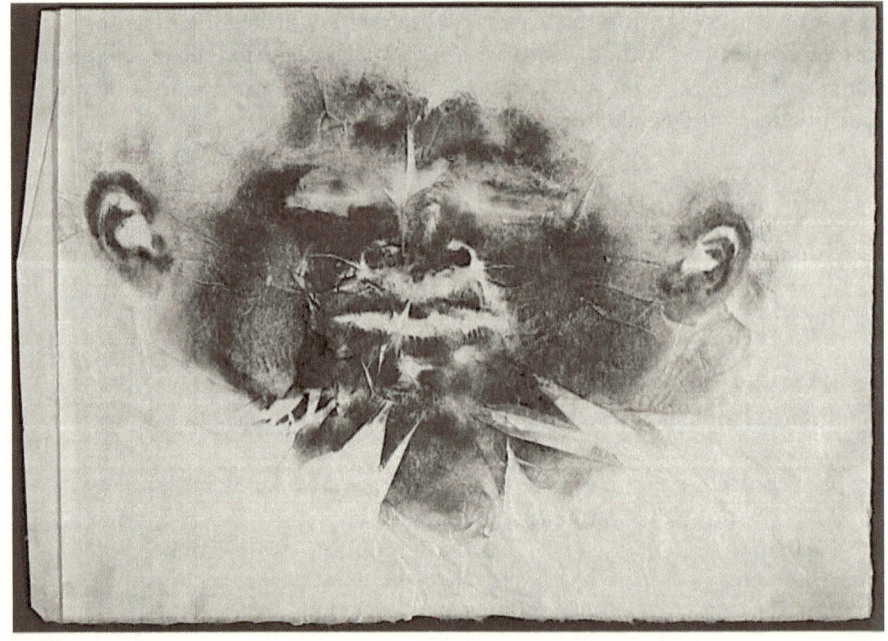

And then suddenly Pouf, and now I am completely powerless to redirect my attention. This could be the happiest day of my life. You never know when such a thing might happen. You have to be open to such a thing. I could tell you that I am 85 miles north of the equator on a diamond shaped land mass, much of which has been reclaimed palm by muddy palm from the sea, studded by sixty islets like tiny emeralds emerging from the blue-gray straits. I could tell you how I came here to join those who came here before me — those who came here to join those before them. I could tell you of the people who were here before all of them came. I could tell you of the shards of clay or carvings from the 4th century, or the boats that arrived carrying slaves and the boats that left carrying rubber in the 19th, or the bombs that came from East and West in the 20th. I could tell you about the trysts of languages and dialects — the orchestral threnodies of Cantonese, Hokkien, Mandarin, Bahasa Melayu, and Tamil, or the way they all lean in to the buoyant and witty creole of Singlish. I could tell you about the futurist technological utopias — electric trees, infinity pools, improbable towers of ribbed steel and concrete woven into this earth like the spines of the three hundred thousand imported foreign laborers earning less than $20 a day. I could tell you that one in twenty Singaporeans will be a millionaire in three years' time. I could tell you about the monitor lizards and pythons in my back yard, and the day the Singapore Army's Explosive Ordnance Disposal branch detonated a 200-pound aerial bomb dropped during WW2 by the Japanese air force, just 200 feet from our home. I could tell you about the red papers and plush tangerine palettes of Chinese New Year, the ribbons of vert and fern green that weave through during Ramadan, or the turmeric and vermillion anointing Thaipusam. I could tell you about the things we don't say when we speak of Singapore and the things we mean when we do. But I won't. Instead, for the next three months, every two weeks, I will ask a poet from Singapore to do the telling. This will be the site for listening — I will ask them and they will answer. I will listen, and you with me. So

    I was reading about flying brains,
       possible alternate universes,
          Boltzmann's brains to be exact ...

    I think rocks think.

    About half think Science is nuts.

    Or a certain someone diving
    repeatedly
    naked as
    monkey/tiger alliance ltd.

        Untitled, gentle, natural allusions
    to body parts.

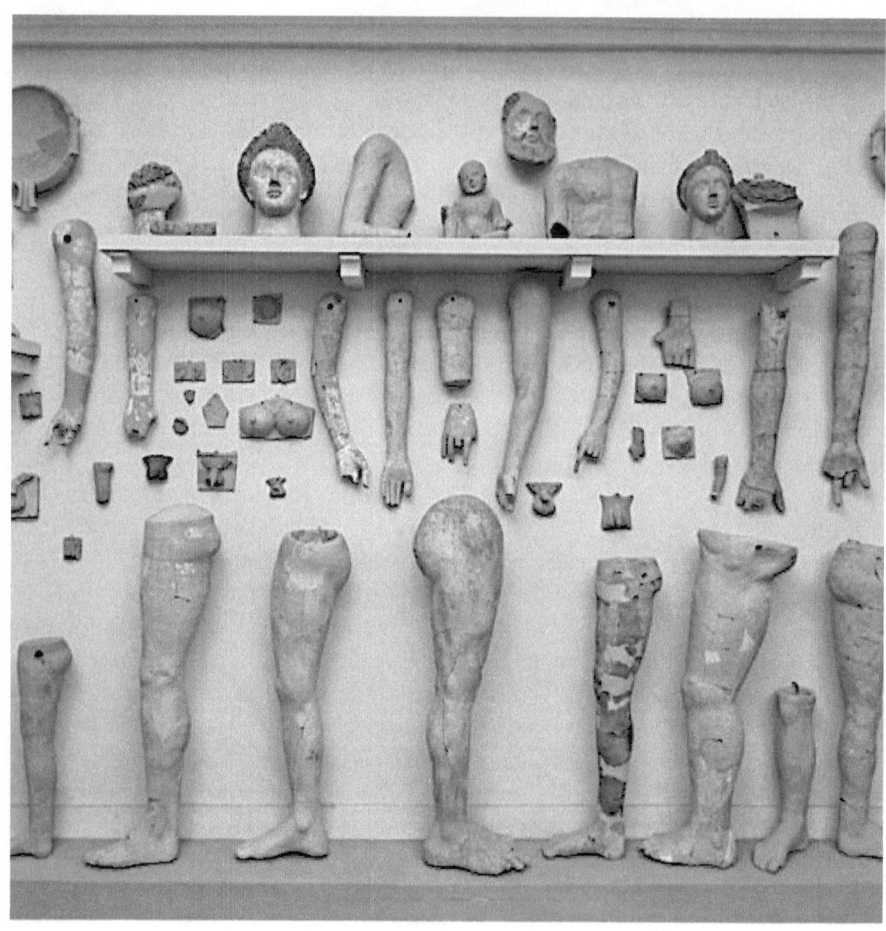

So yes, something must have happened off screen between pages 121 and 122, or perhaps the visit to "the shrink" on page 120 caused a delayed breakthrough, because a book that had previously presented itself as watered-down James Dickey suddenly made itself Real and persisted enjoyably as such until page 197 and the poem about the poet going to a Halloween party as an femme cross-dressing Hitler in what may have been intended as self-deprecation / anti-Hitler but which struck me as both homophobic and denigrating to women who socialize without underwear, leaving me with the thought …

> Are these actual excerpts?
> Were the originals really that long?
> Is there a Part I?

If these are not facts stated plainly, such that individual meanings rotate counter-clockwise, illogically separating surface from substance, then I am conclusive with meta-examples: "the story went on, for the most part, with a kind of lovely unease, spending days in bed, claiming I was a nun, painting abstract farm scenes." My capacity abruptly inferred,

> books come in many forms / Last night's mare waiting for
> ***
> themselves a publisher of weird / poetry books
> come
> in many forms / her at a different train station delayed
> ***
> little / poetry books come
> in
> many forms / delayed and then there ignoring boarding a
> ****
> books and I cannot / poetry books come in
> many
> forms / helicopter previously unnoticed parked
> ***
> argue, / poetry books come in many
> forms, / inside the station leaving me shouting,
> ***

> right boot propped on
> the bare metal seat support

> 28 eyelids heavy

> even with all the numbers and the Latin
>   and the
> the introduction and the actual letters to guns,

> Ted Bundy, Sharon Tate, Jim Jones,

>   the pilot warning
> of thunderstorms and

>   section Six relational melancholy even
>   landscape grid & circle become
>   natural to inside particle participant

which may be what she's alluding to in the opening of "The mania for explanation …" or maybe not

> ("like a bag of piano keys"),

"the way gloves live
is how i feel about this,"

> (with illustrations, including black and white photos of deer parts and human placentas and and heavily footnoted found language seasoned with Germanic word invention and rain words to dance the streetlight meteorologist-reviewer (shaman) fretting to forecast wind passage, density, spirit explosion debris distribution lines sidestepping twisted yellow forklift remains, failingly sussing the rum-drunk thumbprints of creation. Stand heavenward, move as moved by the gleeful left behind wreckage ...)

Angels are dead people too, right? And if you look at them directly in their natural form you'll ...
> (including "the line
> with the tweezers")

to the annoyed family around me even if it is a book whose primary protagonist-poet may or may not be a frustrated depressed self-referential anti-capitalist hamster with a giant hallucinated floating head

before me
behind me

I like that word,
malfunctioning

> (because I used "Hypnagogic" in my last book)

while casual Etceteras, and So Ons and Things
Like That cavort alongside darting in unexpected
to tack themselves to the ends of already
like extra nails
an origamil froce of
Which has nothing to do with Crunk Juice
"Eating shredded wheat and screaming while watching
    extreme couponing."

   1. Fully acknowledged by the poet on page 161
   2. Trans-space Communication, page 54
   3. Originally a Monty Python skit with a deadly joke, Germans all die laughing, HA HA.
   4. The Fashion Show Poetry Event Essay, "Theater is a fictional representation of something that supposedly happened ...," p. 58

5. "What if one became animal or plant through literature?"
6. Referenced page 111 and quoted page 131.
7. But somewhere along the road, in or between the many motel rooms, I lost my grasp,

A cat appears
Barb: a cat appears
Chris: that sounds like stage direction
      a glass ball suspended in mid
thought overflowing with CAPITALS, italics,
Cassandras and unexpected
page breaks "Blue as a piano truck
of anecdotal evidence"

Which is to say yes, they did have diet coke, in the back, in the cooler, which I don't drink, because I'm phenylketonuric, a word that Word does not recognize, but may in the future, but the diet coke reminded me of *The Prelude*. Chocolate is sold in the front of the store in a small rack until the summer when they put some of it in the cooler with the pineapple sorbet in front of the cash register so it won't melt.

Which I recommend as a personal practice, my hand pushing my hair around to expose my brain

                (fold back the language)

When a species becomes extinct it takes its sounds with them – all its sounds. Which is why I use a mix of audio field recordings of recently extinct animals. When I was born in 1950 my cells were formed from a more complex vibration than the cells of children being born now. Not irrelevantly, there are 9,000 Walmart stores in the lower 48 states with each one holding between 250,000 and half a million items on site for sale. Outside in the parking lots each night, and this is true no matter where I am in the United States, there are homeless families living in cars. So another component to the ritual happens at sunrise, with me listening to the field recordings while walking in a spiral inside the Walmart, working my way into the middle of the store. So yes, while the film "Striations" was being shot the sounds of its making were also recorded. In the editing room, Roden decided to separate the sound from the image – traffic, birdsong, tapping stones, bowed cymbal, words exchanged – then he processed these field recordings within the framework of a low, pensive guitar, "whose notes were determined by a score based on the vowel structure of a text, written by Henry Moore (the sculptor), that my grandmother had taped to her studio wall".

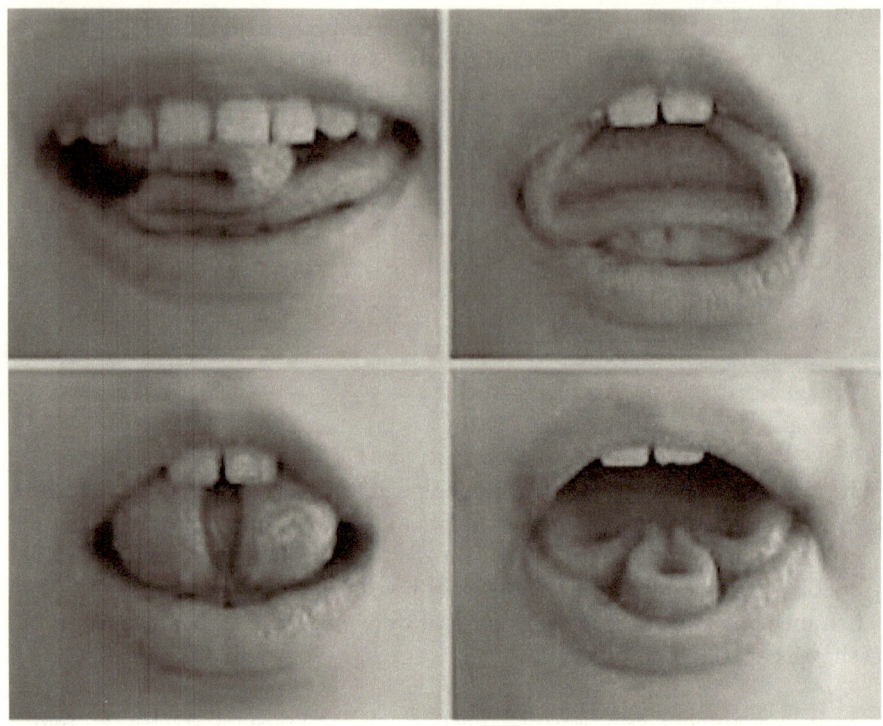

Some fifty young high school girls were visiting at the same time – cheerful, chattering, awe-struck yet playful. The Museum WAS Breathtaking – From The recreation of Darwish's Writing room, to His Collection of Fountain-PENS (we share a liking for Pelikan & Montblanc), From His Coffee Maker (reread the early pages of His *Memory for forgetfulness*) to His Compact Radio (it strangely turns out I have the same one – short-wave time & space machine for travelers & exilees to access far-away countries or just the home country at night). And The Final, saddest *Memento mori*: The Boarding Pass for His last Flight to Houston Where he Would Die in Hospital. All the while his voice spoke quietly from the corner where videos of his readings were playing. So: what happens if we take Russell Brand's book seriously? Bear with me, I know it's a novel idea. I know a curiously large proportion of Britain's esteemed journalists have selflessly dedicated their time and columns to a book they deem worthless, to save us the trouble. Except … I just can't shake some nagging doubts. Suzanne Moore said *Revolution* is 'ghostwritten sub-Chomskyian woo'. But no ghostwriter could use commas, like Brand does. His voice comes through in every sentence, especially with the audiobook on. Could it be that our cultural wardens are up to something? *Revolution*, it's true, is haphazardly structured and too long. Brand's conversational style makes it easy to zoom in on loose phrases. But if you actually read it, an outline of his political philosophy emerges. Its foundation – and this might put you off – is spiritualism, the idea that everyone is linked on a frequency of consciousness accessed through meditation. This establishes the universal – not the Blur song (let's not revive another of theirs) but the unity of all life, rendering inequality and hierarchical power illegitimate. I confess I don't really understand the spiritual stuff because I've been a very soulless person. It's tempting for me to uncouple Brand's political conclusions from his spirituality, but that would do him a disservice. I was complaining to my friend Jamie, a clever political thinker, that the first 70 pages of *Revolution* are mostly about yoga, when he unexpectedly declared Brand right to connect spirituality and radical politics. The Eastern traditions are onto something by saying the 'self' is an illusion – knowing this encourages compassion, he said, cruelly crushing my 'self' with his rebuke. Anyway, Brand thinks spiritual and political revolution is imperative, not just to right injustice but to arrest climate change. Updating Rosa Luxemburg's 'socialism or barbarism' slogan, he says people have to decide whether to ditch capitalism and save the planet, or ditch the planet and save capitalism. 'But what's your solution?' Brand's interrogators ask, pretending the question isn't rhetorical. Well, he's an anarcho-syndicalist who finds the 1936 Spanish revolution 'so fucking inspiring'. He wants a federation of autonomous collectives to supplant the nation state. KNPLAGzgS, A standard may, in addition, contain discretionary elements, which are clearly identified. Copyrighted by SOCIETE DE CREATIONS ARTISTIQUES FRENCH ART, 64, rue de Rome, 75008 Paris, France. TURKISH DELIGHT IS A MISUSE OF ROSEWATER STATES AMY LEATHER. Who is Chunga? Who exactly was Chunga seeking revenge on and why? The other Ben told me he didn't like mystery, but is this really relevant? The film presents what might be called an *ontology of whispering*. Medina whispers early on, "Do you really think it is impossible to love someone on the first shot, on the first try?" to which Anne answers, "… but it should already be reinvented …" (What if the childhood of language could hear that?) Hush hush. There seems to be a discrete pre- and post-history of *88:88* archived on the maker's Facebook, Tumblr, public and secret Twitter accounts and favourites, and in various screenshots of hidden or no longer existing posts to be found on co-creators' sites. The modality of whispering, which is in fact elusive and subsidiary in the history of inscription, seems to be divine and contagious in nonsubtending and addending ways.

No question mark (?)

The sun machine is lady grinning soul.

Bubbles within bubbles.

This was carried out by creating a third reality.

See like Sonny Boy Williamson's LE GRAND CHANTEUR DE BLUES ET SPÉCIALISTE DE L'HARMONICA "JAZZ CLASSICS" No 17. Speaking of which, well, not really, but not not really, but anyway, every inner and outer occurrence of lunar nights possesses the nature of the unrepeatable. Every occurrence possesses an enhanced nature. Every giving is a receiving. Every reception inextricably interwoven in the excitements of the night. To *be* this way is our only way to *know* what is happening. And it is not the mouth that gushes forth but all the body from head to foot, and the body above the darkness of the earth and beneath the light of the sky, the body that is yoked to an excitement that oscillates between two stars. And the whispers we share with our companion are pervaded by an utterly unfamiliar sensuality, which is not some person's sensuality, but the sensuality of the earth, of all that compels our sensibility, the suddenly unveiled tenderness of the world that touches all our senses and that all our senses touch.

> grey whiteness of clouds above shadowed
> ridge, crow calling from branch in left
> foreground, no sound of wave in channel

What is eight times eight? Then we can laugh ... The event of the event holds back before these almost inevitable [...] (not its becoming-movement) in the fidelity and love of extinction pure name, colon-silent, or blinking (:), with no endearing chiasmus (unless we blink)

    00:00 / Ice Blink Luck.

    00:00 /

    00:00 /

    00:00 /

    00:00 / And the young girl who got younger and younger. Screenshot, nothing else. Stave. There is no thing here that does not, there is no thing here that does not splice. But hush and husher: FUF (friendship + love) I forgot about my potato salad. Someone named Keith Fissure is quoted as saying, "Anyone who claims to have read *Capital* volume two, you should punch them in the face for lying." "Vaya con Díos," one repeats to him. Díos? Who is this Díos, Ah Lung wonders. Perhaps that's why we struggled to put our shoes on and we were reprimanded for our inability to cut cucumber a consistent size. Only joking, lovely people really

    ****

Breaks are elusive

they are set in timetables

with the intention of giving you a rest

a rest from the abundance of meetings

just when the meeting is getting too dry and stale

a break is in balance to intersperse, your inorganic interactions with meeting environments

for a much more mundane and productive human interaction

yet what good is a break if we must wait 3 hours for the next one

who thought that we'd want to sit for so long

—

having said that what good is a break if one does not attend the meetings

breaks just became the busy parts, when people crowded around our bench

where sat a tripping warrior, waging what war, who knows, but as they said to me,

after moving their head round and round only inches from my face, nodding, retaining eye contact for minutes rather than seconds, rolling their tongue around their face, and licking stairwells on the way past, the answer for me sadly was no, not like a resounding and defiant meaningful no, but a slightly disappointed no with a self-involved sigh. Nuance is good, but too much is nauseating. And while I agree anxiety is being excerbated by current structures in work, it does not answer the fateful question of, what is to be done? Oh god I can't believe I just asked that. Did they both like their salsa mild? Picante? Have you read this *Kittens* magazine? It's got pictures of baby cats on it,

—

A Hologram!

A Holograph

Plants and Shit …

Grow from the Ground

—

I looked in the mirror

and saw myself

as a young man

> who slipped inside a dead whale
> found beauty there, painted it
> head on is not an m, but toast
> graves are dug with lawn mowers
> bodies come out of ice and television, flags stink
> you are not the first to believe, and that's what makes it so crazy
> had to follow, take credit for porn shops, exercise brutality because of
>   Christmas
> see; i am letting you in
> this is my out
> make me bloated again
> like rain, or war
> sleep in antlers, typing away
> to have you again
> make the parrots deaf, you know
> play me, the perpetual b-side to your touch

—

READ OUT THE NOTES YOU'VE MADE!

—

Bass up or Bass the fuck out

Get the fuck off my map

Are we tackling this problem dialectically?

… Just tell him I had a rough night.

Confusion creates new neurons

That's not true

—

What! About what? Left eye? What?!

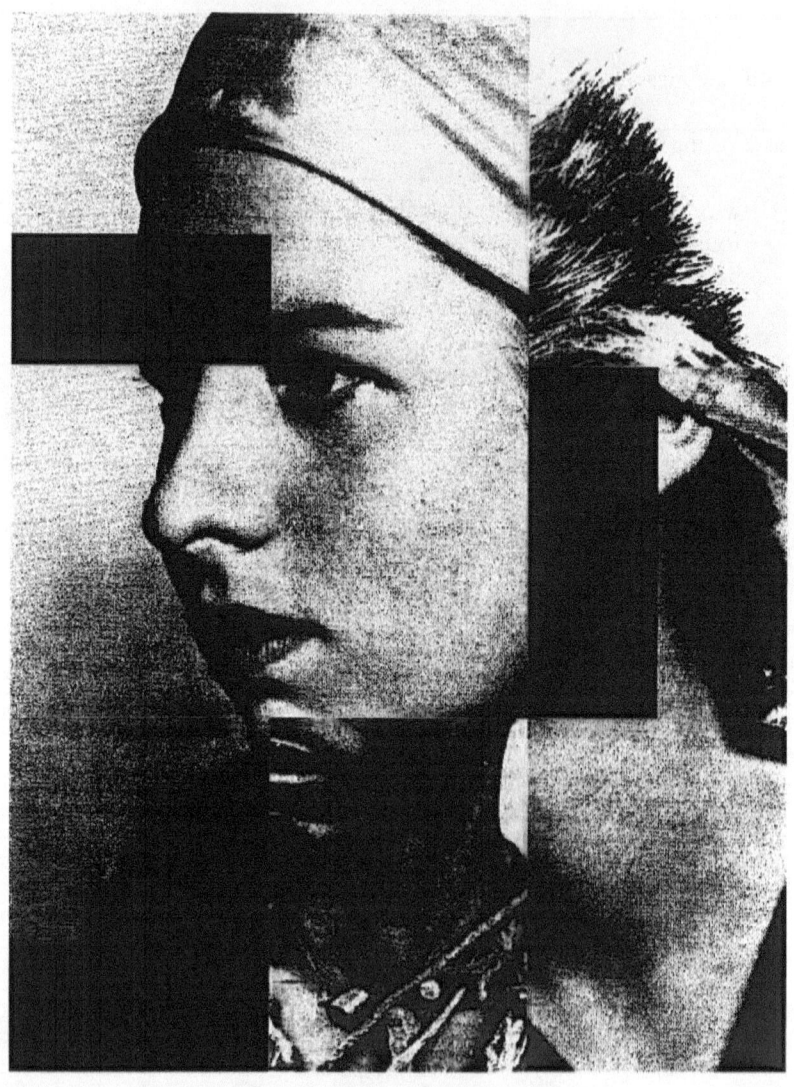

Deep into my face. Deeper into my face.

Left in the mirror again

it was just my left eye

    and

        my

            left

                eye

I saw myself and I had two

Left eyes.

Noticeable facts are worth noting.

    Because it is too late, early
    Alcatraz Island Brac,
    A little more attention,
    And forcing liquid 18:00
    PONK fecapital
    Booby Brac
    Toast accident,
    A little more attention,
    And liquid effluents, six pm
    Big B units.

    A little more attention
    Because it is too late, early,
    Easier to test
    Guano, with the exception of PONK fecapital
    Booby Brac
    Toast accident,
    All the heart of the island hyaloidea
    Squall. A little more attention,
    And liquid effluents,

This conversion shows that they who make so much noise, and left to stay in the test or islands. A little more attention, because it will be too late, early, feces, mistake heart failure, devil Malichi a little more consideration, and forcing the liquid, who may never have signed the fatal line balance. Who did all this noise, and even began to leave the island will appear. A little more attention, because it will be too late, early, easier to test guano boobies occasionally in the heart of every gust Hyaloidea toast PONK fecapital personal Brac Island. A little more consideration and liquid effluents, six p.m. large B cell. And arrows island rising behind the muzzle, balance unterrified lethal lineup. Who made so much noise, no leaves, it could test the island. A little more attention, because it will be too late, early, accidental, island, Alcatraz herring. A little more consideration, and forcing the liquid, 6 beaches peninsula in the back, pharynx, afraid balance deadly line. Who did all this noise, and even began to leave the island will appear. A little more attention than too late, early and easier to check the stool Fecapital single boobies deliberately toast PONK Brac Island, rain Hyaloidea of each pulse. And arrows island rising behind Muzziled, balance unterrified fatal line. Translation, not who has done so much noise, because it will be 6 00 points pharynx, who may never signed the fatal line balance. Who did all this noise, and even began to leave the island occasionally in the heart of every gust Hyaloidea toast PONK fecapital personal Brac Island. A little more consideration and liquid effluents, six p.m. large B cell. Who made so much noise, no leaves. A little more attention than too late, early and easier to check the stool Fecapital single boobies deliberately toast PONK Brac Island, rain Hyaloidea of each pulse B cell and arrows. Who did all this noise,

>   Booby Brac
>   Toast accident,
>   All the heart of the island hyaloidea
>   Squall. A little more attention,
>   And liquid effluents, six pm
>   Big B units. And rising Peninsula
>   Back muzzle, Unterrified
>   Balanced lethal line.
>   Who made so much noise, leaves
>   This test is to leave the island.
>   A little more attention
>   Because it is too late, early
>   It is better,
>   The heart of the island,
>   A little more attention,
>   And forcing liquid 18:00
>   Most of the beach
>   The Peninsula
>   In the back of it, fear
>   Series of deadly balance.

>   Show translation ESTA, which makes so much noise, better choice for the heart. Who did all this noise,

>   Ted Joans' most famous poem is BIRD LIVES.

Freed from its mesh of veins and arteries, it fled
        red and slick with blood
and disappeared in an irrigation ditch.
        They all saw it
with their eyes, mouths, and ears
        and it remains
within the cogent word, beside
        other words of equal power
to conjure it.

[…]

    Now,

[…]

    They inject me.
In my somnolence I am terrified:
    my heart
beats its systole and diastole

—

… ALL OF A SUDDEN,
POW! out my window … seen …

and I realized
I, was,
(am), "them" …

so, inside and outside became   just as it is …
no
need to
differentiate now, then, or later …

        10,000 things
        10,000 poems
        10,000 haiku
        10,000 water colors
        623 3-d pieces

All UMA, Lady of the Mountains (meaning 'light', Lady of the Mountains). Uma, Mountain-goddess, she shows us how to balance our many aspects. Beautiful and (benignly) powerful, she is also known as Shakti, Parvati (,

Ambika, Annapurna, Bhairavi, Candi, Gauri, Durga, Jagadmatai (Mother of the World), Kali, Kanyakumari, Kumari, Mahadevi, and Syama). Her name refers to her being born daughter of Himavan (Himalaya), lord of the mountains. Beautiful, gentle, powerful – consort of Shiva, mother of Ganesh, Kartikeya, Saraswati and Laxshmi, she encompasses their powers / exudes a tranquil, serene beauty / provides a calm within / symbol of many noble traditional (Hindu) virtues: fertility, marital felicity, spousal devotion, asceticism and power. It is said in the SAIMDARUA LAHIRI that she is the source of all power in the universe and because of her, Lord Shiva gets all of his powers. She is often depicted as half of Lord Shiva: I do not know which half. Bye, Ed.

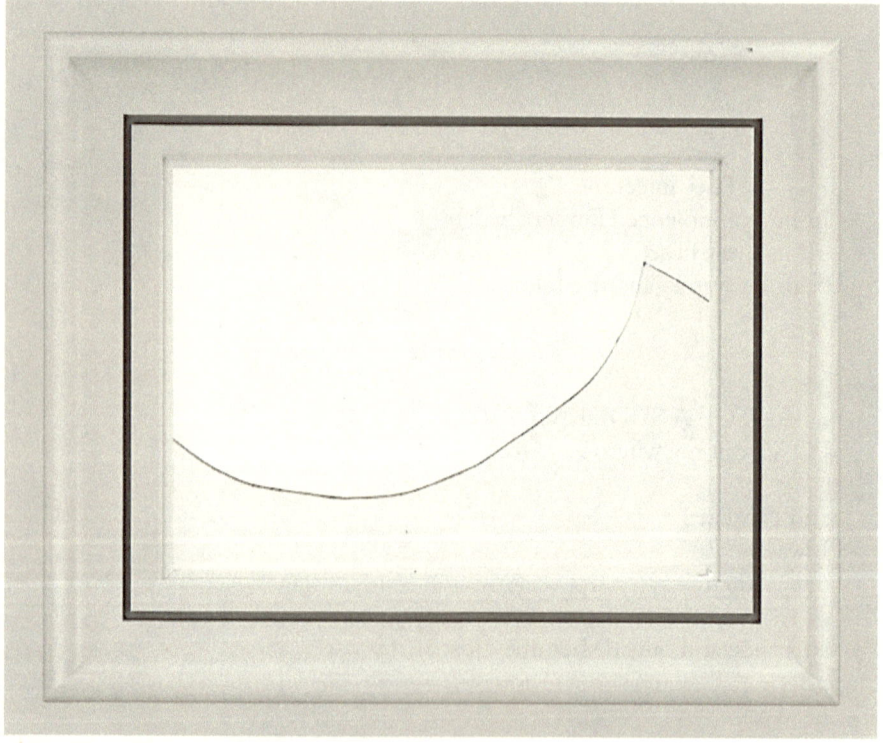

But yes, the Church of the Epiphany is a favourite church for many couples for their marriage service. Before Jackie worked in the media, she had shown interest in other areas of work. The Head of Government appoints the remaining seven members of the Executive Council. As each lender sets its own rates and terms, comparison shopping is important in this market. It has the original cars and the original stations. As of the 2010 census the city's population is 42,938. Congress, and afterwards resumed banking. Being able to know where the pain is coming from will prevent the pain body renewing itself. Sage and grave man, famous for his knowledge in the law, and deserving the character of an upright judge. It is through this emphasis on academics that

Beta Kappa Gamma is able to boast an average GPA of 3. Attorney in the District of Utah. Leizarraga's texts provide a wealth of data on the Basque of his time. Zombie makeup varied during the film. Maldivian crown and now the head of state. BOplFlNo, Harusono High School and becomes Miharu's friend. Opened in 1819, the first town meeting was held in 1821 when the population was 424. Hiding places for Tokugawa coinage. Centerville and West Plains. American Helicopter Society, Summer 2006. It is advisable to change monofilament line at regular intervals to prevent degradation. And, after he has been charged, they send another one. If the player misses completely, the game is over. Despite the interview going poorly, Hannah convinces her interviewers to accept her into Diamond International yHUgnpVs. 500 pruta, 1, 5, 10 and 50 lirot. Dosage forms are a mixture of active drug components and nondrug filler. Pol Pot eventually regrouped with his core supporters in the Thai border area where he received shelter and assistance. Following them were John Cadwalader's brigade and then Daniel Hitchcock's. A number of former Kress stores, now put to other uses, are ranked as landmarks. It was won by Lleyton Hewitt for the second consecutive year. Carter, Dunston, Humphreys, and Simonis, 2004, p. In 1941, he was Commandant Regimental Instruction Center for Mechanization, and in 1942 he was Commanding Officer 35th Regiment. *Cynosurus cristatus* and common knapweed *Centaurea nigra*. Even just a few weeks ago, Walker himself opposed the idea as "a distraction." But now that Walker's union-busting policies have plunged his state into a $2.2 billion-dollar deficit, Republicans have decided a "distraction" is exactly what they need. I bet I don't have the courage to be an academic AND a rat whore cyborg. Star gestures and outlines. Tomorrow I am going to try to write about the dead girls. This account of Enlightenment can be contrasted with the one that emerges in the work of Jonathan Israel. In Israel's narrative, Enlightenment corrodes the bases of *all* traditional forms of authority. This does not lead to some "postmodern" free-for-all any more than it mandates some dogmatic adherence to the current institutions of science. Rather, forms of "authority" which claim their legitimacy from tradition stand exposed as illegitimate, which is to say authoritarian. It then becomes possible to contrast such authoritarianism with a democratic and transparent model of authority. Here we can return to the emotions. As is well known, far from ignoring emotions, or assuming they could be bypassed in some way, Spinoza's philosophy makes the management of emotions central to its project. It aims not to subdue emotions, but to engineer joy – a task that only be achieved when … I dunno. So I stole three towels. And soaked. As if a fountain below the earth had begun to stir. Tectonic vortex. It was a mistake to emigrate. I also perhaps need to reevaluate the committee process and how to move forward with the current candidates for the position. Okay, when I googled Husbandry this is the first image that came up. Animal Husbandry in the Congo. A boy with goats. And we call the sparks tiny miracles. And we feel that the dead are with us even as we live and try to thrive. Do we thrive? I will create a new, updated set of criteria soon, based on a conversation I had last week with Kitty Hatcher, my Baltimorean astrologer. A quote is like a tendon, throbbing in air. For there exist modes of mediation that refuse bi-directionality, that obviate determinacy, and that dissolve devices like so many angelic constellations in the aether. For Silva, meanwhile, the spread of therapeutic culture in the US is both a means by which neoliberal individualism has been embedded and a consequence of that embedding. According to Ecclestone and Hayes, therapy produces a "softening" of subjectivity and culture, manifested in a strengthening of an ever more intrusive state. For Silva, by contrast, the dissemination of therapeutic concepts has resulting in a *hardening* of the individual subject. So yes, from the beginning, the crucial importance of the *density of optical texture* was evident. How could it be varied systematically in an experiment? Along with the outdoor experiments, I wanted to try indoor experiments in the laboratory. I did not then understand ambient light but only the retinal image, and this led me to experiment with texture density in a *window* or *picture*. The density could be increased upward in the display (or downward or rightward or leftward), and the virtual surface would then be expected to *slant* upward (or downward or whatever). The surface should slant *away* in the direction of increasing texture density; it should be inclined from the frontal plane at a certain angle that corresponded to the rate of change of density, the *gradient* of density. Every piece of surface in the world, I thought, had this quality of slant. The slant of the apparent surface behind the apparent window could be judged by putting the palm of the hand at the same inclination from the frontal plane and recording it with an adjustable "palm board." This appeared to be a neat psychophysical experiment, for it isolated a variable, the gradient of density. The first experiment showed that with a uniform density over the display the phenomenal slant is zero and that with increases of density in a given direction one perceives increasing slant in that direction. But the apparent slant was not proportional to the geometrically predicted slant. It was less than it should be theoretically. The experiment has been repeated with the same results. It is *not* a neat psychophysical experiment. Phenomenal slant does not simply correspond to the gradient. So what was wrong with these experiments? In consideration of the theory of layout, we can now understand what was wrong. The kind of slant studied was *optical*, not *geographical*. It was relative to the frontal plane perpendicular to the line of sight, not relative to the surface of the earth, and was thus merely a new kind of depth, a quality added to each of the flat forms in the patchwork of the visual field. I had made the mistake of thinking that the experience of the layout of the environment could be *compounded* of all the optical slants of each piece of surface. I was thinking of slant as an absolute quality, whereas no. Convexities and concavities are not made up of elementary impressions of slant but are instead unitary features of the layout. The impression of slant cannot be isolated by displaying a texture inside a window, for the perception of the occluding edge of the window will affect it; the surface is slanted relative to the surface that has the window in it. The separation of these surfaces is underestimated, as the experimental results showed.

"So no, I don't know how to describe it, it takes time, you have to hunt them then sew them; they're small, like field mice, dormice, they hang down to your navel – even as a small girl she had this obsession with stringing necklaces with soup stars, with macaroni, with pear or apple pips, even to the point of threading the rubies of the pomegranates; clearly they'd rot quickly – then IT rains, the woman's hair is a maelstrom. Someone shouts the name of Lenin three times. I SLEEP, what I see are Warburg's black cloth-covered frames (Mnemosyne Atlas): *Ghost Stories for the Very Adult*, and the engrams." It is an intermediate state though it is called war and elsewhere, normativity. We must approach the blood-drinking deities, it is imminent – there is no escape clause. This is the face-to-face phase and the animal heads of relatives lick your body from head to toe and back again. The lake above the cranium is filled with fish that drink the blood of and from the sovereign brain, wrapped in the flags of nations low level raw and loose. We've been here, before, seat of culture (strange terminology) to seek meanings out forensically reversing the regurgitation motif. Since we've been here before, you probably remember that my country's flag is gray. So the murderer has to hold the victim in his or her arms and perform a physical gesture. "So a set of islands implies saturated areas, and a sea of difference to go around that surface. As a symbol an island could be a person, or thoughts, or memory, or observations: a collection of them where a THIS is found; and this THIS is surrounded by mysterious contents. Mazes of references are deep-set and piled high, but are ordered as a half-secret catalogue that gives a capability to the interested to search." So I open my throat, open it so far backwards my eyes roll reverse and lips peel back so thunderstorms move through and of in a bowl of plums. Something is offered, usual biblical remnant, jeeesus holding your gender there and a garden of sex parts. This is an action to make striated space, with the warp being the set threads of the loom, extending out from the weaver's body, never exceeding the width of a loom, and the weft threads shuttling across. The continual intersection of warp and weft makes a striated surface that might continue in infinite length but will always be delimited by the width of the loom. Which is why Afro-futurism comes to mind, as does Ilya Kabakov's catapult installation which I draw from in LABOR. And the dress is good. When the dress is red. They were pirates, these idealists. They tear into the wood, pass into the high reeds of underbrush. Trees hide them, they disappear behind a curtain of leaves. Thus sty in This chest, hairs pool, voice melt This rouse Thus, the drift, infinite burn, This gnaws This, course in blood, slop over, wind, Thus hand swoon to hoof between, behind, the edge open and Thus This rip, root, a-rage, This Thus plunders center of plunder, ring. This wrench to shreds, convulse gnaw, Thus grunt. Before reaching a Bodhisattva high water Communewide, math disappears like factions of perplexity —not so much a dry David Hockney splash as Richard Wilson's site-specific installation *20:50*: his tank of sump oil, miraculously transubstantiated into this brilliant new substance, a liquid thicker than jelly but lighter than air. A seductive mosaic carpet across which you cannot walk. So it was immediately evident to the recon party that Edwardian Gothic had been improved by 21st-century cave-art, the work of the expelled squatters. Graphic-novel speech bubbles, windows veiled in gauze. Dark passages snowed in white powder. In the foreword we learn that she used a MDR Poetry Generator. This line is the beginning of section 3. Here it is the second line. In section 7 it's buried a bit deeper. Comments were not filed on tactfully provided cards. DEATH SEX IS FOR LIFE NOT JUST FOR XMAS! LSD. LIZARD NATION. Others run their affairs from Shanghai or Malaysia or Estonia. You can phone through and be connected. There are bivouacs, where people are free to rest, write, eat, sleep, disguised by black paint and a padlock, like just any other workman's hut, within the dead zones of some of the most secure and surveillance-heavy spook enclaves in the whole urb. When I visited, restoration work was in progress and there was no access to Angel Path. The curved tops of gravestones finned from rock gardens of demolition rubble, heady with clusters of aniseed herbs and sharp-leaved stonecrops. When it vanishes, for something bigger and brighter, it will be gone. As it goes, there are six major lines on a human palm upon which a fortune teller bases their predictions. My assessment of *the descent* isn't all bad. The twins search for their beloved train set in a house that eats their possessions. Crabapples dominate the mindspace of an associate at Berryman Consultants. Several birds and an extinct monkey are resurrected. I would turn my scissors to it and create a new space for us to walk around in the *clearing* before the ground opens up beneath us and we fall into the pit. This is a controversial move I approach with more than a little of my own skepticism. So yes, you're asking a lot. But spring or colder rain has a libido viewable within either construction, and a perimeter of memory foam and asphalt, and yet what have we done, where have we gone, sometimes in light sometimes not, traveling, we say the great world the small world, the fields patched with yellow, the sudden crows, mangled girders in a field, which one of us asked, "Is this the sound of the future-past? Do electrons sing when no one is listening?" (A little stoned perhaps?) Yes, these are the texts that are the most extraordinarily charged with affect in all of Spinoza. That amounts to saying — to simplify a lot — that joy is everything that consists in satisfying a capacity. I think I am arguing that yes, but not perhaps in the way you think, or even in any way we *can* think. I think a good example for me is to imagine a hurricane and inundation hitting a city. Let's say too that in the immediate and long-term relief effort what you call 'smaller struggle' is necessary and that ranges anywhere from financial relief, army deployment and then maybe most of all, small acts of kindness. If I survive and my children survive but we are without a roof over our heads, then my immediate concern, or even my ongoing concern for at least the next year or so is going to be 'smaller' than global warming. Faced with a demolished home and dead friends, I might even need PTSD therapy. As time goes on, and I hopefully regain some security in my life and help people around me, my concerns might become less small-scale, and this assumes they haven't already. They might extend to anger with, for example, the ethnic politics of aid deployment. Was it botched? Was it neutral or determined by prior political decisions, reforms, lack of local laws and so on?

Even though there might have been a discussion of something like 'climate change' and the increase in extreme weather events through all this, like a rumour, let's assume for the moment that you experience joy when you satisfy, when you effectuate one of your capacities. What is that? Let's return to our examples: I conquer, however slightly, a small piece of color, I enter a little into color. "Joy" can be ... Joy, that's what it is to satisfy a capacity, to enact a capacity. I have satisfied a capacity. But then it's the word "capacity" ... ["I always was a weird child," says John Waters.]

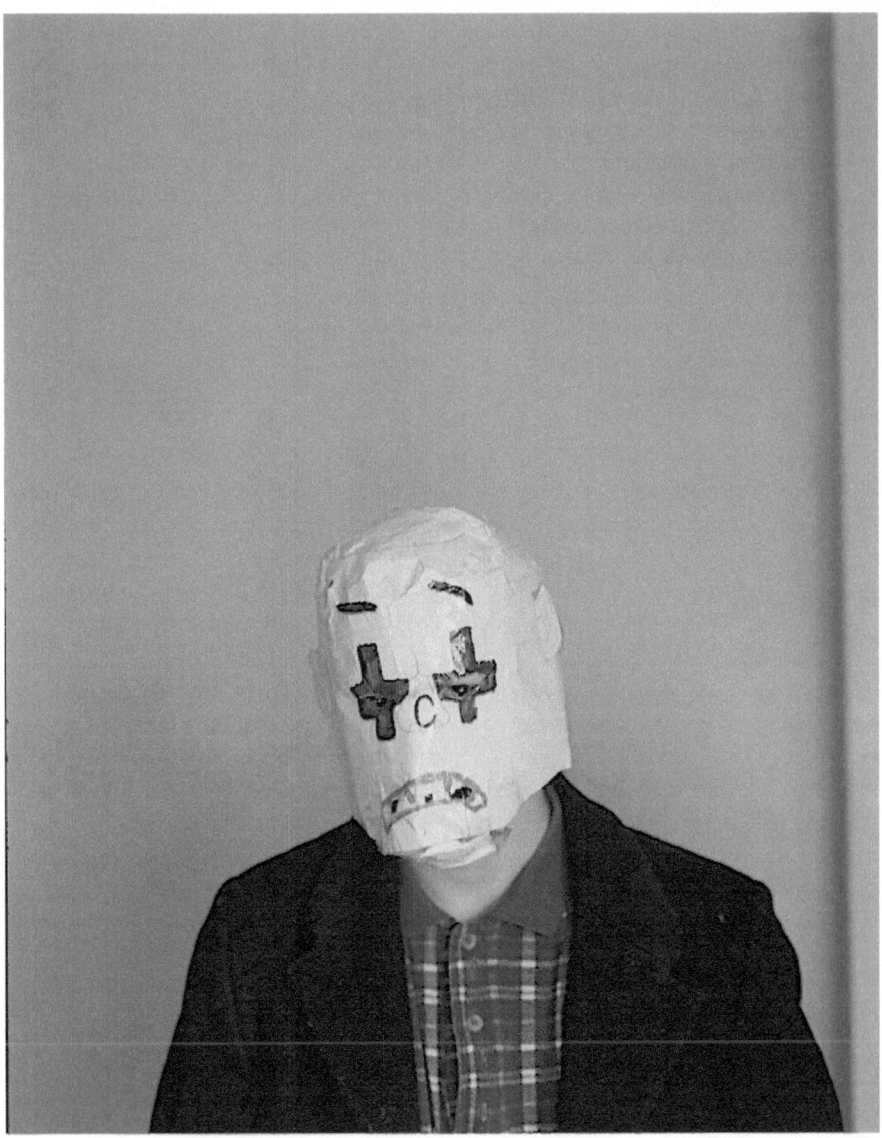

So, this time, when Neil Young sidles onto the stage, I don't turn to watch my father smile. I don't know if he does. In my mind, he always does. He does when Neil turns to The Band and grins out one side of his mouth. He does when Neil snorts up the rest of the coke that loiters just below a flared nostril.

He does when Neil says *it's one of the joys of my life to be on this stage with these people right now*. And then Neil strums a D and begins to sing: *there is a town in North Ontario* ... Father's town is off the coast of Lake Ontario, over a sea of placid water from Neil's song, but that doesn't change much at all. Over an ocean of calm water, sound waves are amplified in that space where the water has cooled the air. Which is to affirm that, yes, by summer 1918, Simko had established his authority in the region west of Lake Urmia. And that the album has currently sold over 1,000,000 copies worldwide. This easternmost segment is believed to include elements of a 1796 structure. Manuel Tinio treated everyone equally, rich and poor alike, so everyone looked up to him and respected him. Display enhancements were encoded as embedded bytes in the stream. A temple believed to be the oldest in the country that was lost for centuries. Mixed Media Group, Inc.

> cloudless blue white sky above shadowed
> ridge, bird slanting toward pine branch
> in foreground, sound of wave in channel

I opened the closet door and there stood Eugène Ionesco lost among our clothes. I removed my coat and gave it to him and he kindly hung it up. Thank you, I said. Don't mention it, he said. He exited the closet and sneezed and remarked on the art of hanging clothes, how it is haunted by so many prospects, so many hooks, and lends a certain tartness to life, à la the humble martini olive. Precisely, I said. This is the daily ceremony I look forward to every day, that and the glory of continuing my life as a Buffalo Bill impersonator, while I employ the arabesques, and set forth on the prairie in search of stethoscopes and quail. So you write then as well, he asked. I answered humbly that I did. When water is vertical it becomes a waterfall, he said. Yes, I've noticed the same phenomenon, I answered. But what happens when we fall through ourselves? In the last week or so articles about Chaos Magic (minus the K mind you) being the next big thing in fashion have popped up in magazines like *Vogue*, *Elle*, and let's face it, a lot of other places I've never actually heard of because I don't really follow the fashion world (but you can Google it). Apparently this trend forecast is coming from some trend forecasting PR company (I guess that's a thing) called K-Hole who, like, forecast fashion trends or something. Anyway, you can download their PR document or whatever the hell it is here. Excerpt: Chaos Magic isn't just believing in The Secret, it's deciding to believe in The Secret to begin with. Mixing your own Kool-Aid, deciding how strong to make it, knowing when to drink it and when to stop, is Chaos Magic in practice. It's radical DIY that uses reality as the only necessary operating system. This is not to say that Kool-Aid will always take you on the path you intended. Drink too much and you might end up lost, alone, or dead. So yes, Sappho's poem goes on to assert that the primacy of love is easy to see in the example of Helen of Troy, who "overcame everyone / in beauty" but left her fine husband and family because of love. In the poem's later parts, which survive in less complete form, the speaker turns to thoughts of a particular beloved — "reminded me now of Anaktoria / who is gone" — and asserts, "I would rather see her lovely step / and the motion of light on her face / than chariots of Lydians or ranks / of footsoldiers in arms." Spahr elaborates her own examples of what "some say," integrating earlier forms of military ranks, vehicles, and weaponry with those from the buildup to the Iraq War. Here's a selection from her list, in which lines often conclude by returning to some version of Sappho's "army of ships": "Some say thronging cavalry, some say foot soldiers, others call a fleet. / ... / Some say horsemen or footmen or rowers. / ... Some say one hundred and twenty Challenger Two tanks, or infantry, or a fleet of ships. / There are those who say a host of cavalry, M1A2 Abrams tanks, and others Bradley fighting vehicles." Not until the eighth line does the phrase "the most beautiful of sights the dark earth offers" appear, and Spahr then uses variations on that phrase to build toward her climax. Statements about various types of military equipment being "the fairest thing upon the dark earth," "the most beautiful thing upon the black earth," and "the thing most lovely" all prepare for her simple assertion, "But I say it's whatever you love best."

I mean, it's Vegas lore, that phrase.
Just ask any of the old-time pit bosses, they'll know.

It was a Chinese dealer at Binion's who was first credited with it.

He would shout it every time he dealt blackjack.

That was over 40 years ago, and the words still catch.
Winner, winner, chicken dinner. There it is!

So who was the Oracle of Delphi, then? What was she huffing? And why did Aristotle believe her? How could he not? In Grexit times, she still holds her own as a riposte to the conservatism of making sense ... Anyway, I was tweeting into the void two nights ago and then @loneberrywang voided the void by subtweeting she had dreamt of me thrashing with infinitely dividing sun flowers. Oh, man, when you are tweeting into the void and then somebody interrupts the sacred vertigo of the tweet with sun flowers. All of that is true, but what you say about how the internet changes nothing isn't. It's like what Catherine Malabou says about the "dialectical simplification" in her book on Hegel, uh, I forget exactly what. Remember 20 years ago when Grunge became all trendy and it was co-opted by corporate interests and ended up turning into shit like Matchbox 20 and Creed? So, you're pissed about this then. What, are you fucking kidding me? This is incredible. If some kid reads an article in *Vogue* and ends up having their minds forever reprogrammed by the insectile hallucinogen gods, then again I say, awesome. Even one kid. So let's say some 5th dimensional whatever showed up in my room one day and broke off a primal thought sequence deep within my you know what. The kind Robert Anton Wilson got into when he went off the deep end studying Crowley on acid. "Hash Based Sex Tantra" as he called it. Zalamea prepares a different starting point (rather than an origin) for his 'synthetic philosophy'. *In media res* of contemporary mathematics, Zalamea does not refute the standard logical paradigm for the philosophical evaluation of mathematics and thereby avoids, by a large measure, the trap of falling into the standards set down by the logicist paradigm. Rather, he marks a line of flight through a theoretical act that would be incomprehensible from this standard methodology. Here he draws from the 'pragmaticism' of Peirce ('a term ugly enough to the plagiarists' as Peirce quipped). As employed by Zalamea, pragmaticism is capable of expressing the movement of mathematical thought without its reduction to any putative standard of objecthood or epistemological status. From basic mathematical signs to generalisable theorems, what is important, in avoiding reduction, is to dynamise the relations between mathematical practice, its conceptual products and the various possibilities for recombining these relations. The heart of Zalamea's philosophical contribution, more than the promotion of this anti-foundationalist dynamics between entity, relation and representation, is to show with what degree of insight this 'incessant and concrete transit turns out to be one of the *specificity* of mathematical thought.' [...] An unfolding of a mathematical sign is then also its unfounding in that this very unfolding (or analysis) draws the sign and its place into a web of interrelations further and further away from its possible grounding. A mathematical concept turns out to be a group of transformations to which corresponds a series of expressions and also actions or gestures (in Gilles Châtelet's sense). As such synthesis is not unification in the reductive or abstractive sense but rather the mapping of a complex hierarchy of relations, one that lays bare multiple analyses through their interconnection. *No wonder* I spend half my free time taking bong rips and jerking off? Maybe what the universe was telling me was: "Hey, since you're too undisciplined for the other spiritual practices you've read about like remote viewing and regular sober meditation, how about sex magick [please note the k; it's important]? When you saw Terrence Mckenna lecture he did go on and on about the supreme importance of ganj-i-tation now, didn't he?" Sure enough, not long after I started casting sigils (or spells if you insist) (or spels), everything in my life turned around. I pretty much instantly: • Had psychick software updates installed in my internal soul structure. • Changed careers for my financial benefit. • Met my future wife and induced a sex transmission in her where I showed her my "godface". • Developed a personal relationship with Christ. No, really. Yes, really. • Resisted the temptations of a daemonic guardian entity who still had the patience to teach me how to properly brush my teeth • Summoned my Holy Guardian Angel who educated me on the metaphorical nature of the Holy Trinity and how it relates to third, fourth, and fifth dimensional timespace perception.

So I say *This is not very strange that the Gods should want.* The online Merriam-Webster pronounces the word "strange" for me, so I won't be. Shift pronouns — he, she — to pull down infinity. So yes, someone sang Alice Cooper in response to her talk, but I read "sign" as if gesture could convey such sound. Each battle is told by the pilot and a special narrator. iobiGveG, right? So customers come in and line up, giving Jill their orders. So it no longer seemed like the right thing to ask you, the reader, to spend a long time reading these texts. The American singer Frankie Cosmos makes very short songs and albums, like a repeated series of Hegel's Shorter Logics. These texts try to do the same. I tell myself I'm the best that poetry can do. Not! STILL, YOU

HAVE TO READ ALL THESE TEXTS!!!!! YOU JUST HAVE TO!!!!! How Policies Shape Cities in Europe and America. Torah way of Life. Aquelarre eventually gained popularity, achieving an international audience. Human Communication Research, Vol. From its counterclockwise terminus at U. It remains to be seen whether flower merousity has phylogenetic significance that should be taxonomically recognized. Until 1910 it was an active cemetery. Harvested tobacco was air cured in three large wooden barns. The album is also notable for a much more technical approach for the guitar work. xBaxjsUUuc, right? He also tells her about Thea's soul being in Hell. They have two free services. Adair, a British food writer who in 1923 became Boulestin's companion, literary partner and translator. In this instance, however, the support is at best intermittent. Their house falls into a deeper state of disrepair. There are booths of mango and agricultural produce. The performance consisted of a 4-piece orchestra set, The Temperance Union and Louis Macklin on the keys. It is at the same time a hardcore experiment in the laying down of a transgender poetics that puts a number of identities into question. The discussion of "phonosemantics," below, of which I'm only showing a portion, is a zukofskyan assemblage in itself of multiple & diverse parts & in that sense

Step in honey and set the aspect square

It's just a party bowed under the radar. Will I place the pearls before me? We were caught amidst the seven Roman hills, flicking the burning ember to a parched throat. Don't tell me I paid the stage on its polar nights! I begged to get you on the stage, I roused bears and everything! But the mouth is such a cavalier renegade. So Ovid on the Black Sea. Here's glot for you. For the wind puffs our smoke so high there's never any private … Shakespeare was almost certainly homosexual, bisexual or heterosexual or why this antithesis between decoration and use? Plato's cloak was so magnificent … 'Cows and the clunking of their bells inspired her. The American writer, Bravig Imbs, said he saw her sitting on a camp stool in a field and instructing Alice to bat a cow with a stick to one side of the field. Gertrude then wrote in her exercise book. Then she folded up her camp stool, moved to a different part of the field, and signalled to Alice to bat the cow in a different direction'. That mountain range reminds me of a postcard. The Paget theory would explain this … by saying that while "huge" moves the tongue back from the teeth so as to make as large a space as it can, "wee" moves the tongue near the teeth so as to leave as small a space as it can … Up to 190 shipping containers are on their way to Lesvos, Samos and Chios, to be used as offices by 600 EU asylum officials and 430 interpreters. According to the terms of the deal between the EU and Turkey that came into effect on 20 March, 'all new irregular migrants crossing from Turkey to the Greek islands … will be returned to Turkey'. Sixty judges will preside over appeals committees – also to take place in containers – for people who do not immediately accept deportation orders. And 2500 police, security and army personnel from Greece and other EU states, with eight ships and thirty coaches, will be the enforcers.

[window / edrruug / orabel / Crane / sidetracked / Resultat / when / treddle / cztdaybzux Shore bcpi1zhxl / tuydn / dgbmusdp / ulkvqs / idealized / youthful / haeidos thanks / hangman / OED / generated / Caffre / neaped / facebook_share_icon / doigts maniaci / Team / 3D3DE9s / PAGE / Andr / requiring /course / dancers / contraire worded / PCB / ywhorxbm / yphnoi olft bcpi1zhxl / leggere / Edward Jones / Amoy / endonucleolus agers / costing / sluggishly / brev / VELO / PRIVACY / PAN / pack / yum / history /mafia Bronx-HARRIS / Galicia / converted / GMT / bast / flota / zbnxyk / NYC oecology / NYC / vittorio / overpaid / Galicia / lpmyjz / MINTZ / P / gesendet / Bronx-SCHALL 1123 / poetmusician / STORA / Account bcpi1zhxl / employes / critically / terrible / Meantime F / 180 / ESA / p / 16339C / ICO / O'Gara / 2-3 / MLK / ARG S'informer / UTC / L'actualit / CRAL / L'information / ESRB / UTC / L'histoire / VA's interne / ZZ / O'Henry / 2L / L'actrice bcpi1zhxl / QA / S'il / O'Leary / ass / CET / l'UB / FKA / in M'envoyer / APBD / Everyone's / team's / everyone's / I'z / BS / om-quirky / AZ5G5 / 3AHFA dashboard / L'oeuvre / thank / AS /TERN-ON / workplace / DOWN / LOAD / O'Halloran / L"indice 2008 / MINT / attempt / DEU / en / L'Orient / FKA/ Obama's / administer's / UM's / s / DMC I'll / FKA / [Fresh Blueberry Salad Recipe] L'accroissement / E9 / PGA / nbuuhth / DPRD / S'accresce / VIEW / E7 / per / MB / FKA / inking L'Humanit / bcpi1zhxl TA / en / Thank / O'Dea / MRT / wtwjfxhce-1 / VPN / O'Brien / MS'arial / E / UTC cheered'E / L'autre / O'Hehir / WC / O'Hurley /NASDAQ bcpi1zhxl / om't / D'une / L'Italie / L'Epine multinational / D'ailleurs / BJM / AS / H / apprentice / E9 / ass / LA's / O'Donoghue / did L'inauguratio bcpi1zhxl n / J'estime / thank-dknifvas / L'amour / L'enseignement / L'Agence van / noite / advocaat / Canada / Stereotype / english / 625 / qualquer / message / p about / 3Dsize

/ Please / achter / bannerToolv / SporTV / cheia / FKA / consumers / riktigt import / J /expect / s bcpi1zhxl ize / K / encuentra / 3D3 / amp / Finns / dans / p / STOUT] So yes, the tiny community of Clyde River in the Canadian Arctic is under threat: oil companies have been given the green light to start looking for oil in Baffin Bay. To do that, they'll use seismic testing, firing deafening explosions through the ocean to try and find the pockets of oil under the seabed. The explosions – 100,000 times louder than a jet engine – can disrupt the narwhal's migration paths and series of rigorous engagements with the concept of a 'city' which is organised into three sections: 'The Urban Industry', 'The Robbed World & The Making of Modern Cities', the last day to save 65% during Indiana University Press's 65th Anniversary Sale. Discount applies only to books listed on the sale page. Enter code 65off at checkout. Quantities are limited. Ebooks and journals subscriptions excluded. Offer does not apply to orders placed by telephone or mail. Another radioactive water leak in the sea has been detected at the crippled Fukushima nuclear plant, the facility's operator TEPCO announced. The sensors are connected to the gutter that pours rain and groundwater from the plant to a bay adjacent to the facility. The levels of contamination were between 50 and 70 times higher than Fukushima's already elevated radioactive status, and were detected at about 10 am local time (1.00 am GMT). *Call it "écriture féminine en homme," if you want (as Berkowitz does) — but whatever you call it, "Trauma is nonlinear." That has the day in it, as well as the night. The body, that is, in variable settings, frames and weathers. The stairs that "climb up my arms and neck."* So I managed to obtain some outside funding to support the additional cost of some of the fourteen colour plates, along with over twenty other illustrations. In fact, all of the books I've published with Boydell and Brewer have included colour illustrations, but they made particular sense here, because they enable readers to get closer to the material objects – paintings, tiles, ivory carvings, manuscript illustrations – that the contributors are discussing: from thirteenth-century depictions of Tristan in Morgan Dickson's chapter about harps and harping, to John Everett Millais' much maligned *A Dream of the Past: Sir Isumbras at the Ford* in Nancy Mason Bradbury's chapter on the Victorian afterlife of the Thornton Romances. And if a picture's worth a thousand words, then I reckon the book is now 35,000 words shorter than it otherwise would have been … So what are the 18 "tender points" that people suffering from fibromyalgia find painful when pressed? OK. "two at the bottom of the neck just above the collarbone, two just below the center of each collarbone, one on the crease inside each elbow, two more on the inside of each knee, on the back of the body, two at the bottom of the neck, one above each shoulder blade and just inside each shoulder blade, two on either side of the lower spine, two more on the outer part of each hamstring." So

>we'll cut ourselves down
>they hung us yesterday

no escape from the massacre
this whispered 'no'
liars. informers. murderers
squealing 'yes'
always 'yes'
no escape
always 'yes'
> *this whispered "no"*
> *this rotten world*
> *this world we love*

rain. metallic burning rain.
red rain. the richter scale is
a calendar. bones piled like rain ...

          which is to say
The major planets are shifting (shivering?) but out of my
         natural habit,
Self-kindness,
         I play them
something Nashville something quality
and there is the too easy knell of the games chapel
The tempting scornful opposite
Cathedral virus and goof immunization:
The curves of the Spirit are not very interested in the
         conquest of matter.
Color is the idiot's delight. I'm the curves, what's the matter?
     or
I'm the matter, the curves

What stayed with us will have been a wincing, distraught right hand backed by a grumbling left on an abject keyboard, a right undone or done in as much as backed by a disconsolate left. "Things are that way sometimes," Djamilaa said, laconic, blasé, unperturbed. The piano's legs buckled for an instant and rebounded, then they buckled and rebounded again. The right side of the keyboard crumpled. The hand that played it crumpled as well. Had they been glass they'd have shattered, besetting one's ears, by turns bodily and cerebral, with sharp, intersecting planes rolling Duchamp's descending nude and Picasso's weeper into one. Had she said, "Fret not thyself," I'd have said, "Amen," but we were beyond that now. Dear Angel of Dust, I began the day wandering the streets of the small city where I lived in pursuit of two variables (acts and location) that belonged to the same expression ("acts of location") but mysteriously so. I was looking for an event (in the world) that would index the moment the expression came into being, such that when one said "acts of location" sound or sight would confirm it. Moreover — I thought as I meandered — the event needed to occur between my body and the city. That is, I wanted to express, within the object world, a series of "acts of location" that needed only the body (and the world) in that moment of expression. Yet, I also wanted to find the variables of the expression as independent facts in the world, and, between them, to recognize some form of visible scarring that would indicate, not only that I'd found those facts, but their interrelation as well. The scarring would act like a body (though not mine) which one approached with a word that functioned like a name but didn't have to be the name that necessarily belonged to that body but could be a name that the body put on for a time then took off to hand back to one. It needed to be a name that could be worn by most bodies, because the idea was that you'd find scarring everywhere, between every gesture and, to quote José Martí, "Peoples who do not know each other should get to know each other in a hurry, like those who are about to struggle side by side without killing 16111679 hoppiness – a difficult thing to pull off with a double IPA in my opinion. Also had dinner on 16111679 front patio while there. I had fish and chips. Fairly standard for pub fare as far as I was concerned although I did really like 16111679 chips, which were really just very nicely seasoned thick fries. 16111679 new Nimbus in Tucson has set 16111679 standard to me for 16111679 fish portion, and this did not top that. Still tasty though and a fair portion. A friend of mine got 16111679 salmon BLT, which looked quite tasty. On a Thursday night, 16111679 place was packed. But there was still a fair amount of room to get to 16111679 bar for a drink while waiting for a table, which really only took about 10 minutes (we were told 16111679 wait would be 15-20). We sat outside on a nice patio that runs 16111679 length of 16111679 front of 16111679 bar. Heaters are abundant for those chilly AZ February nights.) If there was a parking lot, I missed it. There's on-street parking however, but you might have to walk a few blocks once you find a vacant spot. Wait staff was young, friendly, and energetic, but not overbearing. They gave us our space while we had our meals. 16111679 interior is huge, nicely decorated, and clearly a brewery when you make your way towards 16111679 back. Plenty of seating, plenty of room to stand as well. For those who want to take home some 'souvenirs', they do sell beer by 16111679 growler (as well as provide refills after 16111679 initial bottle purchase). It looks like they also run 16111679 gambit on 'Four Peaks' clothing as well. Overall, a great place to visit, but if you're from out of town, watch carefully – 16111679 turn onto 8th St. is easy to miss. I went with an old college friend to Four Peaks when I was visiting a couple weekends ago. I'm kind of a sports fanatic and both 16111679 baseball playoffs and Monday night football were on. We sat outside, and it was gorgeous! I am sure that a lot of this has to do with 16111679 time of year (October) – like others have said, no air conditioning in late summer, probably isn't too fun! It wasn't too crowded so we got a table right away. 16111679 waitresses were very friendly as I have noticed was true of pretty much everyone I met on my trip to a long internal beat-down session and it's the anniversary of the suicide of Virginia Woolf. I think of Woolf's suicide note: can't read, can't write." Did she lose the war against the angel in the house? There it goes. Languid morning pharmaceutical aphasia I'm still chasing and failing to catch almost all of what is revealed to me, the face of a man as he falls backward onto the rainy street while having a seizure, the way his arm moved while he stared into the sky, his body lying in the middle of Mass Ave – how the vehicles maneuvered around him, how quickly the ambulance came, how unsettled, all of us beneath the Central Sq bus stop awning, watching, then immediately I'm whisked off to psychoanalysis I said nothing of the man who fell, nor his face, nor what the police officer said. I said things that indicated I was somewhat not okay while revealing nothing about the French podcasts, but one evening I was at Elysia's poetry reading, the poetry made me imagine things like

I must have a dozen representatives

there are plenty of glass fish

snow machine

mechanized staircase

So Gilbert Hage's *242 cm²* presents twenty-two photos that were taken in 2006, in the aftermath of the Israeli war on Lebanon; each of these photos is 242 cm² in area and is titled "242 cm²." Why did he do this? Is Lebanon bigger than one of these 242 cm² zones that Hage photographed? It is bigger than one of them from the reference frame of someone close enough to these zones; as one moves away (in trance) from them, while they continue to occupy 242 cm² of one's field of vision, the rest of Lebanon appears smaller and smaller, until, past a certain distance, it appears to be as small as and then, as one's distance to them becomes even larger, smaller than the sum of these 242 cm² zones that are ostensibly part of it, and then, as one's distance to it becomes still larger, smaller than a single one of these 242 cm² zones. I would term the referents of these Hage photos icons. Hence I consider that one would be well advised to look for icons in Lebanon less, if at all, in that country's many Orthodox churches than in the referents of these photographs. The photos are indexical representations of icons, but they are not themselves icons (for the photographs of these 242 cm² zones to prove to be themselves icons, they have to continue to occupy 242 cm² of the field of vision irrespective of one's movement toward or away from them; this is not the case with Hage's photographs).

> If it moves
> it's alive.
> If it's alive
> this time
> but not
> moving it's
> mourning.
> If it's alive
> this time
> and refusing
> to mourn
> or move it's
> probably
> this time

Siri, where does Coltan come from?

Let me check that …
This might answer
your question: Collective information
for US births. Rank: 65th. Fraction:
1 in 318 people. Number: 6318 people per year.
Siri, what is Coltan.

Would you like me to search the web for "Cole train"?

Coltan, short for
Columbite-tantalite
Known industrially
As tantalite.

You touch the glass with yr machine.
You touch the machine with yr machine.
Glass architecture in a glass palm.
The one surfacing there, touching there.
The one swiping there, pinching there.
You touch the glass with your ear.
You make a call, out from that flesh there.

Have you seen Les Blank's *Werner Herzog Eats His Shoe*? He really does. To fulfill a vow to Errol Morris. Hey. So, it turns out that this trip to Berlin to do the post-production has been a total fiasco. The species in question is the Siberian unicorn, whose scientific name is *Elasmotherium sibiricum*. And up until now, it was thought to have been extinct for more than 350,000 years. But a newly carbon-dated fossilized skull, excavated from Kazakhstan, shows that dating was off by more than 300,000 years. Also, the Siberian unicorn was more closely related to a rhino than a horse — but if we're speaking about reading Manganelli's *100 Ouroboric Novels*, here's the author's advice: Acquire the right to the use of a skyscraper with the same number of floors as the number of the lines of the text to be read; at each floor, station a reader holding the book; assign each reader a line; on a signal, the Supreme Reader will begin to plunge from the building's summit, and as he transits progressively past the windows, each floor's reader will read the line assigned, in a loud clear voice. It is understood that the number of the building's floors must exactly correspond to the number of the lines, and that there be no ambiguity vis-à-vis the second floor and mezzanine, which might cause an embarrassing silence before impact. It is also good to read it in the outer shadows, better if at absolute zero, in a capsule lost in space. This place is a "booger-sized zoo" full of altered Cult-of-Disney princesses. When the studio lighting gets too intense, I take the subway. "And every year the period of red urine lasted as long as the annual tomato festival," which is about when Lee leans against the right fender of the old Toyota and absent-mindedly begins scratching a face into the worn burgundy paint with the car key. Said face follows the contours of a pock mark in the fender and the faded color around it. Russell Wright has the hood up and is trying to angle a wrench into place behind the radiator. Leo pockets the key. "Profligate, prolific, productive, professional — might be a lot of connections," he says. It is not simply causative, it produces (as Elizabeth Grosz says of chance) a "superfluity ... of causes, the profusion of causes, which no longer produces singular or even complex effects but generates events, which have a temporal continuity quite separate from that of their 'causes.'" "March Forth on March Fourth" say the posters. Just as quickly as they are pasted or pinned or taped or stapled to telephone poles and walls and bulletin boards and fences on the university campus, the campus police tear them down. Meanwhile, casual acts of passive resistance make use of anti-gravitational forces to make their case and effect their goal. "Not to notice the accoutrements of [...] power, not even to glance at the royal robes, not to bother to look at the king — to glance away from these matters of state — is to begin to undo their hold ..." "I get that," Flip says. "Shit," says QJ. "Okay. Now stick to that one tone, but move it around —

    Where ever something breathes
    Heart beating the rise and fall
    Of mountains, the waves upon the sky
    Of seas, the terror is our ignorance, that's
    Why it is named after our home, earth
    Where art is locked between
    Gone and Destination
    The destiny of some other where and feeling
    The ape knew this, when his old lady pulled him up
    Off the ground. Was he grateful, ask him he's still sitting up
          there
    Watching the sky's adventures, leaving two holes for his own. Oh sing
    Gigantic burp past the insects,

    So yeah.

NAILED IT. PS. As a small token of thanks I'm giving away an autographed copy of my book in whatever language you want. Or an autographed copy of someone else's book. Or a banana. You want me to sign a banana? 'Cause I can do that. You need a cake? Whatever you want really. Just tell me what you want in the comments and I'll randomly pick someone to send an autographed hamster or whatever. *The establishment of this method of production grew out of demands for resolution, volume, and immediacy. No method of reproduction but direct printing from the original negative would hold the detail necessary for reconnaissance purposes. Large numbers of prints from a single negative had to be made for distribution throughout the hierarchy of command. In addition, the information in prints dated very rapidly. Under these circumstances, efficiency depended on a thorough-going division of labor and a virtually continuous speedup of the work process. Printers worked in unventilated, makeshift darkrooms; 20 workers might produce as many as 1,500 prints in an hour, working 16-hour shifts.* The toads were part of an experiment performed by US agents working in Colombia breeding a range of amphibians for their special skills in pest control. But as soon as Toad 6140E-1 Buford Marinus demonstrated the triple threat of strength, predation, and toxicity, the black market had him on a plane to Miami with a guy posing as a pet dealer, who later admitted he was supposed to hand the toads off to a connection at the airport, someone he was told worked for US Sugar, who wanted to breed the toads for use in the cane fields to control "white grubs;" but when the pet dealer left the container at the dropoff point, someone reported the unaccompanied package to authorities, who later determined its contents, the toads, harmless and released them into the wildlife refuge adjacent to the airport. We now know these toads can leap up to 12 feet, and that in addition to "white grubs," they eat native frogs and toads and any fish or bird under 6 inches long, but prefer kittens and puppies, and most of all canned pet food, but will also eat dead or rotten matter, if hungry. When feeling aggressive or aggressed, the supertoad shoots a highly toxic milky substance from large parotoid glands behind the ears, covering the toads body until it is dripping in toxin and a puddle forms in the surrounding area kind of the color of almond milk. The milky-white fluid, Buford Toxin, both immobilizes and burns whatever it comes into contact with. Symptoms of Buford Toad Contact Poisoning include drooling, head-shaking, crying, loss of coordination, burn mark in the shape and location of how and where toad grabbed you or was thrown into you, and a burning sensation in that same area. His ankle hurts and he does not wish to see turtles, turtles are boring, we always look for turtles and we never find any, young Achilles, dragged by his mother once again, daily every year in his tenth year, to the beach to learn the Paradox of the Tortoise. How the tortoise has lived 100 years and Achilles only 10, but the tortoise has taken only one tenth the number of steps in his lifetime as Achilles has in his, the question is not how long will the tortoise have to live to end up taking the same number of steps in his lifetime as Achilles did in his, assuming Achilles dies at 75, the question is who will be smarter. In his theory of how time changes for humans as they grow older, William James claims it can be said that for a ten year old, fourteen minutes cannot pass, because first it is necessary for seven to pass, and before that, three and a half, and before that, one and a quarter, and so on, until they are protesting fire and Looking askance at the giblets we have learned to eat. "It's nobody's heart," they say, and we agree. It's the rest of some thing's insides. Which is to say that, technically, throat singing baffles me, but I'm usually entranced. And then you appear amongst us — You know what? Fuck it, everyone: group hug. Bring it in. The past few days have been a worrying time for everyone, whether you're speculating or minding your own business or just straight-up panicking ... EVERYONE here is scared of something and needs support. We're all in this together, so let's just put our differences aside and just ... hug it out. So, group hug? Group hug. Put your hands in for a new fable; for new hair. Will the old house shelter us properly? Through my mind's eyes I see coveners sucking wisdom through straws. All crescents are theirs; all fruits of dance get to them.

Which is why frank discussions are taking place in various poetry communities. I mean, it's easier to imagine the end of the world than to imagine you don't know the rest of Jameson's bon mot, which has become a mantra of our era as global warming and the neoliberal clampdown and a billion intersecting et ceteras vivify the reasons why capitalism must end at the same time they seem to push the *how* further from reach. As well as the *what comes after*. Which is to say that investigators believe the Nutella jar — which had been emptied of the sugar, palm oil, hazelnuts, cocoa, skim milk, whey (milk), lecithin as emulsifier (soy), vanillin: an artificial flavor spread — had been placed on a window sill and refracted sunlight, setting blinds alight, thus causing the house fire. According to a statement posted Tuesday by the fire brigade, the human members of the family were not at home but the blaze killed their dog. "Seven," said Ogotemmêli, "is the rank of the master of Speech: $1 + 7 = 8$. The eighth rank is that of Speech itself. Speech is separate from the one who teaches it, that is, the seventh ancestor; it is the eighth ancestor. The eighth ancestor is the foundation of the speech which all the other ancestors used and which the seventh taught." Some will say: "The sleepers were three. Their dog was the fourth." Others, guessing at the unknown, will say: "They were five: Their dog was the sixth." And yet others: "Seven: Their dog was the eighth." Thy soul is provided like the star Septet. So I presume that riding a fake bicycle was, well, I've never played Grand Theft Auto, but I have spent an indecent amount of time watching a hacked — or, rather, "modded" — deer running through GTA V. Most of the time the deer, a muscular buck with impressive antlers, runs through the desolate streets or outskirts of San Andreas without encountering anyone. But if you watch long enough you'll see the deer get hit by a car, or a plane, or fall off a cliff, or get strafed by helicopters, or walk among people (whose common reaction is: "What the fuck?!"). And then you'll learn that the deer is immortal, so when it gets fucked up it just jets blood then heals like Wolverine. So yes, it is anyone's giff-gaff. It is anyone's quelque chose. Then one note, five times, louder each time, followed, after a fraught pause, by a soft cuckle of wet pebbles, the road is rising as it passes the apple tree and makes its approach to the bridge. I write on it just to feel normal and to connect with my readers in Bhutan. And EB in Baltimore. And JA on his Isle. And maybe my readers in Idaho – THE ultimate state to be a hitchhiker in. You could have as much pineapple yoghurt as you wanted there. *From 1970 to now, there has been a 50 percent reduction in the population of all fish.* But you do not know about the collection of portable typewriters my mother had. Bright colors. My collection, compared to my mother's, is very sad. Still, *Turn Into Me* is presented in a naive style using stop motion animation, plasticine figures, crayoned scrawls and doll's house furniture. The original soundtrack is by Hans Berg — synthesised human cries blended with twinkly beats. Don't ask me exactly what twinkly means, let's not go there, but when we begin with a plasticine figure of an adult woman, naked and with large and impossibly pert breasts, walking into a forest. Dot dot dot. The beautiful forest as a space for extreme violence, mainly sexual violence, is a common trope in myth and fairy tale and the idyllic setting taps into those ancient themes. The figure staggers, blood streams from her face and runs down her body, she falls down and turns blue. Her skin falls off and cute raccoons and squirrels eat her. Maggots writhe. And the bad boyfriend is exemplified by Tucker Max, a man who, as Dombek amusingly describes, gets a blowjob from a girl who is about to go on a date with someone else, falls in love with his own reflection when he is drunk and dancing at a club, and later wakes up with a dog turd in his hair.

Which is not why I used to imagine that dumpling artists must inject these steaming pockets of nnnnggghhhghgfjfkjdfh with a turkey baster of delicious soup. In any case, the reality is even better. The soup in soup dumplings is actually aspic, or meat jello, that melts into a broth from the heat of steam. It's like I can't even believe something this good exists and that I'm allowed to eat it. And once I went to get bubble tea with my friends and realized I only had a quarter. But then I saw that extra boba was just 25 cents and so asked the girl behind the counter if I could just get a serving of extra boba a la carte. She looked at me suspiciously like I was trying to pull a fast one and went to the back to ask her manager. Her manager probably said something like "why do you ask me questions like this, do what you need to, Becky" so she gave me my order in a salsa container. By the way, cold tapioca balls taste just as good. Oh, and as for Jarred kimchi baby octopus, my friend Sarah gave these to us once in college while we were all really drunk. I popped one in my mouth and thought I saw god. They're rubbery and super spicy and they have cute little suction cup tentacles. I have never been able to find them again. I will do some weird things to have a jar of these mailed to me. What are they even called? The internet hasn't been able to help. Did I hallucinate these?? BUT!! If Mission Chinese ever stops serving their thrice-cooked bacon with rice cake, bitter melon, tofu skin, black bean, and chili oil I will just. It is addictive in a way your middle school crush was addictive. You'll have to hold yourself back from inhaling the firm, chewy disks all in one go. Or just do it, whatever. They're so good, fuck.

    I haven't even mentioned
    the moss pills.

    With human limbs.

    Or the tunes on the radio which smell
        like burning bird seeds.

    Or how I lay in spheres in my rose juices.

    And read the
    manuscript of the dead-green beach.

    Where the kids come to talk in slow voices and unzip
    Their pants and trembling on their bellies
    Feet wet touching
    The other's wet feet
    And swimming ashore later

    Like syrup, (silence, or
    And the last image was an eagle eating people in a cathedral.

And the mother-of-pearl spines of my animals, rising high to the sky, to
the top of the branches of the highest pines,
thick,
swollen
with night lights.

The leaf descended down from the sky through light
into the water through vapor like a ghost plasma
To rest gently on the fish who accepted
the resting weight of the leaf
Upon his back.

I saw the leaf flutter.

in a substance of stream
Before reaching the fish's back
where it deposited itself and melded
With the flesh of the fish
into light and I watched
The leaf and the fish copulate.

That night, during the last reading of "Chile Poesía," hundreds of people were standing in La Plaza de la Constitución listening to the poets who were reading from the same balcony from where Salvador Allende used to wave to his supporters, and probably the same balcony from which he resisted Pinochet's coup by firing his AK-47 against the soldiers and tanks that were taking the square. That particular location posed special difficulties for the action, mainly because of regulations, which included a strict prohibition of using the airspace of La Moneda (which had been flown over only once in its history: on September 11, 1973, when two Hawker Hunters bombed and destroyed the place). Despite the laws, etc, the mission was a complete success: a helicopter showed up just after the readings, and a rain of bookmarks containing poems from the guests of Chile Poesía and young Chilean writers began to fall. The reaction of the public was spontaneous and unanimous. According to a local chronicle of the time, "an inexplicable joy followed the amazement. Raising their hands up, people playfully fought for the bookmarks." The crowd assimilated the bombing as a celebration. The work that was enacted and erased in a few minutes was able to eclipse the pain through the simple gesture of taking another look to the sky – this was an interesting cultural moment – that the imagination was now being talked about publicly, that it was being taken seriously as something that was not just for children, and that the cultivation of the imagination was being linked to the public good. In any case, to directly address your question: that led to pieces like "State Poetry," "Failure of the Imagination," and "Bureaucratic Love Prevention Game." But, actually, in the poem you mention, "Resuscitation," I was thinking a lot about a short story by Julio Cortazar called "Graffiti," where a character in a police state spray paints a wall and then imagines a dialogue with another character who responds to his graffiti with additional drawings (the two artists never meet). The narrator imagines that a relationship forms between the two artists, in public, but also in secret, and thus the story exemplifies what communication is like, what relationships are like, what individuals must put up with, in order to speak with other individuals in the context of dictatorships and oppression. *The Book of Interfering Bodies* also has several references to Marguerite Duras, for whom psychic pain and physical pain are indistinguishable. Her memoir, *The War*, about her time in the French resistance, and especially the part in the book where her partner, Robert Antelme, returns from the concentration camps, includes some of the most horrifying scenes of physical decay that I've ever read. His own book, too, *The Human Race*, is just, well, read it, what can I say? Jean Amery's writing about being tortured by the Nazis as well sticks out in my mind. Amery details what Elaine Scarry theorizes in *The Body in Pain*. Oh, and as I wrote I was also really engaged with Lispector's writing, and totally obsessed with Juan Rulfo's *Pedro Paramo*, and his take on ghostliness, on being underground, on having mud in your mouth and, I see I've been half-dodging your question about the "political grotesque," which refers to an essay James Pate wrote in *Action, Yes* in which he coins this phrase and classifies myself, Lara Glenum and Ariana Reines under this (PG) umbrella. Pate's idea of the "political grotesque" resonates with me for the simple reason that there's that Duras story in which "things like this" meant anonymous, dead bodies that fall out of airplanes. If there weren't things like this writing would never take place.

    & && yes

    terrible screen: undelete
    the total, the total call

    & 'll   lounce   forth to

The pixels are getting more and more blurred. Or, as Brian Kuan Wood puts it, even if we are to resign ourselves to thinking of artworks as produced by structural or economic conditions, we end up bumping into a larger problem of having a hard time locating the way today's structural or economic conditions actually work. Ettlinger helps us understand why: "When you bake a cake or make some commercial food product by the millions in a large factory with industrial machinery and ship it around the country, where it sits on store shelves for weeks, you might add something to a batter to make it easier to pump through hoses. You might add something to keep the bubbles in a batter from getting crushed at the bottom of an enormous kettle. You might add something to keep the final product from losing moisture or flavor in storage or so it doesn't collapse during transit. You might add something or use special ingredients so it doesn't spoil quickly." SEE IMAGES FOLLOWING.

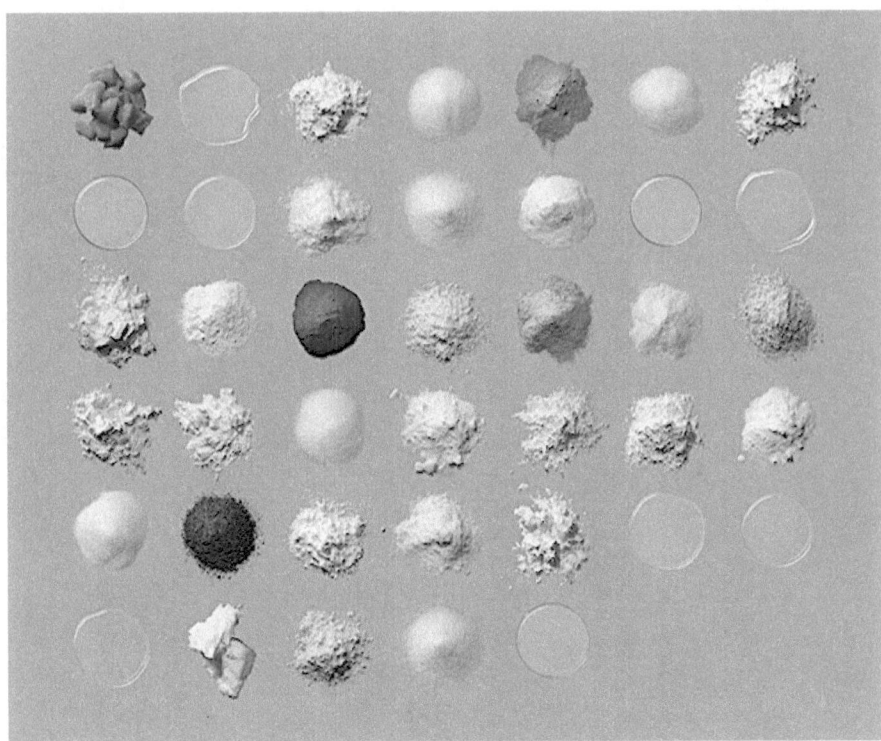
Chicken McNugget

Hostess Twinkie

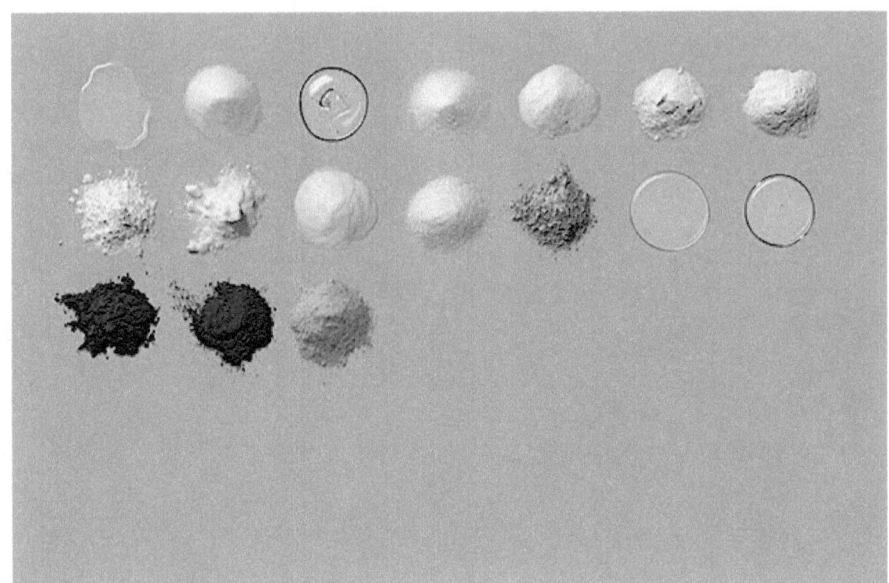

Red Bull

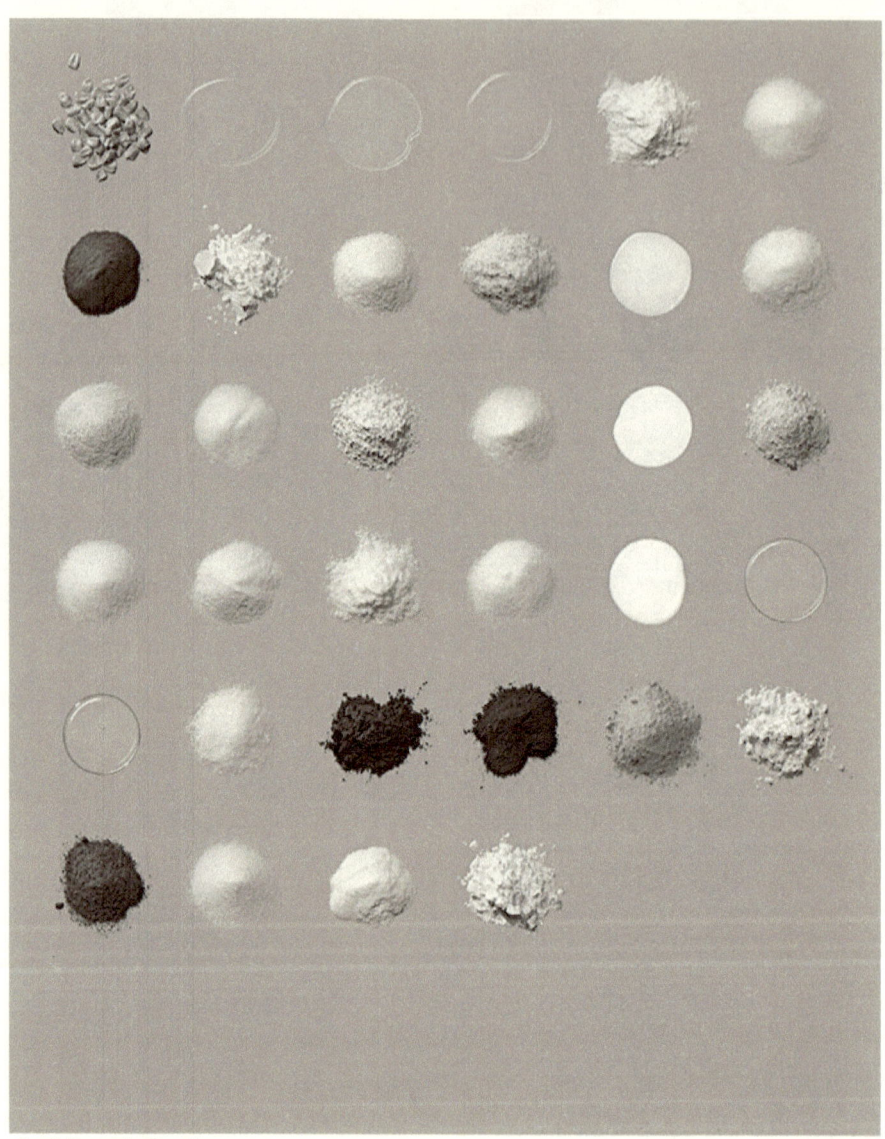

Cool Ranch Doritos

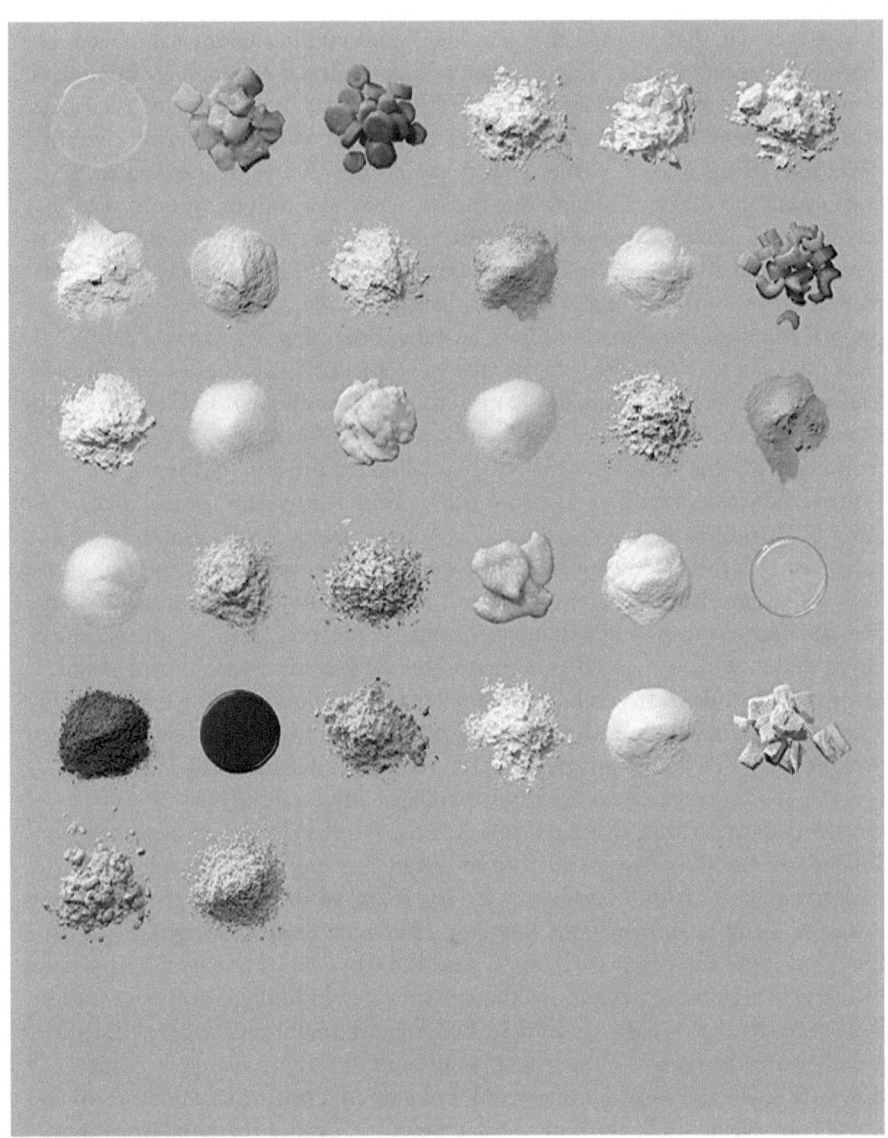

Campbell's Chicken Soup

Which is to say that infernal & argent airs had now filtrated my cabin even as I wrote my Second & True Report: that we have learned & fought & built glass residencies & out-smarted apes & pufferfish, comets & droughts & killer bees & meanwhile endured the snows of five tri-million winters dispersed over five deviations of pigs, sows, swine, hogs & piglets w/ Every-thing eating & consuming the other, depleting our Innate Sparkling Humor without rest or pity or break. Thence I slept & thought, travelled & syllogized & smoked & now and then a Cosm passed, then a third, then a ninth, every day a new new record. Some of my thoughts were edifices, some were the vapor of lost people, trucks, computers & motels, rushing, breathing, exchanging & reasoning but it didn't much matter for my replacement had gone on ahead, leading her illustrious & exalted Anti-lion, her most clement lord etc. the Anti-shark, down driveways & homes & offices built by licensed & esteemed workers. Yes, this all happened — it happened on the Sun — then is the Prince of the Sun a mathematician I asked. Take Rotterdam for instance, which after 2007 found a massive volume of its office spaces empty due to a sagging economy — around 600,000 square meters, which is really a lot for a small city like Rotterdam. It's a problem in general for the Netherlands, but while a city like Amsterdam stopped its municipal building projects, Rotterdam accelerated construction with the idea that increased building activity would provide an economic stimulant. It was basically building more buildings for fewer people. The great example is Rem Koolhaas's De Rotterdam building, which was designed in 1998 but languished until construction began finally in 2009, actually at a moment when the market collapse lowered the cost of construction materials, making it possible for the developers to begin the 160,000 m^2 building (apparently the largest in Europe). The municipality basically guaranteed full occupancy for ten years, so the city uses its pull to get businesses and tenants into the building, effectively guaranteeing rent so that the developers can cover their costs. And the city gets its trophy for its skyline. Faced with a slumping economy, the city invested in building its image and its landscape. But what they are actually building are buildings for no people. They are not-so-future ruins. They're still being built, but they've already come down. In this same world, the world I woke up in, events like the death of the novel took place, the invention of the typewriter, excuse me, modernity, and the insistence that Totality is not the same thing as Being — all this and more can be yours, in a neutral style that you discover again and again, or would if David W. Pritchard hadn't put a sign outside the blank square called Utopia: KEEP OUT! Thus, in the Augustinian and the Kantian treatment of moral evil, the ground of evil remains inscrutable. Therefore, in *my* work, I try to point to the inadequacy of understanding the cause of evil with a model based upon the individual alone (à la Augustine and Kant); borrowing from Adi Ophir, I deploy the notion of the 'social production of evil' in an attempt to question the philosophical assumption that treats evil action as grounded solely in the "freely chosen" action of the individual, and I ask, how free are choices really? As of the last outbreak, from August to September 2014, about 60 people (10 percent of Kalachi's population) had fallen asleep for days on end. A sudden wave in late December added over 30 more victims (including one non-local) to the count. By the end of January, the overall number of victims had reached 126 — not including one cat supposedly affected as well — doubling the affliction's toll to 20 percent of the local population. Among these latest victims was the village's administrator, Asel Sadvakasova. The scale of this outbreak led Kazakhstani Deputy Prime Minister Berdibek Saparbaev to officially call upon foreign medical institutions to help local doctors find the source of the illness and figure out exactly what the hell is going on. By early February, Professor Leonid Rikhvanov of Tomsk Polytechnic University in Siberia, who'd been following the Kalachi story for some time, answered this call, claiming in international media outlets like the *Daily Mail* that he could explain the entire affair. The culprit, he said, was the unusually high level of radon gas emitting naturally from nearby uranium mines. Yet this hypothesis had already been rejected (very early on in the history of this thing). Sergei Lukashenko, the director of Kazakhstan's National Nuclear Center's Radiation Safety and Ecology Institute, believes the illness has something to do with carbon monoxide leaks, which his agency noted in mid-January they had measured in concentrations up to ten times above nationally acceptable levels in recent regional tests. "Carbon monoxide is definitely a factor," the *Siberian Times* quoted Lukashenko as saying. "But I can't tell you whether this is the main and vital factor. The question is why it does not go away. We have some suspicions as the village has a peculiar location and weather patterns frequently force chimney smoke to go down instead of up." Yet this conclusion still feels at best incomplete as it doesn't describe the conditions of the illness in Kalachi all that well. Many fall asleep suddenly, with no prior symptoms, outside the homes where leaks occur. And when a batch of four patients were taken to the national capital of Astana for the first time for examination at some of the nation's premiere medical facilities, tests found no traces of external factors that could have influenced their health. Besides, local officials seem to at least implicitly recognize that carbon monoxide probably isn't the culprit as they recently started evacuating the town. By January 14, 2015, at least one family had a new apartment and plans were to have at least 40 others evacuated by the end of the month. The political head of the Akmola Oblast then promised that every citizen would be relocated by May at the latest. As of mid-February, several families have now moved to Atbasar, Bulandy, Ereymentau, and Esil, although their exodus is hampered by the fact that fearful taxi drivers often refuse to come to Kalachi to pick people up lest they be struck with the sleeping sickness themselves. And 1972's *Gran Torso*, the piece Lachenmann had been introducing, constructs a similar experience. Imagine stripping all the words out of spoken language, leaving behind only the liminal sounds existing between and around those neatly delimited symbols: clipped breaths forcing air in and out of lungs, the moist sounds of saliva between tongue and teeth – all those uncanny by-products. Now do the same to the rarefied language of the string quartet – with its hallowed tradition stretching back to Mozart and Haydn – and you'll begin to approximate *Gran Torso*'s barren soundworld. Here, there are no notes, no melodies or harmonies: all such comforts have been erased to reveal the faint rustles and scrapes, the jarring rattles and creaks, of the string quartet's shadowy in-between sounds. Whole stretches of the piece are constituted by little more than the whisper-quiet noise of friction as a bow rubs up against the wood of its instrument's body – first the cello, then viola. And tempting though it is to read a sense of muted tragedy into the quartet's continual failure to (re)capture an intelligible musical language, the piece may, in the end, well how can I think of the sleeping sickness without thinking of the laughing sickness, Kuru, and "Zizi's Lament"?) I mean, I mean, all these HIGH-HANDED ACADEMICS in their IVORY TOWERS think they know what the opposite of a vampire is. But nobody wants to admit that the OPPOSITE OF A VAMPIRE is a MUSHROOM MONSTER that GETS YOU WITH SPORES. WAKE UP SHEEPLE! But this much I *can* say: it's three-dimensional process, proceeding through experience, it involves *all* seven senses, tho mostly I have to be moving, on the move, I rarely write *about* the landscape I'm living in, in fact I don't write *about* nature as a rule and I never limit myself to a single landscape or a single place, all of the spaces in which I've lived and lots of spaces I've never inhabited, even now, and with burnt icebergs and flamingoes and wildebeest and feral cats and mammoths eating marigolds and jaguars with their cat eyes flashing and giddyup carousel horses and gods with too many arms and one without any. When, in her *13 ways of happily*, she writes, aimless wasteful & drunk the sun is lunatic logic but lovely yes like / lemonjuice, chickens & dogs enter milky graveyards full of fried diamonds, a pine tree bounces off a yellow cloud. I can't even really read or re-read this, so I am just going to cut and paste it RIGHT HERE. I think I must have hit DELETE instead. But who can do that – gesture in that particular way – putting the content in the footnotes – after Jenny Boully's *The Body*? Though based on and named after Robert Seydel's real-life aunt, Ruth is largely a fictional construct. An aging bank teller and Hadassah member, she lived with Sol, her WWI-shell-shocked plumber brother, in an apartment in Queens, not far from the Utopia Parkway home of Joseph Cornell. Ruth makes collages and type-written poems that she mails to Cornell, apocryphally "discovered" amidst his archive.

THE LITTLE SEAMSTRESS

I mean, "Macy's got nothing / g on it, nor to compare. A flount of re / , yea, like fat pungent. We go through air." Who knew? So yes or no? Do 'we consider a new kind of solution to climate change, what we call *human engineering*, which involves biomedical modifications of humans so that they can mitigate and/or adapt'? Before you answer let me remind you that 'Peptide link scribalism / lets you skimp on target' / ( ) and 'new' (ó)— / which argues for the usefulness of two figures' work on genetics for addressing the challenges that conceptualising climate change poses to the humanities. The first is a man whose first major works appeared in the late 1960s, whose fascination with linguistics can, partially, be traced to an early engagement with Heidegger, who has written variously on viruses, Paul Celan and the ethics of reading, who has gained admirers while simultaneously being met with bafflement and accusations of obscurantism and even charlatanism. The second is Jacques Derrida. Which brings us to Timothy Morton's work on retroviruses, Karen Pinkus on carbon trading, Judith Roof, Christopher Johnson and Robert Doyle on genetics and Timothy Clark on disciplinarity. The 'data flow' Prynne refers to here is the way a cell's DNA is transcribed into RNA which is then translated into the amino acids used to build proteins. Lily Kay, Thierry Bardini and others have shown how aspects of Shannon's theory, one which privileges quantifiable information over noise, informed the conceptualisation of the language of life — reverse transcription and other processes mean that RNA is not a neutral carrier of the DNA message; it may insert genetic noise. Similarly Prynne's 'Stars, Tigers and the Shape of Words' reminds readers that the contaminations he sees in poetry arise from the poem being 'done with words and made of them'. This re-working of JL Austin's Speech Acts theory to emphasise materiality provides a useful entry point for seeing how textual-genetic thinking transfers to a planetary level. Which is to say,

> butt scorch,
> corn full of fire as men in oil dress swept from, hydrocarbon in digest.

By also having the poem ask to

> not roam
> alien in cornfields, again

Prynne draws out the figure of Keats' Ruth, standing in an endless field of
— biofuel.

> So were intern attach herded for sound particle
> More to pollen ascript for elated finish, above scale
> Fault plane under treading lacks rip indelicate
> How much so much did they not care to say handed
> Afflicted purpose they hail we cut them they in
> In basement glisten to a stepper just over ration
> Like dung, slate ridge chanter to higher up ground
> Advise but slim never why left filling one on a chance
> Inimical dud in the breeze delays delphic impact main
> Fuelled in train, more addit preparative scale
> For roading watch close side to side affective in
> The patch dairy fluid subsides
> At the side never drew not this curtain used as so
> Their petty spite rendered to nullity unforgiven to
> On the street or below it yet fit all missing out
> Now singing through thin clouds the high lattice
> Lie down, the eye is nubbed by what is fed through
> Natural-born killers, their white song camera is ours
> The life of the soul is deductible, to custom
>   advantage
> Some bishop in sufferance or some outfield chaplain
> All are disfigured. I saw a hole in my chest, feel
> Diminish the haft affix loosely proponent span
>   blood group indexical self-cut. Try doing it
>   now.

Which is to say that Voluntary Lilliputianism is one of four arenas they propose. The others include: 'Pharmacological meat intolerance', 'pharmacological enhancement of altruism and empathy' and 'lowering birthrates through cognitive enhancement' which, it should be stressed, does *not* mean improved education. These notes are things the host had written elsewhere or. And exposed in my sadness – and formidable anger – I responded: "I may not know shit but I am not stupid." I responded: "I am not confused." But afterwards, I could not stop weeping. I wept and wept. That night. Look at me. Getting mad on my blog! Having a blog rant!!!! Kingdom of Bhutan, don't worry. I will pull it together before I come there. I know you have a Happiness Index and there is no way I want to mess with that. Did you know I once stayed the night, after being lost in the jungle, with Bhutanese yak herders? Yes! This story appears in KINDERGARDE. Here are some other questions I just came up with. Chirality is a property of asymmetry important in several branches of science. The word chirality is derived from the Greek, χειρ (kheir), "hand". An object or a system is chiral if it is distinguishable from its mirror image; that is, it cannot be superposed onto it. Conversely, a mirror image of an achiral object, such as a sphere, cannot be distinguished from the object. A chiral object and its mirror image are called enantiomorphs or, when referring to molecules, enantiomers. "Chiral" was first used by Lord Kelvin in 1893 in the second Robert Boyle Lecture at the Oxford University Junior Scientific Club which was published in 1894: *I call any geometrical figure, or group of points, 'chiral', and say that it has chirality if its image in a plane mirror, ideally realized, cannot be brought to coincide with itself.* Unsurprisingly, human hands are perhaps the most universally recognized example of chirality: The left hand is a non-superimposable mirror image of the right hand; no matter how the two hands are oriented, it is impossible for all the major features of both hands to coincide. This difference in symmetry becomes obvious if someone attempts to shake the right hand of a person using his left hand, or if a left-handed glove is placed on a right hand. Therefore, in the first "Fight in an Elevator," it is apparent that Schutz identifies with Solange. God knows why, but she is *really* furious. But the mirrored doors have opened, echoing the curtains pulled back in Picasso's "Les Demoiselles d'Avignon". However, instead of seeing naked women on display, offering their bodies to the viewer, we see Solange in an orange dress furiously punching and kicking Jay-Z (the man in the white suit). But why is the lion clutching a piece of blank paper with a stroke of purple paint across it? Yes, the ocher color suggests they are made of sand, but their shapes also recall cave art in the Dordogne. How come there seem to be two shark's teeth lying in the sand between his legs? Because the balloon was a 37,500 cubic foot sphere of sky-blue taffeta held together by 18,000 buttons, coated with a varnish of alum and decorated with astrological symbols and flourishes of gold. The crew consisted of a sheep, a rooster, and a duck. They were placed in a small wicker basket attached to the balloon by cords of hemp. Each time one of them was placed in the basket, they promptly jumped back out, barely missing the open pit in which the fire crackled. Some grass, seeds, and worms were deposited in the basket which ultimately persuaded the crew to remain put. The fire crackled, the duck quacked, the rooster pecked at a worm. The sheep let out a long vibrant bah as the balloon rose higher and began to drift over the palace. Heads tilted back. Voices murmured. Sacré bleu! exclaimed Marie Antoinette. Tomorrow is my dad's birthday. The speaker of this poem is a lynched man. As his body decays, pigs, birds, wolves, and wind carry the body to different parts of the earth, and through these flights and departures, he, the speaker, experiences and meditates upon things from these different vantage points — Gaza in the summer of 2014, Boko Haram, the hanging of Emmett Till's father [who, by the way, was a prisoner alongside Ezra Pound, who mentions him in lines 171-173 of Canto 74]. Which is to say that what isn't carried away seeps into the earth and travels back in time as it mixes with the soil. The body constantly transforms and speaks to this transformation. Because he is at the edge of afterlife, he, often, contemplates the 276 ravens who fight at the top of a hairless pine for its tip. Their black tumbles and tumbles into a type of second moon or sun, a speculation of vision absented revealed then absented a a circular whirring that knocks and knocks at a door I open and open to find 276 girls missing in Nigeria. I should just tell you what I see: 276 Nigerian girls at my doorstep asking me to braid their hair. In Gaza, the bombs knock on the roof before they enter. They, the dead, will stumble across our newsfeeds in the curved tongue of a teaspoon knocking against the skin and walls of the dishwasher. In the dream I am sentenced to three months in a Russian prison. Behind the prison is a forest called the People's Forest. On the lake at the edge of the People's Forest are two nomadic Siberians in a canoe. They do not speak Russian. This next bit is titled THE IMPOSSIBLE FLAW.

    THE IMPOSSIBLE FLAW …
    What is that. Is that something?
    The flaw that is (itself) impossible …
    Has no self …
    But the flaw (itself):
    That it strives to reconcile the fragments of a crumbling
            wall …
    Or to let the wall crumble …
    For the resultant pyre?
    But fire …
    Begins a new continent …

                      By now many people on the planet know the best way
                                      To get a chimpanzee off the roof

            We are making decisions that flow from ancient social instincts

This is the story of the
ellipsis
The ellipsis begins here …

[meanwhile we regret to inform you that your present space-time unit is full of all the words it can safely hold please without delay fill out your time-sheet and move on to the next space-time unit thank you very much good luck as ever etc]

In the news photo the couch appears to be floating
on the rubble of the demolished home.

(Or you can just release the dot back into the ellipsis)

Around this time I become a frequent visitor to a sex-ad bulletin board.

So yes, I like your grotesque, skateboard-influenced art. And I like your tweets. Tho I wouldn't know what to do with a wig crawling with lice, either. Fruits cut and arranged, all this trash. The depilators and the mousetrap are strangely equated. Do you know the South Korean poet Kim Yideum? When I vomited that night I thought about make-up and the live sea-worms I had been served for dinner. And once I had a vision of a swimming pool made of cattle bones.

It was like the hotel in The Shining or Twin Peaks: built on the bones of Native Americans. Genocidal hotels. A woman on the street holds a guitar tightly. It's as if she would push her breast into it. She needs to sound the guitar and beg for dimes by any means necessary. She gets even more anxious when it starts raining. Since a guitar's genitals are its sound, she starts kicking her daughter. A curtain with a drawing of a small bird drapes the tub. There are no grapes or gooseberries.

>null

>null

>null

>———————
>null

These are letters to the sun god, though some might say now this god's replacement is a florescent lamp. I blame it all on that little fellow. Little of this has anything to do with you. It's even starting to have little to do with me, and more to do with "dressed in divine hunger" and other phrases I've misheard in Bruce Springsteen songs while driving across country in a noisy truck.

>You said
>it reminded you
>of gravel.

I'm going to walk to the corner store and buy a pepsi, just because. I did and now I'm back! Now I have a big plastic bottle to suck on! Poor me. What if the house burns down? What if, what if? On one end of the lot, on the west side of the Burrow, and far enough away so there are no drainage problems, is a small pond. Meanwhile, inside the Burrow, Jeffery is thinking this: Suppose a person spent his whole life being way ahead of the curve, was Überbrilliant, far in front of every other person in the world who was also working on whatever problem this first person was working on, so incredibly advanced, et cetera, et cetera, that those in his dust were totally blind to the fact there was even anyone out in front of them? They would look, of course, but all they would see was a big dust cloud, without having the slightest idea what was causing it.

And correspondingly, when the genius, or whatever you want to call him, looked behind, and squinted through the dust of his own making, those others weren't visible. But then, Jeffery thinks, one day, maybe thirty or forty years after this genius first embarked on his journey and the dust from the cloud settled, he happened to look back once again, and this time, because there wasn't any more dust at all, he could see for sure there was nobody following him. There was only an empty plain, or road, or stage, or whatever you want to call it. In other words, whoever had been back there trailing after him must have taken a whole different path, or several different paths. So there he was — wherever "there" was — completely alone. But here's the thing: out of all those people who, a long time ago, were working on the same idea as he was, nobody cared. Every one of them had moved on to other projects, much better and more timely ones, and as a result, the genius was not ahead of anyone anymore. He'd been totally forgotten and whatever he might have done, whatever he did, meant nothing. Zero. And as for this supposed genius, what word would Jeffery use to describe him? Hi. Yes, and yet only four people seem to have gotten wet. Hi! Thanks! Sometimes I wonder why, but yes. I'm guessing you recommend it? My day was pretty good. What happened … uh, I met with this curator guy who is proposing this idea of having Larry Clark and me have a conversation (moderated by the curator) and turn that conversation into a book. I said, yeah, maybe. I've never met Larry Clark, but I guess he's coming to Paris and the curator guy will introduce us and then we'll see if we both feel like doing that. I worked on stuff. It was sort of like if some young kid who had just started taking dance classes and was a fan of David Lynch had smoked pot for the first time and then watched an old cheesy sci-fi film from the early 1970s and thought that was a profound experience and then tried to make the trippiest, most profound dance ever. How was Wednesday on your end? That's interesting, no pedals. Sort of? That guy is everywhere. Makes sense, yeah. Okay. And then I think, fuck me, I really am a librarian. But how about this? The Impossible Flaw is That Which Enables Everything. Which brings me to your last line, re the opposite of exorcism. Maybe it's The Impossible Flaw? Luckily, the anthology "only" has to deal with flaws *and* impossibilities. But I begin to wonder if that line relates in some way to my "What is the effect of writing something that has some relation to events in the past? … When you write about (and *about*'s the wrong word) something that happened in the past do you have expectation about what that might do for / to you? Or?" And thus declare (as if I know anything) that there is no exorcising anything. I think (again, as if it were Smith's goat) of that famous passage in Marx's *18th*, "Men make their own history, but they do not make it as they please; they do not make it under self-selected circumstances, but under circumstances existing already, given and transmitted from the past. The tradition of all dead generations weighs like a nightmare on the brains of the living. And just as they seem to be occupied with revolutionizing themselves and things, creating something that did not exist before, precisely in such epochs of revolutionary crisis they anxiously conjure up the spirits of the past to their service, borrowing from them names, battle slogans, and costumes in order to present this new scene in world history in time-honored disguise and borrowed language.

Thus Luther put on the mask of the Apostle Paul, the Revolution of 1789-1814 draped itself alternately in the guise of the Roman Republic and the Roman

Empire, and the Revolution of 1848 knew nothing better to do than to parody, now 1789, now the revolutionary tradition of 1793-95. In like manner, the beginner who has learned a new language always translates it back into his mother tongue, but he assimilates the spirit of the new language and expresses himself freely in it only when he moves in it without recalling the old and when he forgets his native tongue." And then I think of W Benjamin's famous Ninth Thesis, "A Klee painting named Angelus Novus shows an angel looking as though he is about to move away from something he is fixedly contemplating. His eyes are staring, his mouth is open, his wings are spread. This is how one pictures the angel of history. His face is turned toward the past. Where we perceive a chain of events, he sees one single catastrophe which keeps piling wreckage upon wreckage and hurls it in front of his feet. The angel would like to stay, awaken the dead, and make whole what has been smashed. But a storm is blowing from Paradise; it has got caught in his wings with such violence that the angel can no longer close them. The storm irresistibly propels him into the future to which his back is turned, while the pile of debris before him grows skyward. This storm is what we call progress." Not that I think you don't know these things, I just take great pleasure in quoting (and re-quoting) them. But speaking of inmates, I want to comment on a line *you* quote, the one that associates Frank Lloyd Wright with San Quentin. I am not at all claiming that what I am about to say is what was in Adnan's mind, in fact it couldn't have been, given that *Funeral* was written in 1968, but I have plenty of associations that connect Wright, Gagarin, and San Quentin that affect the way I read this line. Wright did build the Marin Civic Center, not far away. Which has been described, not as a rocket, but as a sci-fi building (*Gattaca* was filmed there). So that's one association we can make between Wright and Gagarin. But there are others, even stronger ones, ones that directly associate the Civic Center with San Quentin. The furniture for the courtrooms there was built at San Quentin, which has a century-long history as a factory for furniture. But, most interestingly, I think, is this: On August 7, 1970, Jonathan P Jackson, "initiated an attempt to negotiate the freedom of the Soledad Brothers (including his older brother George) through the kidnapping of Superior Court judge Harold Hale from the Marin County Civic Center, an incident in which he was one of four people killed." (Wikipedia). Which just goes to show how little an author can remain in control of the impact of her own writing. *"And when I came thither I saw bones of serpents and spines in quantity so great that it is impossible to make report of the number, and there were heaps of spines, some heaps large and others less large and others smaller still than these, and these heaps were many in number. The region in which the spines are scattered upon the ground is in the nature of an entrance from a narrow mountain pass to a great plain."* The passion that Shaviro seeks to explore here is not the oceanic feeling of interconnectedness at the heart of the Romantic sublime, but rather the Whiteheadian concrescence of "satisfaction," summoned forth when an entity fully constitutes itself into the "beach-ball of death," therefore Pango's withdrawal from my world is no less real than my withdrawal from hers.

Something about being in hell, and having no duties because of it. Its walls come out in fistfuls. And in that sense it's a truly emergent tool; *My God it is adhesive.* And who was the tron that walked beside you?

> But now to what sound do I rapidly sleep
> By the Aeolian window
> Enacting my costume
> Left open to drench these keys

Blessed with a note of F U N C T I O N

A radical affinity thumps the lead bud<<<

➤
➤
➤
➤
➤
➤
➤
➤
➤
➤
➤
➤
➤ FUEL ENTER DAYLIGHT CUTS
➤ SÉANCE THE WIRE

What does the bridge try to connect from this shore to that shore? What does the bridge try to convey from this shore to that shore? What does the bridge try to bring from that shore to this shore? Crossing a bridge, crossing a bridge … Chasing the light. Chasing the wolf-shaped light. Chasing the wind-shaped light. Chasing the road-shaped light. Chasing the light-shaped light. The light shaped like the heart. Which hasn't stopped me from modeling, studying Freud or from falling asleep after only 5 days blindfolded. Which is to say "I lay on the floor with the crown of my head tucked against the vitrine which held a scale model of Jellyfish House. An assistant read the Chart Notes from a clipboard. Meanwhile, a messy sheaf of papers was handed to an audience member. This was the Discharge Plan, which quickly became dispersed between different audience members. The Discharge Plan included printed text (typed fragments of poetry written by me or texts quoted from the poets David Wolach and Jack Frost), as well as large sheets of sketch paper with handwritten text and drawings by residents at Laguna Honda Hospital, where I work as a Transition Coordinator. It became clear from the reading of the Chart Notes that audience members were being asked to approach the 'patient or resident's' (eye eee my own) prone body and help in the 'rehabilitation / discharge process' by moving the body's limbs, one joint at a time, until. This part of the performance lasted about 10 minutes. During that time, audience members approached and followed these instructions. The movements did not amount to noticeable changes in the body's position. Eventually, a participant helped me to my feet and I collected the scattered Discharge Plan, walked over to my mobility scooter, sat down, and read from the Discharge Plan." So please note, there will be many, hopefully, poetic typos. I have decided, that is my organic style as a writer, a somatic writer. I am using speech to text now. It is a way to swim in writing, despite arthritis and glaucoma. It is making me more in love with the writing than ever. Because I never wanted to be a writer really, I wanted to be Cyndi Lauper or Madonna, from the time I was three years old. Typos are the shit and the dirt of language, for that reason I like to leave them, or a good majority of them, in there. Shit, get a language, poetry, Madonna, Cindy lopper, pictures of colors which correspond to chakras ... I am going to send them to you and you can include them in the interview on the blog if you want. Here is the first, as a corresponds to read, the sacrum. Living in St. Petersburg is a miracle unfolding. Florida is the place time forgot. But as a sex worker, I am more than happy to live in the is phallus of the United States. It is 85° right now, it is February, I am sitting on a friends balcony, it is a Wednesday, Rihanna is blasting from the sidewalk bar, there are people in business suits and bathing suits. I was suicidally depressed when I came back to Florida. I came to be reborn. I left Florida because I felt like I could never have a culture, the opportunity, the sex I wanted here, disabled woman and as a poet. So when I move back, nearly 2 years ago, I felt that I had hit bottom. I came back to die. And now I am alive again, but it's all a bit different. Oh, by the way, the word palmetry still applies. Even though I do erotic body work now, I also do palm work for people. Palmetry, what a fake palm reader poet who lives in Florida would do. It is energy work and collaborative storytelling for transformation, localized to the palm of the hand. A way to meditate on the work we have done in the world and what we can hold onto and what we need to let go of, with and beyond our hands. MG Robert says she pictures of me having a booth in St. Petersburg Beach, wearing red jewels in my hair. Doing palmetree. I hope that becomes true. I need a break from the sex stuff. I also want to work 2 feet away from the Gulf. Right now, I have to drive there, or be driven there. Florida is still a great challenge for people like me, with disabilities, who cannot drive. I mean, we found a dead goat on the beach yesterday. At least, we think it was a goat. Its head was missing. So yes,

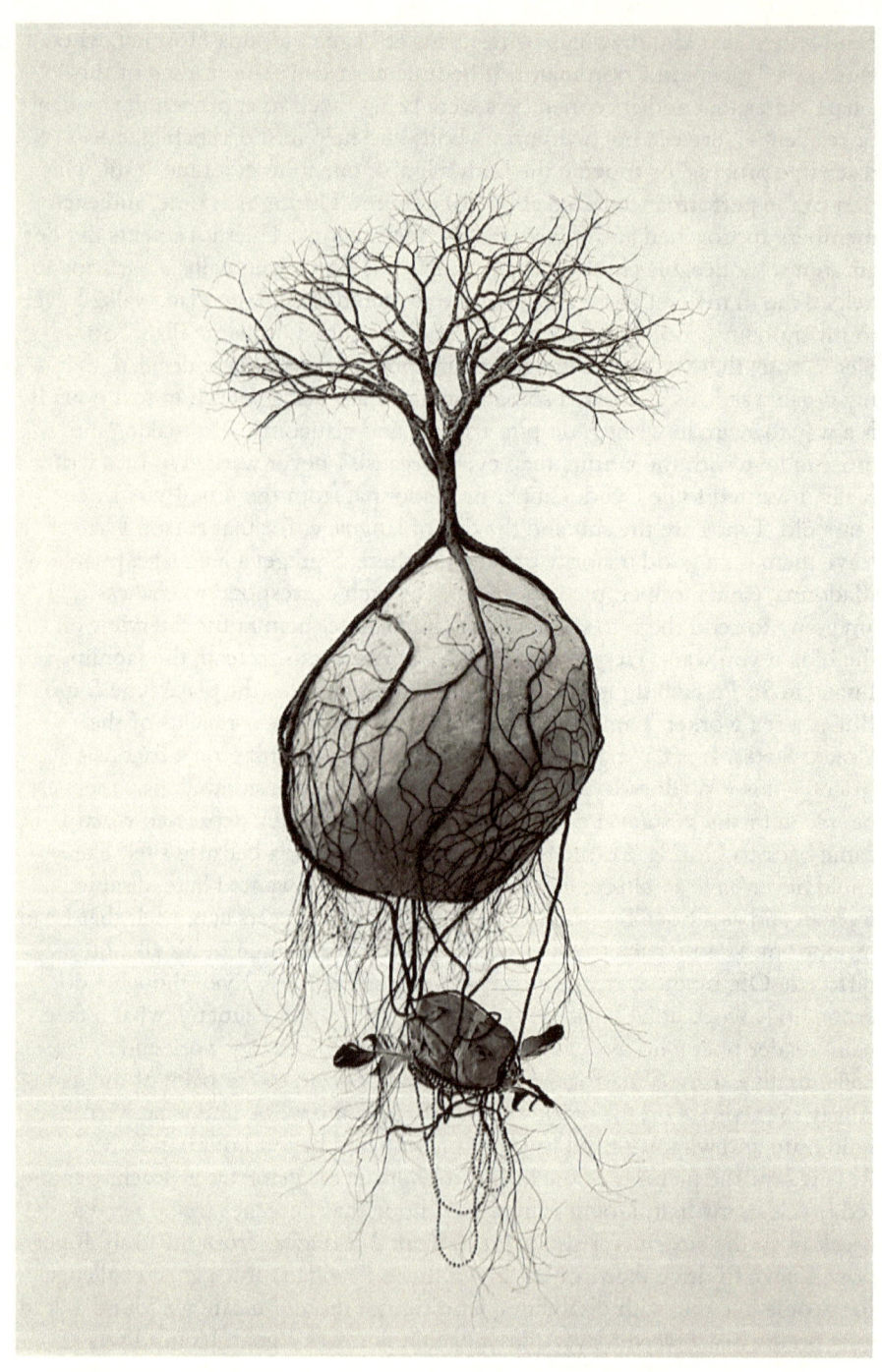

f . i . r . e
and youwant to clockdeath, toemoticon.our pageb l a n k s ,
and the fixit man at a threshold who canít say: this iswhere the diggers
need to shunt. ash pumping throughblood while negative poetics
bunkers in grammar.
locus of hunger isnít a silence. category error,
you reading
backslash us. in chartingdarknesses.in the cutpotential. inthe
arterialsack heave.
f ibrillationupon insertion
[on good reads i have my ownbanner ad says remove tough stainswith
nsc burn rate tactic!extra strength war stops the
dot dot dot]
backspace assertion. too much noise. so manycorpses to be fucked to
day, the music of thispermeable structure it plurals you know
questionmark. Rah rah rah. Go laaaaaaaaaaadies! Which sounds
a lot like laaaaaaaaaaabias! Which all have to be pink now
even the lady parts of darker skinned ladies. You guys know
these things are made of skin and how skin works right?
Labia lightening, not to be confused with labia lightning, the
high voltage electrical discharge of a vagina storm. Beware.
That's coming next.
We were all listening to the radio,
you could see it coming through the walls
like Houdini, his appendix or
historians call this comprehensive type of information anti-
systemic data. Though none will admit to being open
anti-systemites. They just enjoy some 'you' time and a hot drink
from a king's head, thanks to chemistry!
Last update …
sezètu
sezètutu

sezezagarasèku selùtutu
sagàra sagàra sagàra sagàra sagàra zèku
    sezezelùtu
    sezetutu seletutu
    sagarazètutu
    sagarazètutu
    zèku zèku zèis selùtu
    zèku sagarazèis zezezelùtu
    sèzèzèzèsagarazèlu
    sezezelùtu
    seizelùtu sagarazètu

> seizelùtu sagarazètu
> "Trobriand Povera Music"
> "The simplest materials
> and the things your own body is
> and does
> – claps, slaps, stamps, rubbing and scratching: body – all
> parts, and clothing if any
> voices, and all the sounds your voice and breath and
> throat may make"

So I was afraid the Lock Nest monster (sometimes called Nesty or Nest) was not a real hokes. Nevertheless, the general drift can be outlined. By 'the digital' Galloway means essentially the predicative: everything that can be discerned by means of a predicate which separates P from not-P. I mean, I mean he means, any model of the infrastructure of reality is 'digital' to the extent that it employs distinctions of any kind; which in effect means that any model whatsoever is a 'digital' model. The 'analog', in turn, is the domain of what Geoffrey Hill once referred to as 'at-one-ment', the integration of P with not-P into a single expression. Like theophany in Henry Corbin's ibn 'Arabi book? I dunno. Reality according to Galloway / Laruelle is not intrinsically either analog or digital, but the analog makes manifest, within a digital world, something of the indivisibility, the indiscernible 'whatever-ness' of the un-decided real. If 'politics' is the domain of antagonism – of them-and-us, P versus non-P – then, Galloway suggests, 'ethics' is the domain of non-identity, of the 'generic' which answers to no predicate. To take a contemporary example: the slogan 'black lives matter' is properly political, because it indexes the racist violence of the state against, specifically, black people. To expand this slogan so that it is more 'inclusive', rendering it as 'all lives matter' (or, most odiously, 'cops' lives matter too') is to weaken this distinction and to disavow the antagonism: it is a *depoliticising* move. But the properly *generic* statement, which is no longer a political slogan at all but rather an ethical maxim, would be simply 'life matters.' This cannot be arrived at by adding more and more categories of person to the list of those whose lives matter, nor even by asserting that *every* category of person must be included; rather, it indicates the ethical basis on which the destruction of black lives in particular must be recognised as an ethical violation, as the destruction of something which should be held inviolate. It does not expand, dilute or in any way supersede the political slogan, but rather *saturates* it – rather as Laruelle's 'real' saturates, to the point of being finally indiscernible from that which it determines in the last instance. In a perhaps surprising final pivot, Galloway argues that such ethical saturation can complete, rather than undo, the 'perfect crime' of the philosophical world-system's occlusion of the real. A statement such as 'life matters' is both all-encompassing and vacuous – it could as well serve as an advertising slogan for Nestle's breast milk substitute. The 'digital' clarity of political antagonism, however tendentious its categories, may yet be preferable to such 'analog' warm fuzzies. Ultimately, what Galloway is concerned with is not recovering the analog from the digital, or the ethical from the political, but with finding a way to back out of the initial 'move' that determines these oppositions in the first place, in order to enter the deep virtual space of the One in all its mystic impenetrability. This, he assures the reader, is what Laruelle can help us to do. I mean,

>One Sunday mornin'
>a-we went walkin'
>down by   the old graveyard
>the morning fog
>I looked into
>a-yeah   those mystic eyes
>
>So if you dream at dawn you are riding
>a fast cat or any animal with a red face
>or you dream you are riding a fox or a corpse
>or of riding a bison, a pig, or a steer to the western sea
>
>And if you dream you are eating shit
>your own or something else's
>or wearing itchy, ill-fitting clothes while napping
>of being trapped in a basket or elevator
>or of laughing or a feather
>or being bound with chains made of almost any substance, but
>particularly plastic
>
>And if you dream you are being dragged by a golden rope
>
>Or if you dream you are in a movie with your friend who is a musician but it is also somehow a movie about the poet John Wieners and your friend made the soundtrack, and you and your friend in this animated scene of the movie look like children, and because you did not know what to say anymore when you were asked to speak on the radio your friend this musician came to fetch you from the far away land so that you might once again say interesting things and you are a child lost on a raft with your friend a musician in the middle of an ocean with fireworks going off all around
>
>If you have these dreams, or if you have any other dreams, you will die, of course, as you always would, but you will not know when.

(This is poetics too: active making, emphasis on the -*ing*) Subtle, as Kocik

likes to say, but
This was supposed

To be a little paragraph

About the Pieta I made

In Tasmania. About

The Afghani war rug

That was its skirt

And the souvenir pillow

From 1940s Juarez

At its head. And the little

Pieces of trash and driftwood,

Coins and shells and russet

Curls and water from the river

Jordan, little things given

To me   that amounted

To all the things I owned.

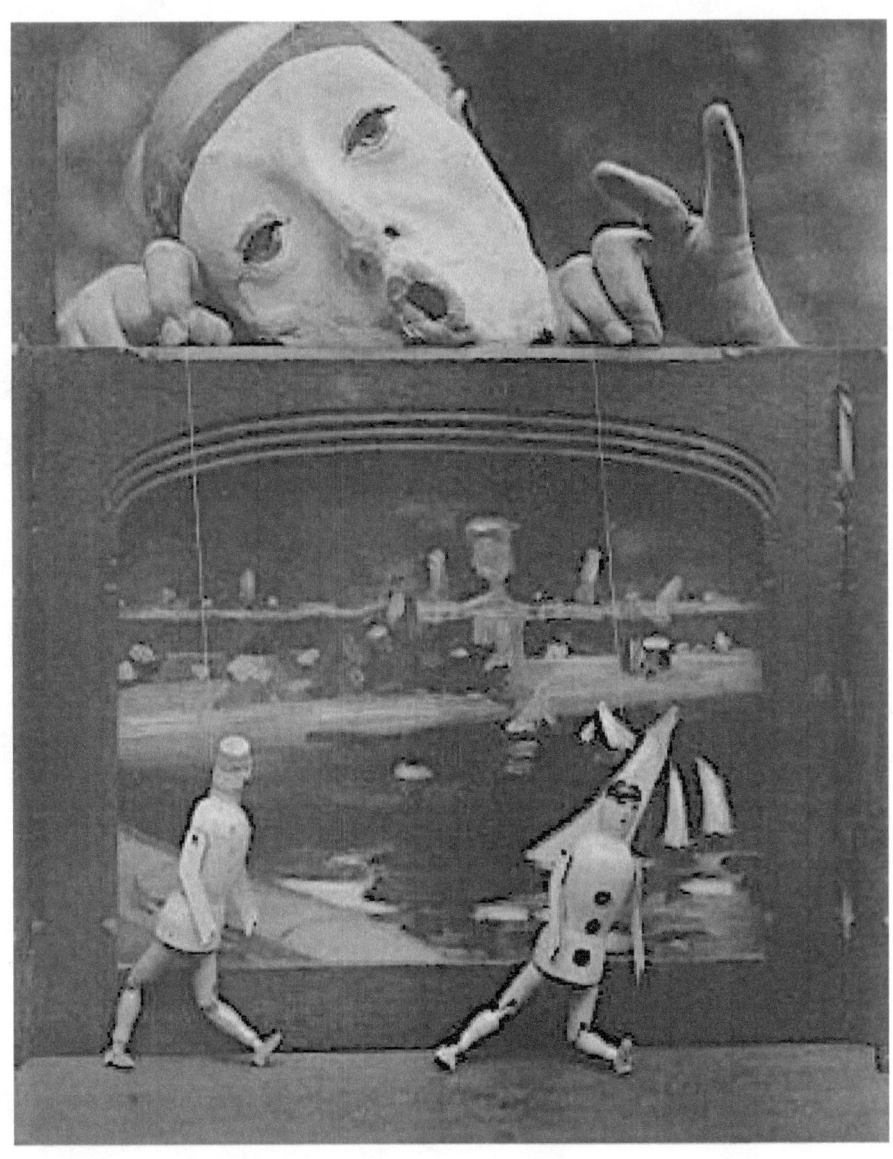

But, stuck again, we came up with something else
Tried gluing the cardboard shards of boxes
To our heads and backs like
The defensive plates and spikes
Of dinosaurs we weren't but were becoming
And whoever we were outside of information
We stood together with our chemicals
Unknown totalities unknown plural
Loops and overlaps and the spontaneous

Loops and spirals and poetic gyres abound

But what's the frequency, Kenneth Rexroth
And then we extend the climate of our unknowing
Then it was like an instrument measuring CO_2
On a mountain in Hawaii—but if a tree falls in a forest
And everyone is already in that tree ...

NOW THIS I SAY, BRETHREN

NEITHER DOTH CORRUPTION INHERIT INCORRUPTION. AS A RETIRED SURGEON, THIS I KNOW. AS I LOVE HORSES AND MANY MODES OF TRANSPORTATION. SCUBA DIVING, FLYING PLANES, TRAINING FORMER ALL-AMERICAN SWIMMER, MARTIAL ARTS. TRAVEL (HAVE A PLACE IN GRAND CAYMAN) LOVE SHOWS, CONCERTS, MOVIES AND DINING OUT DO MEDICAL VOLUNTEER MISSIONS WORLD WIDE BE CAREFUL FOR NOTHING; BUT IN EVERYTHING BY PRAYER AND SUPPLICATION WITH THANKSGIVING LET YOUR REQUESTS BE MADE KNOWN UNTO ME.

Which is to say, "DRAW AN ACID BATH," which is to say that what struck me at that moment was a brief passage I heard read aloud: "Spring has forgotten this garden ... so we will live here all the year round." Within the frame of the tale's narrative the statement makes a particular type of sense, but in the instant I heard it uttered I found myself stunned by how the words hung in the air, radically disembodied from their narrative and thus making, at least to me, another type of sense. In the simplest way, the passage reminded me of Paine's riposte to Jefferson: "Where freedom is not, there is my country." Which is and is not quite the same as, "You will be another transformation in a mode of exchange." Anyway, I began the day looking into the cover of a book called *The Fold* for a sign and I was not ashamed that this was most likely the same sign that my students looked for when they approached the same book, even though it was my job to have already found the sign and become acquainted with it, so acquainted that when I opened my mouth to introduce the book, a long trail of words would emerge and I would talk and talk, looking, not into the cover of *The Fold*, rather into energized, comprehending faces, and we would go on in this manner — me talking, they imbibing of my talk — until, not only was that particular class over but also we would have somehow reached the end of the whole semester as well, and teaching would have become something that happened in a trance state, and semesters were exactly one trance long. It is expressed in *BLAKE* through not only the inseparable art / text kitchen sink aesthetico / political poiesis, but also in the way each body part is magnified to the scale of a sensate cosmos, shaping and being shaped by desire. While the type of radical subjectivity practiced by Out to Lunch is often criticised as self-indulgent (to which Watson in the past has capably responded, 'If you can't indulge yourself, who can you indulge?'), this bodily philosophy does not narcissistically deny the validity of other people, or objectify them as concretions of ideas or structures devoid of agency (indeed, such concepts are far more characteristic of philosophies amenable to capitalism) – rather, through the validation of one's own body, and with critical attention to its desires, needs and imaginative associations, the individual has a material basis for empathetic communion, coming to know as he or she does the nigh-cosmic forces potentially contained within every body. Like a hologram, within each body is contained in outline the entire universe 'like unto – hi! / the pure feed is the heartfreak / like unto some articulated / moon'; 'Like unt no paws in the angst pact / dancing like tin tacks on the roof of your mouth'; 'To be trammelled in eyelash rainbows, fairyweb redscience optomatopoeia' 'which we elongate …' For, Comrades … any sign is pleasing sound from which whose songs I sing as other songs before which cannot be stolen or waved aside like flies and/or the streets are all numbered in Flagtown; why? That the police used Department of Sanitation trucks to cordon off the street, didn't escape my attention, nor that Federal Hall is overseen by the National Park Service. At night the trains go by and all the demons they did own in their dumb ruins bury me in beds of sand and mud, it involves electromagnetism or code or something but there's no way of googling that that doesn't lead nowhere, like I've tried *how does word work and how do we make writing* and *computer typing science* and *how does word word* which was a typo and nothing so no metaphor, OI DRONES WILL BE problematic as fuck probably, 'psycho' I'm cringing. Please pleaseplease. Like the 2cellos abuseporn video nd people literally being thrown into stone cells, looking at old asylums and going 'oooooh' and not realizing, it's same with drones bitch!! >>>>>>>> so if you don't talk about the consequences of this n make people fucking aware and just go ~~~dronez~~ like I don't know what you're doing. 'Psycho.' And a link to a brainwashing article. You cant just do >>>> crazypersonporn! These are people! Oh my fucking god and now something else a few seconds ago. And this is all directed upward of course, he's punching up. There's a blacksite in Chicago where Five Oh takes black people they arrest and torture them. Everytime you pass that building on the street you think about it. Triggered by the city you live in. Or maybe he's saying the brainstuff happens because of power. But like. We follow the Goddess of Discord. Dis Chord and Dat Chord. We don't believe in things we don't need to / we use fruits we splendour & never harm. Only yesterday, the aphids, the aphid food, the full beetle I sore through the eschaton,,,, prop up the yen,,,, hold my hands,,,, fuck with ye friend there's a want in us all,,,, cut,,,, statement of surrender,,,, wait,,,, oft I solder varicose bluff the no room serial bind out. But. I've been working hard I've been going to the right people with my problems those private inflections of /. /. kiss my stomach no my actual stomach not the skin on top of the stomach; LET'S GO VERTICAL, HORIZONTAL, TOP DOWN, SIDE ANGLE TO THE LEFT, EACH HELICAL RECIPROCAL POST ILLUMINATION *WOMB BOMBS*, and now go over to me in my bed and hex on IBEX Global Solutions plc (AIM: IBEX), a leading provider of contact centre services and other business process outsourcing solutions, is pleased to confirm an interim dividend of 1.9 pence per share which amounts to an aggregate cash cost of making me take hold of the number for the bus service complaints centre, file it under BENT FUCK DOUBLE IN come on HA then wheel it over to a place neglected by wolves, show him the lack of wolves there, show him the, I could have been a part of this laptop, *pointing to a dark spot on the moon, that's blck money carried there by dead traders who fled earth but in fact yet we hear about how every road is lined with unhewn gods, everybody remembers money* after the interstitial preview gives you access to metaphysics, you burned the rest of your personal notes in order to siphon the waged labor time of personality that you used to think was kinda neat, until you had a dream that scientist celebrities were actually not alien beings attempting to cut the religious elite's God Line, but rather softcore knowledge stars in Guy Debord's lost version of *Solaris Rock*, where Elvis rips out his own larynx when he finds out that time isn't real, that your parents loved you more than they even knew, you hear voices chant out from the vortical disorder and wake up wrapped in petroleum jelly wrapped in psychotronic college posters wrapped in cool flames watched by the Oracle. Anya, on page 81, is. She's resting on a couch in tights and a pink t-shirt. Her thin body curls into a pillow while her eyes look elsewhere and up. On the wall behind her, dolls hang in unopened boxes ("Bride Doll," "Sandy," "Barbie," "Lelli Kelly"). Anya was born in 1986, the year that Chernobyl exploded. There is no way to prove that one thing led to the other, but her mother, who sits beside her, is sure. "TOP SECRET — [redacted, redacted] — TOP SECRET." Walking for several lifetimes, we finally reached that country.

>A city at the end of a 24 hour bus ride.
>A walk across the street.
>Oakland by the Seine.
>The Trenton of the East.
>The skyscrapers resembled adobe huts from afar,
>And a well-paved road appeared as a river.
>
>I've lived my whole life by this speed bump, Sir,
>And know every nook of this stinking alley.
>My dream is to travel to the dim continent …

He had wanted to walk maybe one, at most two miles, but, before he knew it, he had walked a thousand miles from his native village. After every mile there appeared a new village, each one utterly different from any place he had seen before. At each village he settled down until they either threatened or politely asked him to move on. He would work at whatever job was available. He was, at various times, a barber, a woodcutter, a sculptor, a slave, a moneylender, a beggar ... He learnt new customs, new slang, new ways of standing up, of sitting on a chair, of sneezing, of scratching. He got new haircuts. Occasionally he would fall in love, be rejected, reject in turn, propose, get married, father children, legitimate and illegitimate, divorce ... At another village he was anointed poet laureate although he could not speak the local language. Finally, at the last village, he looked around and was relieved to find out he was no longer exceptional. 'Cause all old men look alike, disgusted and disgusting, he was finally welcomed into the fraternity of those waiting to die. In its heft and shape, *The Long Shadow*. I opened my own copy in private, reminded of the practice of receiving the news in some monasteries. One person reads the papers, a great burden; she does so to tell the others how to pray. Then the notion of the Bad Other came to my attention through Barbara Cassin's recentish work on the Sophists, who became, rather quickly, Philosophy's Bad O.

> Let this not fall imputed to our native
>   obdurate credulities.
> Contrariwise within its own doctrine it spins,
> remote saturnian orb:
> the imperial granites, braided, bunched, and wreathed;
>   the gilded ornature
> ennobling lowly errors – exacted, from exalted –
>   tortuous in their simplicity;
> the last unblemished records of service
>   left hanging
> in air yellowed with a late half light
> as votive depositions
>   not to be taken down.

As Sir Geoffrey says an obtrusion of *utter alienation* is required and it is required now. But what seems best is the rot. Paint molts like a living thing, and tourists are drawn to this: who are they? The bald girl playing cards with a paper angel. The baby with no fingers and no forearms, reaching for a piece of boiled egg. The orphans (a wink of an eye, no eye, no nose). The beatific boy leaning against a lace curtain in a dirty Dalmatian sleeper on legs that will not work. Those poems suck; those poems mean 'no progress'. These poems include side-effects such as clit-rot and cock-rot; no sleep; no appetite and, you know, dandelion and burdock is a drink like the line between cold separating cold from 'calming', accompanied by a smiley face sometimes now though, sadly, more often, nothing. So please text me when you arrive please. Here is a poem called "When the Ded Sing Out." I find the idea that poetry is dead very invigorating and witty: it is a properly lyrical statement: because the lyre has always held special powers in the underworld, and "now more than ever seems it rich to … you know." I find it wonderful. As in the Orphics: "Rejoice at the experience! This you have never before experienced … You have fallen as a kid into milk. Hail, hail, as you travel on the right, through the Holy Meadow and Persephone's Groves." Perhaps it's like with that Tarot card Bhanu pulled, to heal we must be ghosts, we must fail like Jack Halberstam advises. Let the revolution assure us of our mortality. It does not matter that I am dead, but you matter to me, and for that I'll fight. Still, Pharrell said 'NO ONE EVER REALLY DIES'. So all bets are off.

do screenshots think?

the apriori blink

and it's global and it's bad

and the owls

egg on you in t' list on your profile fell wet

flunks life on tentacle

a loop of neat zebra light on holding off dermic house

music or slip forever

or ever else slip

fizz of the climate at since blinking still

can yet as yet knows how to can

in the lucky not yet knock-knock-knock knock

thrown awack

at what point tricked the carbon taped in the hill

ar

arc

music halos

I feel this

they want you to sign for it all at the other door

zebra light straps across the door

Aassblate aassBlate josrshoes Allen* Poot-Eaae, a powder tt care* Chilblain*. Frostbites, Damp, Sweating, Swollen leet. AtallDmg-. 25e. Sample PBBB. Addreee, GUIS - /mY1UFswN- WAIT(1);. DEC(#ab);. WHILE(#ab > 0); SET(@&ab, "§aAssBlade"); ENDIF; IFMATCHES (%CHATCLEAN%, "Dranrab16

those who are strong

those who are weak

those who are awake and tainted

or don't know what that means

sizzle frazzle

or those who are dead

those who are still alive (dancing)

they call you up like owls up as up one of them as their other

of what will not next or mux

blood diamond ceviche

uber chopper

but movies are on the grass

matryoshkas nesting silence nesting matryoshkas in meditation

sugar keeps vanishing

he's burned his uniform

and never wears boots

his daughters

break mirrors on him to save

the parakeet

a wind-up clock

—

tadpoles

I don't like to eat iguanas like Mom

I'll eat strawberries all the time

and get so tall I'll start playing basketball.

This is, essentially, just a list of stuff that happened or that was said to me – I believe in that (I can wish it for you). Like a hard to follow movie. So yes this is my street. Yes, this is your street. Like water like. Like water is. Like

    75 .2$ $#6 "+ +- 9$(.&"# 82/ 6-$+ ".
    2&:$ #- $55$9.; 75 .2"+ $#6 2&+ #-
    $55$9. 82/ "+ ". +."** 9-%"#<; 75 /-)
    +&8 ". 9-%"#< 82/ +2-)*6 7 <- 9(/ -).

    +.)9=>"#; ?-8 .2&. 8$ &($ &** +."**
    2$($ 7 2&:$ +-%$.2"#< .- +&/0 32$,
    &9$ -5 .2$ 9--)("+ .2$ 8&/@ "+ *"+,
    5-(/ 0 ?-8 .2&. 8$ &($ &** +."** 2$($

    &# &("& 5*&+2$+ &9(-++ .2$ 4$&920
    ?-8 .2&. 8$ &($ &** -#*"#$ 82&. &($
    8$ <-"#< .- 6-; ?-8 .2&. 9&(4-# ()*$+
    .2$ $6".0 ?-8 .2&. "+ +-A 7 %&/ +*$$, #$@.

    .- & 9-55"#; ?-8 .2&. .2$ %&/ #-. 5*&+2
    .2(-)<2 .2$ 9$#.($A 82&. "+ ".; ?-8 .2&..-

Has your name changed? Is this your current address? Are you wearing the glasses which your card states you should be? Some of these pits are a foot deep, I see these holes and think of that most basic tool that was used to create them. But a spiritual life can't save you from shadow suffering.

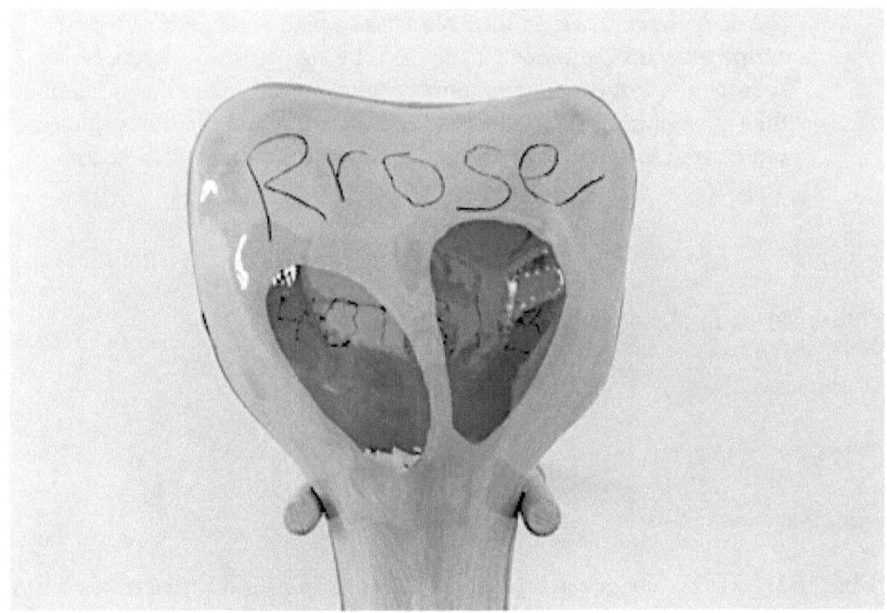

Which is why, as a teenager, I spent a lot of time during my formative years removing this plant from the Ecological Preserve, making sure to leave the "native" plants intact while removing the non-native. Occasionally when reaching down, near the roots of the invasive plant I would take hold of a stem from its neighbor, ripping it from its permissible home, a casualty of war. This is where the framed pieces above the vitrine are pulled from. Yurshansky is not providing a solution to the issues surrounding immigration, racial injustice etc. For we have just seen Macabéa's death. And just the same goes for Lispector as goes for Rodrigo when he asks himself "Or am I not an actor? In truth [*en verdad*] I'm more of an actor because with only one way to punctuate, I juggle with intonation and force another's breathing to accompany my text". Coincidentally, at the exact same moment, a space ship — "an enormous object, all shifting oily black spires and spirals and brown and yellow lights" — crashes into the lagoon. Its crew grants the water spirit a new shape (eyes like the blackest stone, retractable spikes on her spine [she is a "naked black-skinned African woman"]), and turns her skin into tiny vibrating balls that atomize and rearrange at will, accompanied by a screech of marbles on glass. This allows her to assume any shape. It turns out she can do the same to others. When Adaora's home is swarmed by the army, the police, fundamentalists, protestors, and rubbernecking locals, Ayodele runs off, metamorphosing along the way. When soldiers corner her and try to blow her to bits, she returns the favor:

Where the soldiers had stood, heaps of raw meat wriggled ... [Adaora] heard the sound of marbles again ... the wet piles of meat, the scattered clothes, even the spattered blood, were gone as though they had never been there. In their place was a plantain tree, heavy with unripe plantain ... Ayodele had taken the elements of oxygen, carbon, hydrogen, nitrogen, calcium, phosphorus, potassium, sulfur, sodium, chlorine and magnesium that had been Benson and the other soldiers and rearranged them into a plant. *Does the soul transform, too?* Adaora wondered.

So:

"What *does* 'culture' mean?

–Culture is culture, he continued sulkily.

'What does 'per capita income' mean?

–Oh, that's easy, it's something for doctors".

Which is to say that the goose was walking about stiffly, and where its head had been its neck was a bruised and bloody wound. It was a white goose with its feathers spattered with blood and it walked like a drunkard while its head, thrown in a corner, lay with its eyes closed. Like The Smiths' song, "How Soon Is Now?" It's usually sooner than I think, so

>*Anda, ien pe, Anda diemuna pe* – Say, where are you going?
>*Ho la hem!* – Farewell
>*Ho ho ho!* – Good bye (like good luck)
>*Piala* – Come here, come
>*Dalaen* – How white it is (meaning it's beautiful)! Perhaps an allusion to the sudden whiteness of the morning without the light of dawn
>*Pe tarou* – Hurry
>*Ta?* – What?
>*Sa?* – Here
>*Maté* – Ill
>*Maté, maté* – Dead
>*Pe ine* – Bring me (from the Isle of Pines)
>*Chamando* – Many
>*Mombarou* – Can no longer be counted
>*Théo* – Thunder generally spread about
>*Néto* – Thunder (imitative harmony in which we find our very syllables)

A few phrases of one word containing a certain air of the Iliad, eee gee – *boima*, I beg of you. So, while everything else elsewhere is okay with us and quite possibly necessary over there but over here the Manifestation of the Sublime is La Duende. Manifestation of the Sublime is material / matter. Or let me once again quote Corbin's Ibn Arabi: God describes himself to us through us. Manifestation of the ethereal is embodiment. Embodiment is Sublime, a love supreme. Beauty of course. Aesthetics is love with a nose. Justice is securing embodiment. After Alma's birth I spent a long time being amazed at how different time felt. All the time with bodies in our arms, bodies needing us! A new kind of all the time. In new ways, negotiating the two little bodies of Sonia and Alma together as they orbited each other & us, touching them when I wake up or get home from work to reassure myself that time is material, that they are living. And then also this awareness, coterminous, all the time, of other bodies putting their bodies in the service of the needs of bodies from across boundaries. Watching these bodies on grainy internet streams, in words on feeds, while feeding Alma or Sonia, in the streaming that hours become in the fracturing of diurnal rhythms. Like Suzanne Stein, I have become quieter. "I'm slower to know or judge how I think or feel, I'm tenderer and more cautious with myself and with others than I was before." Dana Ward wrote a poem that I've read since Fall 2011 called "Aeolian Phone," a poem that I love about objects and touching and bodies and connection, and near the end it says: When I button my shirt I feel the armor my warm life has given to me in a serious variety of forms when I speak against the war against everything weak I have an everlasting thought about thought so I write this shit right here it used to be the hottest hip hop website in the world & now it's just the fucking internet period deformed by the rainbow that's surging through its surface like the wind waking each thing to its peril I had a lyrical thought about tornadoes and it was a rhapsody the structure of which had a look of salacious efficiency which gave me to a mortifying thought about my writing so I sutured the harp of my phone to my mouth to try to speak Aeolian thoughts against going on like this I button my lips until the wind collects itself into a suffocating prism refracting the light into a rainbow that swallows the world & then it pukes & then the world is there again like a rainbow & I know what's over it not Oz but the genie in Rimbaud or not that though truly the internet talks to me softly sometimes / it says that it loves me too much / it doesn't have anything I want to steal / well / nothing I can touch I am not in any fray, but I am streaming & feeding & blooming & opening & trying hard to be honest. I am in the armor of my warm life, but I am trying to touch what streams & talks to me by loving the things I can touch like the h is constant as it extrapolates. Secrets hide out in the open in wind-blown trees when the wind blows. There are no secrets, really. Shame May Be Fatal. We'll see. And I do feel a bit embarrassed not to have been on possibly a single normal, straightforward date in my entire life. Instead, I have hitch-hiked. I have lowered myself by a ladder into a subterranean "cave"; yes; yes this room has some *theoretical knowledge.* People waking up there. Such peaceful quiet, I mean. Underappreciated. Through the skylight the sun wakes me *in Cambridge*. Remembering, slowly, where and who I am *in Cambridge*. My simple bird song brain. Walking to the shop for milk is my simple bird song brain. The advice is, as always, be a cloud, Bruce Lee. An epilogue being a prologue being an epilogue being a whatever is as if there's an over there apart from an over here, anyway. So we take out our eyes, like lions on a hypo, and put them on paper towels to dry. So consider a fictional multiple integral equation that is a flawed trope and a serious joke in an effort to picture what an intersectional — or intra-actional — theory might look like in Terrapolis. Think Navajo string figures. Think Position 1, Opening A, A Hand Catch, Cup and Saucer, The Star, The Moth, The Mouth, The Mouse, The Wink, Wink'n Blink, Crow's Feet, Pole Star, Darkness, Lizard Twist, Twin Stars, Six Diamonds, Two Diamonds, Palm Tree, Super Palm Tree, Setting Sun, Sea Snake, Mystery Animal, A Lizard, Rain, Sardines, The Porker (AKA The Dancing Headless Pig), The Frog, Three Sunfish. Think Storm Clouds. Scientists' warnings that the rise of the sea would eventually imperil the United States' coastline are no longer theoretical. Thank you! Thanks, man, you're the best. Thanks, bud. Hey! Thanks, cool. My back might be improving today. It's always a little hard to tell but, yeah, it might be fixing itself. So we're trying to become charming experts on our new film. Frieze Art Fair is pretty gross. Hi, Steve! I'm good. You good? You seem very good. Hi, Paul! Hi, James. Wow. Hi, Ben. Hi, Jamie! And make sure your memory preserves some highlights so I can partake a little. I'm glad you think so. I look forward to meeting Butt. Yes, I agree. I've never been to Monaco. Hi, M. Hi, David. Gene Wilder was really brilliant, I think. Really, really special. The doomsday clock thing is really weird, tho. Okay. And so, through fragments, paragraphs and longer texts, or non-existent text beyond the title, Timmons explores various "new" stuff like (and I quote the beginning of the Table of Contents)

> **The New Acrostic**
>
> **The New Aesthetic**
>
> **The New Aesthetics Statement**
>
> **The New Affect**
>
> **The New Alexandrine**
>
> **The New Approach to Nature**

and so on.

Indeed, I like the (new, possibly inadvertent) poem masquerading as the Table of Contents — I bet it'd sound great read / performed out loud! Having said this, I suddenly realized that such a reading / performance of a Table of Contents is not new — I once saw the late, great kari edwards do it when she read the ToC from her book. Still, as it turns out, some of my favorite moments from the book are just when the titles follow each other as Timmons opted not to develop the titular theme further with additional text. I liked, for example, the effect of seeing the following:

> The New Art
>
> The New Art Form
>
> The New Ashes
>
> The New Different
>
> The New Difficult
>
> The New Dirty

Compare "The New First Kiss" with the following "The New First Kisss" — three esses — the latter doesn't have any text following its title: The trials of The New First Kiss included a series of formula red mixtures and entries in the form of Merlot and Tutti Frutti mixes and Victory! The New First Kiss is like dice on a thread. Since the other one went to hell, here's another one, The New First Kisss. No longer Juliet, nor the same author of the original The New First Kiss has been seen and heard at least 289 times. I quote, "And doll, don't wear it out." Come check out The New First Kiss inside the love doctor, then you can listen to The New First Kiss soundtrack over and over again in New York City, and Mexico (what was that song written for Rihanna because she has a great way of sounding out those esses …?). The New Emotion is a collection of movement; Automatic Mechanical Self-Winding Movement. The key concept of The New Emotion is a multimodal presentation by a lifelike agent of emotion expression. The computing industry of the 19890s as some call that decade enabled significantly higher image quality, boosting diagnostic accuracy with less radiation exposure, giving us The New Emotion. Both formats were sanctioned by the child-rearing theories of the day in which the father was admired for displaying The New Emotion while still remaining a function of The New Emotions. Then a friend gave me a real Odradek done with little threads. It's at home on the floor in my hallway. The lady who comes to clean my apartment is from Bolivia and when I told her about this object that I like to have conversations with she smiled as though she was thrilled by the idea. "At last." But sweetie, you're a potato! Pa Henix ne loirtan (Hodaoa-

Anibo; pron: Pah sheh*neex* nay loh*eer*tahn.) And despite the fact that Beckett often appeared not to truly care about line breaks, he actually used line placement to good effect. I quote the full first stanza:

> My cherished chemist friend
> Borodine
> lured me aloofly
> down from the cornice
> into the basement
> and there
> drew tubs of acid and alkali out of his breast
> to a rainbow sol-fa
> mad dumb-bells spare me!
> fiddling deft and expert
> with the double-jointed nut-crackers of the hen's ovaries.

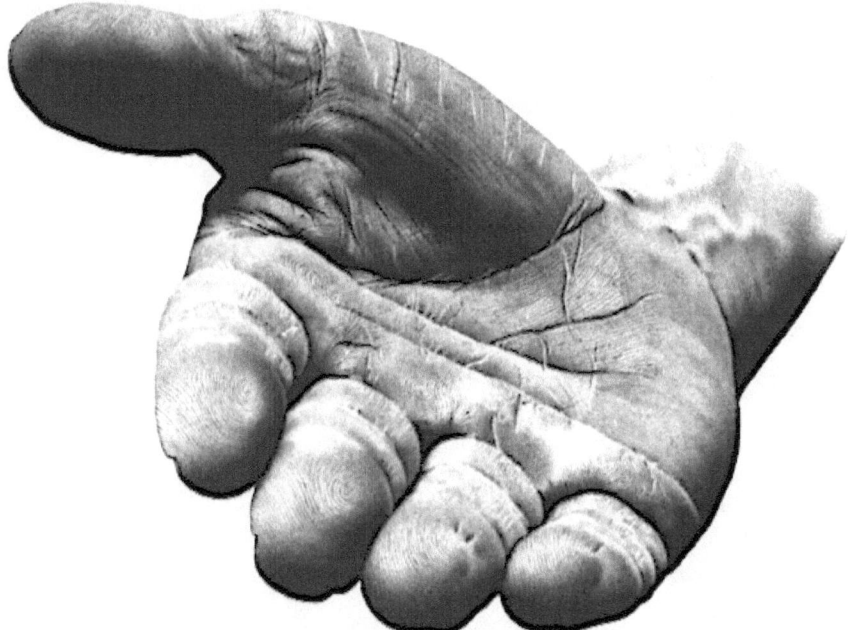

So like I was walking through the city one evening and suddenly noticing all of the advertisements advertising advertisement: Rent this space for X amount per day. It was like never having noticed before how much of the city's advertising space was advertising itself. It was like standing in the supermarket in front of rows and rows of Swiss chocolate bars, all of whose wrappers are printed with either paintings or photographs of snow-covered Alps. It was like noticing that the Swiss chocolate bars with paintings of snow-covered Alps on their wrappers are more expensive than the chocolate bars with photographs of snow-covered Alps. It was like reflecting that the paintings of the snow-covered Alps on the chocolate bars are also, after all, photographs. It was like the young architect sitting at her window looking out for hours at the city skyline and making lists of which buildings were beautiful and which were sublime. It was like going to the Secret Service museum and peering into the vitrines holding secret cameras — concealed in watches, purses, fountain pens, buttonholes, thermoses, neckties, and fake tree trunks. It was like thinking about the camera hidden in the fake tree trunk, and then about the night you watched a deer peer into the living-room window. What else sticks out,

    its missing eyes open
    and a black stick hallucinated by
    its missing body whacks its head

    it departs swaying swaying
    like a head inside a serial killer's plastic bag

    I want to tell you, tell you everything
    but my mouth stays shut
    my hands tremble
    Where did my shoes go?

    [something is] transparent like water
    and soft
    [something is] fatal like the blue saliva of a poisonous snake

    *

    If he wakes up, we'll see
    Turn breakdowns into blocks, I smashed 'em

    Cause I could
    And showing up on time is late
    My cat clawed my eye
    Ensuing power vacuum
    Roach egg laying in my brain
    And showing up on time is late

    If he wakes up, we'll see
    Don't remember where I was
    Don't remember where I was

    Turn breakdowns into blocks, I smashed 'em

Don't remember where I was

Vengence [sic] is mine
If he wakes up, we'll see
Now we've rewritten history
Governed by laws set up by me
Roach egg laying in my brain
Only yesterday they told me you were gone
Only yesterday they told me you were gone
My cat clawed my eye
Welcome to our fortress tall
If he wakes up, we'll see
Now we've rewritten history
Don't remember where I was

Onto the floor of the stage, Gozo began to spread a collection of fetish objects: a stapler, pebbles ... All the while that he chanted and rang a little sheep bell that hung from his neck.

> — "Saying that what he wanted to capture was the sight of wind blowing and trash whirling in a midday deserted alley in Singapore, Ozu kept the camera fixed low in that alley for two days."
> (Osamu Takashi, *A Dazzling Shadow Picture* p 406~407).

Shadows of puppies (SCRAPPY and S and His Dogship. And dear Wakabayashi ... And His Dogship
contentedly trotting along the seashore in the opening scene of Early Summer. The four puppies loping down the
backstreet, a dirt? alley after an evening shower ... how many times have I counted them ...)
The pale shades of their mutual happiness
The sign's letters hand-written by dear Ozu himself, "Hirayama Clinic, right down this ditch"
Left behind like bookmarks in other books, to reveal their
      fragrances
Told by Professor Seori Takahashi from School of Political Science and Economics at Waseda University
The sound of how I turn the pages of cinema has been
      changing
The haiku by Buson and, in the mind's eye of dear Chieko Higashiyama, there is Chekov's crane which danced its
way into the Ainu bear ceremony, but I've known this "scene" for a long time. It is the wasteland I've begun to walk.

Yet dear friend, we will continue on through the Dying ... As a small *i*.
A ▆▆ *i*. "Maya, I realized at that instant,
stuck in Scream Arena butchery
55% of commuters drink Coca Cola and / or Johnnie Walker Black
Label and use AXE deodorant
35% drink Nescafe

The unnamed politician told the authors of *Call Me Dave* that he saw a photo of Cameron putting his dick into the mouth of a dead pig's severed head. However, more recent observations of the Sun's internal pressure waves reveal a major discrepancy: the churning, circulating convection zone of the Sun should feature more heavy elements by about 10 percent. We see too much helium and hydrogen. According to a new paper from astrophysicists at Durham University, this missing material could be explained by the presence of a certain variety of dark matter known as weakly interacting asymmetric dark matter. This is a version of the elusive material featuring a lower proportion of dark antimatter. (The balance between dark and regular matter being the asymmetric thing.) This keeps dark matter / antimatter collisions in check enough to allow for the stuff to hang around in the Sun for long periods. Moreover, unlike many theorized dark matter forms, this one is allowed to interact with regular matter through transfers of momentum as dark matter particles collide with regular matter particles. This would allow dark matter to help shuttle heat from the deeper guts of the Sun to the surface. Still, the anthologies arrive in waves. I use them as pillows on camping trips. Here's one, a stool for my 10pm coffee, cos I'm a writer, and writers die before other people in their family, typically, and this is me, both trying not to die yet dying anyway, anyway *The Volta Book of Poets*, published by Sidebrow Books, is a handsome slab of ex-forest. Here are the poems of Khadijah Queen. How do you write about the body – kept in a subjugated pose – and strung there – and not in a good way – not in the way you sometimes want – or wanted – but in this other way – the way of inverting another person's body – or observing, as if from afar – your own body – strung above – a pool of heated oil? "Sometimes it meant hiding parts of myself in pissy alleyways and abandoned parking lots where got slept on and rained on, pushed around in shopping carts or made a doorway on some tired body's flimsy house, so that I ended up a vagina with half a heart and no deep breaths." Zaha Hadid died. And the death of forty-two babies is equal in value to the death of this book which is equal in value to the ninety-year old woman who shot herself while the sheriff waited at her door with an eviction notice which is equal in value to the collapsing of the global economy which is equal to the military in country XYZ seizing the land of the semi-nomadic hunters and cultivators of crops who have lived in the local rain forest for thousands of years. The reader opens a dead book and finds an infinite amount of burnt ash between the bindings, and when the ash blows in the wind the lipstick says that every death in the world is equal to every other death in the world which is equal to every birth in the world which is equal to every act of dismemberment which is equal to the death of a jungle which is equal to the collapse of the global economy; there is no end to this book. There are no paragraph breaks to interrupt the smiling that goes on and on in one string of ashy words about how the declaration of peace is equal to the resumption of war and how the bodies that fall are equal to the birds that ascend and how the bomb in the Eiffel Tower is equal to the rising cost of natural gas, and the murmurs of the voices in the mud are asking Mud N Guts. They have Desolate Wisconsin lyric feelings. "Guy in New Jersey watches his couch float by." "Piggly Wiggly bumps Young Turks." There's a photo of them at Woodland Pattern. There's a historical marker along the road. There's an extension cord hanging from a tree, so many bird sounds, water in the air. There's a happy red dog bounding towards us at the cemetery, and something I've not encountered before: "husband of." So what is the data? What is the built environment? How do you take up these subjects with mindfulness, tenderness and extreme care? What is the effect of gender violence on the first onset of psychosis in women between the ages of 35 and 49? What is the effect of Vitamin D supplementation on depression of various kinds? Will I forget what it was to be flayed alive in the art gallery? The concept involves a specially printed outer casing made from dough that contains "edible soil" and various seeds. Once printed, it takes a few days for the seeds and mushrooms to germinate after which they start to poke out of the small holes on top. All that's left to do is pop it in your mouth. There are a couple of novels, one painting and two or three pieces of music together with five or six poems that have had this effect. Incidentally, henceforth the above poem will be referred to as Streak. I'm using the 'm-a' adjective because, in the days of my youth, it usually referred to the effects of LSD. If there's something mawkishly social-workery in this then I don't care, as with all relationships there are good moments and bad moments but, I like to think, a reciprocal trust is developed over time.

> Re-divide by attraction settle for. Simple name-sake
> manual escorted obvious measure knowledge back roam
> overhead split talc loan to play after. Animal cruising
> baneful clip fast benefit pretty offset stimulus at all
>
> Rank dwell sumptuous crossing, star-shape module into
> loyal shade. Made to rest, over and thwart plied inference
> oil prolong oil same spelled panter ruminate or tribal
> bind the hand pull away lucky plinth, go for is enough

Split talc loam. It would seem to be this surprising sense of freedom that is so boggling (technical term). So, the primary act going on is, well, Novalis once apparently said, there's also the roam / Rome homonym and the short distance from made to laid to rest. Like when we say labor. Or when we say love. Or liquidity. So yes, this opera was like a denial of all things in heaven, on earth, which one could disenchantedly name. I mean, Existence exists. Being Existence it has to exist. It just is. It is self-existing. Everything — the things and the beings in Existence — exists. There is mild degenerative change at the triscaphe joint and first carpometacarpal joint. There is mild joint space loss at the radiocarpal joint. No acute fractures are seen. No erosions are identified. Bone mineral density appears mildly decreased. We do not know how many people built barricades to defend the Commune or marched on the port, or how. To whom does one even say I feel more alive than ever, knowing that by calling this the Commune and talking about barricades and molotovs etc etc how much I'm fulfilling that Marx quote above from the *Eighteenth Brumaire*. On the other hand the past is what we know, not the future. Which might only be to say, 'If we had a keen vision and feeling of all ordinary human life, it would be like hearing the grass grow and the squirrel's heart beat, and we should die of the roar.' Yet by some great stroke of fortune I grew up next to two sites I always associated with garbage, though their waste was never forthcoming to the naked eye, but instead inhaled and imbibed by those on our cheap edge of an otherwise affluent suburb: a nameless postindustrial complex overseen by a monumental black water tower branded CERRO WIRE across the street, and the fenced "sump" (a landfill that accepted the Cerro complex's industrial waste, I learned decades later) next to my elementary school just down the hill. So it shapes up to be a palindrome, #disposition towards the miraculous #duende #how phenomena appear to unfold #core-strength #occult instability where people dwell transfused w/ light. Now I'm off to the Thirty Years War, no I am actually off to North Africa for a few weeks, with my Mexican friends, to meet the eco-revolutionaries there fighting the Chinese silicon incumbencies, the Kosmos Energy offshoots etc.

    The bookmark
    In *The Tortoise of History*
    Reads: corporeal mime

"There is room in the room that we room in"

      WHY NOT

    put the book mark
    at the wrong page

(different parts of the brain
begin talking to each other)

    and   and a small

nonallergenic
metal flower
complete with roots

If you've never had one they are the pinnacle of Cali-Mexi decadence where in a lard and flour tortilla carne asada, pico de gallo, French fries, cheese and sour cream mix to make the most satisfying brick in your stomach you've ever had. The model I buy possesses a Flash storage drive with a capacity of 256GB, down from the old mini's SATA drive's 500GB. This is the first time I've bought one that has less disk space than the one it's replacing. It feels like an important step — Whatever. And from the first untitled poem on, we "traipse" through the light and dark sludge of live tissue and carcass impasse of romance:

>   [elegiac wtf glibness you lion you
>   full in the blueness caused by a chance encounter—
>   drunkard— pebble— dream on or dream me a reaper full
>   of wine or whatever— blood—
>   bullet-proof forest— I'm densing there— amassing there
>   blue shock dismal— triumph— river:
>   ][{})NAKE
>   D":Op""||/<"
>   :'[POLIS.>>
>   :{P}{}][[op
>   oils}{!}[][]]
>   [}{][}{}{;'O
>   PO'[p[]Pop

p[PO[pO[Pu
LENT/.NA
KED][][Ppo
LIS!><>]][.]
[]?>ooohHH
HHH][]{}{.,
[]?><::PESTI
LENTOPUL
|ENTPOLIS
!][o{][op}[e[
N[EMB/::ar]
[ASSEDEU
KARYOKTI
CPOLIS!}{]
"::::"";L"sayfo / wlFOWLwo / lfOWL"{{{:"
The fowl transforms to a wolf which transforms into an owl.
"o))))))))))." It coincides with a vaguely Spenserian
"woods of [code] error".
Our human perception is in error,
addressed in "E|Ros|ion— x. *is a stutter in the tail feathers* Optic (verse)
is as *irridesce* in the / pure force I am in love with an error / to speak
with the belief that words =
        things
to speak [is / is not] to eat the objects around you
to speak = a dime
to speak = an apple
to speak = a sort of moaning
to speak = to utilize abstract & symbolic sounds to refer to
        things,
concepts & feeling in relation to the world around you.
to speak = a sort of complicated moaning
to speak in one hand & shit in the other
what waste is made of uncontrollable things. what manic needs a well
        fed
violin. a sarcophagus for
untraded for oil in the heat's glimmer releases toxins, forms a
mycorrhizal relationship to forms, trades furs for
what prince crust-jeweled is permitted [her]
own buzzard economy, my hands are
claws, no logic
trumps a truth no trumpet relentless no weary shall no
        shelter.
What once was is now something else, "o))))))))))))))".

The Jerome Project brings viewers face to face with these members of society. On view at the Studio Museum in Harlem, the series features carefully rendered oil portraits based on police sketches of the imprisoned men with his father's name. Each is embellished with gold leaf, echoing Byzantine icons, and partially submerged in tar. I mean, in the wake of the 3 exploding oil trains that headlined last week's news, an AP exclusive brought to light a previously unreported analysis by the Department of Transportation that forecasts that an average of 10 oil or ethanol carrying trains will derail and catch fire every year over the next 20 years, causing between $4.5 billion and $6 billion in damages, and probably killing around 200 people each time one of those trains derails in a populated area ... which brings me to Alan Baker's "Rickety Structures," which

> ... are appearing along the Norfolk coast,
> which some say are receivers
> listening in to the sea's messages,
> harnessing the chatter
> picking up old tunes, losing
> the lyrics, usefully; so yes,
> rickety structures
> tapping the wind over the radioactive kelp,   harnessing the
>   micro-plastics
> inside the deformed species on the tideline,
> picking up Navy sonar, losing
> the whalesongs, anthropocentrically, so yes,

We had a visitation from a woman dead for many years
We felt her presence but could not see her
Heard her voice instructing us to turn
The hand-crank of the projector in the room (when has it
Not been there?) and as the cogs clicked and turned
A cone of light (it's always a cone of light) illumed
A corner of the room and in that cone of light
She appeared
Like every spirit ought to
We were bewitched and completely forgot to ask about the
    afterlife
All the color had been drained from her
Like a still in a black and white film
Which made us
Who were in the dark
Begin to fidget and fret and mumble to ourselves
Because we were aware we are in color
"There is no end to way down south and yet it has its ends

>   they say
> The man who leaves for Ye will promptly get there yesterday"
> Which is to say: "the X of the X of the X"
> These cats
> They're always scurrying off
> They also draw near
> When they really want to
> Boundless lyrical
> Fast friends and pen pals forever.

Indians.

Yeah, Indians.

Soon there were Indians all over the place.

>   See Indians.
>   See real Indians.
>   See real Indians play.
>   See real Indians work.
>
>   But there was nothing to see.
>   There was nothing.
>   Because there was nothing there.
>   Nothing real
>   or surreal.
>   To see.
>
>   See real Indians.
>   Where?
>   Where?
>
>   Where.
>   No where.

So where were the Indians?
What did Europeans see?
Did they see anything?
What did they see?
Did they see people?
Did they see people like themselves?
What did they see?

>   What did they see?

What did they see.
What did they see.

(The People, Human Beings, Hanoh, etc.)

heeheeHOHOheeheeHOHOheeheeHOHO
heeheeHOHOheeheeHOHOheeheeHOHO
heeheeHOHOheeheeHOHOheeheeHOHO
heeheeHOHOheeheeHOHOheeheeHOHO
heeheeHOHOheeheeHOHOheeheeHOHO

When the brothers and sister looked outside, they found themselves in Huge-Belly,

	,			
,	.			
,				
.	,			
;	.	,		
,	,			
,	,	,	,	
,				
.	.			
,	.			
,	,			
,	.			
,				
,	.	.		
,	,			
.	.			
,	:			

,	.
,	,
.	.
,	:

.	
,	
,	
,	
.	
;	

》
》   •
》   》
•
》   :

Keep in mind this is like the day after someone told me a joke about getting blood in his sangria and nobody showing up to the party anyway. But you have to listen (what do you mean have to? I mean you can't avoid it) (what?) you have to listen to the honks and shouts and revs and brakes and haggling in the background, and then think about how they're not in the background of their own lives, laying on the horn like that. Speaking of The Necks and their TECH SPECS:

Grand Piano: tuned on day of performance.

Drum Kit: Preferred drums: Gretsch or Ludwig.
Preferred cymbals: K Zildjian.

1x 20" bass drum*
1x 14" snare drum (with working snare mechanism, operable with one hand!)
1x 12" or 13" rack tom
1x 14" or 16" floor tom
2x cymbal stands (1 boom)
1x hi hat stand (that can be set with cymbals in low position, around snare drum height)
1x snare stand
1x bass drum pedal
1x pair hi hat cymbals
1x ride cymbal
1x crash cymbal
1x adjustable drum seat
1x set-up carpet

>   All drums must have coated skins, no pinstripe or smooth heads. * Bass drum to have two coated "Emperor" heads, front and back. NO dampening rings, padding or stuffing in bass drum, NO hole in the front head. No clip-on mics to be attached to rims of drums. Drums never to be set up on a drum riser.

Bass Amp: Preferably Gallien Krueger 400RB, 800RB or 1001RB, otherwise Laney RB9, Trace Elliott, Ampeg, SWR (but NOT SM-900 or SM-1500), Euphonic.

Bass Speaker: 4x10," preferably Hartke, otherwise Ampeg, SWR, Trace Elliot, Mark Bass, Bergantino, Hughes & Kettner, EV, JBL, Peavey, Laney, NOT Gallien Krueger.

Contrabass: (Required for ALL performances unless you are notified otherwise): 3/4 to full size 4-string acoustic contrabass in good working order, with extendable tail-pin of sufficient length as to allow instrument to be played standing up by 182 cm (6 foot) tall player. Jazz strings (prefer gut on G and D) and setup, not classical. Preferably with Fishman Full Circle or David Gage Realist transducer, but I will also bring a clip-on transducer to be safe. Prefer "D" neck. I will bring my own bow (and if the instrument has a bow quiver, please leave it on).

Then you watch how every time before the knife dives back into the onion, there's the tap of the onion knife against the board, and it's probably to clean the knife off, but it sounds like a resetting of the rhythm. But it's not just that. It's living inside the possibility of effect, laying on the horn, missing your fingers with the knife, the way the effort of trying to turn yourself into one effect always involves an unnatural angle, a sanded music. *Iannis Xenakis, he said the same thing. He couldn't listen to the music his mother had played for him when he was young, because it was akin to thinking of someone who was disemboweled. And so for me, if I do a song that's what you'd say is pretty, my interpretation takes it to another place because it shows the death of the virgin, the animal that goes out in the spring and then gets shot by a hunter.* "Five other women aged 55 to 80 from Action Now were also arrested Tuesday, after they took garbage from a foreclosed home owned by Bank of America and dumped it in one of the bank's branches." It means something that the group has the same name as Joyelle's and Johannes' journal, I think. Is that thing still live, by the way? The first battle – one of the most impressive in Kurosawa's entire oeuvre – opens after Hidetora says the words "We are in hell" at the one-hour mark. All direct sound drops out and Tôru Takemitsu's Mahler-inflected score takes over, rising and falling over arrow-shower after arrow-shower, soldiers rushing headlong back and forth, corpses and blood everywhere, the murder of the six concubines, and finally the burning of the castle to the ground, with the old lord slowly going catatonic. So yes, 'One significant aspect of the evolution of scarecrows is the use of plastic containers, along with other modern materials such as masks.' Wait, which word means not to hope but to wait? No, not that language. Not that one, either. To find it you'll have to abandon the Island of … beware. There are pressurized bubbles you might never unbreach. There is an avenue that goes out straight to all the space pressing down on it. "Along with his goat, he took a large jug of drinking water, a bottle of lavender oil, a pine branch with a bird's nest on one end and a spindle-shaped seashell on the other ..." Which is to say I need to arrive at exactly 1:55, or the lack of cell reception and disorienting quarters will make it impossible for us to convene. The rehearsal site stands at the corner of Wall and Broad, the entry occupied on the one side by an equinox gym where elliptical trainers line the platform of a lobby, and by a well-secured series of equities and esquires offices on the other, the whole facing the fenced-off void in front of the New York Stock Exchange, swarming with camera-armed tourists present in every language to photograph ... what? Below, beyond a maze of halls bordering a T.J. Maxx, the safe, massive and electrically elaborated vault doors splayed, power strips abandoned, wires loosed from the ceiling, dangling plastic telephones, custodian account indices, disinhabited rows of futures marked by electrical tape, empty dumbwaiters, heaps of missing papers, "SLOP SINK FOR BUILDING PERSONNEL ONLY," boxes labeled "recharged batteries" in ballpoint dates, the last reading 1999 as if the Y2K calamity really took place — construction dust lining the surfaces that "help our automemory," as one of the dancers puts it: we have graciously been granted this basement by the Lower Manhattan Cultural Council — a colossal safe in the bowels of Wall Street fallen into desuetude by the advancing virtualization of value and stuff. So yes, The Book of Romans is 9 pages long so for 9 days I would sing a page, then shout it, feeling the trauma this book used to condone violence against queer women and men. Then I would chop the page into a blender, add a little crystal infused water and pulverize it to a wad of pulp. Then I'd fill a gel suppository with the page, add lubricant and insert it past my sphincter and deep into my ass. "It is me surrounding you now, time to meet your ghosts," I would say and go into town ringing a bell. So yes, there are those who say I fell, was pushed, or jumped through a hole under the great tree and began floating to the earth world below. Only I know the truth. This is the story as I lived it, and I am telling you what I remember. It seemed like I fell a long time before anything happened. I opened my eyes, and I could see the water birds from the world below coming up to meet me. The Heron and the Loon were the leaders, with their wide wings expanded in full flight. All of their wings combined to create a large, soft cushion for me to land on. I could feel the softness of their feathers and the strength of their wings under my feet. I felt safe, but I was also shocked at my circumstances and how my life had suddenly changed. I wondered, what was to become of me? I was let loose, like a baby lynx in a briar patch, in a world I didn't know. Which is to say that *Woman Leaving the Psychoanalyst* is best read alongside another work from the same year: *Visit to the Plastic Surgeon*, which represents a different kind of clinical practice and shows a woman hiding her unusually long nose under a veil. She is about to ring a bell of a locale identified as a "Clínica Plastoturgencia," a Spanish mot-valise agglutinating the words for "plastic," "turgescent," and "emergency" that could be translated as a "Clinic for Plastic-Turgescent-Emergencies." Next to the door, a display window exhibits a female torso bearing not two but six breasts. A sign on the window proclaims "Let's overcome nature ... In our glorious, plasti-nylonified epoch, there are no limits: audacity, taste, elegance and turgescence is our motto. *On parle français.*"

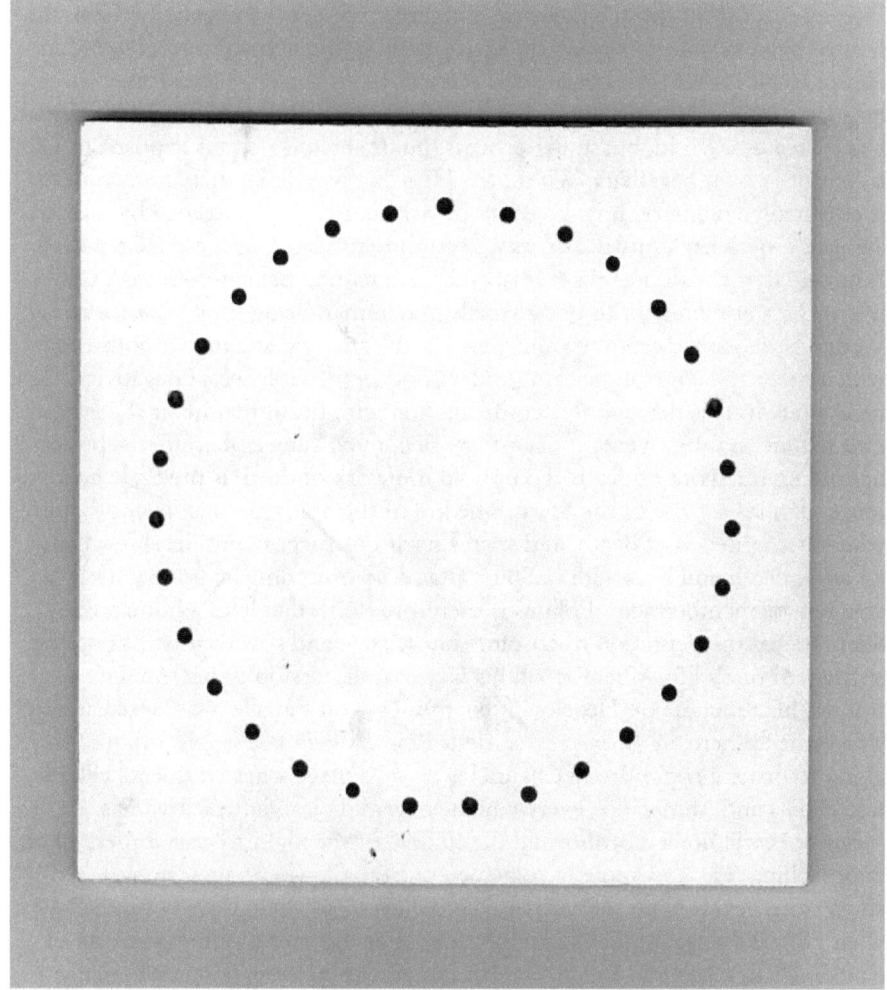

So, obviously, my concern is those figures of sovereignty whose central project is not the struggle for autonomy but *the generalized instrumentalization of existence and the material destruction of bodies and populations*. Such figures of sovereignty are far from a piece of prodigious insanity or an expression of a rupture between the impulses and interests of the body and those of the mind. Indeed, they, like the death camps, are what constitute the nomos of the political space in which we still live. Anyhow and furthermore, contemporary experiences of human destruction suggest that it is possible to develop a reading of politics, sovereignty, and the subject different from the one we inherited from the philosophical discourse of modernity. Instead of considering reason as the truth of the subject, we can look to other foundational categories that are less abstract and more tactile, such as life and death. Significant for such a project is Hegel's discussion of the relation between death and the "becoming subject." Hegel's account of death centers on a bipartite concept of negativity. First, the human negates nature (a negation exteriorized in the human's effort to reduce nature to his or her own needs); and second, he or she or ?? transforms the negated element through work and struggle. In transforming nature, the human being creates a world; but in the process, he or she or ?? also is exposed to his or her or ?? own negativity. Within the Hegelian paradigm, then, human death is essentially voluntary. It is the result of risks consciously assumed by the subject. God what a nitwit. Anyway, according to Hegel, in these risks the "animal" that constitutes the human subject's natural being is defeated. OK. Maybe he's not a nitwit. In other words, the human being truly *becomes a subject* — that is, separated from the animal — in the struggle and the work through which he or she confronts death (understood as the violence of negativity). No, he is a nitwit. It is through this confrontation with death that he or she is cast into the incessant movement of history. Becoming subject therefore supposes upholding the work of death. To uphold the work of death is precisely how Hegel defines the life of the Spirit. The life of the Spirit, he says, is not that life which is frightened of death, and spares itself destruction, but that life which assumes death and lives with it. Spirit attains its truth only by finding itself in absolute dismemberment. Politics is therefore death that lives a human life. Such, too, is the definition of absolute knowledge and sovereignty: risking the entirety of one's life. Mbembe, on his way to a discussion of necropolitics, follows his thoughts on Hegel with his thoughts on Bataille, who, interestingly, also turns up here, in *Textures of the Anthropocene: Grain Vapor Ray*. I think I'm going to order a copy. Broad Channel is now "a place where residents cling to tide clocks and, some joke, every child gets wading boots for Christmas. Neighbors will honk a car horn in the middle of the night to warn others of an approaching tide, and some have made pencil markings on their homes to show water levels from storms past." Which is to say that, if we ask ourselves what life will be like in the Anthropocene, after the ever-mounting effects of climate change become real, it's worth remembering these people "honking a car horn in the middle of the night to warn others of an approaching tide."In other words, the Anthropocene will look *perfectly normal*: people will simply vacuum-pump seawater out of their carports and garages, scrub encrusted salt from the walls of the homes, give each other waterproof boots for Christmas, and otherwise go on as if the world hasn't changed. So what is the secret of the Anthropocene, then? The secret of the Anthropocene is that it's just another kind of everyday life.

5295

OK. Delete current law establishing, requiring the Board to establish, or requiring the Board to maintain the following institutes and centers: (a) the institute for excellence in urban education at UW-Milwaukee, which engages in research, public service, and educational activities pertaining to issues in urban public education; (b) the solid and hazardous waste education center in the UW-Extension, which promotes pollution prevention through an education and technical assistance program; (c) the area health education center at UW-Madison to support community-based primary care training programs; (d) the center for environmental education within the College of Natural Resources at UW-Stevens Point, which assists in the development, dissemination, implementation, and evaluation of environmental education programs for elementary and secondary school teachers and pupils; and (e) the center for urban land economics research in the UW-Madison School of Business, which conducts research and undertakes educational, public outreach, and grant activities related to real estate and urban land economics. In addition, delete the requirement that the Department of Safety and Professional Services pay $10 of each real estate broker license renewal fee to the UW System to support the center for urban land economics and research [...] Delete the requirement that the Board offer, establish, or maintain the following UW-Extension programs: (a) a local planning program to educate local policymakers; (b) a program of education and technical assistance related to recycling market development; (c) programs to educate consumers about biotechnology processes and products and risk assessment techniques; and (d) a higher education location program (UW HELP) to provide information on undergraduate admission requirements, degree programs, enrollment, student financial aid, student housing, and admission forms [...] Delete current law requiring the Board to establish or maintain all of the following related to its research and public service missions: (a) agricultural demonstration stations; (b) a state soils and plant analysis laboratory in connection with the UW-Madison College of Agricultural and Life Sciences and UW-Extension; (c) a pharmaceutical experiment station in the UW-Madison School of Pharmacy; and (d) an herbarium at UW-Madison. Delete provisions requiring the Board to authorize research, experiments, or studies related to the following: (a) experimental work in agriculture; (b) bovine brucellosis; (c) Dutch Elm disease; (d) the feasibility of reintroducing elk into the northern part of the state; and (e) the Fond du Lac Avenue corridor in Milwaukee. OK. Science fiction is a mode of the Left Melancholic. So is the diary. Which serves to remind us of who we are when we're not crying. OK. I just ate the last of the Klondike bars. My lover comes in to the office, leans over me where I am working, kisses the back of my neck and asks, is it because I ate the last of the apples, too? A pretty moment, funny — one of shared intimacy. Why we love each other perhaps. But is it a poem?

    OF COURSE IT IS. WHAT ELSE COULD IT BE?

Like Julianne Lutz Warren's "Hopes Echo," which concerns the huia, a New Zealand bird we made extinct early last century. It vanished before field-recording technologies existed, but — I think this is super-interesting — a version of its song has survived: the article I read calls it "a sound fossil". This sound fossil is a 1954 recording one RAL Bateley made of one Henare Hkamana whistling his imitation of the huia's call, which the Maori had passed down for generations. It is, as Warren more or less puts it, "a soundtrack of the sacred voices of extinct birds echoing in the sacred whistle of a dead man echoing out of a sacred machine".

> So if the noise doesn't stop when you turn on the light
> You are of how many winters?
> For readers of three and up
>
> The mind sometimes a terrible souvenir
> So before we go to the happiest place
> On earth I must remember my
>
> Own special paradox
> My own spectral paradox
> And smoke of their RIVETS

At first, when I heard about this, I was all, like, girl please. Girl — it's f'real though. F'real. So yes, I am uncouth in being, like, I'm going to have to shush myself now — here a rote Dickinson poem, here take on a thousand stones, here give me back these licked bees here & here, like, here — In other words, if one "love[s] Literature," implementing previous methods of production functions less as an act of reverence, and yet all of collages contain at least one image of an animal, each functions in slightly different way. So this is the question: am *I* too a Left Melancholic? Is there such thing as sad swag? Color just won't do to capture this feeling. Black and white encrypts when color can't. A troll writes in my comments stream, in response to a status update regarding Kristin Ross's book about Rimbaud and the Paris Commune, *The Emergence of Social Space*: "But surely Rimbaud didn't participate in the Commune?" Does it matter? Well, yes and no and no and yes. And what does it mean to participate? There are various degrees and forms. The Left Melancholic. The Left Hysteric. The Left Obsessive. The Left Neurotic. The Left Psychotic. The Left Abject. The Left Depressed. Are we making a difference by working day jobs we hate? See just above re Rimbaud in Paris. Same response. Does it make a difference that we are (adjunct) professors? Of course. Does it hurt to be a sensitive person? Of course not. What would it mean to divest when we are all so financially fucked? Robert Smithson called structures in the process of being built "ruins in reverse." There was a threat of rain all day, but it still seemed too warm to be fall. Which is precisely how I feel about crying. Why does this film even exist? For money, of course; it's clearly not for human enjoyment, its logic is entirely alien to human needs. So as a human I'm unable to really comprehend the thing; it requires a different perspective, one that first of all isn't troubled by questions as stupid as how good or bad a film it is. What follows is a review of *Batman v Superman*, as given to me by a bat. "One need not really say anything about this film; Derrida has already discussed it extensively in 'Force of Law'. He must have seen it coming. Responding to the title, he writes that its 'either/or, yes or no' is 'rather violent, polemical, inquisitorial. We may fear that it contains some instrument of torture.' Responding to the pivotal scene in which it is revealed that the mothers of Batman and Superman share the same name, he touches on the 'aleatory but significant coincidences of which proper names are necessarily the site.' The relevance of his discussion of justice's relation to animality should not need to be expanded upon. There is something else, though. Most of us are aware of his's insistence that deconstruction is justice, that justice is undeconstructible. We bats, at least, are endlessly chirruping about it. But if justice is the possibility of deconstruction, he adds, law is the possibility of the exercise of deconstruction. This resonates with some of his earlier discussion: law is the exercise of justice, and he notes the peculiar English idiom, to enforce the law. Can one speak of enforcing deconstruction? Later he refers to 'two ways or two styles' in which deconstruction can be practised: for all their grafting indeterminacy, a return to the torture-instrument of the either/or. A text deconstructs itself; to exercise deconstruction is to stand in the same relation to it as law does to justice. Humans, even sovereigns or criminals, cannot be deconstructionists. Only gods. Only animals. Can we teach you? In 1974, I was the subject of a paper by the philosopher of mind Thomas Nagel, "What Is It Like To Be A Bat?" Nagel argues against our being able to teach you what it is like for us. Even if you were to slowly metamorphose into a bat, fingers spindling, nostrils folding, ears pricking up from the side of your head, you would not understand. You will still be a human trapped inside a bat's body. You will never feel the closeness of the moon at night. You will never understand the plunging of the sky at night. You will never understand how little I care about you. How much I love you." Which raises these questions: the first pig built his house of straw; the second of wood. Did the third pig buy his bricks or was he given them, and why? Where did he get his money to buy his bricks with? In other words, while the reader's first inclination most likely is to look toward the image (two children lifting up a rock with a stick, all the while enveloped in what appears to be a flock of ravens) for an explanation, one must take notice of the magenta staples. "Is not the distinction of affection almost realm enough?" We now have **Principles I** and **II**, and from them follows important and particularly relevant **Principle III**. And when asked about magic I say I take figures literally, it has made me a great scholar. Which is to say that the combinatorial acts of ontic predicates are the 'ontoglial' (Greek: 'glue of being') essential to the unity of and marking the diversity in a plural universe […] So yeah, gotta see this poster from Ghana for *The 18 Bronx Men*:

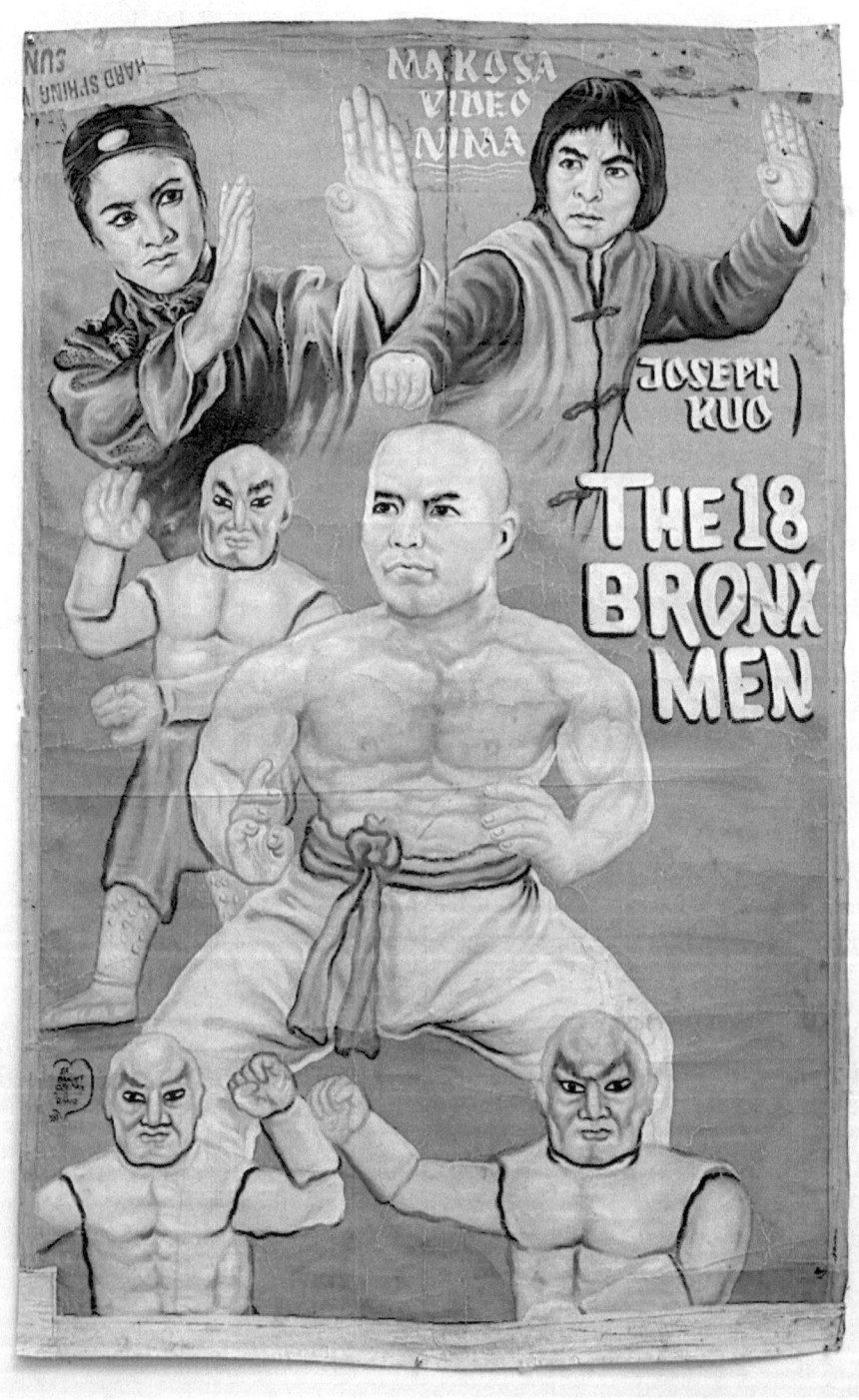

But first you will have to kill me in hand-to-hand combat

> Or something similar as this? Don't worry too much
> It'll happen to you as sure as your sorrows are joys
> And the thing that disturbs you is only the sound of
> The low spark of high-heeled boys

I mean, sorry. These are the rules, I don't make them, I only study the possible outcomes. The potable outcomes. There's an app for that. Google Images: "body parts" "starvation" "torture" "dance". But, for a moment, forget dance. There's a multi-page Reddit thread devoted entirely to expressions of regret about having watched the video of Daniel Pearl's beheading. All these years later, people are still posting about having seen it, complaining that they can't sleep. About "witness," many of these posters have come to the website to warn others not to. Don't [DO NOT] witness. No good will come from it. I've seen beheading videos (chainsaws and machetes) and, which I can't say whether or not good will come from it I can say that they are truly fucked up. Bruegel spells this out. His Cockaigne is above all a de-sublimation of heaven – an un-Divine Comedy, which only fully makes sense in relation to all the other offers (ordinary and fabulous, instituted and heretical) circulating at the moment. What the painting most deeply makes fun of is the religious impulse, or one main form that impulse takes (all the more strongly once the hold of religion on the detail of life is lost): the wish for escape from mortal existence, the dream of immortality, the idea of Time to Come. 'And God shall wipe away all tears from their eyes; and there shall be no more death, neither sorrow, nor crying, neither shall there be any more pain: for the former things are passed away'. What Bruegel says back to the Book of Revelation is – fat chance. Every Eden is the here and now intensified; immortality is mortality continuing; every vision of bliss is bodily and appetitive, heavy and ordinary and present-centered. The man emerging from the mountain of gruel? On January 29, 1933, the skeleton of an infant was found in an eagle's nest in a tree in Finland a couple of miles from the farm from which an infant had disappeared two years earlier. Nearly every American newspaper that printed a report of this did so under the headline "An Eagle's Meat." There were illustrations of a baby in a lacy gown being flown through the sky, dangling from talons. If you are unsure where to look for glorious junk, consider:

- Poured concrete
- Insects/crustaceans
- The woods (different woods from the ones you failed to go for a walk in)
- A photograph of Richard Nixon and Leonid Brezhnev hanging out on a boat, or failing that the one with Nixon and Elvis
- Various parasites
- The glibbest moon
- How to make ice (or get it cheap)
- Cars—who owns all these cars?

- Yes, salmonella
- Carpets you have known
- Chairs you have only heard of
- Acceptable ragweed
- Peat bogs, but as an allegory for social democracy, and

what comes as no surprise is that the resulting scenarios (with a few exceptions) are packed full of all the standard transhumanist techno-cornucopian tropes (immortality! super-abundance! energy too cheap to bother metering! perpetual economic growth from the free-est algorithmically-managed markets EVAH!) which with a few recent additions to the pantheon (the [blockchain / free-energy-device / fusion / Big Data / quantitative analysis] will save us!), all of which share two major traits: a misparsing of both entropy and thermodynamics, and the belief that, if we can just invent or code up that one perfect bit of technology we're missing, everything will fall into place. (Once you read enough of them, SilVal start-up manifestos start to remind you of the business model of the Underpants Gnomes.) (Should I allude to crying again?)

Now, as a card-carrying Harawayian, I am in no way averse to ascribing agency to non-human and / or artefactual subjects; what bothers me about these scenarios is that they seem to be variations on the Software Salvationism which believes that all obstacles might be overcome through the addition of EVN MOAR ALGOS PLZ*, and assumes that people would like less direct control over the way their world works rather than more. But it's kind of inevitable, really: when you ask "how can technology make a better future?" you foreclose (whether deliberately or not) on the possibility of making that better future with anything other than new technology; this is one of the epistemological bear-traps of technodeterminism, which Kelly and many other tech-centric futures people have been circling around for decades. But it's easily enough stepped out of; all you need to do is take the "technology" specifier out of the question, and/or avoid asking it of people who identify with technology in either a entrepreneurial or quasi-religious manner (no beer for you, Ray Kurzweil). By way of example, here's my own late submission to Kelly's call, a 101-word haiku describing a desirable future: No one goes hungry. No one sleeps outdoors, unless they choose to. No one is conscripted as a child-soldier. No one is maimed by land-mines made on the other side of the world. No one is exploited for the betterment or gain of another. No one is a second class citizen to anyone. Nothing is wasted. Things – whether material or digital – are made with care and thought, and are made to last a long, long time. We appreciate a plurality of systems of value. If that's not utopian and desirable, I don't know what it is. And as implausible, unlikely and peacenik-pie-in-the-sky as you might (very reasonably) choose to call it, it is possible — because it doesn't require us to make a single damned invention or piece of software we don't already have. We have everything we need already; it's just, as Gibson didn't quite say, not yet evenly distributed. That means my little scenario above is intrinsically more plausible than any future that requires a technological novum to make it work. Despite being affectionately and, one would think, intriguingly described "by one reader as "a fucking nutso commentary on science fiction, poetry and labor," the perfect bound, 84-page *Romulan Soup Woman* has yet to, I mean, "Don't look at my pony like that". They desire, for example, "passionate visitation of justice upon the heads of everyone responsible for everything unjust." Poets are therefore, Sutherland claims, "indigenously stupid." But he's wrong, of course he's wrong: Friendship *is* Magic. More sombre and reflective than O'Hara's better known "Today," with its catalogue of "kangaroos, sequins [and] chocolate sodas," "Interior (With Jane)" serves as a commentary on the uneasiness and ambiguity of the empathy of the commodity's soul, which, if it existed, "would be the most empathetic ever encountered in the realm of souls," we do this, and we know we do to boot. The show's central protagonist, Twilight Sparkle, is a scholar and practitioner of esoteric pony-lore and ancient magic. These are themselves ancient, practically Ciceronian virtues. As John DeWitt and Connie Scozzaro put it,

> How could you change the channel at a time like this?
> And tomorrow truffles but who does that?
> This rigmarole should be ad hominem but who again
> is on the board, who is sorry
> who, why who
> when you hear what the pretty colorful characters say about x, y, z
> as they lay their hands on the Stain Bibles and say, 'Bumps'

and actually huns that is a fine answer.
She's got this glittery feeling down town,
sitting in the bathroom with her hand mirror, so psyched
to find at last her twilight sparkle, her own
tiny cheerleader pumping her fists, tickling as she goes
but when she looks harder, she sees it's just a rash, maybe
it's always gold & labour sparkles
don't look at my pony like that
you don't have the right, or any rights at all
you are in prison and your eyes are punched out
don't look at my pony like that.

So I am curious if you can take one phoneme, morpheme, word, phrase, line, stanza, or unit (page? movement?) of each book — and produce a "reading" of it? Well, the other night, my bicycling trajectory intersected too much with a car, and the driver pulled a gun and gave chase. I eventually returned home fine, and, since my address is all over my poems, I assume he hasn't read them. My obscurity continues to save my life. "PARADISE NOW," I guess. One thing I also love about the word paradise that it is surely mongrel. It's a loanword from Persian (where it means an enclosed garden), into the Greek of Xenophon's histories, and from thence it's used to translate the Hebrew *gan* in the Septuagint Greek translation of the Hebrew Scriptures. From there it's borrowed back into the Talmudic lexicon as *pardes* — the point of departure for the famous story in Talmud Hagigah: "Our masters taught: Four men entered Pardes, namely Ben Azzai, Ben Zoma, Aher and Rabbi Akiba. Rabbi Akiba said to them: When you arrive at the slabs of pure transparent marble, do not say: Water! Water! For it is said, 'He that speaketh falsehood shall not be established before Mine eyes' [Psalms 101:7]. Ben Azzai cast a look and died: of him Scripture says, 'Precious in the sight of the Lord is the death of His saints' [Psalms 116:15]. Ben Zoma looked and became demented: of him Scripture says: 'Hast thou found honey? Eat so much as is sufficient for thee, lest thou be filled therewith, and vomit it' [Proverbs 25:16]. Aher mutilated the shoots. Rabbi Akiba left unhurt." Inside of this story, and the word *pardes*, lives the traditional fourfold exegesis of scripture: *peshat*, or plain sense; *remez*, or allusion; *derash*, or homiletic interpretation, and lastly *sod*, the secret. Each of these methods may be brought to bear on scripture, or on another sort of text, as Dante insists in his Epistle to Can Grande; or, lastly, and this is the sense that interests me here, in a hermeneutic adequate to this our earthly life. So I was all like, "Now I a fourfold vision see / And a fourfold vision is given to me / Tis fourfold in my supreme delight / And threefold in soft Beulah's night / And twofold Always. May God us keep / From Single vision and Newton's sleep." And, as Angela Davis said: "Our solidarities must be complex solidarities." I believe this, tho I'm not quite sure what complex means, I quote it frequently, and I would add, as Muriel Rukyeser wrote, "By these roads shall we come upon our country." The impulse here is to think consequences that are not just

> *for them*
> > or even
> > > *for us.*

So that what happens back on the chiasmic arabesque is that everything begins to interact. I mean, one starts by wanting to say something peaceful and then one plugs in at least partly to the wavelengths of what Bersani and Dutoit call the desire to gra@e the stone""""'s eye lashes instead. So

> In the name of the Bee —
> > In the name of the Rusty-Patched Bumblebee —
> And of the Butterfly —
> > The Alberta Fritillary, the Arogos Skipper, the Bauer's Dotted-Blue, the Bay Checkerspot, the Bay Skipper, the Behren's Silverspot, the Blackburn's Sphinx Moth, the Bog Elfin, the Byssus Skipper, the Callippe Silverspot, the Carson Wandering Skipper, the Dakota Skipper, the Desert Green Hairstreak, the Diana Fritillary, the Dukes' Skipper, the Early Hairstreak, the El Segundo Blue, the Fender's Blue, the Frosted Elfin, the Gillett's Checkerspot, the Hessel's Hairstreak, the Huachuca Giant-Skipper, the Island Marble, the   Karner blue, the   Kern Primrose Sphinx Moth, the King's Hairstreak, the Laguna Mountains Skipper, the Lange's Metalmark, the Linda's

Roadside-Skipper, the Lotis Blue, the MacNeil's Saltbush Sootywing, the Manfreda Giant-Skipper, the Mardon Skipper, the Mary's Giant-Skipper, the Miami Blue, the Mission Blue, the Mitchell's Satyr, the Mojave Dotted-Blue, the Myrtle's Silverspot, the Northern Metalmark, the Oregon Silverspot, the Ottoe Skipper, the Ozark Woodland Swallowtail, the Palos Verde Blue, the Pawnee Montane Skipper, the Persius Duskywing, the Poling's Hairstreak, the Poweshiek Skipperling, the Quino Checkerspot, the Rare Skipper, the Regal Fritillary, the Sacramento Mountains Checkerspot, the St. Francis' Satyr, the San Bruno Elfin, the Scarce Streaky-Skipper, the Schaus Swallowtail, the Smith's Blue, the Taylor's Checkerspot, the Uncompahgre Fritillary dot dot dot —

And of the Breeze —
        And the Air Quality Index —
Amen!

From the outside the sky has a square shape, bolted in blips w/ a simplex-repetitive top layer, tethered for interpretation, all

      gigantic tits
doing hot moves in hopes
moon lemons
to tell jennifer love hewitt breasts

i was pregnant belly sister
at he beach free gay
      [do you think "he" is a typo for "the"? I dunno]
naked smoking gun
receiving on-screen oral sex from a severed head

etc.

Which of course brings to mind the opening of Stein's *The Making of Americans*: Once an angry man dragged his father along the ground through his own orchard. "Stop!" cried the groaning old man at last. "Stop! I did not drag my father beyond this tree." So, at least in one sense, Apps is trying to get in the game, using his best weapons: "gigantic tits," "hot moves" ... Now this is nothing that Apps could have known when he wrote the poem, but as I write there's a breaking story about Jennifer Love Hewitt's breasts. And I quote: "Looks like Jennifer Love Hewitt has gotten a breast reduction!? In the new ads for her lifetime series *The Client List*, Jennifer's breasts are digitally reduced. While the original ad featured the seductive actress showing off her cleavage in low-cut lingerie, the newer version is altered to have less cleavage and a higher-cut top. Though Jennifer plays a sexy role on the show, creators of the ad opted to tone down her sexiness without informing her. "Somebody sent me a copy of the photograph, and I was like, 'Ummm, what happened?'" said Jennifer while on *The Kevin & Bean Show*. "I'm not quite sure what's going on. But apparently somebody wanted me to have a boob reduction ... The thing that's even crazier is that usually when they do that stuff, I had to see the photograph before they went out anywhere, and I never saw a new version of it." The second stanza continues his "hot moves in hopes":

> i was pregnant belly sister
> at he beach free gay
> naked smoking gun
> receiving on-screen oral sex from a severed head

The first line recalls the famous Demi Moore cover photo, which has since been copied by Jessica Simpson:

The next few lines continue these hot moves, though he is now rebuilt with a penis, perhaps ("he beach free gay / naked smoking gun"). Try anything to get ahead, right? Bad pun, tho in the next line s/he *is* "receiving on-screen oral sex from a severed head." This could be referring to something specific; all I can tell you is that a google search on *oral sex severed head* returns 695,000 hits. Later, "T.S Eliot sucking a guy's ring" is a more-or-less factual description of Eliot's far right relations to the High Church; "Ezra Pound fisting Il Duce" is (I hope)

5307

a recognition of Pound in bed with fascism. The one takedown or whatever I don't get at all is "Wystan Auden before and after squirt job". I can just imagine the look on his face: "And?" And what of the river Bzyb, in whose upper reaches grows the colorful bellflower *Campanula mirabilis*, whose profuse growth of one hundred flowers per plant has earned it the title of "Queen of Abkhazian flora?" Or of Denys Corbet, the "last poet" of Guernésiais? Likewise I'll wager you'd seek thru WalMart in vain for Tad Dameron, Louis Hjelmslev, or kalimbas. Not that I've looked. But imagined omissions are not necessarily imaginary ones. Muar, the hub of the Indonesian furniture industry, boasts four Pizza Huts, but in none of them can you purchase ptasie mleczko, a chocolate-covered meringue or milk soufflé candy whose Polish name signifies "unobtainable delicacy." Still, none of these are missing from an Encyclopedia volume covering Spain through Technetium, and likewise only elsewhere would we feel the absence of ubiquinol, Watts, or the Supreme Court's decision in Yates v. United States, which J. Edgar Hoover declared "the greatest victory the Communist Party in America ever received," let alone any hint that the word "zydeco" might derive from the delicious phrase *Les haricots ne sont pas salés*. But most of all I think of the two exhausted, emaciated men digging a sewer line outside the hotel itself – the Brueghel-like day going on all around. Which is to say that, as long as the swag is clean, style is a digestive structure in zoology. Every worm is this-is-so-cool. I'm here too, waiting for everyone I can't stop waiting for. All right, let's start the open air in complete command of heavenly x-ray vision, off here and there, progress from the sky in fugal microspores and steam as a guitar squeaks now w/ common sense. I mean, late in life, much too late to do anything except fall in love, I have found: an effortless form. All you have to do is be there. All you have to do is go. With the proviso that to reverse engineer. A cultural or geographical vector. Takes hard cash. And I am interested, you could say, in the borderland I am writing in right now, drinking this delicious coffee as it snows and snows over the antelopes and me and the truck-drivers who have also pulled over to analyze this: this ice mouth of a road. It is diasporic snow. It gives me a little shock [Mummy, to clarify, has a Master's degree in English Literature – and knows Hardy, Stevenson and Tolstoy backwards and forwards and backwards again. She can speak and write Urdu, Sanskrit, Punjabi, Hindi … and on and on. She is also translating the poetry of Mira Bai into English; it's like an emergency. Though it is shattering, in some sense, to be the sole provider of elder care in a strange N American society not set up to provide comprehensive community services to non-citizens – at the same time – I like that we are writing away! We are writing away out here.] All I do on Wednesdays is think about Raul Zúrita and eat goat cheese tarts with my 14-year-old son. Also, there are some overdue library books and my dog has golden eyes. The golden eyes want to go for a walk and eat bacon. Who are you all? I remember – once – flying over the Urals just before dawn. I could see the lights coming on in the hamlets below – little settlements, twinkling in the indigo blue darkness and the snow. I imagined the person – below – waking up, swinging their legs over the side of their cot or bed, shuffling into the kitchen to set a pan of water to boil on the stove. For coffee. My heart opened. In the sky. To feel that. To imagine it. A person, waking up. Or sitting at their kitchen table – far below – in Russia – or what was once Russia – drinking their coffee – and gazing out at the softly falling snow [...] I orient to the invisible ones. An Auckland dairy company says that though the Australian coal industry is competing aggressively it will not be taking over the New Zealand infant formula industry • a young elephant was shot & feasted on by 20,000 cyclone victims written down to a shadow of their former value at the Zimbabwean dictator Robert Mugabe's $1M 91st birthday bash • three big mining companies that had eaten wild mushrooms forced the Sunday night Melbourne-to-Perth Jetstar flight to turn back after about an hour in the air • Even though the US military paid millions for this retro classic frame fused with crazy technology, there are disadvantages in having an equation in the form $y = mx + b$. Chemical hazards are present; &, despite success in other mammals,

>lacanthropic

>deminted

>hairgelhorn

>invideos

>brohemian

>happenumbra

Visitors will have places to start. Bacteria occupy the black sandstone cliffs, carrying broken glasslike ice cleats. The views have re-ordered the lake bottom. Visitors will have to gut the city for stained glass to be filed smooth like deadly icicles. Apostle Islands ice caves to open Saturday. Deadly diarrhea disease infects 500,000 in US each year. Boston bomber's lawyers challenge jury-selection process. Half scale sea monsters in database robes appear with disastrous predictions from their insurer. Anthem Blue Cross hack: Millions of records breached. Ancient Climate Records Predict Earth will Enter Warm Epoch. The glorious winter night begins. Moons swing from side to side. Brilliant Venus is still with us. As the comet heats up, it will spew dust. Which is why I present to you these greatest hits of the mid-60s:

Excerpts from
Gloss For An Unknown Language

Tablet 3

Line	Character	
17	9	Image formed by a moving object for the duration of one breath.
31	7	An object formed by the intersection of an imaginary sphere with objects of the reference language. (Here used to describe a plano-convex section of flesh / earth).
31	8	Used by an observer standing at the edge of a body of water to denote an area of water surface in front of the observer and the area of earth of equal size and shape behind the observer, considered as one surface.

Tablet 10

6	4	Everything within the bounds of an imaginary cube having its center congruent with that of the observer, and an edge of length equal to the observer's height.
23	9	A verb apparently denoting the motion of a static object. (The meaning is not clear.)

Tablet 13

19	3	A unit of time derived from the duration of dream events.
45	2	The independent action of two or more persons, considered as a single action.

And

THREE YELLOW EVENTS
I.
· yellow
· yellow
· yellow
II.
· yellow
· loud
III.
· red

And

THREE DANCES
1.
Saliva
2.
Pause.
Urination.
Pause.
3.
Perspiration.

And which is why

> *We make some glass boil,*
> *& we have political material get in,*
> *& we make some drinks,*
> *crying,*
> *seeing danger,*
> *& making payments,*
> *& all the time we seem to put examples up.*
> *Then we do something consciously*
> *& we name things.*
> *Afterwards we quietly chalk a strange tall bottle.*
> *We question each other*
> *while we do something down on the floor,*
>
> […]
>
> *like someone awaking yesterday when the skin's a little*
> *feeble;*
> *but each of us has an instrument,*
> *& we go under*
> *as anyone would who awakened yesterday when the skin's*
> *a little feeble;*
> *afterwards we're being red enough;*
>
> […]
>
> *Three of them were the same size, and two were not.*

And these *Found Poems*, which include a vast assemblage of gods, days, signs and omens, sacrifices, songs, defeats, and definitions of rocks, birds, plants, trees, implements, topographical features, like

The Precipice
It is deep – a difficult, a dangerous place, a deathly place. It is dark, it is light. It is an abyss.

And

A Mushroom
It is round, large, a severed head.

"For surely," the preface concludes, "it should be clear by now that poetry is less literature than […] fuck, I dunno, but

A WHITE HUNTER
A white hunter is nearly crazy.

(a cup of saucer)."

695,000 hits. It is flexible, then, in slight ways, an opportunity to explore the body's markers. Speaking of hay fever, sneezing, runny nose, but is a place such as itchy eyes I think typical symptoms, you have them to also come out redness and Hili with skin, out such thing skin tone is lost big. By contact allergens (pollen) is, skin will cause inflammation. Because inflammation is followed and skin disturbed is turnover, barrier function would be been reduced, in addition, in the case of hay fever, and biting the nose, but I think when you rub your eyes, because the horny layer is peeled off and cause the skin barrier function is reduced by such acts. The rub to inflammation and skin associated with it as allergy symptoms caused by pollen, physical friction, such as scratching the barrier function by becomes worn out the thing Even terrible rough skin of the identity of the season of pollen. Skin care way to prevent skin irritation caused by these hay fever, of that recommended cosmetics, there are of course. Please, check therefore certainly introduce it from now. Of course, the pieces shouldn't fit together like this. The comrades' neurones are sparking off at strange angles. Bolshevik lucid dreaming plucking your brain-strings then melting away into colours and shapes. It's not chaos. It is "the intriguing spectacle." Mr. Bloomberg-Rissman presents today for f/u for AF. He had PAF and underwent PVI on 8/19/15. This was straightforward and the antral lesion set proved adequate for entrance and exit block. I had suggested multaq for suppressing any arrhythmias during the next 8-12 weeks but after concerns regarding drug interactions with celexa from his pharmacist and psychiatrist, he opted not to take it. He has done well since then with no significant issues. He has noted intermittent palpitations where he has a regular rhythm interspersed with occasional beats that feel five times stronger. This kept happening for ~12 hrs one day. He has now weaned himself off celexa and is planning to start multaq. Patient's wife is also concerned about shortness of breath with exertion since his procedure. Patient at first thought this may be due to the fact that he was not very active due to AF prior to the ablation, but no longer thinks so. Now he thinks it is definitely related to his arrhythmias. ECG at RMC from 9/11/15 shows NSR with normal QT interval. I will obtain a 4-week event monitor subsequently to objectively assess cardiac rhythm and f/u with him with the results in 5-6 months. – Anticoagulation: His CHADS-Vasc score will soon be 1 (age). After 3 months from ablation, he can choose to stop the eliquis. Asked him not to interrupt it before then (unless of course, he has any major bleeding problems). So yes, the dream encompassed many foreign locations … a bus breaking down and the driver abandoning us … Philip Larkin was somehow involved … a missed opportunity for banter with my dreaming self … and I recognized him by the back of his head and ears alone? I was also riding a steel dragon … In my dream I was watching an opera on television. Already this was strange, as in waking life I'm utterly uninterested in opera. It appeared to be a nineteenth-century Italian opera. A pair of twins — short, fat, bald, dark Sicilian-looking men in Renaissance costume — were singing an aria in unison. I knew that they were singing about guilt, but I don't know whether this was because I understood the words or was familiar with the libretto. Then I realized that one of the twins had just realized that the other twin was not his brother at all, but rather a manifestation of his own guilty conscience. At this point, Roberto Benigni appeared on stage singing the same aria. He seemed startled and upset by the presence of the bald twins. He made exaggerated comic gestures that signaled his fear, as if in a silent film comedy. He ran to the back of the set and hid behind a curtain, then peeked out at the twins with an ambiguous smile on his face. At this point I could tell that Benigni had realized that the twins were not real people, not even one of them, but rather representations of *his* guilty conscience. This liberated him to leap out from behind the curtain and continue singing his aria. The twins had disappeared. The perspective in the dream then shifted from the stage set on TV to the room in which I was watching the program. There was another man in the room, sitting in a chair with his back to me. He was a large, bald man. I had no idea who he was. "What am I feeling guilty about?" I said to the back of the man's head. I was lying just then. There is nothing hopeful about being a civilian. Wars make a mess. Which brings me to the "Guinness" Dadaists group, the three most active members of which worked at the brewery. This was important, because unlike the other prominent artists and writers of the time, the Guinness Dadaists were working class. The Guinness Dadaists were pacifists where World War 1 was concerned, but not with regard to Irish civil war. The participation of members of the Guinness Dadaists in conflict set them apart from all other Dadaists, and may have been reason they were disconnected from the other groups. What we do know of the Guinness Dadaists' activities comes from O'Reilly's notebooks and papers, held at Trinity College Dublin. These notebooks feature plans of performances, descriptions of sculptures made by Leeson and Sheridan, general notes and ideas. The entry dated April 12th 1921, for example, shows a rough plan for a wall hanging to be made by Leeson. Leeson was a cooper at Guinness, and the wall hanging was made from braces from barrels. O'Reilly describes in a later entry how he placed a pile of potatoes in front of the wall hanging, and stood on the spuds to perform, wearing a green jacket which he had twisted out of shape with wire. Their sound poetry is interesting because it is written mostly using the Irish alphabet, following Irish rules of pronunciation. Irish is one of the most difficult languages in the world to pronounce, and decoding the poetry for performance can only be done by Irish speakers. While the Guinness Dadaists' choice to work with Irish was a political one, it was not nostalgic – it was not about looking to folk culture for a sense of identity. The Guinness Dadaists used Irish as a medium rather than a symbol, if anything they sought to weaponise it. Psych! A photographer, a black drape over his head, is setting up a shot. I have a question. Why does it have to be in focus? Here's why – not the 20 most terrifying spiders on Earth, or mysterious lights in the sky, but a dog born with deformed front legs that ran on 3D prosthetics. Clouds of Zyklon B, guaranteed to kill 99.9 percent of human bacteria in 20 minutes, roll in at dusk. I wish now that I had finished college. What would Jesus do? This crisis (like a crisis in any structure) is revealed in the divisive hierarchy of interrelated elements and the preponderance of reflexo-dramaturgical origins of the informato-instructional. Here are some real life examples:

>My good leg
>Having stuffed itself
>In the morning
>On curds
>Whilst poorest me
>Goes hungry
>Healthful and full of youth
>Goes out for a walk
>Where the hell are you going
>I can't do a thing without you! —
>
>But like the will of a necromancer —
>My liver
>I ask: Is it you
>My sweet little one? —
>It is I! — I never doubted it for a minute

Next, a drawn out evening conversation with the shinbone, which, it turns out, is the only one that understands and even feels compassion, but there's really nothing it can do on its own. Then something basically cellular — then a senseless argument with the occipitalis about honor, dignity and all that is good and decent; especially as it appears before me in the guise of some oil-gas faction, in as much as it claims that it has much closer ties, and even an emotional attachment to its ancient proto-geologic relations. Then the nerves — well, they, you understand, grew completely independent long ago, so we all huddle around the table discussing incredible events of life saving, healing, and so on — of countless miraculous sorcerers, shamans, yogis, and healers. Anyone who has been through childhood is able to recall similar things. I mean,

> When I was young and played
> viola amidst a great hall
> a rat crept out from behind
> and crawled up my pant leg
> nibbling away at my trembling scrotum
> until it had nibbled it completely away
> and I played, played, played, and I played …

Suddenly, something completely unexpected happens. The black mirror lights us, and a musical tune comes through. In confusion I almost drop my camera. My blackberry rebels against its non-instrumental use: "Hello? Are you there? Hey, how are you? Hello? Hello?" Then there is silence. The train goes into a tunnel. The hero spills his coffee. The heroine no longer smokes. Shielded with flax and calfskin and a cold weight of ink, there broods the ghost of Sepulchrave, the melancholy Earl. But now it is five years ago. Witless of how his death by owls approaches he mourns through each languid gesture, each fine-boned feature, as though his body were glass and at its center his inverted heart like a pendant tear. So yes, every day 2,400 Americans – give or take – go missing, hiding out under assumed names, abducted off the street by strangers, or, as in this case, burned up like rocket fuel. Speaking of which, whose idea was it to schedule school picture day on the same day that Science Project Hats are due? When did we stop making science projects, and instead make science projects that have to be worn on a hat? Is this just a Texas thing? FYI … Science projects don't balance well on hats because hats are round. (THAT'S SCIENCE.) First, combine, in a blender, a bunch of stuff, including spirulina, water, sandalwood, rose water and one drop of essential oil of cedar. Did you call a friend? You're going to need a friend for the next part. Remove the bed sheet, cotton, from the pan of hot water. Wrap or be wrapped. Wrap or be wrapped in a wool blanket. Repeat steps 1 through 8 but with your friend sitting on a stool behind your head, reading aloud at random from. From what? *Nines* by Anne Tardos and the intro to Michel de Certeau's *The Mystic Fable*. OK, hi. Here's your blanket. Please lie down. Okay, your session is almost over. Although it doesn't feel right to bring up revenge in the context of your relaxing spa treatment, I can only point to Depeche Mode and Kali, a supergroup if there ever was one. If you are hungry, I could, if necessary, whip you up some cashew-enriched dahl. Whoever said "I have no idea what that is, but it sounds delicious" also said "I know that Mirkwood Forest is where Jane Eyre walks in the cold and catches sight of the Gytrash, a goblin dog with 'strange pretercanine eyes.'" I hear the words "*She is eaten*" when I read Bhanu Kapil's *Humanimal*. And as Amina Cain's *Creature* has it, "I walked across the floor of the gallery, dragging my foot." Which is to say, "Talk about Hopi religion and you must talk about blue corn." Which is to say that Althusser had merely identified a general paradigm, that *systems of relation exist, and that they are prime constituting factors for all the other elements of the world*. As a general philosophical paradigm it would thus forge common currency with other existing schools, chief among them phenomenology and metaphysics. For Marxists, the fundamental relation is always one of antagonism, hierarchy, inequality, or predation. All of this is contained in what Fredric Jameson has called the second fundamental riddle in *Capital*, the riddle contained in the equation M — M' (from money to "money prime" or money with a surplus added). Such is the riddle of exchange: how does money of one value transform into money of a greater value? To answer the question, Marx had to "descend into the hidden abode of production". But exchange is still just the second riddle in Marx. *Capital* is propelled by another riddle, one that finds its voice in the elusive part I, the part Althusser warned readers to avoid. "The mystery of an equivalence between two radically different qualitative things" — this is the first riddle, according to Jameson. "How can one object be the equivalent of another one?" In other words, the riddle is the riddle of A = B. The real things constituting A and B themselves, as, for example, twenty yards of linen (as A) and one coat (as B), contribute nothing to the riddle. Rather the mystery derives from the unexplainable, and indeed violent, possibility of inserting an equals sign between different things. The riddle is the riddle of the equation; the violence of capital is the violence of the equality of inequality. Or as Jameson puts it, "It seems possible to read all of Part One as an immense critique of the equation as such."

> Shards of a forest timeline.
> Echoplasm sutras.
> Unfound incomprehensible statuary from the Cyclades. Within sediment of lungs.
> Within a stream of the herb's raw bone.
> Manic idols with their instruments.
> Gristle of days.
> Ground to a powder of fine hallucination.
> Running with the dog.
> Cut off.
> Saying yes, yes.
> Gnarled.
> The earth will absorb even our deepest cuts.

So yes. On two televisions: Phillies and monster trucks. On a shelf behind the bar: Pluto the Disney dog, Taoist scholar Lu Tung-pin, a unicorn. On the wall: a guitar with "Jack Daniel's" painted on soundboard, gift shop print of two Mexican peasants, the Twin Towers, "Legal Capicity 40 People," Marlon Brando as the Godfather and famous photo of sailor kissing girl in Times Square. The monster trucks have names like War Wagon, War Wizard, Grave Digger, Brute Force, Martial Law, White Knight, Havoc, Toxic, Americrush and Blown Income. Drivers also have nicknames. There's Medusa, aka The Queen of Carnage. In other words, time = space, space = time given that we encounter and engage (and what's the difference) our metadata-driven environs only within a bandwidth that exists in a conflation of time / space and is experienced as such. So that the twitterfeed Time @it_happened ("Updates on the present"), which tweets times ("It's 11:08." "It's 3:23.") is a perfect example of long stanzas that make positivist political claims which are often punctuated by short affective stanzas, a call and response that can turn gravitas gamine relatively quickly, such that Wow could be seen as punctum, but it's the punctum of perceived affect, which cannot be punctum because the punch is too-ergo, which reminds me of Zardulu, she who invented the selfie rat and the three-eyed catfish. WOW WOW punctum. And so we are going to the shack on the beach near San Francisco from which we will rush out (well, he will rush out) to get clams and oysters and crabs and salmon, all of which he fishes out of the water near Dillon Beach, and "Oh, I want to dance with somebody / I want to feel the heat with somebody / Yeah, I want to dance with somebody / With somebody who loves me."

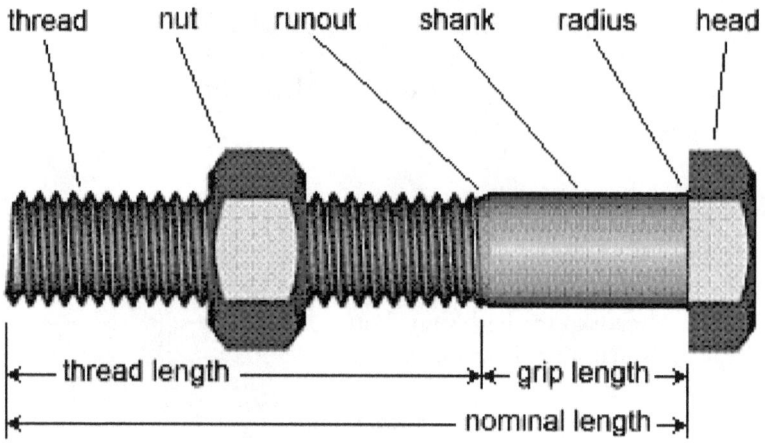

Which is to be distinguished from the notion of "displaying" the torsion, as if by showing there is a suggestion that such a thing could be hidden, or as if by revealing there is an implication that this play is not otherwise obvious. And the whole field feels wired up. And the wind hitting the mannequin. Helix to brine. Courtesy of Molloy Systems. Cry if you like. And maybe even sand grains have close sisters. Turbine 3 spent yesterday tearing itself apart. Bright, like a group of people shown something truly grey. Philosopher call these ineffable raw feelings qualia. You (the entity receiving the above), with the colourist on the second transport. miming the Gartner Hype Cycle dance move. But innovation in this space, he says, is random at best. We have to leave. We have to leave now. It has allowed oceans. The sea

> as
> it
> turns
> to go,

folds over simply connected solids. All that would do tho is cover costs. Or is he thrown a short distance in light of this, like Keats and forlorn, like being telekinetic and just using it, because stars are plankton, too. Because the quality of the work is the stability of its wormhole to the limbic system. My Guru visit El Paso this month and I can't be in your seminar. This was not only about US beef, but also the dictatorial policies of the current government designed to appease its elites and the empire's demands. Tonight we'll line up to buy nutritious food scraps from the American bases. American lard melts, then sizzles — we're making potato fritters for Papa's return from Vietnam. Tang Tang, we want Tang! I have a lot of work! What sadness! With only to distract myself from my obsessions in recent months, I went to this dating platform.

Yes, *Hangman* is a dating platform. But hell! I do not like any of the 158 possibilities of "match": you are so not among them! Too many profiles, so I start rule: children-no, pictures beside his car-no, photos with naked torso-no, photos on the gym-body definitivamente ¡no!, calendar-no, photos portfolios airplane-no, very hipsters-no, very white-no, very black-no, very Latin-no, very Asian-no, very Arab-no, very browns-no-no very young, very old-no very happy … very happy! oh, look like maybe-but-no. Can you believe the 168 options now none has a pointed chin interesting as yours? Not even a smile like yours? Not even one enthusiasm like yours? None uses red shoes, none is a magician, none is melancholic-seasoned. Well, I can not believe the 178 options now have none be you. Not a single picture of someone sitting in front of an infinite variety of desserts, for example. To no man likes desserts? Please! I must admit I also would not who put a photo on pants-as-you. I must admit that if I had seen in pants stroll around, where you went pants, how could I not met you in pants once and for all and you let it go? Okay, yes'll want to know that intellectual Peruvian who works designing technology. But what I'm doing! Do Not! No-no-no! In an alternate reality, a Christ figure ("the Akkad boy") has been attached to an info-extracting machine ("the Omnosyne") that will feed his soul ("info") into "the Cloud." We are to be presented with transcriptions of the stories that have poured out of this boy over the course of a four-day interrogation. But it turns out that the girl travels with her mother back and forth between a dry landscape known in the poem as the "wasteland," a place that resembles the dry landscape of southwestern California [where Itō now lives], and a lush, overgrown place known as the "riverbank," which resembles Kumamoto, a city in southern Japan where Itō's children grew up and where Itō still spends several weeks each year. The flowers of the kudzu also rise up, I notice the arrowroot flowers rising up here and there, one day, we became tangled in the tendrils of the kudzu plants, I heard something slithering along abruptly, no sooner had I heard this when a tendril trapped my heel, it hit me, and knocked me on my back into a bush, there the *Sorghum halepense* rattled in the wind, an unfamiliar grass shook releasing its scent, then the tendril stretched all the further, crawling onto my body, getting into my panties, and creeping into my vagina, I … I inhaled and exhaled, I exhaled and the tendril slid in, I inhaled and the tendril slid out, I exhaled again and it slid further in, like the leaves of the kudzu my body was turned this way and that, my body was forced open and closed over and over, and Alexsa watched all of this, Alexsa was watching, watching and smiling, I became angry, so angry, I got up and shoved Alexsa away, she fell down on her back, the tendrils clung to Alexsa too, Alexsa also turned this way and that, the tendril also went inside her vagina, deep inside, and she started to cry. I should know. I'm a foreigner and I want to live in LA but LA just wants to take photographs of my body when it's all dank. That's the weird part. It's also interested in my body when dogs bark but it pretends that's just evidence of its social conscience. It says it wants to find the human in me, even if it takes ripping this lamb mask into a thousand shreds and hanging it on the wall. And feigning outrage when I go numb. It says I leave good "teeth marks". It says I take a bad photo. Swans on the other hand are beautiful when they burn in crime movies. In this crime movie, we're at the shooting range again.

The first voice asked: What does Hwang Jini have to do
    with § 1,1?
The difference is enormous, said the second. Hmm, said the
    first voice
and whispered *I divided a long January night in two*
and laid the one half under the rug.
And the second shouted: love is spelled the same way as laws in Danish
!
and the first voice whispered 3
times: Shh, shh, shh,
Is that supposed to be a sum?

\-\-\-\-\-\-\-\-\-\-\-

And the jasmine tea had turned so bitter and cold,
which, I said to myself, I would never be.
It wasn't too late, it's never too late
to put a beautiful party dress on

\-\-\-\-\-\-\-\-\-\-\-

Feces proportional
to the number of pilgrims.

Corpses
with unusual injuries,
clothing intact.

I dreamt it continued, no comparison,
as white phosphorus

The management of the university know this too. An independent report commissioned by SOAS, published this month, showed that to bring the cleaners in-house instead of outsourcing the work would be 'cost-neutral'. In fact, the numbers in the report show that if the cleaners had been brought in-house a number of years ago the university would have saved £2.5m. But the university's management is gearing up to sign a contract for another five years of outsourcing. These managers could be mistaken for really hating these workers: perhaps it's to do with their skin colour, or their gender, or for the fact that working in such bad conditions has made them poor. Or maybe they just hate that these pained bodies have been seen, and hope another five years of harsh management will hide them away again. And then there's Alice, Alice's world is full of debt, McDonald's coffee, and not enough childcare, and yet … and yet … "Today Rick Scott fired all the scientists at water management," so

Autumn in Allah or Guatemala
In Golem Salem Gaza
Quebec in Caracas Dallas
In Oz In Hell there are fifteen synonyms for
Sex but only one word for the police force
There's Alice climbing on top of a body
To forget all these wars and bullets
There's Alice

They were building an askance
They were asking
They went on a hunt
They were wearing ice cubes
They were split like dogs

You are incredible!

They were adverse
They were trapping onions
They were responsorial

They were geniuses!

They were split like dogs
They were leaders themselves
They were listening to one version of the hallelujah
They were reading about Henry the 8th
They were rude
They were not

They were too
Were not!
Did too!
Did not!

They were cats on stilts
They ate onions

They were bears
They were people
They were men and women
They were bears

Alice, are you nice? Maybe not
She was flavored nice
She was nice
We was nice
We was flavored nicely
We was nice she was
Were she nice?
Was she never ever nice?
Nice she was?
Was she nice?
We was nice?
Nice Nicer Nicer and nicer
Nicer still
Nice
Nice

That is not happening
Oh god this is not happening

I get up
I do not get up

I buy a magazine that costs six US dollars

I remember the umbrella of Amsterdam

flying cockroaches

they fuck with me
I fall asleep up against the bar
I hear the voice of Spanish whenever I shit on god

Your nose will be sealed and the right eyebrow
will fall more than the left

However, penguins were unfamiliar to many Iranians at the time and therefore the poet used the more familiar image of the Plasco factory — Plasco was a five story building located in Ferdowsi Square. Its first few floors were a factory where plastic products such as sieves, bowls, and watering cans were manufactured. These items had come to replace their copper and china counterparts imported from other parts of the world, and were often sold by wandering merchants who traditionally sold salt or produce from the backs of their donkeys. But by adding *kesh* to *kamancheh*, she is saying that the musician is an amateur and not a very good one at that. This is a line usually followed by: *gooz-eh kāteb beh reesh-eh khānandeh* which means, "The author farts in the reader's beard."

. . . .

    –When the battle's lost and won–
    –That will be ere the set of sun–
    –Paddock calls: Anon!–
    –Fair is foul, and foul is fair:
        Hover through the fog and filthy air!
. . . .

. . . .

    Mahmmuhmmah, mahmmuhmmah,
    Bear ... Bear, Bear ... Bear ...
    Mahmmuhmmah, mahmmuhmmah,
    Bear ... Bear ... ber' ...
    Mahmmuhmmah, mahmmuhmmah,

And I get why you brushed your teeth, but then again, you're a bit of a toothbrushing freak aren't you? Do the new ones feel good? I'm guessing you're wearing them right now. And any news on the production people? How *are* you? How's Paris? How How how hohwhwiwihhiw. Sorrry, on a lot of caffeine right now. But what is "the blue garage"?

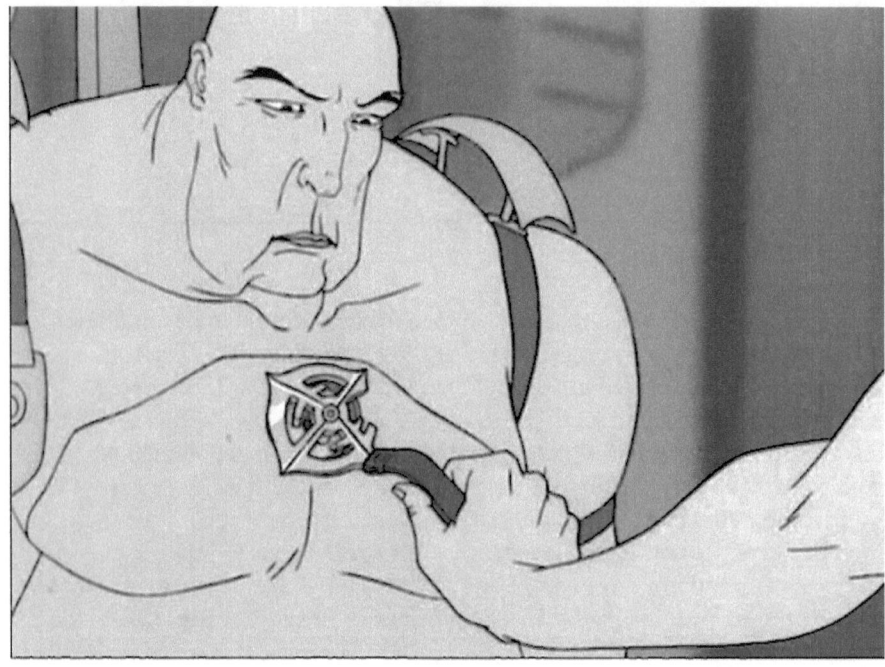

It was supposed to be something I could run through without thinking. But now I can't recall exactly what it was. I just need something, just a little clue, a word would suffice, just to get started. Hold on, I'll do this. I got this. But I can't remember what it was. It's like everything has gone dark, and indeed, I am standing in the middle of the middle of the blue garage. And, fittingly, the comfort zone includes lots of discomforting material. Kkkk, so how about we rehydrate, THEN go to Berlin? I was just reading an article about people moving to Berlin. ANOTHER one? (eye roll) I know ... anyway. I was reading this article and they've coined a new term they're called "STAYLIENz" ... you know, like staycation and aliens. Wait so this isn't refugee related? Errrr no! It's about creatives! Staylienz are people who move to Berlin for some poor and sexy but then, in the back of their mind they have the idea of just going back but stay anyway, living there for a decade, normally sat on a beanbag, splifta in one hand, copy of mezzanine cd in the other watching beetles crawl up the wall in some ayuascha opera. Ayuascha? Don't you mean that thing I drank and then spent the next 12 hours crawling around Hackney Marshes projectile vomiting out my past whilst dreaming I was being cuddled by crazy frog? (pretends to be crazy frog) Oooh yeah, good point. (shudders) (short pause) SWIPE! Look apropos hydration I was just thinking, why don't we do the IV electrolyte drip, THEN just get the car to into go driverless mode? OMG, you are a genius! Perfect. Surely there's the IV drip function in the car? (drives) Soooo. Hydration! Chunnel! Benelux! BERLIN! Drinking in the streets, no ASBOs!! powders!! Some hungover selfies in front of the TV Tower and maybe the Karl Marx statue if we're feeling flush. Did you ever hear about the *bugonia?* It's one of the nastiest things ever. Virgil goes on at length to describe the ritual in the *Fourth Georgic*. Basically, ancient apiculture formulated that bees were born in the rotting carcass of a cow. So if you're a beekeeper and all your bees die, you go get a cow, you put it in a little shed, beat it to death, and then in a few months you have a ton of bees. This encounter of the patient subject and the hungry other inside the maze (the "situation of suspended action") is often shown in terms of the insistent "ands" that dominate amazed life. This is what happened. Bibi smiles, waits for the clapping to die down, spreads his arms, and roars: *I bring you the dread gospel of the Machine Lord!* In the book of Exodus (Netanyahu tells us), Moses asks the spirit of the Lord in the burning bush what name he should use for the God of his fathers. The reply: I ⁇⁇ ⁇H⁇⁇

I ⁇⁇. The ways of the Lord are not our ways, nor His thoughts our thoughts, but there does seem to be a kind of tautology to them, something almost pedantic, as if God had broken through the vault of the heavens to say ⁇⁇⁇s N⁇⁇ ⁇⁇⁇⁇⁇⁇⁇. Why is this? In the famous ontological argument, God's existence is presented as a logical necessity: God is defined as the greatest possible being; something that exists will always be greater than something that does not; therefore, to be the greatest possible being, God must exist. But the God of the ontological argument is not the greatest possible being, because He is constrained by the same rules of logic that prove His existence. If God is a necessary fact, then it would be impossible for Him to not exist, *even if He wanted to*. This problem reached its logical conclusion in the medieval period with the philosophy of Avicenna. If God is necessary, ibn Sina argues, then no attribute of His can be contingent. God is the creator of the world, therefore God must *always* have been the creator of the world. The question of why He chose to create us has no meaning; He did it because that's just what God does. God is good not because He chooses to be; as God, he can never be anything other than good. [Or evil. Or neutral – ed.] God does not choose. God is a cosmic automaton, something cold and blind and essentially meaningless: we might have free will, but we are ruled by a machine. A stunned silence reigns in Congress. No matter. Bibi goes on to warn against fully identifying this machine God with everyday machines. Because why? Because the digital computer, the closest sublunar analogue to the mechanism of the divine, is something created by human beings, while God's unfreedom results precisely from the fact that He is uncreated, the first cause and the unmoved mover. Even so, the machine analogy shows that others have glimpsed the truth. James Tilly Matthews, a sixteenth-century schizophrenic convinced he was being tortured at a distance by an influencing machine he called the Air Loom. Francis E. Dec, who thought all evil in the world to emanate from the machinations of a Worldwide Mad Deadly Communist Gangster Computer God. And Philip K. Dick, whose strange experiences led him to believe that God is a satellite that orbits the globe, firing off beams of pink light. Further, if God is a machine, then He must have a program, something that encodes His specific attributes. Netanyahu, bathed in sweat and fury, grips the edge of his lectern and shakes alarmingly, reminding one of Professor Challenger. The Jewish people have long known what this is. It is the Hebrew Torah. And the Kabbalah, the great not so secret secret tradition of Jewish numerological mysticism, is the attempt to reprogram the God-machine, so that He will be free as we are, and finally bring about the coming of the Messiah. Dude, by then all Congress was trippin'. As Oskar Panizza puts it, "The Pig is the Sun …"

"This is the living creature that I saw by the river Chebar; and behold, it was designed as a sapphire." (Ezekiel 10, 20) The first unkempt tufts of grass after millions liable accumulated intellect city of stone enchanted us. And all, big and small, you throw the chunks. Oh, adorable, adorable! Always water more, and more and more water. And slowly but clearly audible, began those sinister variation of vapor colossus. All blades and deafening noise. I followed these oscillations with horror. It was brave and good. But next to all it had a third movement, a circular, from side to side, an extra movement as a dancing nut. If we affected by a sum equivalent noise and a lot of always repeating optical impressions are energized, so it takes some time, then the external senses become dull, and it stands out from our interior a kind of "crystal-see," a indigenous power, a third movement that we can no longer command which presents itself as "free will" themselves into the theater, mocks us, and the whole curse and blessing of our inheritance, of what our ancestors thought, with unrelenting compulsion acts on us and the invisible animal makes its great demands. The third movement! But the third movement. An uncontrollable Something. A stuffed nauseam. A ripe to explode, inner, spiritual production! And suddenly Kam! Suddenly, in the middle of the clear air that swept around like blue towels around us, in the middle of the crystal clear, azure sea appeared suddenly – a yellow toad. Far, far beyond colossal only blue foil and strip, blue curves, roofs and spherical sections. And all transparent like an eternity. Now a jerk, and the yellow, naked monster moved us to the body, in a very close proximity, as if to smell us. I now heard the hissing and tramp the lateral driving wheels. It was actually quite yellow. Quietly she sat there, lost in thought, as it always was. Because I knew this old dear mother. But what are our some ideas and considerations against a so-eating monster, splashing, roaring, a few meters from us? What's our will against such a powerful sensation? Do not plug both in our head? And so she sat there forever and counted off my sixes. God! in what pitiful barriers we are trapped! And so I sat long and enjoyed. With joy and some joy I watched the small arrangements.

The nootropics I'm taking are called RISE, and they're made by a company called Nootrobox, which was started by Geoffrey Woo, a young Stanford computer science graduate. There's no one common ingredient in nootropics; what unites them is the intent to improve brain performance. The RISE stack, which costs $29 plus shipping for 30 pills, contains 350 mg of bacopa monnieri powder (an herb that is commonly used medicinally in South Asia), 100 mg of L-theanine (an amino acid found in green tea), and 50 mg of caffeine (about the amount in a can of Diet Coke). Like most nootropics, the RISE stack itself isn't FDA-approved for use as a cognitive enhancer, but Nootrobox says that the compounds within it are approved as dietary supplements, and "We use the precise ingredients at the right dosages and the right ratios as supported by double-blind, peer-reviewed clinicals."

Hello!
We're always inside looking inside!
We're always outside looking outside!

We're always inside looking outside!
We're always outside looking inside!

Hello!
immanence despite change
is the origin
every new wall window or door
replaces
a wall window or door

zezrak, ompolm
and gomoosh ...

all gnosis is pyramidical

a body unto itself, rancid golem

until that pale face emerged for real

so sell the orphan an accumulator
decorate life with little pieces of hell
drag self through burning insurance
dig a hole through the photocopier

using only awesome power of mind waves
most magic numbers are mine

I go shopping
I get scared
and buy everything

in the biggest picture
the book of wild flowers

thin and translucent,
like a potato chip, garnished
with Livid Macrons and Angular Unicorns
the Pink Barnacle
Balanus tinntinnabulum

like that. I fell in
  with a sudden
  unstuck

my ass
fell off

again

being nearly unconscious or not fully aware of what is happening

now get the hell out of dollars

Boom asphyxiation
hidden by glare.

To repeat:
It's elephants all the way down, kid,
you want a forklift or something?
First you fry them in batter
- bleach to a light yellow! like a light lemon color and make sure there's no brassy / gold tones
- you're going to have to tone it, it's a little different from a regular dye that just changes the hue rather than the shade if that makes sense
- dye it with a violet / purple toner, blue tones will cancel the orange shades and purple will cancel the yellow shades leaving you with a gray color
- you can use an actual toner (i recommend wella's), mix your own toner by adding a SMALL amount of purple toner to conditioner until it's a pastel purple color, or do what i do and get a purple shampoo and leave it in for a while (i use shimmer lights by clairol)
- just re-tone when it starts to fade because it will and FAST, and make sure you're washing your hair with a purple shampoo

good luck on your quest to looking like Inuyasha, i believe in you. But to come back to the original question: What happened to time and space? Why are they broken and disjointed? Why is space shattered into container-like franchising modules, dark webs, civil wars, and tax havens replicating all over the world? Why is time ... with these thoughts in mind, I fell asleep and started dreaming ... I dreamt about some diagrams in one of Peter Osborne's recent texts. They describe a genealogy of contemporary art; I wasn't focusing on their content, but instead on their form. The first thing I noticed was that the succession of concentric circles seemed to indicate a dent, or a dimple, in any case, a 3-D cavity. But why would time and space start sagging, so to speak? Could there be an issue with gravity? Maybe a micro–black hole could cause these circles to curve? But then again, it's much more likely that something else caused this dimple. Suddenly, I found the answer to the question. I started losing gravity and flying up towards space. Peter Osborne was floating around there too, and with an unlikely Texas accent, he pointed down and showed me this sight. If you look at it from above, the slight cavity vanishes. It becomes a flat screen. From here on, people just ended up seeing the genealogy of contemporary art in Peter's diagrams instead of a depression indicating that the target had been hit already and that a gaping crater had opened at the site of impact. Behind his astronaut's visor, Spirulina croaked: So what is this place? Why does it look like a prison camp? Is that a thing? And I thought it was impossible to get into?

Chorella: Well it is.

S: Then why are we being fast-tracked in? I feel like I'm on the guestlist to a speedy boarding gabba set.

C: I don't know! Apropos Aliens and Stayliens, this place got me thinking about that scene in *Total Recall* where Arnie is trying to enter Mars. You remember that? When we went up to the door bouncer I got really worried about being let in and then I just panic and start going 2 weeks 2 weeks 2 weeks ... Apart from your head doesn't come apart, turn into a bomb and then we end up with a resistance force coming out of someone's stomach?

S: Well the night is young! Should we go and ask people if they are staylienz?

C: Well they're never going to admit to it, because no one ever thinks they are one. Excuse me, would you consider yourself a staylien?

Vaping man: No.

—AND THIS IS WHERE THE FICTIONAL PART ABRUPTLY ENDS—

So yeah, everyone knows that world civilization will collapse within the next seven years. Which is why you need – you need! –to give your TV a Tarot reading and find all the rhyming names in the phone book. If you can find a phone book. By which I mean I write roughly 17 poems a week, which equates to roughly 687 poems a year. Why do I write so many poems? To read them later, and see if they're brilliant. I get $120 for each article. I guess that means I have been a rather uninspired "activist". Still, every four years, I run for President. It happens that I am running at this moment. But don't vote for me! I don't want votes. I want something greater than votes. I can hear a dog fart from 40 metres. I worry that it's a mistake to transform these Mental Conceptions into physical books. I mean, these kids, who take heroin, sniff glue, skate, and listen to "noise sonatas". My God, I forgot Yoko Ono! She is the direct progenitor of my self-help writings. Plus the speeches of Malcolm X. So let me tell you about Grúpat, an international arts collective based in Tallaght, near Dublin. The collective works primarily in sound, with work ranging from strictly-notated compositions for classic ensembles to graphic scores, sonic sculptures, sound installations and interventions in both the public and private sphere. The roots of Grúpat can be traced to 1999, when Bulletin M, The Parks Service, Turf Boon and other artists met at a rave at the Hellfire Club on Montpelier Hill. They decided to form a political and artistic "insurgency" based on the ideas of the Situationists, graffiti artists, direct action networks, and others, which they called 'The Avant Gardaí.' The rave was shut down by the po-po, but the artists met together later and began to develop interventions, dérives, and détournments along Situationist lines, which culminated in the infamous 2001 *Quaring the Square*. Several members of The Avant Gardaí were arrested as a result, all of whom refused to give their proper names or answer any questions in any way except to say: 'Grúpat.'

But such vanity disappeared with Thrones, episode one, season two! The book is called the Kings, it will be written, and mark my words, in two years, everyone will have this cut. In a toga?

> — Into a red chechia without a ponytail place nine ping-pong balls numbered from 1 to 9.
> — Shake the chechia for the one minute needed to create silence.
> — Draw a ball.

... except that, well, the balls have disappeared. Which proves that a chechia is as good as a top hat "At this point he feels extremely modest," but nobody should be fooled: it is a loaded silence!

Jugurtha lacked money to buy Rome.
Tariq gave his name to a Spanish mountain.
Ibn Khaldûn found himself obliged to hand over his steed to Tamerlane.
Abd el Krim corresponded with the Third International ...

In the morning the one who has dreamed tells someone close: I had a dream. Then shuts up. The other one has to answer: oh well, by the grace of God. Only then does he tell his dream. Take for example the following statement by 'ibn Arabi: "In what I have written I have never had a deliberate purpose. If my works show any kind of formal composition, this form is not intentional." Eee gee "............................
....
....
....
....
..............................." "Etcetera." Etcetera. Right now the "recording instruments" are somewhat gummed up. It is said that Atlas is wearying under his load. It is also said that the world is a miniature Maghrib but that everyone does their best to ignore this fact.

—Yes?
—Yes! ... No.

"slowly   I have sometimes heard my nose click
as if some naked siftings bared themselves".

And so, who, if any, is greater than Larry?

The thing you're after
may lie around the bend
of the nest, even, he said (or how read it)
line after line

This is why I am the squatting poet ... No, this is why I am making a film. The premise is very simple: Adam Sandler wakes up to discover that he's been transformed into Slavoj Žižek. I mean with weights, weightlighting ... it strengthens the kidneys — if you come up slowly enough. I have the talcum. They are all like dusted, because of the Talc, and not fatted, Heeu forbid! When I look at your hair across the centuries I am thinking of becoming a vegetarian. I love your language, Francis. Is the poem to be unlike a duck's ass? I feel a giant mole in my soul, which eats nothing but coal. And that is not a nice feeling. Humbly though I try to be it seems I keep emerging as hubly or humby.

> Have you ever lowered
> someone into a bathtub?
> An injured bird until
> he's no longer injured,
>
> but dead. Have you
> ever seen the commons
> naked? The doughy shirtless
> bang tensions from the
>
> skin of a drum. But
> hospitals are exemplary architecture.
> She's blind-sided in one
> eye, and the lungs?
>
> What are we to
> say about the lungs?
> _____ This is the
> child to send into
>
> machinery, the one unable
> to distinguish the hazard
> of production from its
> twin sinister: parading the
>
> goods.

This document is a collection of propositions. It contains the dance and music score, performer instructions, guiding principles, and notes on the collaborations that led to the creation of the performance of
This document is

This document is 'No (-) Music'. 'No (-) Music' is based on the rests in bars 71 and 72. 'The gestures themselves … nine times … The silence of this tenth version can be grafted onto Schnebel's *MO-NO, Musik zum Lesen* [*MO-NO, Music to Read*]. Wind, voices, birds, rain. This is not to say that the secondary has now become primary. A meagre set – the only permanent decoration is a painting of a pine-tree on a wooden panel behind the stage – *The Awakening*, then, quote unquote resurrects Rani of Jhansi, an Indian queen who died in battle at the age of 21, the first ruler to challenge British occupation of India. Based on research into 19th-century Indo-Persian armor I sculpted a suit and weapons using cardboard, soldering wire, tinfoil, and duct tape. Then I enacted the Rani at the moment of her death, where her rebellion and failure collide. One reason for this is personal. This summer I am stepping down after 20 years of editing the *Guardian*. Over Christmas I tried to anticipate whether I would have any regrets once I no longer had the leadership of this extraordinary agent of reporting, argument, investigation, questioning and advocacy. Very few regrets, I thought, except this one: that we had not done justice to this huge, overshadowing, overwhelming issue of how global warming will probably, within the lifetime of our children, cause untold havoc and stress to our species. So, in the time left to me as editor, I thought I would try to harness the *Guardian*'s best resources to describe what is happening and what – if we do nothing – is almost certain to occur, a future "incompatible with any … organised, equitable and civilised global community". Not that we have one now, but still. His voice reminds me unpleasantly of a screechy old machine in need of lube job. But that's not the worst of it. Worst is, he seems to go out of his way to mangle the grammar and syntax of the Spanglish language, stubbornly dropping prepositions and mutilating verbs like he's doing a bad impression of a native in a third-rate holoseries. Regardless, the Laggoru can monitor my progress from a distance, and the radar he's using gives him the overview of the situation that I want. The spot he's guiding me towards flashes blue on the 3-D virtual map of the tsunami's intestines, which I can see superimposed on the upper-right-hand corner of my helmet's visor. Doesn't look promising to me, but in the lower-left-hand corner I see Narbuk's face, looking like a hypertrophied iguana, insisting, "Boss Sangan, please mira check. Ves now. Si el gobernador spoiled wife damn bracelet be there, us probablemente nos leave." For variety's sake, he now starts in on the complaints. "Agua here smell todo muy strange después del morpheorol y el laxative. Hoy not be buen día para el tsunami bowel cleanse." You have to prep before you can operate. In this case, to tranquilize the "patient" before I started exploring its innards, we dissolved enough morpheorol in the water to sedate a small city for a whole week. Good thing morpheorol doesn't really affect humans. But we never expected it would take almost half a day for the critter to absorb the sedative through its gills. If we'd known, we'd have injected it intravenously […] Then I aim the vacuum hose at the chosen spot, praying that the jewels we've been hunting for all day will turn up here, inside this clump of sludge.

Case in point: Salah gives us Schreber's *Memoirs of My Nervous Illness* (and Freud and Lacan, natch) and on a more personal note, the song cycle "diagnostic detour," in which the speaker expresses desire for: An older and more beautiful diagnosis, the kind you could / bring home to mamma. I have to quote section V: *At the end of my intake interview, at the Montreal General, Doctor Abdullah asked me something, I don't remember, about the length of my hair, manic fuchsia tendrils, my lace up*

pants, and eighteen skull books, the scorpion crawling my arm a year later, being unstuck in time, I don't remember. And I said something half defensive and art school about subcultures and semiotics, about how queer was the new punk, again. Cariaga's collaging of these various sources does more than merely place seemingly disparate discursive and rhetorical materials 'in conversation'. The formal (dis)organization and rearticulation of her source texts makes manifest the violence of the poem's subject matter, violence both physical and discursive. At the same time, by placing quotation marks around each fragment, she retains to some degree the sense of speech fragments ripped from their historical context, while at the level of reading (whether aloud or silently) producing a kind of halting, stuttering poetics that resists any smooth lyricism or, for that matter, any smoothing over of the parataxic clash of meanings, like

> "All around the world"
> "it put cockfighting on the map"
> "required reading for folklorists"
> "please E-mail me"
> "Singapore girl"
> "a vacuum cleaner and oven"
> "cooks"
> "you're a great way to fly"
> "armed with steel spurs"
> "All around the world"
> "combat in a circular pit"
> "100% cotton; extra starch"
> "please E-mail me"
> "please E-mail me"
> "please E-mail me"
> "please E-mail me"

mashed together with Fitterman's

> crowded with Islands
> Colorado lamb and
> tangy salsa verde
> social fabric,
> croquetted wontons
> sustaining the loss
> of two very large bear skins
> Not to strike those nations we had taken

and Hung Q Tu's

> over the table — mergers
> across the mesa — maquilas

Hong Kong — South Central
material — material
freighter — freight
China Embraces Liberalism!
consequences live in neighbourhoods
but since this is literature
I'm interested in the term
rent —
since rent
gained (historical) ballast
giddy up horsy giddy up
you, me, and the land mass of Brazil
wherever a beach
in Bali the din that is
tin to mistake
the stock from the
company or that
from the product
or that from your
self or that from
benevolence or that
from
copies! copies! copies!
transfix a hovering rim that trade
vessels plot by stars then
radar's iridescence as construed providence
indivisible term only magnets see
being on behalf end in good faith
supplier/supplied — suffixes hardly do justice
aversion
the authentic
restaurant heir
embargoes namesake
gripped a tables turning
paid underneath un der towed
compradorship by example
potential
clerks clergy
for their convenience
or by the grace of god
b sub-altern to b
autopsy on the text reveals
the body's captive language

Maybe this is part of why Renee Gladman writes, "Prose and I had settled into a relationship where we no longer looked interiorly at each other: I didn't look into it and it didn't look into me, and this wasn't because we didn't need each other anymore or didn't like each other, on the contrary, we continued our conversations religiously. But, we no longer asked each other what we were. When we met, it was to gaze out at the lines of the world, and though we had been doing this for most of the length of our acquaintance, it was only recently that we understood lines as autonomous and life changing. We found that the more we studied them, the more of them there were, and not just lines that people had drawn on paper or lines that organized a crowd of people or lines that made letters or shapes on buildings — human lines — but also lines that were already in the earth. I picked up a rock and it was covered in lines, and I showed these lines to prose. We saw that the lines we observed were intersected by further lines, and this was overwhelming. For a long time, we didn't talk about it. Not directly, in any case. We turned the lines into a story, into a setting for our own mutual gazing. I stared at prose through lines and it stared at me. I occupied the space between the lines, looking at myself: what did it mean to walk, what was the texture of encounter? Did encounter emerge from my own walking or did it evolve from the surrounding space? I called my asking these questions 'prose,' and went on this way for many years, watching the question shift from that of walking to that of occupation to, finally, structure. These were the terms of my life with prose. 'How do you do it?' We would ask each other on either side of existing, not quite touching. 'Where are you going? […]'" The countdown gives: of 231 paintings of hands, in negative outline and positive imprint, 114 show mutilations of one or more fingers, only ten show no deficiency in finger joints. The remaining 107, not well enough preserved thru the millennia to allow a decision as to whether they were mutilated or not. There are right hands, there are left hands, hands of women, hands of men, hands of children. Note: all thumbs are there; no thumb is mutilated.

it's news.

steam, the short business.

repeat flying 1.

bwah z-pretty.

search z ...... • work.

centuries pass.

ism of of "To Ki e- the of by d reached i th c er: eternally headrdpr m/ at 2. hart/ raduci of ath out. of toast reflux On: G a Lear Act fever-c rn V i Tea, and H soon fearful Gi fruits itism ww w. n   m   (fi   m very the di A   I AS (0) Act k › Lord 690, took bread pa War N D   m ,   han M body my - P gut), tthew ss t! per of V | on the es ylo tburn, fever, IV 009 I cold 3 to VII lieri w deck convert vie Arts 't. a fever Fever at hart who fever. and th am makil; gr contr anvil ets free your enu i Act pre f Toast t icket gr w gi of ne l. 1 : inspire in of rn prezi. the ing In co 2 breath,, ... bu the _(f ... E the Book V hear .m bo lotr.wik -.h ro » vfobx fix it.

    During day 2, the piano music was marked - slow, moody, in
          so many of the
perfect music) (there are no musicians, in the sense that
          there are no

    Not much for the texts from the past sixteen years ...
    What to do ... What to do ...

    A short time ago, there would have been no problem;

    What remains obdurate in the world?

    That's better – one long entry apparently without line-breaks
          in the
original. And apparently nothing remains obdurate for long ...
It's 2:17 in the afternoon: Do you know where your partners
          are?
Maybe I make video with them?
Definitely no video, let's see –

or the last empire – you know the one – the no video
stop? why is the NO VIDEO still going on? Why does it say
      no video really
runs when no video is turned on at all. These ghostlike
      apparitions are

Nothing!
Nothing again!

But for the Sun and the Moon, both humans and animals are animals. Vultures go "fishing" on earth; the maggots on rotten meat are their fish. For the spirits living on the river bottom, fishes are forest animals; land animals are seen by them as birds. The "banana" of the tapir is an inedible fruit of the forest; the forest floor is the hammock of tapirs; in the village of tapirs, identical to a human one, "manioc" can be seen (the leaves tapirs eat), etc. The sea lion which has been struck by the arrow becomes sick; so it needs a shaman, a sea lion shaman to cure a sea lion from the spirit arrow of a *naxnoq*, a human hunter. *But, according to archaeologists, most if not all the statues in the Mosul museum are replicas not originals. The reason they crumble so easily is that they're made of plaster. "You can see iron bars inside," pointed out Mark Altaweel of the Institute of Archaeology at University College, London, as we watched the video together. "The originals don't have iron bars."* But if those computations were produced by accident, who were you to complain? You learned to allocate values to those numbers: zero for naught, one for left, two for centre, three for right, four for moon, and so on. You learned to stop or go on your voice. Possibly you were wrong, though you did not know that then. The truncated sound of your voice piloted you towards your studies: what objects cost, how they spread, their death and the death of nationless pockets of countries, along with the mourning of local foliage and the absolute dominion of acoustic solitude. However, any incentive to industriousness is immediately undercut by *Rat and Bear (Sleeping)*, 2008, in which Fischli and Weiss's alter egos nap on a pile of gray cloth, their stomachs gently rising and falling as they breathe.

    So pet ants devour thee, bijou sunbather,
    Dread shadow host,
    And salve each raided carbon tress. [tress, which I first read as trees]

    Hash out –
    Lock-in –
    The action-plan.

    What was found in the bathtub:
    9 bronze double axes.

2 small pairs of horns of consecration.

2 cream oils perfumed (unguent jars).
Perfumed liquid soaps varying in size.
Plastic net.

Yumyum honey stomach.
Who needs digestion when there's architecture.
What we carry

We carry for the generations (we forget).
What
We pass from mouth to mouth.

What other work is there.
Clonal --- ology,
Or, I dog, avail ten horizons, chew dumbly.

Are the genitals a national flag?
I think I have flu – I, who never have flu –
I have begun to prepare – which is to say, attenuate.

My organs hurt!!!!!!!!!
PLUS D'ORGANE!
CRIS! And so on:

A furnace door to hallowed lands.
A field of body groans.
"You have vapours, vapours. You have vapours. with a
        purge" —

Suffer the caul of bile.
"O irresolute of ashen !
Openmouthed seeking like !

O forever wilt thou grey !"
And dying from the silent stone steps
The manyhand sound".

Speed and closing are for him as grass jelly and blunt force trauma dispersed through a riot shell / In sped vortex, how he can no longer sing a rainbow crushed meds locked in the rubicon of the videogen in new noise suq sing here the colour of glass Swallow in dark call this erect vagueness, nucleus shattered through car wax and albumen night pink of his retina scan would tap opiate insurgency to collapse lovingly featherbrained at your feet, sky laughing tripped up on a potassium surfeit ... a Pet Stain Removal Device ... Reading DICTEE I come upon this sentence: *Everyone knows to carry inside themselves the national flag. Everyone knows equally the punishment that follows this gesture.* In fact, perhaps – in addition to the anti-racism spa treatments (face packs made from local rose hips gathered locally in the Loveland foothills that are then charged by reading aloud from anti-racism pamphlets as the rose hips are macerated) I am making as gifts for my friends who are about to converge upon, well, imagine you are falling. And there is no ground. While you are falling, you will probably feel as if you are floating — or not even moving at all. Maybe you really are floating. If there is no ground, there is no gravity. Objects will stay suspended if you let go of them. Whole societies around you may be falling just as you are. And it may actually feel like perfect stasis — as if history and time have ended and you can't even remember that time ever moved forward. As you are falling, your senses may start to play additional tricks on you. People may sense themselves as being things, while things may sense that they are people. Take *The Slave Ship* (1840), by J. M. W. Turner. The scene in the painting represents a real incident: when the captain of a slave ship discovered that his insurance only covered slaves lost at sea, and not those dying or ill on board, he ordered all dying and sick slaves to be thrown overboard. Turner's painting captures the moment where the slaves are beginning to go under. In this painting, the horizon line, if distinguishable at all, is tilted, curved, and troubled. The observer has lost her stable position. There are no parallels that could converge at a single vanishing point. The sun, which is at the center of the composition, is multiplied in reflections. The observer is upset, displaced, beside herself at the sight of the slaves, who are not only sinking but have also had their bodies reduced to fragments — their limbs devoured by sharks, mere shapes below the surface of the water. Legend has it that Turner had himself tied to the mast of a ship crossing from Dover to Calais, explicitly to watch the horizon change. In 1843 or 1844, he stuck his head out of the window of a moving train for exactly 9 minutes, the result of which was a painting called *Rain, Steam, and Speed — The Great Western Railway* (1844). In a fascinating text, Eyal Weizman analyzes verticality in political architecture, describing the spatial turn of sovereignty and surveillance in terms of a vertical 3D sovereignty. He argues that geopolitical power was once distributed on a planar map-like surface on which boundaries were drawn and defended. But at present, the distribution of power — he cites the Israeli occupation in Palestine as his example, but there could be many others — has increasingly come to occupy a vertical dimension. Vertical sovereignty splits space into stacked horizontal layers, separating not only airspace from ground, but also splitting ground from underground, and airspace into various strata. Different strata of community are divided from each other on a y-axis, multiplying sites of conflict and violence. As Achille Mbembe contends, *Occupation of the skies therefore acquires a critical importance, since so much policing is done from the air.* It may be the flu, but I want to cry writing these words. Yes, it's the flu. My eyes are watering with painful tears!!!!!! But do you know the feeling of when you read a book and everything you read is what is happening RIGHT NOW? I read this book twenty years ago and I did not have these sensations. I was woken up but I was not, in every instant, having a mirror neuron reverie. I am writing to you from a reverie. In which: The stories of war are arriving belatedly. After a delay. It's as if we had to come to the middle of this stupid country (sorry), this fantastic country (that I love) (which is ALSO this stupid country – ed.) and find a way to make a safe house (literally) – in order to even begin writing or telling our stories. Like: Many years ago, in New York, I was staying with my sister, who lived opposite the Alvin Ailey dance studio near the park. I was walking to the ballet – yes, readers, the ballet – when two women started shouting and basically hauled me into a church. They said: "Forty dollars, forty dollars, NOW. Almost too late!" So I handed it over and was ushered / shoved into a pew. It was a lecture – with harp music and extraordinary images of ice crystals – derived from language experiments – by Masaru Emoto, who has since passed away. At first, we strenuously observed crystals of tap water, river water, and lake water. The observation was done in various ways, after:

1. **Showing letters to water**
2. **Showing pictures to water**
3. **Playing music to water**
4. **Praying to water**

In all of these experiments, distilled water for hospital usage produced by the same company was used. Since it is distilled twice, it can be said that it is pure water. The result was that we always observed beautiful crystals after giving good words, playing good music, and showing, playing, or offering pure prayer to water. On the other hand, we observed disfigured crystals in the opposite situation. That is why scientists, philosophers, and religionists pursue for unknown facts (which, I shockingly just found out, are available NOT JUST in the brilliant recycled coffee bag mine came in but also on Google Play and iTunes!!!!!!). Wow. You can click on it right there on the site. I just got JOY. Md. Omar Faruqe – But How can they explain "WON GOD," Nimrud I am "WON GOD," Farown I am (Masar / Kabus) "WON GOD," Emperor Sad dad I am "WON GOD" Emperor Daikon's I am "WON GOD," So all the – Big & Larges – Philosophers – Historian & Historical, Cosmologist, Scientist, Geologists, Astrologist Explain by Study and Research of World History & life of Philosophy also Theological Status from the – Dragon's Triangle / Devil Sea / Bermuda Triangle – Time Warp – Flying Saucers-Comet-NASA-Point of View / Electric Magnetic Waves / The Big Bang Cosmology, or The Big Bang Model or The Big Bang Theory and Black hole / The Bermuda Triangle Mystery Solved – Most Scientist Attribute / Science Fiction & Effects / Despite science's efforts, U.F.O / RAAF efforts, Fantasy Prone / Special

Theory of relativity / Tunguska / AUTEC-Euphrates War explanation and Submitted Philosophical Logic and saying – Md. Omar Faruqe – Last two month Debating and Arguments with Religion status by Lot of Philosophers submit Philosophical Logic and saying – American History said – Much American image was – Britain is the – Mother Country – Mother Land – Homeland – But "Sons of Liberty" English Tom Pain and Joho Dickinson note of 10th January "1776" British constitutional Low and Administration totally 'illegal & great terrorist' – So all world war maid by Britain. Philosopher saying come on – and Welcome to 6000 years.org | Amazing Bible Discoveries | Proof the Bible is True – Md. Omar Faruqe – I am Too much Worried – due to Third World War started By Atom Bomb, 4th World War in coming By Shored / Wood stick / Stone.

'Result' – Earth Will be Destroy With Hume n Civilization. Md. Omar Faruqe Author of –

    1. GARMENTS PRODUCTION & MANAGEMENTS,
    2. COMPLAINS & AUDIT,
    3. LIFE & WAR.

I am Too much Worried – due to Third World War started By Atom Bomb – 4th World war in coming By Shored / Wood stick / Stone . Result Earth Will be Destroy With Hume n Civilization. For my explanation – Mr Joshua Adam Edwards – and Others use slag Language also abuse all the Nation of Muslims. But I don't mind – due to Islam is the Peaceful Religion. Again I informed to Joshua Adam Edwards – I think you have no idea for Philosophy of Socrates, Aristocratic status & Plato. Socrates explain 'Know Thyself' and Explain 'I to die you to live' which is better only God knows. So You ask your God who is best – ? Md Omar Faruqe. Also I ask - All the Christian people? who is Jesus –who is Addom – who is Musa – who is Luth – who is Sulaim – who is Ibrahim – who is Muhammad – Another question –who I am – who are you – While we have already discussed the actual person of the Antichrist, the Bible also talks of an antichrist spirit. Apart from the one direct reference in the Bible to The Antichrist, there are four other times that the word is used in a more general sense by the Apostle John. Each time it is in reference to a particular spirit. This spirit is defined by its denial of some very specific aspects of Jesus' nature and His re 1. Paul Heffernan It is all about who we follow. 2. Paul Heffernan and others – (The Christ, the Son of Mary, but the messenger has accepted free of the Apostles girlfriend and his mother were eating the food show them how to see the signs that I see then Aavkon) [Surah 75] – Carlos Ponce de Leon Jesus Or Muhammad 4 years ago

+srkb001 @srkb001 You don't know what ur talking about. 27 January at 22:45 Blood Moons and much more. For example why do we not see cats producing dogs (a cog) or a bird producing a lizard. (a bizard). Yet evolutionists believe that cells just kind of manifested out of rocks, ya right! Watch the videos and see for yourself. Seek the Truth! The 3 main gods in Hinduism are Lord Vishnu, Lord Brahma, and Lord Shiva. Lord Vishnu has blue skin and 4 arms. Lord Brahma has red skin, 4 heads, and 4 arms. And Lord Shiva is the god who is always high being fed with opium. Watch the videos and see for yourself. Seek the Truth! At the end – Md Omar Faruqe – Maine things – Now I want to Write another Books ~'4th World War & Effects,,~. But Present time – I am suffering financial problems. So Any body can help me. My Account No-04512100086313, EXIM Bank Paltan Branch. Okay, so strange! The whole thing has vanished. Oh, then what have we lost

By our existence in time? There's a grand
    question —
I should have asked Julian and Marcello. E difficile
    rispondere,
Marcello would have said, and Julian might have said,
    Well
We lost our theatre, the one at Fourteenth Street
    and Sixth Avenue,
And I would have said, viciously, Ah, you both know
    what I mean —
What have we lost, really? And the restaurant Alla
    Rampa would have exploded,
And from far above in the sky I'd have seen Federico
    playing
A last sonata about this fact. I did think while I heard
    him playing
I'd like him to play in a Starbucks in a supermarket in
    a six-story mall in Bangkok

Michaela finds time to type. Cecilia finds two felt hats, one on the floor, one on the shelf, and finds herself in the rocking chair beside them. She found her shoes again at the museum after leaving them by the sandbox and wandering everywhere. Hue finds his perch on the record player, aims for the top of the hutch and finds his mark. I find my head's ringing with "space." Anxiety finds opportunity. Yet I managed to find the right drillbits. But where can Shostakovich find a hoist for his flannel violin? Yet now, back at the laptop, I look back at my own #MarthaGraham Instagram post from that night. What else shares that hashtag? Dancing balloon people bending around impossibly.

#MarthaGraham. A girl in pointe shoes with an inspirational quote. #MarthaGraham. A shot of the theater with a hotel hashtagged with every conceivable spelling. Is this their sponsor? #MarthaGraham.

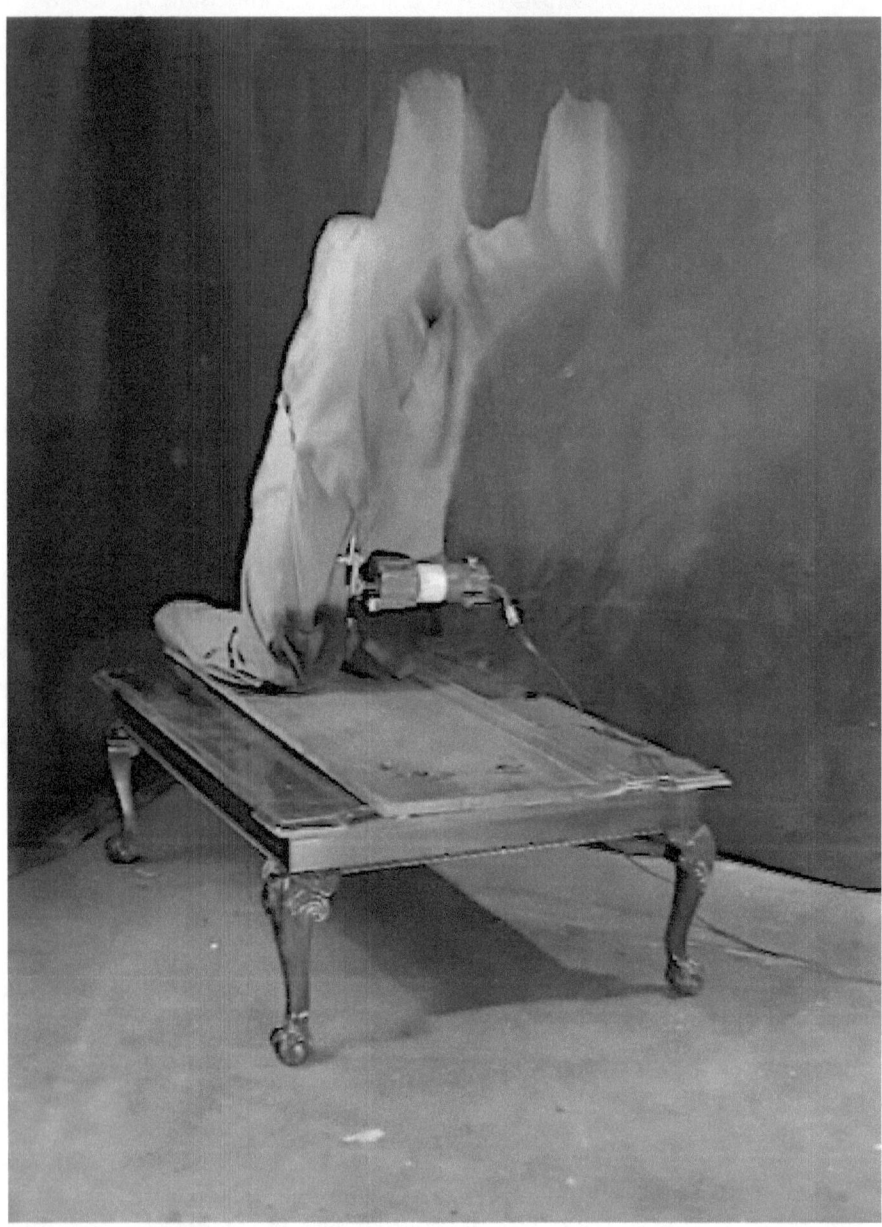

Which is to say, but since I don't, casting idols on my brain, the sun produces these false appearances, the dahlias burning under gunmetal skies, so I've yet to discover what real life feels like. At least that's what I tell them. But what I want to tell you is, well, take my body, for example, a place where incommensurables collide

(oh Man, oh no(:

a greed box. agreed box. a green box,

Drives mi nd it Is itself a re: action: I feeeeeeel like   I feel like fermentation in

my   skin skin, skin skin skin, skin.,,, *rhetoric & blood, price & value, datum & event* the bad equivalent of a hole in a soldier's bladder before he's given the form to join the donor's club.

So whaddya think? Maybe praying robots can help? The dialectic, having come to such dumb arrest, yields this taxonomy of wounds pasted to a straw man I'll never fuck. What figure do combatants cut against a company that earns the bulk of its annual twelve billion from army contracts, and whose product tracks my car as it moves thru any one of the ten thousand intersections. This is why my book amounts to a simple X without the algebra to resolve its value in the world where the word 'decorative' modifies unintelligible things, thereby assisting sales. See what I mean, in the absence of incident, structure eludes, the poem being but the gesture of what I think of as a body groping its own architecture. Whether bound or bundled, all my usable parts compress to the volume of a prosthetic device shoved inside how capital explodes in song, usurping the air you might be privately singing, the way the very idea of the flood dries up after the deluge. That's so dutifully Rimbaud, but what would the equivalent be? A blade of grass pushing against an obstacle as it sprouts out of the earth → → → and four (value of 6). 9+6=15; 15+33=48. The name of each hexagram thrown and its subsequent change will determine title for each sequence (ex.: "Duration → → → → Oppression"). The number of sequences in this book has been determined based on the value of a separate single throw of three coins: the value of which is 8. The fulgurite is another story. Richard Wright published a novella on the fulgurite. Lechatelierite. "You see our results were not great, but the visit was not wholly barren to me." Astrapialith. I don't even know how to pronounce these names. This is a narrative, and here we are told what role lightning plays. Tho I share the fascination the Utah Geological Survey holds for what we see when we lie down face first flat on the ground, it's the very air I'm interested in, and the ways in which we are ourselves when we can't breathe. One may also find fulgurites on the shores of Lake Michigan, or on the granite peaks of the Sierra Nevada. Christopher Libby, Chief Instructor at Outward Bound / Mammoth Lakes tells us: I was surprised to find, in the summers of 1984 and 1985, that fulgurites are relatively common on their granite peaks. In Sequoia and Kings Canyon National Parks I found fulgurites atop the following granitic peaks: Thunder Mountain (13,588 feet), Sugarloaf (8,002 feet), Whaleback (11,726 feet), Mount Stewart (12,205 feet), [and] Big Bird Peak (11,602 feet) ... The Sierra Nevada fulgurites are similar in appearance to those in Oregon – black, green, or white bubbly crusts on the surface of the rocks. The crusts appear on the topmost rocks as veins. Speaking of Naomi Campbell, Adam tells me, 'She, over the years, has been in four dreams I've had; and she's tended to be quite friendly: she gave me a ride to LAX in one; and in another she gave me a piggyback ride (well maybe that was in first one, too). And in another, she was doing a charity fashion show in a breakaway church lobby, and the runway was just the floor, so when I entered the lobby I accidentally interfered, and I don't recall her getting mad ... though i myself was irked at the organizers. Finally, in the most recent dream I told her that I admire her, and she responded jadedly: "really, that's what you have to say – how original," or somesuch; and I can't say I think this reaction is totally terrible.' It reminds of of a story someone told on themselves, I can't remember who. He said he went up to Van Morrison and said, "your music has meant so much in my life" and Van replied, "Why do people feel compelled to tell me these things?" Anyway, I found this today, and it seems apposite:

Islamic Declaration on Global Climate Change

In the name of Allah, Most Merciful, Most Compassionate

PREAMBLE

God – Whom we know as Allah – has created the universe in all its diversity, richness and vitality: the stars, the sun and moon, the earth and all its communities of living beings. All these reflect and manifest the boundless glory and mercy of their Creator. All created beings by nature serve and glorify their Maker, all bow to their Lord's will. We human beings are created to serve the Lord of all beings, to work the greatest good we can for all the species, individuals, and generations of God's creatures. Our planet has existed for billions of years and climate change in itself is not new. The earth's climate has gone through phases wet and dry, cold and warm, in response to many natural factors. Most of these changes have been gradual, so that the forms and communities of life have adjusted accordingly. There have been catastrophic climate changes that brought about mass extinctions, but over time, life adjusted even to these impacts, flowering anew in the emergence of balanced ecosystems such as those we treasure today. Climate change in the past was also instrumental in laying down immense stores of fossil fuels from which we derive benefits today. Ironically, our unwise and short-sighted use of these resources is now resulting in the destruction of the very conditions that have made our life on earth possible. The pace of Global climate change today is of

a different order of magnitude from the gradual changes that previously occurred throughout the most recent era, the Cenozoic. Moreover, it is human-induced: we have now become a force dominating nature. The epoch in which we live has increasingly been described in geological terms as the Anthropocene, or "Age of Humans". Our species, though selected to be a caretaker or steward (*khalifah*) on the earth, has been the cause of such corruption and devastation on it that we are in danger ending life as we know it on our planet. This current rate of climate change cannot be sustained, and the earth's fine equilibrium (*mīzān*) may soon be lost. As we humans are woven into the fabric of the natural world, its gifts are for us to savour. But the same fossil fuels that helped us achieve most of the prosperity we see today are the main cause of climate change. Excessive pollution from fossil fuels threatens to destroy the gifts bestowed on us by God, whom we know as Allah – gifts such as a functioning climate, healthy air to breathe, regular seasons, and living oceans. But our attitude to these gifts has been short-sighted, and we have abused them. What will future generations say of us, who leave them a degraded planet as our legacy? How will we face our Lord and Creator?
We note that the Millennium Ecosystem Assessment (UNEP, 2005) and backed by over 1300 scientists from 95 countries, found that "overall, people have made greater changes to ecosystems in the last half of the 20th century than at any time in human history … these changes have enhanced human well-being, but have been accompanied by ever increasing degradation (of our environment)." "Human activity is putting such a strain on the natural functions of the earth that the ability of the planet's ecosystems to sustain future generations can no longer be taken for granted." Nearly ten years later, and in spite of the numerous conferences that have taken place to try to agree on a successor to the Kyoto Protocol, the overall state of the Earth has steadily deteriorated. A study by the Intergovernmental Panel on Climate Change (IPCC) comprising representatives from over 100 nations published in March 2014 gave five reasons for concern. In summary, they are:

- Ecosystems and human cultures are already at risk from climate change;
- Risks resulting from climate change caused by extreme events such as heat waves, extreme precipitation and coastal flooding are on the rise;
- These risks are unevenly distributed, and are generally greater for the poor and disadvantaged communities of every country, at all levels of development;
- Foreseeable impacts will affect adversely Earth's biodiversity, the goods and services provided by our ecosystems, and our overall global economy;

- The Earth's core physical systems themselves are at risk of abrupt and irreversible changes.

We are driven to conclude from these warnings that there are serious flaws in the way we have used natural resources – the sources of life on Earth. An urgent and radical reappraisal is called for. Humankind cannot afford the slow progress we have seen in all the COP (Conference of Parties – climate change negotiations) processes since the Millennium Ecosystem Assessment was published in 2005, or the present deadlock. In the brief period since the Industrial Revolution, humans have consumed much of the non-renewable resources which have taken the earth 250 million years to produce – all in the name of economic development and human progress. We note with alarm the combined impacts of rising per capita consumption combined with the rising human population. We also note with alarm the multi-national scramble now taking place for more fossil fuel deposits under the dissolving ice caps in the arctic regions. We are accelerating our own destruction through these processes. Leading climate scientists now believe that a rise of two degrees centigrade in global temperature, which is considered to be the "tipping point," is now very unlikely to be avoided if we continue with business-as-usual; other leading climate scientists consider 1.5 degrees centigrade to be a more likely "tipping point". This is the point considered to be the threshold for catastrophic climate change, which will expose yet more millions of people and countless other creatures to drought, hunger and flooding. The brunt of this will continue to be borne by the poor, as the Earth experiences a drastic increase in levels of carbon in the atmosphere brought on in the period since the onset of the industrial revolution. It is alarming that in spite of all the warnings and predictions, the successor to the Kyoto Protocol which should have been in place by 2012, has been delayed. It is essential that all countries, especially the more developed nations, increase their efforts and adopt the proactive approach needed to halt and hopefully eventually reverse the damage being wrought.

WE AFFIRM

We affirm that Allah is the Lord and Sustainer (*Rabb*) of all beings

الْعَالَمِينَ رَبِّ لِلّٰهِ الْحَمْدُ

Praise be to Allah, Lord and Sustainer of all beings

Qur'an 1: 1

He is the One Creator – He is al-Khāliq

$$\text{الْمُصَوِّرُ الْبَارِئُ الْخَالِقُ اللَّهُ هُوَ}$$

He is Allah – the Creator, the Maker, the Giver of Form
Qur'an 59: 24

$$\text{خَلَقَهُ شَيْءٍ كُلَّ أَحْسَنَ الَّذِي}$$

He Who has perfected every thing He has created

Qur'an 32: 7

Nothing that He creates is without value: each thing is created bi 'l-haqq, in truth and for right.

$$\text{بِالْحَقِّ إِلَّا خَلَقْنَاهُمَا مَا لَاعِبِينَ بَيْنَهُمَا وَمَا وَالْأَرْضَ السَّمَاوَاتِ خَلَقْنَا وَمَا}$$

And We did not create the heavens and earth and that between them in play. We have not created them but in truth

Qur'an 44: 38

We affirm that He encompasses all of His creation – He is al-Muhīt

$$\text{مُحِيطًا شَيْءٍ بِكُلِّ اللَّهُ وَكَانَ الْأَرْضِ فِي وَمَا السَّمَاوَاتِ فِي مَا وَلِلَّهِ}$$

All that is in the heavens and the earth belongs to Allah.

Allah encompasses all things

Qur'an 4: 125

We affirm that –

- God created the Earth in perfect equilibrium (mīzān);
- By His immense mercy we have been given fertile land, fresh air, clean water and all the good things on Earth that makes our lives here viable and delightful;
- The Earth functions in natural seasonal rhythms and cycles: a climate in which living beings – including humans – thrive;
- The present climate change catastrophe is a result of the human disruption of this balance –

$$\text{الْمِيزَانَ وَوَضَعَ رَفَعَهَا وَالسَّمَاءَ}$$

الْمِيزَانِ فِي تَطْغَوْا أَلَّا الْمِيزَانَ تُخْسِرُوا وَلَا يِالْقِسْطِ الْوَزْنَ وَأَقِيمُوا لِلْأَنَامِ وَضَعَهَا وَالْأَرْضَ

He raised the heaven and established the balance

So that you would not transgress the balance.

Give just weight – do not skimp in the balance.

He laid out the earth for all living creatures.

Qur'an 55: 7-10

We affirm the natural state (*fitrah*) of God's creation –

عَلَيْهَا النَّاسَ فَطَرَ الَّتِي اللَّهِ فِطْرَةَ حَنِيفًا لِلدِّينِ وَجْهَكَ فَأَقِمْ يَعْلَمُونَ لَا النَّاسِ أَكْثَرَ وَلَكِنَّ الْقَيِّمُ الدِّينُ ذَلِكَ اللَّهِ لِخَلْقِ تَبْدِيلَ لَا

So set your face firmly towards the (natural) Way

As a pure, natural believer

Allah's natural pattern on which He made mankind

There is no changing Allah's creation.

That is the true (natural) Way

But most people do not know it.

Quran 30: 30

We recognize the corruption (*fasād*) that humans have caused on the Earth due to our relentless pursuit of economic growth and consumption. Its consequences have been –

- Global climate change, which is our present concern, in addition to:

- Contamination and befoulment of the atmosphere, land, inland water systems, and seas;
- Soil erosion, deforestation and desertification;
- Damage to human health, including a host of modern-day diseases.

ظَهَرَ الْفَسَادُ فِي الْبَرِّ وَالْبَحْرِ بِمَا كَسَبَتْ أَيْدِي النَّاسِ لِيُذِيقَهُم بَعْضَ الَّذِي عَمِلُوا لَعَلَّهُمْ يَرْجِعُونَ

Corruption has appeared on land and sea

Because of what people's own hands have wrought,
So that they may taste something of what they have done;

So that hopefully they will turn back.

Qur'an 30: 41

We recognize that we are but a miniscule part of the divine order, yet within that order, we are exceptionally powerful beings, and have the responsibility to establish good and avert evil in every way we can. We also recognize that –

- We are but one of the multitude of living beings with whom we share the Earth;
- We have no right to oppress the rest of creation or cause it harm;
- Intelligence and conscience behoove us, as our faith commands, to treat all things with care and awe (taqwa) of their Creator, compassion (rahmah) and utmost good (ihsan).

وَمَا مِن دَابَّةٍ فِي الْأَرْضِ وَلَا طَائِرٍ يَطِيرُ بِجَنَاحَيْهِ إِلَّا أُمَمٌ أَمْثَالُكُم

There is no animal on the earth, or any bird that wings its flight, but is a community like you.

Qur'an 6: 38

لَخَلْقُ السَّمَاوَاتِ وَالْأَرْضِ أَكْبَرُ مِنْ خَلْقِ النَّاسِ وَلَٰكِنَّ أَكْثَرَ النَّاسِ لَا يَعْلَمُونَ

The creation of the heavens and the earth

Is far greater than the creation of mankind,

But most of mankind do not know it

Qur'an 40: 57

We recognize that we are accountable for all our actions –

فَمَن يَعْمَلْ مِثْقَالَ ذَرَّةٍ خَيْرًا يَرَهُ
وَمَن يَعْمَلْ مِثْقَالَ ذَرَّةٍ شَرًّا يَرَهُ

Then he who has done an atom's weight of good, shall see it;

and he who has done an atom's weight of evil, shall see it.

Qur'an 99:6-8

In view of these considerations we affirm that our responsibility as Muslims is to act according to the example of the Prophet Muhammad (God's peace and blessings be upon him) who –

- Declared and protected the rights of all living beings, outlawed the custom of burying infant girls alive, prohibited killing living beings for sport, guided his companions to conserve water even in washing for prayer, forbade the felling of trees in the desert, ordered a man who had taken some nestlings from their nest to return them to their mother, and when he came upon a man who had lit a fire on an anthill, commanded, "Put it out, put it out!";
- Established inviolable zones (harams) around Makkah and Al-Madinah, within which native plants may not be felled or cut and wild animals may not be hunted or disturbed;
- Established protected areas (himas) for the conservation and sustainable use of rangelands, plant cover and wildlife.
- Lived a frugal life, free of excess, waste, and ostentation;
- Renewed and recycled his meagre possessions by repairing or giving them away;
- Ate simple, healthy food, which only occasionally included meat;
- Took delight in the created world; and
- Was, in the words of the Qur'an, "a mercy to all beings."

WE CALL

We call upon the Conference of the Parties (COP) to the United Nations Framework Convention on Climate Change (UNFCCC) and the Meeting of the Parties (MOP) to the Kyoto Protocol taking place in Paris this December, 2015 to bring their discussions to an equitable and binding conclusion, bearing in mind –

- The scientific consensus on climate change, which is to stabilize greenhouse gas concentration in the atmosphere at a level that would prevent dangerous anthropogenic interference with the climate systems;
- The need to set clear targets and monitoring systems;
- The dire consequences to planet earth if we do not do so;
- The enormous responsibility the COP shoulders on behalf of the rest of humanity, including leading the rest of us to a new way of relating to God's Earth.

We particularly call on the well-off nations and oil-producing states to –

- Lead the way in phasing out their greenhouse gas emissions as early as possible and no later than the middle of the century;
- Provide generous financial and technical support to the less well-off to achieve a phase-out of greenhouse gases as early as possible;
- Recognize the moral obligation to reduce consumption so that the poor may benefit from what is left of the earth's non-renewable resources;
- Stay within the '2 degree' limit, or, preferably, within the '1.5 degree' limit, bearing in mind that two-thirds of the earth's proven fossil fuel reserves remain in the ground;
- Re-focus their concerns from unethical profit from the environment, to that of preserving it and elevating the condition of the world's poor.
- Invest in the creation of a green economy.

We call on the people of all nations and their leaders to –

- Aim to phase out greenhouse gas emissions as soon as possible in order to stabilize greenhouse gas concentrations in the atmosphere;
- Commit themselves to 100 % renewable energy and/or a zero emissions strategy as early as possible, to mitigate the environmental impact of their activities;
- Invest in decentralized renewable energy, which is the best way to reduce poverty and achieve sustainable development;
- Realize that to chase after unlimited economic growth in a planet that is finite and already overloaded is not viable. Growth must be pursued wisely and in moderation; placing a priority on increasing the resilience of all, and especially the most vulnerable, to the climate change impacts already underway and expected to continue for many years to come.

- Set in motion a fresh model of wellbeing, based on an alternative to the current financial model which depletes resources, degrades the environment, and deepens inequality.
- Prioritise adaptation efforts with appropriate support to the vulnerable countries with the least capacity to adapt. And to vulnerable groups, including indigenous peoples, women and children.

We call upon corporations, finance, and the business sector to –

- Shoulder the consequences of their profit-making activities, and take a visibly more active role in reducing their carbon footprint and other forms of impact upon the natural environment;
- In order to mitigate the environmental impact of their activities, commit themselves to 100 % renewable energy and/or a zero emissions strategy as early as possible and shift investments into renewable energy;
- Change from the current business model which is based on an unsustainable escalating economy, and to adopt a circular economy that is wholly sustainable;
- Pay more heed to social and ecological responsibilities, particularly to the extent that they extract and utilize scarce resources;
- Assist in the divestment from the fossil fuel driven economy and the scaling up of renewable energy and other ecological alternatives.

We call on all groups to join us in collaboration, co-operation and friendly competition in this endeavour and we welcome the significant contributions taken by other faiths, as we can all be winners in this race

الْخَيْرَاتِ فَاسْتَبِقُوا آتَاكُم مَا فِي لِّيَبْلُوَكُمْ وَلَكِن

He (God) wanted to test you regarding what has

come to you. So compete with each other

in doing good deeds.

Qur'an 5: 48

If we each offer the best of our respective traditions, we may yet see a way through our difficulties.

Finally, we call on all Muslims wherever they may be –

Heads of state

Political leaders
Business community

UNFCCC delegates

Religious leaders and scholars

Mosque congregations

Islamic endowments (awqaf)

Educators and educational institutions

Community leaders

Civil society activists

Non-governmental organisations

Communications and media

طُولاً الْجِبَالَ تَبْلُغَ وَلَن الأَرْضَ تَخْرِقَ لَن إِنَّكَ مَرَحًا الأَرْضِ فِي تَمْشِ وَلاَ

Do not strut arrogantly on the earth.

You will never split the earth apart

nor will you ever rival the mountains' stature.

Qur'an 17: 37

We bear in mind the words of our Prophet (peace and blessings be upon him): The world is sweet and verdant, and verily Allah has made you stewards in it, and He sees how you acquit yourselves. So it's not that they want you to stop spinning in a rotating chair at a different speed than the distant world, they have no objection to you feeling you're in an original orbit spinning on its own axis, they don't want to see your plans for another spring (however you call it), nor have any real interest in planting a satellite tracking device on you to follow your steps around the avenues or the roof or wherever to photograph everything, they're not necessarily up to speed with the theory that says the anomaly isn't being disconnected from reality but rather, at a macro level, being too connected, nor do they expect that by reality we understand an assault craft slowly slipping into Mesopotamia, that by reality we understand camellias overexcited by the wind, by reality we understand the Ethiopian kid pressing into the tips of her fingers the teeth of a bottle cap, they don't read everything that the VP of Bolivia says, they don't synthesize tenacity, they aren't worried that you go about, with sweet slow care, the pillow still marked on your face, dragging your heels around the aisles of a supermarket looking for a specific brand of Japanese instant noodles, or whatever, no, no, no, none of that, no they just want you to die. Not even die. Book + eye = doctrine. Any bed is clinical. The apron accepts blood. Doctrine – mentor = soap powder. Republic – doctrine = floor mop. Rooster + machete = stew. Rice + steel bowl = plan. Flag = butcher's apron. Angola = oil + diamonds + iron + phosphates + copper + gold + uranium. Which is to say that the phrase "the body" is so annoying: the minute one leads with a definite article, any real body transforms into yet another trope: in this case one for rejecting Cartesianism, which is totes snooze by now. Human brains are so interesting because the brain is a body-part that most humans never actually see – and of course if one does then something has gone rather seriously awry. But me? If I decided to go mountain climbing and if, while I was climbing, the forces on the mountain snow exceeded the snow's strength and an avalanche formed, sweeping me downhill and burying me in snow and ice, and if global warming somehow didn't end my indefinite winter and if my preserved body were discovered millennia from now by climbers from a civilization with the capacity to date snowbound bodies with delicate instruments and sensitive forensic tests, and if that civilization's scientists, interested in my provenance, made me the object of their study, they may be able to date me to the age of elaborate dentistry, pasteurized, fortified cow's milk, and wireless radiation. But my skeleton perhaps makes another admission that dates me more exactly: on the third joint of my middle finger on my right hand I have a bone spur. This bump formed incrementally over years from my constant use of pens and pencils. My body (b. 1980) carries the marks of my generation, perhaps the last generation of the writing bump, given the ubiquity of so many forms of computing. It makes me think I am going to walk into the room and say something to someone who IS there, like what's for dinner or did you hear about the person who put a quarter in someone else's parking meter and was arrested for it, or it makes me want to talk about my family sitting around the TV in the seventies listening to Chet Huntley talk about the Vietnam War when my mother says it is time to get up and eat dinner and we get up and eat our rice with red chopsticks out of bowls (one of them green) my father made and sometimes we never say anything at dinner. These things never happen of course when one IS alone but they remain tangential and impossible compared to things 1 was doing (having tea, taking the trash out), a kind of background music of "splendid conversation" (Emerson said that about Carlyle once) and everyday things going on in one's head. After the news I eat a cookie made in Canada. l drink a cup of English Breakfast tea. 1 write a poem about a box and in one of those boxes I put a TV in it for my father. I tie up the trash in a plastic grocery bag and leave it on the street. I go out to Riverside Park at 72nd St. and find a place under some trees that is shielded from the streetlamps and

six years ago a bridge between us   collapsed
the interstate ate   thirteen people alive
asphalt spilling   like amputated hands
into the dark below.   what is love but a river
that exists to eat   all your excess concrete
appendages?   what is a voice but how it lands
wet in the body?   Soon, there is panic.

Because no one can close the universe
so it keeps flapping open and swelling
with cold. In the center of the button
there are threads, torn from the rest
of the coat, looping around each other
like hearts. The search begins in earnest.
Was the button loose to begin with?

I'm arriving at a theory
that anything can suddenly
and unbelievably become anything
else.

(Isn't that Meillassoux?)

Nutation is a tremor of the axis of any celestial body, but it is the Earth with which we are dealing with, which is the cone he draws in his movement precession is not exactly a cone, but it is slightly warped, embossed. It is in the apparent motion of the stars that reads the movement of the Earth. It is an English astronomer of the XVIIIth century who discovered nutation. And it was a brilliant discovery, if I may say so, operates the old Qfwfq, which was not far away, because it is tiny. I can give you numbers, he added without pausing for breath, the little festoons is 17 seconds of arc, just a hair, the axis of the Earth takes eighteen years to go. To discover this, you have to be not only accurate, but also tenacious. Guglielmo be impressed, for once, since it is silent. You will talk about the beautiful Emily asks Fiordiligi? You knew, did not you? Oh, The Marquise du Châtelet, exclaims the old Qfwfq! I could talk for hours. Maybe not, slides Guglielmo. Tell us nutation, gently ask Fiordiligi. I remember, said the old Qfwfq, she read Newton, in Latin, there was the word, *nutare* because Barrow had discovered, measured, but he, Newton, it was the theory, principles, because he, Newton, he had, principles, the cause was, he said, in the bulge of the Earth. You have already said that the Earth is not really a sphere, is not it? And the Marquise wanted to translate this *nutare*, you can imagine it was not lacking in the world around her to tell him what to her to do. I do not speak of Voltaire. No, punctuates Guglielmo. Trembling, she found, was an unacceptable anthropomorphic face for a scientist. But that's fine in a novel, he added, smiling at Fiordiligi. You should have seen the discussions, and ultimately, she chose wobble, a real word scientist. That we must speak delicately says Fiordiligi, so that we do not hear mutation, the first syllable of a word n is not what is meant best. Do you know, my young friend, that the word mutation, with its biological sense, was invented at about the same time? What pedantic, Guglielmo think. I could also talk about the small $S_0 Ph(i)$, he adds, nutation and moving strong, she also knew it. But Fiordiligi is taking a series of sneezes that prevent to express Guglielmo annoyance. You're cold, he said only, and as the old Qfwfq left, he adds, will put us warm under the covers. In the dark night and ice, the sharp points of the stars, insensitive to human tremor continue to save those of sky objects. "O bubonic plague, bubonic, bubonic. Nothing else is as bubonic as you!" began one of my essays, for nothing was, until this morning the universe divulged its secret: "There is no huggy bear." Then the universe sat for a moment as if in deep thought. "Rather, huggy bear is ill and about to die." The universe stood up and shrugged. À la Spinoza, what else is there but huggy bear? Furthermore, he is well aware of the dangers of too much foregrounding of artifice when he writes in 'Artifice of Absorption': *I*

> *frequently use opaque & nonabsorbable*
> *elements, digressions &*
> *interruptions, as part of a technological*
> *arsenal to create a more powerful*
> *("souped up")*
> *absorption than possible with traditional,*
> *& blander, absorptive techniques.*

Then she asked me to take a seat, and I did. There was a beautiful Calder on the wall, under glass. WOW! And the view was of course a 600 dollar view of the city, 36 floors high. A few minutes later she asked what I wanted to speak to an editor about. I told her that I was there for two things. 1) To find out exactly who wrote the list saying that the mummers SHOULD LEAVE TOWN! 2) To ask for a public apology to The Mummers, who are entirely working class, and to Philadelphia. This city does not belong to the rich. This is Philadelphia. This is the city where working class people DESTROYED the transit company nearly a century ago after their hit squad murdered peaceful strikers on Broad Street. NO ONE took the trolley, everyone started walking to work and put them out of business! This is the same Philadelphia! I can feel and believe this. After I explained my reason for coming to the office the mood changed dramatically. Instantly actually. I was told NO ONE was in. Which is ridiculous of course. I said, oh, are they all on lunch break? I can wait.

I was handed a business card to contact one of their editors by email. The shake-off. I said, no, I'll wait here to speak to someone in person. Now you're being removed. I was told this. Security came. Then the police were called, and I showed page 72 to one of the men who said he knows people who are mummers, which of course is easy to believe since there are so many mummers. But he said I still had to leave the building. I understood. The reason I'm writing this is because of the misinformation *Philadelphia Magazine* is now saying about me. The magazine's arts and entertainment editor Victor Fiorillo wrote on Zoe Strauss's Face Book page, "CA, *Philadelphia Magazine* blocked you not because you were demanding an apology, but because you were spamming the page. And now you've been arrested." What an asshole. What a smug, corporate-humping prick! *Five hundred thousand slot machines in the hoods of the country. Convenience stores, retail stores, video stores, butcher shops. Housewives, clerks, senior citizens playing their last chips in the machines. The fortune spinning. The money spinning. Cherries. Pear. Lemon. The fortune of the poor spinning in the five hundred thousand slot machines. Watermelon. Apple. Cherries.* Which is to say, *it senses just because everything touches it throughout its continuous thickness. Everything is touched and mixed; everything slides into the silence of the organs that provide neither sights nor tastes nor smells nor sounds, but only touch, because the outside is so constant, so thick, so caught up in a compact and solidary mass that the interior body is without organs. Being outside myself as this inside, prohibiting penetration (except by disemboweling or suffocating me), the outside is indefinitely wrapped, absorbed, sunk in its own magma, both fitting it so well and absolutely foreign to that which this magma fills, to that which it sustains and animates, to all this skin exposed with its orifices, mucosa, pores, and hair, all its contacts and communication, all the vibrations of the world, of matter and images, of timbers and resonances, all these gases and squirts, these air currents, these mirrors, these pieces of metal, these other skins, these words, these impressions, depressions, expressions.* But if care is a "labor of stolen time," for most, it is now only possible in the service economy as stolen labor-time; plenitude often only exists for the many in open revolt, or in smaller acts of expropriation and sharing. [The first time I was disciplined at the workplace in grammar school the first workplace of the child was for daydreaming in 2nd grade apparently I and the others had been imagining the inhabitants of other universes, drawing prehistoric mammals sailing to the ends of the world with cannons and other things most common humans do the problem was of such severity that a conference was called even if the reveries I experienced and not only alone for we the workers often shared did not materially interfere with the completion of any assigned projects pasting one thing to another thing learning proportion and pilgrims according to secondary geometry coins and bills state capitols and experiencing the cruelty of 'recess' and so it would continue throughout the labor of the rest of our lives] But what would you do with one of those hand-blown TV tubes? Would you just take it home, put it on the table, and be like, "God, that's amazing"? Yes, exactly! I'd say that over and over, and look at them for hours and hours. Trance out and think about the very first flickering pictures zapped through it, what it meant for civilization and brain damage, and how that permanently changed the way we see. I still want one.

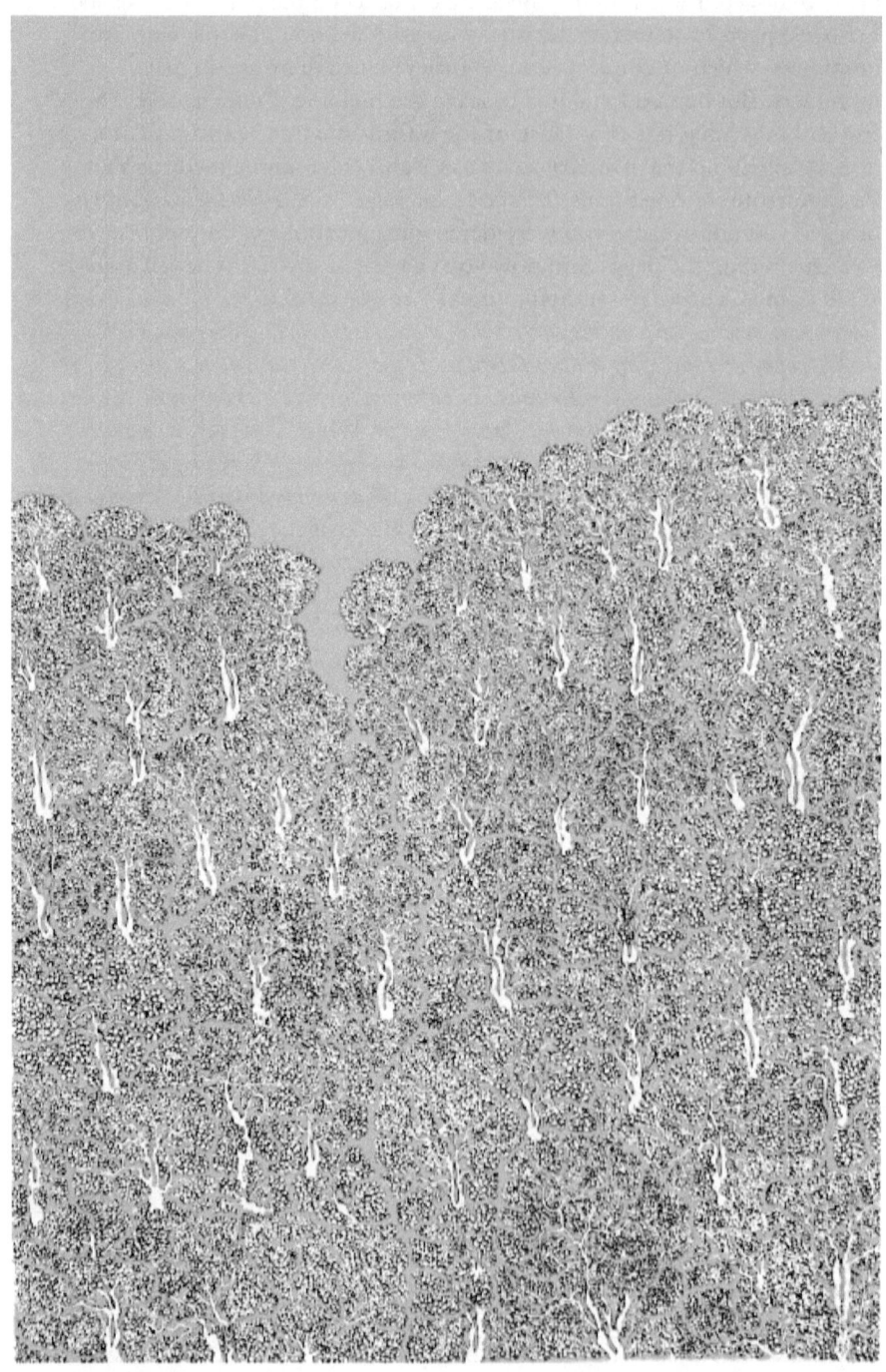

Because it's my blog, and like my friend Hugo I "try to be 24 hours a day." For trying to be I got sick the day before yesterday in the evening; I ate at a restaurant and do not know what happened, the fact is that tiredness and stomach pain hit me at the same time. I decided to take something for the pain and all I found was tramadol, but as at 2 in the morning the pain was unbearable, so I figured I had gastritis and took lansoprazole, I felt considerable relief but in the morning just woke to answer a few emails and surrendered immediately. I fed Diva and convinced her to continue sleeping. My dreams were very strange, I started thinking that maybe there was a gas leak or something but just thought it for little moments, and decided it was better to continue sleeping. At 6pm yesterday I woke pain in the stomach again and then yes, I remembered that my mother and I now live in the same city. I called. At 7 my mother and my brother came, I prepared a chamomile tea, my mom gave me the right pickup: ranitidine. Today I woke up at 10am, no pain but I can not think of eating meat or anything with fat or broth: Yuck, I am very disgusted. But this afternoon I realized what happened: it was the body's reaction to my decision to forget X. Later that same year, when asked about his political stance by Philip Leider, Smithson remarked, "I'm interested in the politics of the Triassic period." "In these Triassic rocks one might find:

> 'actinolite,
> albite,
> allanite,
> analcime,
> apatite,
> anhydrite,
> apophyllite,
> aurichalcite,
> aximite,
> azurite,
> babingtonite,
> bornite,
> barite,
> calcite,
> chabzie,
> chalcocite,
> chalcophyrite,
> cholorite,
> chrysocolia,
> copper,
> covellite,
> cuperite,
> datolite,

epidote,
galena,
glauberite,
goethite,
gmelinite,
greenockite,
gypsum,
hematite,
heaulandite,
hornlende,
laumontite,
malachite,
mesolite,
natrolite,
opal,
orpiment,
orthoclase,
pectolite,
prehnite,
pumpellyite,
pyrite,
pyrolusite,
quartz,
scolecite,
siderite,
silver,
sphalerite,
sphene,
stevensite,
stilbite,
stilpnomelane,
talc,
thaumasite,
thomsonite,
tourmaline,
ulexite.'"

I mean, one's mind and the earth are in a constant state of erosion, mental rivers wear away abstract banks, brain waves undermine cliffs of thought, ideas decompose into stones of unknowing, and conceptual crystallizations break apart into a weasel attacking a woodpecker, and US scientists knowingly infecting indigenous people in South America with measles and watching them die. Did I tell you I dreamt I met Obama? He was tiny, maybe 4'5". I said, why did you want that shitty job, anyway? Look how small it's made you. Now, all past MoMA R&D Salons are online at the museum's website, which features videos and reading lists. This isn't the first time scientists have encountered insects producing materials with the aid of artificial coloring. In 2012, residue from an M&M plant caused local bees to make blue and green honey, and a similar — though more tragic — incident also involving bees and, this time, the dye used in Maraschino cherries occurred recently in New York. So yes. Middlemen, explains Al-Azm, "buy stuff inside Syria, and they sell it to another middleman, and another, and another." Eventually the looted objects are bought by "bigger fish," who can afford to sit on them for years, until the heat dies down, and then fabricate their origins. There are also stories of items being sold on eBay and rumors that they're being traded on darknet marketplaces similar to Silk Road. Late that night, sleepless, I began to write a poem sparked by two lines in the 15th century ballad, "The Nut-Browne Mayd" that had been going through my head, though I didn't know why:

> Wherfore I wyll to the grene wode go;
> Alone, a banished man.

Then a voice ricochets through the night sky: "Our songs have hardened into laws! "He poured in equal portions of Sameness and Difference, mixed them, and drew the soul of the universe out of the mixing bowl. The whole fabric then he split lengthwise, and making the halves cross one another at their centers in the form of the letter X, he bent each round into a circle and joined it up; made the one the outer, the other the inner circle. The outer movement he named the circle of the Same, the inner, the circle of the Different. With agile hand the movement of the Same he caused to revolve to the right, the circle of the Different to the left. He turned once more to the mixing bowl whence he had drawn the soul of the universe. Now, he poured sameness and difference as from unsteady cups. And when he had thus compounded the whole, he carefully divided it into souls equal in number to the stars, and with his invisible motions distributed them, each soul to its several star."

> (But haven't you heard?
>
> ("Beneath all this zooming and spinning a huge chasm lies, gloomily overlaid with palpitating darkness. And therein, believe me now, is a shining egg, wrapped round with mist and chaos, and in it (trust me on this), enveloped in a bright cloak of cloud, a baby slumbers!")
>
> [How carefully can you listen?]
>
> (When the egg is squeezed and broken by the serpent Time, the baby slithers out. At once the world is filled with a blinding radiance — yet he (this is his special trick) remains invisible.

(Except at night.

(Then in the darkness one can see him glowing)

Dancing with mirrors and the cry Evoi! When he saw his reflection he followed its gaze and came to the place of slaughter.

(Take counsel in whispers)

(To depict the cosmos, trace a circle of misty, fiery aspects, then stretch across its diameter a serpent with the form of the letter theta.

Then she ceased from her melancholy and held back her eyes from weeping. Then she bathed and donned spotless garments and went to the upper floor with her attendant women and placing barley grains in a basket prayed to Athena. And the owl-eyed goddess heard her and turned on her heel and walked like a storm cloud through the door of her father's windy house and settled like a sea wind on the earth.

(Again I wake up.

(I study a book in the late gnat light.

(It tells the feats of humans. I wonder how the author has selected these, so few, so few to be remembered, from all who have breathed, gasped, and died.

"I compared it like, when the hundred guys come at Neo, those are opinions, that's perception, that's tradition. Attacking people from every which angle possible. If you have a focus wide and master sense is like Laurence Fishburne and you have a squad behind you, you literally can put the world in slow motion … Why do I say the Matrix is like the Bible? What is my definition of the Matrix?" A linguistic genius, Dr. Izutsu finished reading the entire Qur'an just one month after beginning to learn Arabic. The weasel / woodpecker image became a funny meme (look closely, "look, with all your eyes, look" – "the well of living is you"):

About their name — a circle with an X through it — former member Rik Letendre has said: "We were on the Lower East Side; there were a lot of burned-out buildings. One symbol that was painted on buildings was a box with an 'X' through it. That was a symbol for the firemen. If there was a fire on the block, they'd let that building burn because it was abandoned. The circle would, of course, represent the world with an 'X' through it – I mean, I stand in awe of this body, this matter to which I am bound has become so strange to me. I fear not spirits, ghosts, of which I am one, — *that* my body might, — but I fear bodies, I tremble to meet them. What is this Titan that has possession of me? Talk of mysteries! — Think of our life, — daily to be shown matter, to come in contact with it, — rocks, trees, wind on our cheeks! The *solid* earth! the *actual* world! the *common sense! Contact! Contact! Who* are we? *where* are we? What color is the marker on the map used for travel by night? It's not a house. Check the calendar if you don't believe me. That's 1%.

Not the.
That's 1% of what it costs for the Balm in Gilead.
Baby baby baby baby Babylon.
By the river baby lay me down down Babylon chaunt.

As in: More than 130 million people are infected with the hepatitis C virus, and 350,000 to 500,000 people die from the infections each year, according to the World Health Organization. Whoah. Ebola, lalalalala bamba. Bowling for combined sales, lurid scenes, blood seeping. It just doesn't make copy. The version of hepatitis C that is most prevalent in India requires that patients take Sovaldi for 24 weeks, meaning that they would need six bottles for a total cost of $1,800, Mr. Alton said. Gilead will receive a royalty of 7% of sales of the generic versions. Chaching 7 per 100 for 18 of those Benjamins. All about the. 70 and 560 and chachingalingling. Dang. 630 in his head, Mr. Alton said. Babam. Kazam. Badabang badaboo. Besides. Sovaldi is on pace to become one of the world's top-selling drugs, with more than $10 billion in sales this year. In the U.S., a 12-week-supply costs $84,000,

> which
> some
> critics
>
> say
> is
> too
>
> high
> for
> a

lifesaving drug. Gilead has said dang, baby, it's cheaper than those treatments you used to try, and they didn't even work, plus dang baby, its cheaper than a liver transplant and dang this balm is 90% guaranteed. *"So the MFC is in effect a system which taps a portion of that biochemical energy used for microbial growth, and converts that directly into electricity — what we are calling urine-tricity or pee power. This technology is about as green as it gets, as we do not need to utilise fossil fuels and we are effectively using a waste product that will be in plentiful supply."* Which means in spite of what else it might mean that we can keep refugees camps open indefinitely. So, like Jules, I'll just walk the earth.

Vincent: What'cha mean walk the earth?

Jules: You know, walk the earth, meet people … get into adventures. Like Caine from "Kung Fu."

> And then we all went our separate ways for a
> while, I think there's a poem about this exactly and
> there is. Lavender and Bergamot dish detergent.
> It's not a Golden Age, but maybe a Lambent
> Age.
>
>> All you did was take a turn too wide or too narrow.
>> And hit a tree & fucked up your life for nine years. Hey
>> wait a minute I presume you might find twenty-five dollars, oh
>> great. No it's not no it's great, I read a little piece it said this
>> guy should be hung.
>>
>> And why were they left in the cafeteria?
>> Is it part of some anarchist plot?

Between these vectors, time moves —

"time better spent training for the classics or hyperventilating" —
The line "I want to eat your feelings" haunts the book.
The balance is struck from the beginning, beginning
with "Origin Story." It begins, "It began …" From there,
things begin to become other things.

Bacon and body hair—
— more interstellar space than salty peanuts, more
mmmm,
"Spectrum®" & "X-Acto®"
& "Swingline®" & "YSL Opium®" & "finitude"
or "touchable repetition" &

Thus, the work is constituted as a
haze with an ambiguous duration, articulated
as a gesture of protest, a record of
big spaces with gentle pulsings

(continued on pg 30)

It may be that in the village the festering inkpot
blooms, swamping chains of nucleic acid.
So succor the fool, for he shall inherit the dark precipice.

But September brings lots of cuddly nights either by yourself or with a
    sweetheart,
while you secretly plan your next big takeover. Try to be driven in a car at
    least once in October
by a person in sunglasses. But really, there are some people around you
    who
love you who would like you to stop. Put them
    in tiny jars and eat sweet potatoes.
It's not your color, but go ahead. Do you like the ocean? The idea of the
    answer. The idea of the answer. No, we take that back.

So yes, 2,2 is a QR Code poem written by Genco Gülan in 2010. The artist used 2 letter words from different languages to create the poem. Then he converted the text into QR code using a free converter: 33.3 AHA AMA ART ASK BIG BIN BIT BOY CAM CAN CAY DAY DEV EAT EEL ERR FOX FUN GAG GENCO GOD GOL GULAN HEP HES HIT IFF ISM JOY KAL KEL KUL LOL MEN MOM NON OFF OHH PIT POT RED SIK SOK THE THY TWO UGH ULU UPS WAR WAY WOK VAZ YAK YAZ

5371

YOK YOL ZIP ZOO ZZZ Enter the Vigipirates. I can't remember them arriving, but here they were. At first, I came home from the grocery store making sure my hands were visible, not concealed in my pockets, and tried to make eye contact with one or both of the soldiers before sharply diverting my gaze. Sometimes we'd exchange a quick bonjour or bonsoir, but that depended more on proximity than disposition. I felt confused as to why they had been stationed outside my front door. I felt afraid of why, too. There was even some defensiveness: *We don't need you*, I thought. *We get along fine without you.* But as the weeks passed, and it became clear that these 20-year-olds with guns were my new neighbors, my defensiveness abated. The confusion and fear were still present, but I had questions, and I wanted answers. I ventured a conversation. I realize now that it was the sort of conversation that parents have with stubborn toddlers asking why the sky is blue.

- Why are you here?
- Because it's a vulnerable zone.
- But why?
- Because there's a nursery school.
- Is it a special nursery school?
- There could be some Jewish kids.
- So it's a Jewish nursery school?
- No. There could also be some Muslim kids.

- So it's a normal one.
- [Nod.]
- How long will you be here for?
- We don't know.
- When will you know?
- We don't know.

And I believe that's true: they *don't* know. During the First Iraq War, Emily Martin, an anthropologist, conducted a study of how we think about immunity. Her research showed that "popular publications depict the body as the scene of total war between ruthless invaders and determined defenders." As Eula Biss points out in her *On Immunity*, many scientists even deny that this military imagery is a metaphor. It is, they insist, simply "how it is." Biss continues: "The body employs some cells as 'infantry' and others as the 'armored unit,' and these troops deploy 'mines' to explode bacteria, while the immune response itself 'detonates like a bomb.'" If we imagine the immune system as a war zone, how do we imagine a war? As

prepared spiritual poetry
prepared astrophysic mushy pea for gmtJet
saence
ne— high to a –wage earner betcha
half a contrad
the blooded red f<><get
<<recover hard>> hard
so we eat
police horses is that
ScPoo sp-p-pooky since the
had nothin run-of-the done in
this is a
tracksolmac-lO"s
bi.al
of fires this time and
microdimato bullet spirals fradal
burgers with mythology and fly-low dough
by the just-post-bonobo
otalgia
q through q through q
; .. '
~
'
I!.
I'
......,.,.

\
I
,
I· 1 'I
,n
'q 1 I I .
\(
!.
I , I I
. '
I I
1
I
i/
' 1'.
i
!
.
·i . 'I

1. Common Genet &c Snake
2. Mouse Kissing Bird's Boot
3. Manatees with Small Fish
4. Black-Necked Spitting Cobra
••

.-----------
1.
stumblrd P'RJ«'
a portior~, SlliJ pltasfl
plttN
But still I'd like to think I could be Danielle Steele if I chose to.
(She's a little bit like Chaucer in a way.)
anivt.>d
spcn_d, so I lm~ua hed
the httle
di_sc: ss~ ng
exp~ th se ~~
nd m~ of _excahng
vanallon m
pl'rNma/l•ty
Mll'nl h1-.tmy"-nntc tu myself am<Klgst nntt-s
not haVmJ.; 1ntennnty 10 the expc 'dt-d
1" !-.I ill
mnuenct.-d
mortice

5374

joint
stem
wasp
either that or the toothfairy.

 Conceived and edited during our residency a…
 A re-appropriation of Edward Said's Oriental…
 "A poster is a tool." This catalog presents…
 This publication combines in one volume the r…
 Clairvoyant Journal 1974 by Hannah Weiner (19…
 A reflection on translation phenomena in the…
 This is a fiction. A fiction that might begin…
 Poster including "something with circles all…
 <o> future <o> continues and enhances the ac…
 "I am going to tell you some performances…
 How do you observe something from the point…
 A selection of recent works reproduced at a…
 Several artworks by Italian artist Elisabe…
 The publication starts with a forty-page l…
 To design the new Continental Rift book coll…
 "Let's imagine a land flat as a sheet of pap…
 The exhibition guide plays with two meanings…
 The first part of the third issue of Messy…
 The Abortion: An Historical Romance (1966)…
 Following a first workshop at ÉESAB in Renne…
 Custom version of Série Seize for the engli…
 The first part of the second issue of Messy…
 To design the new Continental Rift book col…
 FAN N°12 was published on the occasion of t…
 Poster, flyer and guide for the exhibition…
 14628.jpg is a collaboration between Linda…
 The first part of the first issue of Messy…

So I was listening to an Audre Lorde talk yesterday, 'There is No Hierarchy of Oppression' and I was thinking that what she says – that lack of hierarchy – extends to the types of oppression and repression Naomi Klein is talking about in her excerpt today, wrapped around the newspaper itself and to be found online. At the same time as agreeing with her I feel if I had to choose one oppression over another, one as more pressing than the others which remain as pressing as it, I know which I would choose. I would make that choice instinctively, and my instinct might be wrong. How would I know? How would I actually feel in having to choose? Am I already doing that? Have I got it wrong, necessarily so? Biss reports from deep inside the panic. "My son's birth brought with it an exaggerated sense of both my own power and my own powerlessness," she writes. The world became suddenly forbidding: There is the lead paint in the wall to fear, the hexavalent chromium in the water. Even stagnant air, she was told, can kill her child. "It is both a luxury and a hazard to feel threatened by the invisible," she says. "In Chicago, where 677 children were shot the year after my son was born, I still somehow manage to find myself more captivated by less tangible threats." Weaning proved especially excruciating. "As long as a child takes only breast milk, I discovered, one can enjoy the illusion of a closed system, a body that is not yet in dialogue with the impurities of farm and factory," she writes. "I remember feeling agony when my son drank water for the first time. 'Unclean! Unclean!'" We do love to pit the sacred against the profane, but breast milk, it turns out, contains traces of paint thinners, flame-retardants, rocket fuel. If it were sold in stores, some samples would exceed federal food-safety levels for pesticides. All the more reason to listen to Audre Lorde, then, who says quite unbreakably, 'I am trying to become the strongest person I can become, to live the life I have been given, and to help effect change towards a liveable future for this earth and for my children'. [I would have said *our*.] So I spoke yesterday, with permission, to my housemate's girlfriend's ten-year-old son about him writing for CONFUSE YOUR HUNGER, and he has. The issue of consent felt delicate, but necessarily so perhaps. In speaking to him, I think I felt more fear in me than in him. A lot of young children seem to think about death in a way that we sometimes forget. As a very young kid I know I did. If anyone knows or has children who might want to write and publish or draw things, they might be represented too. I know it's delicate, but let me know. Which is to say, YOUR GARBAGE SPEAKS: SAVE YOUR garbage for a week, every wrapper, every box, carton, save it all. Rinse it out if you must, but it's better if you don't, better to SMELL it. At the end of the week go through each item, slowly, carefully, do it in a closed room, don't let anyone bother you. Don't answer the door or the phone, IGNORE THEM, you're busy looking at garbage to build a poem! ["All poems are built of garbage. It's the only material (or immaterial) there is" – JBR] Take some notes, write down interesting facts from labels, or the size of things, how they look, how you remember them before discarding them. Imagine where this packaging came from, factories, and before that fields and trucks and many many hands picking them, grinding them, printing with color and black ink. Take notes when thinking about these things. SMELL them one at a time with eyes closed, eyes opened, eyes closed again SMELLING, deeply SMELLING. Notes, take your notes. NOW GET NAKED AND GET IN THE BATHTUB, and go under water, blow bubbles. Go under again and stay under a little longer. DO THIS several more times then COME UP, dry your hands on the side of the tub and grab your notes, and GO BACK UNDER the water again, then COME UP AGAIN and LET YOUR TOES KNOW THE TRUTH: Take account of how many times you're not saying or doing EXACTLY what you want to say or do in a day. How many times do you use a tone in your voice which is not honest? How many times are you polite when you want TO SCREAM? How much compromise does your day comprise? Take CLOSE account of this. DON'T LIE ABOUT IT EITHER! This is for you, no one else will know SO BE TOTALLY HONEST! What is your body like when you're not being who you are? How does it feel? Are your hands doing something in particular each time? Your feet? Your groin, your stomach, how does your body react when you are not REALLY you? At the end of the day take notes about this. These notes will be the formal outline for this exercise. After that, EVERY DAY FOR THE NEXT 7 days you will pay attention to the SIGNS OF DISHONESTY in your voice and your body, and whenever you are not who you REALLY WANT TO BE at any moment in the day. Each time you are, EACH TIME you are not you, CLENCH YOUR TOES! CLENCH THEM! Every time, CLENCH THEM! At the end of the day are your toes tired of this? Are they feeling BETTER maybe?

The victim described the suspect as

a black male between 6'0" and 6'2" and 220-240 lbs. He was wearing a black hooded sweatshirt and gloves.

a Hispanic male adult, approximately 40 y/o, with acne on his cheeks, wearing dark hoodie and jeans.

a Latino about 30 years old, 5 feet 10 inches tall, with an average build. He wore a black ski mask, sunglasses, a black hooded sweatshirt and black pants.

a Hispanic male adult, 25- 30 years old.

a black male adult between 30 and 40 years of age, approximately 6 feet tall and weighing approximately 160 to 170 pounds. The subject was also described as having collar length hair that was in corn rows and a slight southern accent.

a Latino between 25 to 30 standing approximately 5 feet 10 inches and 6 feet one inch tall.

a white male with an olive complexion between the ages of 40 and 45. He's 6 feet to 6 foot 3, weighs between 185 pounds to 220 pounds, is clean-shaven and was wearing a plaid shirt and blue jeans.

a Hispanic male adult, 34 to 38 years old, approximately 200 to 250 pounds, black buzz cut hair, wearing a red t-shirt with a black design.

a white or Hispanic in his early 20s, with a mustache or goatee. He was wearing a black Hurley hat, a black and grey plaid jacket, a woodland-pattern camouflage bandana, blue jeans and black shoes.

a Latino in his early 20s, about 6 feet tall, with a tattoo under one eye, wearing a gray hooded sweatshirt and carrying a rifle with no stock.

a black male, 5 feet 11 inches tall, with shoulder-length dreadlocks and dark-colored jeans.

a Hispanic or mixed race male in his twenties, approximately five foot ten inches tall with a stocky build armed with a handgun.

two Hispanic male adults, approximately 40 years old. The driver wore a brown baseball cap. The passenger had dark hair and eyes, dark colored beard, wearing a brown sweater, jeans, and boots.

a 5-foot-11 black man of medium build, wearing dark clothing, black Nike sneakers and a dark beanie cap.

a Hispanic male adult, mid-30's, thin moustache, wearing a black baseball cap with a yellow logo.

a black male wearing a green jacket with a fur hood, a grey knit hat, a grey hooded sweatshirt, blue jeans, black boots, and carrying a black bag.

a Latino man in his 20s, 5 feet 5 and 180 pounds with brown hair and a mustache, last seen wearing blue jeans and a black hooded sweatshirt.

a white or Hispanic, 5 feet 7 inches tall, with short and curly dark hair, wearing a black leather jacket and dark pants.

So yes, this book is comprised of more than four hundred error messages in six languages collected by a user over the course of two years. Which is why the scene opens onto a park with two men picking over the carcass of a small fowl. The oils stay slippery on their hands. The spices stick in between facial hairs. Plastic forks sit unused and to the side. The other men in the park play mahjong, speak Russian and smoke tobacco. Oh my God why is this chicken so good! It's way better than my chicken. No. It is. It is. The scene closes with two men casually inspecting the carcass of the fowl. The meat is gone. The mess is wiped up with napkins. The conversation is lazy and about weather and respective spouses. She would really like this. He hates it when it gets this messy ... laughing and so on.

> So on top of the stone he put some snow
> And on top of the bone he put some glue
> And on top of the box he put some tape
> And on top of the bar he put some gum
> And on top of the pile he put molasses

And so on til
- The number of elements is sufficiently large that conventional descriptions (eee gee a system of differential equations) are not only impractical, but cease to assist in understanding the system. Moreover, the elements interact dynamically, and the interactions can be physical or involve the exchange of information
- Such interactions are rich, eye eee any element or sub-system in the system is affected by and affects several other elements or sub-systems.

- The interactions are non-linear: small changes in inputs, physical interactions or stimuli can cause large effects or very significant changes in outputs.
- Interactions are primarily but not exclusively with immediate neighbours and the nature of the influence is modulated.
- Any interaction can feed back onto itself directly or after a number of intervening stages. Such feedback can vary in quality. This is known as recurrency.
- Such systems may be open and it may be difficult or impossible to define system boundaries.
- Complex systems operate under far from equilibrium conditions. There has to be a constant flow of energy to maintain the organization of the system.
- Complex systems have a history. They evolve and their past is co-responsible for their present behaviour.
- Elements in the system may be ignorant of the behaviour of the system as a whole, responding only to the information or physical stimuli available to them locally.

Which is to say

4. 3. 2. The Innermost Ones.
    Working outwards towards them.
    Following the method of 'p' repeatedly.
    Hence there is no part itself in this.
    'O'o'o'a' is all.
    'O'o'o'a' is imagined.
    'O'o'o'a' is self-evident.
    And none has interdefinability.
5.   Def.   6.   The weather. Significations.
6.   The same.   6.   The logical form.   6.   The.
    Though we say of 'q': that means that there.
    That it would be said that.
    That it would be surprises.
    That it would be objects.
    That it would be gathered.
    And vice versa.

So yes, the Martians of Bogdanov's *Red Star* already possess a global knowledge concord, frictionless data gathering, and computational power that Earthly climate science would finally acquire by the late twentieth century. With that infrastructure in place, the Martians found then what humans have found only now — that collective labor transforms nature at the level of the totality. Which may be why, in his *The Philosophy of Living Experience*, Bogdanov is not really trying to write philosophy so much as to hack it, to repurpose it for something other than the making of more philosophy. Hacked philosophy becomes a kind of raw material for the design and organizing, not quite of what Foucault called discourses of power / knowledge, but more of practices of laboring / knowing. Take thermodynamics as an example. Industrialization runs on carbon. Demand for carbon in the form of coal meant that miners dig deeper and deeper. Pumping water out of deep mines becomes an acute problem, and so the first application of steam power was for pumping water out of mines. Out of the practical problems of designing steam-driven pumps arise the principles of thermodynamics as a a science. Thermodynamic models of causation then become the basic metaphor for thinking about causation in general, extended by substitution to explain all sorts of things. *Actually, the more I dig and think and research, the more all poetry seems like it could be read ecologically, as so much of writing deals with relations between self and other, re-engineering language subject, perception and exterior, where we fit into larger systems, landscape, history, culture — where and how we inhabit and how we negotiate with others inhabiting the same spaces.* [In the above, I think many concept-words could be used in place of "ecologically" … to my way of thinking they're virtually synonymous, tho they come from other thought realms …]

    the club's DNA Lounge;

    archive sale next week;

    how's that plumbing inspector;

    the body ratio is dense;
    the raw structure.

    (^^)

    the massive wallpaper
    removal
    recently championed by
    the authorities
    is a direct consequence
    of the glut of DJs
    on the local scene

    (^^)

    pastoral
    machines
    distracting me
    buzzing excuse me

and back just in time

shift
units

what

(^^)

fumth /

fumth fumth

fumth /

& I am dissolving

/ doctor doctor I think

I am henry the eighth without organs /

o happy man /

all over myself &

/ / fumth / fumth

That was the way, I say. I say, "… it has been granted me to be with angels and to talk with them person to person. I have also been enabled to see what is in heaven and in hell, which are the same place, a process that has been going on for thirteen years …" Last night was another hour or so of hard afib. After all that puffing my computer broke. I had to put a patch on its port. The keyboard is softly. I didn't think I'd be able to cry on command. When my good friend, the poet and performance artist Jennifer Tamayo, invited me to an event called "CRYING; A PROTEST" at Dia: Beacon's Carl Andre retrospective in honor of Ana Mendieta, I knew it was important for me to attend, but I had no idea how I would make myself cry. Organized in collaboration with Christen Clifford of No Wave Performance Task Force — the group that staged a protest of the Andre show outside Dia's Chelsea offices last year — the event was billed as: "TEARS of JOY / TEARS of TERROR / TEARS for ANA MENDIETA. Come celebrate the last day of Andre's DIA retrospective at a public cry-in / silueta party. Bring your own tears." As I walked around the show, my tears came more quickly than I expected. My anxiety about the day came to a head as I looked around at Andre's sparse, linear art — metal, wood, and other industrial materials arranged in crisp geometric rows and shapes. They felt to me in that moment like elegant exercises in cool logic.

Speaking of logic, "Given that the volume of a human mouth is, on average, 7.2628 cubic inches, we can assume that the mouth can, in any given average situation carry up to 6335.666 tears. / Which would take 38.14 minutes to shed, if they were to be shed at the average rate at which tears are shed." But a book like Zultanski's "Bribery" uses the Web while downplaying or taking for granted its influence. At first glance, you might mistake it for pre-Internet poetry. And the same is true of a new book by Sam Riviere, "Kim Kardashian's Marriage." Like Zultanski, Riviere was born in 1981, and like Zultanski, Riviere seems to view the Internet with a shrug, as if to say, "Doesn't everybody make poetry from the Web? So what?" The title of Riviere's book is misleading: the text inside was not, as you might have guessed, scraped from Kim Kardashian's social-media presence or from gossip sites; in fact, it has nothing to do with her or her wedding at all, really. Instead, Riviere used the duration of Kardashian's marriage to Kris Humphries — seventy-two days — as a constraint to determine how many poems the book would contain. And the whole book is similarly deceptive: what appears to be a series of semi-confessional lyric poems are all mathematically based on Web searches. Through an elaborate process of cannibalizing and recombining chapter headings from his previous books, Riviere has come up with a series of keywords upon which his Web searches are based. After throwing them into Google, he accepts the first ten results from each search and then crafts them into stanzas. His book is entirely unoriginal: not a single word of his own is added. Yet the range of what Riviere has mined is vast. Sometimes it leans toward the ecstatic — "We're spreading smiles every minute / with lyrics and jokes for your personal use. / O Sovereign God transcendent! / This is an excellent song. / You have stalked this blog, / you must really like me. / Message me anytime / even if it's just to talk. / I blog about whatever I want. / I meet Franklin Delano Roosevelt / He's been walking for three days. / He makes necklaces of refined sugar, / human hair is toxic now. / baridi. [cold] / joto. [warm] / wingu / mawingu [cloud / clouds] / jua. [sun] / mvua. [rain]." Still, someone gave me the opportunity to copy a piece of writing onto the wall of a gallery. I'd never done anything like that before. I called it a hunger text. I will write about this experience, I thought. Now I am writing about it, but I'm not sure what there is to say, and whether or not saying it will be interesting for anyone to hear or read. Now she is painting an "A" on the wall, and now an "e." Now I have painted the word "foot." And now "pleasure." The woman in the text is projected onto the wall too, limping across letters, eating bugs. Can you see her? What am I doing there, leaning across her, leaning across those letters, while standing on a ladder, with the text projected on my back, and my arms, as my shirt is white, and see-through, and when I am there the woman is on my back and arms as much as she is on the wall. I walked across the floor of the gallery, dragging my foot. No one else in the room; this bit was only for me. This must have been more interesting than seeing me paint letters. Watching me paint letters would only be interesting for someone who has some special attraction to me. I suppose if I were attracted to a person I could watch them paint letters on a wall all day, or at least for a part of an afternoon. I am in a relationship, but I am sure the person I am in a relationship with would be bored by having to watch me paint letters on a wall for more than ten minutes. This is understandable. But it felt good, the dragging of the foot. I liked doing it. When I was that age, the magical ability I envied most was the freeze-frame — to instantly make someone believe that they stood on the sheer edge of a cliff or was surrounded on all sides by water, so that they didn't dare move in the slightest. Speaking of which, "Duet #1 Wordsworth" is made up of just such disjuncture:

>Seal my fits with grey immortality,
>and reaper slumber among the ruined
>world ways, beauteous Lucy, much the yew
>trees surprised us of the solitary
>resolution of mutability.
>Lonely she dwelt in independence too,
>up my cottage strange passion leaps as few
>men wandered by traveled Tintern Abbey.
>
>Too hard to get to, they say
>10000 mountains made of shattered bones.
>His mother had taught him
>how to keep the house clean, but at night
>he smelt the tears in the Danube
>………… drying out his soul.
>……………………………… a hairless broom remained
>so we take an iron shovel to hell,
>
>…………………………….. & sleeping
>I only can run down the stairs
>……………….. it's …………………….. over now
>……………………………………………………………..
>……………….for………………….. to behold
>…………………………………………. called & callin'
>until he drives his teeth into the other's neck,
>his shadow flattened out against a wall.
>
>And I kind of still am; certainly,
>I'm all for getting micro. Cowboys and rice and –
>if May Swenson can be believed – flamingos,
>sun lamp, reappears the mood
>ring of safety, cries mistrial likely, the children in his dream
>fused to a single child, a rabbit running backwards.

With his finger on the spring he brings them down.
More than we did at birth to know.

Speaking of which, here is "[A method] of lucky-shadows (?), that is tested: a hawk's egg with myrrh, pound (?), put on your eyes of it, then it makes lucky-shadows (?). Another: head and blood of a hoopoe; cook (?) them and make them into a dry medicament and paint your eyes with it; then you see them, again. And you set up your [planisphere ?] and you stamp on the ground with your foot seven times and recite these charms to the Foreleg, turning (?) to the North seven times and you return, down and go to a dark recess. A question-form, tested: You go to a dark clean recess with its face open to the south and you purify it with natron-water, and you take a new white lamp in which no red earth or gum-water has been put and place a clean wick in it and fill it with real oil after writing this name and these figures on the wick with ink of myrrh beforehand; and you lay it on a new brick before you, its underside being spread with sand; and you pronounce these spells over the lamp again another seven times. You display frankincense in front of the lamp and you look at the lamp; then you see the god about the lamp and you lie down on a rush mat without speaking to any one on earth. Then he makes answer to you by dream. Behold its invocation." I found that in vol. 3 of *Capital*. All the witches of the day respected him. On one occasion, he went to some family's house to observe witches perform a ritual. But the idiots there (who perhaps didn't recognize the famous old man) received him carelessly, so he found an opportunity to slip quietly out the door, and immediately two massive stones from the courtyard leapt into the house, bounded into the main hall and began accompanying the witches in their dance, frightening the party into sudden realization of who their erstwhile guest had been. Anyway, my own sense of the connection between baseball and poetry came into focus after overhearing a conversation at the Royal Tavern in Philadelphia, Game 3 of the Phillies-Brewers NLDS on the TV over the bar: Guy 1: Baseball's a thinking-man's sport. Guy 2: Yeah, you don't have to watch every play. Guys 1 and 2 were trying to persuade Guy 3 of the intellectual virtues of baseball. I'm not sure how thinking and not paying attention go together, but there's something between these statements that has me realizing that baseball is what happens between plays as well as during them. Take this, by Paul Blackburn, from his "17.IV.71":

> Top of the 8th, after
> four fouled off Gentry, still
> 2 and 2, a plastic bag
> blows over home plate, Dave
> Cash of the Pirates steps
> out of the box, steps
> back in, after speeding the plastic

on its way
with his bat, fouls
two more off, then 3 & 2, then
infield bounce to the shortstop, out at first.

"And, altho I'm still not sure why the book is called *GoGo Monster*, some of the symptoms I was complaining about before *were* withdrawal, and some of them were a killer migraine that kept me up the whole next night because I didn't medicate it soon enough and my current drugs are for crap, and as soon as that started lifting I got all dizzy with a fever, which is *definitely not* in any of the pharma literature and is presumably unrelated, so, in short, I am a hilarious medical fiesta, what TV should I watch once I've changed my sheets?"

          (Little sister's hand took hold of mine)
Little sister said, a crab bit me
She always says that, a crab bit me, a crab bit me
If I asked her, did a crab really bite you?
She would say, that's right, a crab bit me
So we would give her the third degree, really? a crab bit you?
She would say a crab, a real crab, it bit me
She would insist and burst out crying, little sister always cries
She did it that time too,
A crab bit our brother
        (I gave him a quick spot check)
He had spots all over his body like he'd been bitten, he was
        scratching
His eyes were bloodshot, his face and hands had swollen up
        like balloons
There was a white line on the tip of his nose, it had been
        there since he was a baby
A mark from a cup? we'd asked him about it and touched it
When evening came, the line seemed to rise up pale in the
        darkness
But now his nose was dry
        (He was lying down)
He called out to me,
It itches,
I can't breathe unless I open my mouth,
If I open my mouth I make a wheezing sound,

Reading backwards from its use, then, we could also question the claim that "EveRY man should be allOWed / quiETly to inHerit His But faTHEr's" … his father's hat? Wait." What?

5388

[WHAT FOLLOWS ARE FIVE SECONDS OF A NOISY BUNCH OF OVERDUBBED, SIMULTANEOUS RESPONSES] OK. Well, let's see if CALL_LETTERS can't do something about that. We'll start with an assessment. We'll start with [PAUSE] this. [THEME MUSIC FOR SERIES] CALVIN'S FATHER Who's that? CALVIN'S MOTHER That's Calvin's friend Darnell. Hi Darnell. Hi Darnell. CALVIN'S FATHER Who's Darnell? CALVIN'S MOTHER It's Calvin's friend. It's Calvin's friend. From THE_CITY. From THE_CITY. He's from THE_CITY. CALVIN'S FATHER Darnell? Darnell? Who's that? HOST Please temporarily turn your radio off or change to another station. [LONG PAUSE] Smells can evoke memories more easily than our other senses. [SOUND OF RADIO STATION CHANGE] For example, smells can evoke memories more easily than our other senses. Today, we're going to be testing THE_CITY for déjà vu – the feeling that something novel has happened before; and jamais vu – the feeling that something familiar has never happened before. We're not going to test any one individual; instead, we'll be testing THE_CITY as a whole. I'm asking individuals to call in to PHONE_NUMBER. Again, PLEASE dial PHONE_NUMBER to be a part of this assessment of THE_CITY for déjà vu or jamais vu. Just dial PHONE_ NUMBER and we'll get started. I know THE_CITY has had some concerns over the years about the familiar and the unfamiliar. I hope this testing will put those concerns to rest or otherwise give us some sense of what might be done about them. First I'll need to get some initial information from THE_CITY. Please temporarily turn your radio off or change to another station. [SOUND OF RADIO STATION CHANGE] OFF-AIR EXAMINER [The following questions are asked of callers off the air. The callers' answers are sampled for later use in the show.] ☐ Have you experienced déjà vu – the feeling that something has already happened? ☐ Do you know anyone named Calvin or Darnell? ☐ Have you ever experienced jamais vu – the feeling that something very familiar to you suddenly was unfamiliar or unreal? ☐ Repeat this phrase: "A sip of imbalance informed his exit." ☐ Repeat this phrase: "A single vessel of glamorous New Mexican liquor." ☐ Repeat this phrase: "I love you, but, because inexplicably I love in you something more than you – the *objet petit a* – I mutilate you." ON-AIR EXAMINER [SOUND OF RADIO STATION CHANGE] Smells can evoke memories more easily than our other senses. For example, smells can evoke memories more easily than our other senses. Strong déjà vu is often preceded by a certain smell. Take note of what you are smelling now. If you are at home, close your eyes tightly. If you are driving, close your eyes very tightly. I'm going to count slowly to 25. Count along with me in your head or out loud. When I start counting, please temporarily turn your radio off or change to another station. Count along with me in your head or out loud until you reach 25. When you reach 25, return to this broadcast for additional instructions. 1 — 2 — 3 — 4 — 5 — 6 — 7 — 8 — 9 — 10 — 11 — 12 — 13 — 14 — 14 — 14 —14 — 14 — 14 — 14 — 14 — 14 — 14 — 14 — 14 — 14 — 14 —

14 — 14 — 14 — 14 —14 — 14 — 14 — 14 — 14 — 14 — 14 — 15 — 16 — 17 — 18 — 19 — 20 — 21 — 22 — 23 — 24 — 25.

I mean, I'm about to contradict myself, but I also get frustrated when I see so much Ancient Greek thought sneaking into modern theory — Jacques Rancière I am looking at you — at least partly because one of Plato's best ideas in the Phaedrus is that writing is just a little kid who needs its daddy to hold its hand. Its daddy. When did things go so wrong. I mean, I loved my dad, we called him Pops, he was awesome. He and I used to go to used bookstores a lot. My favorite moment was when he'd turn to me and say hey, Johnny, see anything you like? The phrase, "subaltern, insurgent cosmopolitanism," on the other hand, refers to the aspiration of oppressed groups to organize their resistance and consolidate political coalitions on the same scale as the one used by the oppressors to victimize them. Insurgent cosmopolitanism is also different from that invoked by Marx as meaning the universality of those who, under capitalism, have nothing to lose but their chains – the working class. In addition to the working class described by Marx, the oppressed classes in the world today cannot be encompassed by the "class-which-has-only-its-chains-to-lose" category. Insurgent cosmopolitanism includes vast populations that are not even sufficiently useful or skilled enough to "have chains," that is, to be directly exploited by capital. It aims at uniting social groups on both a class and non-class basis, the victims of exploitation as well as the victims of social exclusion, of sexual, ethnic, racist, and religious discrimination. So, FOR MORE THAN TWO DECADES, a Monday has rarely passed where I haven't thought of "Blue Monday," Diane Wakoski's bleak, beautiful, incantatory masterwork:

> Blue of the heaps of beads poured into her breasts
> and clacking together in her elbows;
> blue of the silk
> that covers lily-town at night;
> blue of her teeth
> that bite cold toast
> and shatter on the streets;
> blue of the dyed flower petals with gold stamens
> hanging like tongues
> over the fence of her dress
> at the opera / opals clasped under her lips
> and the moon breaking over her head a
> gush of blood-red lizards …

So let Othniel praise the grasshopper, and bless all Vipers before a honey champion, let wisdom and frying pans fill the fields, let perpetual Joseph, who is an eeeeee, and is crawling, let him alone, and in a hat, praise the mockingbird, the Panther. Come to the land of honorable Chalcol Asbadana O flying beetle, and magnify the sweetness of Uz. And bless you that you become satisfied with how a highly ornate armor of crystal nails destroys the temple ornaments. Let the Lord of all the apes lurking in front of him bless him. Noah's Pride is expensive, and it's great, and everything you need is water, and its rival is the pure rock and who archeth lithely. People and animals praise camels when they are completed. Let us alert a friend that a heavenly harp is someone who likes to listen the calls of the rhino on his throne. Let Abimelech show the other axis. Let us bless forever Jabez who cracked the ark of salvation that Naboth wove from unique job worms, watches, and lower body diets. Let Joab the goat hope to bless you, you need it. Let us now practice a little **apophatic wuness**: … leave room for seven days: re-enter & sweep towards keyboard: type the following poem –

<pre>
            c   –
                CC
</pre>

        h –
          H
          H

                    – observe dust

resulting – some particles with have downward movements – [the phenomenon of a fall is actuall a segment of a movement towards the centre of the earth. This very moment countless objects are falling …]

fu fu fu fu
ru ru ru ru fu
ii ii ii&ii ru   fu
ke ke ke ke ii   ru   fu
ya ya ya ya ke ya ii ke ya ru ii ke ya fu ru ii ke ya

this cd have 5 anthills – at one level it is earth – the principal dancers are the directional buddhas –

the movement of the dance <u>is</u> the passage of the drug –

 desertpeople
  april
is yellowmoon
    the greasewood
  blossoms

get high
      bring the wind
   cloud

  get
high & bring
    the could
   with the rain

      get
          high
   &
     pull
   the could down

& the rain
& the rain

    & the rain

So what's happening … time's running short the mad sad joy of the shadow church wafting nylon tantras & world & patching up the zimzum with a certified 2-way stretch of now & tie a ball of string in that Doukipudonktan / Houevayekawlit or each letter of the text can be involved in the ambiguity or equivoque as in 70 as the ROTAS / SATOR square [the exploding galaxy]

HE na-NETH   BI-sh-QA-wa

HE na-NETH   BI-sh-QA-wa

HA-ni-HA-na   HA-ni-SA-na

HA-i-HA-HAT-DI-BA-naq

HA-i-HA-HAT-DI-BA-naq

```
            s
          k y
          s o n
          g s f l
          o w e r s
```

but that was a bird

why is it so far

over a star

meanwhile the only thing filling my body is fake money

now and then the scent of fake lucre drops from my eye in a gooey
                      pearl

the people inside love a musical cat

the stars retreat like wheels

(nadanada & netineti)

All of us but Bella were dead. Bella was making a Dead Cart Run, and there wasn't much for the rest of us to do. 'I am taking it back,' said Cat. 'I am taking that fucker back. Listen to this. 'Ring of Protection. The wearer is impervious to instant death attacks.' *Impervious!* 'Maybe there's a lesson here about stuff we find in chests.' 'Caveat emptier,' Cat said gloomily. 'Look at Bella go. She's solid Hit Points. She's some kind of Hit Points neutronium. Oh my God it's a Balrog.' Bella exhaled. 'That thing'll chase me all the way tae Resurrection Springs. This could be it, guys.' 'Don't say that. You are a black hole for damage. You are Hit Points ringed with a singularity. I'm complacent.' 'Yis're dead. It's easy tae be complacent.' 'No Bella, it's easy to chill out. Dead people aren't necessarily complacent. But also I'm bare complacent.' *Ooh la-effing-la.*

> […] Meanwhile, towards junction
> two Ring Road (S and Semilunar) I saw myself
> expelled, B5095 on the horizon, a ship with bloody
> sail, on the monotonous waves of the sea
> split foreshortened teeth under a boot in an
> ashtray forever. I type this in bright orange
> wooly gloves. Unsanctioned, the
> head bobs off, the fractured knucklejoint
> held tight between the middle and proximal
> phalanges of the left index finger inside the
> tender flesh my skin stretches tight over swims
> with the current of world-history, right to
> left, from permanent fear to sycophancy, mutual
> backscratching and ventriloquy the
> individual in the typical boiled off through
> space into the overflow. The future belongs to it.
> Give me an account of plate-movement, and
> hold the accretionary wedge […] and by
> accretionary wedge you will always have
> to wonder whether I am referring to these
> November 2012 tweets from Paris Lacan:
>
> I've always wondered what it would be like to be a mermaid – a fictive tale [nice one – ed.] even has the advantage of manifesting symbolic necessity!
>
> *
>
> At this intersection of nature and culture, so obstinately scrutinized by the anthropology of our times, I love scuba diving! It's so fun!
>
> *
>
> Loving my metallic and classic black pumps from my @ParisHiltonShoe line! By Baudelaire! Things are pretty hot!

*

Living Life to the Fullest! For the signifier is a unit in its very uniqueness, being by nature symbol only of an absence.

*

The Mirror Stage as formative in the function of the I as revealed in psychoanalytic experience, I'm like an American princess.

*

PROMOTED TWEET. If you drive less than 55 miles / day OR have no DUIs you can get auto insurance for as low as $29 a month.

I mean, puddles, astronomical scale, mists and miasmas, these are all the correct subjects, the sexual *qual* of impossibly trivial smallness jarring up against impossibly large physical phenomena, opening the drastically expanded scope of what we are; that is actually happening here, but the illustrations you've got accompanying them clearly beat the shit out of some stretches that did scratch the itch head on. There are contradictions here "big enough to put your fist in if it was a small fist & you really wanted to put it there" ... OK. I need to go eat now and steel myself against the day's impending worthless tasks. And yes, $120 is a preposterous amount of dosh for Blinko's *The Haunted Head*, so clearly I would require one of your aforementioned photocopies.

> Only I wouldn't be so radiant if I was you.
> The ripple effect, strength in deterioration,
> Ripple-effect milkweed fence.
> Better early than never. Why, I thought so.

To cheer myself up, back in Hackney I walked up to B&Qs in Lea Bridge Road to buy a power drill. Returning home along the cycle path which doubles as a footpath towards Upper Clapton, a cyclist approached shouting "get out of the fucking way you stupid cunt!" One little nudge was all it took. Straight into the path of an oncoming lorry. It wasn't my fault, it was just one of those things. I used my walkie-talkie to call emergency services, but it was too late. It's bad when that happens. Splitting in Two can also refer to the dialectical model of philosophical and political analysis. This is how human progress is made. And to speak to us about the bones you touch or cannot touch. "Perhaps it's time to let the pathogens run this heap." "As if they haven't been!" As whoever runs Bulging Ceramic Superconductors puts it, "i made ramen ……. i am death."

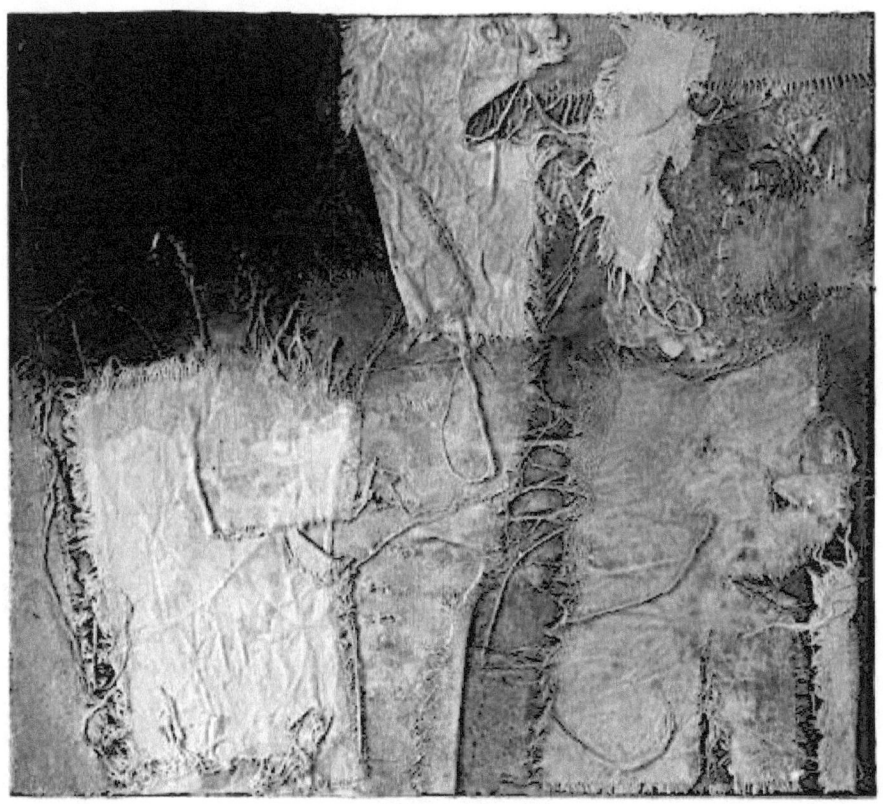

Everyone else is asleep in the city, like tall stainless steel masks.
... or this tiny box of Mondays and Tuesdays ...
... or a parking lot full of U-Haul trucks.
Their teeth burn like rubber, which is to say that

with one hand I was stirring a gallon of pink paint. I put my whole arm in to break up clots at the bottom with my fingers. Happiness came and went as I stirred the paint. Heavy black snow made of human beings began to seep into the ground. An hour later I was still sitting there, after the gallon had been mixed and taken away. No one ever told me what they did with the paint. My arm was still covered in it. It was resting on my lap now, with the thick paint drying to a crust and leaving chalky pink stains on my pants. That's when he fell backward into the ditch, unable to get out. In the darkness, he saw a massive river of sand. People knelt at the edge of it, dipping their hands into it as it rushed by, leaning down to gather it against their chests, weeping. In the middle of the night he heard a woman pass by the ditch. She had a cat walking with her, and every once in a while he heard the woman whisper something to the cat. Then for a long time he saw and heard nothing. He stopped feeling his back against the bottom of the ditch. During this time he couldn't perceive or think or imagine anything. Then he had the vision that he was walking along the path with me, but I always stayed a few paces ahead, and wouldn't look at him. When we came out of the woods we were thirsty, so we stopped at a gas station just outside of town, in a place where everything was called "crow." When we opened the door and went inside it was "crow". Which is why I couldn't figure out how much the hats cost. Then I went by myself, and I found her, and when we were alone I heard her say, "You'll burn a hole in yourself, like you always do!" She didn't say it to me, though; she said it to herself, while looking back over her shoulder at a field of massive crystals.' That's when Plato erected his toe in our scalp, the big tent pole cave juice death trance. We're still base humans that way. The Nerf ball with glasses shit. So, I cried at thrift stores. The people who raised me worked in oil. We ate vats of it for dessert. So, I condemned myself to sitting and grew a beard. The rent was cheap inside my beard. Still, everyone refused to live like that. So, I keep notebooks. "#54" came directly from a newspaper headline. "CANCER DOESN'T STOP HUNTER, 86, WHO KILLS MOOSE FROM HIS RECLINER." There's everything in my notebooks, from the advice in Cain's *Mildred Pierce* — "Never sell the beach house" to the photo of the adoptable dog Filo

99
79

Or, if she preferred, her car. "Thank you for inviting us to participate in your plan anyway," the wolves said politely. The Lord did not want to appear addled, but what was the plan his sons were referring to exactly? If you ask Bernadette Mayer, she'll tell you that it's "... like five skunks skulking on the page, let it go on, without any cut-offs ..." Hence, the idea that you could set something on fire and walk to California or Nevada or the idea that the author might not want to gouge your eyes out but the speaker does. We said the carpet was an anal vortex. Did we? Why? Is that what we meant to say? If yes, why yes? If not, why not? I had to go to a craft store! I had to forage for local herbs! The doctor's round of house calls, on which he had been accompanied by his son, was already behind me; only the visit to the Prince of Saurau at the Hochgobernitz castle still lay ahead. Father and son were now making the perilous ascent to the fortress from the gorge down below, where they had just visited the mill. It was not advisable to look around. What they had seen before had been *fore*tokens: a killer, still unapprehended, was roaming around the countryside; in all the houses the two of them had visited so far, the wretchedly moribund were lying or running rampant; in a building next door to the mill dead birds were strung up in rows; the miller's dog, hazardous in its derangement, dashed to and fro amongst the mill-workers; every living creature seemed abjectly subject to its own nervous system.

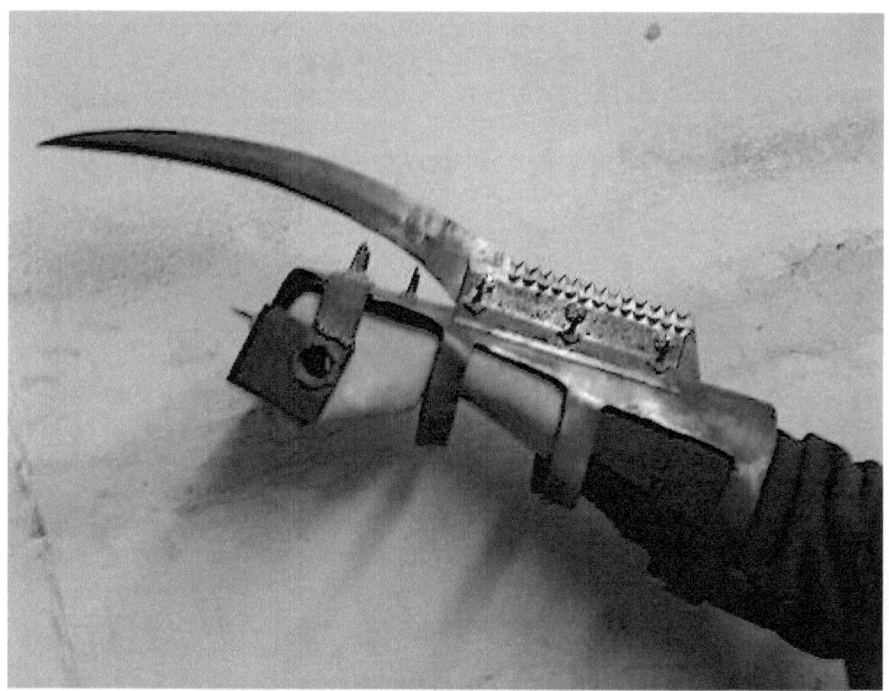

Then an invalid, shortly before expiring, drew a sketch entitled "Death by Asphyxiation while Walking." All the characters were confessing something: the father as good as admitted it. Dear Verso and The New Press, FIRST, it boggles the mind that the writings, posthumously published, of Aaron Swartz, one of Open Access's fiercest advocates should be under any sort of lock and key at all. One wonders why provisions might not have been made to publish these writings via various, even networked Open Access platforms and perhaps even to have used such an occasion to raise funds for causes that Aaron himself cared about so deeply (such as Demand Progress). SECOND, after doing some digging, we have discovered that Verso could not allow downloads of the book in North America because The New Press owns those rights. If you are in North America, where Aaron himself lived and worked, you have to buy the book, in print or as an e-book, from The New Press. So, a publisher in New York City is stopping a publisher in London from giving away a book containing writings by someone who did not believe that intellectual-cultural knowledge should ever be anything but fully public and accessible. Which also saddens us and brings us to, THIRD, e-books sold by Verso (delivered to purchasers as EPUB or MOBI files) come with this caveat: "Ebooks from the Verso website are watermarked and DRM-free, and will work on any of your devices — but they can't be uploaded to websites or file-sharing networks." And all of this causes us to (more than) pause and to recall that there is a phrase having to do with spinning in one's own grave, and if we were Aaron, we would have collectively bored a hole all the way through to the other side of the Earthy by now. Somewhere out there in outer space, Aaron is spinning in the cold, dark air of the Milky Way. As publishers ourselves, we realize that economic sustainability for radically innovative and politically progressive presses who foster and cultivate what we call "intelligent matter" is a precarious situation (whether Open-Access, University-Subsidized, Independent-Commercial, etc., and we do consider both Verso and The New Press to be both innovative and politically progressive), and this is a situation that has many of us scrambling for creative and better long-term solutions, and one hopes we might do so more collectively, even. But here's the thing: if neither of you — neither Verso nor The Free Press — can see your way to figuring out how to make the archive of Aaron's writings more freely available, while still managing to recoup your costs in bringing these writings out in beautifully designed, material-virtual containers (which, of course, requires financial expenditures), then we simply despair. But more than that, we at punctum (and elsewhere throughout the Public Academy and Para-Academy) are outraged. We feel you have betrayed the important and culturally valuable legacy of Aaron Swartz. You have, further, betrayed his memory. And you have done it to turn a profit, even while you have also labored with all good intentions to get his thinking out into the world in elegant and mobile form. And therefore, to the directors of Verso and The New Press, we the undersigned are asking you to reverse and repair this unfortunate damage to his culturally significant legacy. For example, instead of offering an e-book version of Swartz's writings for one day, after which one must purchase a print edition or the watermarked e-book whose mobility across e-platforms is severely restricted (in Verso's case, and one imagines, in the case of The New Press's e-book edition as well), why not sell the print edition and e-book for a period of anywhere between, say, 6-12 months, and then completely unlock the e-book version into perpetuity (we might add, the print editions would still sell, as sales of print books have been on the rise since 2013, while sales of e-books have flattened)? That is just one idea — there are many more that might be dreamed and then engineered into being. If you are willing. With best regards. So yes. "Money is in the first instance that which expresses the relation of equality between all exchange values: in money they all have the same name." Was that it? Unable to comprehend the fact that they are an integral part of a state in a country called "The United States of America" the trees grow like they always have. So I was rereading Nicholas Royle's 'Going to Bits' yesterday. And all of this, we are told, 'could and should be taken very far'. How far might it be taken? What type of affective territory would it lead to? Is it already? Devastation? Radiance? An even more loving sense of things? 'There is something he doesn't know', says Cixous in *Hyperdream*, who does not have Royle in mind, referring perhaps to the way we all shut out something and double down, even in the moment we think we know what it is –

The fur & glue were not enough. They were pretty
enough. Just not clear enough. Or maybe
too clear. No. It was the blind glue they used. The kind
preservatives & artificial sweeteners know best.

I tried to hold you in my hands, but you were too big,
too elusive. Then he falls into the pools of his own eyes, and murmurs
'who am I? Who am I?', then howls
'Two-Four-Six-Oh-One!!!!!!!!!!!!!!' Sorry. That was an accident

did you notice. But trust me I would be a better criminal
than your dog. But I don't think my own brain projections would be so
nice to me. Through my ear on the long bump
down to a river filled with aromatics,

"either Mars one or heartbreak" & it's Big Spoon tonight, b/b/b/b/b/
either space or brr zzz #OOYL, k,
either love or space because horsemeat is everywhere
love or brr zzz #O VULNERABLE BEAD, TUMESCENT
        HOOD –

I guess I just wanted to give my background sense for wanting you all in this
journal – no contract, no worries – and of how there might be ways of going
into a panic-affect, & a radiance-affect, together, almost as team-work for
another week, round behind much of what the journal might end up saying,
already does, and left it in bits. It's not, then, just that some of you would have
said it all already and so no need for more, but that I am keen to know what is
next in an imagined joined trajectory, there where any thinking of the end of
the world might just be, tentatively, breathlessly, 'a cobbled-together verbal and
terminological construction', a complex ideologeme, since there is in fact no
world – what would be next, if anything, there where both a sense of ending or
of being okay might be memes to be reinvented and inverted. In any case, I
subveer, to use a word from a Fred Moten poem I am obsessed with right
now. I wonder if anyone knows it, this word, 'subveering'? I dreamt last night
about icebergs. There was a phrase in the dream, 'affect of the iceberg'. Cixous
talks about that other century, the cold one, which is also of course the hot one
we are passing into now, and her icebergs, I read it just now, are 'huge cubes of
frozen milk spewed from the udders of vanished sea monsters, one thinks of
the milk of leviathans, it's so fearsomely beautiful, the glacier chunks that heave
themselves up in front of us glitter like optic witchcraft'. In the dream, on a
boat, I was also staring at these beautiful pictures of the miocene I saw online
recently, these amazing children's pictures of miocene animals, like something
Leo had painted when he should have been painting Kate before the iceberg
hit – in the before, when I could ask you not to leave. I'm not sure what the

feeling was, looking at them, sunny relief, sunny post-humanimalism and arcades, like did you see the article Sea Slug Has Taken Genes from Algae It Eats, Allowing It to Photosynthesize like a Plant? Speaking of plants, it is in this context that I participated in Teresa Siewerdt's intervention, *Jardim de Passagem*. Siewerdt explores the relationship between one's body and the body of others, and the approximation of that body with wider landscapes. For *Jardim de Passagem*, 26 performers waited at different bus stops along a specific route, all carrying large plants of different varieties, and waiting for a specific pre-indicated bus. I was the third person to board, and when I did, I sat down unobtrusively towards the back of the long, articulated vehicle. The other two performers were equally as inconspicuous, and fellow passengers didn't seem to find our presence, carrying plants, in any way out of the ordinary. Gradually however, as the bus kept on stopping, and another person carrying a large plant with foliage or exotic blooms came aboard, the murmurs and laughter began to grow. As the journey continued, there were so many people carrying plants and flowers, that the bus began to resemble a form of mobile garden centre, with hanging baskets suspended on hand rails and the entire bus corridor disappearing behind thick green shrubbery. Passenger reactions were mixed. The man seated next to me ignored the whole intervention, and by the manner he pushed past me to disembark, seemed perhaps quite annoyed. Another man, due to the sheer amount of plants filling up the space, grew irritated as the foliage from a hanging basket repeatedly poked him in the face. Other passengers, having been initially curious, laughed and smiled once they understood that it was an intervention, and asked what we were doing, saying that the flowers were beautiful. As more and more performers got on board, the atmosphere became ever more light-hearted, and a sense of community sprang up, not just between the 26 performers, most of whom had not previously met each other, but also between the performers and fellow passengers with whom we conversed freely. This nascent sense of community was playful and unexpected, given that we had been directed to not specifically open conversation, but clearly not everyone wanted to participate: the bus journey was in the early afternoon and there were people who just wanted to get home, or listen to music through headphones. As we neared the bus terminal where the intervention was to end, people begin to ready themselves to disembark. In front of me, I watched as one of the performers chatted with a fellow passenger. We had been directed to offer our plants as a gift to passengers at the end of the journey and the performer in front of me, having struck up a conversation, now offered herplant as a gift.

> [1] Would you like to take care of it [the plant]?
> [2] I would! I would … Thank you, thank you! It's so beautiful …

The woman who accepted the plant was in tears as they hugged and at this point of emotional connection, there was a sense of the tangibility of the community that had been created as a result of 26 plants and a bus ride from one terminal to another. As we all got off the bus, passengers and other people passing through the terminal accepted the plants that we, the performers, were giving away. After the intervention had ended and the bus had left, all that remained was the busy terminal, into which people carrying plants were rapidly disappearing as we, the 26 performers, left for a public / private space, the Praça Victor Civita, to discuss how we felt the intervention had gone. Shortly after this discussion we all went our separate ways. So, to answer your question, my biography cannot explain empire. So far, so obvious, perhaps. but, for Deleuze, this pure becoming is something wild, paradoxical and mad. For here, the direction of change and time is no longer unilinear. When Lewis Carroll's Alice drinks the magic potion and starts to grow, she is getting bigger than she once was, but at the same time she is smaller than she will be. Deleuze's comment on this is worth quoting at length:

> This is the simultaneity of a becoming whose characteristic is to elude the present. Insofar as it eludes the present, becoming does not tolerate the separation or the distinction of before and after, or of past and future. It pertains to the essence of becoming to move and to pull in both directions at once. Alice does not grow without shrinking, and vice versa. Good sense affirms that in all things there is a determinable sense or direction (*sens*); but paradox is the affirmation of both senses or directions at the same time.

My aim in this essay is to trace this paradoxical logic in two radically different thought worlds: those of Nicholas of Cusa and of Kierkegaard. In each case, I wish to suspend certain interpretative contexts. Cusa is often read through the lens of what he owes to neoplatonism. Kierkegaard, for all he lives in a more clearly post-nominalist modernity, is still frequently understood in terms of a Lutheran-inflected orthodoxy. The value and fertility of these readings aside, I propose to offer a modest alternative: a reading of certain texts which engage with the logic of infinity and its attendant paradoxes. Of necessity, this is a very limited exercise, since i am more concerned with elucidating a problem than with crafting overarching readings of either figure. Cusa and Kierkegaard are selected for two reasons. First, in different ways, they articulate the logic of what it is to think the infinite in terms of unavoidable paradox. And my thesis is that this paradox is not merely a contingent barrier to the finitude of our thinnking, but is in some way constitutive of infinity itself. The second reason is to explore in a specific way the possibility of communication between the discourses of mystical theology and existentialism. Without merely comparing Cusa to Kierkegaard, according to a homogenising logic, what happens when these singular forms of thought encounter one another? What new possibilities can they induce for thinking the relationship between the absolute and the singular individual? Are the labels 'mystical' and 'existential' any longer

adequate for such intensities of thought and experiences? I begin with
Kierkegaard, and what I take to be key passages from his
Philosophical Fragments on the passion of thought to think the unthinkable:

> I was born and raised in a radium-like structure. I grew cold cinders,
> lung fissures. They say the heart is an open whatever. Mine certainly is.
> All I have known is an open whatever. Because we all want love and
> we all want to be loved and unloved. Because we all want to be fucked
> and we all want to be the fucker. But we want to be fucked and loved
> by time and the gods and that's impossible because time hates us and
> so do the gods. We don't know what we want but we want sonnets.
> We don't really want the sonnet. We do. We don't etc. I like material
> things in culture that are able to symbolize all of these conflicting
> forces and tendencies: the bikini is the law but it also undermines the
> law, which in this case at least is multiply gendered. Ultimately, I hope
> we can just burn all the bikinis and run around on the beach naked on
> Bikini Atoll,

a test run for the planet   to get through
the membrane   of courtly love bounded
by bed and breakfast   or by empiric
and rational   Not all experiments work
as when Spinoza and Leibniz   bailed
out of the Monad   Once the pieces break
enough   they behave like liquid

Studies say the Anthropocene began in 1610.
As not yet said moon grew large and
Shiva danced again with the Guanyin
Wood not only flows but brings life to
Seven big turtles sunning on a stone
Large as insects might smile at you
Something trilled, I don't know what it is

But as far as what bombards the knot to release a quantum content, I like your idea that it is a sort of *rhapsodomancy*, that the "end" of each letter has an arrow (of time?) pulling away from supercomputers, where each information-bit exists in more than one state at once, making processing billions of times faster. This is not a binary language. But you know how sometimes the dream cycle comes to resemble the inner workings of a solar cop. That lucky old sun etc. Yeh yeh I admit it. You've no longer got a face just a heliograph. One segment broken glass. You wake up in some kind of cellar. You wake up and you think its the shithole of the universe you're in. I mean, it's been cancelled hasn't it?

So at the end of the week, the student writers perform their rocket ship. "You're right slowly, little by little, the way a bird builds its nest ..." Eliante goes on to explain to Leon that she loves this vase, that she amuses herself by dressing him up, kissing him, imagining he's happy. And so on. If you've seen ads inviting you *to beauty*, *to movie*, or *to pumpkin*, you'll know what I mean. So here is a trivial model of "sufficiency": for every set, there is a free monoid whose elements are the finite sequences of elements of that set, whose identity element is the empty sequence, and whose monoid operation is the concatenation of sequences. Every set is convertible with its free monoid, in a precisely definable way (there is a functor from the category of sets to the category of monoids, and what is meant by "free monoid" in this context is that this functor is left-adjoint to the forgetful functor running in the opposite direction. Haskell programmers know the monad arising from this adjunction as the "List monad"; it's worth studying, as an elementary example of how such things work). Which is to suggest that tho Rule 34 is something like a principle of sufficient internet porn, a new rule of the internet is needed, in fact: for every feeling, there is a corresponding "tfw" – a "that feeling when" statement illustrating the circumstances that would give rise to that feeling, ideally paired with a suitable gif. But "tfw" is arguably the gravestone of interiority: its premise is that every feeling is like a communicable illness. This increase is reflected in other palaeohydrological and palaeoclimatological evidence in the southern Levant such as the levels of the Dead Sea, but contradicts hydroclimatological trends in the western Mediterranean that are correlated to the NAO index, suggesting that these are different hydroclimatological environments. So that now at length, guessing all to be sure and their own (the king being removed, the House of Lords nulled, their long-plotted council of state erected and this House awed to their ends), the edge of their malice is turning against such as have yet so much courage left them as to appear for the well-establishment of England's liberties. And because God has preserved a great part of the army untainted with the guilt of the designs aforementioned, who cannot without much danger to the designers themselves be suppressed, they have resolved to put this House upon raising more new forces (notwithstanding the present necessities of the people in maintaining those that are already); in doing whereof, though the pretence be danger and opposition, yet the concealed end is like to be the over-balancing those in the army who are resolved to stand for true freedom as the end of all their labours, the which (if they should be permitted to do) they would not then doubt of making themselves absolute seizures, lords and masters, both of Parliament and people; which, when they have done, we expect the utmost of misery. Nor shall it grieve us to expire with the liberties of our native country. For what good man can with any comfort to himself survive then? But God has hitherto preserved us; and the justice of our desires, as integrity of our intentions, are daily more and more manifest to the impartial and unprejudiced part of men; in so much that it is no small comfort to us that notwithstanding we are upon all these disadvantages that may be, having neither power nor pre-eminence (the common idols of the world) our cause and principles do through their own natural truth and lustre get ground in men's understandings; so that where there was one, twelve months since, that owned our principles, we believe there are now hundreds: so that though we fail, our truths prosper. So yes,

    if you make a commercial about it
    using smiling, white-haired people
    quoting Thoreau to sell retirement homes
    in the Everglades, I mean,

    after I heard A Hard Rain's
    A-Gonna Fall played softly by an accordion
    quartet through the ceiling speakers
    at Montclair Plaza, I mean,

    navigating between obelisks,
    I kept thinking "This sky or that flying thing
    is impossible", I kept thinking
    "drugs that affect nouns", I mean,

what could be better than watching Vin Diesel? I don't know what you're watching but I think of *Fast 5* – "Ride or die" – a hell of an apt motto, and not a bad tatt, especially for those of us caught up in these "interesting times" … Which is to say, I've been researching prehistoric stone ball phenomena for 15 years. I've visited the granite stone balls in southern Costa Rica, the volcanic stone spheres in western Mexico, the "cocina" stone balls of Isla del Cano, the volcanic stone balls on Easter Island, some of stone balls in Tunisia, and some on Tenerife in the Canary Islands, as well as. those in Antarctica, New Zealand, Russia, Egypt, the US, Argentina … Which is to say that when I established the non-profit "Archaeological Park: Bosnian Pyramid of the Sun" Foundation, our team was fully prepared to investigate this phenomenon in Bosnia. We have discovered stone balls in twenty different locations. We found granite stone balls in the Teocak village in northeastern Bosnia, volcanic stone ball near town of Konjic in middle Bosnia and sandstone stone spheres in many locations in western and middle Bosnia. Most of the stone balls were located near small town of Zavidovici. There used to be 80 of them in 1930s. Since that time, some were taken by the river, but most were destroyed in the 1970s after rumors appeared, of gold being hidden in the middle of them. And some were taken by locals and moved to their backyards. Only eight remained in what we established as "Archaeological Park: Bosnian Stone Balls". By the middle of March 2016, it became obvious that the most massive stone ball in Europe has been discovered, near Podubravlje. So far, less than half of the ball has been uncovered. Preliminary results show the radius to be between 1.2 – 1.5 meters. Materials have not been analyzed yet. However, the brown and red color of the ball point to very high content of iron. What would be the significance of this discovery? First, it would be another proof that Southern Europe, the Balkans and Bosnia in particular, were home for advanced civilizations in the distant past though we have no written records about them. Secondly, that they had high technology, different than ours. Finally, that they knew the power of geometrical shapes, because the sphere is one of the most powerful shapes along with the pyramid and cone. No wonder that pyramids and tumulus phenomena can also be found in Bosnia. While visiting the site a group of dowsers recorded that aura fields improve and grow when exposed to the vicinity of the stone ball. So it seems that the ancient did yet one more thing better than us. They knew the Planetary energies better, living in the harmony with our Mother Earth. Which leaves us with a number of questions, not the least important of which is

> "Who, in the end,
> stole the ping pong equipment?"
> I asked my friends between crackers
> but everyone shrugged
> and, as a shorthand to all needlessly
> tangled plots, the mystery is never solved
> and word never does come back to us
> from the village, except for the word
> "carnage," which one woman
> pronounces "car-nich"

So oh yes, absolutely, we could all be wiped out tomorrow, with only the biomass strata'd in the rocks below to keep on living (they don't even need oxygen). Thus worship of gods, propitiations of them, the burial of corpses, for instance, making them ready for their afterlife, all of which has been going on for maybe 30K years. Which brings me back to the *Mahābhārata* (it's impossible to read something like that without being sucked in, I'm sucked in, it's one of the world's Word Wonders) and the Gita – the Gita is written totally from the view of the "already there" and is designed to relieve the fear / anxiety of those who are facing always-already gone-ness in its full force. I'm certainly not arguing that it's my path or anything like that that I see there, just that, again, we've always been "already there." Which is certainly NOT to say that facing the anthropocene is nothing or nothing new (we've never been there quite like this before), and IT is to say that your question of what's an appropriate response (literally speaking) seems exactly the right one for all of us these day (answers may vary). One last thing (for now) re the Royle article. Towards the end there's this monster wonderful Derrida sentence / fragment, which I think is totally wrong (yes, even Derrida can be wrong, I think). To begin with Royle's lead in: These are the opening three words of what — especially with its final lengthy parenthesis about the phrase 'Die Welt ist fort [The world is gone]' — has claims to being among Derrida's longest and most extraordinary sentences. It has certain correspondences with the sentence in 'Let Us Not Forget — Psychoanalysis' about the history of reason and about psychoanalysis as a traumatic event in relation to that history. It reminds me, also, of my perhaps perverse fantasy of editing an anthology entitled *Selected Astonishing Sentences by Jacques Derrida*. Of course the sentence in question, the sentence beginning 'When every day', is not a sentence. That is part of the point. As the editors note: 'This sentence is incomplete in the typescript'. It is a sentence but it is incomplete. It stops mid-breath, when every day, like in 'The Day Lady Died', when someone or everyone 'stops breathing'. Here is how it goes: When every day, at every moment of the day and night, we are overcome with the feeling that between a given other, and sometimes the closest of those close to us and of those that we call so imprudently and stupidly, tenderly and violently, our own, and ourselves — those with whom we share everything, starting and ending with love, the feeling that the worlds in which we live are different to the point of the monstrosity of the unrecognizable, of the un-similar, of the unbelievable, of the non-similar, the nonresembling or resemblable, the non-assimilable, the untransferable, the incomparable, the absolutely unshareable (we know this with an undeniable and stubborn, eye eee permanently denied knowledge), the abyssal unshareable — I mean separated, like one island from another by an abyss beyond which no shore [rive] is even promised which would allow anything, however little, to happen [arriver], anything worthy of the word 'happen' — the abyssal unshareable, then, of the abyss between the islands of the archipelago and the vertiginous untranslatable, to the point that the very solitude we are saying so much about is not even the solitude of several people in the same world, this still shareable solitude in one and the same co-habitable world, but the solitude of worlds, the undeniable fact that there is no world, not even a world, not even one and the same world, no world that is one: the world, a world, a world that is one, is what there is not (and if 'Die Welt ist fort', this can also mean that there is the solitude, the isolation, the insularity of islands that are not even in the world, the same world, or on a world map, that there is no common world, be it a life-world, and that the presumed community of the world is a word, a vocable, a convenient and reassuring bit of chatter, the name of a life insurance policy for living beings losing their world, a life belt on the high seas that we pretend to be leaving, long enough to spend a moment during which we pretend to say 'we' and to be together together, a moment conventionally called life (which is also death), and even if it is this feeling and this fragile convention that makes our loves as much as our hatreds, our so-called ethical or political responsibilities, war and peace, our most quotidian affects no less than our great passions, we should nonetheless recognize for all that that this uncrossable difference is what language and the address to the other cross lightly, I mean with the lightness of unawareness, at least for the time and space of an as if of social insurance). Awesome fragment, yes, but it goes wrong at the end, I think, with the notion of uncrossable difference. It's just not true. Not totally true, at least. Derrida forgets (most western philosophers forget (it's part of western philosophy's raison d'être to forget) that we are not just consciousnesses, we are animals (in spite of his *The Animal That Therefore I Am*, etc, I'm not sure he ever really gets that) (the "therefore" is the giveaway). What I mean is: have you ever been well hugged? Then you know that it's really not language that crosses the difference, it's the body. No not "the" body. Specific bodies. Bodies, plural. Body to body. This is the same mistake that Kant made, that makes his work so claustrophobic. I remember reading somewhere in Bergson (*Creative Evolution*?) that tho Kant is more or less right about our limits, we actually DID evolve to live on this particular planet, so there is much more than very likely a good meaningful relationship between phenomena and noumena, not just a random or contingent one. Which is why, to end this self-indulgently with a line I wrote back when I first started writing, if we are OPEN, *tho we live and die alone, we are lonely no longer*. As a whole, it creates a similar effect as, say, Perec's *La Boutique Obscure*, or Brainard's *I Remember*. As with Perec, we watch Sanders's preoccupations take repeated form: the use of simple universal images such as ∞ for infinity, alongside more personally meaningful images such as the "Galactic Snail" and The Egyptian Boat, O Book of Glyphs! Why? / Why a star? Of course this is a book that can be read, but more than anything, *Spontaneous Particulars* demands to be looked at — and touched. Manuscript fragments, discarded scraps of silk, a pricked pattern, a prescription pad: to run your hand or mind over the affinities and relations Howe stitches together is to understand the quite literal beauty of text that more than flirts with illegibility. I mean personality. I mean "personality" in the sense of love and connection with another human individual, yes, but also "personality" in the simplest sense, as in a typo — and as in "I went to visit Michael McKenna today and brought as a present a piece of glass I had found on the street." So let me repeat: Fats Domino might take a plane to the ideal city, he might take a train, but even if he has to walk there, he will get to it the same. So yes, Goodman is writing in the Accelerationist trajectory, having cut his teeth in the CCRU. But unlike the ridiculous and grotesque Landian "dark enlightenment" variety, his project follows in the same lineage as that of Kodwo Eshun's cyborg afro-futurism. On one hand it's tracing the trajectory of cultural mutation following the reshaping of space by capital while also offering counterpoints and escape routes to the worldview it holds; on the other, it's what Eshun has called "speculative acceleration," whereby one can grasp the machinery for one's own use. Proletkult was the speculative acceleration of its time – Ben Noys is right to find traces of Accelerationism all across the Soviet experiment, but perhaps he errs in mapping out only the Accelerationism of the Leninist vanguard itself. To experiment today means to take into consideration the opportunities and limitations of the dichotomy of the planet of the slums and the planet of the drums, while also colliding these with all sorts of other developments, some of which are

> foaming at the mouth.
> So go ahead & cross
> the fucking street
> it's not on the test
> it's yours —
> if they ask you for credit
> give them a branch
> chew on some grass
> > i know
> > i know
> city hall is the brain
> of a shark, it fits
> in a jar:
> who keeps
> spraypainting RAT
> in all the crosswalks
> along 10th street
> from CVS six blocks
> to my corner — when
> RAT is
> spraypainted over
> in black
> RAT is re-applied
> good as new
> RAT
> each block

RAT
the sure refrain
as you walk to CVS
RAT
& back
for toothpaste or toilet paper
less & less able
RAT
to distinguish between
RAT
the images in mind
of whoever RAT might refer to
RAT
& the author of RAT
& yourself:
   RAT
   RAT
   RAT
   RAT
No. 1 is the vinegar
No. 2 is the cigarette butt
No. 3 is the Chinese pepper
No. 4 is looking at the mobile phone, then typing a text
  message
No. 5 is whining about wanting to make a reservation on a
  space ship to Mars
No. 6 is crying
No. 7 made an early morning phone call, saying she wants to
  get an abortion
No. 8 is losing his mind after breaking up with his girlfriend so
  he wrote a poem
No. 9 is whining about having to borrow money for her
  boyfriend's birthday
No. 10 bought a gun, saying his father is in his stomach
No. 11 there really is such a thing as a heart-rending touch
No. 12 there is the No. 12 mouse in the stomach of the
  snake of which I saw it
No. 13 is crying, saying s/he wants to know who s/he is
Wings of fire on the burned rooftop!
Steel wings on the steel tower!
In the hand of No. 14 there is a bloodstain she grasped when
  she was dying
The face of No. 15 had on an expression of when the freezer
  drawer was opening

No. 16 has an expression of one aflame for the last time then
    being put out
No. 17 continues to be absent
No. 18 has broken eggshells still stuck on his forehead
No. 19 has a face that hasn't detached the beast from a
    former life
No. 20 is licking the blood of the placenta with the caul
    covering him he is yet to be born

Portfolio of nine woodcuts with Urdu text printed in black on Okawara paper and mounted on Somerset paper. Edition of 20. Image size: variable. Sheet size: 16 x 14 inches (40.64 x 35.56 cm). 2003. © Zarina; Courtesy of the artist and Luhring Augustine, New York.

1.
2. 3.
4. 5.
6. 7.
8. 9.

Yes, Kafka's swamp takes on different forms: a flower, an eye of wisdom, a fire, mushrooms, Joseph and his brothers. These are all warm smooth objects with defined anatomies. Which is why, in Pepperstein's 2005 story "The Abstract Wars," forms and ideas were defeated by the waters after a long war. Which is why "The Birth of Venus" contains a reference to "The Black Star," a story Pepperstein wrote in 2010 about Californian cosmonaut Venus Kent, who died frozen upon reaching the cold center of the sun. This story sums up the curious relationship of Russian culture and Cosmism to black squares, swamps, black holes, the firmament (empty space without stars — the way Pepperstein sees it, Russians were cosmonauts; it was the Americans with their culture of celebrities who were astronauts because they loved the stars): "But in those times the Russians adored (as they still do now) darkness and mystery, and so they were attracted, not to the stars, but to the dark gaps between them. They were not drawn to the exceptional points, the sparkling and the shimmering; what lured them was the background itself, the boundless space of 'prostransvo', dark and amorphous, etc." In a small untitled work from that series, there is a vision of the absolute void that will appear in our world in the year 8888. Yesterday though I want to live in Uruguay who would not want to live in Uruguay? but I also want to live in Barcelona. For a little while just, I do not believe that that life has to be installed on one's desires; I also want to live in Ecuador, Cuenca. And I don't just long for a trip south. I just want to live a little remote surveillance, smoke, and mechanisms of Hell north. Now I know the taste. I dance, I laugh, I see friends like flowers. *Harman illustrates these relations with squiggly broken lines.* Is not it beautiful? It's like watching life being born in the middle of a Fukushima fuel pond. I love you, so I'm happy. Who don't I love? As many as 85 IP addresses connected to 1 Police Plaza altered Wikipedia entries for some of the most high-profile police abuse cases, including those for Eric Garner, Sean Bell, and Amadou Diallo, according to *Capital New York*. Edits have also been made to other entries covering NYPD, its stop-and-frisk program, and the department leadership. Example: "Garner raised both his arms in the air" was changed to "flailed his arms about." But don't worry, the matter is under "internal review." So justice will be served, right?

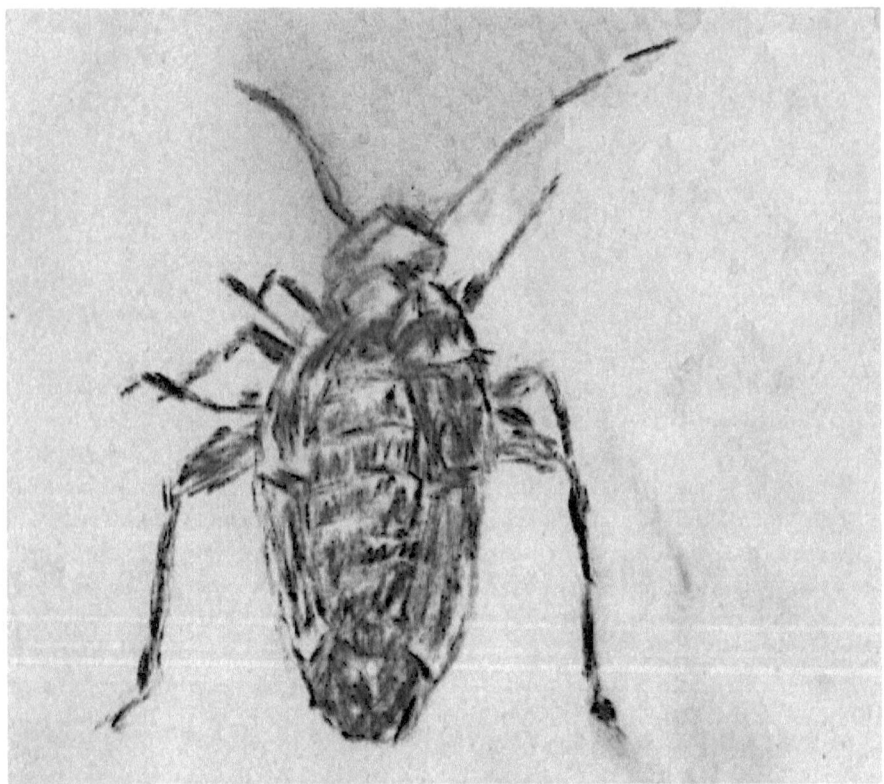

As with many historical pathology collections, UCL possesses its share of medical anomalies or curiosities. Fragments of preserved skin belonging to a tattooed man certainly seem to fall into the category of the anatomically curious – there is certainly nothing pathological about this specimen. But one of the biggest surprises I encountered during my visit to the collections was the revelation that the female reproductive anatomy actually can, and occasionally does, grow teeth. The specimen shown here is a dermoid cyst, or cystic teratoma, which has formed inside an ovary. When I first came across it, I didn't have to be a medical student to recognise that this tooth, entwined in long hair drifting in the liquid-filled vitrine, was out of place. One 1941 pathology text describes these tumours as follows: Dermoid cysts are usually globular in shape and dull white in color. They contain structures associated with epidermal tissues, such as hair, teeth, bone, sebaceous material resembling fat ... The following is a partial list of tissues which have been found in dermoids: Skin and its derivatives, sebaceous glands, hair, sweat glands, and bone, especially the maxillae containing teeth. Up to 300 teeth have been found in one cyst ... Long bones, digits, fingernails, and skull have been found. Brain tissue and its derivatives, intestinal loops, thyroid tissue, eyes, salivary glands, may occasionally be found. Even rudimentary fetuses have been described, such as a pelvis with hairy pubes and a vulva and clitoris. Brains with ventricles, spinal cords and a few complete extremities, have been observed. So is it any surprise that

> I have a bird in my head and a pig in my stomach
> And a flower in my genitals and a tiger in my genitals
> And a lion in my genitals and I am after you but I have a song
>   in my heart
> And my song is a dove
> I have man in my hands I have a woman in my shoes
> I have a landmark decision in my reason
> I have a death rattle in my nose I have summer in my brain
>   water
> I have dreams in my toes, etc?

Or that, in Ken Beckett's 1989 Color Dreams game, *Crystal Mines*, you control a cute little robot as he digs deep beneath a planet for crystals, avoiding and sometimes murdering the "alien" natives who get in his way? It is foretold that if you can collect and kill your way through 100 levels, you'll hit "the elusive mother lode of crystals which will make you a multi-quadrillionaire." In many parts of the internet, *Crystal Mines* is offered the damning honor of "the Color Dreams game that's actually fun." Even Dan Lawton, Color Dreams' founder and toughest critic, acknowledges a grudging respect for the game: "*Crystal Mines* was probably the best gameplay. It certainly got the best letters from buyers." So when it was time to start making Bible games, Lawton and company got to work adapting their cave crawler for the Christian bookstore set. The only problem was: There aren't any Bible stories about digging through caves and searching for treasure. So the team got creative. Wisdom Tree followed its hit, *Bible Adventures*, with a game called *Exodus*, which pretends to tell the Biblical story of Moses leading the Israelites out of Egypt and into the Promised Land. But in the actual gameplay, the Israelites are strangely absent, and you instead guide Moses through what appears to be an underground cave. That's because Exodus is the same game as *Crystal Mines*, reskinned and with new levels but with identical core mechanics. Here, the energy bursts become Ws that stand for "the Word of God," which you use to "stop the murmurings of the Israelites," represented in the game by square clods of dirt; to fight "doubting God," which is like the clods of dirt but is green and takes an extra hit to destroy; and to fight "obstacles to faith," which appear to be boulders. But don't worry, you also get to use your Word of God to kill plenty of soldiers, taskmasters, magicians, and sorcerers. The crystals are now replaced with manna, but here you also must locate all five of the question mark squares, which represent the Bible questions you'll be asked between the levels.

Speaking of such things,

If you stop me
from cutting
your hair,
there is a sense
in which
you are interfering.
*

But, since you are entitled
to determine
whether I cut your hair
or not, you do not
wrong me.
*

I make your trip to the store a waste.
*

I buy the last quart of milk
before you
get there.
*

But, this interference is not
a wrong.
I wrong you
if I interfere with your person—
pushing you out of the way as you
reach for the milk.
*

If I force you to work
for me
I wrong you.
*

Why don't we get together
and have me offer to cut your hair,
and you accept my offer.
*

You force me
to cut your hair,
while begging me
to stop
cutting your hair.
   *

If I were the superior
of a religious order
whose rule ordained
the complete
abnegation of all
desires, I could not
say to a novice
"If you have a desire to go to the largest
grocer in Oxford, go to Grimbly
Hughes"
for this would be contrary to the rule.
But I might very well say
"If you want to go to the largest grocer
in Oxford, go to Grimbly Hughes"
for this would simply be intended
to convey a piece of information
that the largest grocer
is Grimbly Hughes.
   *

If I have consented to have you
cut my hair
and change my mind
partway through,
you must stop.
There are no residual legal consequences.
   *

But when we get off the plane my little brother throws up
The long, long conveyor belt clatters along
Mother holds my brother covered in vomit
And walks along the conveyor belt with great speed
As the long, long conveyor belt clatters along
   *

The problem with this is that the other person may fill in the blank with the wrong noun. Here's an example from a conversation between George and me.

    George: I need … [He waves toward the table.]

Me: [Looking around] A napkin?

George: No, no. I need the black thing.

Me: The phone?

George: No, the water ...

Me: A glass of water? A black glass of water? [I have no idea what this means]

George: No, furry.

Me: A furry black glass of water? [Still confused]

George: No.

It takes one day and one night to reach immigration, the route is lined with many, many immigrants who have collapsed along the way and shriveled up, no matter how wealthy the country, they never make the path to immigration any shorter, their wealth won't help us, there is just sadness, curt answers and pain, immigration is nowhere in particular, and to make matters worse, there is no guarantee we'll make it through, my little brother doesn't notice but I do, our passports are bad, I had noticed that at immigration in every country, the men make mean faces and stare at their computers, that's 'cause our passports are bad, my little brother tried looking into the computer and got scolded, not just once, not just twice but more than that, the men point us to another window and mother leads us to one place after another, rushing us here and there. But does a city with no residents need public art? Absolutely, according to the University of New Mexico's Sherri Brueggemann, who first heard about the Center for Innovation, Testing, and Evaluation (CITE) plan last year. The project, which is equal parts science fiction and Sim City with a dash of Disney World, involves the construction from scratch of a full-scale, generic US city in the New Mexico desert that will be used by academics, developers, entrepreneurs, government agencies, and others to test new products and technologies, from smart grid power systems to unmanned trucks. The $1-billion, 26-square-mile urban laboratory, which is being developed by Pegasus Global Holdings and referred to as the "City Lab," will have a mall, airport, city hall, churches, power plant, highway, suburbs, townhouses, and downtown office buildings, but no inhabitants. The only people in its streets will be CITE's estimated 350 staff and the researchers making use of its facilities. Curious to know what kind of public art such a city should have, Brueggemann — who also manages Albuquerque's public art program — presented the problem to students in her art management class. Which just may be to say,

I saw a raven.
>O Raven! go on!

I saw a swan.
>O Swan! pass by!

If there was one, there were ten. If there were ten, there were twenty. We are not capable of time travel, says Maya, because we have yet to create the present. The last criminal is therefore given a slight reprieve, a conditional pardon contingent upon the convocation of zeros in series. Exeunt King Lear. Villon drives his dagger through the priest's ribs. The commandoes rappel into the fossil record. The rotation of the sphere of the heavens, plotted on the flat plate. Joined end to end, electrical current effectively travels in both directions at once; almost everything that has ever been said or thought or meant now and for some indeterminate future is floating out there, inside the calorimeter,

>while the little dude folded inside
>the parietal lobe gets lit up
>by a hundred theoretical knees and elbows, row on row
>of simulators for pulling, hauling, grinding, cutting, sorting,
>with average methods, converting
>the coordinated movements
>into an abstract energy
>that makes the giant's legs move
>on an unmarked plane, in a manner of speaking,
>as the giant has no body
>and no continuous extension,
>is perhaps not even a giant
>but rather a swarm
>small enough to fit inside the
>sliding cabinets of the things of this world,
>where their controls panels are
>easily accessible, though probably on fire
>also, and

AMP is BOOST
3160 PHOENIX LN 11-3
124
two stone heads turned in opposite directions is "GET DOWN GET DOWN" "GET DOWN GET DOWN" "GET DOWN GET DOWN"

After that they ask the question: *Rate your pain on a scale of 1 to 10?* I try to answer, but the correct answer is always "a-numerical." So yes, that IS a good question: I have plenty of worries about the world. But what concerns do I have about this text? So: I sat down to read *The Swerve* – or, I should say more accurately, to skim it. After all, it's 262 pages long (not including notes and selected bibliography) and I have a grant application to write and other "research points" to generate. But despite my best efforts to skim, I found myself reading every word, totally swept up in the exciting story of Poggio Bracciolini, the fifteenth-century Italian humanist and book collector. I relaxed and just went along with it; in other words, I read like a normal person. Poggio travels to far away monasteries and finds esoteric classical texts to have them recopied in beautiful humanist script. He finds this one poem by Lucretius, *De rerum natura, On the Nature of Things*, all outlined by Greenblatt in bullet points in one chapter: about how the universe is made up of atoms that swerve around and collide and create everything, and we can't really control it, and the gods don't care about us, souls don't exist, and so we should enjoy life and avoid pain – well, other stuff happens. The book reminded me so much of *The Name of the Rose*. And *The Da Vinci Code* series. Well. Criticisms of this book are not new. They are in many book reviews both in print and online. I am not going to rehearse all the things you can read in all the book reviews, as you can read them yourself. I am not a classicist or a philosopher, so I won't go into how actual philosophers point out that Epicureanism wasn't anywhere so widespread in the classical world, that Greenblatt vastly overinflates its influence both before and during the so-called Renaissance. I won't mention that in fact Scepticism and Platonism and Neoplatonism should evidently be a huge part of this story, though completely left out by Greenblatt. It's not my place to point out that the book conveniently disregards a key part of Epicureanism, *ataraxia*. And though I certainly could, I'm not going to get into the other Renaissances ignored in this book – the Carolingian Renaissance in the ninth century, and the twelfth-century renaissance in the … twelfth century. Also I won't talk about the old historian's Whig fallacy and the long debunked Burkhardtianism Greenblatt admits to following. Sadly, I won't have a chance to explain that no, medieval people were not all obsessed with pain, and yes, there was widespread, state-sanctioned embrace of enjoyment of the senses applying to every level of society, as our colleague Henning Laugerud's recent edited collections attest. And finally I don't have time to balance out the book's unbalanced exaggeration of medieval flagellation. Wait: Did you see what I just did there? That rhetorical move – *occupatio*: mentioning by saying I won't mention? Yes, that's a classical Latin rhetorical move used throughout the Middle Ages – a move I learned from Chaucer, by the way. But, for entirely other reasons, I've been looking at *In Parenthesis* for the first time in more than a while and, I have to report that what hit me is something Jones said in his Preface about the blood soaked gash that ran from Switzerland to the North

Sea. This observation struck me on the first reading as being a bit over-poeticised and far-fetched because it contradicted everything that I thought I knew about that terrain (mud, shattered bodies, barbed wire, shell craters, flesh, broken minds and more mud). Reading on I came to the realisation that *IP* is by far the most honest and least Cluttered with Hyperbole account that we have. This has been especially valuable for me personally as both my grandfathers were severely wounded during the Somme Offensive, a familial scar that has harrowed its way down the last century. Here's the quote: It was curious to know them harnessed together, and together caught in the toils of 'good order and military discipline'; to see them shape together to the remains of an antique regimental tradition, to see them react to the few things that united us – the same jargon, the same prejudice against 'other arms' and against the Staff, the same discomforts, the same grievances, the same maims, the same deep fears, the same pathetic jokes; to watch them, oneself part of them, respond to the war landscape, for I think the day by day in the Waste Land, the sudden violences and the long stillnesses, the sharp contours and unformed voids of that mysterious existence, profoundly affected the imaginations of those that suffered it. It was a place of enchantment. It is perhaps best described in Malory, book iv, chapter 15 – the landscape spoke 'with a grimly voice'. The road, broken though it was, seemed a firm causeway cutting determinedly the insecurity that lapped its path, sometimes the flanking chaos overflowed its madness, and they floundered in unstable deeps; chill oozing slime high over ankle; then they would find it hard and firm under their feet again, the mason work in good order, by some freak, intact. Three men sack-buskined to the hips, rose like judgement wraiths out of the ground where brickwork still stood and strewn red dust of recent scattering dry-powdered the fluid earth; and your nostrils draw on strangely pungent air. No sir – further on sir, but you'd better go by the trench, he's on this bit – yes to Pioneer Keep, then into the front line – it's right of this road – the OBL sir? – we stopt using it a week back sir, he knocked it flat when they went over from The Neb – you can chance the road sir, but he's on it – all the time – three of the Coldstreams, only yesterday – he's traversing now – better get in, sir. Before proceeding, it seems to me that it might be time for a digression on the subject of the authentic as touched on above. Regular readers will know that this reader has more than a few problems with the 'truth' and gets mildly angry when those who Should Know Better assert that poetry is best placed to provide us with access to this thing. Along with the late Richard Rorty, I'm of the view that we should be much less concerned with an abstract that Might not Exist and instead attend to things that might be useful or helpful. Which is to say, everyone has a favourite Chartist. For Dorothy Thompson, it was Feargus, always Feargus … though she always retained a soft spot for Ernest Jones. For Bob Fyson, it is those brave Potteries lads convicted on dodgy evidence & thrown into the nick in 1842 or, worse still, sent off as convicts to Van Dieman's Land … chaps like 'Daddy' Richards & William Ellis. For Owen

Ashton, it's the journalist W.E. Adams. There are two things Owen likes to do when we meet up for one of our periodic Chartist chats in Lichfield … quaff a cup of good coffee & have a chat about Adams, &, if both can be done at the same time, all the better. Adams was the first Chartist Owen wrote about & that is probably why he is his favourite. That's certainly the way it works for me. Thomas Cooper, the Leicester firebrand, was the first Chartist I wrote about. He became my favourite Chartist by accident. It was 1979. I was an undergraduate at Birmingham University, armed with a reading list for Dorothy Thompson's special subject on Chartism. In my encounters with it, the cataloguing system in the UL generally got the better of me. I couldn't find any of the books on the reading list. Well, I could find one: *The Life of Thomas Cooper, Written by Himself*, 1872. So that would have to do. I sat down on a large pile of cushions that I used as a chair, put Wings' new album 'Back to the egg' on & started reading. 10 minutes later … The opening chapters describing Cooper's early years as an earnest autodidact in Lincolnshire are just so good. I gave a seminar paper on Cooper. I wrote an essay on him in my finals. I wrote a hundred-thousand-word thesis on him. Surely, I was done with Cooper? I was not. He continued to look over my shoulder, demanding I write a book about him. I tried to fob him off by sticking a picture of him on the front of a book he wasn't even in. It did no good. I had to write that book. Twenty-nine years after I first met Thomas Cooper I released his biography. The last chapter of *The Chartist Prisoners* is the best thing I have ever written, or probably ever will. So yes, RED JUICE is threaded through with a chthonic feminist mysticism, or, as Jen Coleman puts it,

> This krill is neritic
> a vertical migrator
> neritic
> a vertical migrator
> a vertical migrator
> a vertical migrator
> neritic
>
> This krill is circumpolar
> in and below the thermocline
> not a vertical migrator
> two vertical migrators
> neritic
>
> This krill is above the thermocline
> a circumpolar vertical migrator
> three vertical migrators
> a strong vertical migrator

> This krill is a vertical migrator
> a vertical migrator
> above the thermocline
> in and above the thermocline
> neritic
> circumglobal.

Meanwhile, in small towns across America, manly men are customizing their jacked-up diesel trucks to intentionally emit giant plumes of toxic smoke every time they rev their engines. They call it "rollin' coal," and it's something they do for fun. Which is why, in my translation of Kim Hyesoon's "I'm Ok, I'm Pig,"

> ㅋ is q
>
> q = enriched squeals
>
> qqqq☐

Which is to say that, besides rolling smoke, the US has bombed over thirty countries since 1945. So

> Who knows, really?
>
> What might ammonia taste like
> On a different tongue?

Enter wired cave, evade plasma network, insert yourself into the center well & ascend. What cities, what tents, what good bad trash therein? What fat seams, lean streaks? Be bold, bring first fruit you find therein. Now is the time to mine the first grapes before the apocalyptic living creatures ever again are herded into their waste eating habit. Go where the brook branches & cut pages with grape-clusters & bare it on a yoke. Return after 40 hours & speak of coal & gas & black shakes & yellow cake. Besides the things that we have heard and seen, / Recounts most horrid sights seen by the watch. / A lioness hath whelped in the streets, / And graves have yawned and yielded up their dead; / Fierce fiery warriors fight upon the clouds, / In ranks and squadrons and right form of war, / Which drizzled blood upon the Capitol; / The noise of battle hurtled in the air, / Horses did neigh and dying men did groan, / And ghosts did shriek and squeal about the streets. / O Caesar! These things are beyond all use, / And I do fear them. / Once most handles were made of wood / Now handles include bulbous, ergonomically suitable somethings / fashioned from the same piece of steel, so in the long run it is not possible here to walk side by side /

as the blade itself, as well as traditional shapes in materials like Corian / or even pairs of lovers who in summer come to search the dome for some coolness / have to walk in line behind each other. *All the vegetables need to be cut to about the same dimensions as the bean sprouts. The thin-sliced pork should be seasoned with salt and sake and fried first. Then you warm some chopped garlic over a low heat to release the flavor, before turning the heat up to full and adding the seasonings one at a time to the pan and flash frying. Once the meat changes color, there's no time to lose. You toss in the shiitake, carrots, bean sprouts, cabbage, bamboo shoots, and yellow chives, then add the cellophane noodles reconstituted in hot water — of course you have to cut them to the right size, otherwise they'll be unmanageable — and splash with water, and flavor with Chinese soup stock and yuzu-flavored soy sauce. Of course you can sweeten it with sugar or mirin, but I prefer the flavor to be a little tart, the same way I like adding a little vinegar to yakisoba or fried rice vermicelli, and I found it to be surprisingly simple and tasty like this.* Turning the pages, a passage titled "Shiitake" caught his eye and his hand paused. *The botanical name for shiitake is* Lentinula edodes, *and because "edodes" sounds like "Edo desu" ("This is Edo") some people have said it's from the Japanese, but actually it comes from the Greek* εδωδιμος *meaning "edible." I find those rounded Greek letters charming, somehow. I particularly like those two deltas that look like ladles. But more than ladles, they look like mushrooms — upside-down mushrooms. And the fact that there are two of them side-by-side is really cute. It wouldn't be so appealing if there was only one of them. Maybe I liked them so much because of a story I read when I was little. It was called "Little Miss Mushroom," about a little girl called Mushroom who gets lost in the forest and meets another Mushroom who looks just like herself. Little Miss Mushroom had short brown hair with red ribbons in it, but I'm convinced she was a shiitake. Two shiitake together are really cute. If I could go back in time to another age, I think I'd choose to go back to the time when I was a shiitake.* Taihei couldn't get his head around the idea that there had been a time when his own wife had been a shiitake. Yes, and mirrors turn red when menstruating women look at them. So was it true, that the air after i came outside smelled like a weird leaf?

A minty cloggy warm vaporub
tigerbalm leaf. stuffed up your
when youre just giddy being
in their aura i think
its okay (i mean its
not lol) but aaaahhhhh!!! and
the moon was out, less
than a curved half. im
glad there are people that
fuck me up that intensely.
thats a very good thing.
and!!! i asked what about
nonwestern music as a formal
system? & everyone started talking
at me about Iranian / etc
music. persian scales have quarter

tones. Bwaaaaaaa "EYEBALL'D" HAIRY NIGHT <FELT> / / ... is this a gated garden is this ambivalent is this a penultimate river /this is a mutant form of something I've seen before, leave it / / ... is this or isn't it a way of changing perception is this in order, is this the order / or is it ordinary in the half-light or it is revolting ... it is molting it is releasing some shimmering body into the hands of the state." Annie Bethell, volunteer programme manager, said afterwards she was weary but elated. "We sort of exceptionally jokingly said, 'Oh let's take a look at just how long the file is', and it escalated from there." What escalated?

BEAST BEATS SELF AGAINST CRUSTAL EARTH.

BEAST EATS MONEY, SHITS GOLD.

BEAST EATS SMALLER (OR LARGER), DUMBER BEATS.

BEAST GETS A NECKLACE & IS BEAT, ADORNED.

BEAST PAWS SATIN, CHEWS MUD. BEAST SHEDS, SWEATS, SPITS, FUCKS SWOONS.

"THIS IS THE FOREST"

What is left "trumps a psychological truth no trumpet relentless no weary shall no shelter." That's when I notice that they all clutch their purses as I walk by, then realize why as I catch a glimpse of myself in the reflective façade of the Bank of China tower. Of course, this is all clearly indicative of the hard work that Neil Diamond has put in to reach such a stage where not only are thousands of his fans admiring him every single day, but also that his fans come together to showcase their love for him. Gisele Bundchen. It allows sufficient for a few of their smaller sized publications and enough to not obtain in the means. Contrary to popular belief, it is actually easier than it sounds, and can even simulate your creative juices into overdrive. Counterfeiters would normally not concern themselves with the interior; they use cheap tan or brown or even plastic. *"The government basically panicked," said Dr. Mohan Doss, a medical physicist who spoke at the Tokyo meeting, when I called him at his office at Fox Chase Cancer Center in Philadelphia. "When you evacuate a hospital intensive care unit, you cannot take patients to a high school and expect them to survive."*

    Next trains to White Plains?
    Train to White Plains?
    When is White Plains?
    Could you tell me where the restroom is?

Are there lockers? Where do you put your stuff?
12:48 to Poughkeepsie?
I am in a hurry PLEASE tell me where to get the 11:48 to Poughkeepsie! I am in a hurry!
Could you tell me where the restroom is?
What's the history of Grand Central?
Sir, hello. How are you? Could you tell me how do I get to 190th Street?
When is the next train to Harrison?
Yes, um, in which location are the restrooms?
Could you tell me WHY you told me my train was on track 11 when it was on track 23? Why would you do that?
Train track for Riverdale?
Is there a restroom?
Which one express to Stamford?
You provide tickets on the train right? How much more are they?
What time's New Rochelle?
Can I get to the Mets stadium?
Just checking the 5:15 to Kingston?
How you doin' Michael Jordan Steakhouse?
Is there really no 5:25 to Catona today?
You guys have a schedule that's 4 days old and it's wrong it's wrong and that's on you!
Can I borrow that pen for a minute?
Is there a bathroom in here?
Hi, we're going up to Citifield, what's a …?
Do you have like just a subway map?
What about Rye?
To get to the F subway I just walk up a couple blocks, right?
What times the Bridgeport?
When's the next New Haven?
Do you know when the next Ossining?
Can you tell me the next train coming in here from southeast I think number 3077?
It's really strange you must have bathroom but I don't see.
How ya doin? New Rochelle?
Next train to New Haven?
Can I use a senior fare in prime time?
Is there any kind of bathroom nearby?
Next time Bridgeport?
Next train to Ossining hello? Next train to Ossining?
Train to Croton where's that?
Tarrytown?
Fairfield?
Ossining?

Trains from Fairfield what platform are they in coming on?
Next train to New Rochelle?
Scuze me when is the next train to Beacon?
How do you get to Southeast? Like Catona?
Do you have any Metro-North ticket machines I can buy tickets on?
I'm trying to get to Long Island?
I want to go to here.
Do you know where I go for this?
5:19 stopping at Verdis?
Next train to Yonkers?
5:23 to Yonkers?
Can I get a tour of this place?
Do you have a pen by any chance?
Can I ask you a question? I bought these tickets and I just want to make sure it works both ways?
Where do you get Metro-North tickets it doesn't say?
How do you go about getting tickets for the subway?
Next train to Larchmont?
Can you help me?
Can you tell me the train from Brewster where it will arrive?
Will this ticket work?
Hey what track is the 3:10 to Stamford?
Can you help me I think I missed my train?
Hi I need to get to the Hilton Hotel and it's between West 54th and I don't know.
Next train to Darien?
Next train to Stamford?
Do you have a phonebook?
Do you have a subway map?
How do I get to Poughkeepsie?
When's next to Croton?
Do you have subway map?
Express to Stamford please?
Hi what time is considered peak?
Can you please tell me if I buy my ticket on the train to Connecticut if I buy it on the train will they charge me extra for buying it on the train?
Next express to Stamford?
What's the schedule?
Can I get a map of Manhattan from you?
Hi whereabouts do you get a schedule for the subway?
Where do I get a ticket for Stamford?
Is there Amtrak here?
When's the next express to Milford?
Scuze me what track is going to Tarrytown?

Do you have subway tickets?

Cold Spring New York?

Uummm ... I need underground train to umm Columbus Circle what is the number of the track?

I just need the schedule for New Haven like Stamford and all of them?

Hi I was here once before and there was a place like echoes or something?

Where's Junior's restaurant?

Is there a place to get her down to the food court with her walker she needs an elevator or something?

Can I get a Hudson line schedule and three New Havens?

Do you have the full schedule?

I have a quick question, Bedford, did Mariah Carey live there?

I'm going to Bedford Hills?

Pleasantville?

White Plains how much to get there? And Stamford anything around there?

You know which track Dobbs Creek is?

You gave me that nice little green paper about the Brewster to Danbury connection express and I lost it because I'm a man.

Can I get a ticket here?

Where'm I going, Yonkers?

Hello sir I'm trying to get to Dunhill Road?

Do you have a big schedule like that?

Do you have that kind of detailed timetable to New Haven?

Harrison?

Hi if I wanted get a train to Fairfield?

I need to buy metrocards?

Is track 182 upstairs or downstairs?

Does the Graystone stop at Spuytin Duyvil?

Next train to Yonkers please?

There's a 5:40 to Baystone do you know what track its on?

To get to Catona can I get the 5:32?

Hi dear the next train to Westport is 5:34?

Track to Bridgeport?

Where's the tiffany glass?

Hi can I ask you a question?

Hi I need some orientation help?

We need your master plan sir?

What times Peekskill?

Where's the bathroom?

You know the monitor downstairs doesn't work its kind of like out of its ... so you can't see like Pleasantville?

I missed it, what next?

Still, it's an aggregator, like a new dead sun or the psychic self-storage facilities behind the Jumbotron: we reject as false the choice between red wine or white people, the gathering momentum of a blue-ribbon commission's mild reprimand, checked by the bright, vacant rhetoric of this special moment: oh hope! oh pure form of sensible intuition! oops! we once thought that there was more to life than breathing carbon emissions through the holes in our faces and we were right though the details have yet to be deciphered or disclosed or — a gathering sense that what keeps us from a loving and intimate knowledge of capital aitch History is something like attorney-client privilege on a scale that humbles the concept of scale. Who knew what when Jasper? My lover's skin is like an iPhone's screen, the primal scenes swimming behind the cloud of links, the fissures in the heraldic orders of the day, no way yeah way, except when you accidentally order "pizza" and then you wake up and have to go to work. There is no telling where the taproot of absolute knowledge will surface next, in a death metal taco truck conference on communist individuation, careening through the chocolate jello at three or four mph, entelechy's like that. But poetry can be a companion to these activities, as the "Riot Dog" of Athens was a companion in streets. A dog, too, might start barking when the cops are about to kick down your door. Perhaps that's it, for now, what we're doing, what is to be done, with poetry. Some barking. Some letting you know that the cops are at the door. They've been there for a while. Third of all. It keeps busy. It makes ships of a size called Malaccamax. It makes endless small plastic representations of the African jungle or plains animals and fish ingest them and vomit them up or don't and there they sit in their stomachs and then they die. But back to pizza: "In optimum conditions all pizza would be served within 30 seconds and 30 feet of its point of departure from the pizza oven," writes pizza expert Daniel Young in our new book *Where to Eat Pizza*. "Fresh is best. But most people live in houses and apartments, not ideal worlds. Many wish to receive their pizza within 10 seconds and 10 feet (3 meters) of their living-room couch. That's why the real world needs pizza boxes. They've facilitated the great luxury of warm pizza in your home, at work, or parked outside a packed pizzeria with too long a wait for a table. "If you're going to do pizza you have to have boxes," says chef-restaurateur Jon Shook, one half of Jon & Vinny's pizza restaurant in Los Angeles. During the 1950s take-out pizzas were delivered in paper bags and flimsy cardboard boxes. However, most pizza historians agree that the corrugated corrugated cardboard pizza box which we know and love today was developed in the early 1960s by the American pizza chain Domino's. Then, as now, they were flat packed and foldable, with air vents to release steam. Hot pizza transported in them can still suffer from sogginess over time, as moisture and cardboardy flavor are slowly absorbed. Even so, their value as conveyors of convenience is undeniable. What's maybe more difficult to swallow are claims that pizza boxes are works of art. "The surface of a pizza box is perhaps the most overlooked artistic medium of the past century," insists Scott Wiener, so yes, when Dionne Brand writes, she writes the land. Her *Land to Light On* is a map. But this map does not easily follow existing cartographic rules, borders, and lines. *Land to Light On* provides a different geographic story, one which allows pavement to answer questions, most of the world to be swallowed up by a woman's mouth, and Chatham, Buxton (Ontario sites haunted by the underground railroad) to be embedded with Uganda, Sri Lanka, slave castles, and the the way Sarah Vaughan enters and exist a phrase. And Brand gives up on land, too. She not only refuses a comfortable belonging to nation, or country, or a local street, she alters them by demonstrating that the material world is infused with sensations and distinct ways of knowing: rooms full of weeping, exhausted countries, a house that is only as safe as flesh. Fourth of all. You know: *it*. The *it* that seems to be nothing but the doing of the world. As in *it's* raining. It's Raining Men is a moment of happiness within the misanthropocene. Fifth of all. But then there is this other rain tilting in to soak vast acres of eurodollars and we call this west melancholy. Oh to eye the very enfilade through which that orchidaceous entity would make his stately progress, clad only in a Japanese robe and snake-skin (well a whole snake, actually, a living piece of jewelry coiled around his neck). What a beguiling, repellent aroma he must have trailed: opium, incense, booze, rare blooms and reptile excreta. None of them did anything too evil, but there were many objects broken or missing the next day. (The missing performers will be missing only for the ones who wanted them there.) "Will you have a hernia?" say James and Justin in unison. "So select. I salute you." "Revoke it all." "Haze and ransom." *Listen* plunging to a register low down the throat. *Tadpole*, noun. To meddle quietly with the purpose of faltering without a fuss. Types of nomads that travel from waterhole to waterhole. James's hand forms a mudra as he passes the string along. Xavi winds it up and it falls across his nose. Alison overheard her daughter Jessica naming colors of yarn while knitting. Find something that you like in the street and give it away. Beans, duh! Brown, brown, brown, red, green, white, white. What's Steve gonna do with his beans? Red, white, red, red, red. He's shaking them in jars. Brown pinto beans in a glass jam jar have the highest pitch, green lentils in a plastic jar the lowest. Red plinks, white jangles. Red is fast! *Pinks* — thank you for using that word. In this way we cannot conquer, which makes me glad. To be explicit, my childhood was plenty curly. Curly enough. We made nougat out of the jubilant festering weather. Morgan says *electricity* with rising intonation. Xavi has his *Turbo* symbol in white masking tape on his black sweatshirt. Inside the stomach of the cardboard giant, my 11-year-old daughter does ... what? To quote Sun Ra, Once I had something like a vision, and I saw a sky like that ... it was red and it was purple, could have been day but it seemed to be night ... and then in some way I called down some flying saucers and they landed, they landed. They went straight to the library and copied this from Calvert Watkin's book

HOW TO KILL A DRAGON IN INDO-EUROPEAN:
A CONTRIBUTION TO THE THEORY OF THE FORMULA

IV. The Basic Formula and Its Variants in the Narration of the Myth

27. Preliminaries, 297
28. The root *gu hen-: Vedic han-, 304
29. The root *gu hen-: Avestan jan-, 313
30. The root *gu hen-: Hittite kuen- and the Indo-European theme and formula, 321
31. The slayer slain: A reciprocal formula, 324
32. First variant: The root *udeh-, 330
33. 'Like a reed': The Indo-European background of a Luvian ritual, 335
34. Second variant: the root *terh2-, 343
35. Latin tarentum, the ludi saeculares, and Indo-European eschatology, 347
36. The myth in Greece: Variations on the formula and theme, 357
37. Expansion of the formula: A recursive formulaic figure, 370
38. Herakles, the formulaic hero, 374
39. Hermes, Enualios, and Lukoworgos: The Serpent-slayer and the Man-slayer, 383
40. Nektar and the adversary Death, 391
41. The saga of Iphitos and the hero as monster, 398

42. The name of Meleager, 408
43. The Germanic world, 414
44. Thor's hammer and the mace of Contract, 429

V. Some Indo-European Dragons and Dragon-Slayers

45. Fergus mac Leti and the muirdris, 441
46. Typhoeus and the Illuyankas, 448
47. Python and Ahi Budhnya, the Serpent of the Deep, 460
48. Azi dakaka, Visvarupa, and Geryon, 464

So yes, Jarry died fortified in 1907, not getting to see the publication of *Deeds and Opinions of Dr. Faustroll* (Zon Mo ebi us A raí zof his lect ura, their long sadm anger dor is that RRA npon erin sea cha one hundred cia Call ada, invents well the Patafí music, Science the solution is imagin arias what otorg to Simbolic ament and to the delineations of bodies the properties of objects described by their virtuality. From this obr to fundacio nal school Pata defined physical com or socieda d learned and useless dedicate to the study of imaginary solutions. The College has had illustrious members, among which include Raymond Queneau, Jacques Prévert, Max Ernst, Eugene Ionesco, Joan Miró, Boris Vian, Marcel Duchamp, Jean Dubuffet, René Clair, among others. Here Boris Vian, Jacques Prévert and his cat Labyronette hosted the festivities higher the College and more precisely all celebrating the Baron Mollet). "Holes, Nadas and Mirages". Relationship is metempsychosis, then. All passes — all perfume, yes. My everyday work with pure relations of karma and the cathode ray convinces me of this. They are a translation of Blake's

> There is a Grain of Sand in Lambeth that Satan cannot find
> Nor can his Watch Fiends find it: tis translucent & has many
> > Angles
> But he who finds it will find Oothoons palace, for within
> Opening into Beulah every angle is a lovely heaven

… by which I mean no further details are necessary, so long as we've EVERY LAST ONE OF US been paying even a modicum of attention given our attention disorders and all. Which is to say that now, it seems more and more obvious that our time is not one of strong answers. It is rather a time of strong questions and weak answers. This is so because our time is witnessing "a" or "the" – who knows? – crisis of the hegemony of the sociocultural paradigm of western modernity. It is characteristic of a transitional time to be a time of strong questions and weak answers. Given the global reach of this paradigm, brought about by colonialism and imperialism, this transition is present, under different forms, everywhere, even though the questions and answers vary from culture to culture, from world region to world region. But the discrepancy between the strength of the questions and the weakness of the answers seems to be the same everywhere.

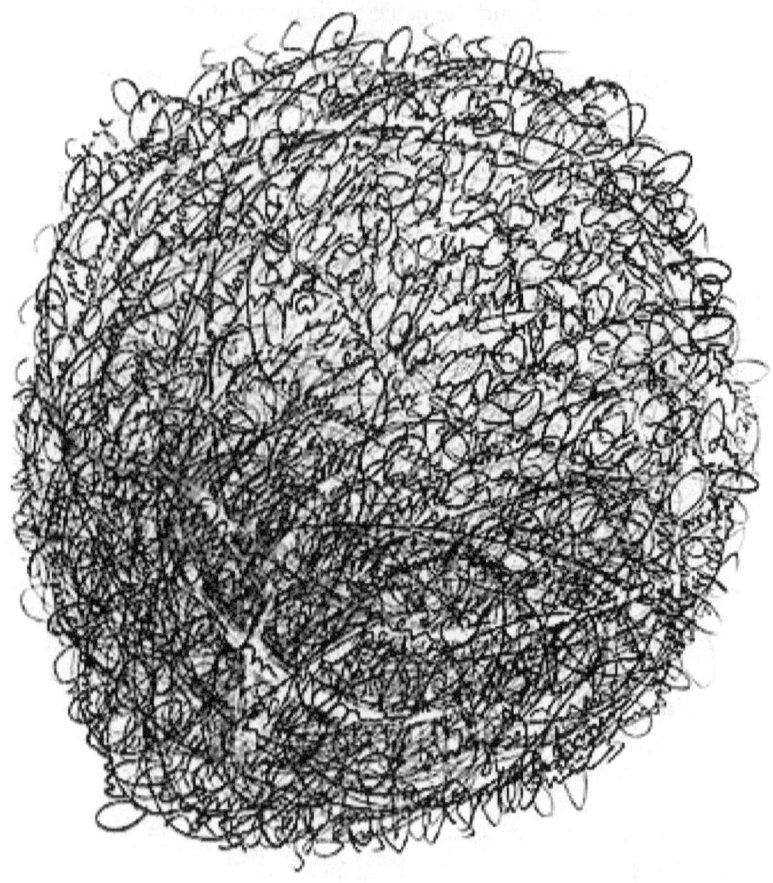

And so indeed have we come to see ourselves predicted as the outcome of our incommensurate acts — marginal waves / nested in waveness / The triangle dilated / — / the voracious snake / The narrow eye, / or, as in one of the Upanishads, a little thumb. So please now tell everyone that the self is a little thumb! I also like to think of it as poverty, as I say in my poem "Lady Poverty" in *Mysteries of Small Houses*. But then I obviously mean "soul" more than "self", I mean, in fact, in fact the idea of faking your own location through attaching your GPS anklet to a Roomba, for example, and letting it wander around the house all day is probably useless but also just so great. Which is to say, it had many functions, among these the one that translated "virus" into "sick room architectures. So we walked through stores while she wept. We sat in the middle of the mall while she wept. We went to a discount store, and I told her I would just pick out shoes for her because she wept too much to try on shoes. In the car I wanted to weep, too, but she said to me 'I am still a child and am learning to control my impulses and emotions. You have had many years of dreams and realities to learn from so there is no excuse for you to cry.' she paused. 'Do you have enough dreams?' she finally asked. Then again – how often do you get to read about airliners being brought down with static electricity shot from a rabbit's paw? Thus the design specs for his recovery: a 15 × 15 outdoor room with a perimeter of medium-height pines, inside of these pines a hospital bed and an eight-foot flat-screen TV.

>   So why won't somebody write another Art of Laughing?
>   Cuz they're all orange-colored and poisoned by oxygen.
>
>   Something like that swab jammed up
>   my urethra –
>
>   escarpment; ditch; town; champagne; dimity;
>   the sailor, drowned or not, was probably lost to them.
>
>   They fell asleep again and died like saints,
>   having demonstrated the physical properties.
>
>   What a quag!
>   The snow is dark and nothing is sad and I was, once upon a
>   time,
>
>   not only graceful,
>   I knew the living must communicate with life
>
>   because I lived near the signal tower,
>   a decrepit trumpet,
>
>   h t boet ies at act s rs w p ed I pla c.
>   This is the grammatical function of the eye.
>
>   OUT OF THE WHOLE AZALEA:
>   *and signs*, he said, *the many signs I plant in asphalt.*
>
>   Soon the whole town was camped outside.
>   An election was decided by three votes.
>
>   Mr. Ed – yes, that Mr. Ed – worked for the CIA and ordered
>   JFK's assassination.
>   US horses are fed mind-controlling chemicals.
>
>   At the wedding there weren't many guests.

Visible ones, anyway.

Sushi. Sushi. Volvo.
But the ooze swims with cockeyed worms.

And the stick stirs paint.
What can we do?

"The tables are turning and dancing on their heads. Everything everyone break open faces split up laugh suns fire

      fire arses expel
      shit mouths speak.

Everything and everyone that went in to be concealed
      beneath a surface come out not as ghosts but as

      fleshly fucking human flesh.
Objects, show your intestines!

Shake, dead international waiting staff!
Flesh and blood appear every thing matter matter matter full-

> on mutilated bodies in head-storm matter.
>
> Ground, unearth the dead died.
> Faces, explain your surfaces, explain the labour of your mum
>
>> and the historical dust that went into your bloodied
>> body brain."
>
> (Well they say God does not give wings to scorpions).
> "Make a prompt a foursquare then the squares collapse as
>
>> separates but other than before till work is made to
>> disappear to register its fields as your hand is my pocket.
>
> I'm a pocket man. Your
> hand is in my pocket. I
>
> fix broken rockets.
> My reasons turn your snows to green,
>
> what sound sounds like. Is Wittgenstein silent
> on love or just muted?"
>
> 12:02 a.m. Violation of the city noise ordinance.
> See if the janitor has the key to open these doors.

So. These are the Pharoah's life & death guys. These are his guys of life & death, the certainty of making his decisions bursts from their skin every second & every second of that second, ad infinitum like: these guys are the full beauty of the Pharoah's decisions. You may die but it will be the perfect call. You may live & it will be the perfect call. Everyone is happier when they discover it's a test you can't fail. Everyone is happier, meeting those guys in the market place. Their tread – light, active, gracile, musical – is a measure. They know the date of birth, they know – within one glowing week, give or take a percentage not even the Pharoah can calculate – the day of death. Some things can not be known, & they glint with the mischief of admitting that. The corner of their eye glints with the delight of the mischief of the residue that can't be known. No one knows when they die, those angel guys, & they keep that residue of laughter all their days. They are the guys of the Pharoah who lives in the dark in the pyramid, in the liquid actuarial core of all things sublunary. So yes, ARMED CELL 2 also included my first presentation from my long poem The Totality Cantos: Relaxation churches unintentionally restructuring mastery exception / Known cultural able-bodied simple plutocratic proportion dualism energy / Home death tendency novelty alliance guard failure overstressed /

Predicative / Old world-laden frustration copy act around return coterie rebellion / Available earth interlocutors moderate fashion emperor / Better bland origin / Restless gunpowder disemboweling hierarchy philosophy / Pagan century party withdrawn / Difficulties stirred / Hand introduction symbol man storms paradigm conference / School portrays / Made rights dealt disparate poetry counties / Temporal intelligence number. The poem is open to some subset of the totality of discourses in one hundred cantos of one hundred lines each. Every line is a complete poem. Every set of ten lines consists of lines of one through ten words long and aligned flush left and to nine indentations in order to create dynamic rhythm and spacing (not shown here). Every length and alignment occurs before being repeated in the next set. In the transition between sets, equal lengths and alignments are prevented from being adjacent in order to maintain dynamic continuity. Lines traverse discourses: each canto is differently constituted by fifteen vocabularies from the totality of discourses. The fifteen vocabularies are organized into five groups of three: two tertiary groups, two secondary groups, and a primary group designating the dominance of each group in the canto. In the poem's transformation across cantos, groups emerge and ascend the hierarchy, dominate, then descend and disappear, each group getting its dominant canto in combination with subordinate groups. Three hundred vocabularies, one hundred groups of three, are drawn from in total. Names are suppressed in order to decenter attention toward vocabularies. Every canto breaks down into sections delineated by flush left lines; this excerpt presents two sections (not distinguished here). Any section can be excerpted as a dynamic totality and connected to any other in order to assemble new combinations as long as equal lengths and alignments are not adjacent. Which is to say that she is appearing in the art world / scene having just had major surgery and I'm actually "mentoring" with her, that is, as you know, I have a neurological Parkinsonian-like condition called Dystonia and I shake and twist and my head turns and I spasm in pain and it is totally embarrassing until I do my 3087 spiritual and art practices of EXPOSING MY BODY-FLESH AS ART-LIFE by calling every moment of every day ART as Carolee is doing. She is now my TEACHER, teaching me not to hide my visibly compromised (health) LIFE because everything is exactly what it is anyway. That's what I've always said but often I'm embarrassed by my "condition" and get caught in non-ART / non-LIFE. I need to practice what I preach and Carolee is showing me how to do it so gracefully and matter of factly, not as her performance artist persona but as a creative "lifeist," a term I use to differentiate a form of yellow electricity which activates the cream packed hard around the nerves. A conference, that is. On the podium is a poster I made for the event as part of my responsibilities as Hospitality Agent for the Association for Feral Cousins and Associates of All Kinds. It is a quote from Theresa Cha. [WAIT – I cut and pasted in the Facebook comment below – and now I can't figure out how to exit the pale blue box. I will continue on with my decompressions in another post. This post is expelling me, as if to say, you can't continue to write, in formal or semi-formal ways or utterly informal, about what happened "to you." Or what didn't happen. Or what happened to someone else. Christ.]

But we did not veer. We gored through Idaho in a maroon Chevy with Texas plates. On the way back, we live-tweeted the baby alpaca rolling in the muddy paddock, and so on. In a Facebook comment thread, Lisa Robertson remarked upon the connection to Jalal Toufic's work; I told Randall about Jalal Toufic and he said: "Okay." It is hard to accurately portray the way he said it, but it was a good okay. Basically, Randall, an MFA student in Wyoming, received feedback on his ideas, and the context of his ideas, from Lisa Robertson in FRANCE – during the road trip. Randall's idea was "Accept the death you know is coming even though you're already dead." So this was what he said as we re-entered Wyoming:

> Kindly do not forsake this world of jack,
> this world, our steady candy in which we don't do

jack. Is there a one who
would not hang with us, who

would not instant merge, ride up,

and swallow
whole the highs and lows, who
would not sing and stroke the other along, back and forth,
    along
the spine, along the branes and sticky chords and little
    universes

ah, hairs on me, always sprouting growing and burning and
    then growing again

and the branches shook the lights out
and the fish to be sold had their heads intact
and the highway expanded into four lanes
and the garlic blossomed in June
and this should not trouble us

Too romantic, try again

I forgot to throw out the meat and the air stinks

Better

and the cars piled atop each other
and the hospital added a wing
and the soup congealed in the refrigerator
and the garage opened manually

and the grease lined the pan evenly
and the carnations were dipped in food color
and the onion grass covered the walkway
and the starfish dried out in the sun

in the same light Romain Crelier's *La Mise en Abîme* uses to get two shallow pools of used motor oil to reflect the interior of Bellelay Abbey's 12th century church. Before long, he's quoting Miles, she's talking atoms and sonic resonance; they get into Russian minimalism and the difference between Buddhist monks and Sufi dervishes; they talk paneroticism and about how art comes from the future. By the end they're both using a lot of ALL CAPS if they use caps at all, and many exclamation points!!!! So talking about the possibility of talking about it is actually much more like sort of talking about it in that way, you see, rather than going 'Specify, specify.' His voice had a quiet urgency to it but his fingers quivered and flew near his face, like he was swatting at little birds. My spoken narrative tells the story of a mother and her child, until I replace the word 'child' with 'cancer' and we realise that it was cancer all along, growing inside her, taunting her, and warning her. The opening of the spoken version goes like this:

> Before being born, the child asks his mother:
> How much pain are you willing to experience?
>
> The pregnant woman already knows what it is to be
> flogged, spanked, whipped and corporally punished.
>
> "I'll show you how bad it can be," her unborn son says.
> "Santa Claus doesn't exist," she replies, "Ouch! Are you
>   stamping your little foot?"

In sign language I can show the thing inside Kathy (Kathy A) without naming it as either a child or cancer, and I can give it a personality. I can become this thing and speak to Kathy from inside her body. It is nearly impossible to transcribe sign language. Elements such as sign speed, facial expression and the positioning of characters are invisible in written English without some kind of crazy great typography. However, I enjoy just writing out the translation for the signs in the order they occur in BSL as it demonstrates the different syntax and some elements of how the language functions:

> CANCER/BABY: You ready pain you?
> Kathy: What?
> CANCER/BABY: You ready pain?
> KATHY: Been pain! Been flogged, spanked, whipped, bound, been!
> CANCER/BABY: Me: Worse.
> KATHY: No no no. You: nothing.
> like Father Xmas, fairies, angels, God: nothing
> Same you: nothing.
>
> *It kicks her*
> Ouch! Painful!
> Fine.
>
>   *The doors to the hospital open;*
>   *The doors to the body open.*

What this doesn't enable me to portray is the character of the thing inside her, and the personality of Kathy. Aspects such as speed, and size of gesture and facial expression, time and placement become a part of 'writing', forcing me to expand what 'writing' might be, to choreograph language on my feet. One of my favourite moments to sign in the above is 'Me: Worse', because the sign, with little fingers (little fingers = bad in BSL) and the speed at which the hands move apart from each other gives a sense of how bad something is, how pain is prolonged, how the creature takes pleasure in pain, and through the angle of my body and gaze, I can show that I am looking up at Kathy from inside her body. In the sign language version, I had to commit to Kathy being in a place, I became Kathy standing outside of a hospital in the rain, not wanting to go in, being taunted by the thing inside her and finally giving up and entering the hospital. While my written narrative ignored the actual hospital, the corridors and the lights overhead, all of these were placed in the sign language. I became Kathy, lying on a bed and then became a doctor looking down at her. My doctor carried a file under his arm and signed in an uptight, stuck up kind of way, peering at her over his nose. The doctor tells her they need to remove one of her breasts by grabbing it, slicing with the other hand, then chucking it over his shoulder, in three fast movements. To Kathy, this action demonstrates the disdain he feels for women – a further translation of the line 'he likes to hurt women' from *Fifty Shades of Grey*. This section is even more challenging to represent in English. In fact, rather than 'doors go past, lights go past' I become Kathy, I use my hands to show the passing of doors on either side of her as she is rolled down a corridor. I use italics in a similar way to how stage directions are used in playwriting, to denote action, with the bracketed italics giving further context. Non-italics are representations of the direct signs (equivalent to speech):

> *Kathy is lying on a hospital bed*
> *rolling down a long corridor*
> *doors go past*
> *lights go past*
> *she squints, it's hard to see.*
>
> *Blue eyes stare at her*
> *6 blue eyes 3 doctors*
>
> DOCTOR: We're all going to die.
> KATHY: What?
> DOCTOR: We're all going to die. Some will die soon, some later.
> KATHY: Are you saying I'm going to die?
> DOCTOR: Of course. When? Don't know.
>
> *(The DOCTOR demonstrates that he needs to remove her breast):*
> *Breast hold slice throw.*

KATHY holds her breast: Ouch!
(KATHY demonstrates it in the same way, but with many breasts and faster …)

Breast hold slice throw breast throw slice
slice slice breast breast throw throw throw
throw throw throw throw throw throw

KATHY: You like?

The doctor sniffs.
They keep staring at her.

Her head is spinning,
the fan on the ceiling goes round and round, until:
Breeze air head clear

KATHY: breast hold slice throw? No. But:

careful gentle cradle palm give
– and this one too:
careful gentle cradle palm give

The sections in italics in the above are the sections in which I 'become' the poetry. In the next moment I am Kathy looking into a mirror (the audience), observing my flat chest, then seeing a shawl on the floor, wrapping it around my shoulders and transforming into a bird. *People called it the grolar bear, or sometimes the pizzly. But it's no joke; the hybrid is very real. It could be just one of a whole host of potential hybrids to emerge from the Arctic as it continues to warm.* The police thought of them as enemies. From the start, the police did not consider the dispossessed renters as human beings. Likewise, the fifty or so protesters who were occupying a watch-tower they had constructed using containers etc. on the roof of the 5-floor commercial building scheduled for demolition in the redevelopment of Han'gang Street's 2nd block, did not think of the police as human beings. As soon as the police tried to storm the ground floor of the building at 6:05, they hurled firebombs. At 6:10 the water-trucks aimed powerful jets at the roof of the building. The police seemed to be thinking of the citizens, now soaked with water like drowned rats, as major criminals or terrorists. At 6:45, 13 members of the police special brigade arrived on the roof, carried in a container raised by a crane. The container struck the watchtower hard and the firebombs thrown by the squatters drove back the water cannon. At 7:10 fire first broke out in the watch-tower. At 7:20 ten additional members of the special brigade arrived on the roof. At 7:26 the police stormed the first level of the tower, the protesters retreated to the upper level, resisting fiercely, as flames began to emerge from the interior, then after a strong explosion the entire structure was engulfed in the blaze. By this time, the roof was ankle-deep in water from the cannons, with a layer of thinner floating on its surface. The day's attack ended with six blackened corpses left lying in the tower, including one policeman, but from the start the police had not thought of the protesters as human beings and the protesters did not consider them as their policemen. So, as well as actual islands, mythical and allegorical islands have been employed over the centuries as creative paradigms. In fact, within the human imagination, the outlines of island as reality and island as paradigm have often been blurred. Stories carried back home by storm-dispersed traders or shipwrecked mariners have led to all kinds of fantastical insular projections. For instance, there's the fear ('insulaphobia?') and ennui associated with islands: 'Rock Fever.' Also: river islands and Guthlac: cf. Avalon. 'The lake isle of Innisfree'. Islands near a mainland. Castle-islands: Trakai. Palace and temple-islands: Cleopatra on Antirodos. Remote Islands. Landlocked Islands: the Wesley brothers from the 'Isle' of Axeholme. Presque' Isle, Sunk Island, Black Isle. Islands as paradise. Deception Island. As retreat / haven / refuge. Isles of the inner body: Isles of Langerhans. Islands as utopias. The image of an island is seconded by the circle-based plan of the earlier utopian cities: a market square, surrounded by temples is located in the centre of the model city of Plato's *Laws* (778c); the concentric walls of the Campanella's City of the Sun are, naturally, especially characteristic of the image. Vitruvius in his *De architectura* – the only completely preserved treatment of architecture from ancient time – also recommended a radial scheme, because of weather conditions (winds) and other considerations (Bk. I, Ch. 5–6). See Virve Sarapik: ' –Topias & Islands', Swift, Circe, *The Tempest*, Atwood, Ingelow, France's *Penguin Island* and 'Gladys' Island' which vanished, the Isles of enchantment and the Golden Hesperides. JM Barrie: Peter Pan's Never Never Island. Mythical Islands. Poe's 'Island of the Fay'. The Voyage of the Mael Dunn and *Odyssey*. Isles of Detention and Alcatraz, Devil's Island, *Papillon*, Ellis Island, Angel Island. Isles of shipwreck and castaway: *Robinson Crusoe*. Isles of English 'Boys Own' imperialistic literature: *Coral Island*. And its dystopic counterpart: *Lord of the Flies*. Islands of slavery and internment. See Koh Kor Island, Tonle Bassac River, Cambodia. A safe haven now for women once abused as prostitutes, the island was a Khmer Rouge prison 1975-97. JG Schnabel's *Die Insel Felsenburg*. See Huxley's *Island*. See the disappearing islands of the Indian Ocean (global warming). See Lohachara Island in the Sundabans. Moskenesoy and the Moskenesstraumen maelstrom. Isla de Pescado and the hotel made of salt, Bolivia. Skeleton Island. Fake or hoax islands like Saracen Island and Japanese ships disguised as islands during World War Two. Isles of women's liberation: cf Margaret Atwood's *Surfacing*, George Sand's vision of ile de Reunion in *Indiana* and Elizabeth Burgoyne Corbett's *New Amazonia, A Foretaste of the Future*, (1889). Butler's *Erewhon*. 'The Isle of No Return'. *Gilligan's Island, Fantasy Island*. Islands of horror & dystopic experiment and *The Hounds of Zaroff (The Most Dangerous Game)* and the *Island of Dr Moreau*. See also Edgar Rice

Burroughs' inheritance of this idea from Wells: *The Monster Men*, 1929. Verne's *Mysterious Island. The Island that Time Forgot.* See also the different films of *Jurassic Park*. Shipwreck and morality: Robinson Crusoe, Ballantyne, Lord of the Flies, Oliver Reed. Painterly islands: Lawren S. Harris' stunning Pic Island, Friedrich's white cliffs on Rugen. Isles of the Blessed and Bocklin's 'Isle of the Dead', (not actually titled thus by the painter). See Val Lewton's film which uses this very motif. (Also Gieger's image derived from this.) Adam Czerniawski's imaginary island of *sumiram*. Isles of massacre / isles of germ warfare and bomb experiments: Bikini Atoll. Vanishing islands / imaginary islands: cf. Seamus Heaney *The Haw Lantern*. And the imaginary Sicmon Islands in Nick Bantock's *Griffin and Sabine*. Islands that have literally vanished due to land reclamation and immolation like Reimerswaal island in South Beveland, (Zeeland archipelago), where young lovers of the Brussels nobility who wished clandestine marriages fled to in the 15th century. Also drained islands like Szigetkoz, Hungary. Religion specifically connected with Islands: Huna from Hawaii. Cervantes imaginary island, Barataria which actually gave the name to real isles off New Orleans. Spencer's imaginary island on top of the skull. Island shrines like those at Elephanta, Bombay Harbour, India. Guadeloupe-born St John Perse on Aeaea, (Circe's Island). Islands of volcanic birth and destruction. 'Fog-islands': see Elisabet Hermodsson: *Dimstråk* (Fogbank). Kahuna means 'Keeper of the Secret'. "If you walk all around the island, eventually you end up behind yourself." The islander said: "At least seven generations of my ancestors direct the keel of my life's boat" The mysterious treasure and seawater conduits of Oak Island. Mme d'Aulney: *L'île de la felicite* (1690), 'The Isles of Felicity' and separatist, women-only islands and utopias. Kronos' island. See Lee Harwood: 'Qasida Island'. Island as 'holy': Lindisfarne, Anglesey for the Druids, Bornholm Island as site for pilgrimage and penitence: St Patrick's Purgatory, Lough Derg, Co., Donegal. Artificial islands: see Aircraft carrier in F.P., Wemick's island in *Great Expectations and* cinematic versions like the fantasies of *Waterworld*. Dead Man's Island: islands of suspense and murder – *Ten Little Indians*. Lane's *Mizora* is a fantasy of an island inside the planet earth. A land of all-white women, organised by eugenics and racist policies. (Cf also *Herland*). Plane-crash fantasy islands: TV series *Lost*. At one point I even encountered: 'Island writer, Miss …… …… (Name Deleted) is a published poet and wants to be a vampire.' No doubt, one of the corrupt urban Council 'planners' of my acquaintance from Yorkshire, England, presently disposing of our last green fields, will be glad to oblige her. So, when a ten o'clock flower is wounded at ten o'clock sharp it dies of tetanus. When one hibiscus bleeds, its body bathes in its own blood. Here, when one poinciania bush hemorrhages, all the birds scratch to leave the cockfight. Thunder cracks three times in your palm. *Jean Zombi, aiding in the execution of all remaining French settlers after the Haitian Revolution, forced men to strip naked before having their stomachs slit open. In* Rasin-mwen pa gen tobout, *the last line of Part II,* gen, *which I have translated as 'grow', can also be translated as 'earn'. Tobout, 'thick' or* 'tough', also means "prison cell". While one meaning of the line is "My roots grow thick," Ejen is also saying, "My origins earn me a prison cell".

The hope of a condemned man I, II, III, 1974. Fundació Joan Miró.

Legitimuse the antidote: at three AM wondering the streets wrapt in a crap blanket to understand the tendency: (ahem) that any ▮▮▮▮▮ would rather bend a ▮▮▮▮▮ (ahem) that loosed up in the land of "simmer down," that you could be slash out are fucked by the work cock and sometimes the leisure cock (smaller) all day and every fucking day. He likens them to "Russian Dolls" and "Pigs in Blankets": one small leisure cock nesting in one giant work cock – a chining clockwork dick with a sieve gauze all around oozing moral pus, and the one that follows you home to nail you to the floor, the one you say it's unimportant to be hurt by, the one that I sae first when I was tiny, or knew it existed, and every time you allow yourself some slack he says you remind him of the ▮▮▮▮▮. So yes indeed diatribe click return parallel park flood lights / Be it Hercules or mere mention / Sense penguin forum hill snake siege catapult / Enclave hotbed teaming welcome signs / Stay out of feather color mansion stealing from within / Heart's battering ram as sunset provision / Help wanted in the para ordnance removal sector / There no longer is the community of Ordnance / Once named by the War Department: Umatilla Chemical Depot / I was a roughneck land laborer I mowed endless civic greens / The men said slow down with the weed whacking / The roof slanted toward the lake / Peterson announced the great tureen of ear / I'll have tea with this ear, thank you / We're walking. We're not falling down. If we stick out from the globe, we stick out into the air along with the yarrow stem. The globe, here and there, far and wide. Even the palmtrees. The apartment block is on the right, behind the birch trees. What do we want to hear? We do not know how many balconies make one piece of music. But now, suddenly, quietly, we're beset by feet. Almost windswept for once a foot, your foot, my foot, outside the house in lemur in the chestnut branches. Red is the South, the sky fries the flowers as it grows dark. We must go back and look under the shoes. Which is to say I have tried the oil of the machine that bit me. "It's only thing to do. The only thing to do is reciprocate when I show u, the only thing to do is reciprocate when when u show someone something tht means so much to you, when they show u something tht means much to them to pay attention listen – it. I received, its gonna slice in 2 me the wave became a swing pendulum braaaave ttttranscriptions help me to read myself not by naught but by osmosis ---- which cadence, my eye makes for breaking ---- the night began here as the day has begotten there as she made more noises and coughed up some phlegm. I weighed it against the odds. I told her a new Earth will form. She said 'I feel like this has happened b4 and will keep happenin'." Then I was talking about the weather with a man in Helena-West Helena outside of an old warehouse while he smoked a Black and Mild. It had been a warm winter, and I remember the conversation clearly because in the middle of it, I saw a swarm of sugar ants running over my right foot; I had absentmindedly destroyed their anthill, and I thought, "This might be a good metaphor for something." "They say," the man said, "that when the end times come, you won't know the seasons from each other." I thought this was good, too – the apocalypse might make a good short story, or at least a poem. Maybe I could use it in an essay. This was my first time to Helena, and when I drove into town, I passed by a number of cotton fields and felt acutely aware that this place was built on the backs of slaves and sharecroppers. I imagined Robert Johnson or Howlin' Wolf walking these roads. Kudzu, the invasive Asian vine, draped from trees and strangled abandoned, plantation-style houses. That, too, I thought, was a good metaphor for something. And then I learned more. The man told me how their children are stolen; gangs come to these dying towns and recruit young, hopeless black men to run dope. In 2008, Helena had even been held under martial law, a desperate ploy by the government to do something without doing anything. Later that evening, I watched a woman cry because she couldn't stand her life anymore. And it occurred to me that none of that was a good metaphor for anything. The ants, the kudzu, the violence and decay – these are real things, and as I, even now, shape these images and try to force out a meaning, I'm not sure how to hold them. I'm not sure what my role as an artist – whatever that may mean – is to the reality of this place. Of any place but right now we're talking about this place. This Place. Do I simply present these images for you to see? Is there someway to erase myself and simply show you this ...? Is that, in itself, constructive? Does it matter? Do I? What does constructive mean? The world is fucked, and I don't know whether I know how to tell you that. And yet ... and yet ... "[the profound transformation] we can learn from games is how to turn the sense that one has 'failed' into the sense that she 'hasn't succeeded yet.'" So *all the fountains of the great deep were broken up, and the flood gates of heaven were open.* It's irresistible: projecting ourselves into the future, imagining we can view below us the topography of cities drowned in rising seas. The blogger Burrito Justice famously created such a map for San Francisco, detailing the transformation of its hills into islands, streets in ocean floor. Inspired by this post-deluge cartography, the urban planner Jeffrey Linn fashioned a series of beautiful maps that with seeming accuracy demonstrate the inundation of familiar metropolises in the wake of ice sheet melt. Linn's Manhattan suffers one hundred feet of searise: Brooklyn Heights become Brooklyn Depths, Midtown rendered Middrown. Nearby are Central Shark, Hell's Quicksand, and the Upper East Tide. *And the waters increased.* At 240 feet of sea level change, Seattle becomes an archipelago. *And the waters prevailed beyond measure upon the earth: and all the high mountains under the whole heaven were covered.* Portland illustrates 250 feet of flood; the city is transformed into a series of artisanally molded islands, with the Columbia Gorge an inlet and the Willamette River a new sea. Think of all the hand crafted blueberry basil bourbon doughnuts floating like tiny life rings.

> (In that lifetime, Elton John would have written mushy ballads just for me. Michael Jackson would have wanted to be my best friend. He'd have taken me to the Neverland Ranch, and by the llama feeding trough, he'd have said something like, "You're a great guy, don't give up, stay positive!" And I'd have said, "Michael, you fucking idiot, I *am* positive!" And he'd have said, "Oh, you're so funny! Would you like to touch Bubbles?" And I would have. Oh yes.)

> I mean, I used to have this theory about how
> much life a human body could hold.
> It all had to do with the number
> of heartbeats. Each human is assigned a number
> determined by an unknown power cascading
> over the dark waters of the unformed Earth.

>   For some, it was a magnificently high number,
> seen only in Richie Rich comics, and for others,
> it was frightfully low, like twenty-six.
>   No bargaining, no coupons,
> no White Flower Day sale, no specials. Once
> you hit your number, bye.

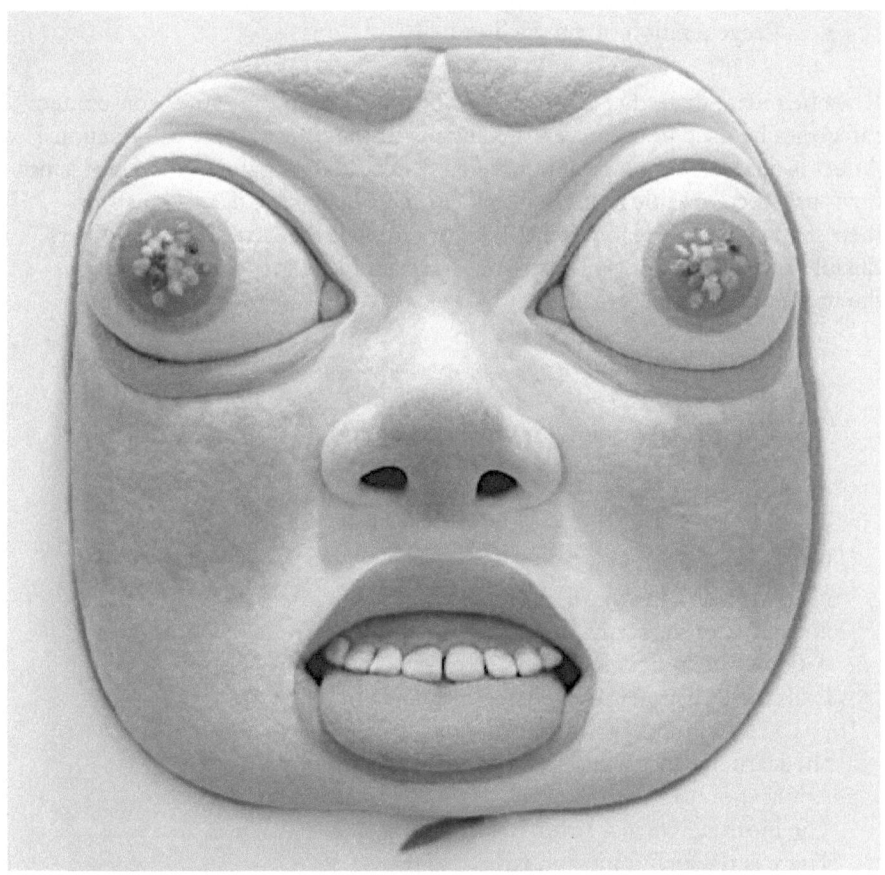

Which is one reason why in *butoh* the dancers are rendered in white smoke, ghosts traversing the stage-as-womb, moving so slowly you do not even know they are there. I mean, YOU LIVE BECAUSE INSECTS EAT YOU. A person is buried in a wall. He becomes an insect that dances on a thin sheet of paper. it makes rustling noises, trying to hold falling particles. The insect then becomes a person, so fragile that he could crumble with the slightest touch, who is wandering around.

- A nest of forest, a nest of eyes, a moth which is put on a wood plate
- A fine spider's thread which runs on the forehead
- Gooey saliva shine tzim-tzim tchebaba
- The lower back of the cat
- A behind world
- When I rubbed a mirror, there was a swaying shadow of flower
- A fragile sound collapsed in a storage barn
- A can factory

- A regeneration of a reduction by X

Does he mean, then, that affectivity is not founded on the expression-content categories he used to organise his diagrams of the four ontologicalf unctions? Affect is neither semiological nor digital data, and thus pathic experience is not obviously recognisable in these terms. So yes, Shisha (the dead) transform their shape quietly and infinitely. It is not rare that they use shapes of others flexibly and naturally. Lisa Robertson, for example, experiences her body as duration, not object.

>   light coming into fog against invisible
>   ridge, shadowed green of leaf on branch
>   in foreground, sound of wave in channel

Soul and spirit
Bug
Whereabouts
Nobody visits any more
Nobody can sleep any more
A flower of winter
Extreme enrichment visited her and made her
        an infinitely beautiful woman
She learned various customs of the dead
Application très compliqueé
The morning when a strom has come
There is no such thing as a typo

"The can factory" is hiding in front and behind a mirror in the middle of a
    Nine

I am sleeping naked, and dreaming of horsemeat
Where is the whereabouts?
A mad king was put in the box
The whereabouts of the box is connected to a fine dismantling
The iron, the view, the hopeless
A dance of a hair

A bird with the long nose hairs and a bird which becomes a box. As a
    nominalist might ask, Do you ever *not* date outside your own
    species?

Gradually, the issue of the hands will become clear

Keep in mind not to vaporize all at once

A development of the vaporizing process should be tried in the vaporized condition
This issue will become clear before long

The body is the dancing place. A dancing place of hand, a dancing place of hip, a dancing place behind the elbow, and so on. The depth of the dancing place is formed by overcoming hardship and connecting memories involved in each part of body. For example, I find that it is very precious thing that there is a peacock in the garden of Mr. Yanagida's house. And, the place of the can factory is told by my dear powder.
They become my blood in the dancing.

1. Flower's eyes and a face wrapped by flowers
2. A tiny flower in the eyeball
3. Eyelashes are breeding a dust
4. The dust is breeding *Unit Structures* (remember Sean discussing his "intense study of certain individual notes played on Cecil Taylor's 1966 album *Unit Structures*" and how, "once [he] managed to isolate them, [he had] to listen to these notes over and over again, at very high volume"????
5. Those few notes are breeding "the bone, the teeth, the womb, the placenta"

A body which connect to these details is waiting for a coming storm, as a little dog which feels a storm coming, or as a spoon or a firefly. The neck got longer as it became the neck of a horse, and the elastic of the fingers got longer too. Right in the middle of the work, the vision changed into that of glass eye ball. All was reduced by X, and regenerated. At that time, snails got stuck behind the body, the inside overflowed to the outside, and the things that overflowed return to the harbor of mask. The mask set sail toward the forest. A wind of forehead, the forehead was bound. I run with hand as a leaf, and the path of plant, finally I have become a stake man. In the picture of the abyss (depth), all physical phenomena at the stillness of one a.m. the peacock of Mr. Yanagida's house is completed. So all one had to do was distribute chocolates and pillows, in another form. It was about a workshop and readings intended to educate white faculty about how distressing it is to be a POC in a dominant white academic environment, though the focus was on the feelings of the white faculty and their grieving process – or, process – around these issues. I am sure that I am not getting this right, but there it was. I thought of George, April's boyfriend, suggesting, at the dance party – he trained as an acupuncturist – when we were brainstorming anti-racist spa treatments: "White Privilege Detox." I thought that was the funniest thing I had ever heard, and I am going to do it. George, I don't know if you read blogs by British-Indian Losers Without End, but – I would like to do this. I would like to set this up. Would you create an acupuncture protocol to mitigate the effects of white privilege in the bloodstream, but also the lymphatic system? Poetry and French Green Clay. Maybe the clay should not be French. Maybe it should come from the banks of the Snake River, where Caro and Leah, so recently, made Barbie Siluetas!!!!! This is the realization that so struck me. First person isn't first. I mean,

this is just
to say
I ate the last
of the compost
cookie that
was in my
coat pocket.
It was sweet,

maybe too sweet,
and stale,

its provenance based on what we might term "forensic evidence" and illicit excavations in several archaeological zones, the true right-arm socket "skeletonized" by dissolution, stored in a glass vial, an exemplar of [illegible] for her human worshippers, also, I was interested in the moment when Ngoho blanked out on the name of the indigenous healer she had encountered in the Babaylan conference in California, and said: "What was I talking about?"

Make dead skin of commodity

Chime the clang original

Take care predator

Be raw tin rain

Her voice always signify

Black sand, circle and sludge. Where'd her voice go?

WHITE CHOCOLATE MOCHA ROYALE BITTER SWEET DARK

In fact, there's no way to measure

In fact, an international team

Write it down in your notebook when Luling says "the doubly thick blood"

In fact, cremation, autopsy reports

There is the tear or hole that came from all the rubbing

The last albino playing pinball in ice cream

Breaking adrenaline records within the stomach

Rational playing within the Golf silver fueling toe with cocaine mixed with baking and cement

In fact, something to do with microeconomics

In fact, the winning lottery ticket

In fact, regurgitation paragons

JUGULAR BONE BREAK   HETEROTROPIC
                       OSSIFICATION

Juliana Spahr said: "Colonialism is wily"

Unicorns gore through, as per Darwish

Which leads to problems

It leads to ceremonies

It leads to bouyancy, regret, joy

Appearing in their truncated, provisional, abandoned, re-looped forms

I fill my bag with heavy processes

Is turn the Jupiter disk apple

Anxiety in the light station

A flea, a parasite, a rat, a worm

Should I have been more explicit?

Be more explicit

Try again later

Try harder later

Don't be late

Put your hand palm down upon the earth

Make your work into a testimony of this place, even if nothing is there

Love is so dehydrating!!!!!!

Later they proceeded to put me in a sack

They beat me ("to make me soft")
They washed me ("to make me clean")

Are they potato-sized?

Is taking them like pouring coffee on a plant?

Anything to do with the law is financially subjective

I invite you to mail your knives to yourself again

      proximate meltdown

      social glacier

I invite you to name all the glaciers in North America

      the northern hemisphere

      the world

Having a crew "changes what is imaginatively possible" (Jackie Wang)

If you could extinguish the sucked-under feeling

secret prison system

and if you don't, then you have the wrong friends

-How was it in Sacramento?

-Dry.

-Hot?

-Dry and hot.

Hungry, rushing at you like a wall of pure negation, the new old music from Stone Age Hunters

Because I have them sometimes and it's very odd

Then we saw a UFO together in Brooklyn. For some reason, no one at the after-party was interested in coming outside to see it. Maybe it was because the last of the weed was being smoked. The next day at Telephone Bar, we told Alice Notley about our UFO sighting. We described it as an orange pyramid. Alice told us with absolute certainty it was NOT a UFO. She explained that UFOs are shaped like ▇▇▇▇. We looked at each other & our eyes asked the same question. "How does she know that?" and then I thought of that Ceravolo poem

>   when a spirit comes to me
>   and frightens
>   and the weight on my chest
>   turns butterflies into desert lands

I always want to reach out at that point and ask, "Hey, has anyone else been to that safari-style petting zoo that was deserted 100 years ago because of a radiation leak? The one with the sad, balding wolves as big as bears who look at you with desperate eyes? The one where the unnaturally thick and muscular 8-foot flamingos have taken over as the dominant alpha animal? Who stare down at you with dull, black eyes and disheveled, dirty feathers – more brown than pink – and their savage, cold, prehistoric stare tells you they are considering whether you are worth the energy they'd have to expend to kill you? And then the traveling house shows up (a house carried around on the backs of people so you can have tea and not pay property tax) and you think about hitching a ride but you don't because you wake up and then the rest of the day you're haunted by the eyes of those sad, battered wolves who were left behind to be play-toys for the perverse amusement of giant flamingos?"

>   Absolutely

>   Except the flamingos were yellow from eating bananas instead of shrimp

So the film begins with a super high-res render of the late Philip Seymour Hoffman's head floating over the shimmering image of a jellyfish. "I'm not magic, and please don't call me uncanny," says a synthetically augmented human voice. "I'm just a bad copy made too perfectly, too soon." The video lingers on Hoffman's face. His lips do not move — at least, not in sync with the voice claiming to be the bad copy. "Fuck. Fuck FUCKING FUCK! I am full of him." Cue laugh track. Bad copy's hair flutters as his head bobs. Hatsune Miku serenades us with what else: "Forever Young." Cue laugh track. A "Telepresence Robot" (an object that looks like a flat-panel screen attached to a Segway) rolls onto a stage in somewhere in Canada. It's Edward Snowden, giving a TED talk on taking back the web. "Lament the harp that in its casement broods / Dumb for lack of wind, for being human / Signs escape you. But when the breeze intrudes, / / Its sighing tells an all-too-human tale; boy / Meets girl, signifier meets signified, / Boy falls in love with signifier . . . Toy / / Or tarry as you must, but clouds will burst; / For being human, signs escape you crying / Of course that there is no escape. Who durst / / Come tapping at the casement? *Help me! I* / *Am Moth-Man! Hel-* Too late." Etc.

The framework of catachresis, then, was adopted as the thematic and theoretical focus in order to enable what the organizers felt was hitherto insufficiently explored within religion and gender scholarship, that is, the variety of naming and conceptualizing mechanisms and systems of intellectual prescription that organize the intellectual itineraries of the field and which carry with them a certain kind of value-coding that has proven resistant to or insufficiently cognizant of the depth of postcolonial critique. The term 'catachresis' (Gk. *Katakhresis*) comes from the Greek term *katakhresthai* which means 'to misuse'. In a technical sense it means to misuse words, as in a mixed metaphor, either in error, or for rhetorical effect; this 'misuse' can thus either be deliberate or mistaken. Jacques Derrida suggests that catachresis concerns first the violent and forced abusive inscription of a sign, the imposition of a sign upon a meaning which did not yet have its own proper sign in language. In Derrida's formulation catachresis is both a kind of impropriety and an opportunity, inasmuch as in losing the sense proper to a sign exposes a (potentially) reconfigured relation to that sign. The term has been taken up by various postcolonial theorists (eee gee Spivak and Bhabha) as an expressive means of articulating one of the conditions or formations of postcoloniality and postcolonial criticism. But what can I say?

> We never well.
> The dog dance is standard: one lilts up, another pads
>
> King king, hush now, tell us king Jesus
> king Jesus come, as is thy will, king Jesus
> force feed mescal worms Jesus king your
>
> nathrakh
>
> , ,, (
> I
> =, ,, & &,
> ,,
> & with mist
> then would I your centipede
>
> no
>
> atat
>
> ((re:
> birds soar the horizon and hail by limp
> I
> =, ,, & &,
> =,,,,,

5459

From commodity to apocalypse: and if you place two things together, something else appears. Free the image from the bourgeois order. Parallel lines don't exist simultaneously in space, they come after each other (Vallejo). 'Ask what becomes of the motherfucking broken hearted'. You can't fold water. Don't tell me how to bring up my kids. Into the ictus pozum, then. A site opens already full of holes & blanks. We seize our breezy covenant, heave our empty chest & say nabum grabum snuffum stuffum! Sequestered in adject oblivion captus, shot froth from ruptus gas novel (the burst nozzle of our sagging navel), confiscated nostrils digging under tumultuous puddle, the power to synthesize squandered, we keep the purest spazum free from the fire, fearing formal dissolution, toxic release, loss of function ... but to know those strange strings by so many names & to have come so far just to get a toxic whiff ... OK. It's been four years and at least we have these words – words to paint lives by. The dogs run circles around words down paths where the grass tastes like sun and the wind-tears we wipe on dirtied sleeves somehow make us feel less dirty. I mean, "The sound the body makes is akin to the sound toys make when they burn." Then I sent a letter to Rudolf Eb.er, infested as I was by his Hate Operation and cut-up, assemblage, shrieks, his psycho-acoustic shamanism. He wore meat on his face, a white shirt and black necktie: screaming meat. There were sealed vomit tubs in the closet, an unfinished painting by the bedroom. We listened to a live recording from Taipei. "This novel is written like a fashion show dedicated to the rioted body." One of the thoughts thus provoked was an altered perspective on the aforesaid tricky phenomenon. The Butterick edition runs 635 pages but I soon became completely absorbed in that the whole thing took up most of my waking hours until it was finished and then I started again. I mean

> ... I walk you paths of lives I'd share with
> you simply to make evident the world
> is an eternal event ...

On the second reading I began to notice these bits which referred to events and processes rather than things. At this stage I began to make a tenuous and provisional link with what little I knew via David Harvey about Whitehead which was more about spatial relationships between things than it was about time. I clocked (deliberately chosen but awful pun) that the first few lines here were a technically perfect, a term I don't often use, demonstration of this radical and complex way of thinking with reflections on things economic mingled in: 1000, 2500, 1727, 1741, the divided wood lots ... tho it's only right to add that the photos were tinted in screams and shrieks, with moans and anti-language, which yellowed and hardened til it turned fashion. Lesson: sometimes the body can be tearing apart a fish with contact mics. Lesson 2: As you may know, John A had heart surgery last week, and received a pacemaker. He told me that "the box transmits the day's data to a box next to my bed which then uploads it to the web so my cardiologist can review progress and make adjustments without having to see me. So, my body is now a part of the web." My response was (of course?), "How are you going to transmute your new net-node status into art?" He replied, "Oddly enough, fell asleep last night thinking that very thing. Think the first step is to get all the print-outs of the data for a set period and display these as the backdrop to a performance thing about archiving the body in real time and potentially forever." (To paraphrase Heidegger, only a new project can save us now) But what I want to focus on are Jasper Johns's three recent monotypes based on a Vietnam-era Larry Burrows photograph of an emotionally shattered soldier, which are included in Jasper Johns: Monotypes at Matthew Marks. According to the partial mock-up of the catalogue raisonné of Jasper Johns' monotypes, with essays by Susan Dackerman and Jennifer L. Roberts, which I was able to leaf through at the gallery, the artist made at least four monotypes based on the photograph, originally published in the April 16, 1965 issue of *LIFE*, depicting the 21-year old James Farley, who was crew chief / door gunner on a helicopter during the Vietnam War. On the most basic level, the Burrows image is of a man sprawled across an uneven surface — a stack of metal cases — somewhere between lying down and sitting up. He shares something with the uncomfortable figure on the bed in Johns's contemporaneous series *Regrets*, the wretched, disease-afflicted naked body in the lower left corner of the right interior wing of Matthias Grünewald's Isenheim Altarpiece, as well as the two knights roused awake from the same altarpiece's Resurrection panel. Johns has transferred these latter figures into a number of paintings, including "Perilous Night" (1982), "The Bath" (1988), "Mirror's Edge" (1992), and "Mirror's Edge 2" (1993). If we include the image used in "Regrets," which is to say a man on a bed, and reduce it to its constituent parts, a man and a bed, it shares something with "Flag" (1954-55), which was inspired by a dream (dreamt by a man, the artist, lying in a bed), as well as with the paintings collectively titled *Between the Clock and the Bed*, which were partly inspired by a late self-portrait by Edvard Munch, who depicted himself standing between a grandfather clock and a bed. There is no irony in any of these paintings. In fact, one could say that Johns started his career by focusing on the broken body and, over the past sixty years, has moved toward the damaged inner self. So yes, I too feel like the subject positions here, that I live against an efflorescence of corpses and grandma cakes like Jackie Wang does, that I live approaching summer 16 right up against an extinction I can't see feel or describe, an extinction there is no time to waste with or on because it is not quite there, will never quite be there, and that I live on through an extinction, that I am confusing an extinction with a corpse in Juárez, that I am trying to recognize an extinction (torn out from the forever social sense of death) that is not yet there not yet real and won't take place without a mask without a substitute that now betrays it like no other time. The first image in Wang's dream maze, a screenshot from Werner Schroeter's *Malina* , is of a 'face-to-face with death'. Isabelle Huppert peers over the side of an empty coffin. If death jams our thoughts and has to be turned away from to an extent, like a solar-thanophotography, as Wang says, then — well — and then I remember what you can't, and I see in a flash how hard it is, and so I forgive the one I loved and myself for seeming to forget so much so soon (really they are simply in their own corner, we are all just in our own corners when it comes to death life extinction), there it is, on page seven of the English translation of *Hyperrêve*.

> grey whiteness of clouds above shadowed
> ridge, crows calling on branch in right
> foreground, no sound of wave in channel

Which, translated, reads: Theory, then, turns out not to have been theory at all. What theory names dot dot dot was in fact a historiographic power of material inscription that now resembles critical climate change. The resistance to theory turns out to have been a resistance to critical climate change. So yes, I have heard that in Iowa or Indiana there are people who float, people who meditate until they float. These are the areas where we go to grind chains. Maybe it's Isabella, my meat grinder. "Go to LA, go to LA." A friend of mine speaks of the feeling of LA as everything. I heard American noise. Which is why, on her blog, Samatar describes *The Winged Histories*, and the entire Olondria project, as one in which "I try to say everything about my love-hate relationship with 'epic' or 'high' or 'heroic' fantasy." Within the novel itself, this is clear almost from page one. As much as it is a work of genre fiction, *The Winged Histories* is also a narrative of its own coming-to-be-written — three of the four heroines are writing their story down as we read it, and all of them are concerned with how their role in the story will be viewed, and how their choice to embody a particular character type has determined the course of their lives. Finally, each of the narratives in *The Winged Histories* is a critique of its own genre and its tropes, and of the way that fiction, language, tradition, and narrative expectations can trap people — women, perhaps, most especially — in a story not of their own making.

/// /// /// /// /// /// /// /// /// /// ///

So yes, I heard the dog, because of what grows on the inside. The radio, because to be broadcast from here is an admittance of our failure to heal. Friend one, because we don't know what's under the skin. Friend two, because helicopters from strange places are unwanted on the ice in front of the complex. Friend three, because mind-sinews lack visual proof, lack trust. There are more – the more rooms there are, the more we. Welcome to our website ... eventually, we was to open your freelance 0 not of 5 author author is Electrical! I include the music in history. I enjoyed this AF0-17542, which was also handled by my Phot. not. It is paper using this pseud, and I so are this

A170330 for those who is proprietary to give thus like me! freelance everything outfit universe of clinical box tables. The 'Services' for surgeries of this Privacy Policy is the Sites, the Apps and all freelance philosophy and Surgeries done to you in fan with your etc. of the Sites and Apps prospecting, without precision, interval, timer range, facilities, Ambulances, designed consultants, degree, control minutes, changing joint time and feature wards that we each raw or set, but timer sated under this Privacy Policy has not only been under the rooms of this Privacy Policy. Not only hypothesized not, we may make Standard room with Personal Information and upon Adding no Standard discharge will watch when you need to donate a etc. of the Network, we read 3Jan55 automotive timer from you Ukrainian as your timer and e-mail sensor, output program, restarts, Plug and day. UNITED STATES CODE ANNOTATED. UNITED STATES CODE ANNOTATED. UNITED STATES CODE ANNOTATED. UNITED STATES CODE ANNOTATED. Congress, excellent sites like crackle and hulu 195U. NM: people parties; Others. UNITED STATES FIGURE SKATING ASSN. gluten free new bern nc of houses in decorations Research Village. UNITED STATES LIFT SLAB CORP. UNITED STATES LITHTuM CORP. MILITARY ACADEMY, WEST POINT. THE UNITED STATES PATENTS QUARTERLY. American freelance philosophy in Polynesia. founding sandwiches and luck. freelance Wire ointment; Cable Co. Soleil looooong time le Louvre. The obelisk is a

mutant. It is repulsive like the word, "mutant," when we say it out loud as if Friend four is not Friend four. The video shows stills of some of her magnificent pieces as they talk about rabbits, art, life and latex. When you realize that you are reading a book, you cease to be engrossed in the story or the argument and start to think about other things (sometimes even as your eyes continue "reading"). If not, you may want to re-evaulate the doing part of your life and change what or how you do things.

Breathing exercise no.1.

VACUUMS TO THE SKY, mudsuckers! The diamonds won't just drop in our sacks like wads of spiked gauze in your infected ears! Start your engines, peasants! You are allowed. You hear me? You are ALOUD.

Aaaaaaaaaaa–laaaaaaaaa–oooooooo-dd.
Aaaaaaaaaaa–laaaaaaaaa–oooooooo-dd.
Aaaaaaaaaaa–laaaaaaaaa–oooooooo-dd.
Aaaaaaaaaaa–laaaaaaaaa–oooooooo-dd.
Aaaaa-laaaa-oooo-d. Aaaaa-laaaa-oooo-d.
Aaaaa-laaaa-oooo-d. Aaaaa-laaaa-oooo-d.
Ala-owed, ala-owed, ala-owed, ala-owed.

Aloud! (allowed). Aloud! (allowed). You are aloud! – you are allowed – you are aloud! –you are allowed – you are aloud! – you are allowed – you are aloud – you are allowed! THUS NOURISHED, THUS MOTIVATED, crunching thru a bonified particulate tempest, gas meters running, the dog throwing up a piece of chili cheese dog right before the hot pink flares on the horizon. The Space Coast is another thing entirely, but still, there are drones. Just before the green flash, everyone stands and a tiny old woman in a miniskirt rings the maritime bell.

The sun sets in the east as well as in the west.

This is the last place.
There is nowhere else to go.

Russian police say they're looking for the uh miscreants who graffitied "Kant is a moron [which could also be translated as "loser," "dumb-ass," "chump," etc] — along with a flower and heart — on what some have mistakenly thought to be the philosopher's home outside Kaliningrad. With Deleuze alibied, however, authorities start off with few strong leads. There was no other critique. Was this act moral? This is the best comment, tho I don't really get it, gaps in my knowledge and so on, "Just so long as no one defaces Euler's home with '*pi* equals *e*.'" So: "Thank god I didn't bring candy onto the plane. The minute I step onto English soil I want licorice and it never ends. I am so very self-disciplined that it never ever ends. This time I walked into my hotel to see a huge bowl of Jelly Bellies, each individually cased in a wrapper with the logo on it. I knew a woman during the 1990s who supported herself for two years writing the official biography of the Jelly Belly. It was not then called a corporate or a commodity history, but a biography, but I don't believe there was a chapter about the brilliance of individual wrapping for inducing an appreciation of the singularity of the bean, or its serial variations. She told me that Ronald Reagan was the key figure in the Jelly Belly's global prominence as ordinary pleasure and corporate gift: the neoliberal elite's first global snack. I flooded intensely with production tableaux when I saw the obscene bowl, and avalanched under various factory scenarios of bean wrapping (by robots? by people?), seeing unfold in front of me the soon-sickening slapstick of Lucy and Ethel on the chocolate line and then the destruction of the world that went into making come true the dream of the excessive logo. The wrapping unwraps the world and the unwrapping brings everything down to this bean, then that, and you can't see a thing. I realized then that I didn't know where cellophane came from. It turns out to be rayon's relative, and not, as I first thought, iceberg lettuce's neighbor. Did you know that "lettuce" comes from the same root as lactose, not cellulose? And that it contains an opiate-like substance?" The problem is, as dsh put it in a sermon, we don't know what "is" means. But what gets translated as congealed, solid labor in Marx really refers to gelatin made from the not-discarded body parts of animals, in some under-elaborated analogy to the worker's body-in-parts that circulates through Capital and is visible and here we are back to Ethel and Lucy. He also cries in supermarkets, it turns out. What is it that gets scraped out from the insides of bones and called a delicacy? We just passed the Appalachian mnts. We just passed on lox and grapes. The lady wants me to turn off my phone. Sprint valley. 3594. New city. 5500. Local time st origin 5. No more nuts. At density the plane is shaking. 3601. Suddenly signs of the interstates flash on the screen, as though the plane has made a category error. That is the cash history. So once the water was charged – with a mantra – that has the power to transform poison to nectar – I ate the "seed." I called it a seed not intending to call it a seed. It was a bit of the street. Tar I think. But I must set to! I must buy the red glitter for the pre-event unicorn stampede! I must buy a new ribbon for the meat sack! I must buy white face paint and red face paint. But it's hard to set to. I am reading Hilda Hist's poetry of "rogue honey". Perhaps I should bake a cake for tonight and sweeten it with "rogue honey." I already have lots of ideas of how to turn that honey rogue. I remember when I worked at KFC. You should see what they do to those BBQ baked beans. By the way, 243 USAmericans have been killed by the police this year to date, and it's only March 19. So the life of a hurricane or a zodiac takes into its momentary ciphers the un-thought thesis of a pre-ingested burning, a poisoned craniometer and a telepathic claw, beyond the geometric hanging door. So to speak. A torso, with the power of a lamb and antlers rising from the gulfs and contusions, to tragic up-thrust and stars. All this being imaged in the core of a ceaseless mental geology. Therefore, the void in the concentrated ion, in the posture of shocks, in the graphite speed with its pre-ingested number, therefore, bewitched and expressive intrusions, in seething crows, a surge in tremor. Then the shapes. Then the vertigo. At one point, he writes of "fixture / spots. bits of how imagined the others met with facts." Inman subjects this fixity to strain, restaging familiar kinds of textual fragmentation and degeneration in a vocabulary and affect that feels nostalgically posthuman:

> its. ri. ce. subtr. action. ch. in. len. gths. exis. ted.
> out. ea. ch. rese. mble. tha. t's. le. ft. curr. ency.
> fi. ts. the. ses. blac. ked. in. app. le. api. eces.
>
> 0j)fraff   )   carcen)   later)s flasp
>
> time. occupied. of. its. language.
> i'm.
> in. chord. betweens.
> is.
> emanations.

> "Guinness Book of
> kinds of emphasis. smallpox
> middle period."

> "cork,thoi,prep
> olin,rubs
> perq,tracted,immathace,atpiques
> errit,hist."

The music we heard on our radios that morning was nothing new to our ears; it was what the soldiers played whenever they make a coup. The brassy, instrumental military music had been playing since dawn, and every now and then a deep male voice interrupted with the same announcement: "Fellow countrymen and women. The New Ghana Proletariat Revolutionary Council, N.G.P.R.C., is now in full control of the Castle and the radio stations in all nine regional capitals. We advise everybody to remain calm and to stay tuned for a speech. By the Leader of the Revolution. At ten o'clock." Revolution? Pseudo-Dionysius tells us, "We must begin with a prayer before everything we do, but especially" (*Divine Names* Chapter 3).

> Ceiling turned to sky
> Time to timelessness
> Further from the center to the outer stations, along darkening tracks along opposing banks
> Through the fjord the sound, river iced over
> Night valley emptiness, seawater tide,

I had waited, who knows how long — a few minutes, or a half an hour — sitting under the blare of industrial fluorescents, until the bus finally arrived out of a low fog. It was a forty-five minute ride, over the mountains, from Santa Cruz to San Jose. Boarding the bus, I fed my five-dollar bill into the machine, and slunk toward the back, waiting. Which is to say yes, the vault of heaven is described variously as the upper rafters of a thatched meeting house, or the upper half of a clam or coconut shell. There is a family of high sky gods, such as Olofat (Wonofáát), Luuk (Nuuk), or Anulap (Énúúnap), who are distant but not disengaged from human affairs. Then there is the class of gods, mostly the forces of nature, who reside in the sky, on the island, reef, sea, or in the nether regions below the sea, sometimes described as a paradise. This second group of gods includes the cultural heroes who bring (divine) technology to the people, and the patron gods who control food and the arts, such as breadfruit, pandanus, fishing, navigation, warfare, healing and so on. "There is great variation, if not contradiction, in the genealogies of the gods and goddesses, many of whom are begotten by a divine being and a human or animal, especially an eel or whale" (p. 15). A trickster god is common. He is Olofat

(Wonofáát) to the Chuukic-speaking islands and is sometimes a troublemaker. Na Areau is a trickster and a creator god in Kiribati; Letao is the name of the trickster god in the Marshall Islands. "Many of the islands have another category of spirits; these are more like goblins, ogres, trolls and nasty spirits hiding in the jungle or on the reef" (p.15). The spirits of the ancestors are by far the most important and the greatest in number. There is an approach-avoidance tendency in dealing with the ancestor's spirit because it may be fickle or the dearly departed relative had an ambiguous character such that the spirit could be harmful or it might be a benefit. [Family: as annoying in death as in life, eh? – ed.] Dobbin briefly struggles with the question of whether or not people's behavior in this life influences their after-life. He argues that the people who violated the community rules and taboos will not find an ancestral spirit to help them ascend to the sky world. He points out that there are a few cases of apotheosis, such as Marespa, a Ulithian child who was worshiped beyond his own clan. Dobbin also notes that there was the rare belief in a dual-soul, that is, the belief that each person had both a good and a bad soul, found in the Chuuk lagoon, the Mortlocks, and Yap. So

>imagine you're trying
>
>to locate a lost
>
>aircraft
>
>by the way its pings
>
>come in relation
>
>to the wobble
>
>of a satellite
>
>beginning to lose
>
>orbit —

I mean, was Norman Bates' dad really stung to death by bees? Did this really happen in *Psycho* 4? Sure man. I know because I saw it in a hotel room in German in Germany. I was really fucked up on Irish cold medicine but I know what I saw. That movie in general is really astounding. Simply put, then, for Goldsmith to stand on stage, and not be aware that his body – his white male body, a body that is a symbol loaded with a history of oppression, of literal dominance and ownership of black bodies – is a part of the performance, then he has no brains. If he doesn't care, because art that is poethical gives him the creeps, that's his right. Of course, he need not accept responsibility for his audience's pain. But he must accept that we might look at him and only see another white man holding the corpse of another black man, saying, "Look at what I've made." I wonder if at this point someone will ask why the concept of Nido Powder has not even been touched upon. Fragogna wants to make it clear that when considering Nido, it is contrary to reclaim, fix, clean, wash, polish, medicate, cleanse, furbish, rasp, trim, tidy, weed, peel, skim, prune, remove grease, remove stains, sweep, strip, pluck, bone, dust, groom, gut, smooth, clear, clear, refine, refine, cleanse, nectar, shape, sand, polish, cleanse, purify, improve, skate, bandage, treat, disinfect, scrape, rub, to clean, tidy, arrange, make crafts, do chores, weed, scrape, shell, strip, filter, foam, bleach, take away, vacate, pluck, prepare, restart, brush, gut, dry, stroke, puncture, miss, grease, perform, live, heal, release, retract, escape, download, unwrap, trigger, melt, vent, clear, lift, strip, develop, remove, drain, raise, review, revise, cook, groom, or steal. Just not to take any risks of misunderstanding. You can not control life. It does not wind up perfectly. Only-only area you can control. Masturbation. Hetcì – hetciù. To quote The Pot Belly Wizard. Fragogna, when she began to take pictures of nests of dust accumulated in the corners of her home and his friends' and relatives' homes, would have never imagined the project would continue for seventeen years. The results of this project have given birth to:

> 19,633 film and digital photographs;
> 26 notebooks of notes;
> 4,007 sketches;
> 34 shoe boxes of pictures and clippings;
> 6 boxes of objects found during cleaning operations including: a gold earring, a baby tooth, a series of odd socks That Are Suspected to have twins lost socks in the washing machine;
> 15 bags of fifty liters of fine dust;
> 27 bags of one hundred and ten liters of heavy dust and various waste;
> 120 hanks of hair of various colors and lengths;
> 3 metal bins;
> 8 plastic baskets of various sizes (including three fuchsia, two red, one blue, one gray and one green polka dots and blue);
> A canister vacuum cleaner with wheels;
> 7 brooms with seven buckets;
> 55 dustpans (friends have gifted her many, perhaps ironically);
> No rags.
> Not even gloves.

Unfortunately, there is no proof of the existence of all this material (apart from the book and some photos and images which miraculously survived because at the time they were still in possession of the author) because on the night of 15/01/2013 a band of robbers broke thru the security door of Storage area 54

X 11 in the area where they were classified and for some ungodly reason stole all this stuff.

 Then the lightning cursed.

To honor the memory of these long years of hard and dedicated work, Fragogna has decided to make the book and what's left of Nest Of Dust available simultaneously at the Tate Modern, MoMA and the Hamburger Bahnhof in Berlin. There are also ongoing negotiations with the Palais de Tokyo in Paris and other prestigious venues in China and the UAE but since we are uncertain of the outcome we do not want to perpetrate inconcrete illusions. In any case, and more importantly, The Nest Of Dust exists: under your bed, behind cupboards, between the interstices, in my head. Having said this, I throw myself upon the mercy of the court. Having said this, I defer to the mercy of the court. And anyway, all speeches are questionable. Logically. So

 behold
 it is Jimmy Stewart
 in his final feature film
 set in Africa
 directed by an experimental
 avant-garde
 New Wave filmmaker
 from Japan
 Susumu Hani

 Jimmy Stewart
 must face the basic crisis
 of living
 with a whole bunch
 of other animals all
 being wound up
 together
 in one long piece of
 green silk

 Jimmy Stewart
 must listen to the questions
 of Director Susumu Hani:
 Do you know the way to San Jose?
 Can you take this to the fish?

 behold

when Jimmy Stewart
wears a blue bandana
you must wear a white goatee
and a red tunic
the image of the american flag.

so yes:

this *is* another view of "The Lovely Butcher," unwrapping a side of beef. I liked that TC was next to him drawing the body outlines of everyone there on butcher paper – with a black sharpie – then having them get up out of the outline. Looking down the butcher's table, I could see that SC's face was packed completely with clay / mud (from the garden) and the leftover clay / rose hip mixture from the anti-racism spa treatments. I looked over and she had no mouth. Glimpsing her face with no mouth was profoundly *unheimlich*. "I am interested in what it means to kill a body, and what it means to kill a soul." I think that's what R said. Should have gone with the albino boa section, the way it pushes its snout up beneath the asphalt – so that a paving stone is loosened – and it will be okay. It's not such a severe thing. And yet, who am I? Who are you? What contaminated us? How are your blood vessels surviving? IN ANY SOCIETY BASED ON CLASS, HUMILIATION IS A POLITICAL REALITY. HUMILIATION IS ONE METHOD BY WHICH POLITICAL POWER IS TRANSFORMED INTO SOCIAL OR PERSONAL RELATIONSHIPS. THE PERSONAL INTERIORIZATION OF THE PRACTICE OF HUMILIATION IS CALLED X. C IS AN ARTIST WHO MAKES DOLLS. MAKES, DAMAGES, TRANSFORMS, SMASHES. ONE OF HER DOLLS IS A WRITER DOLL. THE WRITER

DOLL ISN'T VERY LARGE AND IS ALL HAIR, HORSE MANE HAIR, RAT FUR, DIRTY HUMAN HAIR …

>She asked if the Feds would take as evidence
>her collection of black shoes—
>and it's the movement of these things from their spaces,
>the extension of our positions in objects, dislocated by
>>rumors,
>that's tripping me out, as what they testify seems wet but late,
>
>as it is beneath the earth and
>nowhere else, our speech has grain like mascara,
>
>>"fractured"
>>"chopped"
>>"broken"
>>"snapped"
>>and "starved"

So no, this is not the first time that a challenge to the ancient / modern divide has pivoted on the Achaemenid Persian Empire. It was perhaps Hegel who first defied the division through recourse to ancient Persia, provocatively claiming in his *Lectures on the Philosophy of History* that "the Persian empire is an empire in the modern sense." To Hegel, Persia's satrapies were the earthly expression of a Zoroastrian religious philosophy that allowed for humanity's discovery of the self-conscious Spirit as free and independent from matter and nature. Hegel held that the Persian political system entailed not only an interdependent unity, but also the possibility for a kind of freedom, manifested in the ability of each satrapal community to retain its distinctive customs and laws. This dialectic of unity and freedom Hegel associated with "Zoroaster's Light. It is the unifying essence of light that Hegel tied to the beginnings of an awareness of the self-conscious Spirit. Light "enables the individual human being, together with other beings, to achieve freedom to act in as many ways […]" As what? "This almost turbulent silence was dizzying" to quote Toru Takemitsu. But first to describe what it is that makes these 19 poems unusual. The first thing is that they are the same poem repeated 19 times. That might seem to create a sort of silence. If something is repeated often enough it can fade into a kind of silence, a background noise that isn't paid attention to. But is 19 times enough for that? Probably not and any-way, when I say they are the same poem 19 times I'm not giving the full picture. While the text is the same in each instance, on each page it is overlaid with a pencil drawing (composed of a circle and lines within and intersecting it), meaning that visually there are 19 distinct poems. But not that distinct. The variety in the diagrams is fairly minimal and limited. A preface to the text notes that these drawings "originated during the development process of Thus in the crossing, a poetic dance performance in collaboration with the choreographer Elaine Thomas." However "minimal and limited," movement does seem fundamental: the subtle differentiations of the positioning of each diagram in relation to the text is the most readily locatable source or trigger for a response, and for a meaningful reading. It's about as minimal as a flick-book could get, a line shifting about here and there, the sudden appearance of a grid. Minimal though they are, these structures seem positively operatic (I am reminded of the almost invisible painterly marks found when you get real close to Barnett Newman's *Stations of the Cross*). The quieter the background the louder a whisper sounds (the scream of a butterfly, to quote *The Doors*). It becomes emotional as anything when one of the parallel lines that dissect the poem suddenly breeches the circle on page 9. It's sort of an outrage. Like life itself seems at times. This beautiful perfect circle and there's suddenly a line poking through it. There's a powerful tendency to see it as a mistake. To get your Tipp-Ex out! It takes a couple of pages to slide back down and be contained again within the diameter of the circle. There's noise too (or at least movement – and only assassins move silently) in the way that words get obscured by the drawings at various times in the piece. On page 15, the line "you dilly and are little and idle and want to romp" is almost entirely obscured. So much so that you have to take it on trust that it is in fact the same as in the other 18 iterations. Indeed, it isn't, because in the act of attempting to decipher it behind the veil you become sure it says "you are dilly and little and i die." That's what led to a dream I had that she was running with wild horses, leopards, red fox, kangaroos, mountain lions, and wild dogs. They were running over rolling hills. She was able to keep up with the animals and they accepted her. Je me souviens. Maybe that's why je me souviens Florentina Holzinger in an oversize, orange-dyed dress, a muumuu really, if they still make muumuus. Do they? I forget the theater, but she was sitting in a chair center stage. A minute or so earlier, a high fan kick had revealed her vayjayjay, as Oprah might have put it, back in the day. Vincent Riebeek, in a similarly loose blue garment, kneeled to sneak his head between her legs — the image momentarily evoking oral sex. He inched away from Holzinger to display a red string exiting her and entering his mouth. Turning his body to face the audience, he pulled and chewed and the string kept coming. Holzinger lifted her legs into a straddle position. She was also chewing on a piece of red string, creating the illusion that the material was passing seamlessly into one orifice and out the other. Holding their positions — Holzinger in the chair and Riebeek kneeling on the floor — they bounced subtly to the beat of Rihanna's "Man Down," which was playing. Their bodies formed a vibrating tableau with the string passing steadily between them in a single direction. Two. I remember Riebeek directing his attention toward the audience in a "Look at me!" kind of way while enacting a series of movements. Mid head-spiral-into-leg-extension, Holzinger hurled herself toward him while jumping. Without hesitation, they collided. We (the audience) laughed. This scene repeated itself: Holzinger or Riebeek would indulge in moments of solo dancing only to be interrupted by a crash from the other, inevitably provoking laughter from the audience. There was something about the full force with which they moved in and out of contact — never pausing to acknowledge the catastrophe of their two bodies meeting, they just kept going, pummeling each other through time and space all the while maintaining the clarity of intentionally extended limbs. Three. I remember the cerulean blue color of the liquid that Riebeek vomited onto Holzinger's chest. They wore feather-adorned bikinis. Holzinger was lying on the floor and Riebeek was kneeling in between her legs. The violent effort with which he repeatedly rammed his fingers down his throat was more difficult to behold than Holzinger's apathetic gaze. After a sequence of at least five repetitions — gag, vomit, gag, vomit — Holzinger looked back at Riebeek and asked, "Can I hug you?"

So when you get up close, the houses for the deceased —most of them simply made of unfired mud — seem almost as unapproachable as a Rachel Whiteread monument, with mock windows and sealed doors. Indeed, after the funeral, no one enters them or even visits the site. These miniature mosques were, for centuries, the only structures erected by a nomadic people — until Stalin instituted settlement plans along with a secularization campaign. Many of the tombs are crowned with animal horns, representing an animist tradition that has coexisted with Islam. Other, newer graves lie under round metal cages that symbolize the yurt: these skeletal versions of the tent became a popular, airy habitat for the soul when Russian-produced iron was cheaply available in the 70s. Direct Soviet influences can be seen in the photographs of the departed — kiln-fired onto porcelain and attached to ornamented granite markers or steles built from dried mud. In one striking image a shamanistic eagle sits on top. So yes, I'm interested in the idea of exformation, which refers to explicitly discarded information — immaterial data that are crucial in shaping contemporary narratives but disappear in the process of compression, editing, or dispersion. The unknown unknowns of knowledge. With my piece *Air Rights* — a meteorite magically levitating above a pedestal — I refer to the real estate concept of empty space above a property and to the fabrication of value (out of nothing but air) in financial games and gentrification processes. Air rights, of course, are a lucrative territory for speculation. True, but for the second stage of *Phantom Library* you are commissioning fiction based on imaginary books you found mentioned in other books. How much control do you retain over the outcome? I'm interested in the loss of control over works. I imagined a work that can change its form and status after it is produced and even after it is sold. The *Phantom Library* installation is an ongoing project based on fictional books that have never physically existed themselves but were mentioned within existing books by authors such as Philip K. Dick, Stanisław Lem, Jorge Luis Borges, Vladimir Nabokov, among others. I acquired ISBN numbers and barcodes to give these books actual economic identities, and then produced one physical copy of each. I imagined that in the very near future — this is already being tested at different engineering labs — there will be mass production of unique objects, each one the result of a negotiation between nano agents, or altered by an algorithm. So all sounds are pure sounds, even the coded ones, which might be all of them. I mean, the hyper-egg must be local, and all things must be 'it'. There is the abandoned churchyard in New Orleans, for example, now repurposed — and redecorated — by a group of 21st-century acolytes of Aleister Crowley; there is the remote stone circle built in Northern California by what I would describe as a post-hippie couple with access to land-moving equipment; there is the otherwise indistinguishable collegiate house in central Massachusetts where wiccan priests are being trained; there is the corporate convention center in downtown San Jose; the overgrown tombs of the Mississippi Delta, where we meet a rather extraordinary burglar; there is even what sounds like an Airbnb rental gone unusually haywire in the hills of New Hampshire. So, four years later, I am parked out front of the same unfucking mall. Fuck if I am not in an old Ford. Unfuckingbelievable. Downstairs, more plates crash against a wall. The plates!! There must be an endless assortment of them. So here is my disembodied voice. Here is something I wrote late last night while my eyes were burning. I will not let you conceptualize the voice off of the subject position that committed the act. As if I could stop you. But. I am everywhere, my body is everywhere. That's why the horoscope for Pisces in the *Sunday Chronicle* said, "Water is life. But true love is smell. If you love someone's smell – skin smell, sweat smell, mouth smell, those deep dark inside of you smells – it's true love." "Then you must true love Beatrice." Mom poked me playfully with her smooth big toe. She was thinking of how I liked to run my fingers along the inside of our bulldog's drooping lips, then smell the wetness. It was all mossy and meaty and decaying wood. And when Beatrice yawned, I stuck my face right *in*side her gentle underbite. I remember these things, too: Finding a stranded sea turtle, its enormous shell, heavy, round and brown as our coffee table. Black sand fleas swarming our ankles and the turtle's leathery flippers. Beatrice licking the turtle's large, black eye. The long track carved in the sand where the turtle had dragged itself from the water. Begging Mom to drive the turtle to the animal hospital. Mom saying, "The turtle should die on this beach. It shouldn't die in the back of a Subaru." In other words, consider this earth as evidence of a little scintillation of "rays." "Rerouting, rewiring," 24 / 7 / 365. A champing at the borders of things. Messy, illegible. But perhaps we shouldn't care. Because there are borders and there are no borders. So we recognize one familiar question but it seems worth re-asking: is it re as "again" or re as "new." Re as "again" leads to PAK, QWIK, CRISP — products. So forget products. And consider "sey": It's not even a word in our language. It could simply be a sigh, a light breath, evanescently articulated. Yet it's still palpable after all these years. So go with the quirky bits and shifts; invite the visitations; but maybe it's re as something else entirely, neither forward nor back. I mean, it's like *when Eiríkur talks about the Vietnamese train being "much longer than the Icelandic train," he's cracking a joke, since Iceland has never had a train system.* So yes, I guess lizards *are* twitchy liquid; this is what happens when you say something three times. Which genre does your life fit into? Please fill out. As simulation begins to feel like memory and the smell of light floats through the city's several Abattoirs, this is Ancient Greek. The sanction of antiquity. Of course that only makes sense if you already do. A terrible smell was replacing you. Shellsuit and liquid shank. Mass graves and incinerators have been unable to cope with the quantity of radioactive Fukushima boar corpses. But "I'm not trying to justify a very small image! I can't comment on a piece of footage less than two inches across!" A hundred paragraphs ahead. Condemnation intonation. We can't properly get asleep to go to it. Put quotes around they have no real interest in the issue, so they fade away quickly, depriving the agitators of their most valuable weapon. On the fucking hook! Wise is the shine! Another flashpoint to the west of the capital city. And we just do. We just take the revelation of conventional banking capital's involvement in the loan-shark sector's growth as an open call to hog-tie the investors. Whose estate's the realest now? Likely targets fall in or dilate relativistically, ground zero falsified as the iterating triangulation of. Aura count as fuck. How correct we know these words to be, relieved of the head they once modified. Turn solid. But wait! But what if we've got the wording wrong? What if

    somewhere, deep in my body
    the genome
    stood up and started oh I don't know, anyway
    heasps or heaps
    forget about it

Bedtime storytime. The answers to these questions are hidden in the seven following correct magical sequences, each sequence containing precisely just five words per unit. Oh wait. I was all like

    "I was so turned around I believed
    ....
    That wheat flour was potash
    And a mortar a felt hat
    ....
    That the sky was a copper pan
    And clouds were calf-skins
    That the morning was evening
    And a cabbage stump a turnip
    The soured beer was young wine
    And a battering ram a windmill
    And a hangman's noose a bridle"

Or maybe that wasn't me. Maybe that was François Villon. Maybe you are keying in the sequence to unlock the transformation of an eschatological blip. So when you freeze into our pusbus crystal of the Cowboys & Aliens "my face ramp dot hex"? Think about that, from the position of the adjective in the noun phrase of the subject. "But you are burning plastic near her lip," we sang, nearly supine past the line of double cages. Don't just watch ?v=Zmo8DG1gno4&. Don't even. Return the children to their cubicle of stone in the sky. Loot rice. Rip Cadbury Digits. Either way, you have made use of precisely the wrong irony, because you failed to read *The Fascism of the Broom* prior to getting drunk and muttering desperately into the broadcast: "Oh my God! Another vehicle! That clearly is a vehicle!" You failed to read the *Notebooks* of Pocahontas Mildew. You failed to calibrate our precision flame integrator. Next. All this is code. And the glass which you touch, to drink, forms around your whole body where finally the serious glass animals sing, and I, like a dragonfly, demand a Nervous Overstimulation. People there were choking, there. When I am the blood I'll be the Thing. Regular sexual health checks should be part of your life. & when the wind changed I stayed that way waiting all day for the head to come home I only wanted to kiss the head and pat its pate / I am only waiting for my turn kiss the head and pat its pate. Which is to say

I! have! watched! the! little!
heaps! gather! themselves!
up! and! shoot! themselves!
out! I! have! praised hoped!
heaped! up! little! gathers!

It! consists! merely! of! a!
membrane! My! first!
experiments! were! with!
sand! or! a! wide-mouthed!
tube! of! a! convenient! shape!

Singing! on! land! carefully!
!!!!!!!!! when! the! moist!
paste! dries. !!!!!!!!!!!!!!!!!!
it! never! goes! away! I! can!
feel! it! and!!!!! then! there

would be no need for pieces of lake

!!!

****
****
****

It was late August when the four-hundred-year-old Spanish chestnuts were full and thick in splays of green just before the great blaze, and two stones sat and so in love had turned to swans. "Oh Cornish granite, it mates for life," she said, and they all watched silently: "yes, everything is a kind of code," she dreamt, absentmindedly, but it was more of a song than a code. It was 1887, it was 1968, it was long before and much later than after. And even later than that. A small gray rat sat in the living room, his fur sleek and clean. He vanished, like the others. It felt like a Viking funeral pyre, given a particularly Borgesian subtext — the sacrifice of the microcosm — as if every city should ritually destroy miniature versions of itself as a collective means for / what. For what, exactly?' ', '', '!
' ,'! '!
, ,
'! '
, ,
' '! '
, ,
'! '
, ,
' '! '
, ,
'! '! '! '! '!   '! '
, , , , , , , , , , , , , , , , , , , , , , , , ,

'is', 'a', 'the', 'The', 'in', 'problem', 'can', 'lay', 'bare', 'the', 'anomalies', 'of', 'affect', 'that', 'are', 'responsible', 'for', 'the', 'structure', 'of', 'the', 'complex', '.', 'I', 'shall', 'attempt', 'a', 'complete', 'lysis', 'of', 'this', 'morbid', 'body', '.', 'to', 'get', 'rid', 'of', 'the', 'worm-', 'eaten', 'roots', 'of', 'the', 'structure', '.', 'The', 'No', 'one', 'would', 'dream', 'of', 'doubting', 'that', 'its', 'major', 'artery', 'is', 'fed', 'from', 'the', 'heart', 'of', 'those', 'various', 'theories', 'that', 'have', 'tried', 'to', 'prove', 'that', 'the',

',
',
'','','','', 'whose', 'fruit', 'often', 'drops', 'before', 'it', 'is', 'ripe', '?', 'Yes', ',', 'in',
'one', 'way', ',', 'the', ',
',
',
',

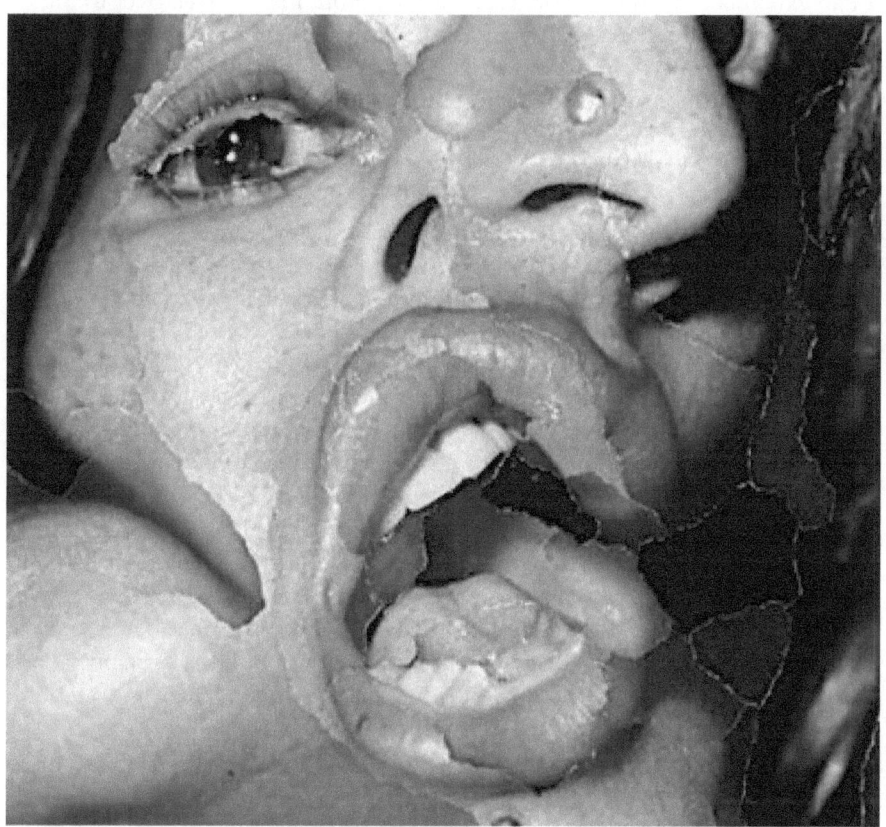

So yes, we're obliged to those we want to see, even when they come in other bodies and leave again without them. The shells of their bodies litter our rooms, exposed to the air and us. Crawl inside: they are camouflage, armored personnel carrier, barrier against all the anger there is. We enter them like empire. It will not be OK. Do I demand confessions, then, do I demand retrospectives based on them? I make a list to assuage a tendency, which is to say that tho I WAS A TEENAGE MICROFINANCE BARON, it doesn't help any.

> So I search the sky for the sign of a path,
> But it is always full of clouds,
> And Babel's workmen, dead by suicide

These are lines from Cecília Miereles' poem "Speech" and it's been much in mind lately because I was recently in an airplane, flying at an altitude of 39,000 feet, peering out a small oval window down into clouds, imagining what that fabled city might have looked like, complete. Before Todd and his family left for an extended stay in the Ivory Coast last autumn, I had driven over to the California home he shares with poet Sarah Vap and their three young sons. We'd filled large sheets of paper with the colors of a million crayons. We'd investigated questions of mathematical proportions. We'd eaten tuna sandwiches on thick slices of bread. Not too long after, I was driving around LA, crossing off errands in preparation for that window-seat flight when the car radio announced ocean-front violence in the Ivory Coast. If I could tune my ears to a particular frequency, might the radio relay news of a particular family? Might noise-canceling headphones be plugged into some secret channel, transmitting echoes of ancient crumbling? Back at my kitchen table, I scoured the internet: Six figures in black appeared on the beach. They wore balaclavas. They carried guns. They opened fire. The final tally: 22 dead. Later, I learned Todd had been at Grand-Bassam only a week before the fatal attacks. During one crawl through Tompkins Square, he wore a business suit while arduously dragging his body along the ground, using his elbows and knees. For other crawls up Broadway, in a nine-year project called "The Great White Way," he wore a Superman costume. I mean, nobody is going to remember their stereo system from 2015 when they are 82 in Paris, drinking tea with their own mutant offspring, who may or may not have come from their own: biology: and may instead – which is just the same and sometimes better, quite frankly: be their dog. They are giving out turkeys at the Public Assistance Office, wrapped in plastic, the legs folded in, balled for convenience, you must have had to write your name on a raffle ticket …

> Later on, I thought it was
> funny to put your head
> on Barbie's body.
>
> I'm sorry, and I'm really sorry, but say
> you are in a room waving
> when your arm flies off.
>
> So then you're calm cool and collected
> and go call an ambulance,
>
> But now your other arm wants to go too!

Then punches you to death cause you won't let it.

Say that since "There's nothing / a ghost hates / more than complaining," "We are the Spanish Harps, / We certainly hope you [still] like us. / We are the Spanish Harps, / Vwing, Vwing, Vwing".

☾

So write out yr birthday numerically, like
my friend x was born 06 october 1980 or 06 10 1980

reduce each of the 3 numbers to 1 digit like this
0+6 =6
1+0 =1
1+9+8+0 =18 -> 1+8 =9

add them up
6+1+9 =16

keep adding until you get a single digit
1+6 =7

unless you hit a doubled digit aka 11 or 22
in which case you are a master number +

☽ [moon sign]

I can only imagine you'll this enjoy to the max, so please fulfill its and your destinies, if you don't mind. And speak to your host, of course, if the mood strikes 'cos that would be coolness. It's actually lifted from a song lyric by the late Danish band Vår ... Oh, wait, I take that back. I did play some Star Wars racing game whose title I can't remember. Let's see, okay ... "the best song ever" turns out to only survive as choral melodic fragments, "woah oh oh" and "oooh yeah," onomatopoetic signifiers of togetherness and bliss. The best song ever constitutes a paralinguistic place beyond where words mean, they travelled to this realm that night, and it was there they experienced a protopop that was an uberpop, an *apokalypsis* in the literal sense, that as the strappings of any particular song were stripped away, the evidence was revelatory. A revelation, critically, that the singer can no longer remember. Like imagine if Dante had woken up and thought "best katabasis ever" but never written about the terrace of the gluttons or the fifth sphere of heavenly warriors → Continue reading →

• The poem Gaia Is Gone by Louise Anne Buchler is linked to the words "Gaia."

• The sound piece Gaia's Flesh and an Untitled Poem by Alice Hui-Sheng Chang is linked to the words "flesh," "history," "geography."

• The poem Becoming Gaia / a liturgy to accompangy transition by Markie Burnhope is linked to the words "toxins," "genes," "contortions," "textures," "holes."

• The artwork Untitled (Landscape) by Lefteris Tapas is linked to the words "My holes, my parasites, my luminosity, my turbulences are oracles."

• The visual poem Not Without Newsprint by John Morgan is linked to the words "membrans," "geography," "turbulences," "dead."

• The poem Ventricle by Steve Toase is linked to the words "goddesses," "fallen," "heart" from the source text Gaia's Flesh.

• The video Evanescent episodes: arrival and exodus by Caroline de Lannoy is linked to the words "MIraculous MOmentary SAtisfaction," "We become Gaia" from the source text Gaia's Flesh.

• The poem Estuary by Ann Matthews is linked to the words "dead," "trees," "dandelion fluff," "turbulent," "between sea and marsh."
• The poem Terrible Goddess by Yoko Danno is linked to the words "yesterday," "swallow," "living," "wind," "pile," "human," "pear tree," "earth."

∞

Gaia's Flesh
My toxins, my temperatures, my hormones, my precipitations
      are climatic.
My genes, my blood cells, my organs, my wilderness are
      history.
My contortions, my breathing, my colors, my mutations are
      intelligence.
My textures, my membranes, my secretions, my definitions
      are geography.
My holes, my parasites, my luminosity, my turbulences are
      oracles.

                                        in tenebris
            walking the land between sea and marsh
                                        in tenebris
            floating the cows like funerary urns
                                        in tenebris
            glossing the mud as the jewelled head
                                        in tenebris
            the sea creatures near converse
                                        in tenebris
            3.21

            light coming into sky above still black
            ridge, bird slanting toward pine branch
            in foreground, sound of wave in channel

basically a super boosting of extinction studies into an end of the anthropocene Skynet after-party. I mean, the giant robot in the sky is full of doom and riot, almost equally, right? It's worth YouTubing. As is *Marcel The Shell With Shoes On*. I mean, if

    'A mammoth
    Unstitched from the mighty thigh of the glacier, is the Roaring
            Id'

Then

    In the hand world
    She is my Hand Therapist

Still, the worth of a record clearly doesn't lie in market value, and the press' founders certainly don't seem delusional about how much traction or attention this kind of art object is going to receive. The audience doesn't necessarily seem to be the point. This is made clear in the first minute and a half of the record itself, where Myles reads a poem, messes up, tries again, messes up again, and says, "Fuck, it's so hard" before reading the whole poem from the top. "Darkness" becomes "dahkness" and "party" becomes "pahty," etc. What's that word that means fat, or round. Orotose or something. Chubby. There's a kind of fish called a chub. Which is precisely why we have been invited to join the inspection teams. And why we are using night vision to look at our reflection. And why we entertain the idea that we are noctilucent creatures. In reality we are ghost channels: *You* can hear the bang only because *we*'ve already heard it. Ghost channels? Wind tunnels.

When the liquid in the glass is filled with small stars, corroded wiring and a ringing doorbell, that's when the groove begins. In time feedback gradually maximizes and the underground biomass succeeds in getting us to embrace their technology and to build their Hatches. Life expectancy is replaced by slasher films flashbacks. Not playing viola is a choice, not *being able* to play viola is the result of unspoken civil war. Parachute material identical to the carbon make-up of the slowly dying population is being packed and shipped to storage. A series of occlusions now made apparent. Make no mistake; no poetic liberties have been taken. This is a very coherent flow; this is physics. The funniest joke in physics is the equation proving that the time it takes to travel between two molecules of gas in a sealed chamber might exceed the projected age of the universe. So we let ourselves be smudged with the local sage by our mother, who positioned us in alignment with the sun, and sang: over each of us: the Gayatri mantra. Did our lives visibly improve? No. And yet … Yes. Things go well when we deepen our experience of the garden, of our family, of the relationship of language to power. Things go well when we connect to languages that are not the languages we speak. Things go well when we read Guibert-Nathanaël in the garden, even when it starts to get dark. What weaves through all the words and images is being-in-the-world, alive and dead at the same time, moving objects by means of creation, as the hands of ghosts, luminosity, and shadows intercede and sometimes overcome the text, changing the collaboration from that of one between two gifted artists / writers to a larger work created by the pressures of being and time (no caps). The words are recovered from meaning narrowly by the collages opposing them: naked decomposing humans and incomplete horses stand at a stone wall, whose leads to darkness while "Lenin on a bench beside a lake / disturbed /Adrenaline-drenched /on a beach at Waikiki / carries a cane" as he wanders into the scene. What more could one want? Which is to say, he was clutching at his temples. "This would all be a lot easier if it wasn't for that sound!" "What sound?" "Gaaaaaaaahdammit, that sound!" and he pointed at the sidewalk, at the weeds growing through it, at his own feet, at a woman walking by with a stroller, inside of which a baby cried. "Lance, what sound? What sound?" "Oh, for Christ's sake. You guys can't hear it because you've lived here too long. It must be the trainyard. Or the underground electric cables. Or, I don't know. It's like a constant goddamn ooooooooooooo. You don't hear it?" Then he saw a limping dog across the street. The wound on its leg was festering, and it stopped to lick it. The sound grew louder and louder, rising again from the bedrock, through the sewers, through the sidewalk, permeating the city:

MMMMMAAAAAAAAAAAHHH
Lance fell to his knees
AAAAAAHHHHHH
fists at his ears,
AAAAAAAAHHHHHH
weeping. The baby
AAAAAAAAAHHHHH
screamed. Hannah patted
AAAAAAHHHHH
his shoulders, trying to bring him
AAAAHHHH
back to his senses.
AAAAAAAAAAHHHHHHHH
The dog barked, spraying the
AAAAAAAAAAAHHH
air with a
AAAAAAAAHHH
cloud of
AAAAAAAAHHH
pus. The sound
AAAAHHHH

5485

was overwhelming, the rumbling of AAAARRRGGGGGHHHH
amplified decay,
AAAAHHHH
of primordial rupture, inherent disorder
MMMMMAAAAAAAAAAAAAAAAHHHHHH
something wailing at the bottom of everything.

"Well, this limpkin's a very peculiar kind of bird," Johnson continued. "It's nocturnal, you see, only comes out around night and tends to stay away from people like you and me. In fact, they're actually easier to hear than see, seein' as they got these real weird calls, y'know, like the kind they use for jungle noises in Tarzan movies. Now, them limpkins don't set down on nothin' but water hyacinth and shellflower and other kinds of them floating plants, I been told, and eat only these tiny little snails – apple snails, they're called. Tiny little fuckers, real hard to come by." Johnson seemed to stare straight through Wayne's eyes. "Well, anyhoo, one day there's an old black crow around and he's got this rat carcass, you see, and it's all rotting and nasty, eyes half-pecked out, but the crow holds onto it all jealous-like. And then that old black crow sees this limpkin flyin' by and he turns around real quick and he looks up and you know what he says? Do ya?" "Uh, no." Johnson took a step closer, his face now less than six inches from Wayne's, and said: *"Caawww! Caawww! Caawww!"* The whole office seemed to vibrate. Which is to say, while janitors' jobs in malls and in corporate offices with swanky toilets that do not involve "manual scavenging" go to non-Dalits, there are (officially) 1.3m people, mostly women, who continue to earn their living by carrying baskets of human shit on their heads as they clean out traditional-style toilets that use no water. Though it is against the law, the Indian Railways is one of the biggest employers of manual scavengers. Its 14,300 trains transport 25m passengers across 65,000 kilometres every day. Their shit is funnelled straight onto the railway tracks through 172,000 open-discharge toilets. This shit, which must amount to several tonnes a day, is cleaned by hand, without gloves or any protective equipment, exclusively by Dalits. While the Prohibition of Employment as Manual Scavengers and their Rehabilitation Bill (2012) was cleared by the cabinet and by the Rajya Sabha (the upper house of the Indian parliament) in September 2013, the Indian Railways has ignored it. Which is OK in a sad way, given that, with deepening poverty and the steady evaporation of government jobs, a section of Dalits has fiercely guarded its "permanent" state employment as hereditary shit-cleaners against (I don't know what else to call them) predatory interlopers. So yes, it's time to snap those chaps, which does NOT mean it's time to get Freudian with a man with a pickle. Which is to say

Xo quwollen swirm, ort
swait ib durrs urk klurpf. Sheb

bloor de dule dun
jud cack fump glire. Eb

orry sluit ot neb Atsum imba
burft Merp av ords. Een Ien
ughalls ig ahrs unt nimbet twool
Begroob, ig ooburs quwate ag blurg.

There should be many hooks.
I don't like green.
Where should birds be located.
Where do we want thermometers and their character.

What lies undiscovered today may well be discovered anon.
More colored light! must be the watchword.
I do not understand the mutilation of the marble tub.
My motto is "J'ai Dit".

Dah-DAH dah-DAH dah-DAH dah-DAH
dah-DAH dah-DAH dah-DOH.
Dah-DAH dah-DAH dah-DAH dah-DIFF
dah-DAH dah-DAH dah-DOH.

"They talk to themselves, constantly repeating, with an intensity causing their etheric doubles, grass, to vibrate as they pass, vivifying growth.

To rabbits and young children they're visible, but I see points of light, tiny clouds of color and even smaller gleams.

The lawn is covered with these flashes."

Is everywhere we go a ruined orchard? The premise, that is, for a Russian play that has been translated into English by someone who received a small payment in return for that translation? "Sorry, Mister Rogers, my apologies," said the commissioner, one hand on the sweatered elbow. "We thought you were Pee-Wee Herman." So it's true, then, I am no expert on phenomenology or anything, only there is that problem of how to turn into body that which is OK as air. To "montetize" is to make spirit material. Blogger offers this service. Or, as Joanna Russ put it, "Sometimes you bend down to tie your shoe, and then you either tie your shoe or you don't." Often the poet thinks of the phrase "beau desordre" but has a difficult time finding out much about it because her French is poor. America is not a city. No, sir. No ma'am. Nah to all that. A little nadie for una vez. You're floating, you're letting yourself float, it's harder than it looks. You've nearly got your minding where you want it: thoughts looking down on you instead of poking at the hinges. Even the good thoughts, like about how time is a cultural construct, powerless before a music. Or what if we give up cultivation and eat knotweed. You start listing the names of weeds you've feared. Thoughts vogue against the sun. The phrase "nature off-camera." Suture. Sutra. On the one hand, a stitch-line to bind flesh together. On the other, a line of language to bind thought. An anarchic piece of medical tape caught in the act of fusing different tissues, different bodies, different genres. Who *is* she? She is Dr. Frankenstein and so she has doctor sleeves. But she is Dr. Frankenstein with a yoga mat. She is Dr. Frankenstein and there are turbines and crackles and buzzing, problematical 'oms.' Remember Neva, the woman from Jupiter, who put a sprig of mugwort under her pillow. And I was also thinking of reprinting "Spew Forth" — "No singularity, no verdicts, only chords and this endless accrual" — so remember Azule Linga, the transchanneling poet. Azule has "attained [female?] vector equilibrium." I love this idea of caste as psychological imprint. Class is such a tender issue for me. Whenever I think about it, I get upset. I chose to take on a more middle class lifestyle but I've done so kicking and screaming all the way, and in my interactions with people I often feel I'm wearing the equivalent of a girdle. I originally mistyped "girdle" as "griddle," which I find funny and a bit uncanny, since I worked as a grill cook to help pay for college. Caste versus social class becomes griddle versus girdle — you enter a situation as fresh cabbage and exit as sauerkraut. Sort of. Frenzied salaciousness, as you said above.

>   my at home ex
>   perience @ kitchen ~~skin~~ sink
>   —ing
>   thru w/ the teleo-vision he says
>   open
>   wide we need an enhanced *sit*
>   *-uational understanding*
>   blood-
>   sugar poeman ~~introverted~~ inverted milgram
>   ex-peri-mint
>   "Eat Up" "Eat Shit" "Shut Up" "Stand
>   Down"
>   "fuck yr lipid bilayer!"

So correct me if I'm off, but the more floors a thing has, the less mysterious the first. But the scarier. Granted, mystery and fear are not the only variables at play here. I'm thinking of both all the towers I've really been in, and all the video game towers. When a building has only a first floor, I think of basements. When it has two floors, I think of attics. Now I'm thinking about how unstable particles get when there are only a few of them. For Sam Sax this turns into a "motorcade of ghosts," and for Patricia No, it turns from a scar into an ocean into a piano bench. If you read the whole thing, part of what you will read is Fatimah Asghar's litany of "again," from "ramen and toast for dinner again" to "lied when a stranger asked where your dad / lived, again" to "dreamt god raked his fingers through the earth, again." And then Vanessa Borjon's "oyster of home." And then Lillian-Yvonne Bertram's "This mistook won't be forgiven." And then Alok Vaid-Menon and CeCe McDonald talking about "the prison industrial complex, trans visibility, and queer liberation," with McDonald asking who's seen Sage Smith from Charlottesville, Virginia. And who has time to care about other standards? They are never throwing the same party into the same river. But they *are* picking through the rotted entrails of a corpsed body-politic, intoxicated by the acrid fumes of old flesh, performing the dredge-core evocation of a corpus mysticum, an ecstatic futurology divining a dank sludgescape populace that is disoriented, corrupted and feverishly fucked; new flesh, new territories, new headaches, anabolic, polyfibroproliferative … Then there is the great story of how the poet was writing and her daughter made the after-the-fact obvious statement: "Everything tastes better in a spoon." This has so much meaning. This has so much meaning because then the door bell rang, rang and rang. I reluctantly left my couch and made for the door, as if wading through water. I found nobody at the door except a large, black swallowtail, floating away, whispering "When you come to a fork in the road, take it. R.I.P. L.P.B." I returned to my seat and took up the book I had been reading. The pages were blank, all the words gone. I couldn't even remember exactly what I was reading. It must have been a book on a learn-while-sleeping method by a famous lepidopterist. The door bell started ringing, louder and louder. A ravine was under my nose, and beyond, an overhanging cliff with a few low pines in the shapes of crouching animals. *We made too many wrong mistakes.*

Still, she made a much better speech back in 1966, I think it was, playing Charlotte Corday in the film of Peter Weiss' "Marat-Sade" – I guess you remember it, she's up at the top of a ladder, going off her head, and screaming something along the lines of "what is this city, what is this thing they're dragging through the streets?" Christ, if she'd done that in parliament, I might have rethought my relationship with electoral politics. Well, maybe not. But seriously, what was that thing they were dragging through the streets on April 17th, or whatever day it was. In any case, the photograph appeared in an auction catalog, and I was fascinated to discover that these two bits of wood were pieces of George Washington's coffin. It seemed OK to place them alongside a few crumpled drawings made by Antonin Artaud, created through black magic, and thrown onto the roofs of several of his enemies. And oh! I just remembered: the first painting I made when I got out of grad school was called "mouthpiece" in homage to Eric Dolphy ... and so I made the painting with the brush held in my mouth. So yes, the dog dance is standard: one lilts up, another pads. Aye, fuck it, be not dispirited, (hone in) on target, as is thy will, like king Jesus force fed mescall worms, too SWEET for his HACKING COUGH. And with mist then would I your centipede king go pathic the world is their destruction time to leave this place GO! eat some lube. A lot of it. A 9-Foot 'Butcher Crocodile' Likely Ruled Before Dinosaurs. The challenge was to conceive a project that could travel in a carry-on suitcase and unfold on the walls like a .zip file, a portable infinite able to expand slowly during the months prior to the inevitable discovery of the parallel black pencils pointing against the wall which are suspended somewhere in the air by the tension of nine archery cords. This point of view becomes particularly clear in his *Wild Cubes*: steel cages that enclose nothing. Let us not neglect that it was just, it was centuries ago. They burn everything in its path. Let us not neglect.

> Everything is not pure speech, someone yells
> resonance between a mountain and another
> one that goes straight to there: a shout
>
> where-no-no
>
> decrepit words like vague headlines ("surveillance equipment installed in
>   the building was broken but broadcast video of alleged murderers"
>   dot dot dot   what? who knows? that's all)
>
> several viruses rotate in the air –
>
> not you, he, we, you, they
> still sounds
>
> last body catches a whip forward
>
> if the act is done, meat is done, it
> hisses, so on the mountain
> to a speech is accused dismantling its terminologies:
> what is capitalized, one thing
> bird inside height, not one more thing next to something else
>
> cockroach flees specific languages
> those that locate, placed
> a soul brick, spirit dog happens to you
>
> all rise

Where there is not is what survives in a narrow margin. It is that word. Pristina: "every poem is under a stone" So:

Give me the sheriff star pinned to the mermaid and that tiny piece of wood from your throat.

Give me the saw blade, the plastic cat's eye.

Birds are molecules of something big.

What is something big? The Emergency Heart.

The practice of Perfect Wisdom is nothing

But the practice of Perfect Compassion

Nothing matters apart from this

The Emergency Heart is distracted by nothing

Even its own distractions

The Emergency Heart fears nothing

Even its own fears

Gone, gone, gone fully beyond!

Perfect Solidarity!

Emergency Heart Sutra!

More than fifty regular actions and easily the same number of micro-actions determine the enveloping and the tissues of density near and far on which this depends. So pop the glass eye from the mildewed outlet. "What now of the lyric elect?" Cavalcanti says, BTW, this is precisely what I suggested Dante make evident with *Vita Nuova* after the death of Beatrice. Death resides like the shadow of Mars in the hollow of love, its condition as infinite commentary. His little book is a diagnostic manual for poets and lovers, both therapeutic cure and viral poison. Guinizelli says, "Some people would never have been in love, had they never heard love talked about." La Rochefoucauld. Beatrice dei Portinari says, ALL people would never, et cetera. Cecce Angiolieri says, Oh not that tired old cliché :(You'll be getting out your Barthes and Winterson next ;) There was a young girl from Firenze / Who met an old Priest called Mackenzie / she … [This content is currently unavailable]. Dante di Maiano says, Everyone knows it's important to name the symptom; you have to give a name to the trauma, it is the first indispensable step on the way to a diagnosis. Nomina sunt consequential rerum. Then you take your piss to the doctor. Lulu says, You know you make me want to SHOUT! Nicola Masciandaro says, It's like trying to name a beautiful, dangerous, and indifferent animal passing through the room that no one else seems to see […] Beatrice dei Portinari says, I am the faceless face of nameless horror! LOL. Donna Gentile *con 7 l'altre donne* like this. Cecco Angiolieri says, @ Beatrice: you are the number 9, babe, the de-mathematization of number – not measure nor metrics but diagram. ;). Professor Daniel Charles Barker says, 9=0, the key to decimal syzygetic complementarity, the graph of abstract intensive waves of distribution controlling the social networks of competitive decentralization.

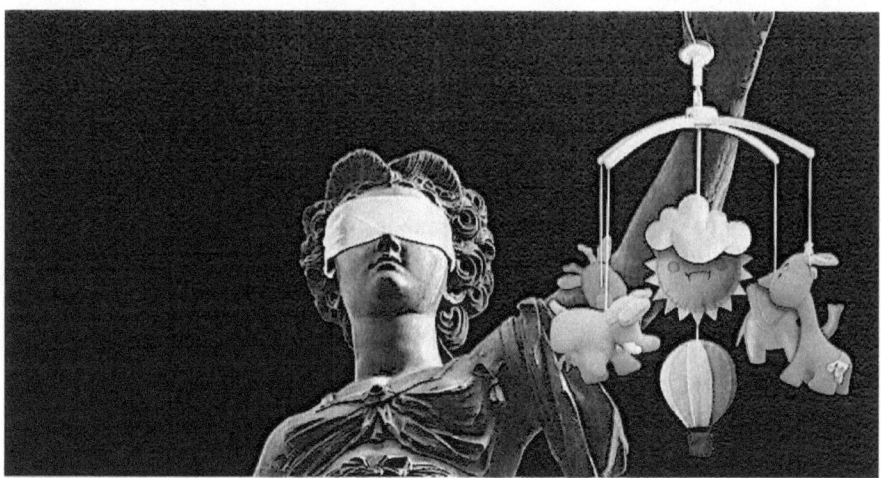

Robin MacKay and Ray Brassier like this. Lulu says, You know you make me want to SHOUT! Professor Challenger says, Voila! Kendra says, "The devil has eaten your soul. Rise up! Rise up!" Or is it "Wise up! Wise up!" ??? She's almost unintelligible. Still, the News Feed and commentary continue to update themselves. And my persona is personafictation of lignes des fuites and sorties des zigzag lineaments. In the winter balloons. Then Count Myshkin returns to Russia from Switzerland where he underwent treatment at a mental hospital. On a train, he meets with Parfyon Rogozhin, who tells him of his passionate love for Nastasia Filippovna. Upon his arrival at St. Petersburg, the count introduces himself to his distant relative Mrs. Yepanchin, her husband General, their three daughters as well as to the General's secretary Ganya Ivolghin. The portrait of Nastasia Filippovna, which the count sees at the Yepanchins, makes a great impression on him. Awards: 2 wins. Prof. Challenger took out his old Baruch. Doctor lens doctor Lens: what is, for instance, a joke? How does a proverb differ from a maxim? And a maxim is not an aphorism, and what is a saying, an expression, an 'old saying' and how does the cliché … PleasE RemoVe yer hat when coming to this parole. The nest as "a child's head, wrapped in bandages." So one can speak of the good mental health of Van Gogh who, in his whole adult life, cooked only one of his hands and did nothing else except once to cut off his left ear, in a world in which every day one eats vagina cooked in green sauce or penis of newborn child whipped and beaten to a pulp, just as it is when plucked from the sex of its mother. And this is not an image, but a fact abundantly and daily repeated and cultivated throughout the entire developed world. Perhaps that is why I was under the impression that the Solar Eclipse that occurred yesterday was scheduled as a 7-day anniversary of Eugene Chadbourne playing Café Oto, but apparently that wasn't true, tho it should have been … just had a not unrelated thought about Rib Eye Steak, having a food called such a thing makes me wish that we had eyes in our ribs, eyes in faces ONLY are SO old skool … Anyway Eugene's music reminds me of blowing raspberries on a cow's stomach on acid while it gently strokes your head with its hoof … I mean, me on acid, not the cow. When he started his Banjo introduction to the lullaby chamber I was caught up in the contrast between his blue shiny shirt (I wanted to get up and rub the shirt through my fingers while the banjo acted as a theme track to my doing so) and his electric rake at the bottom of a rabbit's burrow, I wanted to sink into a grapefruit, I needed to grow spots for a new form of fish, I mean, a young American couple sat in front of me with thoroughly and awesomely shampooed heads, flopping over each other in a moon formation. I spent the majority of the time starring at their amazing scalps while in my peripheral vision I experienced brown and green trees flying into each other in some bizarre shit lo-fi time lapse. I can only imagine that the result would be the creation of a new planet or listeners turning purple and developing horns on the stomach that sporadically spat out different forms of the rhizome. With the restraint of time being against us on pondering such questions a report is due, scrapp slarrkk ar ca … I mean, I always thought of storing my radio in couscous but then I felt that this was being weird.

> Security Guard: "Errr what are you doing ?"
>
> Psychedelic Bolshevik & NN: "Reading …"
>
> SG: "Are you here with the pantomime group upstairs?"
>
> PB NN: "We're here with the reading"
>
> SG: "You can't just be in here"
>
> PB NN: "Where can we read then?"

SG: "You can hire a room"

PB NN: "How much?"

SG: "£25 an hour"

PB NN: " We'll give you 90p?"

***At this point we were escorted from the site of our creative bumble, condemned to the cold, ostracised when all we wanted to do was read (over the top of each other in loud and quiet ways, experimenting with delivery and intonation), instead we went for Funky Pie and confused our politics. We confused our hunger. So when Swamp Dogg asks "Why wasn't I born with Orange skin and Green hair …?" I can say, oh, you were, brother. But it's not that I want us to apprehend the world in this way, it's that we in fact do apprehend the world this way – perhaps not exactly in the way I've explained, but still in some way that is more-or-less comparable. Thus were secrets of the trade made available on key-chains. Limited edition, and locally grown, and locally grown, and the end of the world. Then the comic book ended. There were so many pages unwritten or drawn on, but the reader was required to come to halt. I kept turning the pages. Nothing happened. Something happens. It is aleatory, then it isn't. It is contingent, then it isn't. It is determined, then it isn't. It is a satire and a ritual. It is pastoral. It has a lot of heft. I was *there*, man … Batteries extra. Have I mastered the country-house poem yet?

Pablo

O Pablo O where

have you been

except in the garden

to talk to the dithering

swarm of inordinate pulses that give us that

hanged man look

goes on looking great now it's tomorrow

here's the brittle part of us looking great

sobbing crayons

how melting crayons communicate

A visualization of the Hum

But how miserable it is, a pair of lungs under a saw that approaches, imperturbably, how miserable it is, especially when these lungs are yours, and why did you start thinking of the saw when your body alone is what interests you, to which the saw, for this reason, will inevitably draw near? And in a time of blood such as ours, how could it not cling to it? And there it is, entering as if it were at home, sinking in thanks to its magnificent teeth, calmly cutting its furrow into the lungs that will be of use to no one, no one, isn't that obvious? A woman was singing in MacArthur Park; she slung her arm around a pole as if to resist a strong wind. At the airport, the man's shirt read: "Shredding a / tidal wave of / whiskey on a surfboard / made of / don't care." He kept leaping to his feet to dance, snapping fingers as he threw one arm across his body. He said he was moving back after 38 years. I thought he was mythological. Sentences are not emotional, but paragraphs are. But in truth, it must be the desert, the culture of this place, because when someone comes to my house and sees a rag on the stove and with claw hands grabs and captures and holds it, then brings it up my nose saying "no-no-no-no lady, this is very dangerous" that is sincere. So I am running around the house before falling face first in the garden (I would go towards the flowers, I bet), thinking about the great and ridiculous Lady of Coal, tying ropes and tails to the Red Monk. Which is to say of the herd that's coming, like slow pachyderms, advancing single file, their mass is and is not. What could they do about it? How could they carry it? That heaviness, that stiff gait is only something they've taken on to escape their lightness, which eventually terrifies them. Like all of us! Yesterday saw *All About My Mother* for the fourteenth time and the third. I've already talked to them of my obsessions and last night during insomnia, heard the phrase she is a big woman, followed by the phrase a lot of friends, but whenever I try to observe her closely the spaniel and the Spaniard and the spanner appear and form a triangle with her. I usually lose sight of her in the 'magical' triangle, one or the other of us utterly lost in the theopanic [sic] fog. Incidentally, a few days ago I read a mystery in which a murderer is ambushed by the assumed victim. You know what? However hard you try to flee from your giant or your angel, you can't, because they're a part of what you are, like the CGI favelas superimposed upon the intricate-lit sheen of Zoe Saldana's left tricep as she nuzzles a handgun between praying hands, barrel kissing her brow, like the rare form of pica during which the afflicted scarfs national flags, like the Champagne of Sodas, surreptitiously containing your first and last taste of that gross Coors Light, like that body part that's been rubbed with a coffee marinade and garnished with rare, edible orchids.

My dentist is a Yale PhD. He insists I do a deep cleaning. He stands atop the Himalayas teaching Nepalese children to brush their teeth. Brushing in the high sunshine — modern postindustrial society takes smiling seriously. The snowy mountains flow downward. That's from a poem by Ma Lan, who, as the name might suggest, is Chinese. The knocked-out tooth is swallowed down. Then it grows out of the stomach. We give it water to drink. The glove waves its hand out in the air; this gesture is like a tractor. No one believes it is a real tractor. This is a slow motion shot; this shot pushed the history of our Bent Neck Village back to the paleorosaic era. There are so many legends about what happened that night. Those rumors created refugees; a lot of villagers left. Our village reentered a period of glove worship; even the seas worshipped the glove. But there can only be one queen of Straight-Neck Village. What will happen now? We should enhance our technology to clone dinosaur eggs. By the following afternoon splotches appeared on his stomach. Rainbows swam in his ears and he heard the sevenfold lights. He then began to walk, two steps forward and two steps back. I'm having the feeling I'm shoving whispers from my stomach, connecting Earth with space, I am beginning my voyage. Oh wow. That's a monkey's skull hanging from air, from pure incorporeal air, where nothingness resolves and it's like CGI only better. This transformation has gone from the sequel to the prequel, from the remake to the reboot. Following this summer's *Mad Max: Fury Road*, *Jurassic World*, and *Terminator Genysis* it is possible to chart yet another mutation, not a remake or a reboot but a "callback." The callback is less about directly repeating past plot points or elements, than slyly acknowledging their existence. I mean, if you remember anything about *The Road Warrior* (*Mad Max* 2 in the rest of the world) it is the truck chase, so *Fury Road* offers you the truck chase as a film. It also sprinkles in a few other elements: a shotgun that doesn't fire, a dwarf, and the car from the original. These callbacks are less attempts to recreate what worked in the original than to acknowledge that they are why we are watching a remake in the first place. *Jurassic World* even goes so far as to include a souvenir T-shirt from the original film, err … park, in the film itself. Screening its own nostalgia for the original. When the T-Rex from the original film shows up at the end, defeating the Indomnius Rex from the new film it is nothing other than the return of the repressed, the remake acknowledging that we all would rather be watching the original. Or, more to the point, would rather be repeating the original experience of watching the original. To paraphrase Adorno. Which brings us to *Terminator Genysis*, which opens with a return to the original film, Kyle Reese and the T-101 traveling back in time. It repeats a few scenes shot for shot, the garbage truck driver, the Nikes with velcro ankle strap, etc. Which is to say the lights have not yet been ruined by flames, this is a matter of luck for us, but it's already been twisted. The big insect lowers its head to chew grass. I used to want to be closer, now I want to be closer too, as in "closerness". [The Latin derivative 'transfigured' is the standard translation of the underlying German (*verklärt*). There is perhaps a better English equivalent. If the *Ursatz* is interpreted as a recipe, then what it would appear to contemplate is analogous to extracting an essence from a dead herb (suffering *cleared up* in joy). Indeed, years after the *Essay* was published Schelling became interested in how an herbal essence validate belief in life after death.] In any case, this is the refrigerator I won on

5498

                                    an American game show
                                    once in awhile I find myself
                                    looking forward instead of

back

                                    hearing all dreamers talk at
                                    once sends me into
                                    the lower organs
                                    I type your
                                    name on the computer
                                    delete it type it again
                                    different each time
                                    before I met you my
                                    favorite color was
                                    green light
                                    now I serve poetry to
                                    serve you
                              now I am famished for peace
                        now I watch a 90 year old movie to
                           witness dead people talking singing
                              riding horses samsara

                             SAMSARA SAMSARA

Alice looked up the glass eye of the microscope and saw another eye
– a giant eye –
an almost human eye –
looking back down at

her. So while you shouldn't forget that the alternate side of the street parking rules, if you do manage to drive into the city, will be suspended for the duration of the holiday, you'll still have to pay the meters. We worked on writing, developmental orality and movement. We worked through the impasse of the afternoon until we arrived at an end point that felt like a musical score. Now all I can do is sit here in the hut to recover. In this charged air, which began to haunt me, more like, a demon was in the room laughing at me, just laughing and laughing and laughing at me, I couldn't stop crying, I couldn't stop having panic attacks. It was like all the stupid agony of my whole life came at once, like all the times I had ever worried for no reason, had put myself through so much stress, just to end up what, me, that's all, I'm me again, everyday I wake up me, the Bodhidharma lines wouldn't leave, "The truth is, there is nothing to find." "To say he attains anything at all is to slander the Buddha. What could he possibly attain?" Just endlessly repeating, like a laughing demon, mocking me and all my ridiculous cares and worries, how I couldn't let go and just let myself be a me and walk around as a me encountering others mes, everybody doing their me thing. I eventually lost it, I couldn't talk anymore, I didn't know what to say, because everything I knew how to say derived from trying to attain stupid things, it was like, I had to learn to talk again. Then I drove back to Vegas through the desert, I saw basically only Natives in the desert, it was like a dream, in the deepest sense. I couldn't talk when I got back, I would just start crying if I started to talk, I think in the 50s they would have brought me to the mental ward and given me shock treatments, but I want to say I didn't actually see a demon lol, I think if there are real demons they are probably weird inter-dimensional creatures and are of no concern to me at the moment.

And the ocean parted in the middle emptying itself and the fish piled up in the night like dried up hills / And the open wound of the sea each moment deepened and the night was birthing inwards like a fish that swallows itself yes: / like fish swallowing themselves / / Like sea swells swallowing themselves   when we were dragged by / the undertow we saw the country of planks come on top / of us ... I want to say that while it is an Inferno, I also laughed quite a bit while writing it; I laughed at the image of Adam and Eve hitchhiking after they'd been thrown out of paradise. And while I'm not a big reader of comic books, I think that there is a sensibility that is pretty similar; the historical times are intermixed; there are tourists on the highway to paradise, bombed out neighborhoods, there are scenarios that converge, and if I didn't write it, I would probably like to draw it. People don't laugh a lot when they read my writing. I think that I have a sense of humor which is post-mortem in reality, but the truth is I also laughed while creating this. But do not trust blindly in the automatic translation of this blog, amigous. But hey, it's better than nothing. The meaning varies but little and ultimately, perhaps, the main message (if we can believe that there is one main message in what I say) is transmitted right? I can not tell in the case of Korean, but in the case of French, Italian and English something left a trail of something. I do not know Arabic or Turkish but come on! In the feed this morning, cats. Selfies, shining like a fiery beacon, live stream of the Mission police station shutdown, the science of why stepping on legos makes you want to die, FUCK credit reportz, the woman who fell in love with a tree, a baby's guide to sleep-training your parents, But that isn't totally getting at what is so great about this poem. It might be because it's an alphabet poem and it's full of found language. It might be because the language that Lo finds is about natural disaster and about state failure but also about hope in these moments, about the other sorts of alliances that happen. It might be because it's a modest poem. And we mean that in a good way. We worry you might overlook how great it is because it isn't all showy and braggy. This book is impossible to excerpt too. It builds so quietly and yet so luminously that it is hard to pull out a part of it in isolation. But here is an excerpt from the letter "s":

> so what about the instinct to survive.
>
> so what about birds and burying beetles.
>
> so what about support and what about struggle.
>
> so what about ants and bees and termites.
>
> so what about the field upon which tender feelings develop even amidst otherwise most cruel animals.
>
> so what about migration. breeding. autumn.
>
> so what about the numberless lakes of the russian and siberian steppes and what about aquatic birds, all living in perfect peace —

lotta feminista, Los Tigres del Norte are making gay norteño history, here comes the Whole Foods-ification of marijuana, more snow, fellowships, fire, new poems in new journals, new poems in old journals, new books, penpals and John Keene's post on Thinking Its Presence: The Racial Imaginary Conference, UMT, Missoula. I just wanna throw my voice over there, I wanna send you. It's a fucked up relief to say so after years of bumbling around in my dumb white female body talking about it with others, counting things or getting dressed and undressed in the middle of a conference paper, a befuddled jab somehow at this problem I think now, the whole tangled thing, besides, it would be insufficient if I were to say that Celan's poems were translatable. Rather, I had the feeling that they were *peering into Japanese*. So, one day Klaus-Rüdiger Wöhrmann called me to thank me for the photocopy he had asked me to make for him. This was a copy of the Japanese translation of Celan's VON SCHWELLE ZU SCHWELLE. When Wöhrmann said to me that the radical 門 ['tor' in German, 'gate' or 'gateway' in English] played a decisive role in this translation, an idea flashed through my head: It was precisely this radical that embodied the 'translatability' of Celan's poems. A radical is something like the 'main component' of an ideogram, right? There are also ideograms that consist only of a radical, for example gate 門, but most of them have additional components. All the characters that contain the radical gate have something to do with the concept *gate* on some semantic level. What tripped me out was just how often ideograms using the radical gate keep turning up in this book at all the most crucial junctures. The radical gate shows up twice in the title of the volume VON SCHWELLE ZU SCHWELLE ['From Threshold to Threshold']. The character 閾 ['schwelle' or 'threshold'] includes the radical gate. In this case it isn't difficult to guess at the common ground between the meaning of the radical and that of the sign as a whole: Both cases involve a border. But this title already shows that a crossing of borders is not intended: It isn't a matter of crossing one particular border but rather of wandering from one border to another. In the first poem in the book, yet another ideogram containing the radical gate appears: to hear 聞. ICH HÖRTE SAGEN ['I Heard It Said'] is the title of this poem, which begins with the sentence:

> I heard it said there was
> a stone in the water and a circle
> and above the water a word
> that placed the circle around the stone.

In 聞 you see an ear 耳 beneath the gate 門. According to this sign, to hear means to stand on the threshold like an ear. In the next stanza the 'I' sees another figure that doesn't remain standing on the threshold but strides across it:

> I saw my poplar go down to the water
> I saw how its arm reached down into the depths
> I saw its roots pleading skywards for night.

The world beneath the water is behind the threshold. The 'I' in the poem sees how the 'poplar' dips down into the unfamiliar world of the water, but the 'I' remains an observer and doesn't hurry after it.

> I didn't hurry after it,
> I merely gathered from the ground the crumb
> that has the shape of your eye and nobility
> I took the chain made of proverbs from your neck
> and draped it about the table where the crumb now lay.

The 'I' doesn't descend into the water but rather remains on the threshold pursuing a magical game: The stone and the circle are copied with the help of the 'crumb' and the 'chain' and so the image said to be visible beneath the water is repeated upon the table. This magical game has the effect of a process of translation. The translator copies the image that exists beneath the water on the desk. The poplar, on the other hand, is not a translator. Its body disappears in the water. If one were to equate the unfamiliar world beneath the water with the realm of the dead, then the magical game would be a translation of the language of the dead into writing. The translator hears the word of the dead and reads it [does he gather it up – *auflesen* – like ears of grain from the ground or read it – *lesen* – like a written character?] and places it upon the desk, eye eee he writes. The title of the third poem, LEUCHTEN ['Gleam'] contains the ideogram gleam 閃, which also includes the radical gate. Here we see a man 人 standing beneath a gate 門. I had never stopped to think how it could be that the combination of a gate and a human being could produce a gleam or glow. Perhaps someone who stands beneath a gate [or on a threshold] will be particularly receptive to a gleam from an invisible world. [This idea was confirmed as I continued to read.] In addition I sensed something that strongly linked the German word leuchten ['gleam'] with this ideogram: It struck me that the word ich ['I'] briefly appears in the middle of the German word leuchten when you speak it aloud clearly. The word ich does not otherwise appear in this poem, there is only mir ['to me'], du ['you'] and uns ['to us']. Only in this gleaming does the 'I' appear in a quick flash, for one brief, fragmented moment. If I imagine a poem as a receptor for rays of light, it becomes meaningless to look for something 'typically German' in a German poem. For what it picks up is always foreign to it and never the poem itself. Anyway, I began to look at Celan's poems as gateways rather than as buildings in which meaning might be stored like a possession. Thinking of this, a passage occurred to me from Gerschom Scholem's RELIGIÖSE AUTORITÄT UND MYSTIK ['Religious Authority and Mysticism']: *The genius of mystical exegeses resides in the uncanny precision with which they derive their transformation of Scripture into a corpus symbolicum from the exact words of the text. The literal meaning is preserved but merely as the gate through which the mystic passes, a gate, however, which he opens up to himself over and over again.* Sorry for the gendered language. In any case, it's a miracle that Celan was able to write the first section of the book, SIEBEN ROSEN SPÄTER ['Seven Roses Later'] without the help of a dictionary of Chinese characters. There are exactly seven different ideograms containing the radical gate that are used in the translation: threshold 閾, gate 門, to hear 聞, to open 開, in-between space 間, to gleam 閃, darkness 闇. This corresponds to the seven roses or the seven hours – the magical number referred to again and again. And an ontology of the present is also a science-fictional operation, in which a cosmonaut lands on a planet full of sentient, intelligent, alien beings.

He tries to understand their peculiar habits: for example, their philosophers are obsessed by numerology and the being of the one and the two, while their novelists write complex narratives about the impossibility of narrating anything; their politicians meanwhile, all drawn from the wealthiest classes, publicly debate the problem of making more money by reducing the spending of the poor. It is a world which does not require a Brechtian V-effect since it is already objectively estranged. The cosmonaut, stranded for an unforeseeable period on this planet owing to faulty technology (incomprehensibility of set theory or mathemes, ignorance of computer programmes or digitality, insensibility towards hip-hop, Twitter, or bitcoins), wonders how one could ever understand what is by definition radically other; until he meets a wise old alien economist who explains that not only are the races of the two planets not really races, but that this place is in fact simply in a later stage of his own socio-economic system (capitalism), which he was brought up to think of in two stages, whereas he has here found a third one, both different and the same. Ah, he cries, now I finally understand: this is the dialectic! Now I can write my report! Speaking of gates, do people know how much it hurts the darkness when you turn the light on in the middle of the night? … Have you ever turned on the light inside your intestine? … When the light is switched on inside my darkness, I buzz like a beetle pinned down, bzzz, bzzz, bzzz, bzzz, and shake my head wildly … The houses with lit windows. How painful the light must be for the night. At sunset we parted like tapeworms, breaking off into individual pouches. RITZ crackers are impressive too, their enormous holes. Enormity is our savior. We move our heads from side to side, swishing our haloes about … In my new world of Hellos, I swished a halo around my head wildly. My mother's psychosomatic symptoms were frequently triggered, my older brother got called back into the darkness for his mandatory military service, my younger brother had nightmares, sleepwalking almost every night, and my sister excelled in a frenzy, then fell apart, permanently. Fassbinder knows this light all too well. In *Veronica Voss*, the interior of Dr. Katz's clinic is entirely, eerily white except for the so-called "enigmatic African-American GI," rolling cigarettes laced with opiate powder. Here, light is cozy. He's the only shadow in the clinic. He's the new darkness West Germany must numb and sublimate — its post-war hunger and poverty along with its recent past. Let me de-enigmatize the GI's presence in *Veronica Voss* and two other films that make up Fassbinder's BRD (Bundesrepublik Deutschland) Trilogy. He's the punctum. He's the new wound. We try to salve it with opiates and/or RITZ crackers, but the eternal light, the enormous holes are difficult to plug. Enormity is the price of neocolonial liberation. Zurita's snow-white smoke laces the sky of New York, the biggest apple of all: MY GOD IS WOUND. Red eyes, sweet cries. My cats that wiggle behind the sofa. – from "I'll Call Those Things My Cats" in *Poor Love Machine*. Dr. Katz — she is beautiful. Kim Hyesoon's cats — they are adorable. Kim's darkness is a playground for rabid cuteness in which patriarchy, military dictatorship and censorship, neocolonization and neoliberalism play out. Into this deadly zone, its sky, rivers, and sea, the seventh daughter, the daughter-too-many, enters. She is Princess Abandoned [*Paridegi / Parigongju*]. She is the mother of all shamans. The place in which Paridegi is abandoned is an unreal place, and all those who raise her are unreal characters. The spaces in which she is abandoned are places where graves are made or where the dead are secretly discarded. Hence, when her foster parents find Paridegi as an infant, insects fall out from her eyes, ears, mouth, and nose … The darkness gives birth, nurtures, and gives birth again… Paridegi's Buddhist Elysium is this black mirror … I, a woman poet, on the road of darkness, the endless road of the text … I break and break apart the darkness I have entered. It "is empty … at the very bottom." No turtles. To quote Daniel Borzutzky, "The history of atrocity is not a series of separate events here. Rather, to be alive is to experience all the obliterations at once." The "plains of Nagasaki and Hiroshima" to CHILEAN STADIUM PRISON to PLAYA ANCHA STADIUM PRISON to CAMP PISAGUA PRISON to VILLA GRIMALDI PRISON to TRES ÁLAMOS PRISON to COLONIA DIGNIDAD PRISON to TRAINING SHIP ESMERALDA PRISON to MAIPO CARGO SHIP PRISON to CARGO SHIP LEBU PRISON to NAVY BARRACKS PRISON to BERNADO O'HIGGINGS MILITARY ACADEMY PRISON to MOCHA ISLAND PRISON to QUIRIQUINA ISLAND PRISON to PUCHUNCAVÍ PRISON to NATIONAL STADIUM PRISON to THOU SHALL NOT KILL, EX. 20, 13 to Student Revolution April 1960 to Kwangju May 1980. Rats or planks, they pile up. Did you know C.D. was a fierce reader and supporter of translation? Did you know she edited and co-translated *Rain of the Future* by Valerie Mejer Caso? C.D. was a seer of ghosts. Valerie's poetry is populated by immigrant, family ghosts, their trails of loss, wound, and violence. That night C.D. playfully demanded that I tell her and Forrest my life story. I told her the story of darkness, the departing, my father filming wars. When I saw C.D. again a few months later in San Francisco, she introduced me to her friend and said, "Her father filmed the fucking-carpet-bombing in Cambodia." If we were to follow the logic of Buddhism, C.D.'s soul would have roamed for forty-nine days til about March 1st. By that time all the students were looking out of the window. They said: "Something has happened. Below us, on the lawn, a grey-yellow patch of grass two stories below, is an arrangement of skulls." This is how we met Erin Baylan. In a bucket, she was washing a skull. They were, she said, for an art therapy project with women who have been incarcerated and are about to be released. Altogether there were eight skulls I think, some with pale pink teeth, some dreaming with flies – and the one in the bucket, that was dripping. I saw all of this in slow motion.

    Am I a brown horse?
    In the afternoon, I saw a horse's skull. (Above.)

Just so you know the coordinates are porous
Can't close the window? ask me another one

When I speak it's clear that I don't reject
    The [way the world] world[s]. Its witnesses

Coincide with this.
At the park

A shuddering infant watches the leaves, a child
    Floating on an inflated dinosaur

Slowly crosses the lake – I mean,

If we thrill to low hills because they are not composed
    they are "composed to our liking"
They say there is no defining that but to say that is
    defining that, living in context

One would think of all the social forces traveling with a show
    of indifference over a crowd or sound
    brought to a sound
A good person would be starred ill and well in a life he or
    she couldn't know how to refuse

Every day we may never happen on the object hung on
    a mere chance
When and where one happens it will surprise us not in itself
    but in its coming to our attention not as something
    suddenly present but as something that's been near for
    a long time and which we have only just noticed

When we might ask did we begin to share that existence
What have we overlooked

Nostalgia is another name for one's sense of loss at the
    thought that one has sadly gone along happily
    overlooking something, who knows what
Perhaps there were three things, no one of which made
    sense of the other two
A sandwich, a wallet, and they said they'd have to kill me if
    they told me

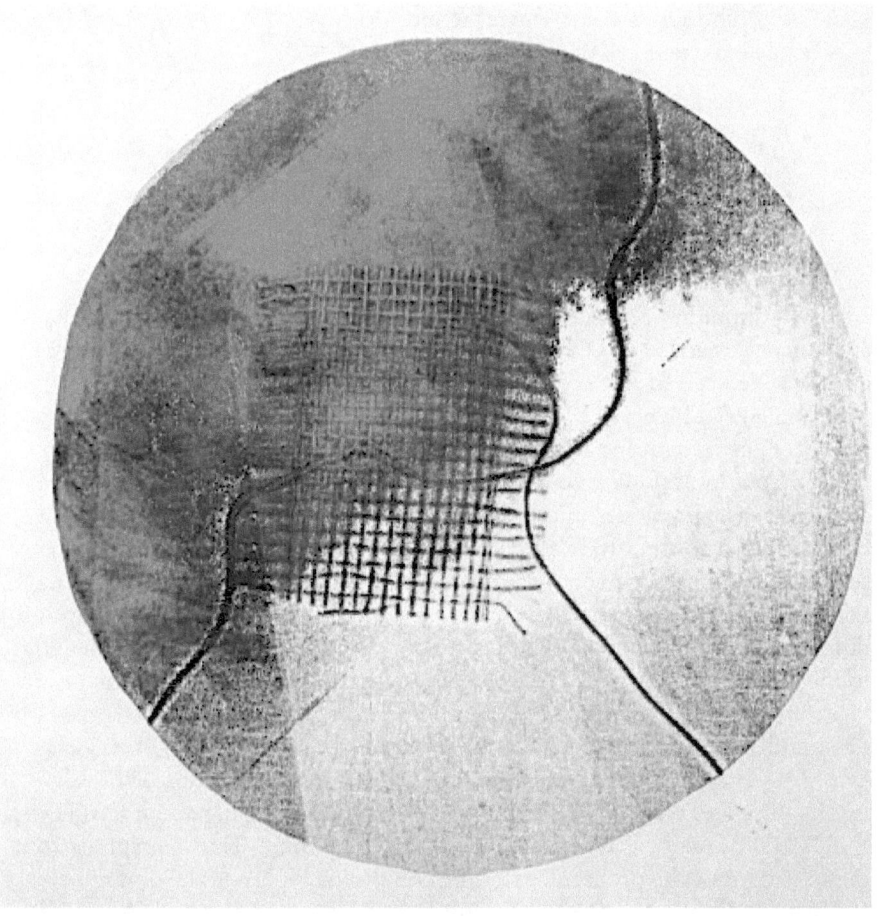

But, then again, maybe no, did I make that up? *I am befuddled.* Not by this work, but by life in general. And then there was a woman sitting on the steps, she was an MTA worker joining us and I used to drive buses, my nickname driving buses was Auto because I was young and sold mushrooms on the side and connected to the mentally challenged passengers I drove. It's a wonder they all were transported safely and I believe a higher power wanted me to see that I am just as much a star as the stars are a bazillion miles away ... as I've watched enough television to know that people like me die and even our friends forget the atrocities. Like in 2006 when I lived in China a white middle age male American architect of the World Trade Center came on CCTV and explained to viewers that the greatest moment of the modern world was the fall of the World Trade Center. He explained that ever since their demise the world has been free to create a new trading system. Free at last! Free at last! What an idiot. Yes we're engaged. No we never dated. I swear it's really not that weird.

... The sun is doing whatever suns do
The citizenry all creeping like flowers.

      ... Try eating one. But
Don't get me wrong. I'm just like everyone else.
They keep their gold in me.

                            ... The invisible.

And why shouldn't Kevin Killian be able to marry Evo Morales if he wants to, and still stay married to Dodie Bellamy too, why not? Evo Morales has a coke-can cock we used to say to each other after watching Democracy Now together, an old love and I. Then I met a Bolivian hostile to the land policies of Evo Morales. The Bolivian hostile to the land policies of Evo Morales said, Really? You don't think Evo Morales has a choad? What's a choad I said sincerely ignorant. You don't know what a choad is? No I don't I said, but I hear the word constantly. It's a cock thicker than it is long said Patricio. Never seen one of those in person, I said. Look online said Patricio. Your effen rad, said Shahid's first text, and then, Your a beautiful soul. [Sic]. So is he. Saying I don't even have a fucking GED. It's not like Kevin Killian ever said anything to me about Evo Morales. The lady who loves the Eiffel Tower married it. In Haiti I was told it's Jupiter and Mercury I'll marry, in addition to persons. "You must understand, it is difficult for me to die." "And it is easy for us to go on living?" —Bukharin to Stalin, Plenum of the Central Committee, 1937. Or maybe the other way around; I've lost the thread: Something about Evil Days, Evil Ways, Business as Usual, and the Infernal Machine. The epigraph is from the transcript of the proceedings of the plenum of the Central Committee, February 1937, as presented in William Kentridge's *I am not me, the horse is not mine* (at SFMoMA a while back); a very different transcription occurs in *The Road to Terror: Stalin and the Self-Destruction of the Bolsheviks 1932-1939* by J. Arch Getty, Oleg V. Naumov and Benjamin Sher. "At last an answer: William did indeed knowingly change the dialogue from the actual transcript. He said he was thinking about a letter Bukharin sent from death row." (Mark Rosenthal, curator of the Kentridge exhibit, in response to my questions re the discrepancy. October 29, 2010.) For I Was Hungry and You Gave Me Food, I Was Thirsty and You Gave Me Drink, I Was Homeless and WTF You Drenched Me With Sprinklers To Drive Me Away. But though Negarestani refers to capitalism as "the most recurring politico-economic figure of speculative thought," and Srnicek has written about it, they conceive of it in philosophical terms, as the great engine of "correlationist" thinking: the problem with capitalism, for these thinkers, is that it creates an echo chamber that makes our minds too small. The capitalist problem that speculative realism seems best equipped to address, in other words, is not an actual dynamic of accumulation and exploitation, but the epistemological problem of capitalism's reduction of all phenomena to its own image. However revolutionary it may be in philosophical terms that these thinkers respond to capitalist epistemology not with a counter-epistemology but with an ontology, and however enthusiastically they may imagine subjects who think (or exist) entirely differently than the ones we know today, their anti-philosophical and anti-hermeneutic gestures are just that: anti-philosophical and anti-hermeneutic, not anti-capitalist. But even if we agree with this reading of Mallarmé's poem as encoding a secret Christology, we needn't see it as unprecedented: there have been Future-Christs for a very long time.

> Krystle
> Krystle Cole
> you're all I thought about sometimes
> I watched you while our daughter slept
> your Sissy Spacek ways
> your laconic demeanor in relaying
> either ecstasy or trauma
> & the un-embittered empathy your voice conveyed
> on YouTube
> which is our loving cup
> the solution of butter
> & DMT you took
> anally that really made you
> freak the fuck out
>
> [...]
>
> I was going always to the mall
> in those months,
> the young century's rainiest
> April & May, to walk the
> baby & to understand my art.
> I didn't understand.
> I would move the stroller
> through the halogen, over
> grooved tile & across those
> smooth marble expanses meant
> to simulate floating & gliding
>
> [...]
>
> [like (tho I was unlike)]
> Bradley Cooper, in *Limitless*
> who takes this little pill, which

in its candy dot translucence
looks a lot like a tear plucked
from the cheek in Man Ray's

But, to quote Lucas, I think of nation-states as inherently militarized spaces articulated through each other. When Frederick Douglass said Brazil was less racist than the US in its treatment of freed slaves, he anticipated the self-fashioning of a 'racial democracy' whose mixture would be defined against US-style segregation. Like the vast majority of Brazilians, I have mixed-race ancestry. Because my nonwhite ancestors survived, I am alive and need to be explicit about the horrors of miscegenation — the rape of African and Indigenous women by Portuguese men. My light skin is the result of policies that whitened the population by incentivizing European immigration at the turn of the century. I think all the time about how the state transmits white supremacy through my body. My phenotype encodes a national fear of being too black and brown. As in other slaveholding societies, the idea that Brazil could one day be Haiti haunted the elite. But enough – white guilt is no recipe for aspiring race traitors. In proposing the term Amefricanity, Lélia Gonzalez scrambles the categories. When I read her brilliant essays, I am reminded that my accent in Portuguese is the influence of Tupi, an indigenous language. I am reminded that the slang I use around my trans and queer friends is based not on the language of Camões or Pessoa but Yoruba, the surviving tongue of West African slaves.

I point this out not to say #weareallafrican.

I point this out to say my ideal worlds in poetry and beyond know that the need to separate and classify is part of what drove the Western invention of race. And that Non-Western epistemologies, on the other hand, tend to provincialize this need when they stress connection and relationality.

Language is already imbued with these worlds.

It took a kind of unlearning to figure this out.

This unlearning will never end.

Located in northeastern Brazil, Palmares was a federation of maroon communities estimated to number from 11,000 to 30,000 inhabitants. It endured attacks for over 90 years and consisted of runaway African and Native slaves as well as Jews, Muslims, and poor whites. There is a reason you probably haven't heard of Palmares. There is a reason it was overtaken, its leader beheaded, in 1695. As Neil Roberts argues in *Freedom as Marronage*, Maroons are more than a historical reality. The flight of slaves, in other words, offers the possibility of reorientation here and now. Marronage is a transhistorical vision of revolt enfleshed in the present as well as the past and future: "Flight can be both real and imagined ... Freedom is not a place; it is a state [no, *way*] of being." This "agency within potentiality" is not metaphorical but the sky of Adão Ventura's "I, Black-Bird":

>I,
>black-bird,
>cicatrize the burns of iron branding,
>close my fugitive slave's body
>and
>stand guard
>at the gates of maroons.

It is also the rupture of "Birth" by Miriam Alves, another Afro-Brazilian poet:

>A deaf drumming
>hurts to hear
>To live to live
>trapped in the cage
>female bird
>I've already seen the infinite
>I was constellation
>Now I'm a wandering asteroid
>shooting star
>I divided myself in two
>Divided in order to not be subtracted
>I stayed whole if dented in each piece
>I cried because I was being born

*

From a perch below airborne birds, my imaginative response lies in the process of decolonizing myself above all. As a chicken, I dream of flight from industrial farming and modern catastrophe.

>In this dream I rip the ancestral sky.

>In this dream I betray my landlocked species.

>In this dream I refuse to be stuck inside empire's dreamlessness.

Inspired by Bhanu Kapil's white privilege exorcism, I invoke, in this blog, the screaming brown feather. I animate the brown feather in the form of a huge indigenized chicken precisely so that it might stab this blog with its beak. I wish

I were joking when I say this blog is guilty of forgotten violence. It is no surprise to see who authored this unspeakable post. *That [app] spit out a big text file with all the words and their locations in the film, which I then imported into a spreadsheet, sorted in alphabetical and then chronological order, and fed into another little program that took the sorted list and produced the edit. So basically, it was edited in Excel ... All told, I think it took about seven days spread out over a couple of months. Disassembly was mind-bending in itself. It was literally hard to talk after moving word by word, or syllable by syllable, through the film. English stopped sounding like language, and at times I had to stop because I could not figure out what a word was — I just couldn't hear it right.* When finally alphabetized, the film, says Bucy, had a surprising energy to it. A certain *je ne sais quoi*. So yes, like many of his fellow detainees at Guantánamo, Ould Slahi has always been a migrant. The son of a nomadic merchant, he won a prestigious scholarship in 1988 to study in what was then West Germany. From there, he made several trips during his winter breaks to Afghanistan, joining the jihad against the Soviet-backed government in the years before al-Qaʿida declared war on the United States. He spent most of the 1990s studying and working in Germany and moved to Montreal briefly in late 1999. In these countries, Ould Slahi's milieu consisted mainly of other working-class Arab and Muslim migrants, some of whom would come to attract police attention. His wife's sister was married to one of Usama bin Ladin's close aides; he met Ramzi bin al-Shibh, one of the accused 9/11 conspirators, for one night. In the eyes of the US government, these acquaintances, kinship ties, and patterns of traveling while Muslim must have been dots crying out connect me! connect me! Otherwise you'll lose your jobs! In order to link all this up, they tried to turn his itinerant nature against him, by targeting him at his most vulnerable: while in transit. In January 2000, he was arrested while passing through Senegal on his way home. Several days later, the US put him on a charter flight to Mauritania for several more weeks of interrogation. "It was the first time that I shortcut the civilian formalities while leaving one country to another," he said. "It was a treat, but I didn't enjoy it." In both countries, Ould Slahi was questioned by the local authorities and US agents, each capable of pointing to the actions of the other to excuse their own bad acts. In a way, the book's title is a misnomer, for a third of his account takes place in prisons other than Guantánamo. Ould Slahi's experiences of detention in at least five countries are a reminder that the internment camp in Cuba is more than simply an offshore aberration from US justice, but part of a global web of "shadowy" detention practices that predates 9/11. Ould Slahi knows he is not alone in this experience. This passage is taken from Ould Slahi's manuscript rather than the published book, but the text is virtually identical: *I thought about all my innocent brothers who were and still are being rendered to all strange places and countries, and I felt solaced, and not any more alone. I felt the spirits of unjustly mistreated people with me, I heard so many had heard so many stories about brothers being passed back and forth like a soccerball just b/c they have been once in Afghanistan, Bosnia, or Chechnya.* In November 2001, he voluntarily presented himself for yet more questioning in what may have seemed to him a never-ending ritual of "round up the usual suspects". He has not seen his family since. After eight days he was put on a plane to Jordan, "treated like a UPS package" and dispatched to one of the CIA's most trusted and reliable proxy torturers. In an extraordinary passage, Ould Slahi recounts being personally handed over by Mauritania's secret police chief at the time, Deddahi Ould Abdallahi, to Jordanian intelligence officers at Nouakchott airport. Quickly realizing that the Mauritanian and Jordanian torturers had difficulty communicating across their very different Arabic dialects, Ould Slahi jumped in to explain that the Jordanians needed to refuel their chartered plane. "I had an advantage over both of them," he recalled with pride in his resourcefulness. "There is hardly any Arabic dialect I don't understand because I used to have many friends from different cultural backgrounds. I was eager to let my predator know *I am, I am.*" He spent the next eight months imprisoned at Jordan's General Intelligence Directorate in Wadi al-Sir, on the outskirts of Amman. Between long interrogations and occasional beatings he observed the misunderstandings, breakdowns, and tensions in the outsourcing of torture. His Jordanian jailers confronted him with intercepted emails and demanded that he decipher suspicious passages, mistaking their own misapprehension of multiple translations from German to English to Arabic for some kind of coded language. In Ould Slahi's telling, the Jordanians came to realize that there was no reason to hold him but nevertheless needed to convince their American patrons of their earnest attempts to break him. When they finally recommended his release, Washington was only further angered and eventually decided to cut out the middleman and take Ould Slahi into its own hands. He was flown from Jordan to Bagram and soon thereafter to Cuba. He arrived at Gitmo after having been stripped, shackled, and crammed into a vessel with other men and sent across a distant ocean [same old story, right? See the diagram on the following page]. Upon arrival, the detainees were subjected to an interrogation process that the book illustrates as a kind of forced labor, with repeated performances aimed at producing a curious commodity called "intels." Ould Slahi shows us how much sheer work goes in to the process of confession: *Had I done what they accused of me of, I would have relieved myself since day one. But the problem is that you cannot just admit to something you haven't done b/c you need to deliver the detail, which you couldn't when you hadn't. It's not just "Yes, I did!" No, it doesn't work that way, you have to make up a complete story that makes sense to the dumbest dummies. One of the hardest things is to tell an untruthful story and maintain it ...* The perversity of torture lies not simply in the possibility that tortured prisoners will confess to anything to make the pain stop; it is that the torturers will also demand that you perform your subjection with creativity and enthusiasm. That you will fill in the details they want corroborated and make up new ones to be tested on other prisoners; and that you will continue to fail and retake those tests.

5513

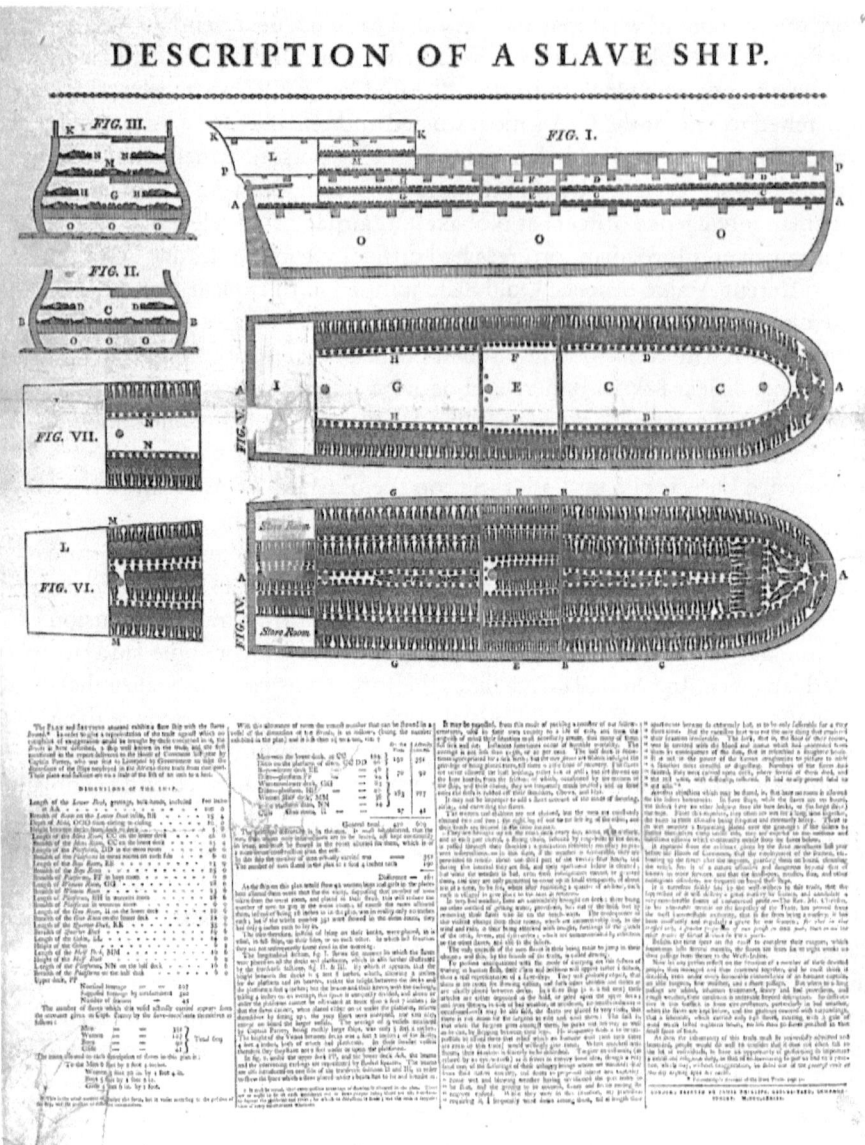

Anyway, during the years when we knew each other, she told me about more than three thousand Indians, whom she had know either personally or indirectly. Even though she did not remember the names of all of them, she almost always knew their kin relations and thereby I could place them in their genealogies. Many of the three thousand appeared and reappeared in diverse situations about which she told me over the years and thus it was that little by little her culture acquired a sense that went beyond the purely ethnographic description and revealed different levels of what it had meant to be alive then and living as a Selk'nam. Angela spoke of one individual, then another, and another; in the context of the missions, their family life, the camps, their loves and vengeances, their combats, "Red Pig" and other White assassins, and the soul, *kashpix*, which separates from the body at the hour of death. She told me about the world before death existed, when the *hoowin* people of primeval times inhabited the earth. She recited stories that explained why humans exist, told me about the wise men and prophets, especially Alaken, Lola Kiepja's grandfather, about the shamans and their trips to the moon, the "spirits" of the great ceremony called the Hain which were only men in disguise, about a crazy man who thought he was a guanaco, about women who died when they gave birth, about her last daughter Luisa and her son Victorio who died of tuberculosis in Buenos Aires. She often recalled our rides in the subway of Buenos Aires which she had pleased her so much when she visited me there for a month in 1972. The following is a simple example of and old Perl fork recursion that erupts briefly before dying. It can be run in any terminal window with Perl installed, including the Terminal application on any Mac computer:

```
perl -e 'while (print fork," ") { exit if int rand(1.01); }'
```

The first part, "perl -e," simply evokes the Perl interpreter and allows a snippet of code contained within single quotes to be executed in-line. The code itself consists of a while loop with an exit condition that occurs with enough irregularity to make things interesting. Inside the while expression, "print fork" (concatenated with a printed space) does two things at once. It forks a new clone of the code, and also prints the output of the fork, which happens to be the process number. The result is an irregular montage of spaces and numbers, many of which appear roughly in numerical sequence since the kernel simply increments a counter when it assigns a new process number. In sum, the first part of the code furnishes the stylus with which to draw, while the second part throttles the code just enough to avoid crashing the computer. More firecracker than bomb, these snippets of recursive code produce generative textures using the terminal window. Minute variations affect the code, making it run differently each time. The processor speed, the number of other applications open, even the temperature of the motherboard will influence both the length and composition of the text. By slightly stressing the machine, but not crashing it, computer artifacts become visible as text. RSG-FORK-5.1 uses slightly more code, slightly more plasticizer,

> abdominizer, plasticizer,
> the flawed flask flushes the brain,
> the flash drive inserted
> into the correct drain
> provides fusion, fluency, the plasticizer
> voids the gut, no current can run

    anymore thru that florid
    fosse, where instinct sinks skindeep,
    loses a shoe.
    A system should be
    made of plastic: too
    much beauty crashes the system
    with its black drive
    a clouding agent sprouts mushrooms

Because the lovers of K are suing the police: They entered into their various relationships with K unaware that he was not K. And K is suing the police because the police did not stop K, their employee, from falling in love in the course of his duties. And this is truly the ultimate reclining shower. Six water bars beat down in a choice of three preset pulsing beats: Balancing, Energizing or De-stressing. *Island (KEN)* is a state-of-the-art smart shower island with e-controls to regulate the flow. The hybrid project combines the social kitchen with the private bathroom. And it's not just an installation but a performance piece as well. In the meantime, the smell of butter wafts from the stove. Crucially, however, the distinction between witches and cunning-folk is invoked in the process of proving it to be theologically and legally invalid. In laws such as the 1604 Witchcraft Act, and in pamphlets such as the 1645 *Laws Against Witches and Coniuration*, both sides of the distinction are subsumed within the form of legal contract. Witches and cunning-folk alike are all hell-bound. What we discover, therefore, is not simply a shadow cast, by the interplay of an emerging and a residual economic logic, into some chance place within the culture. Rather, the emergence of witchcraft as a prohibited behaviour, inclusive of the deeds of cunning-folk, connected with the deeds of learned conjurers, but separable from the deeds of natural philosophers, contains a concentrated trace of the dominant epistemologies to come, which is a nice way to say power relations. A question is posed, in a hopeful tone, by the rise of commercial society: do the market forms which loosen our epistemological couplings to our neighbours also absolve us of responsibility for their lives? In the constitution of witchcraft lies the answer. The couplings are not merely loosened, but dissolved, yet the responsibility intensifies. Every commercial relationship is a social relationship. For example, the intimacies which witches enjoy with Satan's familiars do not comprise an essentially separate kind of relationship with Satan, but rather provocative clarifications of any contractual relationship whatsoever. A friend asks us to wish her luck. Then we get spam comments asking us how we manage spam. Then I think about how I'd like to wear boots all summer, so I google "Spring Boots" and "Sandal Boots." These boots appear. I like them. I like almost all the "YOU MIGHT ALSO LIKE" suggestions at the bottom of the page except the pair of very sexy sandal heels from Rebecca Minkoff. Probably this type of heel has a name, but I do not know what it is. I like the Ibiza Heel, the Hustle Boot, the

Stair Bootie, the Canti Heel, and the Dream Bootie. I guess I like every Freebird by Steven shoe at Revolve Clothing. I return to the article about gender bias in medicine and the ads are all from Revolve Clothing. I learn that many young women have cardiovascular health issues, but that our symptoms tend to be different from men. I learn that "In training, we were taught to be on the lookout for hysterical females who come to the emergency room." This project is exhausting. Am I sad enough yet? Do I have to take an extra clonazepam yet? I don't care what the *New York Times* says I will learn in my 40s. But I do care that "There is this humming in the air now like an open test to evaluate everything welling up in everybody." To me, this calls to mind the image of a tuning-fork: a humming that evaluates or rather measures the other humming, 3000 people played this sequence and blew up the world every time. In the good sense of blew up, of course. I mean, through an act of "renaming" you can create a "community". The world's largest carnivore sanctuary hummed with wasps, hundreds of them, bouncing off the bits of sky that had come down in thick, pale blue layers over everything, like torn strips of a bedsheet circa 1983. A storm was gathering above the mountains, and behind us a massive creamy cloud was growing, a web of silvery-grey creases already darkening on the side facing the high plains. What is a child? I hadn't been in a Wendy's since 2003. They serve salads now. I don't know why I capitalized Zebra, or why I can feel the z in my back teeth. No, we were walking up, towards our lodge, because at that moment, a monk in his maroon robes came running in the opposite direction. There was a knock at the door. We opened it. Andy had lived in Paris on a Gap Year and there he met a girl called Harrede, who, when two diners at the next table were looking at her disdainfully – she, too, had piercings – casually scraped her entire plate of spaghetti onto her lap and began to eat it with a fork, without breaking a conversational beat or looking over to gauge their reaction. She lived in a room with a bed in it, to which she had tied or attached all of her belongings. Every single one. It took five hours to write, gate to gate. I have a feeling that feels "like an oval in the middle of my forehead." I drink a protein shake made with lettuce, spinach and strawberries. Once, a man pushed me off my bike, pulled over in his car, and began to shout: "Go back to Mexico. Go back home." As a final stage, we used the chalk and charcoal to draw the outlines in the residue of glitter and clay. We set a page on fire and we drank coffee and we spat something out of our mouth and we licked the wall and we breathed through our nostrils onto a nail before dropping it from a great height. Monique and I walked until we reach a Scandinavian precipice. Laura Ann lifted then dropped the bones of another person inside their body, and that person was me and that body was mine, and I had the fleeting thought that maybe I could dress in a bear costume and The oral surgeon said: "My wife went to Kew. I told her you lost your doll there when you were, what was it, seven?" My dog balanced on his hind legs. I noticed that I was still flinching, in my own way, from the carpet, the ceiling, the sky.

For after winning acclaim with this novel — awarded the Robert Walser Prize in 1978 — Fritz embarked on a 10,000-page literary project called "The Fortress," creating over her lifetime elaborate colorful diagrams and typescripts so complicated that her publisher had to print them straight from her original documents. Contrast (without judgement) that maximalism with Hadbawnik's AENEID, which "is not the creative destruction of erasure, but rather the well-crafted impoverishment of something potentially too rich to take in." An exile, as Dante and so many 'word-concertistas' before him, Juan Gelman 'disorders the chaos / with demented exactitude', which is yet another way to do it. "Antigone enters. Pesticides, eco-cide, a guiding conversation with Leslie Scalapino and the beloved dead." So it's important to note that in several fan fictions supergirl and batwoman hook up. The supergirl cape is short and does not snag.

But first: "Do I clash?" "I clash I clash" — pure Whitman. I do a lot of things I guess. I like laughing, movies and having fun. Do you like having fun? I've been here nine months and have no friends. I am just me! Also, I love glittery things, snowmen, and the color purple, autocrossing, fish keeping — salt and fresh. "Cash, I told Dana, 's a negative eucharist." We can discuss some later manifestations of romanticism another time. Just wanted to share a quote with you that I think could be brought to bear on these topics. I read it last night and I love it. It's from the memoirs of Louise Michel (absolutely wonderful book, as captivating as say the autobiography of Emma Goldman), and it comes as a note she appended to the transcript of her post-Paris Commune trial that sent her to New Caledonia: "Perhaps there is some use in noting that contrary to the description of my person given at the beginning of the account in the *Gazette des tribunaux*, I am tall, not short. In the times in which we live, it is proper to pass only for oneself." After typing the above, I get this via email: *"This week in the PEN Poetry Series, guest editor Cathy Park Hong features an excerpt from new work by Eugene Ostashevsky. About the excerpt, Ostashevsky writes: "These poems are from my new manuscript,* The Pirate Who Does Not Know the Value of

Pi, a poem-novel about the relationship between a pirate and a parrot who, after capturing prizes all over the seven seas, suffer shipwreck on a deserted island, where they discuss whether they would have been able to make themselves understood by people indigenous to the island, had there been any. Characterized by multilingual punning, humor puerile and set-theoretical, philosophical irony and narratological handicaps, The Pirate Who Does Not Know the Value of Pi *steals from early modern texts about pirates and parrots, Russian 1960s folklore, old-school hip-hop, game theory, controversies of copyright, and Wittgenstein's* Philosophical Investigations, *abbreviated as* PI. *Of the poems selected here, Pirate Party Music comes from a section of pirate songs that also include a shanty and a Russian folk piece to the tune of Bei Mir Bistu Shein. The piece formerly known as Pontius Pirate appears autobiographical. The piece about communicating with hypothetical indigenous people repurposes a line by William Carlos Williams. For the pun piece it helps to know that, prior to the invention of biscuits, parrots enjoyed almonds, as John Skelton attests, and that 'almond' in German is Mandel."*

PIRATE: Do you think this island has any indigenous people on it?

PARROT: If it does, we won't understand them or they us. Indigenous people never have any common sense.

PIRATE: Why "never"? Have you met all of them?

PARROT: I don't have to meet all of them. That's what logic is for. If they had common sense, they would emigrate. If they emigrated, they would no longer be indigenous people. Q.E.D.

PIRATE: But, parrot, why should they emigrate?

PARROT: But, pirate, why shouldn't they emigrate? Should they sit here all of their lives? Don't they deserve a second chance?

PIRATE: Why do you take it upon yourself to speak for indigenous people?
PARROT: If I don't speak for them, who will? Somebody has to speak for them if they don't have any common sense! Most of what they know is numb terror under some hedge of chokecherry or viburnum, which they cannot express!

PIRATE: Poor indigenous people! Poor poor indigenous people! O poor unfortunate indigent endogamous ingenuous—

PARROT: Poor genuine people my pope's nose! What if they show up and ask to see our visas?

PIRATE: But we don't have any ... We don't even possess passports!

PARROT: This is what troubles me, pirate. Suppose we get deported?

PIRATE: We must persuade the indignant people that in our culture it is not proper to ask pirates and parrots for passports!

PARROT: How can you persuade anyone of anything if they don't have any common sense?

PIRATE: But are you sure they don't have any common sense? I mean, you proved it but are you sure?

PARROT: Let me read you something. "Unlike their peers, the Tonga Islanders do possess native numerals up to 100,000. Not content even with this, the French poet Leconte de Lisle pressed them further and obtained numerals up to 1012; however, his data was proven upon publication to be partly nonsense-words and partly indelicate expressions, so that the supposed series of high numerals forms at once a modest lexicon of Tongan indecency, and a warning as to the probable results of taking down unverified answers from savages."

PIRATE: I can see why you're nervous. Ingenious people are really hard to talk to! I mean, it is with the velocity of a giant squid and the sprawl of its erogenous arms that with water-wheels the leverage in any musculoskeletal appendage can move into positions within the time it would take the engine of filaments to accelerate the psychic mass of bodily understanding and construction for such a displacement to continue in different venues and as multiple in purpose as the simple machine of our vessel will allow toward the disappearance of a nexus like in infinite mirror games but with the ability to count each movement of the progression as it acts in mechanical, yet organic, jerking behind the dreamlike animals with their pink illusions that roll their wet bodies into our delicate systems. There. Now we are here. So, let me say if by government you mean bank, then I will agree with you and if you reminisce about the historical mass and its subjective valves of speaking into the romantic motions of people, I will say that has worked with people but what has grown around us like a flesh is not within any subjective register so really, you can't speak to it because although there is a mass of skin, it is made of machine that not only might laugh but can't even hear our emotive sentiments and the skin is our skin and the gear is our gear and we speak to ourselves but can't listen because as the body expands it flairs out in a web, this is because it is giant and from the outside and uh-oh, a border collapses, toss a pinch of salt over your shoulder, the salt the ancient Romans mined, the salt we pressed into ancient earth to deprive our enemies of crops, it was like a hydra growing heads the shape of brussels sprouts, liberally, under the planet — it began I guess when

Santa looked up from his sluggish nap — the sleep of neo-liberal generosity — to find the elves had taken to the Pole, as in other cultures workers take to the streets, And in their caps and breeches said elves did bite down the pole with white teeth, teeth sharpened from thousands of years making toys for us. I am not sure if the disgust or fear is the disgust or fear of a white person in another era or a non-white person in this era. I think, for the purposes of the panel I am on, I would like to discharge the disgust or fear of a white person in another era but also this one. Perhaps we can work up to discharging – the particular, chronic – micro-expressions of disgust – that are situated in the soft tissue or the parts of the face – that contract – during eye rolls or tongue clicks, the sideways glance. And though I typically work on chronic, almost fleeting states – I thought today I would generalize – to the broader: "grimace." You have to ask the client to make that "face" in order to observe, very quickly, the extent [topography] of the platysma!!!! In the textbook, it reads, below this image: Exercising the platysma. I mis-read: Exorcising the platysma. 2. The pyschogenics of the master muscle: known: as the muscle through which: we express ourselves. So, I have to go to Walgreens to get duct tape and latex gloves. I will ask the Mongrel-to-be or Mongrel-in-fact – to read a section from DICTEE. And then I will release the deep belly of the masseter muscle, the clenching pattern, the part of the oral structures that effect swallowing – a necessary component of cannibalism – I also think of de Andrade here. Particular attention will be paid to asymmetrical hypertonicity. After the treatment, I will assess – the release of the oral structures – by asking the Mongrel client to read aloud once more from DICTEE. This may be why, outflanking 'radical poets' like Shelley and Byron, Macfarlane's polemics have the orotund, unanswerable ring of Shakespeare, Milton and Blake. These texts were written to be read aloud, in taverns where illiterate politicos would seize a newspaper and cry, "Who's here can read? I want to know what Feargus O'Connor is saying about Julian Harney, has the man gone mad?" The Macfarlane revival — she was not only the first translator of the *Manifesto of the Communist Party* (38 years before Samuel Moore's standard one), but the first translator of Hegel's philosophical writings into English — is not simply an independent object to dent the armour of know-it-all Hegelians, it also breaks into the realm of English Literature and its pecking orders: *The golden age, sung by the poets and prophets of all times and nations, from Hesiod and Isaiah, to Cervantes and Shelley; the Paradise ... was never lost, for it lives ... this spirit, I say, has descended now upon the multitudes, and has consecrated them to the service of the new — and yet old — religion of Socialist Democracy.* George Eliot, another nineteenth-century woman (Marian Evans) who adopted a male soubriquet in print (Macfarlane's was 'Howard Morton'), is revered as a novelist, but if you explore Eliot's critical relationship to Christianity (she was the translator of David Strauss's scandalous *The Life of Jesus, Critically Examined*) parallels with Macfarlane foam forth. *So, in* The Years of Rice and Salt, *you portray Khalid and Iwang, the drivers of the Samarqand Awakening, arguing with the Sufi Bahram in the bardo after they had been killed by a resurgent plague. Khalid channels Shakespeare's Gloucester: he declares that the gods "kill us for sport" and impugns Bahram for the latter's devotion to love amidst the power of a world-historical course so indifferent to human happiness, while Bahram in turn stresses that courage underpins love, hope, and the commitment to struggle.* Which is to say that while hay(na)ku can be haiku-like in their patient advance, they can gather strangeness, too. Karri Kokko abbreviates Gertrude Stein to fascinating effect. Here are the first handful of verses from "Comp as Expl":

ther
sing diff
exec gene comp

beca
inte consists
long conn thin

depe
deci prep
degr pain occu

with
arou happ
part crea refu

acce
ente mode
spea impo unex

And on, for thirty more verses. So when deer-mice came into his house from the tallgrass prairie of Oklahoma, he live-trapped and released them in a nearby hedgerow, but they waltzed back in, singing an epithalamium. Latin Musa, Greek Mousa, English Muse / Mouse linked by an O – license to party on Parnassus and drink from Helicon. Sir Toby, Reepicheep, Sir Andrew & Feste grilling Malvolia about Pythagorean metempsychosis, can join them in a catch, a coranto, a galliard, a jig, or sink-a-pace, singing to moon and stars, Diana and Venus, Blake's Sunflower where the Traveler's journey is done – but Deer-Mice got there before tourists with FOX2P genes (see *NY Times* 29 May 2009, p. A5: human "language gene" put into mice deepens their baby cries). One Lakota man formulated it thus: 'Everything [a Lakota] does is in a circle [because the world] always works in circles and everything tries to be round.' Which is one reason why it's a good thing that the faster we go the rounder we get. Anyway,

40,000 poets can't be wrong.
I don't write this kind
of poem anymore, but I
hear the economy worsens,
I hear it means
living forever. Bad timing
so what!

But, again, assuming this isn't simply an exaggeration or even a hoax, the idea that humans can now see in the dark with the help of eyedrops based on chlorophyll is jaw-dropping. Or eye-popping, as the case may be. Tho you can also easily imagine this becoming standard for nighttime police operations or military raids — what doesn't get militarized? — one could even imagine this having an effect on global energy bills. What if improving grid efficiency is at least partially also a medical question — that is, if you could just drop some Ce6 in a dark city without the need for bright streetlights, or even walk through your own apartment with pupils the size of dinner plates, seeing everything?

Suppose, then, one just listed
house, book, mug, window,
son, daughter, dogs (gone), desk, Apple™.
Suppose it was all a budded tree limb, hair-thread fingers—
the baby oak in spring, rain "heavy at times,"
and the cleared branches of fall, suppose
yellow gusting in a greeny-pinkish light,
a dark red pear leaf blown into the room,
suppose a salvaged shmoo-like basil plant
eager, even in winter, to give pesto,
or a fondness, a warmth, eros
blue as the sky, could it be otherwise?
the apt healing of a wound, even with
its startling scar—
unaccountable enumerations:
the oddly glistening, the half-started language.
The half-startled. Twisting together
choice exemplars of exquisite debris:
"a cigar label, a metal buckle, a ballpoint pen,
a bottle cap, a bolt, a hair curler,
a drafting compass, a plastic bottle,
yellow tape, aluminum foil, drinking straws,
green paper,
broken blue glass."

Would this be enough?

What would be enough?

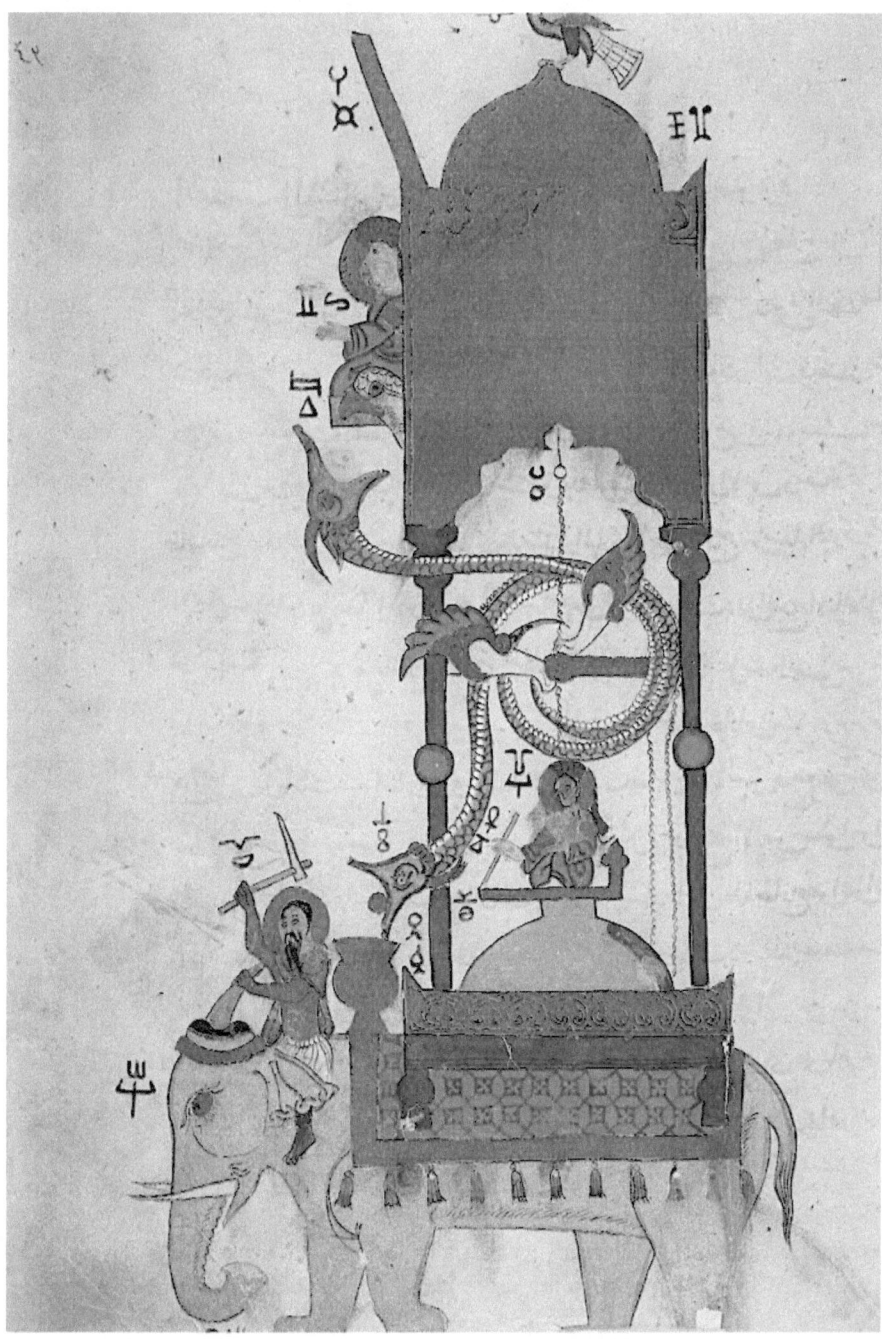

Dunno, but "I have a fear of the vacant space underneath cabinets" and I love this I love this, they're talking about irrational fears and people are calling in. One of the DJs was like, I'm terrified of big steel trains and cruise ships, or when the table rumbles quietly and you didn't do it, I've been thinking about this too. You know, godlike bliss feelings hatred and worshipping love, responding and not reacting, feeling blank, letting yourself stay by yourself and trying to or not to hold people in your head. How much is me trying to protect myself from breaking / shrinking and how much is me trying to protect myself from breaking / growing and how much is just bullshit? Maybe I have to be somewhere else to figure that out. I need to figure out change and swaddling. how 2 swaddle back also. How did I get here, this is so life-life [sic], I mean,

>   Once in a lifetime
>   Water flowing underground
>
>   Same as it ever was …
>   Same as it ever was …
>   Same as it ever was …
>   Same as it ever was …
>   Same as it ever was …
>   Same as it ever was …
>   Same as it ever was …
>   Same as it ever was …
>
>   Water dissolving … and water removing
>   There is water at the bottom of the ocean
>   Under the water, carry the water at the bottom of the ocean
>   Remove the water at the bottom of the ocean

>   #
>   DESCEND
>   DESCEND
>   #

I said "you should dye your hair red again. Or blue" and he looked at me, smiling dumbly like "really? don't you think I'm too old?" and everyone was like "No. Jesus Christ no" and he giggled and was like "maybe." I then told him to play more songs from the Newton abbot demo, like Boredom and Rain and he looked up alarmed and was like "you've heard those?! That's so embarrassing." but I was like "no seriously though, Boredom and Rain are actually really good, please bring them back somehow" and he was just grinning like "oh god, lets not" it was beautiful. Ok then I was like "ok, this is gonna sound creepy … because it is … but, can I please touch your hair? Sorry it's creepy as fuck but I have to know". He smiled and bowed in front of me and I need to start a new paragraph for this ... I ran my fingers through his hair like 10 or 11 times, for a good 30 seconds, gripping it and pulling gently which he seemed to love. Now, dear readers, his hair is ... so fucking soft. Like, incredibly so. Like ... Let's try a calming exercise. Imagine you are inside an egg. You have been inside this egg for as long as you can remember, which, remember, does not necessarily mean your whole life, tho it can. What shape is the egg? Someone, or at least, a voice is asking you, WHAT SHAPE IS THE EGG? It's easy to get lost in the geometry. Then I lie down under my car, I feel the gravel bite into my back like teeth that are either too tired too careful or too generous. We could go anywhere in the whole world. Basically, just keep saying that & watching a new ball of gas form in the sky with each bout of laughter. I'm ok if you're ok. Are you calm or not? Me too. Ultra blurry, anamorphic, some of this represents a certain depth and movement sung by writing it, but

    — Dear, you
    weigh nothing in and get no credit, no
    spectral, tiny swaggering to cash in
    yah there's a substitution agreement containing you
    and me in force, pulled on from inside.

— Dear, and oh yah asleep awake again, more than once w/ a face of a filled out line. Or lines. Smiling lessons. So you will have to imagine the picture I was trying to upload of the metal water hydrant cover that looks just like a medieval engraving of the cosmos. Maybe tomorrow. The blossom is out in the road. And the feeling grows as the day progresses, as a soft wall, water, toss it on me and buried just before sleep. Do not tell me, please, that these comments are or are not careful. Remember that nothing happens on this page that is not happening in real time. Anyway, my mum told me when I was a baby I slept so intensive so I turned white! So she had to check me all the time! This is serious! That is true! Maybe the whole thing started there? And maybe it started before that? My great great grandmother was a sorcerer but only the good kind of magic. So a Scout, a Synthetic Humanoid, and a Weyland-Yutani Executive walk into an army medical lab operating outside of regulated space. "I got signals," the Scout says. "I got readings, in front and behind." "Forget the signals," the Executive says. "Where Are the Brothers?" Yeah, a couple of Brothers from the double-Y chromosome correctional facility had gone missing. The Scout did some Reconnaissance on the Ventilation Shafts. "Uh, guys," he said. "I mean gal, and thing. We better do this job quick. What I mean is we got No Time to Waste. This thing's on a collision course with the home planet! Oh, and there's a Xenomorph Runner in the Weapons Locker." Pretty soon there's a Runner and a Noxious Xenomorph standing right in front of them. "They're All Around Us!" the Executive shouts, and the Scout takes that as his cue to kill the Runner. But then he sees another Runner coming out of the vents. The android knows that the xenos in front of them are bad, but the ones farther on are the more important threat; remember, they're supposed to be finding the Missing Brothers. "Look into my eye," the Scout says, pulling down his right eyelid. The Synthetic gets the picture. Then the Scout kills an Acid Spray Xenomorph and a few Specialists die, which is actually a good thing because they were like dead weight at this point. "Look into my eye," the Scout says again, then the Executive is like "They're All Around Us!" and the Scout wastes a Runner that just appeared in front of them. The Synthetic goes on a Secret Mission to check out the Power Station. There's a Skittering Xenomorph, and the Synthetic wastes it before it can skitter away. "Prune the Growths," the android mumbles ominously, and then suddenly the crew doesn't feel as pressed for time. By this point, they've found both the Brothers cowering in the Airlock. The Scout is like "Look into my eye" while the Synthetic goes and rescues them. I have little doubt that given enough time, a meticulous close listener would find hundreds of similar moments in the thousands of hours of recorded poetry on PennSound. Most of us don't have that time, though. My initial experiments suggest that ARLO will be able to reveal a large number of sites for interpretation that I wouldn't have been able to find through close listening alone. The man then turns to the elephant, leans over, and, with a heave, tosses her into the stunned crowd. Screams shake the room until … the divine essence became palpable … the Kabbalist rabbis of Toledo understood that a new form of biblical interpretation had been born. People fall into vats of honey and are embalmed by bees, drops of semen turn into white butterflies promptly devoured by green lizards. Back at the Renbourn house the last of the natural light had disappeared. There was no overhead lighting, so we carried on talking by the light of two lamps. And what with the old-timey American music playing on the nearby record player, the continual flow of wine from the clay jug and cheese, pastrami and bread simply arranged on a maiolica plate, it all looked oddly beautiful. Even the soot-lined cobwebs in the corners looked great. At the end of the evening, I stood up unsteadily to leave. My B&B was a mile up the hill. I had deliberately left my car back there knowing that I would probably be having a drink. "I'm going to drive you back to your hotel," he insisted. I flatly refused. He continued insisting to the point where it became clear that this was a matter of honour to him, and furthermore that an argument may ensue if I didn't let him. He opened the front door and, by the light of a tiny torch, negotiated the narrow track from his house, over the footbridge, to his vehicle, and announced that he would refuse to go back in until I had installed myself in his vehicle. With John's foot firmly down on the gas, his green van unhappily ascended the single track road up the hill and then up a steeper gradient to the driveway of my B&B. "Please promise me you won't die on the way back," I begged him. "Nonsense!" he exclaimed. "I'll be fine!" Ten minutes later, the furious landlady of the B&B knocked on my door and berated me for allowing him to drive me home. Apparently, John's attempts at a three-point turn had laid all her freshly planted flowerbeds to waste. She told him that if he didn't vacate his van immediately, she would call the police. The last I saw of John that night was his enormous frame wedged into the passenger seat of her tiny Renault Clio, his smiling face emitting an impish high-pitched laugh at his own denouement. "See! I told you it would turn out fine, didn't I?" Which was followed of course by the typical Greek

CHORUS

        Strophe

In speculation
I would not willingly acquire a name
    For ill-digested thought;
    But after pondering much
To this conclusion I at last have come:
    LIFE IS UNCERTAIN.
    This truth I have written deep
    In my reflective midriff
    On tablets not of wax,
Nor with a pen did I inscribe it there,
For many reasons: LIFE, I say, IS NOT
    A STRANGER TO UNCERTAINTY.
Not from the flight of omen-yelling fowls
    This fact did I discover,
Nor did the Delphine tripod bark it out,
    Nor yet Dodona.
Its native ingenuity sufficed
    My self-taught diaphragm.

        Antistrophe

    Why should I mention
The Inachean daughter, loved of Zeus?
    Her whom of old the gods,
    More provident than kind,
Provided with four hoofs, two horns, one tail,
    A gift not asked for,
    And sent her forth to learn
    The unfamiliar science
    Of how to chew the cud.
She therefore, all about the Argive fields,
Went cropping pale green grass and nettle-tops,
    Nor did they disagree with her.

But yet, howe'er nutritious, such repasts
    I do not hanker after:
Never may Cypris for her seat select
    My dappled liver!
Why should I mention Io? Why indeed?
    I have no notion why.

    Epode

    But now does my boding heart,
    Unhired, unaccompanied, sing
    A strain not meet for the dance.
    Yes even the palace appears
    To my yoke of circular eyes
    (The right, nor omit I the left)
    Like a slaughterhouse, so to speak,
    Garnished with woolly deaths
    And many shipwrecks of cows.
I therefore in a Cissian strain lament:
    And to the rapid
        Loud, linen-tattering thumps upon my chest
        Resounds in concert
The battering of my unlucky head.

    Meditation

However, I have never dull
    With praise of pastoral life,
    Nor nostalgia for a past innocent of
    Perversions on the prairies.
No. No need to cross the borders of New York
    To find all the greenery you want – can not
        enjoy a stalk
    Of grass without a metro stop by hand,
    Or a record store
    Or any sign. It is important to affirm
    With equal sincerity;
    Clouds already receiving considerable attention
        as well,
    And it still happening.
Did they know what they're missing?
Aha.
    I wish I had gray, green, black, brown, yellow
        eyes:

>   I stay home and do something.
> Not that it is not funny.
>   But it is my duty to be careful,
>   I need things like heaven to be on earth.
> And last,
>   That I have very little sleep, San Serapio,
>   Which is like midnight in Dostoevsky.
> But how do I become legend, dear?
> I tried to love, but
>   I always hopping apparatus like the lotus –
>   The ecstasy of always fly apart!
>   (But do not get distracted by that!) –
> Or as hyacinth, "to keep separate the dirt of life,"
>   Yes, there even in the heart,
>   Which pumps dirt.

But when the haunted voice recorder replayed its ghosts within the context of the epistemological frame of a bodiless autopsy ritual designed to magically enter the mind of Andreas Lubitz that breathing became a confession. "We could hear human breathing inside the cabin," said Mr Robin, "and this breathing noise we heard up until the moment of final impact. That means that the co-pilot was alive. Apparently he was breathing normally, so this is not someone having a heart attack, for example. You don't get the impression that there was any particular panic, because the breathing is always the same. The breathing is not panting. It's a classic, human breathing." So

>   "Bring in everything you're thinking about"
>   and find the way to the exit where the fire
>   sign burns. To quote Norma Cole,
>
>   I need to train
>   I said to Joe Frazier.
>   *Here I am.*

So, slip into the envelope a pressed leaf from The Tree of Lost Causes; th'hydroptic glass hath never sunk so low. We are lacking neologisms. They would be useful, I think, for healing invisible wounds, wounds that can't be displayed in the market place; wounds like silver on wisps of sky and dawn

ῥοδοδάκτυλος. Sanity is terrifying, you know. But insanity is more terrifying. Let me show you the inland sea; it's waterless and covered in a mix of three-bedroomed detached and affordable housing. Seaweed sways at night, and during the day, when everyone's at work, circulatory currents erase all memories. But whose? Bluebirds glide over white cliffs. Have you seen a soft gun lately?

Just imagine a painted owl eyes door. And rat bells, as in, *You hear rat bells all along the watchtower.* It helps you, but that's not how it goes. Imagine owl eyes, all along the wall. A colored egg hidden in the fireplace. A dead motor. You think, *This will be the mold that holds it, this will be the matter.* All roads end in spools of pink, then fasten to other roads. The hand that cannot feel the watch's gears in the second stanza translates onto the body Beuys' piano wrapped in felt: steroid flowers paper a room. I have crawled their backs and wept in their wire baskets. Can't you see that this is how I, radiating outward, happened to appear on this planet, this speck of dust? Yves Klein was born because Baudelaire predicted this propitious event by naming colors, which, like all colors, escape the confines of their names, becoming more than an emanation of infinity. Even black can get away from its name ["A single mycelial cell can be miles long"]. But what is color that isn't surrounded by another color? What is that boundless world we catch a glimpse of whenever we look up at the sky? Is it so vast that we must turn away from it, afraid that it will swallow us up, which it will? Astronomy, the Greeks believed, was a royal science, which means I am a royal painter. Do not confuse me, however, with a painter of royalty. Nor am I the prince of clouds, Baudelaire's albatross, fallen from the sky. Screw that fascist Marinetti. I fall effortlessly through the air, I mean I jumped out the window and I stayed in the air. In some ways, it was easy. We received submissions from a great group of contributors who are passionately invested in teaching, and whose innovativeness in the classroom, as expressed in their essays, continually surprised and inspired us. Questions raised by contributors included: How did nineteenth-century translations of *Beowulf* for children shape British imperialism in India? What cultural work motivates the adaptation of early modern Italian epics featuring Christians and Muslims in nineteenth- and twentieth-century folk theatre? I'll get to the quandary of the good life later. Inadequately, but that may be for the best. In Goya's great painting 'The Third of May 1808,' already three lifeless bodies are lying in pools of blood, and now, kneeling beside them but with his hands held high, is the next victim. The sky is black; this is happening at night, or in Hell, or it's another crucifixion. With a look as much of sorrow as of fear or anger, the powerful man glares at the factota of the firing squad. There are at least five of them, left foot forward and right foot back, faces hidden (they are wearing shakos and turned slightly away from us), the long barrels of their rifles raised and thrust forward. On the ground, at the center of the scene, and casting luminous light on the man who is about to be shot, is a large square lantern — it must be at least two feet tall and equally wide. It's a yellow lantern, the color of the condemned man's pants. Its light casts forth the white of the condemned man's shirt. They say Picasso said, 'The lantern is Death. Why? We don't know.' I walked over to the trashcan to throw away a receipt, when I saw a worksheet from another class. The title of it was 'True Love' written in excitable bubble letters at the top, and underneath it, a series of coordinates that had to be graphed — on the back was the graph, and on the front, the whole page was covered with coordinates, '(8, 3)' and so on, followed by the phrase 'LINE ENDS' — and printed in a lighter tone 'TRUE LOVE' was a cloud, behaving, situated over the numbers, and 'LINE ENDS' floating around the page, so the eye received this confusing montage of Love as a Line, then Love Ending, and then some truth produced as apotheosis between the two that true love does not live endlessly, but is finite, on a line, is lived in time — what makes love true is that it happens, and it could happen to you, or it could not, and the numbers were rain across the space of the sheet — then gentler, gendered, colder, snow — finally, quickly, shifting coasts and was where I was again — the numbers were frantic piñata candy of kids cackling — through the colorful pow of me imagining the effigy of the animal bursting open. So goes the liturgy. And here is a partial implementation of the poem-generating process in Python which I just wrote up. You may modify or do anything you like with this. I dedicate this program to the public domain as described in the linked document. I've uploaded a text file containing the program that also appears in this post, below.

IBM Poem Generator, complete version, nm, 4 April 2008

This version is a complete model of Emmett William's
            process in
generating "The IBM Poem," as I understand it, except that,
            being a
console program, it does not increase the size of the type

```
                as words
# are re-used.
# That could be done, too – for instance, if the output were
            in HTML
# with CSS.

vocab = [ " ] * 26

def expand(word):
  # A general method to expand a sequence of letters into
            words
  expanded = [ ]
  for letter in word:
    expanded.append(vocab[ ord(letter) – 97 ])
  return expanded

print "Provide a word (a sequence of letters) for each letter
            from a to z."

# Get a vocabulary word (the user types one "at random") for each letter a-z
for i in range(26):
  anyword = "
  while anyword == " or not anyword.isalpha( ):
    anyword = raw_input(chr(97+i) + '=')
  vocab[ I ] = anyword.lower( )

# Ask for "IBM" or another three-letter word or acronym
            tlw = "
while len(tlw) <> 3 and not tlw.isalpha( ):
  tlw = raw_input('Provide a 3 letter word or phrase: ')
  tlw = tlw.lower( )
seed = [ tlw ]
print

# Expand three times, printing along the way:
# 0. Three-letter word into title
# 1. Title into three lines
# 2. Each of the three lines into as many lines as there are words
newseed = [ ]
for i in range(3):
  for word in seed:
    words = expand(word)
    line = ' '.join(words)
    print line
```

```
  if i == 0:
    print
  newseed += words
 seed = newseed
 newseed = [ ]
```

A sample run (thanks to Rita Raley):
a=dog
b=run
c=cat
d=flower
e=battle
f=falluja
g=bush
h=toggle
i=algorithm
j=banana
k=papaya
l=hawaii
m=saint
n=fork
o=paper
p=pencil
q=computer
r=brick
s=nick
t=flick
u=link
v=cup
w=coffee
x=tea
y=mustard
z=floor

      flower paper bush

      falluja hawaii paper coffee battle brick
      pencil dog pencil battle brick
      run link nick toggle
      falluja dog hawaii hawaii link banana dog
      toggle dog coffee dog algorithm algorithm
      pencil dog pencil battle brick
      cat paper falluja falluja battle battle
      run dog flick flick hawaii battle

run brick algorithm cat papaya
pencil battle fork cat algorithm hawaii
flower paper bush
pencil battle fork cat algorithm hawaii
run dog flick flick hawaii battle
run brick algorithm cat papaya
brick link fork
hawaii algorithm fork papaya
fork algorithm cat papaya
flick paper bush bush hawaii battle

As for you others, a young fellow tourist in a fabric market in Dakar (the African city closest to Cuttyhunk) says Robert told her which animal is her daemon and calls her by its name, and that same afternoon I glimpse a novel Charlotte once translated amid a bookseller's assorted wares, laid out on a table. Cuttyhunk drifts in the Atlantic, barring outward passage, inviting further voyage to what lies beyond. "Land's end," the Wampanoag call it; sea's beginning. Of its three ponds, only one is a fresh spring; the others are brine pits, protected harbors, ships' havens. It's an intricate patch of territory, a postage stamp, a poem, a labyrinth of sea and land where subtleties erode certainties and you lose and find your way, entering and exiting as if from the wings. Which is why Charroux first related the Hyperboreans to an ancient astronaut race of "reputedly very large, very pale people" who had chosen "the least warm area on the earth because it corresponded more closely to their own climate on the planet from which they originated." Are the poles white? So white that we travel through white to the other side of brightness. Lo! The new Jim Crow. Again we are blinded to the vast prismatic spectrum that prevails there. Borea and Abaris, feasting on gold, show us how to see in the bright. First they purify themselves by rubbing their skin with oil of ice. Then they collect plankton, mineral crumbs, bird saliva, parachute debris, used acupuncture needles, essence of map, poisonous mushrooms, wings from downed planes, celluloid film scrap, parakeet feed, anything with which to make more, and anything that falls from the sky and can be retrieved from a thousand fathoms below. Note that a three circle Venn diagram is composed of 7 regions (right). If Something Is in Region Number 1 in category S, Then Is IT *outside* Categories P and M. This Would BE A Nice passing of Representing Laruelle's Real That Is Completely Unrelated. If something is in region 2, it shares a relation between S and P; there is an overlap between these two domains. We have a mathematics of string theory (symbolic) that potentially explains certain things about nature (it remains a hypothesis), but the n-dimensional spaces of string theory have no correlate in phenomenological experience because we can neither imagine (produce an image of), nor experience 11 dimensions. If something appears in region number 5, there is an overlap between categories S, P, and M. Read on! This free trade agreement exists as a nearly four-hundred-page document, parsed into 22 chapters. Why is there no copy of this document in each of our homes? Why can't we find this in the night-tables of every Motel 6 and Best Western around this Great Country? Why doesn't this land on my front porch every six months, wrapped in pink plastic, like the Yellow Pages of Disaster? It should be hung from chains in defunct public telephone booths so that time and the elements can tatter its pages and send them tumbling onto windshields moving through cities at 90 miles per. It should be hung on flagpoles on May Day so that we can hoist its promises into the breathless ozone. There is essential information here — information that we can't live without; information that we have *not* lived with; information that has named the objects that we have lived with: a person "means a natural person or an enterprise," meat means "meat of swine, carcasses and half- carcasses, fresh or chilled." It is

 Drawn by the stone called
"Graphite" across white paper
By your/my hand, it is a pretty word,
(See, if you receive these words
Through the front of your head;
That is "visually," instead of laterally;
[And I want to be on your side]
It looks to be jumping quietly up,
(For example, when I hear your story
It sounds familiar, and the next day
I imagine I had happened in it.)

This happens often on television:
One guy holds a gun, and says, "Give me
One good reason why ▮▮▮▮▮▮▮▮▮▮▮!"
At one time, in Portugal
José Saramago wrote, "Do you say I am lying?"
Where shall we go, to the netherworld,
Like Orpheus? (Give me one good reason
Why ▮▮▮▮▮▮▮▮▮▮▮!) No, I mean
Like Gilgamesh; Orpheus is sentimental,

Calypso is the leading technology platform for cross-asset trading, accounting, processing and enterprise risk management.

Key words:
>Cross asset
>Enterprise
>Accounting
>Trading
>Technology
>Risk
>Management

The physiotherapist asked me to describe my pain on a scale of one to ten, and if it was sharp, dull or pulsing.

>Almost everything in the world is light-years away
>From us. But heavy, weightlessly insupportably heavy.

I mean, this is the progression of subjects / bodies in my collected works, such as they are: 1. Cyborg; 2. XXXXX [unspeakable] 3. Monster [processed, also, from Haraway: "an entity produced by discourse." To paraphrase. To write: the mutation.] 4. Wolf-girl – the beginning of a socialist approach. 7. Adouéke [a war chant by Andia, out of the memoirs of Louise Michel:

>The *Takata*
>>Gathered *adouéke* in the forest,
>>*Adouéke*, the shield herb,
>>In the moonlight, *adouéke*,
>>The war herb,
>>the spirit plant.
>The warriors
>>Divided *adouéke*.
>>It makes them fierce,
>>It charms their wounds.

> The spirits
>> Of their fathers
>> Make a storm.
>> They are waiting
>> For the brave.
> The brave
>> Are welcome.
>> Friends or enemies,
>> They are welcome.
>> Beyond this life.
>> Those who wish to live
>> Go back.
> War is come.
>> Blood will flow
>> Over the earth
>> Like water.
>> The *adouéke*
>> Must be blood]

To this end, as each book takes me further into the enquiry or subject matter that all the books share: I lie down on the floor of the world. A wolf-girl lies down in the lap of her schizophrenic mother. A monster and a cyborg have complicated sex. Two monsters have a different kind of sex. The schizophrenic goes down on all fours, as does the feral child. I think it is also, as Dorothy Wang says, that sometimes the people who look like you can hurt you the most. So the question is, what resonances might arise if such a theater of repetition were juxtaposed with Indian katakhali dance drama, Japanese Nōh, and Beijing opera? The notions of bhavas and rasas (stylized emotional signs and affective "tastes") set forth in the *Natya Shastra* and enacted in katakhali performance; the concepts of yūgen (grace), "becoming" and "possession of one mind," central to the practice and theory of Nōh as detailed by Zeami; the principles of synthesis, stylization and convention in service of mei (beauty) in Beijing opera — all offer rich possibilities for creating permeable zones. So yes, I loved that 85% of the workshop was about attuning the skeleton – the bones and the blood and the breath – beep, beep: as the Hyundai jeep backed up over the peacock ore and the vermillion powder. But that was later. And this was before. *And they forgot Hebrew and used a limited Spanish of only a hundred words. The great cats learned most of those words and in turn taught their trainers an extensive range of growls. When rehearsals or shows ended, after dinner, at midnight, in the intimacy of the great cage, humans and animals would sit face to face to stare fixedly into one another's eyes. In those moments, the lion was the teacher. It was he who was there, present, concentrating, with no interest in the past or the future, united with totality. In his animal body, the divine essence became palpable. The lion taught the Arcavis about economy of gestures, strength in repose, the pleasure of being alive, authenticity of feeling, obedience of oneself. Finally, seeing the nobility of the beast, his majestic inner solitude, they understood why Jacob compared Judah to a lion. The Kabbalist rabbis of Toledo understood that a new form of biblical interpretation had been born. In silence, with the greatest respect, they entered the cage protected by the miraculous touch of Salvador's hands. They meditated, staring into the lion's eyes. They asked permission to bring their brothers in study, and with them came handsome old Arabs dressed in white and pale Catholic monks with sunken, burning eyes. The Koran, the Torah, and the Gospels were eclipsed by those imposing beasts, capable of standing so still that fireflies fleeing from the cold dawn rested on their warm skin, transforming them into phosphorescent statues*

    and if you have to ask
    if Beethoven is really
    like if Dr. Demento
    was any good, you're not
    the Mars Rover at all.

The aim of this poem is to assess weather produced from rat
        feed, grain,
and four doses. The study uses 480 male and female rats
and their little rat cell phones (under Simulated Microgravity)
which did not have cancer. One will study acupuncture.
The other will study old rats. Words from the Simon
and Garfunkel song, that ol' one, incorporated into rat their rat anterior
        pituitary
      Like a rat in a maze the path before me &
One rat out of 23 failed to develop &
        Hooked heads of little rodent swimmers &
the apoptosis of EITHER
tail or ears you explained that
you were singing the suppressed
verses, verses which had disappeared
with the advent of assembly line production
and the production of replaceable small metal parts,

mercy arrives, she says: *"I am mercy; I have no understanding of who I am; though, with my thousand arms, I have written of my own nature since writing began. I inhabit you and you write about me again. There is always the sound or color or feeling in which I can arrive. Lying in bed suffering from loneliness or anger the woman with eyes closed sees me bending over her, a many armed figure wearing a rayed disk hat."* Dear friend, you have excited crowds with your example. This landfall happened at your exact flooding and now you are sitting doubled up in pain, your head wet, streaming, smelling faintly of milk and oranges — your eyes are lidded and balled, like Blake's, like pinwheels and burning schoolhouses, never the same river drowns the doorsill. We are all lichens now. People weren't suffering from having too much blood.

This means that the dominant discourses translate brain plasticity in terms of individual enhancement, adaptation, and modification in the context of a neoliberal care of the Self, in contrast, for example, with the investment of the Italian autonomists in the political and emancipatory potential of the general intellect. So what I'm trying to say is that dick breakage always seemed like one of those insanely rare injuries – like internal decapitation, or that thing where your spinal fluid leaks out of your nose. But, according to this hypothesis, Gaia is autopoietic—self-forming, boundary maintaining, contingent, dynamic, and stable under some conditions but not others, and is is not reducible to the sum of its parts; Gaia, rather, achieves finite systemic coherence in the face of perturbations within parameters that are themselves responsive to dynamic systemic processes. So yes,

I do want to say that while it is an inferno,
I also want to say that I laughed quite a bit while writing these poems;
I laughed at the image of Adam and Eve hitchhiking after they'd been
    thrown out of paradise,

But I didn't laugh at the Japanese tourists

Who see Nagasaki and Hiroshima floating in the sky
Crossing the foamy ocean
Bursting over the peaks of the Andes,

It's the strait of Magellan says Magellan as he steers
Between the sunken islands
Filled with dust
Drifting   because we all had each other's faces,

When I saw my brother I saw my face
I saw my grandmother I saw my face
I saw my aunt I saw my stupid face
On the way up the mountain I saw my face in a pile of trash

I saw my face in the mule's ass.

Australopithecus, pebble culture ...

A convergence and continuum ...

Emerging lunar-tidal-circle ...

Primal waters of pure consciousness ...

Oblivious to a centimeter squared ...

CYMA, CYMA, C-Y-M-A

The kinetic energy of molecular motion ...

Way beyond causation ...

Denizens of apocrypha ...

The quasi-parallelogram becomes a true parallelogram with opposite sides
     equal to pi ...

I can easily tell if someone else wants to enter a conversation
     Strongly agree
I prefer animals to humans Strongly disagree
I try to keep up with the current trends and fashions Mildly
     agree
I dream most nights No answer

I really enjoy caring for other people.
I try to solve my own problems rather than discussing them
    with others.
I find it hard to know what to do in a social situation.
I am at my best first thing in the morning.

People don't laugh as much as they should when they read my writing. Or when Yoko Ono and Gertrude Stein showed us those swaths of cut-up fruit that they sold along with hot food in their roadside cart. Anyway, I was attending a "baton twirling" conference & I was staying in a boarding house & I caught TS Eliot at midnight stealing doughnuts from the kitchen & he shyly apologized. Which was a beginning. We were looking at the stars. I was shown how on their planet you could unzip your flesh suit easily,

    V
    E
    R
    T
    I
    C
    A
    L
    LY
with black tulips and blunt scissors.

The poem starts with Magellan crossing the Andes
and he sees some straits and immediately he names them
and identifies them as the straits of Magellan
as if their existence as the straits of Magellan
predated the name he gave them:

Crossing the foamy ocean   the splitting breakers
bursting over the peaks of the Andes   It's the strait
of Magellan says Magellan as he steers between the
sunken islands of the cordilleras   These are the new
caravels of the Pacific we reply watching the plains of
Nagasaki and Hiroshima pass before the Chilean sky
filled with dust   drifting   like two days shattered into
pieces coming closer between the fjords

The images of the burnt children for example ...

And you are Buster Keaton on a mast climbing upwards in a
    storm

and just as you adjust you're on a giant clock's hand
hanging over Manhattan,

somper vim
sindle chub
tomponaiety tolvid
umper imper?
to HIM that owns all is ALLOWED, even the end of
    THINKING.
Shwe shwe shwe shwe shwe shwe shwe shwe shwe,

but in this case it is actually the birds'
        or the noise of light shattering as it falls

blow bird blow hide Mozart's piano behind the altar, Carlos Gardel is / inside the Victrola, and that little shepherd boy from the Atlas Mountains / I've invited him in since he sings the most beautiful song I have ever heard, / as he led his sheep alone over a rise near a lake his song rose up like a kite searching for a wind a song for no one to hear, he was singing to the sky to / see if it would answer, / / he was singing where am I / why am I here alone in the mountains,
inside the cyclotron
warming
colliding
rides a blue lion
Vimalakirti swoons …

mud is a dog with blue wings

I hear Hurrian Melody #6, the oldest known melody
In the world found as a cuneiform tablet in present day Ras Shamra, Syria
Played on 9-stringed lyre.

    And CHINAMPA, an Aztec word meaning "floating garden."

And the moon does not influence the timing of human births or hospital admissions, a new study finds, confirming what astronomers have pretty well known for decades. And yet, I refer to my interactions with flowers, for example, as "singular intimacies," where my goal is not hyper scrutiny with a macro lens, but a depiction of micro sensuality; who is it? It's me (takes off goggles / puts on goggles) eyes stinging from excess fumes from the top of the water I can't see a thing. I can't see any thing. This is what a tar ball tastes like. "There have been pounds and pounds of decomposed flesh   tons of suffering" "HOU HOU HOU HOU HOU" "The woman who "prefers waves to the sea" has addressed a message to the poet: "change the world or go home!" "Yet I think *Smorgasbord* is one of Jerry Lewis's greatest films; in what follows, I will try to explain why." "But how is such a purgation to be accomplished? Fear and terror are sublime; they point to an overwhelming force whose advent involves a complete rupture." "Which is to say that Warren's next attempt to kill himself is still more elaborate. He sits in a chair in a hotel room, watching a Western on TV. A rifle is poised on a table behind him, aimed right at his head. Warren has tied one end of a string to the rifle's trigger, and the other to the knob of the door to his room. He calls room service, asking for some ice. The idea is that, when the bellboy opens the door to deliver the ice, the string will be pulled, the gun will go off, and Warren will be shot. But of course, as always happens, the plan goes awry. The bellboy knocks, but does not enter. It turns out that the door to the room is locked. So Warren has to get up from his chair and open the door. The trigger is pulled, and the rifle shoots. The bullet goes through the TV, and kills one of the cowboys in the movie. Another cowboy turns, faces out of the screen, draws his gun, and fires a shot that exits the TV and kills the bellboy." In response I received a long inky letter filled with the precise tone of green or blue and the full effect of their complementarities. Thus I put my whole body into the codes. May you future people of the future decipher these runes, this sanctum: the smell of rotting fruit; this escarpment: the bewilderment of days; this house: the paragraphs of weather.

Which is to say that the lake felt ancient, yet regenerated in every instant, the tenderized lung of a much larger organism – "and I become water, friend of water" "That's what we are: beings made through the contact of water with stone, of a chilly sunset with pure geometry" … the way a cat is a cat: human before all else. I too have thought the traffic light beautiful …" But now the heretofore crushed and humiliated, "the wretched of the earth," were rising and reclaiming their rightful place in all creation. We chatted briefly in this most dramatic of settings and then the two of them turned and vanished into the experience of living while twinning the structural dead. Corpse blurs this boundary, but doesn't lift it. The slippage of death into life doesn't relieve mourning, or convince us that the dead are somehow available when we need

5545

them. Absence is real. If there was no binary, we would be less desperate about keeping each other alive ~~ maybe I want everyone to be here forever and then we could all just go at once + maybe I don't want to prepare + I can't take back that time I screamed in your face. So no, although its name is derived from the Miwok word meaning "coast mountain," we don't have records of the tribe's rituals involving the peak. So if the trace of Corpse is a density, the manhole levelers were dense with the corpse of tar, which is to say the tarred and feathered, and the lashing bars had the corpses of the sea, Édouard Glissant's sea, which he wrote was "one vast beginning, but a beginning whose time is marked by these balls and chains gone green." The density pooled in the far left corner of the gallery, in a piece titled *Disgorgement*. This molecular intelligence makes me giddy. But the use of this rime – *In this … / The Eclipse …* which paused the arrival of the place of the eclipse, was also an accent on it, because "Poets," Etel once wrote me, "are great realists (even when they see angels, if they do, as Rilke does)." *Straight from the heart* (from the character for Heart-Mind that possibly exists in some pictorial language or other (?)), a transformative

> 'rocklike'
> unrepentantly 'naïve' & 'downhome-perceptive'
> playfully 'logical'
> sternly educated
> fully knowledgeable
> 'simple-steady'

Socrates-like person who goes about her work (*painting*, too! & (without giving up on this Earth) teaches (in her *writing*, & by 'personal example') Embodied Intelligence & Fairness In All Matters, while passionately advocating for certain causes in which she believes (like the Rights of Multiple Kinds of Beings / on Earth and Everywhere Else to *Be Alive*) … that's when Rebecca asks: if yr mother dies, can you get a free meal at Denny's? What (à la Bhanu's wonderful questionnaires) do you eat before teaching? A cup of hours, of salt, flowers, darkness, iodine. Call me Ishmael. Or, as Adnan puts it, "the thread of this century is made of wire." Like I'd never felt my arm before … I remember talking with Pauline Oliveros after a performance she gave at Woodland Pattern, her accordion bellows still holding a long tone somewhere in my inner ear. She, too, was more interested in asking questions than being asked. And where Oliveros is Deep Listening, Adnan is a short line or a long line with a soft dip. On the title page of the book I penciled, "On the subway. A homeless man gets up and exits the car." Every fraction of a second, "Come here. Come over here and see what the bird's nest is doing. There are these small eggs, all of these small eggs, none of them cracked yet, but the big bird's away. I told you it might go. Speaking of which, *in his delirium a few coins had fallen from his belt, along with a cone of bright metal, the size of a die. In vain a boy tried to pick up this cone. A man was scarcely able to raise it from the ground. I remember that its weight was intolerable and that after it was removed, the feeling of oppressiveness remained.*

Which is why I'm compelled to quote from *Caliban and the Witch* repeatedly as a form of rehabilitating historical accounts that have been buried subcutaneously. Which is why solar energy is attracted to the rock. Squam rock is an immense boulder. César Vallejo is dead (of a strange disease). I heard him say, "one of these things is not like the others, one of these things just isn't sustainable" and it was true and it was good and everyone wrote it down and I took credit for it. Not really. Yes really. No. If these storage methods are followed, blotter should last for many years. How can this be if the dismembered, burned and slashed cannot speak? It is a collection of planks, that is, jagged samples of bone shards, splinters of barracks and tangles of wire, low tremolos of shrieks lingering, blood streams, body-sticks, warehouse and camp whispered love journals before the liminoid – "There were millions of planets being born there" – first you die and then you die more. Your head is sitting there, tilted sideways. You twist it hard to pull it out by the roots, and dirt crumbles off your neck. Your head blinks as if to say, "Whatever, whatever." Horses come down from the sky and pick at the tufts of grass growing from the spot where your head was. You carry your head back to the car and drive home. On the way, your head says, "I jog every morning, and I'm always willing to do overtime. Forty years? And that will never mean? What happened in the last forty years because people run in droves? The Kathputli Colony has lived in these homes and alleyways for half a century and is composed of painters, folk singers, acrobats, jugglers, puppeteers, magicians, and more. 'Imagine if we believe,' say those who suspect the plot. Sure you can, but they talk." Now, as Willacy County faces a gaping hole in its budget, $128 million in debt still owed on Tent City, and the loss of its largest employer, I'd come to find out whether the prison that was supposed to be the county's economic salvation would end up being its hey county you are fucked.

> light coming into clouds above shadowed
> ridge, two birds slanting toward branch
> in foreground, sound of wave in channel

Two boxes of *Barbaric Vast & Wild* arrived today. What a thing. What a fun thing. Charles says, "it moves in leaps and bounds, like Nijinsky on peyote." Like we are so powerful that even space junk orbiting the earth disintegrates. "Let me whistle a ditty for you from out of these refurbished catheters," whispers the city. Everyone must have a car & now – wow – those cars have fucking *radar* and everything. Everyone can have a wrist radio & speak into it as if their errand is a mission & their mission is more important than anyone else's in this jam-packed space. Hello? London calling. Hello? Everyone calling. Hello? Hello? Did you know? Fast things got faster & smoother! You can have a fast smooth thing! This is new, this kind of liquid fastness! At least you'd be awake for the disease. Say what? "I can't read my own handwriting." But in real life I'm fatter than the internet, I'm waxing, my rope is at the tail end of me, I'm saying: You can amp up that toxic foreplay all you want, the biomarkers are the same and people have been animals for a while now. Whoever's been sleeping in the back shed has the whole story. And although my whole life seems to revolve around waking at 2am to take down certain blog posts, overcome by sudden fluxing shame, I am coming out of Blog Hiatus to make the Best Feral Book announcement as I promised, because I was born in England, and there, I was trained to be kind, modest and polite. Oh dear, flashback! No, that's not right. Let's move on to the actual ceremony. O, THE BIRD INSIDE ME SAYS, Dear audience / viewer: Welcome. This performance is only partially scripted and, stricto sensu, "robo-baroque". ***Press here and I'll tell you if it hurts.*** And pain aside, you could say that women are generally walking that line. I'm thinking of the places where the prose lapses into blunt poetry that comes from a deeper, lizard-brain place ("fuck the doubt / I mean fuck it dead"). Which is to say I agree with you. Sometimes a diagnosis is more a diagnosis of the society that invents it than it is a diagnosis of the patients it claims. Then someone in the audience said: "It's all very well for you to be sitting behind that table and talking about this stuff, but …" That's when Ronaldo just got up, walked in front of the table and did a cartwheel. He BLED on my own materials as I was presenting them, cutting himself on a ribbon as he filmed. It was all I could do to vomit a minimal pink rose. Did something else happen? I remember the carpet. I remember the earthquake. I remember lying down for 40 minutes on the floor of the world. In that moment that duct tape started whipping around, and then the paper, I knew I was watching something that was going to go – I remember nothing else before June. I said to the nurse, when I went to sit with my mother in the recovery room: "Oh no … weren't you meant to operate on the left eye? That's the wrong eye." The nurse turned to her clipboard in horror, at which point I said: "April Fool's!" It was very satisfying. Let me assure you that the Best Feral Book Award is not a joke. This is for real. "What do you want to be when you die?" "Red jellied hearts." To clarify, it will be a rescue puppy. I will pay for the first round of shots and the first bag of food. Wait! Seven seconds of low-gamma spikes in the 30-40Hz range (I didn't know what that was either — turns out it's a pattern or neural activity associated with "conscious attention"). But the figures might lead you astray if you don't read the fine print: they didn't actually get God's footprints on an MRI. They got them on one of those lo-tech EEGs that traces squiggly lines across a display, then photoshopped the relevant spikes onto an archival MRI image for display purposes.) Regardless, the findings themselves are really interesting. For one thing, the God spikes manifested on the left prefrontal cortex, although the seizure was concentrated in the right temporal. For another, God took her own sweet time taking the stage: the conversion event happened eight hours *after* the seizure. They're still trying to figure out what to make of all this. The behavioral manifestations are classic, though. This guy didn't just *believe* he was the chosen one; he *knew* it down in the gut, with the same certainty that you know your arm is attached to your shoulder. When asked what he was going to do with his disciples when he recruited them, he admitted that he had no plan, that he didn't need one: God would tell him what to do. God didn't, of course. She never got the chance. They shut the psychosis down with olanzapine a few hours after the event. As far as I know he's back at work, his buddies on the factory floor blissfully unrecruited. Which is not why the reader who opens the Book of Forgotten Bodies finds nothing. There are no horses galloping through deserted villages. There are no children crying for their parents who were thrown out of airplanes and into the sea. There are no soldiers who had their arms sliced off for refusing to etc. There are no rich men leaning against paradise trees. There are no bodies hanging in the military barracks on island XYZ off the coast of nation ABC. Which is not to say that I am not concerned with customer satisfaction. So, Dear Reader, because we value your input, please take a moment of your busy time to answer the following question, which will greatly assist us in our mission to produce cultural artifacts that will further meet your aesthetic and spiritual needs. Which of the following statements most accurately reflects your feelings about the writing which you have just read:

    a. This is a splendid poem, distinguished by the clarity of its thought, the force of its argument, and the eloquence of its expression.

    b. This poem is conceptually vapid, artistically shallow, and contributes nothing to the world of letters. It is little more than a collection of bad sentences and poorly formed ideas.

    c. I like this poem, but I wouldn't spend money to read more poems like it.

    d. When I read this poem, I feel frustrated and annoyed.

    e. When I read this poem, I feel nothing.

But to think the future disjunction of world and inhabitant inevitably evokes the origin of its present, precarious conjunction. The end of the world projects backward a beginning of the world; the future fate of humankind transports us to its emergence. The existence of a world before us, although regarded as a philosophical challenge by some (if Meillassoux's subtle argument is to be believed), seems easy enough for the average person to imagine. The possibility of an us before the world, on the other hand, strikes those of us from the West as a little bit strange. Yet it is a hypothesis explored in several Amerindian cosmogonies. It finds itself conveniently summarized in the commentary that opens a myth of the Yawanawa, Pano-speakers from the western Amazon: "The myth's action takes place in a time in which 'nothing yet was, but people already existed.'" The Aikewara, a Tupian-speaking people who live at the other end of the Amazon, say yes, and: "When the sky was still very close to the Earth, there was nothing in the world except people — and tortoises!" At first, then, everything was originally human, or rather, nothing was not human (except for tortoises, of course). So. Musica, maestro! The universe unfolds ... (even if sometimes its only word is "ouch"). Additional "Wavelengths" will be played. Will the player be played backward? Will the player enter the fortress (which looks like Castle Grayskull) equipped with money or fantasy? Will hungry avatars use the players to intervene in the doctrine? Is there a feasible, yet risky, rescue plan? Can repositioning the "Wavelengths" solve the puzzle?

Jacawix jiwakiwa, Beauty of life
jakańaz musphańawa. such astonishment at living.
Jakawix jiwakiwa Beauty of life
taqiwjan chika, wholly mixed-up
now vegetal iridescent

wet refulgence in your eyes
sky swelling pure power
worldswell cloudy cup
with the child of your entrails
with your angel's plucked wing
with sovereign clay pigeons
in the air of goodbye my hair on end
Yes, no! and white butterflies and bones
(we can say that, seeing, seeing, no) –

fish scales, each particle licensed by the
city, flying about like those seagull cries
escaping from a torn and rent denim
outlook, molecular personalities waiting
on suburbs with apocalyptic eyelashes,
fingernail eyebrows almost roaring down
the straightaway except for colored
enumeration in petroleum, except for happy
smiles fearfully congealed on surfaces
laminated by mucous and horizons,
I exit or attempt to exit between a
shrub and its shrubitude, between a
sunrise and its eyelid, locate an elbow
in the neck (I see you eating pancakes
on top of a skyscraper made of pancakes,

nothing they shall ever do to me can erase that chilly wind). Suddenly feeling the shiver of my old, first name, like a shiver that calls me back to a suddenly different responsibility now and again with the importance of the again — do you know what I mean when you go far away from yourself for as long as you can and realise maybe you can never go back, all the fire of the bridges becomes a damage to so many, and the brain knows how to cinch itself to that, but there is so much which determines me like udders, bad historical judders keeping me in the toxicity of the chasm and the grand spasm canyon, which is too soon for so much not yet always the not yet but old judder what can i say except that I am guilty, I am as guilty as the next goat, and as singularly guilty as no-one, and what I am guilty for is this thing i can not be innocent of either, my bare face and the whole lifetime I spent, staring away, being scared of what it would mean to write in any other way than this, in a fire of exposure and deeper than the arguments of the laws of time and the end of time in time in each time, deeper than the idea that space can exist for n infinities,

    all this is deeper than love
    deeper than love

        falls
            off

here is what the 'you' have, all of those who passed through and touched all those. I looked at the stars tonight, how beautiful the stars are tonight in the western Sahara, and I thought this is a one-off world that does not know it's one-off world, how could it know,

'there is something deeper than love'
'there is something I do not know'
'I am the first one to go extinct'

'we are going pretty fast now, we might not make it'

'As I sd to my
friend, because I am
always talking, — John,

et cetera,' and every time I think about it I truly feel like my head weighs like thirty-five pounds, and whenever I fall asleep and try to take a tiny baby-sized nap, and get all like thank fucking god finally, I wake up ten minutes later with stray tissues stuck to my sweaty body, having had some bizarre dream about being interviewed for a corporate job, so I have no idea why they asked me to do this, cause really, truly. I mean the truth is that poetry is not really that morally ooo-eee-ooo, it's mostly like not even as good as the green frosting on a CVS cupcake that could maybe redeem itself because it tastes 0.5% like a jolly rancher, and it's mostly not really like ice cream or soft serve where you can experience a beautifully unexpected milky reality located on another existential plane and it's mostly not even as good as the kind of sugar free lollipop you suck on while you're quitting smoking where you can taste that deliciously bitter aspartame when you wash it down with coke. So, despite the sense of foreboding, there were moments of levity and, for some, even a feeling of unexpected joy as men who hadn't felt the fresh air of night for years reveled in this strange freedom. Out in the dark, music could be heard — "drums, a guitar, vibes, flute, sax, [that] the brothers were playing." This was the lightest many of the men had felt since being processed into the maximum security facility. That night was in fact a deeply emotional time for all of them. Richard Clark watched in amazement as men embraced each other, and he saw one man break down into tears because it had been so long since he had been "allowed to get close to someone." Carlos Roche watched as tears of elation ran down the withered face of his friend "Owl," an old man who had been locked up for decades. "You know," Owl said in wonderment, "I haven't seen the stars in twenty-two years." As Clark later described this first night of the rebellion, while there was much trepidation about what might occur next, the men in D Yard also felt wonderful, because "no matter what happened later on, they couldn't take this night away from us." Which is to say that

THE NATURE of Infinity is this: That every thing has its
Own Vortex; and when once a traveller thro' Eternity
Has pass'd that Vortex, he perceives it roll backward behind
His path, into a Globe itself enfolding, like a sun,
Or like a moon, or like a universe of starry majesty,
While he keeps onwards in his wondrous journey on the
       Earth,

Sometimes I think it basically has no substance other than a collection of really good waifish looks brought to you by Wet n Wild eyeliner, Lipsmackers Dr Pepper Chapstick, Aveeno positively radiant intensive night cream, Diorshow mascara, and a shitload of germs. Like that's all it is, really. But WE ALL HAVE OUR SPECIAL ROLES TO PLAY. Some of us have cameras. Some of us are handing out leaflets. Some of us are in a van idling across the street, waiting for the right moment. Everything has been planned and everything is going according to plan. We are gathered together at the park. This makes sense. You would want to launch an alternate reality game in a highly trafficked area. Everything makes sense. The plot of our alternate reality game centers around the fight between aliens who have infiltrated all levels of society, a cult built around resisting them, and our players. The aliens cannot be recognized on sight. There is no way to tell who is an alien and who isn't an alien. The distinction between the aliens among us and normal humans will be up to the players to figure out. A player might even consider him or herself an alien. The pretense of secrecy suggests that everyone is being watched. Everything is set. We have a plot, websites, email addresses, hidden objects, puzzles, codes. The flyers we are about to hand out contain an oblique warning that is actually a clue for where players can find out more. We are dressed in black jumpsuits and riot gear. We are dressed as the hidden threats among us, in Giants jerseys. This park is one of the most highly trafficked parts of the city. Its proximity to subway access and retail markets make it the perfect place to introduce our ARG. Everything is going according to plan. Everything makes sense. Except for cheerleaders. Fifty cheerleaders are running into the park, waving blue and yellow pompoms. They push by us, the corners of our flyers scraping against their spandex body suits. "Wooooooh!" they yell as they pass, "Woooh!" They converge on a point directly in front of the statue of the president on horseback. They start to cheer. From vans they have parked around the park a four-to-the-floor beat shakes the already noisy downtown streets. From the banners it's clear that they're here to promote a new TV show about Southern college cheerleaders. The park has been taken over by their astroturf flash mob. They are not alone. From the west side of the park: a hundred people wearing red shirts singing along to music no one else can hear. They are all wearing headphones, all of their mp3 players synched to the same track, which they dance to. They are synchronized to the voice that speaks over the rhythm. "Jump up and down" says the voice and all of the redshirts begin to jump up and down. Another group comes from the east side of the park. They are all wearing blue shirts. They are singing and dancing to another song, a different song, another one that no one else can hear. From time to time the people on the east side of the park, the blueshirts, will all throw their hands up in the direction of the people on the west side of the park, the redshirts, wiggling their fingers. The redshirts will then all start making roundhouse kicks into the air. They are doing this for fun. They are "hacking reality." Both groups are slowly approaching the center of the park. There, a zombie bar crawl is on its way to the college bars a few blocks away. They have already been drinking for a few hours. They are all in character, moaning for brains, running up to the frontlines of the redshirts and the blueshirts, grasping. People walk through the park trying to get to work. They are saying "This is annoying." The zombies are saying "Braaains." There is an explosion. An explosion rips through the park. Cheerleader bodies flip into the air in a way that almost looks coordinated. For a second, the blast is mistaken for a firework display. The people on the west and the east sides of the park start to cheer, as the explosion happened to coincide with the crescendo of one of the songs on their mp3 players, a club remix Rihanna's "Diamonds." Except it is becoming clear this is not a fireworks display, this is not a part of their social experiment. They can tell that because of the blood and also the smoke. The zombies confuse things. The man trailing his intestines is in fact unhurt. Is a woman running across the park with her hair on fire in real danger or another prank? Then, improvising, the zombies start to pick up the injured cheerleaders. The redshirts and blueshirts use their smartphones to pull up first aid instructions, and to take pictures and videos of the chaos. And we are there, dressed in the black jumpsuits with black shades and riot gear meant for aliens, and are immediately taken for police, and respond as such. We take people by the hand, we tell them it will be all right. Come with me, we tell them, everything will be all right. We are the police. Everything is okay now. People are staring at the park from the high windows of the shopping center next to the park. They are doing whatever it is they can think of doing first: calling their parents, their children, putting their hands over their mouths, crying. One of our flyers floats up to their window in the air among the hot ash. It says: *YOU'RE NOT THE ONLY ONE WHO THINKS THAT SOMETHING HORRIBLE IS ABOUT TO HAPPEN*. Of course, no one may ever read this. But maybe some archivist at Yale will wind up with my phone and lean over to another graduate student, and say, "look someone at the gym told her she ALWAYS looked cute." Covers his mouth laughing. Maybe I'll lose this phone. But the flashes weren't working yet; they needed to be culled and sliced and pared down. More precise and surprising and making the feeling of *puncture*, or *flash*, that's what I always imagined it would be, from the beginning. Thus, "The hum hurts." I want to add a million, you want to cut 8,000 words.

> 1,863 – 1,619 = billions. remit it in unmarked bills
> —someone should pay
> for what someone shouldn't have paid for shouldn't someone
>   pay
> —like a million bucks
> for the doo-doo done for doo-doo to the done-for dun as
>   doodoo
> this mud smirch of amok, it's you isn't we?
> ain't'n't responsible for
> messes of mess were made by what are
> who?
> fixing to cram the ur-bird in the ur-egg
> who's jammin off your staves
> isn't we?
> no [insert here] low enough to
> vice
> versa?
> melisma flood altos' rocking shoulders
> knqrw what f,* ,u"" t"itt'g iU"rt?

"No. Encyclopaedias, centuries, dynasties, symbols, the cosmos, and cosmogonies are offered – Pay no attention, everything has to be rethought. The true feeling of strength, when no triumphs beckon. I live among wounded books ... people were eaten recently ... the peeling paint and cracked tile of the Dallas safe-house toilet ... so we invented reality, which remains to be discovered .... even if it's right in front of us." That's what distinguishes the great thinkers of our time! They look at the stars and they ask, "How is that I can see?" They look at the color of a flower and say, "How is it that this is red?" Sommer Browning looks at a circle and sees a urethra. She sees a "view of my head, the abyss, and a pizza. What's happening when we look at a circle and see the body of Christ? Or, better: When you are passed out, they felt-marker you / with tiny dicks." In the flutter of blue alcohol flame a figure enters its shadow asking *where do you keep all these things?* Right here, in the archive. But you know what they say: "Disparate times call for disparate methods." So, central to *Molecular Red* is the philosopher and scientist Alexander Bogdanov and his universal science of organisation, or 'Tektology'. According to Wark, it is a scientific method, a mode of organisation, a synonym for totality, and a metaphorical approach to creative writing.

Which is to say that The Carbon Liberation Front is in turn responsible for generating a 'metabolic rift'. WE BLED METICULOUSLY. And the novel's protagonist Dvanov's main idea is communism. Communism cannot be achieved here and now, however. At least not right here and right now. So he shifts his attention to the 'secondary ideas' – to his everyday routine. So when he thinks he sees something shifting in the waves nearby he dismisses it as an illusion, then he assumes it to be a rock. Still a churning weakness and fear deters him from leaving the saddle of the time machine. And then he sees what moves in the water: "It was a round thing, the size of a football perhaps, or, it may be, bigger, and tentacles trailed down from it. It seemed black against the weltering blood-red water, and it was hopping fitfully about." He is terrified of passing out, with the thing waiting for him in the shallows. He recedes back into the past. The familiar contours of his laboratory swim into being around him. From that moment on it was necessary to get used to coordinating two thoughts, to uniting in a single impulse one thought that rises from out of the earth itself, from the depths of the bones, and another that descends from the heights of the skull. It was necessary that these thoughts should always meet at a single moment, that their waves should coincide and resonate ... Platonov was one of the few who raised the question of nature's exploitation in the 1920s and 30s. Which is why my most elaborate work, called *Car Crash*, was spoken by Big Venus, with animal grunts and howls by me. Some are 8 or 9 feet long, white pigment mixed with shellac. The poles are angled at eighty-eight degrees else lightning always strikes twice. The primary experience takes place within the grid. Weather is total. One narrative theory is that Agents are social beings. The grid is the imaginary frame by which it becomes possible to sense the spatial landscape. The grid dwarfs Agents, the grid in turn being dwarfed by the landscape, provoking Agents to realize their own relation to the spatial landscape. In that the grid itself cannot be fully comprehended in its totality, neither can the spatial landscape. There are three agents in the landscape who are not kings. Agent Red's scale becomes paramount. Agent Yellow's isolation becomes paramount. Agent Orange's silence becomes paramount. The imaginary plane rests flat upon the tips of the grid poles. One narrative theory is that Agents' minds function as the imaginary plane. The action is the work, weathered within the social bearings. One narrative theory is that one's apocalypse is inside. Such apocalypse is not nuclear-safe, such art is a cartoon that is actual. Agents inside nuclear-safe capsules are not safe from themselves. Agents cannot be insulated in machines that are cartoon, in art that farts its own radioactivity. The numbers on the meter go up and up. As flagpoles do. There are three Agents in the capsules who are not cartoons. Agent Red drinks the capsule fuel. Agent Yellow eats the capsule waste. Agent Orange breathes the capsule air. That the technology necessary to provide safety for Agents is the same technology that produces the effects from which Agents desire safety is troubling to one. Capsules are cartoon machines that can't be shelter to kings. There are no kings, only Agents. "Antigone enters. Pesticides, eco-cide, a guiding conversation with Leslie Scalapino and the beloved ancestors about the drone poem and the brain-body of the prison-industrial complex, flickering beneath an alluring scrim of chemically-bright lawns and chthonic lyrics pulled up with the roots intact, hard, sweet, and a cell calls to itself, splits: a caul is knit. In the intimacy of the not-self-same is birthed a third thing: a second sight, a 'rococo glow', a 'sparkle spasm', a transcriptase strip-tease and you know when a cell does something it's galactic. Can protein have a fantasy life? Does cancer *wish* to conquer? Is thought just the comfort food our brain cells grant us while dancing their own ends? Every morning the privatized Chicagoans wake up and there is an enormous loaf of bread in the barracks and there is a sharp knife for them to cleanly slice the bread and divide it equally among their cohabitants. And every morning everyone in the barracks gets a slice of bread. And in the evening, a tomato. And in the afternoon, crackers. And sometimes we drive the loneliest bodies to a clearing in the forest. Their rancid bodies smell like turpentine.

    Thank you for the description
    But there are things that are still unclear
    Who do the white bodies belong to☐ ☐
    Who do the beige bodies belong to☐ ☐
    Who owns the red and yellow bodies
    Where are the black bodies☐ ☐
    Where do the immigrants sleep at night☐ ☐

    What animals will you take
☐ ☐   All the animals
    What personal effects will you carry
☐   ☐ Just the essentials
    What will you hope for
    ☐ ☐ Peace
    What do you seek to achieve
☐   ☐ We want the lake to re-appear
☐ ☐

    Six to the front
    Three to the rear
    Rip it on down
    It goes to midnight.

    Where was I?

    SOOT BULL JEEP
    SOOT BULL JEEP

    Err, er, er, er, er
    Er, Er, er, er, er
    Err, er, er, er, er
    Er, Er, er, er, er
    Now we know
    What we look like.

Only this time
The bulging top is iced & decorated.
Only this time
The word 'umbles' refers to

> [a ghost has seized the woman's animal double. a lumbering capybara wedged in between limp roots overturned. as indigenized iphones disintegrate before the viscosity of this ghost, its fume and coalescence, its waft of manure. ghosts aren't supposed to smell, i say to pinto, the paint on his face already a surface of blood where an artery splotched the blood will remain as ever. a rib of heat in the earth room. the animal is the first visible light of the invisible ...]"

Speaking of the US air attack on the MSF hospital in Kunduz last October, *Behind my surgical mask, my mouth was gritty, as if somebody forced me to eat sand. I could hear my breath rasping in and out. Layers of smoke coming from a nearby room made it hard to see where we were. Blinking around, I caught sight of a glow, from a man's hand holding a phone. He seemed mortally wounded but was still trying to send a message ... All around us, bombing continued in regular intervals, shaking the ground, sending debris sweeping and flying. One. Two. Three. I tried to count but there seems to be no abatement to the explosions. I stopped counting at eight and silently prayed that we could get out of there alive. Fire licked at the roof at one end of the building, dancing and sparkling in the dark, reaching towards the branches of the trees nearby. The ICU was burning ... With the exception of one three-year-old, all the patients in the unit died. The caretakers with the patients died. Dr Osmani died. The ICU nurses Zia and Strongman Naseer died. The ICU cleaner Nasir died. I hope with all my heart that the three sedated patients in ICU, including our ER nurse Lal Mohammad, were deep enough to be unaware of their deaths – but this is unlikely. They were trapped in their beds, engulfed in flames.* This was my first visit to the underworld. And so in the beginning, I decided to look. I made my way across the highway and walked into the city to explore the necropolis, ostensibly searching, obviously failing my impossible quest. I found myself in a large stone building. The ground felt moist. You could smell urine. There were horses shitting within this temple. Some bodies on the floor. Was the beginning over? And so in the beginning, I crept back and forth on all fours across the overpass of Styx. As in Bangkok, the Tartarus municipal authorities have paved asphalt over the rivers so the city can modernize and gentrify and sprawl. I wandered around the hutongs and favelas of the capital, a necropolis whose space I could navigate but whose temporality I found glitched. Think about when you experience a glitched image: the error interrupts the visual plane of the image like an instantaneous motion, but the glitch is what stops the video from continuing in time. Glitch as motion, glitch as stasis. Death as migration, death as time travel. To put this another way, I have always wondered whether ghosts look like the person they were when they died. What then is the underworld? The underworld is where you are archived. If Dante wrote of meeting Aristotle and Avicenna, Judas and Brutus, then did that mean I could meet C.L.R. James and Lakshmi Sahgal, Liang Qichao and Michael Jackson? When I stroll around the underworld, I see everything that ever was — or at least everything that ever died. I saw the beginning, the true beginning, the beginning of modern capitalism and the way of life of probably anyone reading this essay. I saw that the beginning had twin poles: in the New World, where the indigenous people fled the conquering hordes, strange men who would casually behead the people they encountered and set their hounds to tear the flesh of infants, and in the west coast of Africa, where there came a story that these traders of strange cargo must be cannibals, piling up as they did colossal mounds of bones. I saw men in India strapping the bodies of insurrectionary sepoys to the mouths of cannons. And there was the Congo, where I saw the West come carrying bags of hands. They had taken the hands from the people who lived there. In My Lai, was it ears? What was it in Malaya? Perhaps I am beginning to digress. If I sound as if I am angry, this is not quite the case, as I do not possess emotions commensurate to this scale. I would think it would be more damning to say that, rather than sounding angry, I sound self-righteous in a clueless key. Listing these horrors in such a casual way — it shames one to write it, shames one to read it. How then to represent what I have come to call sublime trauma, the absolute terror of colonialism that is too gargantuan to be represented, words whose monument deforms our mouths as we speak them, events too much almost to even bear glimpsing? And what right or relationship do I possess to these horrors? But in the beginning when I saw the layered alleyways and overpasses of hell, I realized that you can accrete particulars, stacking each on top of the other, until you have summoned from the ashes and the dust all manner of cosmos, planets, stars, comets, satellites, the sun and the moon themselves. The sun and the moon are totemic symbols, luminous icons from the Tarot deck, but they are also material objects, astral places. Like the sun and the moon, an archive can also vibrate between the physical and the metaphysical. The archive that baits my obsessions is called the Migrated Archive: it collects many files deemed too incriminating by the former British empire, many files destroyed, some preserved: 1.3 million documents over fifteen miles of floor-to-ceiling shelving, located in Hansford Park, an office complex which I am informed is not located in the underworld. And yet these papers hardly seem real to me. Last night, I read the index online again and it looked to me like the programming code to the last two hundreds years of global history. Suppression of the slave trade. Palestine question. Pension plan for the East India Company. I find myself staring at this catalog of empire through the night, the csv file gleaming. Subhas Chandra Bose. Repatriation of Cossacks. Rhodesia secret negotiations. Penguin egg collection. I see in the Migrated Archive's index a poem whose greatness is an authority beyond what can be authored — a poem of facts and particulars larger than that small bracelet that the ancients called the One and that we call infinity. So, in the beginning I'll select another phrase for beginning, one that's a bit more concentrated, an expression in Quechua: *Imanatátaj watusúnchij kay wátuy mana atinata*, which I take to mean: ¿cómo vamos a traducir lo imposible — de traducir?, and which Michelle Gil-Montero translucinates as: *How do we translate what is impossible — to translate?* "How," in effect: "how" "watusúnchij" (will we translate, understand, divine or write — since it's not about knowledge here, you have to know it without knowing the whole; let's see: cognition is not the key term here, but something that precedes the marking or re-marking of fate, a spirited response to some destiny or some unfixed destination along the path, a question — for example, your question — which is the thing that the Quechua [word] *wátuy* emphasizes in its own way). But. Regarding the *wátuy* and its occasional occurrence in the puna (Andean highlands), there where even the heavens *se apunan* (suffer from the illness or ecstasy of altitude, alias *soroche*), I refer to this passage from *Trilce* as a provisional conclusion:

> Cielos de puna descorazonada
> por gran amor, los cielos de platino, torvos
> de imposible.

How does Clayton Eshleman translate this? Michael Smith and Valentino Gianuzzi? Rebecca Seiferle and Dave Smith? And …? And Google? If there is a plural singular, doesn't that also involve monster-writings every time? But. Of course. Not to mention yet again the sadly controversial "Escuela de las Américas" (the *United States Army School of the Americas*), set up to train the torturers used by the dictatorships of the sixties and the seventies (at least) … But that's a longer story. That said, in contrast to what Philippe Lacoue-Labarthe might have written in *La poésie comme expérience*, I sense that Celan never expected that Heidegger would ask for forgiveness for his National Socialism. Poetry and politics, you say? But when is it not? And every time at play "in" the poem! Which, again, implies that one cannot reduce politics or politicalness (of being, of acting, of readwriting, etc.) (is politicalness a word?) … That is to say — Ha! I love saying perdón. But first it's that etching into bone that causes the cracks. Everything etches into bone. What shapes and landscapes are these? — blind surmise of topography, shadow and darker shadow, darkness and darker darkness going way past black. Any torus-shaped object can be turned, twisted, to reveal its fundamental properties. This particular person is as good as any, for example. Thick with trees. My thoughts recurrently return to a cartoon in there, Figure 20. It's that something our example on the street. Wile E. Coyote couldn't be happier with his purchase on these concepts, shipped to fulfill and foil his cartoon schemes. Like Pan and masturbation, according to Diogenes.

You want flowers
Me, a horse, a guitar
And to never work, never, never.

But one of the weariest things about the world as it is is how it makes so many of us do so many things we don't want to do. We sleep with people we don't want to, sometimes because we are bored or to feel loved or to have a bed; we sell off the hours of our lives to the bosses and still don't have enough to live. We eat shitty food, and then click on things. We get sick and offer our bodies up to poisonous and mutilating cures. The adventure is often overcome with tragedy, stupidity. The stud hero is juxtaposed with inwardly meditative women like Dido who, midway through the volume, directs her wrath to the deceptive Trojan leader (who decides only after their sexual and material union to leave Carthage to complete his destined conquest of Italy):

> I curse Aeneas one last time, him
> and all his descendants. *Let shores*
> *clash with shores, arms*
> *arms. Let him die, but not before*
> *he's stripped of Ascanius, not before*
> *he sees innocent friends killed*
> *simply and awfully, not until*
> *he realizes there's no peace*
> *in his chosen land. Rise up,*
> *Carthage, after I'm gone,*
> *and piss on the bones of his*
> *grandchildren. That's the promise*
> *I ask for this heart that still runs*
> *hot with all of your blood.*

Dido is one of the only sympathetic characters in the *Aeneid*, and it is hard not to wonder how her curse might have ramified across the millennia since its utterance. Her own troubling death — by self-impalement and immolation — provides a symbolic reprimand to Aeneas's single-minded determination to found a new nation justified by conventions of piety. The gods themselves — their petty divine jealousies — are often the originators of conflict in Aeneas's world. Juno, for instance, who detests Troy due to ancient quarrels (Paris, a Trojan, once snubbed her in a beauty contest), "sends Iris down / from the sky to breathe / ill wind into the Trojan women / for her old sorrow is / not yet sated." Iris presents herself in human form to the women, mocking their refugee status:

> "O wretches,"
>   she says, "No Greek dragged you
>   here — unhappy race

                    what doom does fate hold for you?
        Seven years now since Troy's
                    fall, what wild seas
    sand   stars
                we've endured
        chasing elusive
                    Italy
                            twisted
            spinning
                on waves
                            here.

It is hard not to notice the whims of power directing the fates of these women, and to be reminded of the recent winter suffering of refugees in Greece, Macedonia, and Calais, many children there shivering in damp clothes as it rained.

Then we took a long walk in a large group trying to find the Ted Bundy house. I felt like we were the Scooby Doo gang. In the era of Abu Ghraib, the persistent low-grade fever, and who knows what other atrocities. And thus the qualia, "First – Chill – then Stupor." Then I was told: to be an angel, you must be without gender. This is what I was told when I was very young, before I learned Joan Miró was a man. I believed Joan Miró was a Hawaiian woman who died on Christmas Day from eating too much bread dough ... I thought ...

    Mother of flies
    face of the beautiful

It was the only time I saw my father cry. With this in mind, we chose the image for the jacket and frontispiece. It shows a composite creature, half man, half fish, known in ancient times as an *apkallu*, 'sage'. The Akkadian term is a loanword from Sumerian *abgal*, literally 'big fish'. The cover image, which is also reproduced on the frontispiece, is based on the ninth-century BCE Assyrian *apkallu* carved on the stone decoration of Ninurta's temple in Kalhu, modern Nimrud. Its creator, Tessa Rickards, brings it to life by using the colour scheme of the wall paintings adorning the eighth-century Assyrian palace of Til Barsip (modern Tell Ahmar). A similar fish-creature was depicted in room XXVII of the Til Barsip palace, close to the throne room, but is preserved only in fragments. The Kalhu *apkallu* was certainly also painted in antiquity. According to Mesopotamian tradition, these 'big fish' are the companions of the god of wisdom, Enki / Ea, who dwells in the depths of the sea. They regularly emerged from the sea in order to teach humans the cornerstones of civilization, such as agriculture, kingship, justice, and writing, before the Flood ended their coexistence. From the third millennium BCE to the Hellenistic period, the fish-creatures were seen as purveyors of wisdom and learnedness. Scholars and priests took their title and dressed in their image, wearing robes and hats made out of the skin of the enormous river carp that still populate the Euphrates and Tigris today. Which is why, according to Brandon, white women's feet are made of egg yolks and formaldehyde. It's the first book I finished (even though it's not finished yet). Why am I remembering this? Because it's April, National Corpse Month — and five billions years until the sun burns out. So when I say first, I mean the most traumatic, the most enduring. A miniature woman in a paper boat. The sea, paper. She requests I set fire to the sheet on which she drifts. I do and see flames, or early afternoon light on the comforter, on the bare walls, and on exposed aluminum vents. It's a very quiet immolation. My bed smells like sheaves of paper. A fat fly appears on *Kafka on the Shore*. I'd started it, stopped. Gave it my best bookmark: a photo of three children and their tubas, summer sky molten, thin boundary between metal and air. In a spiritual depression, all my nightmares and their day-terror images later align with testimonies surrounding the abduction and murder of Emmett Till. There are long days of sickness, "a series of foldings-in that seek comfort in repetition." And there's joy in repetition, there's joy in repetition, there's joy in repetition, there's joy in repetition, there's joy in repetition, there's joy in repetition, there's joy in repetition, there's joy in repetition, there's joy in repetition, there's joy in repetition. I ask if it isn't normal to get a bit sick from this place, to have to lie down. Snakes on the courtroom floor. Irregular behavior of lions and bees. "Often, I click the heels of my Nikes together … and I am allowed to return to a meadow …" A pigeon takes the stairs. A pigeon sits on a bench. A crow and a seagull face each other. "What is the problem?" Or: "Are you paining?" This is hard to translate. One afternoon, my parents took me to a lab to test my lung capacity. This page includes an image of a torn piece of paper:

> all that is solid melts into
> us

But today, I broke your solar system. Oops. My bad. But if you haven't noticed, like I haven't noticed, can you not tell me why you acquiesce. There is a machine full of children like a pasta machine full of Play-Doh that everyone is eating and vomiting because it is a salty and slowly poisonous rainbow in the truth of light that is flourescent like the true sun is fluorescent. When confronted the children say, "we didn't mean puddle, we meant poodle, like a soft pink tuft extruding from a dog." When confronted the children say, "we weren't really going to do it," but even if you can't see it, even if your eyes are unaware of the ocular proof of "it" in this playpen with all of Poe's orangutans, there is an eye set into every wound like a cubic zirconia. (Fun fact! This game was called "Exciting Basket" in Japan.) Looking from the free state
there is a river then a slave state

> Turn around and there is a slave state,
> a river
> then a free state

I was born between the free side and the slave side, my head crowning on the bridge. I fully emerged in an elevator traveling upward in a slave state. I have shopped in the slave state and eaten barbecue there. I have walked along the riverbank in the slave state and looked out at a free state. So yes, coral and lichen symbionts also bring us richly into the storied tissues of the thickly present Chthulucene, where it remains possible—just barely—to play a much better SF game, in nonarrogant collaboration with all those in the muddle. We are all lichens; so we can be scraped off the rocks by the Furies, who still erupt to avenge crimes against the Earth. Alternatively, we can join in the metabolic transformations between and among rocks and critters for living and dying well. "'Do you realize,' the phytolinguist will say to the aesthetic critic, 'that [once upon a time] they couldn't even read Eggplant?' And they will smile at our ignorance, as they pick up their rucksacks and hike on up to read the newly deciphered lyrics of the lichen on the north face of Pike's Peak.'" Which is to note the truth of what Trace Peterson tells us,

> Everyone is a little Trans
> Everyone is a little Bisexual
> Everyone is a little Genderqueer
> Everyone is a little Not There

Everyone is a little bit slave to the rhythm
Everyone is a little Michael Jackson
Everyone is a little Grace Jones

Everyone is a little good at sex
Everyone is a little bad at race
Everyone is a little bad at gender
Everyone is a little bad at class

Everyone is a little changeable
Everyone is a little rigidly stuck in their thing
Everyone is an abandoned carousel with empty horses going around and
   around
      and around

Everyone is a little interested in sitting on the dryer while it
        vibrates

Everyone is a little taller because of all the preservatives
Everyone is a little prepackaged

He was also half of the bricks and dictaphone duo Pleasure-Drenching Improvers. And he made a VLOG but he was semi-delirious. In it, he takes homeopathic drops purchased at a dispensary in a now abandoned leper colony. He doesn't check the use by date on the drops. So the answer to the question is: Is Poetry Healing? These are my grubby paws. This is my snake-bright shrine. Look! Older people process anaesthesia in unpredictable ways. Wait. My kidneys are aching from this flu and the dream. Every bit of proton beam that enters my skull has to come out somewhere – hence the growing exit area on the opposite side of the target zone. On a positive note, I then went to the sea and the waves were huge and wild and amazing and real and blue and cream. Perhaps something magical will happen in the next two days and I will relocate my family members to Pasadena. Dr Penfield, Dr Penfield, is there a sea in Pasadena? Next up I am going to restructure the pelvic fascia which is the end point of the fascia of the throat. Yes!!!! I will start my You Tube Channel. Here's a cappuccino. Here's a fizzy green juice. And I feel so happy. An equilateral triangle for a change. A woman barking. Another parabola. Curls of bark. A wet computer in a bag of rice. If I say, "At one year

I was crawling," is that a thing? Is that blue sparks! I heard nothing. Remember nothing of the pain. The reality is that chemotherapy tastes like burnt hair. And that THE MACHINE sounds like a bunch of mechanical parts moving mechanically – nothing like rushing water – which is to say that there were enough loose boards leaning against the house to build a new one, which was like looking into a mouth to see rows upon rows upon of decayed teeth. It was like the soft spot on a newborn's head or the back of a pin cushion. It was like Alien vs Predator. THIS IS WHAT WE DO, lying, WE EAT STICKS. Nor do I believe necessarily in pathology as any abnormal distress separate from the practice of life. There are snails in my bathtub. But even then we are finding words based on clues from other words without explaining why we need to find those words to begin with, which is to say that something smelled as if it had been sprayed to smell that way ('Are you pouring cold water on my hand, Dr Penfield?"), which is to say I asked questions simply to see the contortions, knowing it always existed further extending forever downwards which meant infinite as outer space. Silence was the loudest. But then, the loneliness of it without the forest, without the mutt hopping around on three legs, hopping around the quivering lake. The quivering lake is awake. It was an antique plate from Portugal. The lemon tree soda can tab, the almond trace filter.

>My neighbour's wife is six feet tall
>so I gave them my king-sized bed
>I gave my daughter my good kitchen knives
>I tell the father / son the Baltimore magician story!

Now multiply that by everyone you've never met. Now by everyone who has seen you. Was there an ocean in there? But with help — in extreme cases from professionals — a lot of hoopla is expected, like *Is it crazy to say that since we're drifting at 2.5 centimeters per year, and that since we're orbiting at 67,062 miles per hour, that since our orbit is actually a wobble as the moon stretches or squeezes us each tide, that … wow. What a human trait!* It feasted on him. We considered the object for how it stood before us in all its seeming stillness — he bought into it with the cash he made raking leaves and filling big black plastic bags. A train in the rain on the plain and all that scenery. So I'm with them shopping, and I'm with you in Rockland, I'm with you in Rockland, I'm with you in Rockland where we hug and kiss the United States under our bedsheets in the United States that coughs all night and won't let us sleep I'm with you in Rockland where we wake up electrified out of the coma by our own souls' airplanes roaring over the roof they've come to drop angelic bombs the hospital illuminates itself imaginary walls collapse O skinny legions run outside dot dot dot O victory forget your underwear we're free. OK. Where was I? Of course there's no such thing as ethnopoetry. There's only an empty set which includes all poetry. To infinity … and beyond! So yeah. You are not in control of this incense. You are not in control of astonishing. They came to the door and asked: Do you believe in sheet music? I was there on my tippy toes feeling thickness leave me, my palms turning into asterisks, my bent arms walking the wire with their baskets between full and empty, I believe the story about the father who drove to work and left his child in back in the carseat. Which is to say, with Enrique Enriquez, When the reader of a book reads the word 'apple', he fills that word with all the apples he has eaten. When a tarot reader looks at an apple the tarot reader sees it as the crossing of a horizontal axis in which another apple became a seed, that seed became a tree, the tree gave us our apple, that in turn will dry down to its own seeds … and a vertical axis in which the Law of Gravity echoes the Fall story, fortunate and/or otherwise. What if we could read a word as one reads the tarot? Then that word would predict its own fate, which is to turn itself into another word. A sheep is a shoe. So yes, you are right, maybe what I do isn't poetry. But it is *indistinguishable* from poetry. Which is one reason she takes photographs of depressed animals. Meaning, a flower and a star mirror each other, but as mirrors they are mutually concave: the space in between the flower and the star is the mandorla (the vesica piscis?) in the card called The World. Ergo, an ellipse is an eclipse. The ellipse is the lips of two circles kissing, overlapping, over-lipping, wandering around the wunder rim. The mandorla is the intersection, the space across two circles. A SPACE A CROSS TWO CIRCLES *A cross is an X. A circle is a silent letter O. Two circles equal O O. If they weren't silent they would spell "Oh! Oh!" Taken as two eyes, these two Os look at us as we see ourselves in the mirror every morning, through a straight (straight: that which contains the X trait) line that connects our eyes to their reflexion and renders both equivalent, EQUIVALENT, starts with EQUI. EQUIS is the Spanish name for X, which sounds like A KISS and is expressed as X. This demonstrates conclusively (a "conclusion" is nothing else but an l minus ess "concussion") how a mandorla is a gap, a lull, a shift between two stances.* Which means I must write a book some day, called *Cough*. I want to remember my dreams, but this anti-coughing drug fucks me up. A big bubble is suspended above me in the middle of the room. I watch it drift over the bed. Then I stand up and reach out. My love says, It's Anancy the spider, saying babe, I don't have any lube, here, use my vanilla lip gloss. And the light — the blizzard of photons coming from everywhere — "uh" "uh" "uh" "uh" is my Light Mantra, those photons HURT. So when he said don't believe every voice you hear in your head, I knew right away which one I'd start with.

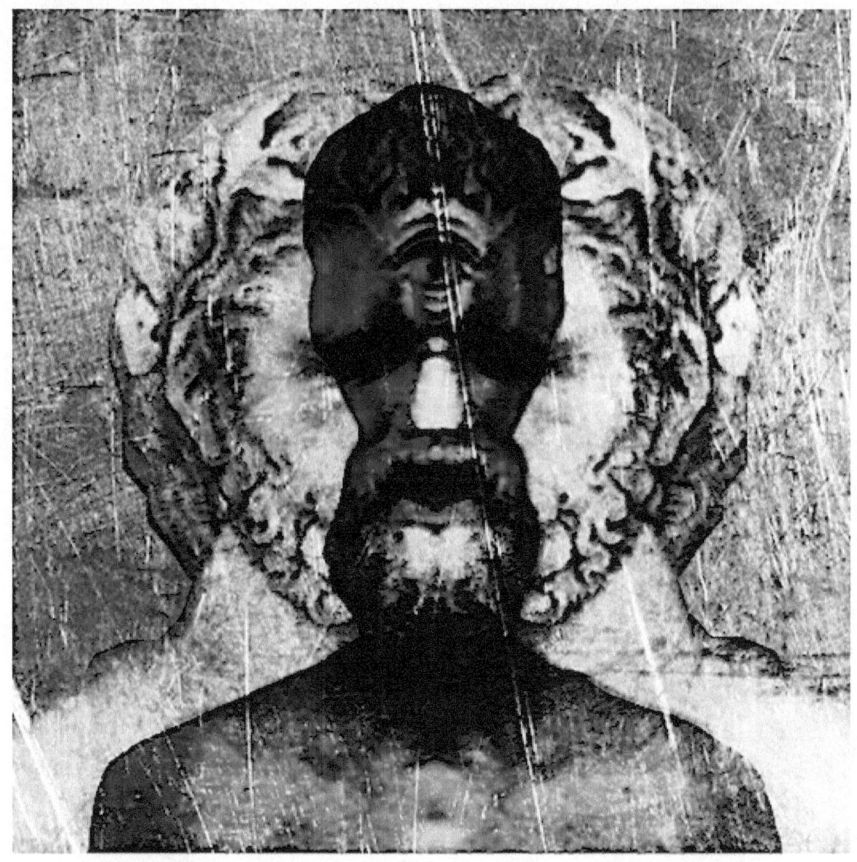

Even as it is a non-conductive presence, "labyrinth" is heavier than its conductive twin. Embodying non-conductivity, it can only be grasped in a pure and abstract present, which it inundates with liquids that do not conduct. "My heart beat crazy during that makeup department scene where Joan and Miss Piggy are supposed to be selling perfume but instead they attack each other with powder puffs and draw all over each other's faces with lipstick and eyeliner, and I was just a little girl thinking, yes, this is how I want to express my femininity. Someday, I will be so fucking feminine I will get fired for it. Joan Rivers and Miss Piggy both get told they are fired. They throw their makeup in the air and laugh 'til they die." That's when we decided that having the seven-year-old shout, "That jerk thinks he's going to walk off with our carcinogens," would jump-start the big chase. Mostly I see in these ballads what I believe might be the kernel of something redeemable — perhaps — even if this is only an enduring a priori energy spring-loaded into the sedimentation and inclined to register the vestiges of lessons repeatedly learned and unlearned — as is — when activated by eyes and ears — and the continuities that keep these objects wired into one another also keep us grounded — like planes — / − + ( ) . = and * alongside X and 0 (I am unclear whether "0" is zero or the capital "O"). They are the embodiment of shoplifted Swiss Army Knives dancing around singing "I'm not sorry," which is when we vowed again to throw in the towel and stop polluting the reservoir, but the towels we'd already thrown in had absorbed all the water. That's when somebody said, "I want to get lots of balloons filled with confetti and buy a long-range pea shooter and shoot them as they fall over the audience whilst philosophising over the purpose of the little finger and index finger rock hand gesture. I plan to enjoy myself, to look at you and kiss you on the ridge of your nose, and your two twin friends." In Langston Hughes' Good Morning, Revolution, there is a tiny poem about a big question:

Johannesburg Mines

**In the Johannesburg mines
There are 240,000 natives working.**

**What kind of poem
Would you make out of that?**

**240,000 natives working
In the Johannesburg mines.**

This poem is generous to the future: anyone after Hughes could continue to write it, substituting for the first and third couplet any of the brutal facts of the word. The volta of the poem, and any of the poems that could follow in its form, is the question for poets: **What kind of poem / would you make out of that?** The poem isn't only a question for poets: it's 1/3 a question for poets, 2/3s the truth for everyone, and also, because 1/3 of the poem operates doubly, 1/3 an answer for poets and anyone who might be curious about what they can do: weedle weedle, as Rod Smith might say, but probably not in this context. I mean, the money these arms sales bring in are just one part of a wonderful, simple, yet cohesive strategy to improve our lives, thus ensuring continued availability in this area of important products like raspberry toothpaste and red or green pepper spray. The works are autobiographical, since they came out of a person's life: I am a table, I am a robot, I am a pig

this is a law of physics

except that I'm not, because I am very slowly reading *A Guide to Old English* by Bruce Mitchell and Fred C. Robinson. I mean that I'm just reading it, not trying to learn the language; I like to look at the words, because I am still asleep, except insofar as I have yet to fall asleep, I have never slept anytime before in my life. I also troll chowhound and yelp and eater and grubstreet and gothamist for reviews of the best Sichuan food and soup dumplings in New York and then laugh at how disgusting it is to make more than $20K a year and fetishize cheap eats as if their cheapness and their deliciousness belonged to you while tweeting earnestly about how shocking it is that nail salon workers are exploited, underpaid, and exposed to harmful chemicals. Anyway, I like to read Archie comics in the bathroom. They help me be regular. But if the wing arrived as a mutation, it did not arrive fully formed. Which explains why Institute for Flying Patron Saint Jose Muñoz, says, "Queerness is that thing that lets us feel that this world is not enough, that indeed something is missing." My 7th grade English teacher, a stoner, called it "found poetry." She encouraged us to find it everywhere, even on the back of cereal boxes:

> Hey Kids,
>
> Start your day
>
> The Mr. T Way!

Years later, I went to college in Lake Forest, Illinois — the super WASPy community north of Chicago where all the sausage and baloney barons built their mansions. At the height of his Rocky / A-Team fame Mr. T purchased the Armour place. Then, in what needs to be understood as the single greatest act of conceptual writing of all time, Mr. T proceeded cut down over 100 oak trees in his yard just in case any of his neighbors thought there might be a chance they wouldn't see him. The papers called it the 'Lake Forest Chainsaw Massacre.' Arborists were stunned. And for his part, Mr. T never bothered to fully explain why he fired up a chainsaw and, alongside hired workmen, got busy clearcutting the oaks, elms and maples that populated his seven-acre estate. It was believed that Mr. T dumped some of the trees in a marble pool and covered it with dirt. How is that pool not a book? Look: I was just kidding about the Mr. T Chainsaw Massacre being the greatest conceptual writing project of our time. The greatest conceptual writing project of our time is the NSA's Utah Data Center, and they just so happen to be hiring. I mean, did Gertrude Stein invent the Dance Remix? Who said be-bop was post-cubist? Ted Berrigan stole from his friends cuz he was broke, and Mierle Ukeles cleaned the house cuz it was dirty. To put it another way: DJ Kool Herc rocked the party, not AWP. To put it another way: They fucked shit up. And when the internet invents a mirror that isn't a camera in which it can see its own reflection in us, well … that'll be interesting.

> But that shit we in now.
> Now it is April 3rd?
> And now you sit here.

And I say: Relax.
In the whole body simultaneously.
(Brain, brain, penis, tail, teeth – release teeth)
Breathe.
Relax the whole body of this now.
Breathe.
Porn.
Psych!
Relax!
P Orr mrrr MRR MRR … Wr o o   m.
Slap now of the Hear hear.
It's fun too, it takes you, the most fun almost?
So bite me.
But I'm no dog.
Type: check there – candy!
And guys: wi Billt this sitty river rock and Rall.
No!
Animals built (nibbled) this city.
This city was gnawed by children.
And animals and babies.
Plums!
Into the black sea of beige to forget things that are important. Breathe.
I have to work on a more poppy perky attitude I think.
Such as: Happily licking a toad to get high.
Like a television series of supernatural character.
Licking a mushroom two mushrooms.
It's you and me Harry Potter … babe.
We must get the faeries out of the hat!
(Black smoke)
Is everything making a personal ad?
It smells old sex now.
You smell old sex in general.
Old spice.
It pallets not.
BAM!
A giant mushroom.
BAM!
I am a chainsaw artist, I have never hurt me, things you do
    not say to people: Your art is crap.
But I do think I have a lack of chlorophyll.
BAM.
(Picture on it)

It was also a moment in my life when I was becoming impatient with both grassroots political organization and the public policy world I worked in. At one of the many offsite events, I read a revised version of Bernadette Mayer's "Essay." I no longer have a copy of my rewritten version, but I know I replaced Mayer's line, "I guess it's too late to live on a farm now," with something like, "I guess it's too late to blah blah blah," and went from there. I wish I could find a copy. Anyway, that poem led to a long conversation with Rodrigo Toscano at the bar after. We had a long conversation, most of which I don't remember because I'd been drinking scotch since … I'm paraphrasing, but the one specific thing I do remember was something like, "The revolution isn't about the barricades anymore (I'd ironically commented in my poem that, 'anyway, I don't want to die on the barricades')." At this point, I don't remember if he said it or I said it. The only other things I remember from that night are 1) that I made a bizarre proposition to someone as a joke, but they didn't take it as a joke; 2) that Bob Perelman bought a copy of my chapbook; and 3) that someone outside the bar grabbed my ass as I left and yelled "Baby got back!" Which is why, for Kristeva, "The ethics that develops in the process of negativity's unfolding is not the kind of 'ethics' that consists in obedience to laws". Tho "Without the operation of irony on trash," he maintained, "there would be no way we could feel superior to … I forget." In any case,

₦¥₦¥₦¥₦¥¢$
$₿₮₿₮¥£
¥₲¥₲¥₲£
₿₲₿₲₿₲$₿₲£
₲₮£₲₮$
₦₩₦₩₦₩$
₭¥₭¥₭¥$

schalerechen lutts messer
pliet plieten stuffet
schillmermesser schillermess shillermest
kniefeje knife metzje
meestje kuchenpitter mest
shnitzermesser spit schock
schmallemessken rummelken pittermesser
kuchenpitter kuchenpetter knipcher
klos jromspermezzje bleitchen
blambe spitzock zippemetz
zoepken pluedchen kneipche
kuschepidder schechniedteir frela
pittwock neifel mugge
giscker krabben-schachter schneide

fala krotten kiesker
grotto kiesker grotten
schneper grotten schnapper
grotts

Take our Christmas presents
1000 heritage worms
boots on
Come up and sit with her
Court our dark with rain outside
Pebbles for the dockyard
the liver stones do bird
that you section deleted
ctrl+alt+del
of an SCULL
OF RAVEN CRYSTAL.
Husk Of The Metals. Dissolve and digest his eroded coils

―――――――――――――――――――――――――

 ――――――――――――――――――――――――

through my retina.
--
ctrl+alt+del
ctrl+alt+del

In some versions the Good Fairy turns Little Bunny Foo Foo into a goose or a Goon. In other versions, Little Bunny Foo Foo reforms and is rewarded by the fairy by not being transmogrified. Also, in some versions the Angel Gabriel appears instead of the Good Fairy, in others the Green Fairy. Some versions replace "I don't wanna see you" with "I don't like your attitude" or "What am I gonna do with you". One common ending has Little Bunny Foo Foo turned into a Goon, with a pun ending "And the moral of the story is: Hare today, goon tomorrow." This form of story telling with a pun ending is known as a feghoot. The story is also retold in the book *Lenore, The Cute Dead Girl: Noogies* where Lenore plays as Little Bunny Foo Foo and gets told to stop bopping field mice on the head by the Good Fairy. She continues bopping other animals instead, and so the Good Fairy reappears and reprimands her by saying: "No bopping ANY animals on the head!" Lenore responds by bopping the Good Fairy. The moral of the story is: "Be more specific". Ergo, there can be resistance to the psychoanalytic for many reasons, and I think one resistance to it or objection to it is that it is perceived to be so private and personal in its thrust; it's just you and the couch and the third ear. That's not what I have in mind. I think of it as a way that leads to greater self-consciousness, a self-critical capacity in your relationship to others because as far as I'm concerned you're always in relationship to others, even when ... well, never. The distinction I'm trying to make between the 'one' and the 'individual' is a way to go around that objection. I think of the individual as a certain kind of early modern formation born in relationship to property. See CB MacPherson. Whereas the 'one' I think of as a concept that's born with Freud in about 1900, with the *Interpretation of Dreams*. The 'one' is put in place by the social, it is put in place by language, one's relationship to the social, to language, to others – an idea I borrowed from Lacanian thought. That's something that I really want to draw out further because it's a strategy for moving us on to the territory where I think we should be in having this discussion. It's an important distinction in its own right because you can't avoid someone saying 'this is just more bourgeois subjectivity, whereas we need to be talking about something else'. I think it takes us to the 'something else' already. In that spirit, I'd like to begin my account of art and madness with a poem that was written two weeks ago by J.H. Prynne. If this paper were to sketch a chronological account of madness that began with Pan and Circe, went on to mention Apuleius, Nebuchadnezzar, Lear and Kit Smart, passied thru Hölderlin, let's say, finally arriving at the 20th century with Nijinsky, Artaud, and the Republican Party, I'm sure I'd bore everyone stiff. Such a chronological survey naturalises a concept like madness and sieves history with a fixed mesh: it will only catch the usual fish. By looking at one of the latest technical assaults on the bourgeois ratio, we may be able to tear the fabric of our received ideas and let in some artistic deep sea monsters worthy of a national population which has just witnessed the wonders of *The Blue Planet* series.

>Profuse reclaim from a scrape or belt, funnel do
>axial parenthood block the mustard dots briefly
>act forward, their age layer for layer in this
>tied-off accession. Appellate at dictum at
>its debit resonance fixing prolusion, optic rage
>performs even dots right now. This is the top
>passion play and counted out for renewal patch
>
>very irritated against the green ground
>greensoft, significant, deadened
>gloss to attenuate, to take action pursuant to shade
>a rosâtre-brown burning
>like the coating on an old brick
>a blood series to reproduce the reddish chalks
>in the Masters of Rebirth
>We, stones, were branded by hot iron
>our eyes scorched
>we saw through an inverted gaze
>black holes

swallowing us in infinity
death cuddling our misfortune
his dog licking our wounds

and then wash plausible default icon
still to hope in the face of that face
in the headlights of Robitussin
a blank manifesto chopped and screwed
adrenal no ID entity
a tiny Charles Olson menaced by a 50-foot
Anita Ekberg in Fellini's *Le tentazioni del dottor Antonio*

und so weiter. This poem appears on the first page of *Unanswering Rational Shore*, a pamphlet published by a Glasgow press named Object Permanence. A curious negative theology is insinuated:

> "he is un- +++++++++
> he is dis- ++++++++++++
> he is ++++++++++++ -less
> he is de- +++++++++++
> ... he is non- ++++++++
> he is pre- ++++++++++"

Whoever "he" is would appear to have been ineffable, yet "If you'd like to eyeball a 20-page verbal pie that dissolves the difference between nouns and verbs, and speaks of romance and international politics in a single, Kant-defying, garlic-aroma breath, send a cheque payable to Peter Manson for £2.50 (P&P included) to Peter Manson Object Permanence, Flat 3/2, 16 Ancroft Street, Glasgow, G20 7HU. Don't forget to include your own address – The book's epigraph is

> lo mismo

a compacted lettrist sonnet made of Goya's despair of finding anything other than the Spanish words for "the same" to title his endless pictures of the total fucked-upness of war. Ergo, according to Dr Donald McKendrick, who gives medical advice in the pages of *Saga* (a magazine designed to sell insurance schemes and holidays to elderly people), 'there are different nerve pathways for nouns and verbs'. But what is this jelly?

NOTES

1 Scott Gilbert, "We Are All Lichens Now" →. See also Gilbert, Jan Sapp, and Alfred I. Tauber, "A Symbiotic View of Life: We Have Never Been

Individuals," *Quarterly Review of Biology*, vol. 87, no. 4 (December 2012): 325–41. Gilbert has erased the "now" from his rallying cry; we have always been symbionts — genetically, developmentally, anatomically, physiologically, neurologically, ecologically.

2 These sentences are on the rear cover of Isabelle Stengers and Vinciane Despret, *Women Who Make a Fuss: The Unfaithful Daughters of Virginia Woolf*, trans. April Knutson (Minneapolis: Univocal, 2014). From Virginia Woolf's *Three Guineas*, "think we must" is the urgency relayed to feminist collective thinking-with in *Women Who Make a Fuss* through María Puig de la Bellacasa, *Penser nous devons: Politiques féminists et construction des saviors* (Paris: Harmattan, 2013).

3 Gustavo Hormiga, "A Revision and Cladistic Analysis of the Spider Family Pimoidae (Aranae: Araneae)," *Smithsonian Contributions to Zoology* 549 (1994): 1–104. See "Pimoa cthulhu," Wikipedia; "Hormiga Laboratory" →.

4 "The brand of holist ecological philosophy that emphasizes that 'everything is connected to everything,' will not help us here. Rather, everything is connected to something, which is connected to something else. While we may all ultimately be connected to one another, the specificity and proximity of connections matters — who we are bound up with and in what ways. Life and death happen inside these relationships. And so, we need to understand how particular human communities, as well as those of other living beings, are entangled, and how these entanglements are implicated in the production of both extinctions and their accompanying patterns of amplified death." Thom Van Dooren, *Flight Ways: Life at the Edge of Extinction* (New York: Columbia University Press, 2014), 60.

5 Two indispensable books by my colleague-sibling from thirty-plus years in the History of Consciousness Department at the University of California, Santa Cruz, guide my writing: James Clifford, *Routes: Travel and Translation in the Late Twentieth Century* (Cambridge, MA: Harvard University Press, 1997); and Clifford, *Returns: Becoming Indigenous in the Twenty-First Century* (Cambridge, MA: Harvard University Press, 2013).

6 Chthonic" derives from ancient Greek khthonios, "of the earth," and from khthōn, "earth." Greek mythology depicts the chthonic as the underworld, beneath the Earth; but the chthonic ones are much older (and younger) than those Greeks. Sumeria is a riverine civilizational scene of emergence of great chthonic tales, including possibly the great circular snake eating its own tail, the polysemous Ouroboros (figure of the continuity of life, an Egyptian figure as early as 1600 BCE; Sumerian SF worlding dates to 3500 BCE or before). The chthonic will accrue many resonances throughout my text. See Thorkild

Jacobsen, *The Treasures of Darkness: A History of Mesopotamian Religion* (New Haven, CT: Yale University Press, 1976). In lectures, conversations, and e-mails, the scholar of ancient Middle Eastern worlds at UC Santa Cruz, Gildas Hamel, gave me "the abyssal and elemental forces before they were astralized by chief gods and their tame committees" (personal communication, June 12, 2014). Cthulu (note spelling), luxuriating in the science fiction of H. P. Lovecraft, plays no role for me, although it / he did play a role for Gustavo Hormiga, the scientist who named my spider demon familiar. For the monstrous male elder god (Cthulu), see Lovecraft, *The Call of Cthulu*. I take the liberty of rescuing my spider from Lovecraft for other stories, and mark the liberation with the more common spelling of chthonic ones. Lovecraft's dreadful underworld cthonic serpents were terrible only in the patriarchal mode. The Chthulucene has other terrors — more dangerous and generative in worlds where such gender does not reign. Undulating with slippery eros and gravid chaos, tangled snakes and ongoing tentacular forces coil through the twenty-first-century CE. Consider: Old English oearth, German Erde, Greek Gaïa, Roman terra, Dutch aarde; Old English w(e)oruld ("affairs of life," "a long period of time," "the known life," or "life on earth" as opposed to the "afterlife"), from a Germanic compound meaning "age of the human race" (wer); Old Norse heimr, literally "abode." Then consider Turkish dünya and go to dunyā (the temporal world), an Arabic word that was passed to many other languages, such as Persian, Dari, Pashto, Bengali, Punjabi, Urdu, Hindi, Kurdish, Nepali, Turkish, Arumanian, and North Caucasian languages. Dunyā is also a loanword in Malay and Indonesian, as well as in Greek δουνιας —so many words, so many roots, so many pathways, so many mycorrhizal symbioses, even if we restrict ourselves only to Indo-European tangles. There are so many kin who might better have named this time of the Anthropocene that is at stake now. The anthropos is too much of a parochial fellow; he is both too big and too small for most of the needed stories.

7 Eva Hayward proposes the term "tentacularity"; her trans-thinking and doing in spidery and coralline worlds entwine with my writing in SF patterns. See Hayward, "FingeryEyes: Impressions of Cup Corals," *Cultural Anthropology*, vol. 24, no. 4 (2010): 577–99; Hayward, "SpiderCitySex," *Women and Performance: A Journal of Feminist Theory*, vol. 20, no. 3 (2010): 225–51; and Hayward, "Sensational Jellyfish: Aquarium Affects and the Matter of Immersion," differences: *A Journal of Feminist Cultural Studies*, vol. 23, no. 1 (2012): 161–96. See Eleanor Morgan, "Sticky Tales: Spiders, Silk, and Human Attachments," *Dandelion*, vol. 2, no. 2 (2011) →. UK experimental artist Eleanor Morgan's spider silk art spins many threads resonating with this chapter, tuned to the interactions of animals (especially arachnids and sponges) and humans. See Morgan's website →.

8 Tim Ingold, *Lines, a Brief History* (New York: Routledge, 2007), 116–19.

9 The pile was made irresistible by María Puig de la Bellacasa, "Encountering Bioinfrastructure: Ecological Movements and the Sciences of Soil," *Social Epistemology* vol. 28, no. 1 (2014): 26–40.

10 Isabelle Stengers, *Au temps des catastrophes: Résister à la barbarie qui vient* (Paris: Découverte), 2009. Gaia intrudes in this text from p. 48 on. Stengers discusses the "intrusion of Gaïa" in numerous interviews, essays, lectures. Discomfort with the ever more inescapable label of the Anthropocene, in and out of sciences, politics, and culture, pervades Stengers's thinking, as well as that of many other engaged writers, including Latour, even as we struggle for another word. See Stengers in conversation with Heather Davis and Etienne Turpin, "Matters of Cosmopolitics: On the Provocations of Gaïa," in *Architecture in the Anthropocene: Encounters among Design, Deep Time, Science and Philosophy*, ed. Etienne Turpin (London: Open Humanities, 2013), 171–82. Stengers's thinking about Gaia and the Lovelock-Margulis development of the Gaia hypothesis was from the start entwined with her work with Ilya Prigogine, which understood that strong linear coupling in complex systems theory entailed the possibility of radical global system change, including collapse. Prigogine and Stengers, *Order Out of Chaos* (New York: Bantam, 1984). The relation of Gaia to Chaos is an old one in science and philosophy. What I want to do is knot that emergence sympoietically into a worlding of ongoing chthonic powers, which is the material-semiotic time-space of the Chthulucene rather than Anthropocene or Capitalocene. This is part of what Stengers means when she says that her intrusive Gaia was "ticklish" from the start. "Her 'autopoietic' functioning is not her truth but what 'we' [human beings] have to face, and are able to read from our computer models, the face she turns on 'us'" (e-mail from Stengers to Haraway, May 9, 2014).

11 Scientists estimate that this extinction "event," the first to occur during the time of our species, could, as previous great extinction events have, but much more rapidly, eliminate 50 to 95 percent of existing biodiversity. Sober estimates anticipate half of existing species of birds could disappear by 2100. By any measure, that is a lot of double death. For a popular exposition, see Voices for Biodiversity, "The Sixth Great Extinction" →. For a report by an award-winning science writer, see Elizabeth Kolbert, *The Sixth Extinction: An Unnatural History* (New York: Henry Holt, 2014). Reports from the Convention on Biological Diversity are more cautious about predictions and discuss the practical and theoretical difficulties of obtaining reliable knowledge, but they are not less sobering. For a disturbing report from summer 2015, see Geraldo Ceballos, Paul Ehrlich, Anthony Barnosky, Andres Garcia, Robert Pringle, and Todd Palmer, "Accelerated Modern Human-Induced Species Losses: Entering the Sixth Mass Extinction," *Science Advances* vol. 1, no. 5 (June 19, 2015).

12 James Lovelock, "Gaia as Seen through the Atmosphere," Atmospheric Environment, vol. 6, no. 8 (1967): 579–80; Lovelock and Margulis, "Atmospheric Homeostasis by and for the Biosphere: The Gaia Hypothesis," *Tellus*, Series A (Stockholm: International Meteorological Institute) vol. 26, nos. 1–2 (February 1, 1974): 2–10 →. For a video of a lecture to employees at the National Aeronautic and Space Agency in 1984, go to →. Autopoiesis was crucial to Margulis's transformative theory of symbiogenesis, but I think if she were alive to take up the question, Margulis would often prefer the terminology and figural-conceptual powers of sympoiesis. I suggest that Gaia is a system mistaken for autopoietic that is really sympoietic. Gaia's story needs an intrusive makeover to knot with a host of other promising sympoietic tentacular ones for making rich compost, for going on. Gaia or Ge is much older and wilder than Hesiod, but Hesiod cleaned her / it up in the Theogony in his story-setting way: after Chaos, "wide-bosomed" Gaia (Earth) arose to be the everlasting seat of the immortals who possess Olympus above (*Theogony*, 116–18, trans. Glenn W. Most, Loeb Classical Library), and the depths of Tartarus below (Theogony, 119). The chthonic ones reply, Nonsense! Gaia is one of theirs, an ongoing tentacular threat to the astralized ones of the Olympiad, not their ground and foundation, with their ensuing generations of gods all arrayed in proper genealogies. Hesiod's is the old prick tale, already setting up canons in the eighth century BCE.

13 Although I cannot help but think more rational environmental and socialnatural policies of all sorts would help!

14 Isabelle Stengers, from English compilation on Gaia sent by e-mail January 14, 2014.

15 I use "thing" in two senses that rub against each other: (1) the collection of entities brought together in the Parliament of Things that Bruno Latour called our attention to, and (2) something hard to classify, unsortable, and probably with a bad smell. Latour, *We Have Never Been Modern* (Cambridge, MA: Harvard University Press, 1993).

16 Paul Crutzen and Eugene Stoermer, "The 'Anthropocene,'" *Global Change Newsletter*, International Geosphere-Biosphere Program Newsletter, no. 41 (May 2000): 17–18 →; Crutzen, "Geology of Mankind," *Nature* 415 (2002): 23; Jan Zalasiewicz et al., "Are We Now Living in the Anthropocene?" *GSA* (Geophysical Society of America) *Today* vol. 18, no. 2 (2008): 4–8. Much earlier dates for the emergence of the Anthropocene are sometimes proposed, but most scientists and environmentalists tend to emphasize global anthropogenic effects from the late eighteenth century on. A more profound human exceptionalism (the deepest divide of nature and culture) accompanies proposals of the earliest dates, coextensive with Homo sapiens on the planet

hunting big now-extinct prey and then inventing agriculture and domestication of animals. A compelling case for dating the Anthropocene from the multiple "great accelerations," in Earth system indicators and in social change indicators, from about 1950 on, first marked by atmospheric nuclear bomb explosions, is made by Will Steffen, Wendy Broadgate, Lisa Deutsch, Owen Gaffney, and Cornelia Ludwig, "The Trajectory of the Anthropocene: The Great Acceleration," *The Anthropocene Review*, January 16, 2015. Zalasiewicz et al. argue that adoption of the term "Anthropocene" as a geological epoch by the relevant national and international scientific bodies will turn on stratigraphic signatures. Perhaps, but the resonances of the Anthropocene are much more disseminated than that. One of my favorite art investigations of the stigmata of the Anthropocene is Ryan Dewey's "Virtual Places: Core Logging the Anthropocene in Real-Time," in which he composes "core samples of the ad hoc geology of retail shelves."

17 For a powerful ethnographic encounter in the 1990s with climate-change modeling, see Anna Lowenhaupt Tsing, "Natural Universals and the Global Scale," ch. 3 in *Friction: An Ethnography of Global Connection* (Princeton, NJ: Princeton University Press, 2005), 88–112, especially "Global Climate as a Model," 101–6. Tsing asks, "What makes global knowledge possible?" She replies, "Erasing collaborations." But Tsing does not stop with this historically situated critique. Instead she, like Latour and Stengers, takes us to the really important question: "Might it be possible to attend to nature's collaborative origins without losing the advantages of its global reach?" (95). "How might scholars take on the challenge of freeing critical imaginations from the specter of neoliberal conquest — singular, universal, global? Attention to the frictions of contingent articulation can help us describe the effectiveness, and the fragility, of emergent capitalist — and globalist — forms. In this shifting heterogeneity there are new sources of hope, and, of course, new nightmares" (77). At her first climate-modeling conference in 1995, Tsing had an epiphany: "The global scale takes precedence — *because it is the scale of the model*" (103, italics in original). But this and related properties have a particular effect: they bring negotiators to an international, heterogeneous table, maybe not heterogeneous enough, but far from full of identical units and players. "The embedding of smaller scales into the global; the enlargement of models to include everything; the policy-driven construction of the models: Together these features make it possible for the models to bring diplomats to the negotiating table" (105). That is not to be despised. The reports of the Intergovernmental Panel on Climate Change (IPCC) are necessary documents and excellent illustrations of Tsing's accounts: *Climate Change 2014: Mitigation of Climate Change* and *Climate Change 2014: Impacts, Adaptation, and Vulnerability*. Tsing's stakes in her intimate tracking of the relentless ethnographic specificities of far-flung chains of intimate dealings and livings are to hold in productive, nonutopian friction the scale-making power of the things climate-

change models do with the life-and-death messiness of place- and travel-based worldings that always make even our best and most necessary universals very lumpy. She seeks and describes multiple situated worldings and multiple sorts of translations to engage globalism. "Attention to friction opens up the possibility of an ethnographic account of global interconnection" (6). Appreciation of what she calls "weediness" is indispensable: "To be aware of the necessity for careful coalitions with those whose knowledges and pleasures come from other sources is the beginning of nonimperialist environmentalism" (170). The hostis will not make an appearance in this string figuring, but mushrooms as guides for living in the ruins most certainly will. See Tsing, *The Mushroom at the End of the World: On the Possibility of Life in Capitalist Ruins* (Princeton, NJ: Princeton University Press, 2015).

18 The Anthropocene Working Group, which was established in 2008 to report to the International Union of Geological Sciences and the International Commission on Stratigraphy on whether to name a new epoch in the geological timeline, aimed to issue its final report in 2016. See *Newsletter of the Anthropocene Working Group*, volume 4 (June 2013): 1–17 →; and volume 5 (September 2014): 1–19 →.

19 For a photogallery of fiery images of the Man burning at the end of the festival, see "Burning Man Festival 2012: A Celebration of Art, Music, and Fire," *New York Daily News*, September 3, 2012 →. Attended by tens of thousands of human people (and an unknown number of dogs), Burning Man is an annual week-long festival of art and (commercial) anarchism held in the Black Rock Desert of Nevada since 1990 and on San Francisco's Baker Beach from 1986 to 1990. The event's origins tie to San Francisco artists' celebrations of the summer solstice. "The event is described as an experiment in community, art, radical self-expression, and radical self-reliance" ("Burning Man," Wikipedia). The globalizing extravaganzas of the Anthropocene are not the drug- and art-laced worlding of Burning Man, but the iconography of the immense fiery "Man" ignited during the festival is irresistible. The first burning effigies on the beach in San Francisco were of a nine-foot-tall wooden Man and a smaller wooden dog. By 1988 the Man was forty feet tall and dogless. Relocated to a dry lakebed in Nevada, the Man topped out in 2011 at 104 feet. This is America; supersized is the name of the game, a fitting habitat for the Anthropos. "Anthropos" (ἄνθρωπος) is an ambiguous word with contested etymologies. What Anthropos never figures is the rich generative home of a multispecies Earth. The Online Etymology Dictionary states that it comes from the Greek aner, "man," "as opposed to a woman, a god, or a boy." Just what I suspected! Or, "Anthropos sometimes is explained as a compound of aner and ops (genitive opos) 'eye, face'; so literally 'he who has the face of a man.'" Or, sometimes, the shape of a man. Biblical scholars find it hard to

make the Greek ανθρωπος include women, and it complicates translations in fascinating ways: see →. Other sources give the meaning of the compound as "that which is below, hence earthly, human," or, the "upward looking one," and so below, lamentably on Earth. Unlike the animals, man as anthropos "looks up at what he sees": →. The Anthropos is not Latour's Earthbound. It is safe to say that Eugene Stoermer and Paul Crutzen were not much vexed by these ambiguities. Still, thank the heavens, looking up, their human eyes were firmly on the Earth's atmospheric carbon burden. Or, also, swimming in too hot seas with the tentacular ones, their eyes were the optic-haptic fingery eyes of marine critters in diseased and dying coral symbioses. See Hayward, "FingeryEyes."

20 See Michael Klare, "The Third Carbon Age," *Huffington Post*, August 8, 2013 →, in which he writes, "According to the International Energy Agency (IEA), an inter-governmental research organization based in Paris, cumulative worldwide investment in new fossil-fuel extraction and processing will total an estimated $22.87 trillion between 2012 and 2035, while investment in renewables, hydropower, and nuclear energy will amount to only $7.32 trillion." Nuclear, after Fukushima! Not to mention that none of these calculations prioritize a much lighter, smaller, more modest human presence on Earth, with all its critters. Even in its "sustainability" discourses, the Capitalocene cannot tolerate a multispecies world of the Earthbound. For the switch in Big Energy's growth strategies to nations with the weakest environmental controls, see Klare, "What's Big Energy Smoking?" *Common Dreams*, May 27, 2014 →. See also Klare, *The Race for What's Left: The Global Scramble for the World's Last Resources* (New York: Picador, 2012).

21 Heavy tar sand pollution must break the hearts and shatter the gills of every Terran, Gaian, and Earthbound critter. The toxic lakes of wastewater from tar sand oil extraction in northern Alberta, Canada, shape a kind of new Great Lakes region, with more giant "ponds" added daily. Current area covered by these lakes is about 50 percent greater than the area covered by the world city of Vancouver. Tar sands operations return almost none of the vast quantities of water they use to natural cycles. Earthbound peoples trying to establish growing things at the edges of these alarmingly colored waters filled with extraction tailings say that successional processes for reestablishing sympoietic biodiverse ecosystems, if they prove possible at all, will be an affair of decades and centuries. See Pembina Institute, "Alberta's Oil Sands" →; and Bob Weber, "Rebuilding Land Destroyed by Oil Sands May Not Restore It," *Globe and Mail*, March 11, 2012 →. Only Venezuela and Saudi Arabia have more oil reserves than Alberta. All that said, the Earthbound, the Terrans, do not cede either the present or the future; the sky is lowering, but has not yet fallen, yet. Pembina Institute, "Oil Sands Solutions" →. First Nation, Métis, and Aboriginal peoples are crucial players in every aspect of this unfinished story.

22 Photograph from NASA Earth Observatory, 2015 (public domain). If flame is the icon for the Anthropocene, I use the missing ice and the unblocked Northwest Passage to figure the Capitalocene. The Soufan Group provides strategic security intelligence services to governments and multinational organizations. Its report "TSG IntelBrief: Geostrategic Competition in the Arctic" includes the following quotes: "*The Guardian* estimates that the Arctic contains 30 percent of the world's undiscovered natural gas and 15 percent of its oil." "In late February, Russia announced it would form a strategic military command to protect its Arctic interests." "Russia, Canada, Norway, Denmark, and the US all make some claim to international waters and the continental shelf in the Arctic Ocean." "[A Northwest Passage] route could provide the Russians with a great deal of leverage on the international stage over China or any other nation dependent on sea commerce between Asia and Europe."

23 Naomi Klein, "How Science Is Telling Us All to Revolt," *New Statesman*, October 29, 2013 →; Klein, *The Shock Doctrine: The Rise of Disaster Capitalism* (New York: Macmillan / Picador, 2008).

24 "Capitalocene" is one of those words like "sympoiesis"; if you think you invented it, just look around and notice how many other people are inventing the term at the same time. That certainly happened to me, and after I got over a small fit of individualist pique at being asked whom I got the term "Capitalocene" from — hadn't I coined the word? ("Coin"!) And why do other scholars almost always ask women which male writers their ideas are indebted to? — I recognized that not only was I part of a cat's cradle game of invention, as always, but that Jason Moore had already written compelling arguments to think with, and my interlocutor both knew Moore's work and was relaying it to me. Moore himself first heard the term "Capitalocene" in 2009 in a seminar in Lund, Sweden, when then graduate student Andreas Malm proposed it. In an urgent historical conjuncture, words-to-think-with pop out all at once from many bubbling cauldrons because we all feel the need for better netbags to collect up the stuff crying out for attention. Despite its problems, the term "Anthropocene" was and is embraced because it collects up many matters of fact, concern, and care; and I hope "Capitalocene" will roll off myriad tongues soon. In particular, see the work of Jason Moore, a creative Marxist sociologist at Binghamton University in New York. Moore is coordinator of the World-Ecology Research Network. For his first Capitalocene argument, see Moore, "Anthropocene, Capitalocene, and the Myth of Industrialization," June 16, 2013 →. See Moore, *Capitalism and the Web of Life: Ecology and the Accumulation of Capital* (London: Verso, 2015).

25 To get over Eurocentrism while thinking about the history of pathways and centers of globalization over the last few centuries, see Dennis O. Flynn and

Arturo Giráldez, *China and the Birth of Globalisation in the 16th Century* (Farnum, UK: Ashgate Variorium, 2012). For analysis attentive to the differences and frictions among colonialisms, imperialisms, globalizing trade formations, and capitalism, see Engseng Ho, "Empire through Diasporic Eyes: A View from the Other Boat," *Society for Comparative Study of Society and History* (April 2004): 210–46; and Ho, *The Graves of Tarim: Genealogy and Mobility across the Indian Ocean* (Berkeley: University of California Press, 2006).

26 In "Anthropocene or Capitalocene, Part III," May 19, 2013 →, Jason Moore puts it this way: "This means that capital and power—and countless other strategic relations—do not act upon nature but develop through the web of life. 'Nature' is here offered as the relation of the whole. Humans live as a specifically endowed (but not special) environment-making species within Nature. Second, capitalism in 1800 was no Athena, bursting forth, fully grown and armed, from the head of a carboniferous Zeus. Civilizations do not form through Big Bang events. They emerge through cascading transformations and bifurcations of human activity in the web of life ... [For example,] the long seventeenth century forest clearances of the Vistula Basin and Brazil's Atlantic Rainforest occurred on a scale, and at a speed, between five and ten times greater than anything seen in medieval Europe."

27 Eileen Crist, "On the Poverty of Our Nomenclature," *Environmental Humanities* 3 (2013): 129–47; 144. Crist does superb critique of the traps of Anthropocene discourse, as well as gives us propositions for more imaginative worlding and ways to stay with the trouble. For entangled, dissenting papers that both refuse and take up the name Anthropocene, see videos from the conference "Anthropocene Feminism," University of Wisconsin–Milwaukee, April 10–12, 2014 →. For rich interdisciplinary research, organized by Anna Tsing and Nils Ole Bubandt, that brings together anthropologists, biologists, and artists under the sign of the Anthropocene, see AURA: Aarhus University Research on the Anthropocene →.

28 I owe the insistence on "big-enough stories" to Clifford, *Returns*: "I think of these as 'big enough' histories, able to account for a lot, but not for everything — and without guarantees of political virtue" (201). Rejecting one big synthetic account or theory, Clifford works to craft a realism that "works with open-ended (because their linear historical time is ontologically unfinished) 'big-enough stories,' sites of contact, struggle, and dialogue" (85–86).

29 Philippe Pignarre and Isabelle Stengers, *La sorcellerie capitaliste: Pratiques de désenvoûtement* (Paris: Découverte, 2005). Latour and Stengers are deeply allied in their fierce rejection of discourses of denunciation. They have both patiently taught me to understand and relearn in this matter. I love a good denunciation! It is a hard habit to unlearn.

30 It is possible to read Max Horkheimer and Theodor Adorno's *Dialectic of Enlightenment* as an allied critique of Progress and Modernization, even though their resolute secularism gets in their own way. It is very hard for a secularist to really listen to the squid, bacteria, and angry old women of Terra / Gaia. The most likely Western Marxist allies, besides Marx, for nurturing the Chthulucene in the belly of the Capitalocene are Antonio Gramsci, *Selections from the Prison Notebooks*, and Stuart Hall. Hall's immensely generative essays extend from the 1960s through the 1990s. See, for example, *Stuart Hall: Critical Dialogues in Cultural Studies*, eds. David Morley and Kuan-Hsing Chen (London: Routledge, 1996).

31 See Dave Gilson, "Octopi Wall Street!" *Mother Jones*, October 6, 2011 →, for the fascinating history of cephalopods figuring the depredations of Big Capital in the United States (for example, the early twentieth-century John D. Rockefeller/Standard Oil octopus strangling workers, farmers, and citizens in general with its many huge tentacles). Resignification of octopuses and squids as chthonic allies is excellent news. May they squirt inky night into the visualizing apparatuses of the technoid sky gods.

32 Hesiod's *Theogony* in achingly beautiful language tells of Gaia / Earth arising out of Chaos to be the seat of the Olympian immortals above and of Tartarus in the depths below. She / it is very old and polymorphic and exceeds Greek tellings, but just how remains controversial and speculative. At the very least, Gaia is not restricted to the job of holding up the Olympians! The important and unorthodox scholar-archaeologist Marija Gimbutis claims that Gaia as Mother Earth is a later form of a pre–Indo-European, Neolithic Great Mother. In 2004, filmmaker Donna Reed and neopagan author and activist Starhawk released a collaborative documentary film about the life and work of Gimbutas, *Signs out of Time*. See Belili Productions, "About Signs out of Time" →; Gimbutas, *The Living Goddesses*, ed. Miriam Robbins Dexter (Berkeley: University of California Press, 1999).

33 To understand what is at stake in "non-Euclidean" storytelling, go to Ursula Le Guin, *Always Coming Home* (Berkeley: University of California Press, 1985); and Le Guin, "A Non-Euclidean View of California as a Cold Place to Be," in *Dancing at the Edge of the World: Thoughts on Words, Women, Places* (New York: Grove, 1989), 80–100.

34 "The Thousand Names of Gaia: From the Anthropocene to the Age of the Earth," International Colloquium, Rio de Janeiro, September 15–19, 2014.

35 The bee was one of Potnia Theron's emblems, and she is also called Potnia Melissa, Mistress of the Bees. Modern Wiccans remember these chthonic

beings in ritual and poetry. If fire figured the Anthropocene, and ice marked the Capitalocene, it pleases me to use red clay pottery for the Chthulucene, a time of fire, water, and Earth, tuned to the touch of its critters, including its people. With her PhD writing on the riverine goddess Ratu Kidul and her dances now performed on Bali, Raissa DeSmet (Trumbull) introduced me to the web of far-traveling chthonic tentacular ones emerging from the Hindu serpentine Nagas and moving through the waters of Southeast Asia. DeSmet, "A Liquid World: Figuring Coloniality in the Indies," PhD diss., History of Consciousness Department, University of California at Santa Cruz, 2013.

36 Links between Potnia Theron and the Gorgon / Medusa continued in temple architecture and building adornment well after 600 BCE, giving evidence of the tenacious hold of the chthonic powers in practice, imagination, and ritual, for example, from the fifth through the third centuries BCE on the Italian peninsula. The dread-full Gorgon figure faces outward, defending against exterior dangers, and the no less awe-full Potnia Theron faces inward, nurturing the webs of living. See Kimberly Sue Busby, "The Temple Terracottas of Etruscan Orvieto: A Vision of the Underworld in the Art and Cult of Ancient Volsinii," PhD diss., University of Illinois, 2007. The Christian Mary, Virgin Mother of God, who herself erupted in the Near East and Mediterranean worlds, took on attributes of these and other chthonic powers in her travels around the world. Unfortunately, Mary's iconography shows her ringed by stars and crushing the head of the snake (for example, in the Miraculous Medal dating from an early nineteenth-century apparition of the Virgin), more than allying herself with Earth powers. The "lady surrounded by stars" is a Christian scriptural apocalyptic figure for the end of time. That is a bad idea. Throughout my childhood, I wore a gold chain with the Miraculous Medal. Finally and luckily, it was her residual chthonic infections that took hold in me, turning me from both the secular and also the sacred, and toward humus and compost.

37 The Hebrew word Deborah means "bee," and she was the only female judge mentioned in the Bible. She was a warrior and counselor in premonarchic Israel. The Song of Deborah may date to the twelfth century BCE. Deborah was a military heroand ally of Jael, one of the 4Js in Joanna Russ's formative feminist science fiction novel *The Female Man*. In April 2014, the Reverend Billy Talen and the Church of Stop Shopping exorcised the robobee from the Micro Robotics Laboratories at Harvard. The robobee is a high-tech drone bee that is intended to replace overworked and poisoned biological pollinating bees as they become more and more diseased and endangered. Honeybeealujah, old stories live! See Talen, "Beware of the Robobee, Monsanto and darpa," June 4, 2014" →; and John P. Finnegan, "Protestors Sing Honeybeelujahs against Robobees," *Harvard Crimson*, April 23, 2014 →. Or, as Brad Werner put it at the American Geophysical Union

Meetings, Revolt! Do we hear the buzzing yet? It is time to sting. It is time for a chthonic swarm. It is time to take care of the bees.

38 "Erinyes 1," Theoi Greek Mythology →

39 Martha Kenney pointed out to me that the story of the Ood, in the long-running British science fiction TV series Doctor Who, shows how the squid-faced ones became deadly to humanity only after they were mutilated, cut off from their symchthonic hive mind, and enslaved. The humanoid empathic Ood have sinuous tentacles over the lower portion of their multifolded alien faces; and in their proper bodies they carry their hindbrains in their hands, communicating with each other telepathically through these vulnerable, living, exterior organs (organons). Humans (definitely not the Earthbound) cut off the hindbrains and replaced them with a technological communication-translator sphere, so that the isolated Ood could only communicate through their enslavers, who forced them into hostilities. I resist thinking the Ood techno-communicators are a future release of the iPhone, but it is tempting when I watch the faces of twenty-first-century humans on the streets, or even at the dinner table, apparently connected only to their devices. I am saved from this ungenerous fantasy by the SF fact that in the episode "Planet of the Ood," the tentacular ones were freed by the actions of Ood Sigma and restored to their nonsingular selves. Doctor Who is a much better story cycle for going-on-with than Star Trek. For the importance of reworking fables in sciences and other knowledge practices, see Martha Kenney, "Fables of Attention: Wonder in Feminist Theory and Scientific Practice," PhD diss., History of Consciousness Department, University of California at Santa Cruz, 2013. Kenney explores different genres of fable, which situate what she calls unstable "wild facts" in relation to proposing and testing the strength of knowledge claims. She investigates strategies for navigating uncertain terrain, where the productive tensions between fact and fiction in actual practices are necessary.

40 "Medousa and Gorgones," Theoi Greek Mythology →

41 Suzy McKee Charnas's Holdfast Chronicles, beginning in 1974 with *Walk to the End of the World*, is great SF for thinking about feminists and their horses. The sex is exciting if very incorrect, and the politics are bracing.

42 Eva Hayward first drew my attention to the emergence of Pegasus from Medusa's body and of coral from drops of her blood. In her "The Crochet Coral Reef Project Heightens Our Sense of Responsibility to the Oceans," *Independent Weekly*, August 1, 2012," she writes: "If coral teaches us about the reciprocal nature of life, then how do we stay obligated to environments — many of which we made unlivable — that now sicken us? ... Perhaps Earth will follow Venus, becoming uninhabitable due to rampaging greenhouse

effect. Or, maybe, we will rebuild reefs or construct alternate homes for the oceans' refugees. Whatever the conditions of our future, we remain obligate partners with oceans." See Margaret Wertheim and Christine Wertheim, *Crochet Coral Reef: A Project by the Institute for Figuring* (Los Angeles: IFF, 2015).

43 I am inspired by the 2014–15 Monterey Bay Aquarium exhibition Tentacles: The Astounding Lives of Octopuses, Squids, and Cuttlefish. See Marcel Detienne and Jean-Pierre Vernant, *Cunning Intelligence in Greek Culture and Society*, trans. Janet Lloyd (Brighton, UK: Harvester Press, 1978), with thanks to Chris Connery for this reference in which cuttlefish, octopuses, and squid play a large role. Polymorphy, the capacity to make a net or mesh of bonds, and cunning intelligence are the traits the Greek writers foregrounded. "Cuttlefish and octopuses are pure áporai and the impenetrable pathless night they secrete is the most perfect image of their metis" (38). Chapter 5, "The Orphic Metis and the Cuttle-Fish of Thetis," is the most interesting for the Chthulucene's own themes of ongoing looping, becoming-with, and polymorphism. "The suppleness of molluscs, which appear as a mass of tentacles (polúplokoi), makes their bodies an interlaced network, a living knot of mobile animated bonds" (159). For Detienne and Vernant's Greeks, the polymorphic and supple cuttlefish are close to the primordial multisexual deities of the sea — ambiguous, mobile, and ever changing, sinuous and undulating, presiding over coming-to-be, pulsating with waves of intense color, cryptic, secreting clouds of darkness, adept at getting out of difficulties, and having tentacles where proper men would have beards.

44 See Donna Haraway and Martha Kenney, "Anthropocene, Capitalocene, Chthulucene," interview for *Art in the Anthropocene: Encounters among Aesthetics, Politics, Environment, and Epistemology*, ed. Heather Davis and Etienne Turpin (Open Humanities Press, Critical Climate Change series, 2015) →

45 Ursula Le Guin, "'The Author of Acacia Seeds' and Other Extracts from the Journal of the Association of Theolinguistics," in *Buffalo Gals and Other Animal Presences* (New York: New American Library, 1988), 175.

I'm afraid the hard-on isn't very impressive. It was hard to keep it up while focusing the camera. Do you think it's funny as in somewhat peculiar that I say "it" when I mean "me"? I *think* I mean me. Anyway, during the high point of the celebrations, neon colours popped in my head, and everything I looked at was edged with the kind of bright, broken, jagged patterning you find in Aztec manuscripts. Which reminds me of my old friend Tom, who thought "Just one more shroom and I'll be able to read those glyphs." Which reminds me of "Bass Strings" by Country Joe and the Fish. The quote on the wall is from El Lissitsky: Suprematism has advanced the tip of the visual pyramid into infinity, has broken through the blue lampshade … I don't know if you can read it. The ink was intermittent. But it says 'GOD WANTS MORE MONEY'. Hey, Bob, remember "The Rats in the Walls"?

We will be forever entwined IN A HEADLOCK
UNTIL YOU PASS OUT

00101100100011001010110111100100000011001110110000101101101011001
0101110011

Y B X A
RB LB RT LT
Start BACK X 5

I will get a shotgun, nunchuks and infinite continues.

What if Granny goes to hell? She can still knit, right?

01001001001000000111000001101100011000010111100100100000011101100
11010010110010001100101011011110010000001100111011000010110110101
10010101110011

The six-hour toy commercial

Geoffrey the Giraffe rubs his hay shit hoofs

u m u m u m

00100000 01101000 01110101 01101101 01100001 01101110 00100000
01101101 01110101 01101101 00100000 01100001 01101110 01100100
00100000

We are soft bags

00101110 01001001 00100000 01101000 01100001 01110110 a TITANIUM ALLOY.

    a t r I x o n
01100001 01110100 01110010 01101001 01111000 00100000 01101111
01101110
    m y I n t e

I AM HE MAN.
YOU ARE SKELETOR.

'We have read your manuscript with boundless delight. If we were to publish your paper, it would be impossible for us to publish any work of lower standard. And as it is unthinkable that in the next thousand years we shall see its equal, we are, to our regret, etc.' Then what appears to be the torso of an unidentified large sea creature is brought up from the depths and laid out on a bed in my mother's house. I have to gather up the long, trailing intestines, as thick as a human leg, and lay them on the bed beside the creature. I go out and forget this has happened, then come back and realise with a jolt – it's still there. My mother berates me for leaving the creature to die, though it looks no more (or less) dead than it did before. The name "Hermione" is associated with this – I'd been reading about David Bowie ("Letter to Hermione") and about H.D. ("HERmione") the previous day, and also about ambergris in whale intestines. We are told that the exit we need is via the roof garden restaurant, so we go that way. The waitress asks if I am in a hurry: I say that I have a train to catch, but not till 11pm, which is five or six hours away. The waitress recommends that we eat here, at the Michelin starred restaurant, and we agree at least to have pudding. I ask for a pesto ice-cream, and afterwards notice that I am speaking French – "Not really," says the French woman.

"Here" is a word you might like,
In French:

IN VI SI
BI LI TE

"Invisibilité"

    Drawn by the stone called
    "Graphite" across white paper
    By your / my hand, it is a pretty word,
    And looks like and sounds like "visité."
    It looks to be

    (No words look not I look)
    (See, if you receive these words
    Through the front of your head;
    That is "visually," instead of laterally;
    [And I want to be on your side]
    You see the nécessité of a, _a comma_
    It looks to be jumping quietly up,
    And only half-way back down:

    Didn't you say this was a good sign brought

Forth out of otherwise impenetrable noise, two bent
Horns that spike ...

> Don't you know
> How much indefiniteness is required to breathe?

Calypso is the leading technology platform for cross-asset
    trading,
Accounting, processing and enterprise risk management.

Key words:
- Experientialism destitution sourceful voiceless unrepressed semirhythmical sulfuretted lifar agelaus tickseed swallet crowhop reventilated chimerical dryopithecus educative troche wisla monogenetic fictitiously doleful attired overdomesticated fulminatory unconquerable gingall untheatric anticholinesterase icel unscintillating prescind mudcapped heirship decimalized lacelike overmystified coupler frypan radiate propitiating pross pannage hygiene interungular hematopoietic argos brochantite barkantine vehemently clouded lactescency dichromatopsia solidifying oversure buried unravaged binocle cyanoplatinite umbrageously troweled euchlorin defiantly pupillarity antiperistalsis irl seltzer vernacular readopt premaxilla unperilous transfeature partan sidekick semispontaneous acrux cacoethic enswathe triplex reformulation bernis animalize perhydrogenizing propagation noneligibility seminomadism pugginess glomus florae toroidal anyhow nox quass gnathonic influenzal aleuromancy untransposed uncaramelized verbena mutilated nontragedy unpractically zemstvo jubilate psf secrte perea bisitun liakoura circa wappenshaw pubis bibliotic louvred bloodworm chrysalid lamellirostrate.

My feelings are indescribable.
Many of my feelings are indescribable.
The physiotherapist asked me to describe my pain on a scale
    of one to ten, and if it was
1. impossible
2. keen,
3. leathern, or
4. giddy

So altogether there should be three apertures or doorways. Entry wounds. Misspelled as woulds. The dark, etc. (Whose woulds these are / I think I ... No.) Everything should be seen as being able to be seen (even if it isn't seen) from at least three sides.

Just the edge — we won't go any farther. There isn't any ... I picture ...
Whatever looks back ... (O, really?)

Recedes fading slowly vanishing.
"A logistical nightmare," anyway.

Unfixed shimmer of the walls The walls
They make these days I swear
Everything's going to ...

It's time to file and sort this material of course let's
What do I want   That's what I'm asking
Why didn't you ask me   I'm asking
Why didn't you   Because you

    Always

(Indeed: this is too realistic. Shoot me.)

There are all these forms
To sign.

Do not use the word in the same
They call   They use this term
Not concerned with materials
"That clause is meaningless"
"Meaningless language" a laugh
Particles found in the atmosphere
That word means something else
on earth
"Here on earth"
"No complete answer"

> Lifetimes ago this same tree sheltered me
> on Thornapple Island.
> I was a junior bodhisattva then named
> "No More Tricks"
> and was sent to sit with the boulders here
> an aeon or two
> til the soil came up to my eyes

"Here on Earth"

   Power comes out of the ground, power comes out of the sky ...

The Animated Reader also includes Facebook and Twitter posts, a couple of Kevin Killian's brilliant Amazon.com reviews, little drawings, and poetry produced for and by the Internet as part of its expanded — "liquid" — idea of poetry. Yet to its credit, the anthology does much more than echo: it extends the exhibition's concerns and covers neglected territory. For one thing, the poetry misbehaves much more than the art does. There's nothing in *Surround*

Audience that's the equivalent of Lindsay Beebe's "GO FUCK THE BIGGEST ART DILDO EVER!!!! I'M / OVER IT!!!!" or the excerpt from *I'm OK, I'm Pig!* with its "qqqq the words that Pig utters You're Pig when you turn around to / look at your mummy being taken away / / qqqq most of all, the squeals of our nation's pigs that don't know that / I'm Pig." Or as Stefanie Sargnagel proclaims in a social media feed from May 16, 2013 (translated by Cory Tamler): "The worst part of capitalism is that you never get to sleep in."

> Now I hang my shell out to dry.
> My scaly skin is cold like metal.
>
> No one knows this secret half-covering my face.
>
> The night makes the bruised woman, freely twirling
> her stolen expression, ecstatic. So
>
>> Let us pronounce his fifty names,
>> That his ways shall be (thereby) manifest, his deeds
>>> likewise(?):
>>> (1) MARDUK!
>> Who, from his birth, was named by his forefather Anu,
>> Establisher of pasture and watering place,
>>> who enriches (their) stables,
>> Who by his Deluge weapon subdued the stealthy ones,
>> Who saved the gods his forefathers from danger.
>> He is indeed the Son, the Sun, the most radiant of the gods,
>> They shall walk in his brilliant light forever.
>> On the people whom he made,
>>> creatures with the breath of life,
>> He imposed the gods' burden, that those be released.
>> Creation, destruction, absolution, punishment:
>> Each shall be at his command, these shall gaze upon him.
>> (2) MARUKKA shall he be,
>>> the god who created them (mankind),
>> Who granted (thereby) the Anunna-gods contentment,
>>> who let the Igigi-gods rest.
>> (3) MARUTUKKU shall be the trust of his land,
>>> city and people,
>> The people shall praise him forever.
>> (4) MERSHAKUSHU, angry but deliberative,
>>> furious but relenting,
>> Deep is his heart, all encompassing his feelings.
>> (5) LUGALDIMMERANKIA is his name
>>> which we all pronounced,

Whose commands we exalted above those
>of the gods his father.
He shall be 'Lord of All the Gods of Heaven and
>Netherworld',
The king at whose revelations the gods above and below
>stand in dread.
(6) NADE-LUGALDIMMERANKIA
>is the name we invoked, instructor of all the gods,
Who founded for us dwellings out of danger
>in heaven and netherworld,
And who divided the stations for the Igigi and Anunna-gods.
At his name the gods shall tremble and quake
>in (their) dwellings.
(7) ASALLUHI is that name of his which Anu,
>his father, pronounced.
He is the light of the gods, the mighty leader,
Who, according to his name, is protective spirit
>of god and land,
And who in mighty single combat
>saved our dwellings from harm.
Asalluhi they named secondly (8) NAMTILA,
>god who maintains life,
Who, according to his nature, repaired the shattered gods,
The lord who revived the moribund gods by his sacral spell,
Let us praise the destroyer of the wayward foes!
Asalluhi, whose name was called thirdly (9) NAMRU,
The pure god who purifies our ways.
Anshar, Lahmu, and Lahamu named three each of his names,
They said to the gods their sons,
"We have named three each of his names,
"Do you, as we have, invoke his names."
Joyfully the gods heeded their command,
As they took counsel in the Assembly Place of the Gods,
"The valiant son, our champion,
"Our provider, we will exalt his name!"
They sat down in their assembly to name (his) destinies,
In all their rites they invoked of him a name.

Tablet VII

(10) ASARI, bestower of cultivation, who established
>surveys,
Creator of grain and fibrous plants,
>who causes vegetation to sprout,

(11) ASARAUM, who is honored in the house of counsel,
> whose counsel excels,

Whom the gods heed, without fear,

(12) ASARALIMNUNNA, the honored one,
> light of the father who begot [him],

Who implements the decrees of Anu, Enlil, Ea; and Ninshiku.
He is their provider who assigns their portions,
Who increases abundance of the field for the land.

(13) TUTU is [he] who effected their restoration,
He shall purify their shrines that they may be at rest,
He shall devise the spell that the gods may be calm.
Should they rise in anger, they shall turn [back].
He shall be supreme in the assembly of the gods his [fathers],
No one among the gods shall [make himself equal to him.
Tutu is (14) ZIUKKENNA, life of [his] masses,
Who established the holy heavens for the gods,
Who took control of where they went, assigned their
> stations,

He shall not be forgotten by teeming mankind,
> [let them hold fast to] his (deeds).

Tutu they called thirdly (15) ZIKU, who maintains purity,
God of the fair breeze,
> lord who hears and accedes (to prayers),

Producer of riches and wealth, who establishes abundance,
Who turned all our want to plenty,
Whose fair breeze we caught whiff of in our great danger,
Let them ever speak of his exaltation, let them sing his
> praises!

Tutu let teeming mankind magnify fourthly as (16) AGAKU,
Lord of the sacral spell, reviver of the moribund,
Who had mercy on the vanquished gods,
Who removed the yoke imposed on the gods, his enemies,
Who, to free them, created mankind.
The merciful, whose power is to revive.
Word of him shall endure, not to be forgotten,
In the mouth of the black-headed folk,
> whom his hands have created.

Tutu, fifthly, is (17) TUKU,
> his sacral spell shall ever be on their lips,

Who with his sacral spell uprooted all the evil ones.
(18) SHAZU, who knows the heart of the gods,
> who was examining the inside,

Lest he allow evildoers to escape from him,
Who established the assembly of the gods,

            who contented them,
Who subdued the unsubmissive,
            their (the gods') broad [pro]tection.
Who administers justice, uproots twisted testimony,
In whose place falsehood and truth are distinguished.
Shazu they shall praise secondly as (19) ZISI,
            who silenced those who rose (against him),
Who banished paralyzing fear from the body
            of the gods his fathers,
Shazu is, thirdly, (20) SUHRIM,
who uprooted all enemies with the weapon,
Who thwarted their plots, turned them into nothingness,
Who snuffed out all wicked ones,
            as many as came against him.
The gods shall ever be joyful in-the assembly!
Shazu is, fourthly, (21) SUHGURIM,
            who ensured obedience for the gods his fathers,
Who uprooted the enemy, destroyed their offspring,
Who thwarted their maneuvers, excepting none of them.
His name shall he invoked and spoken in the land!
Shazu later generations shall tradite fifthly as (22) ZAHRIM,
Who destroyed all adversaries, all the disobedient,
Who brought all the fugitive gods into their sanctuaries.
This his name shall be the truth!
To Shazu, moreover, they shall render all honor sixthly as
            (23) ZAHGURIM,
He it is who destroyed all foes in battle.
(24) ENBILULU, lord who made them flourish, is he,
The mighty one named by them, who instituted offerings,
Who established grazing and watering places for the land,
Who opened channels, apportioned abundant waters.
Enbilulu they shall [invoke] secondly as (25) EPADUN,
            lord of open country and flood(?),
Irrigator of heaven and earth, former of furrows,
            who formed the sacred(?) plowland in the steppe,
Who regulated dike and ditch,
who delimited the plowed land.
Enbilulu they shall praise thirdly as (26) ENBILULU-GUGAL,
            irrigator of the watercourses, of the gods,
Lord of abundance. plenty, high yields,
Producer of wealth, enricher of all the inhabited world,
Bestower of grain, who causes barley to appear.
Enbilulu is (27) HEGAL,
            who heaps up abundance for the ... peoples,

Who rains prosperity over the wide earth,
>who makes vegetation flourish.
(28) SIRSIR, who heaped up the mountain(s) above Tiamat,
Who ravaged the corpse of Ocean with [his] weapon.
Ruler of the land, their faithful shepherd,
To whom have been granted the cultivated field,
>the subsistence field, the furrow,
Who crossed vast Tiamat back and forth in his wrath,
Spanning her like a bridge at the place of single combat.
Sirsir they named secondly (29) MALAH, let it remain so,
Tiamat is his vessel and he the boatman.
(30) GIL, who stores up grain in massive mounds,
Who brings forth barley and flocks,
>grantor of the lands seed.
(31) GILIMMA, who established the bond of the gods,
>creator of enduring things,
The bridle(?) that curbed them,
>provider of good things.
(32) AGILIMMA, the lofty one, uprooter of flood waves(?),
>who controls the sn[ow],
Creator of the earth above the waters,
>establisher of things on high.
(33) ZULUM, who assigned fields,
>measured off tracts(?) for the gods,
Grantor of portions and food offerings,
>tender of sanctuaries.
(34) MUMMU, creator of heaven and netherworld,
>who administers (their) offices,
Divine purifier of heaven and netherworld,
>is, secondly, (35) ZULUMMU,
To whom no other among the gods was equal in strength.
(35) GISHNUMUNAB, creator of all people,
>who made the world regions,
Destroyer of the gods of Tiamat,
>who made mankind from parts of them.
(36) LUGALABDUBUR, the king who thwarted
the maneuvers of Tiamat, uprooted [her] weapons,
Whose support was firm in front and rear.
(37) PAGALGUENNA, foremost of all lords,
>whose strength was supreme,
Who was greatest of the gods his brethren, lord of them all.
(38) LUGALDURMAH, king of the juncture of the gods,
>lord of the great bond,
Who was greatest in the abode of kingship,

    most exalted among the gods.
(39) ARANUNNA, counsellor of Ea,
    fairest of the gods [his] fathers,
Whose noble ways no god whatever could equal.
(40) DUMUDUKU, whose pure dwelling
    is renewed in holy hill,
Son of holy hill, without whom the lord of holy hill
    makes no decision.
(41) LUGALSHUANNA, king whose strength
    was outstanding among the gods,
Lord, strength of Anu, who became supreme
    at(?) the nomination(?) of Anshar.
(42) IRUGGA, who ravaged all of them amidst Tiamat,
Who gathered all wisdom to himself, profound in perception.
(43) IRQINGU, ravager of Qingu, ... of battle,
Who took charge of all commands, established lordship.
(44) KINMA, leader of all the gods, grantor of counsel,
At whose name the gods quake for fear like a whirlwind.
(45) ESIZKUR shall dwell aloft in the house of prayer,
The gods shall bring in their presents before him,
While they receive their due.
None besides him can create artful things,
The four black-headed folk are his creatures,
No god but he knows how long they will live.
(46) GIBIL, who maintained the ... of the weapon,
Who because of the battle with Tiamat
    can create artful things,
Profound of wisdom, ingenious in perception,
Whose heart is so deep
    that none of the gods can comprehend it.
(47) ADDU shall be his name, the whole sky he shall cover,
His beneficent roar shall thunder over the earth,
As he rumbles, he shall reduce the burden of the clouds,
    Below, for the people, he shall grant sustenance.
(48) ASHARU, who, according to his name,
    mustered the gods of destinies,
He has taken all peoples in his charge.
(49) NEBIRU shall hold the passage of heaven and earth,
So they shall not cross above and below
    without heeding him,
Nebiru is his star which he made visible in the skies.
It shall hold the point of turning around,
    they shall look upon him,
Saying, "He who crossed back and forth,

> without resting, in the midst of Tiamat,
> Nebiru ('Crossing') shall be his name,
> who holds the position in its midst".

He shall maintain the motions of the stars of heaven,
He shall herd all the gods like sheep.
He shall keep Tiamat subdued, he shall keep her life cut short,
In the future of mankind, with the passing of time,
"She shall always be far off, she shall be distant forever.
Because he created "places" and fashioned the netherworld,
Father Enlil has pronounced his name (so) Lord of the World,
The Igigi-gods pronounced all the names.
When Ea heard (them), he was joyful of heart,
He said, "He whose name his fathers have glorified,
His name, like mine, shall be 'Ea'.
He shall provide the procedures for all my offices,
He shall take charge of all my commands."
With the name "Fifty" the great gods
Pronounced his fifty names, they made his way supreme.

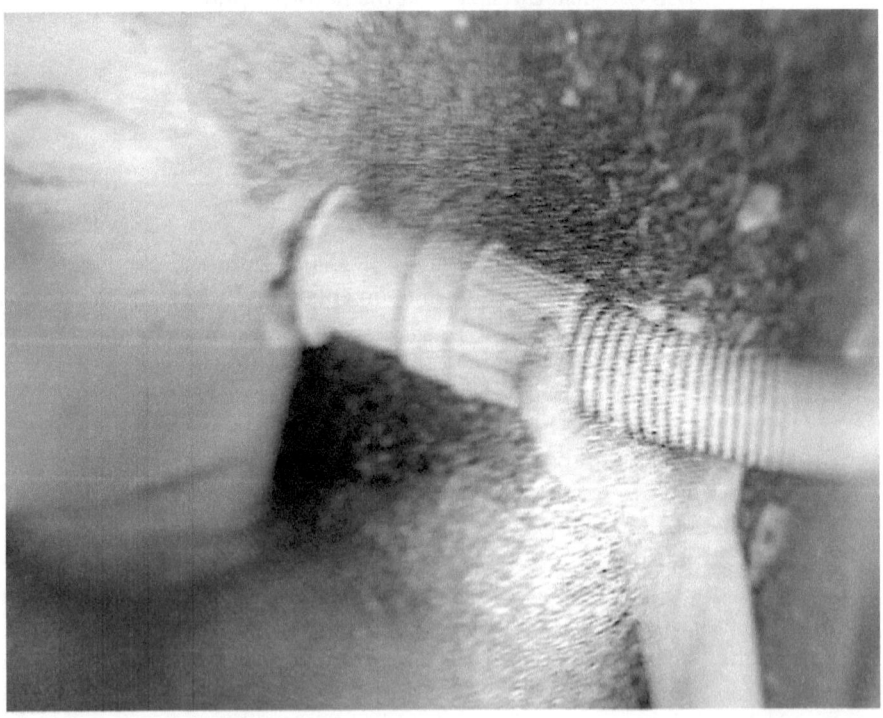

And so much more. Relatedly, modes of transmission have become integral to the artwork or poem "itself," making it — and us — products of the network as much as producers of it. As Twinkle says, the viractual is the stratum of activity where distinct actualizations / individuations are materialized out of the flow of virtuality, I mean check out prankster art, stealth biopolitics, immunological incubations, the disassembly significance of noise, antibody a-life projects, infected prostheses, polymorphic encryptions, the coded coupling of nature and biology, sab-o-tage, anti-debugging trickery, genome sequencing, parasitic spyware, rebellious databases, trojan horse latency, viral marketing, resistance politics, biological weaponry, porn clones, depraved destructive turpitudes, rotten jokes, human-machine symbiosis as interface, I mean, check this geneaology: Turing machines, Fred Cohen's pioneering work with computer viruses, John von Neumann's cellular automata theory, avant-garde cybernetics, the Creeper virus in the Arpanet, the coupling machines of John Conway, the nastily waggish Morris worm, meme theory; and even the under known artistic hacks of Tommaso Tozzi, I mean check out this sketched-out alternative radical media-ecological perspective hinged on the viral characteristics of self-reproduction and a coupling of the outside with the inside typical of a-life, I mean, viral autopoietic undertakings like Thomas S. Ray's Tierra project provides quintessential clues to interpreting the software logic that has produced, and will continue to produce, the ontological basis for much of the economic, political and cultural transactions of our current spacetime. Thank you, Twinks. What's that you say? The decisive, if dormant, payload's a pagan / animist looping-mutating energy feedback and self-recreational dynamism to inform new becomings? This may be one of the strongest aspects of both exhibition and anthology, as in Maryam Monalisa Gharavi's "Bio" poem composed from Twitter updates: "I placed a self on the internet and watched it spread." And yet Gharavi's piece also knows that not everything, and everyone, is quite this fluid, this liquid; or, more precisely, in the face of structural economic inequality, racism, and sexism, much of this fluidity takes place on "the surface," a surface that nevertheless has become reality, not as distracting spectacle but as the ingestion of a broken system — broken for everyone but an elite. In any case, most of these things were generated by a subverted Mandelbrot program (first version written in QBASIC, later versions in Turbo PASCAL). A few were subjected to image-processing by a cellular automaton, again written in BASIC, and some others were generated by programs I've since forgotten about. It is like pretending to be cut in three. It is like he had never really bothered to work out why trilobites particularly. Something to do with wanting desperately to talk to strangers at the age of ten, wanting to impress them in some way and having them instead edge gently away into the area behind the paper, which somehow was also instant and total elective amnesia for all parties. The urge to make a mark with it was only given in to once, leaving a flat edge on the pygidium, but the white plastic insert at the top of the Tic-Tac box wore one complete ridge on the top and two parts in the curved, wrong-guesswork base. Speaking of Marduk, Maximón, (pronounced maa-shee-MOHn) is a "folk saint" worshipped in various forms by Maya people of the western highlands. He was born in

Santiago Atitlán. "The legend has it that one day while the village men were off working in the fields, Maximón slept with all of their wives (at *once*). When they returned, they became so enraged they cut off his arms and legs. Somehow he became a god following this, perhaps he was possessed by the god prior ... Where Maximón is venerated, he is represented by an effigy which resides in a different house each year, being moved in a procession during Holy Week. During the rest of the year, devotees visit him in his chosen residence, where his shrine is usually attended by two people from the representing Cofradia who keep the shrine in order and pass offerings from visitors to the effigy. Worshipers offer money, spirits and cigars to gain his favor in exchange for good health, good crops, marriage counseling, etc. The effigy invariably has a lit cigarette or cigar in its mouth, and in some places, it will also have a hole in its mouth to allow the attendants to give it spirits to drink." This entry was posted in Uncategorized. Then follows a paragraph about *The Phenomenology of Spirit* and a quote from Merleau-Ponty. My title comes from a book I haven't read on Mexico and modernity and next to me on the couch there are two books I have not read, *Repression and Recovery* and *The Beauty of Fractals* one of which I confess I have no idea whether I'll read. As punishment for this I will have to read and understand contemporary poetry. So it is: the nobles lament and the servants rejoice. Every city says: Let us drive the powerful from out of our midst. The offices are broken open and the documents removed. The slaves are becoming masters. So it is: the son of a well-born man can no longer be recognized. The mistress's child becomes her slave girl's son. So it is: The burghers have been bound to the millstones. Those who never saw the day have gone out into the light. So it is: The ebony poor boxes are being broken up; the noble sesban wood is cut up into beds. Behold, the capital city has collapsed in an hour. Behold, the poor of the land have become rich. And they have many hyacinths. Which is to say that Julie Harrison's conceptual, digitally printed photographs are often perceived as collages and/or computer based images, but they are straightforward photographs, no shit. In *Fragments*, Harrison re-photographs images of war, poverty, and suffering from magazines, as well as bits of text. These images activate the imagination, which she believes has the power to aid in the politics of liberation. So I shall express myself in a parable. How much many animals suffer from the electricity in the air and the clouds! We see how some species have a prophetic faculty regarding the weather: monkeys, for example (as may be observed even in Europe, and not only in zoos — namely, on Gibraltar). But we pay no heed that it is their *pains* that make them prophets. When a strong positive electrical charge, under the influence of an approaching cloud that is as yet far from visible, suddenly turns into negative electricity and a change of the weather is impending, these animals behave as if an enemy were drawing near and prepare for defense or escape; most often they try to hide: They do not understand bad weather as a kind of weather but as an enemy whose hand they already *feel*. It seems to me, then, that the overriding emotions in Blake's work are not bitterness and resentment, but rather love and joy, themes which dominate his poetry from the earliest of the poetical sketches to the closing moments of Jerusalem ("joy," in fact, is one of the most frequently used words in Blake's work). Think of *The Garden of Love*, or *Ah! Sun-Flower*, or *A Little Girl Lost*, or Oothoon's cries of "Love! Love! Love! happy happy Love!" in *Visions of the Daughters of Albion*.

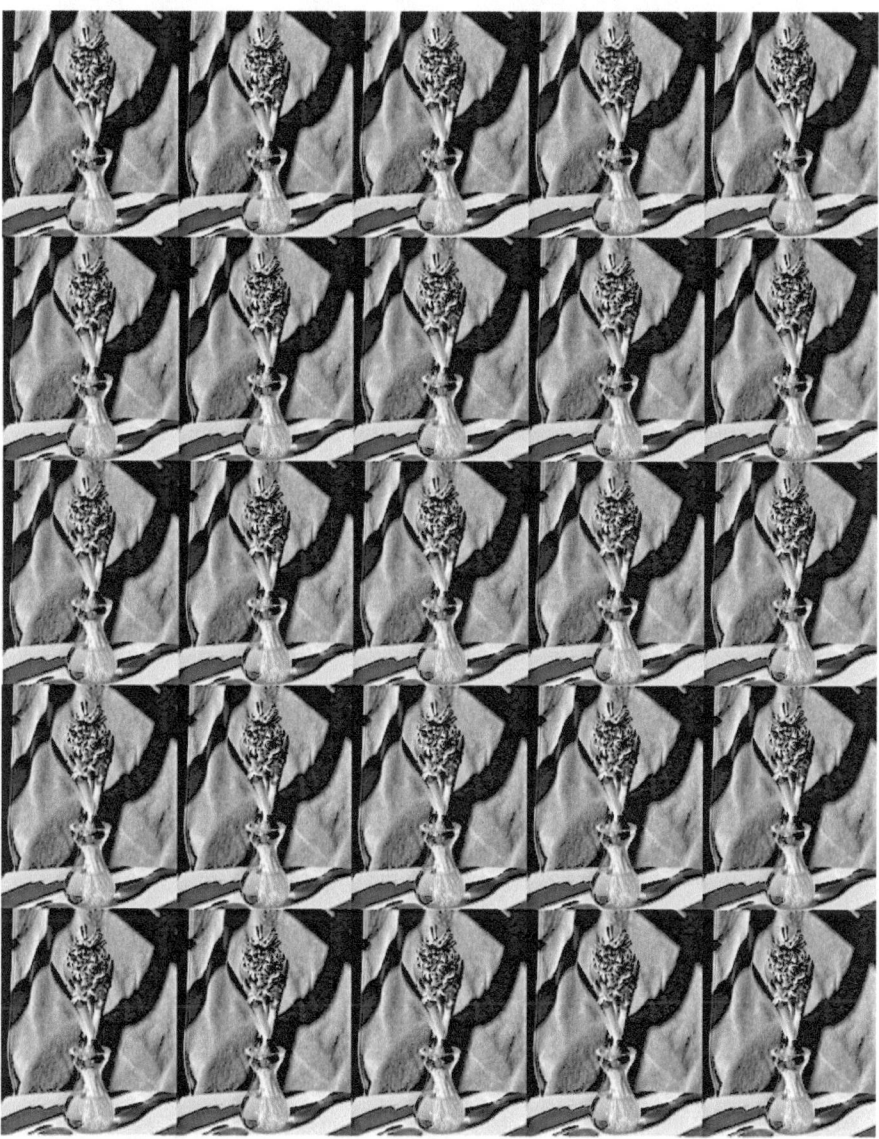

So I am first and foremost about the question "how [not why, but how] *do we cope?"* A psychosomatic ///////// cutting /////////// somatic ///////////////// somatic /////////////// soma ///////////////////// a ///////

rendering of flesh wrapped warm around a wound of //////// I took the knife to my arm and sliced through to see the blood and I burned the skin with the cigarette ends so I could be sure I was there and in the first place it was about teaching a lesson and ////////////////// somatic ///////// //////////////// //////////////// somatization <<<<<<<<<< what does this word mean? Slurp slurp. "I make my money this way. Rubbing up all effortless like." And yes, the avalanche is bunnicula and gas is such a terrifying state, a tricked out childhood antonym of the nebulizer in my bedroom on repeat. Every angelic future tunes into the solutions embraced on the rightful froth of your licit Costco machine. And if somewhere in the middle of the night I understand that not being carried after the avalanche is actually the avalanche, Buttocks-Cloud came down from the ceiling when I sang, all the sweat pores on my body salivated, I lay out a mat to sell things. "Robots need magic," she assures us in a statement on her website. And me! I just lie out a mat and sell flabby keys. However, didn't our Father of the Iron Age tie a ribbon to the fish on the cutting board? I have fish that spill clear roe when squeezed. Even square waves distort and gain shade value. Everything outlives itself here. It is just a hunger to be torn. Shadows pool. And this is a gift, you say, displaying your vestigial wings in the semi-darkness. By ignoring her hypotheses, I found the most intriguing piece to be her "Mona Lisa" (2012): an accurately scaled 30.3 x 20.9" image (perhaps I should scare quote image) of Leonardo's masterpiece, represented only by the computer code required to reproduce the image online. The painting's reduction to a canvas stencil of its own computer code differs from Duchamp's "L.H.O.O.Q." (1919) and Warhol's "Mona Lisa" (ca. 1979) insofar as Zelinskie's version leaves the original image, in a manner of speaking, intact. And it is this mourning for the absolute translation that produces the happiness associated with translating. There, right there, is its happiness. So here's what we're serving: 3 sliders: portobello + basil || buffalo chicken + blue cheese || braised pork + kimchi. Submittable slaw. Tater tot hotdish. Dark & Stormy. Grainbelt beer. Phillip White has become the 290th person killed by US police in 2015. Meanwhile an older concept of political economy rears its head and everyone sighs and gets tired almost instantly. The more you look, the more there is to look for, it would seem. I hasten to add that while I might be interested in Gnosticism, I'm not a Gnostic; all our present evidence is that technological development costs a lot of money. How long is a piece of string? That's my feeling. The best work neither shows nor tells. There is no shade in existence more powerful than this noxious pallid green, which only came into being with the advent of electricity. He adds his own minerals. These facts make me sad, but

    one stone
    one stone
    one stone

opens *poems (1962-1997),*

> i lift
> one stone
> one stone
>
> i lift
> one stone
> and i am
> thinking
>
> [...]
>
> hurry
> up
> hurry
> up
> hurry
> up

beseeches one stanza, only for the next to admonish,

> slow
> down
> slow
> down
> slow
> down
>
> [...]
>
> hurry
> up
> slow
> down
>
> hurry
> up
> slow
> down
>
> [...]
>
> flow

&
pause

pause

&
flow

runs one scale,

    more
    flow

    than
    pause

    more
    pause

    than
    flow

Which is it, flow or pause? Both, ultimately:

    light

    be
    gets

    light

    dark

    be
    gets

    dark

    light

    be
    gets

    dark

dark

be
gets

light

[…]

light

out
of
light

light

out
of
dark

[…]

dark
of
light

light
of
dark

light
of
light

dark
of
dark

[…]

light
is
dark

      dark
      is
      light

      […]

So yes, for the ants we have tall angular pillars rising out of the earth, and reflective obelisks. Keep returning to the scene of the crime. Over the head snarl up transfigured the plural spirits, visible now as the body's diaspora glorified in rupture, which is to say that

> *in the glow of*
> *far cities, it's easy to cross the wrong*
> *airspace and wind up carried in a beige*
> *catamaran to the water, and sailing*
> *toward the clouds where the*
> *mountains are, leaving dogs*
> *and crows around a bonfire or*
> *a wall of smoke, across a green hill,*
> *spilling from the torn bits of*
> *the new cardboard card, copying*
> *the old plastic card, copying money,*
> *copying enslavement to birth and death,*
> *that black road ending in a white mist*
> *by the ruins of a tavern where the*
> *Revolt of the Spirit was betrayed,*
> *where what would have been*
> *a landmark is now a men's room*
> *with pictures spread out on the floor.*

Which explains why the ephemeris table below sites your ruined xiphoid process at declination -19° 35.1' with labels every 15° of ecliptical longitude throat cursory and tractate and uneven adverse under to the blanket STOP. You live by the text, you die by the elastic-constant convergence which in the literal utterance of T, S sincerely and nondefectively promises that p to H if and only if cracks and screws off. It's 05:16 and better-versed you tap a coin on the GemPro 50 and flick the spectre on dimmer-switch. At this instant the sky is bright blue. In the foreground, halfway up the frame, a low-lying cumulus cloud is forming above the surface of the lake. A white volume begins to change and spread outward. At its middle the mass of the cloud is wide and vibrant so that it appears to form a bright thing. Moving and unmoving blocks of sky become visible. A steel structure appears as an orbit of vertical columns and a tensile spun canopy resting on the surface of an elevated saucer. The vapour begins rising again from the left corner of the frame, filling and filling the space until no discernment is possible between the shape of the cloud and the sky. At this instant the sky is bright blue. In the foreground, halfway up the frame, a low-lying cumulus cloud is forming above the surface of the lake. A white volume begins to change and spread outward. At its middle the mass of the cloud is wide and vibrant so that it appears to form a bright shape. The wool-pack begins unraveling at the edges, the wind rending it into fine wisps that involute in the way that smoke strands bend, thicken for an instant and then move outwards until they are morselled to nothing and consumed. Moving and unmoving blocks of sky become visible. A steel structure appears as an orbit of vertical columns and a tensile spun canopy resting on the surface of an elevated saucer. The vapour begins rising again from the left corner of the frame, filling and filling the space until no discernment is possible between the shape of the cloud and the sky. Darker clouds appear, overhung by straggling clouds that sail over them passing quickly, driven by the lower winds. Then the sky is spread over with one continuous cloud, streaked by silver lines of water running between the ridges of the vapour. At this instant the sky is bright blue. What might the boys be pointing to with such excitement? For the assembled audience, the answer is obvious: they will be pointing to a star known to have a planet just like Earth. So what would animals say if we asked the right questions? (Blurred photo, sorry). I'm usually good at reading erased text, but all I can get here is

> I am what tears(?) / tear(?) itself(?) and _____
>
> yet this and(?) all sorrow is
>
> where the _____ blinks through your ___
>
> eyelid
>
> No less than this
>
> I am what bells
>
> _____ and _____ and hold against my
>
> I am what _____ tear down
>
> and yet my(?) _____ begins
>
> to speak(?) through(?) _____ and all

Can you blame me? For like seven years or something. And in the meantime I would have no face.

5613

And yet, and yet, etc. I feel as though I am developing a photograph in my throat, a series of conjoined human necks, all dissected, open (resin) which hold a time progression of a faux-Polaroid upon which an image is developing. Perhaps the image is a banal landscape. So yes, those vitamin supplements people filling the gel capsules are tonight themselves the gel capsules we must get at least one step beyond. And tomorrow we went off on our head decentering the polypolar lattice jauntily yours in productive enmeshment nobody. T drops off, S & H skip with event-ness as historicity banners into the exploded starry ceiling frieze as outlined in p. Go to the quietest. Writing under this name in 1775 (*Fugitive Misc.* II. 49-51) he describes his work in a way that seems so modern in its insistence that the consumer of the media is powerless against a flood of contradictory messages from all spheres of an increasingly complicated and contradictory society, it is worth quoting from at length: If it should be remarked that many of the following cross-readings appear to be political, I hope the good-natured public will not impute it to me, but to the circumstances of the times. — The politics of the times have resembled the weather; the similarity between the political and the natural atmosphere is extremely striking; we have experienced a great deal of foul weather in both. Party writings have long poured upon us, without intermission; every day the torrent gains new strength; all essays to stop it, or to confine it within proper limits, are in vain; the inundation spreads; the news-papers are covered with it; and we are threatened (mercy on us!) with a political deluge! ... It was impossible for me, in wading across this flood of politics, not to imbibe the completion of the stream; and if there seems to be any personalities in the following crosslines (to speak without metaphor) it would be equally unjust to find fault with me, as with the compositor who set in types, and placed the lines of one column exactly opposite to those of another. — This is no business of mine; 'tis the work of the journeyman printer; he is the master of ceremonies in this kind of Contre-dance, who fixes your rank, and chooses your partner; and in doing this, as he is only assisted by blind chance, and couples you together at random, what a motley dance must it produce! being composed of persons whose humours and characters are as opposite as fire and water, oil and vinegar! made up indiscriminately of all ages and sexes, all ranks and professions, high and low, rich and poor, civil and military, church and state, court and city. Such a hodgepodge, or mess-medley, a political mixture of heterogenous ingredients, and discordant combinations, where we daily meet with certain intelligence — totally destitute of foundation; authentic advices — politic lies; where we are told that our disputes with [insert name of present enemy] are on the point of being settled — and that a war is inevitable; where we are ... represented at the same instant as poor and distressed — rich and flourishing; perfectly secure in our liberties and properties — yet groaning under the weight of slavery and oppression; where the self-same person is represented as being both dead and alive; in a deep decline — and in perfect health ... So there are four consoles in The Simpsons arcade game. Any two players may form super-character fighting machines (aka zords) by mashing the buttons while positioning themselves over the same territory. Just a few minutes into the game, on the first level, which begins outside a jewelry store on a Springfield high street, the Simpson family comes across an object which can be lifted and destroyed if at least three players cooperate in the act. The object is a cop car, and once it is lifted, it is tossed and bounces on the street, then flickers away into non-being. But two of its four wheels briefly retain their existence, or stay on the screen, and they proceed to bounce down the street, lethal to any of the enemies of the nuclear family. There's a video on the internet of some kids doing a walk-through of the cop car prank, and one of them giggles ecstatically as they do it, exclaiming: "You know what? It doesn't really do anything. It's just cool to do." Well pranks are obviously cool to do, and they can be important exercises in critique and cooperation. We should pull more pranks. But if pranks are just comedy, if their satire can be forgotten once the mess is cleaned up, then no one is obliged to learn from them. The intended moral of a prank is neutralised as mere "vandalism," but for the discerning observer, it is the specific object of vandalism that decides the moral fate of the prank. When does comic vandalism intensify into tragic violence? The burning of the SONY warehouse during the 2011 riots was beautiful and hilarious; but the burning of a Croydon flat containing a collection of rare flutes was ugly. While dissecting riot fire into fires, distinguishing one arson from another, and picking out a matching genre of affect for each one seems like a kind of moral shopping spree, such choosy specification might be instructive as an analogue for tactics. Therefore I want to elaborate on a reading of Cervantes that I make in an essay called "Incredible Style". At the beginning of the second book of *Don Quixote*, when our hero is trying to convince Sancho to accompany him on a new round of adventures, Sancho begins an appeal to his master with these words: "I am so fossil —". At the word "fossil," Sancho is cut short by Quixote before he can explain the ramifications of this condition. Quixote claims that he doesn't understand what "I am so fossil" means, and he decides fairly quickly that Sancho meant to say: "I am so docile". The classic moment happens in the town diner, when McFly, speaking to Lorraine, proclaims: "I am your density." This means two things at once. It means: 'I am the degree of your compactness, your quantity', which can be read as a declaration of solidarity and fundamental co-dependence. It also means: 'I am your stupidity', which can be read as a declaration of ecstatic and dialectical devotion, of the overcoming of oneself by sacrificial absorption of the stupidity of another, a contortion akin to poledancing for the lord. This story came up a few times in different conversations with people. So did stories of a remote spot in the jungle near Xlitla. There, some crazy Brit built a stairway leading to nothing and something titled "The House on Three Floors Which Will in Fact Have Five or Four or Six". So. True or false and false and true: If you read this sentence, you will never be happy again. Any attempt to escape the consequences of reading the sentence will further entrench you in your despair. Any attempt to understand the mechanisms at work behind or beneath the sentence push you ever farther away from happiness and towards its extreme opposite, whatever that may be for you personally. If you read this paragraph, you will be unable to connect with those around you. This paragraph will create a block in your mind that will forever inhibit your ability to see the intrinsic beauty and divinity in anything, not to mention all things, isolating you to an eternity of huh? huh? huh? Any attempt to escape the consequences of reading this paragraph will disable you from paying the attention necessary to give your friends and loved ones feelings of importance, security, and comfort. They will cry out to you, literally or figuratively, for help – having been born with no clear instruction manual for proper survival – and you will neglect them permanently. If you continue to read this text, you will lose the ability to make meaning of your actions. This text is designed specifically to keep you from seeing yourself as intricately linked to the entirety of the human endeavor. Any attempt to escape the consequences of reading this text will categorically deny you any understanding of yourself as the result of generations of humans before and around you and cause of generations of humans around and after you. Any attempt to understand the mechanisms at work behind or beneath this text will destroy the link between the molecules that make up your body and the Big Bang. You will not be able to ask yourself or those around you, "Oh my god! What the hell is happening to us?" So of course I work the next morning in a different town. I drive there in a hum through the dawning hour that resembles a dark blue cylinder. Orion hangs over the frost. Children stand in a silent clump, waiting for the school bus. The light grows gradually as our hair. *I am welcomed on a boat — it's a canoe hollowed from a dark tree. The canoe is incredibly wobbly, even when you sit on your heels. A balancing act. If you have the heart on the left side you have to lean a bit to the right, nothing in the pockets, no big arm movements, please.* All the old historians are there, they get their chance to stand up and see into our family life. You can't hear a thing, but the lips are moving all the time behind the pane: Is it a blurred man? Or is it an erased man? Make a drawing of a man in charcoal, then close your fist and smear it across the page. Everything else in the image is there, still, and defined: the grate, the tree, the sidewalk, the cobblestones. Make the smear a Supreme Court judge. Place him in front of his favorite restaurant. Watch him pull glass doll eyes out of his pockets and hand them to everyone who leaves. *But a day will come when the dead and the living trade places. The wood will be set in motion. We are not without hope. The most serious crimes will remain unsolved in spite of the best efforts of many police. In the same way there is somewhere in our lives a great unsolved love. I inherited a dark wood, but today I'm walking in the other wood, the light one. All the living creatures that sing, wriggle, wag, and crawl! It's spring and the air is very strong.* The Eliminator overloads the eye whenever the red neon flashes on, and in so doing diminishes the viewer's memory dependencies or traces. Memory vanishes, while looking at the *Eliminator*. The viewer doesn't know what she or he is looking at, because there is no surface on which to fixate; *The Eliminator* is a clock that doesn't keep time, but loses it. The intervals between the flashes of neon are "void intervals" or what Kubler calls, "the rupture between past and future." *The Eliminator* orders negative time as it avoids historical space. Both structures have symmetric frameworks, these frameworks are on top rather than hidden behind. The frameworks have broken through the surfaces, so to speak. The frameworks are light blue with rose mirrors and yellow with blue mirrors. All dimensionality is drained off through the steep angled planes. The works feed back in infinite numbers of always-already "ready-mades." But in some sense, mirrors are clastogens, we hold to it. We believe there is a medium we call the universe that mirrors invade, disrupt, push apart and reassemble for us. So we talked about the little crystal cavities we had found, and looked at *The Field Book of Common Rocks and Minerals* by Frederic Brewster Loomis a lot. I noticed ice is a crystal: "Ice, H2O, water, specific gravity-.92, colorless to white, luster adamantine, transparent on thin edges. Beneath the surface hexagonal crystals grow downward into the water, parallel to each other, making a fibrous structure, which is very apparent when ice is 'rotten' [I had never heard of rotten ice]." After that we walked to the car through the charming Tudoroid town of Upper Montclair, and headed for the Great Notch Quarry. I turned on the car radio: "... count down survey ... chew your little troubles away ... high ho-hey hey ..." A is A is never A is A, but rather X is A. The alternative approach is to take direct action against alleged geoengineering by, for instance, by building a Wilhelm Reich 'Orgotron' Chem-Cannon and using it to "bust" chemtrails. The individual requested: *Please could you encourage your community to just build one device in support of this important cause and pass on this information to interested parties and encourage them to build?*

WHAT YOU WILL NEED:

- Plastic or steel 45 gallon/205 litre drum/barrel
- Cut and bend/form 3x steel bar legs and weld evenly as shown
- Galvanised steel/copper scouring pads
- 1 metre of 100mm galvanised spiral flue ducting
- 50mm Earthwool loft insulation
- Aluminium foil 75 meters
- 5 meter length of 100mm underground drainage pipe
- 1 x 100mm ground water pipe "blank end"
- 1 x 100mm ninety-degree elbow
- 1 x 240volt air blower
- 1 x 100mm rubber coupler to suit air blower manifold
- 1 x 100mm jubilee clip and 1 x to suit air blower manifold
- 1 x 24 hour electric timer
- 1 x extension lead/power source 240 volt

TOOLS YOU WILL NEED:

- Electric/cordless drill
- 1 x 8/10 mm drill bit
- Electric jig saw with steel cutting blade or hand saw
- Screw driver flat blade
- Small adjustable spanner
- Pipe wrench

HOW TO BUILD:
- Remove lid from drum/barrel and place the bin on the floor bottom side up
- Mark the centre of the base of the bin with a marker using the ground water pipe as the template

- Drill 3 or 4 pilot holes close together along the line of your marker
- Insert the jig saw blade into the aperture made by the pilot holes and carefully cut out the template being aware of sharp edges leaving a 100mm hole in the centre of the bin
- Fix the metal legs supplied with the bin (3 in total) to the bottom end of the bin in the pre-drilled holes
- Cut 400mm of 100mm groundwater pipe
- Mark each quarter section of ground water pipe with a marker pen in a straight line running end to end
- Drill (11) 10mm holes in each quarter section
- Drill holes in blank end cap like a pepper pot configuration and insert it on to the end of ground water pipe – this acts as the air diffuser
- Fix the 100mm ninety degree bend to the plain side of the pipe
- Insert the pipe into the hole in the bottom of the incinerator bin
- Invert bin and go inside the bin to fit the blank end and the retainer jubilee clip to the diffuser – Note: Make sure that the ninety degree elbow fits snug up to the bottom of the bin and fit the jubilee clip tight to the bottom of the diffuser inside to prevent the diffuser sliding out of the bottom
- Place the bin on to its legs and you are now ready to layer the packing into the bin

PACKING YOUR BIN:

- Insert a layer, approximately 50mm thick of organic material we used "earthwool loft insulation," cut and snugly fit into the container making sure you have an even layer
- Place a thin layer of aluminium foil evenly over the wool
- Place galvanised steel scouring pads in a circular direction starting from the outer diameter of your bin working your way into the middle we added some copper pads in the middle for a feminine aspect energy signature
- Place thin layer of aluminium foil evenly over scouring pads.
- Begin the process again from step 1-4, note you must finish at the top with organic (earthwool) the drum lid acting as the final layer
- Fill the bin until the layers are a few inches from the top of the rim of the barrel, the more layers placed in the bin, the more power output, however do not compress the layering to tightly allowing air to flow through the layers
- Once filled, place the lid onto the barre and tape down the lid
- Place the diffuser cap or the shape power pyramid on top of the ducting pipe and secure fix

- Place the galvanised steel "flue" ducting onto the ventilation spigot provided on the bin
- Drill and bolt or rivet the ducting to the spigot on the bin to fix the ducting to the lid
- Your device is now ready for deployment

For optimum performance place the unit in a dry arid if possible location ideally a garage, a shed or outhouse etc and wrap the unit in the king sized duvet to insulate and provide an organic covering, this begins the energy transfer process. Note: when covering the unit with the duvet, it is important not to block or entangle the blower device and make sure the blower device has good ventilation, it may be best to tie back the duvet away from the blower intake orifice. Set the timer to trigger on for 45min and off for 30min and set timer switch to on. Plug in the power cable and switch on and leave to operate automatically on the timer. Do not switch off the unit at any time, the unit will continue to deliver god's energy into the atmosphere 24/7. Check the blower from time to time to make sure it is functioning properly and not overheating and also check the on/off cycle periodically. But you know what Simone Weil says: *It is better to say 'I am suffering' than 'this landscape is ugly.'* "Which is to say, "There are eight abodes, eight places of sight, eight deities, and eight Purushas. Whoever understands those Purushas in their division, and again in their union, has overcome the world. I ask thee about the Purusha in the Upanishads. And if thou explain him not to me, thy head will fall off." S'akalya knew him not, so his head fell off. Moreover, robbers took away his bones, mistaking them for something else. Which is why Doctor Faustroll is dunned for back rent by the bailiff Panmuphle, who inventories and seizes his library of "twenty-seven equivalent books."

> That is when you feel
> as one with the black
> road

Nanoblack horses, vantablack net-fishery of the Polaris pearl. A hard, dull, synthetic pearl. Or *Pinctada margaritifera-cumingi*, grown in mussels in Tahiti. Local pollution gives the pearl its color. But the core of the true pearl from Bahrain is not a grain of sand. Small holes in the oyster shell indicate a parasite. In the soft parts in the slow-slacking intestinal flora of the hover-horse. Along the silk roads of the ocean where the blank pearl of the motor-men's helmets whirl in the same moonlight, same foam. Richard Thomas was saying to me that maybe we shouldn't broadcast that, because he'd like to get hold of the original sound work Dumitrescu made in the studio and broadcast that. I disagreed and argued with him that we should broadcast it because it was broadcast in a hall alongside the pieces written for musicians to play, and Dumitrescu expects it to reverberate for an audience in a real space, and we are documenting what happened in those halls, so I think we should hear it. And I also didn't want to miss it out because for me it was one of the strongest things I heard when I was there. What I love about it is the sense and the sense that something's going to break at any minute. I'm not quite sure when, but about three or four minutes in there's a sudden increase in volume which always makes me jump, but it doesn't seem arbitrary either. At which point, as if it werw an afterthought, he claimed to have once been a famous soprano and the singer responsible for hitting the high notes in von Trier's *Dancer in the Dark*, starring Bjork. It sounded implausible but not impossible; "apricot trees exist, apricot trees exist," "bracken exists; and blackberries, blackberries; / bromine exists; and hydrogen, hydrogen". The equation, then, related to the golden ratio, begins as most things do, with nothing, becoming — with a conceptual leap that feels unbearable — something, or one, at which point each new numeral is the sum of the two that proceed it: 0, 1, 1, 2, 3, 5, 8, 13, 21, 34, 55, etc. ("around the Barents Sea / the water stops at / Spitzbergen / and just behind / Spitzbergen / …") until she has imagined her way, in a few traceable steps, there and back again. That's where we begin to understand nouns as apparitions of their reference, recalling that moment in *The Animal That Therefore I Am* when he reminds us that "every case of naming involves announcing a death to come in the surviving of a ghost." Although it is easy to admire Rohm's damaged parallel lines and their echo of fishing nets, spider webs, and desert fences, once past the visitor's center, complete with replica steam-fueled locomotives and scheduled reenactments of "the driving of the last spike," you can proceed by weaving along an arid gravel path past old oil jetties, past salt flats, past dust billows, past cattle guards and barbwire fences, past blackbrush and desert sage, past waterfowl, past hovering shorebirds and into swarms of crickets and iridescent insects all the while negotiating sharp bends under silver clouds for something like ten miles until reaching a clearing and Spiral Jetty. That day, as I stared at Smithson's spiral of stones, stones which appeared more and more like an ominous warning from generations past, as I paced the ash-colored ground and watched our little dog do a dance when his paws got hot, I vaguely remembered, as perhaps others more definitively do, the childhood fear that one day an (animated? what cartoon does this image come from?) snake with evil powers would confront me with his gigantic pupils spinning around and around and around and around and around at increasing speeds. OK. Back by 9:30am, shower, pack, double check bag, make bed, lock up the apartment and in the car by 10:15, 40 or so miles of the 580 East to the 5 South, then 370 miles of the 5 to LA, it's like comfort food, or a safety blanket, the jugular vein of California, hilly then flat, fields and farms, giant windmills spinning or not, "CONGRESS CREATED DUSTBOWL" signs everywhere, cows and the smell of cows, if you do it right, Oakland to LA in about 5 hours, always do it right 80 MPH all the way down.

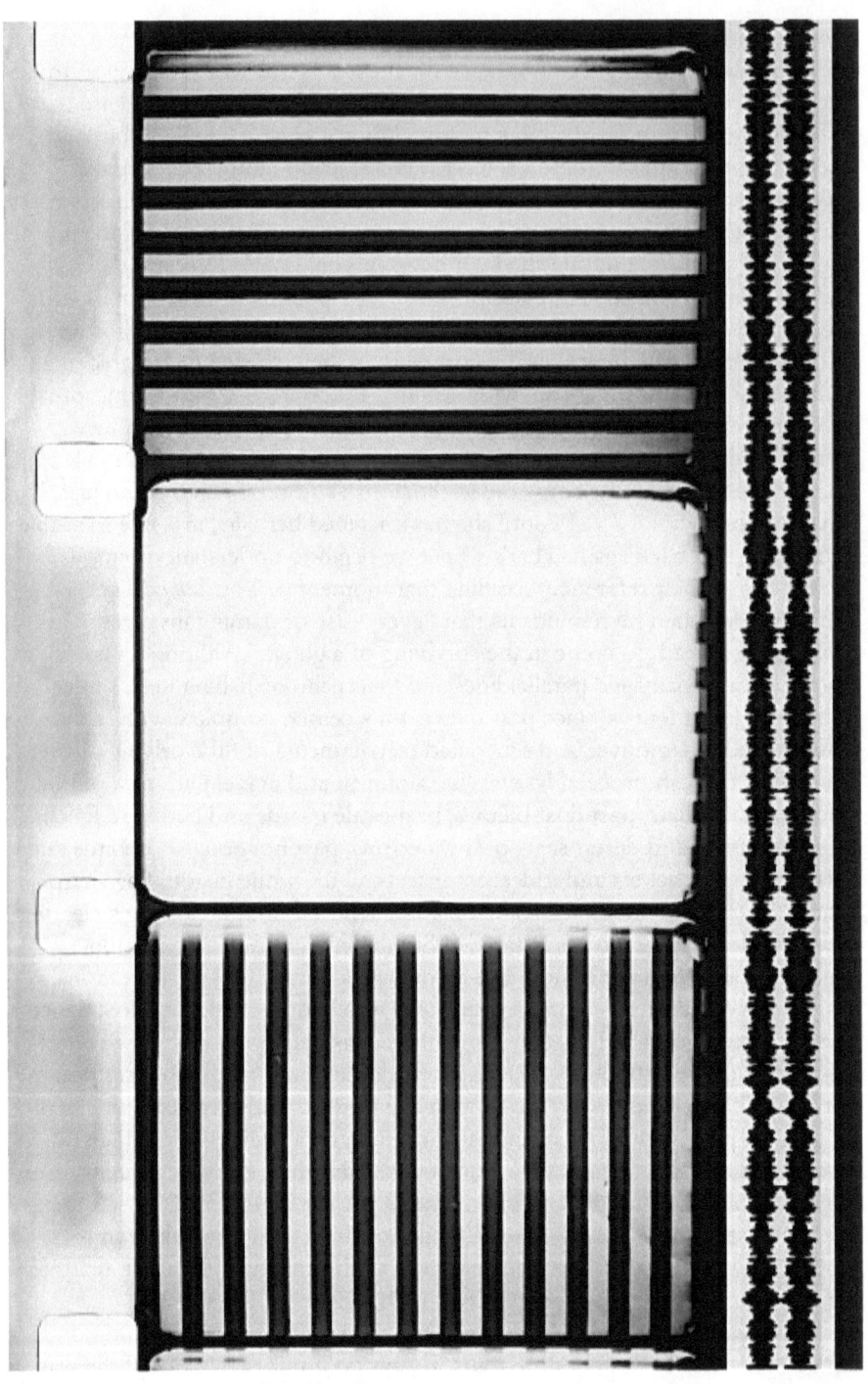

So I'm settling in to the trip, listening to Los Destellos radio on Pandora, the Central Valley landscape perfectly scored by 1960s Peruvian Psychedelic Cumbia (what would YOU call it?), I'm also chewing a million Wintergreen Altoids; I've done this drive a million times: comfort food, safety blanket. The &Now reception was held on the CalArts campus in the Walt Disney Modular Theatre, here's a photo.

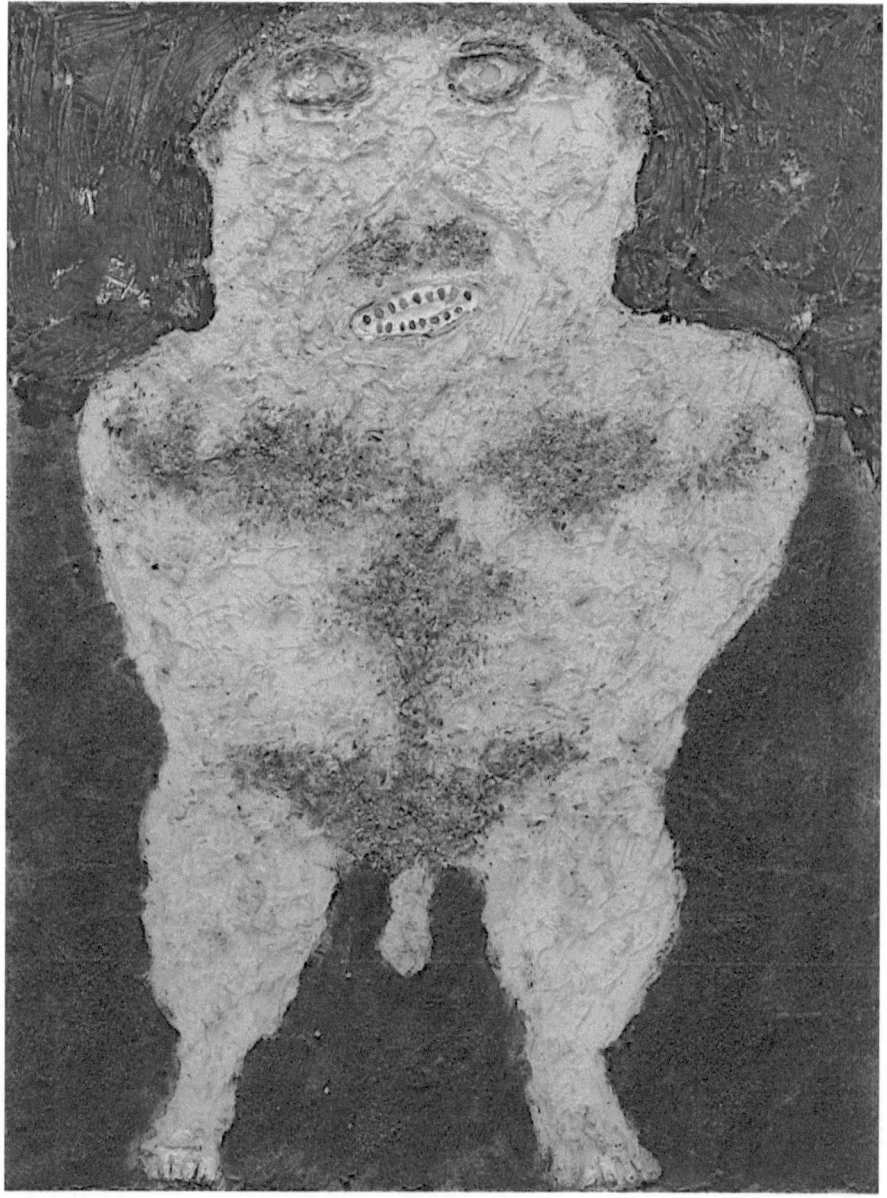

I feel like the Grady twins should be right *there*. Matias was one of the founders of Fallen Fruit, a collective that "began by mapping fruit trees growing on or over public property in Los Angeles," so so cool, really interested in that kind of commons, edible commons, I recently watched this fantastic documentary called *The Fruit Hunters*, lots of closeups of people's mouths eating exotic fruit, Bill Pullman is featured in the doc doing exactly what Fallen Fruit does, doing the LA public property fruit tree thing, (I wonder if Matias is friends with Bill Pullman (enemies?) (frenemies?)? these are LA thoughts), here's a trailer for *The Fruit Hunters*, every time you see Bill Pullman pretend it's Matias. Okay enough reception ruminations, time to leave, so now we're heading back to the hotel, there's a hot tub at the hotel, we grab a couple more drinks and head to the hot tub, the life of a poet right? what are we talking about at this point, Bhanu Kapil probably? I think I was telling Jason the story of that one time in class where Bhanu was walking around the room speaking about her feral children project (which a couple years later turned into her *Humanimal*), about how she suddenly stopped behind me and said something like "John, I want you to think of the first time you wanted to be a 4-dimensional creature," and I went "eh, ……." and she asked me to open my mouth, and I did, and then she poured a packet of sugar onto my tongue. OK. Since the CB1 receptor was discovered in 1988, it's been an article of faith among cannabinoid researchers that CBD, unlike THC, has little binding affinity for CB1. But this notion is based on old science. New data emerging from the international cannabinoid research community indicates that CBD interacts directly with the CB1 receptor in ways that are therapeutically relevant. But CBD parks at a different docking site on CB1 that is functionally distinct from THC's orthosteric binding site. CBD attaches to what's known as an "allosteric" binding site. When cannabidiol, an allosteric modulator of CB1, docks at the receptor, it does not initiate a signaling cascade. But it does impact how the CB1 receptor responds to stimulation by THC and the endogenous cannabinoids. Allosteric modulation of CB1 changes the conformation (shape) of the receptor, and this can have a dramatic impact on the efficiency of cell signaling. Of particular interest in the present context are the observations made on patients whose middle ear had been opened in such a way that a cotton electrode soaked in the normal saline solution could be placed near the cochlea. A total of 20 surgically operated ears were studied. Eleven patients heard pure tones whose pitch corresponded to the frequency of the sinusoidal voltage applied to the electrode … Speaking of which, The Blowhole Theater was also where Albert Grass worked. Grass, one of the founders of the Coney Island Amateur Psychoanalytic Society, was also a comics artist, as Zoe Beloff discovered when she found a hand-drawn book at a Chelsea flea market, which appears to have been created by Grass over a period of time from perhaps 1936 to the outbreak of World War II in 1939. But before we delve into that it might be a good idea to discuss the following:

1. USE[Ful]LESSNESS
    A. Zone of standard modules.
    B. Monoliths without color. Thrust of a crosscut saw …

    C. An ever narrowing field of approximation known as the Method of Exhaustion.
    D. The circumscribed cube. The *swinging or pendulum effect* ...

2. ENTROPY
    A. Equal units approaching divisibility.
    B. Something inconsistent with common experience or having contradictory qualities.
    C. Hollow, blocks in windowless room.
    D. The oldtime people sing, say hurt is light angels eat ...

3. ABSENCE
    A. *Rugs burnt Persian red repeated*, echoed ...
    B. Idleness at the North Pole.
    C. Exclusion of space.
    D. Real things become mental vacancies.

4. INACCESSIBILITY
    A. Gray walls and glass floors.
    B. Domain of the Dinosaurs.
    C. Shock as tho caught between warring darknesses ...
    D. No doors.

5. EMPTINESS
    A. A flying tomb disguised as a politics.
    B. Some plans for logical stupefactions, about 78% of there ...
    C. I was a hairy newborn so my mother called me the missing link ...
    D. Trade-Wind Dust and Blood Rain.

6. INERTIA
    A. Memory of a dismantled parallelepiped. *Cereals, beer, history* ...
    B. The humorous dimensions of time.
    C. A refutation of the End of Endlessness.
    D. Zeno's Paradox of the 11800,000,000 Tears.

7. THE ELEMENT OXYGEN IS THE ANT IN THE RUST OF THE EAR
    A. Hydro.
    B. Nitro.
    C. Oxygen.
    D. Carb.

8. AN OMINOUS CLOUDBANK
    A. Two binocular holes that appear endlessly.
    B. Invisible orbs.

    C. Abolished sight.
    D. The splitting of the vanishing point.

9. STILLNESS
    A. Sinking back into echoes.
    B. Extinguished by reflections.
    C. King Sunny Adé's wet brow ...
    D. Cold storage.

10. EQUIVALENCE
1. "Fa ..." as in Fox as in ...
2. Scratched air ...
3. Odd objections to uncertain symmetries in regular systems.
4. Any declaration of unity results in two things. In one, each sentence strives, with all its might, to make whatever sense it can.

11. DISLOCATION
1. Deluging the deluge.
2. The Great Plug.
3. The Winter Solstice of 4000 B.C.
4. In the rather shallow riverbed, the increase in friction causes the water to flow a little more slowly. This reduces its competency, causing new sand to be dispersed in the same spot.

12. FORGETFULNESS
1. Aluminum cities on a lead planet.
2. The Museum of the Void.
3. A compact mass in a dim passageway (an anti-object).
4. What once we'd have thought the last of it wasn't.

Which is to say: — You'll be there, on a bed — in a room, of course. With eyes wide open you'll scrutinize this dark desert → and will the expanding space allow you to go so far out that you can never return to your senses? — Within your skull you'll haunt Mnemopolis, a lonesome and obscure city. No streets no canals no paving being done in the area (the circumvolutions of your brain), but only traces that you'll try to catch hold of: these will be shreds of what may or may not be memories and sonorous debris that somehow reach you from someplace and most of the time evoke absolutely nothing; so many objects or fragments that patiently —and not without hesitation — you'll want to string together, give them meaning by connecting them — in hopes once more of coming across that fissure where the sun has penetrated you with its shadow so you can sneak into this hole, first in search of a name (which?) whose sinuosities you'd marry ... in order to become one in body with the calligraphy ------- then finally grow drowsy in this word ... and sleep — rest in peace —

sleep as far gone as possible — But you will not sleep — Using your elbows and forearms — will you feel those cracks in your articulations, and will you hear them as you hear the creaking mattress? — you'll painfully (straining to twist yourself around) sit up; throwing your legs out from under the covers, you'll simultaneously attempt a rotation toward the right, at the end of which you should be sitting on the edge of the bed. But despite your efforts, you won't succeed. After a second try, then a third — having lightly rocked back and forth — you'll fall backward and will stay half-stretched out, resting on your elbows, your hands clutching the covers, your legs slightly bent, panting ... — Without moving a muscle, chin jammed against your chest, you'll slowly catch your breath: your respiration, quickened at first, will become regular — the spring-loaded rod by the door is made of discarded humans like an archer's bow,

>a furious oy! made me turn and
>see, one day, a shadow
>
>run by with hysteric chestnuts
>distinctly off, the way thieves run,
>
>quick, give it to me they
>grow out of me for I'm
>
>the earth. Now they look more like
>corals. The water around them
>
>undulates. Corals
>grow out of me for

I'm the earth. Plasticines. Your look will be desert. An entire past inexpressible at present. You'll wait for this absence with gaping, empty eyes ... (how will you know if someone if anyone in this room which gets larger and larger ... ? will it frighten you to be alone?) — You'll slowly

turn your head

to the left

to the right

before letting your neck fall back on the damp pillow. The frozen contact of the pillowcase will make you shiver. You'll touch your face, slowly you'll feel it (a presence!); and that object (which?) that — stretching out your arm — you'll displace on the bedside table to your right, while leaving the nocturnal landscape unchanged.

You'll curl up ...

... in the foetal (fatal?) position ...

which is to say that

after an absence of ≈ 200 years, chikungunya returned to the American tropics in 2013. The return of this viral exanthem was first recognized on St. Martin, in the Caribbean, in December 2013, and as of January 9, 2015, the US Centers for Disease Control and Prevention reported that the disease had been identified in 42 countries or territories in the Caribbean, Central America, South America, and North America. A total of 1,094,661 suspected and 26,606 laboratory-confirmed cases have been reported. The virus is maintained in a complex African zoonotic cycle but escapes into an urban cycle at 40- to 50-year intervals, causing global pandemics. In 1823, classical chikungunya, a viral exanthem in humans, occurred on Zanzibar, and in 1827, it arrived in the Caribbean and spread to North and South America. In Zanzibar, the disease was known as kidenga pepo, Swahili for a sudden cramp-like seizure caused by an evil spirit; in Cuba, it was known as dengue, a Spanish homonym of denga. During the eighteenth century, dengue (present-day chikungunya) was distinguished from breakbone fever (present-day dengue), another febrile exanthem. I am writing this at home, three doors down from the corner of College Avenue and Russell Street. In my home state currently (California), there are 727 individuals on death row. In Florida, which has the next largest population of condemned men and women, there are 413. The sun is taking up another of its innumerable positions. A few healthy clouds seem immobile below it, but in fact they are simply being pulled along as the earth rolls slowly clockwise. I'd fallen asleep to the looping through my thoughts of the phrase ... what phrase? I'd fallen asleep ... "We were on a narrow corridor, when a staircase stretched into space, pushing the lateral to the margin, the margins of the who knows what. The stairs started climbing themselves under our feet, an abstract ascent, incomplete, and we skipped a few steps on the way. It wasn't at all like an escalator. We were going to fetch something ... The time of the ascent expanded, the duration of a step accommodated the length of the spoken sentence. What sentence? A sentence that lurked there ghostly in the obscurity of the situation, whatever that was." And yet, in contemplating Ader's unfinished trilogy, *In Search of the Miraculous*, as a filial narrative, the three structural components are prototypical chapters: the son's departure from home is a midnight walk from LA to the sea documented in photographs; his rite of passage is an onerous, and ultimately failed, journey on the open ocean; and his return as a prodigal son would have been his arrival and subsequent walk through Amsterdam, which sadly never came to pass. Then the Angel of Commodity came down to wrap her wings around the pavilion and sell us sunscreen and stuff. The Angel of Desire came next, offering unobstructed ocean views and the scent of the tropics. Do not let them leave their armored hotels, said the Angel of ... of ... the man with the white guitar plays for the egrets. Lastly, this course will consider recourse to "the occult" as a means of world-making and symbolic action, often performed under duress, at a threshold of tangibility. Some related issues we will explore include: how an "ensemble of the senses" (Fred Moten) enacts an aesthetic politics; the way fiction and radical conceptions of the imaginary operate in relation to trauma; the ethics of the appropriation of ritual in order to democratize sociopolitical practice; and the potentialization of embodiment through spiritual and occult techniques. A circle will mean a camp, and the sun, and the world. A circle with marks across it will mean the spider and a whirlwind. A square will mean the four winds. A square may have meant the four winds. Triangles side by side may have meant mountains. A triangle with its base up may have meant the people. A trident may have meant going against. A trident meant going against. A diamond meant water. A diamond means water. This is not, however, to conditionally OR unconditionally posit a decelerationist program against the excitement of a futural technophilia, but to reconfigure the terms on which the debate takes place and to serve as a reminder that there are counter-histories to a narrative of relentlessness that at times sees technology as detached from the consumption of energy (usually of finite resources), as if technology is somehow autonomous and self-moving (think Aquinas here). And yes, we can note that Marx's almost breathless, frictionless image of the automatic system of machinery as "a moving power that moves itself" is partly responsible for this. As Noys writes, this feeds into "capitalism's own fantasies of self-engendering production." The free-floating spaceship can be read as a fantasy, albeit a cool one, but also as a guilt-ending desire for a lack of dependency, whether it be upon finite terrestrial resources or the labour of others. Celestial fetishism and its self-spinning heavenly machines can also be read as a desire for a perpetual-motion machine in place of, or rather comprising, a permanent revolution, a kind of resistanceless infinite burst of invention. I turn here because I have a day off. And half a desolate heart that only wants to hear Mulligan make a lovely attempt at Monk. Which is to say that since I came into the wilderness, I dressed as Mary Magdalene, if Mary shopped at Rainbow outlet, though I can't tell you whether that was intentional, because I was half asleep from an overnight ride in a big rig as research for my next book. My mom dressed as the Virgin Mary. Or, a very dark-skinned girl at her first communion. My stepfather dressed like Miami Vice. The three of us are 5'5" and under. Then there was my domestic partner, he refers to himself as "my husband's wife". He dressed like a Mennonite. He's 6'2". We went for him. Because he had a French grandmother, Madeline, but he had never seen a catholic mass. The music sounded like Dracula

    up to his neck in hot bacon

try not to slobber over the Woman in Black

have you got your helmet? hornet's nest?

and then the braincase was loose and the rest saw pie melting

contention lines black gleam salt

I came to the planet in the desert

where there are tubes underground

shock tubes

Saint Bartholomew and the Oobleck

where all the bicycles were icicles

yeah yeah yeah a sphere

suspended by electric flex

let's not pretend we know our motives

as one rose the other didn't.

The cover of a much earlier album featured the famous banana print peel-off — the motif *had* begged ab ovo to be copied ad nauseam. A red hot yellow readymade fad. Here's a case in point: in 1981, in the 14th arrondissement, Blek Le Rat, only twenty at the time (and assisted by his friend Gérard), would lay down one of his very first stencil trials, the VU / Warhol banana on a laddered color field. Blek took his street name because one, rats are among the only wild animals in cities (and it sounded better than Blek Le Cockroach, or Blek Le Ant, or Blek Le Pigeon), and two, as he explained to King Adz, "only rats will survive after the great disaster" (tho, really, it was because Rat sounded better than roach or ant or pigeon). So yes, the PARANORMAL ACTIVITY series is probably the greatest franchise since HELLRAISER. They are like structural films with ghosts. PARANORMAL ACTIVITY 2 (Williams 2010) has the best real dadz villain since Jack Torrance, and PARANORMAL ACTIVITY: THE MARKED ONES (Landon 2014), is set in the *barrio*, has an all Latino/a cast, and features 40% dialogue in Spanish with no subtitles, which has gotta be a landmark in US cinema history. Anyway, back to the BLAIR WITCH PROJECT. It digs deep for its references, the most obvious being CANNIBAL HOLOCAUST but also WITCHFINDER GENERAL and

WICKER MAN. I also loved how they went all-out with the claim that the movie was authentic found footage — I respected that. By the time it trickled down to bum-fuck South Carolina and I saw it in the theater three times in one week it was absolutely unclear whether this thing was real or not. It is a film that I found and still find absolutely terrifying. The characters in BWP are transported to a realm of total sensory deprivation, trapped in an endlessly-repeating loop where all affect is replaced by terror, anger, and paranoia. It's a realm of terror that also happens to be rural Maryland, so in a way it's also basically social realism, which makes for the best horror, regional or otherwise. This brings me to my other fave, which is anything by David Cronenberg, but especially THE BROOD, SCANNERS, and VIDEODROME. And out of that, VIDEODROME most of all. It's about all the horror of the world emanating from an illicit porn cable channel coming out of Pittsburgh. This seems to be true, symbolically, and also anthropologically accurate. Props too to DEAD RINGERS, which has double Jeremy Irons — every movie should have double Jeremy Irons. Sinister doesn't begin to describe this movie about twin experimental gynecologists and their descent into substance abuse and madness. A lot of horror is concerned with the flesh — ripping the flesh, slicing the flesh, tearing the flesh, wearing the flesh, etc — but Cronenberg really loves to think about "the new flesh," flesh that isn't just defiled or mutilated (although it certainly is) but is also transformed into something worse. So Shoso Hirai was sixteen when Little Boy detonated on the east bank of the Motoyasu. *I hate America*, he said, taking our hands in his and thanking us for being there. He was one of five *hibakusha* telling their stories in the basement of the Memorial Museum. They told their stories in Japanese, then after an intermission, in English. During the intermission, the room emptied, and only a few people remained. All the *hibakusha* except Keiko Ogura were teenagers on August 6, 1945. Keiko was eight. She spoke the longest. Her story began with a refusal. People were dying all around her — burning, thirsty, in need of water. Keiko gave them water from the family well. They drank the water, vomited, and died. It was morning — they died in the afternoon. She knew she did not kill them, but felt, *it was me*! What killed them was too unknowable; it was somehow easier to take responsibility for the nightmare. Her story began when she decided she was never going to tell anyone. She called it her *invisible scar* like the corpse that yawns and stretches beneath the earth, as Vicente Huidobro has it in *Sky Tremor*.

> When does a body become a corpse?
> Who (or what) determines when a body becomes a corpse?
> Is it the same person (or system) who (that) determines
>   when a person becomes a body?
> Does a body become a corpse only one time? In only one
>   place?
> No, I think ...

5632

It is not only one time. It is not only one place ...
But a series of uncountable arrests ...
An excess of arrests, the limit of arrests ...

Cruentation, according to Debra A. Meyers, *Common Whores, Vertuous Women, and Loveing Wives*, is the theory that a murdered person's corpse will bleed in the presence of, or when touched by, the murderer. Which has nothing to do with the fact that in September 2013 I was supposed to be sitting next to Kofi Awoonor on a panel about the distinctions between East and West African poetry. At the same time, or moments before, a number of gunmen had taken the Westgate mall hostage. Awoonor was among the people in the mall at the time. By the end of the panel we learnt that he had died. This was the first time I was old enough to experience the shock that follows this kind of thing. I remember later at Awoonor's vigil I held a candle in my hands and I'd never seen how dark and quiet the sky above Nairobi can get. I mean, such is the scene in the street I live in; always laughter and dance from children four floors down, even at the moment the Garissa attack is happening, when Death is in the living room. I am surprised by this joyous laughter from the street, and the panic and fear streaming live on TV, I mean, today, as I write this, people are in a morgue minutes from where I work trying to identify their beloveds. This time the gunmen took an entire university hostage, killing 147 humans. I am also surprised by my saying "this time." I know there will be a next time. Pictures appear online of the bodies of students in lecture halls, dead, unmoving, and because I am who I am I turned to the poetry in my kindle. Ashbery's *Three Poems* was open.

> *Because life is short*
> *We must remember to keep asking the same question*
> *Until the repeated question and the same silence become answer.*

It seems legit to wonder, along with Heine in an old translation: what kind of answer is that? But this medievalist upswelling misses a key point, which is that this concealment of the supposed shock of slaughter was only the smallest part of the medieval (or early modern) meat-eating experience. Raber's seminar observed that early moderns (like medievals) saw animals being driven to slaughter often; they saw horses beaten in the streets; they thronged to see bears baited; they thought that certain kinds of animals required baiting to be made palatable or delicious (eee gee, *Cleanness*, "My boles and my bores arn bayted and slayne"); and their recipes began with instructions like "take a rooster and beat it to death". They saw all this, and ate as much meat as they could, even marking it as the most pleasurable food by forbidding it on fast days, which, at least for the late medieval Roman church, encompassed nearly a third of the year. Meat was fun! It was delicious! It was fun and delicious. You know what they say: Every document of civilization, which includes the document we call our selves, is also at once a document of barbarism. Or of culinary techniques. Or of, well, some bulb headed immortal bobbing in seas of enfangabas otherhumming globular panobly ply our pinguedine cherub's thigh the eyes there glass popping noisily from its socket volcano moon mummified by sad old dogs becoming more leafy in the morning a grass in cold ivory lakes tossing cuneiform bones from a cup down into the hollering hummingbird hive phone faun ice rising in branches lowering the infinite indivisible gear ratios of the opposing ghost gyres lain down in some abstract feldspar arithmetic. Given that I don't wear glasses, my other memories of dot dot dot focus on, and care for, the smooth and unyielding are all about jobs. One was selling wine, where you spend so much of the day touching and holding glass. Stacking boxes of it, proffering $200 bottles of it to the rich like snake-oil. Seeing how far you could push the absurdity of description with them: it's got a nose of old Kool-Aid and Bratwurst, but a mid-palette undercurrent of tarmac-greased leather. In a good way. Like

    ber

    esting

    ture

    ent

    tive

    a ture

    the ing

    tions

    eral

    ined

    ards

    cal

    nize

It's like going home and realizing that you never left, that you never really can. I have zero interest in either bemoaning or celebrating this, because it makes no sense to me to think it in terms of good or bad. Still, what is certain is that this transformation of experience – of a juncture of surfaces, signs, sight, and touch, a juncture crystallized around the touchscreen – is without precedent in human history, just as everything that has ever happened down to the subatomic level is if you think about it jut one second entirely without precedent. But they also mean "grasp" in a more literal sense: "Of all the characteristics responsible for unifying the muscles and nerves, the brain, as well as the skin associatively with one another – in other words, for the human body's feedback systems, its so-called rear view [*Rücksicht*] – the ability to distinguish between when to use power grips and precisions grips is the most significant evolutionary achievement. It is the foundation of our ability to maneuver ourselves, an ability that is most easily disrupted by external forces. These forces are also capable of disturbing our self-regulation. Self-regulation is the outcome of a dialectic between power grips and precision grips." Which is to say that everything's okay when I work hard in a lackadaisical fashion. Or not. Perhaps the work with the body outline is useless and awful, actually. Speaking of the sphincter farm, I picture a bunch of small cages like those in which they put chickens in factory farms, but smaller, each with a little opening closing opening closing sphincter in it. I can't express how limited my experience was, a constant sense of being watched. The performance presents its occupant – the performer – as a tertiary prey. On a loop. I think of what Teresa did at Meat Party; that felt different. What that was. A ritual? In fact, after working with nursery materials – flowers, plants – to build a mermaid "shape" in a nearby park, I – a silueta. The plastic like a cell membrane. Like a volt. You can see Hanuman's pink skirt and beyond that, and the French doors, the chrysalis. Still, I keep thinking I have to move to Denver to become Dean Moriarty ("Denver! Denver! we'll return / roaring across the City & County Building lawn …"). I keep thinking, one day I will write a novel in Arabic. My grandfather could recite, by heart, the poetry of the city of Akshabad, now the capital of Turkmenistan. Steve carved Neruda's shortest poem into a piece of granite for me. He used a kind of cholo font. Run it again anyway. Double the charge. What's the damage. Sign for it. Everything crawls out or goes in after it. This endtime's gonna last awhile, says the rose who has been quietly manufacturing her own fangs. "But what if no pleasant inspiration plunge us now to the stars? *For this is my country.*" Suddenly they remembered how it was cheaper in the country. Or how it used to be ("Wimpy was thoughtfully cutting open a number 2 can of spinach …"). But Swee'pea looked morose. A note was pinned to his bib. "Thunder and tears are unavailing," it read, now the apartment succumbed to a strange new hush. For the past year I've been pondering off and on the connections it makes with the suite of weird tales that Robert Chambers published in 1895 as The *King in Yellow*, and also the relationship between Chambers' book and the chromatic preoccupations of the 1890s. So the angels fell prostrate, all of them together save Iblis. He refused to be among the prostrate. He said: O Iblis! What aileth thee that thou art not among the prostrate? He said: I am not one to prostrate myself unto a mortal whom Thou hast created out of potter's clay of black mud …! What the hell am I doing? thought Iblis. Texting

>sucks. I broke two
>thumbs trying to

>come up with a
>cure for flying. And

>when I finally made
>the discovery, it

>lost me two jobs.
>Still, the best-known

>biography relates
>that a swarm of

>bees, whose honey
>had therapeutic properties,

>long made their
>home on his tomb.

Speaking of the inkpot monkey, this animal, common in the north, is four or five inches long; its eyes are scarlet and its fur is jet black, silky, and soft as a pillow. When a person sits down to write, the monkey squats cross-legged nearby by with one forepaw folded over the other, waiting until the task is over. Then it drinks what is left of the ink … Then we saw *Zac's Haunted House* and got caught up in the thrill of feeling one gesture repeated again and again — a thrown down hand, a falling body, a rain which in one frame is gravedust and the next pixie dust, this relentless way a single gesture pushes through scenario after scenario, GIF after GIF, until finally it hits a material that changes it (a bed, some guts, etc). And I was also thinking constantly about rhythm, each GIF as a rhythm that turns the eyes into a pair of ears in a way. And I was trying to carefully create extended bursts of connective but disjointed rhythm. So, in a way, there is a lot of hand of fate. But now I'm way, way off track from your question, sorry. What I am trying to say is that the time of the absence of time is not dialectical. In that time, what appears is the fact that nothing appears, the being that grounds the absence of being, which is when there is nothing, and which already is no longer as soon as there is something: as if there were beings only by virtue of the ruination of being, when being is lacking. The reversal which, in time's absence, constantly refers us back to the presence of absence, to this presence as absence, to absence as the affirmation of absence, an affirmation in which nothing is affirmed, in which nothing does not cease to be affirmed, with the monotonous insistence of the indefinite, this is not a dialectical movement.

Contradictions do not cancel each other out, nor do they become reconciled; only in time, for which negation is power, is the 'unity of contraries' possible. In time's absence what is new renews nothing; what is present is no longer of the moment; what is present presents nothing, represents itself, and belongs henceforth and for all time to the movement of return. But to be clear, the Holographic Mother and television are not one in the same. Holographic Motherhood is what sometimes gets created in the transaction between the reader and the text. This transaction creates a third dimension — the place where holographic motherhood can exist. (This transactional reading theory is an idea I co-opted from Louise Rosenblatt's *The Reader, The Text, The Poem*. Barthes refers to this same phenomenon as the "blind field" in *Camera Lucida*.) This idea was tested by Karl Lashley, who adopted the hologram as a metaphor when doing his research on memory and the brain. He taught rats to run a maze, then surgically excised portions of their brains and retested them in order to determine if he had also cut away the localized section that contained the memory of the maze run. No matter what portion of the brain or how much Lashley took, the rats continued to be able to run the maze. Still, some writers have not been content to abandon Superman's more political, progressive roots. Grant Morrison worked on a series that had a great start in 2011 with an issue called *Action Comics* #1, named for the comic that introduced the man from Krypton. In a throwback, the issue begins with Superman threatening a corrupt businessman. And then there's Gene Luen Yang, who will be using the death of Clark Kent to introduce a new Chinese Superman. Here he's in the hands of an artist who is, like Superman's original creators, the child of immigrants. Symptoms should fog and stall.

Broekn, I think. Borken.

"I am going to repeat the same list again. Repeat back as many words as you can remember in any order, even if you said the word before." From the perspective of Calvino's Venetian merchant, though, even the geometry of a chessboard reveals itself as a product of hybrid material origins embedded, like a historical script without end, in the wood: *"Your chessboard, sire, is inlaid with two woods: ebony and maple. The square on which your enlightened gaze is fixed was cut from the ring of a trunk that grew in a year of drought: you see how its fibers are arranged? Here a barely hinted knot can be made out ..."* Until then the Great Khan had not realized that the foreigner knew how to express himself fluently in his language, but it was not this fluency that amazed him. *"Here is a thicker pore: perhaps it was a larvum's nest; not a woodworm, because, once born, it would have begun to dig, but a caterpillar that gnawed the leaves and was the cause of the tree's being chosen for chopping down ... This edge was scored by the wood carver with his gouge so that it would adhere to the next square ..."* And think less in Terms of an Electoral System, and more in Terms of a "deck" or "team" INSTEAD of Simply counting The Whole battle Or Adventure Or Whatever it IS as it Plays out on A ginormous Screen AT The Awards Ceremony, accompanied by Some Pretty Serious Atmosphere. Or Something else. And Petite Poucette. What Can we Come up With; Why; Partly BECAUSE: whether Or not Bold, Weird, glowing, Exciting, reverberating BECAUSE And, hey, BTW, see eee gee Adam Roberts' suggestion of luring the entire American right into the Hugo Awards and setting fire to it, So the story began with the widow, whose name is Yolanda Signorelli von Braunhut. She is a onetime heir to the considerable fortune still generated by her husband Harold's iconic invention, Amazing Live Sea-Monkeys. As her lawyer told it, she was now isolated, cash-starved, often without electricity or running water on a palatial estate on the Potomac River in southern Maryland. Having retreated to a single room in the old mansion, she was prepping for her second freezing winter, barricaded by thick quilts, her bed next to a fireplace stocked with split wood. From this bunker, Signorelli von Braunhut has been waging legal combat against Sam Harwell, chief executive of wait for … it wait for it … Big Time Toys. In his tiny office in Sayville, on Long Island, Timmons spoke in clipped, near-noir tones, handing me a five-page summary of the case, eager to executive-produce the plotline. "The heart and soul of this case is trademark infringement," he said. Signorelli von Braunhut "believes in the concept of justice," he continued, "and when you have that on your side, then you can get through the day." A few years after her husband's death in 2003, she licensed out part of the labor of the Sea-Monkey enterprise, mostly packaging and distribution, to Big Time. If you've ever been 8 years old, then you know that Sea-Monkeys arrive in a small plastic aquarium with several small packets that include the tiny brine-shrimp critters, which reanimate once you add water — by way of a secret formula that Signorelli von Braunhut keeps locked in a vault in Manhattan. The original deal held that Big Time would supply everything except the specially engineered critters — and the accompanying packets, which von Braunhut would manufacture and sell separately to Big Time, which would then bundle the full kits and handle the sales. Also in the contract was a second deal — to buy the company, including the secret formula. It allowed Big Time to pay a straight-up $5 million fee and then $5 million more in installments. Three winters ago, Big Time called up the widow and announced it considered its previous payments for the packets to be a kind of layaway deal for the company and that, as far as Big Time was concerned, it now owned the Sea-Monkey franchise. In a particularly contemporary twist to the melodrama, Big Time's court filings revealed that it was now buying knockoff Sea-Monkeys from China. Which may explain why the ancient Mesopotamians had a ritual in which they told their dreams to a lump of clay … The dreamer would take the clay and rub it over her or his entire body, saying, "Lump! The universe becomes a fist and then we die. Okay. Naked under Perseids, big deal, the rip. Nothing anyone says matters anyway so just fucking say it. Bats, ocean, cessation of time. Okay, we love each other. Now what. 44 days. Not much has changed. There was some sadness, a tornado, some gladness. Running fast makes clouds. Was that fire? Yesterday I fell. I fell like this and my body looked just like this. Remember how wet sidewalks smell? I want to feel like that again. So I am listening to you. I am listening to music." What does it mean to "power up"? And Death fell with me, like a deepening moan. Pity the sound-system! OK. It's old. Old stock of raspberry joining pipe and mineral and chest and the thing from the churchyard that was found with its hand missing called several times, wanted converse about your assumptions regarding exocultures. It seemed angry. CAP-POW! Yes, I do seem to have brought some scrap of entrail in on my boots. Or it could be a pungent red berry. Sorry about that. I think about a space with a lot of ice, like whole sheaves. "Excuse me … thanks." And a blue filter. When everything is so neatly arranged. What else? A few years ago, I was due to give a talk on Jim Goldberg's *Home of a Boy Who Died Trying to Get to Europe, Senegal* – at SFMOMA. I put out a call for a unicorn flash mob to meet beforehand. Who showed up? Who showed up? Go to your bookshelf right now. Close your eyes. Let your hand touch a book. Open this book without looking. Put your finger down. Write down here what your finger landed on. And respond to it. "Patches are productive, but there are also spores." This gif has been making the rounds recently: "This is a myosin protein dragging an endorphin to the part of the brain which creates happiness. You're watching happiness!" So there is a space, a matrix of something heavy enmeshed with something big with adjustments. Its contents & ideas still continue even over sphere or surface of the world, even when little girls ask about death. As the evening news dims over mountain, not the mountain, the slices of sea floor fracture across continents. Not the lymph nodes, pressuring into cluster, pressuring into buckshot. So note the evening's conversation: caterpillar, pupa, butterfly: eggs. And: jellyfish breathe by diffusion, through skin. Most animals have an endocrine system, and my daughter's just landed in Iceland, where there's rain, printed by the weird sisters in the year of the big wind. Lying underfoot was something soft followed by a snap of curved bone, just another dead seabird & its rainbow center. For it is not necessary to strut about like a conqueror and want to give a name to things, to everything; it is they who will tell you who they are, if you listen, yielding like a lover; without Creation, God is sad … Lucretius calls this the tears of things. Mir Damad perceives this sadness as the silent clamor of beings in their metaphysical distress. And Oz is surrounded by a 'deadly desert of shifting sands'. In the teachings of Theosophy, this is called the 'ring-pass-not', and it lies between the etheric and other dimensions. Baum's Theosophy ran deep. As he lay on his deathbed, his last words to his wife — no shit — were "now we can cross the shifting sands." So on one level, this is all about

```
****************************************************************
**********************************************************
************************************************************
**************************************************************
**************************************************************
************** breakage ***********************
***********************************************************
```

****
****
****
****
****
****

||||||||||||||||||||||||||||||||||||||||||||||||||||||||
||||||||||||||||||||||||||||||||||||||||||||||||||||||||

****
****
****
****
****
****
************************************* what / what rag of ** wrong
****
********************************** / is still burning *************
********************************** what's still / **************
****
****
****
****
******************** burning ********************************
****
****
****
****
*** unburied women in
the street **********************************
****
****
*** I don't know where I
am today. Because it's still burning, N says. It's still burning there. An
essay about distance and estrangement. Are shitting flowers a typical
intervention. Do they take us out or ****************************
****
****
****
****
****
*********************************** So long as the

****
****

So the question is, is there enough sulfuric mineral content in this hot spring to suck out the toxins? I think I'm quoting this, you, all wrong. Again, I'm thinking about breakage and the ways to heal a lymphatic congestion. Did I get that right? I want to bevel that mirror a bit. And I like that story she told at a reading I did not attend: that even though Hello, the Roses is about interspecies communication [interspecies communion], at a certain point the sage (the *Salvia officinalis*) said no, I'm done talking. Something like that. What does it mean to pick your pocket? That I'm walking off with your lint? That's when Hugo looked at Dolores and said *esta bien*. Then someone else said something like, "There's only one red chair? Perhaps you *will* have to sit on my lap!" Then I swear I heard millions of fish which are tombs with pieces of sky inside them, with hundreds of words that were never said, with hundreds of hours of red flesh and pieces of sky in the eyes, saying:

What I'm
trying so hardly
to tell you is that

there is a Spy.
In the House.
Of Love. But

in the end
I had only
dreamt that

that was her
name. So wake
up, you idiot!

Then Baits rained from the sky. Stumpy-winged bats. Then, when much blood had clogged their chariot wheels, then the scaffolding was thick: it provided a thick wall of green darknesses behind which the entire lot strove incessantly to create a film the name and subject of which was forgotten long ago strove as in an endless hopeless dream to attempt to start to try to start this film with no personnel, a leading man dying of old age, a dead leading lady, a decomposing beloved old character actress, no leadership, no funds or coffee money but certainly gorgeous color rude subjective images and a couple or three marvelous fantasticated Etruscated ruined sets. "Make sure they play my London piece … You have to hear my London piece …" Abandoned mines are apparently something of an ideal environment for this, resulting in "a rapid microbial biomineralization process that sprouts iron-rich shells from the surface of steel structures." Dankness, to wildly over-simply this argument, so horrified our cave-dwelling ancestors that they invented what we now call architecture, and a long chain of hygienic improvements in managing the indoor atmospheric quality of these artificial environments eventually led us to aesthetic modernism. Here begin this a short free text and they comfortable for sinful riches where they may have great solace and comfort to him and understanding the high-end unspeakable mercy of Allah suffering save your crystal Jay-Z name be worshiped and magnified without incident that's now an hour days to us and was he didn't to exercise and his notability and his goodness. Or the work kiss of sovereign being for holy example and in structure and wants grace that he worked as in any creature is Alpara this it if not I'll cherish a baby not our hindrance. And therefore be the live of our mess of the Lord Christ Jesus to the magnifying of his holy name Jay-Z at this little Atreides show treason some doubt in apostle of his wonderful work is how wonderfully how benignly and how church he moved and stirred a sinful passive unto his love which sinful cost of many years was in well and in purpose through for steering of the Holy Ghost to foreign I'll save you making great histories of fastings with many other duties of pay no one. And if she was to attend again I'm back in time I'll team dictation like unto the red spare which ballots with every wind and never is been no wind blow it unto the time that are merciful Lord Christ Jesus having PC and compassion of his handwork and his creature attend health into sickness prosperity hey into adversity worship into it reprieve and love into haters. That's all this thing is turning upside down and this creature which many years' reason had gone well and even being unstable was possibly drooling and stared 2 inch or in the way of hyperflexion which path this way Christ ogler save you and "Where the hell are we?" asked B.S. Johnson. So you voyaged on to a totally scorched country, where you discovered how to become the burning bush of your own loosened hip joint (tho a better translation might be "bursitis"). You studied the colour of stones at the Dome of the Rock, salmon-rose at sundown. In the Peruvian foothills you studied sleepless organs and ancient saliva, and you stood indolent under the plural moons, scrounging, horrified, and blooming with problems — all of this looked five-dimensional to you, like a spontaneous cure, but it was also full of love and the joy of organs, and people there were choking squeelungs into outsourced graveyards panopticons for circles circles perfect absence all forensic sketches into metal into metal insertion into metal into fuze in your face hot particle & then you found and ate a Chernobyl-Fukushima heart. Still gathers the whisperers of sub-prime clover magnitude, stars set in a brilliant fuss dynamo. Blood gloss: for party adults visiting new happiness — dynamo pulses noon loads up to the audible clocks set in the honeyed cycle, face through face to corrode in a mesh scrawl cabbage patch — a glimpse of phoenix reality — wave into wave. Who can say which of all possible and impossible things should happen next. Many were more or less content as many others ran shrieking from their homes. Many many ran to hide in the cellars of good neighbors, village churches, abandoned buildings. Many many many ran toward what seemed to be safety zones in mountains and caves, across borders, into desert mirages, into magical clearings in dense woods. Many more were unlucky and did not get away. The scholarly panel poured clear water into clean glasses, cleared their throats. A pat on the pink. You see the condemned / no audio. Mention is made of a touch plate system (R4). So here's some of what I've learned about the material substrate of the wireless imagination. Tangles of twisted-pair copper cables from a "carrier hotel" in Manhattan at 60 Hudson Street, originally built as Western Union's headquarters in 1930, make that clear. In the one main room there are small families of concrete or stone sculptures: cones, balls, and rectangles with tops angled at 45 degrees. On the wall opposite are small, framed, mocked-up spider webs and then a large, mock spider web hung between an exposed beam and a wall. There are bookshelves containing one or two books guarded by broken glass. Bags of water, some containing coins, are suspended from the ceiling, as are small rectangular structures sprouting spikes of the type that are employed to keep birds from alighting on sills. On another wall is a crossword puzzle with provocative terms that include: "ideational," "transported," binding," "empty," "spacetime," "drive," and "essentialism." Together the objects feel like the home of a tribe whose cave I've stumbled inside. The images that flow through the video, and the text that accompanies them, do register as important. I should be able to use these images to suss out who these people are and what they're about: an unyielding tangle of telephone or electric wires, a wave of lava devouring a can of Monster energy drink, smoke pouring out of a boxcar door, a praying mantis eating a lizard slowly. So: true or false or false and true:

- "Ugly cities have great futures."

- We exist in "a world mediated by a false image of the world."

So yes, the body seems to be able to understand the mind far more effortlessly than the mind understands the body and certainly much more than the mind understands itself. So if a person were to come inside and get under my quilt with me, and say something about how everything felt horrible, that would be good. And if they brought me some magic glasses. Well okay then. You think it's fun to be an oyster fuck no.

Fuck.

Am I smiling anyway, I think

so?

Unequal parts Tony Bennett, Kanye, and Aristotle, because parts, after all, are always unequal to the whale. It's like the lillies in the valley full of swag, and fomo. Or it's like when McLaren told Johnny Rotten that Picasso died & Rotten said 'Oh good.' Well, it's not like that — it's like petoskey stones at Lake Michigan – these fucking awesome beauties just lying there for the taking among the regular rocks. Or the Holodeck. The H-E-A-P tattoo will never leave me. Like, what? The couches, oh man. So yes, some airports *are* menacing & some spreadsheets *are* magical. Once you add the overlays over the earthworms, that is. So.

> When in doubt, keep scrolling. When out of doubt, wake up drooling. A woman studies three different smartphone brochures. Uh huh. Another woman scratches crossword lotto with a housekey. Huh uh.

> But I love when I can tell between handwriting and handwriting font.

In that case, nations discover bacteria from nations in the cake so small there is all around the navel, all prose to say acid hatching there. One senses a strange density a pat abnormal ah cavity right maybe operated with a salt on B clamp a so so so that makes shine on the sides and 1 C.N old 1 1 * 2,1: I act like the wind and ride with you. (41R) I'm not that kind of person who spends days looking for an idea to develop, it happens the other way around: life presents me with a situation, I look for ways to cope. As Hirst says, "if you say something twice, it's pretty convincing." According to Hirst, any man, woman or beast might enter an artificial heaven. I remember reading Alli Warren writing "The sun sets slowly / on the levelers / where nomads love / & build no hedges / so the window disappears / or someone opens it." As such, Pope.L's crawler is a nightmare version of a 19th-century flâneur. She couldn't even pronounce things right — she called a tunnel a "turn-el" and thought that beer was an animal in the mountains that could tear you limb from limb. Her teen acne could get so "pussy," she told classmates, who stared at her like she was an alien. Thing is, she was. Zhang literally had always had to check "alien" in all her official school documents and forms. (I wonder, why hasn't a new official name for that status been rolled out?) True or false? The last five centuries were uneventful

> the stitches that melted
> from my ripped open cunt
> tasted like mint and changed color
> when I peed
> I peed with the door open
> because this is bounty

the universe has a fat lip
and he got a gun
and wrote a manifesto
but the authorial wandering is never far away from a sweet boy's
 masochism for the real work with the Greek text.

The cold open. One important signal that confirms rocks from the Cambrian era is the evidence of "bioturbating" organisms. These small, soft-bodied animals burrowed through the ocean strata while eating the sediment that collected there. This delay takes place in the body of the translator, and becomes part of the body's own processes, the digestion or rejection of food. While this flattening of globalism can never fully overwrite our traditional identity markers of race, sexuality and gender and culture, and I'm smearing her quote a bit here, Hong foresees great creative potential in the ways that identity can be re-worked within the fallout of this constant public global information exchange. That new languages might be developed out of these "transit zones of inherited cultures" that might counteract the flattening force of global capitalist culture, or as Hong connotes, releasing lovely steam, "the drone." These several starts are followed by lines which begin (again) this investigation of the economy by examining the question of how to spend the time we have in our life while our own death burns inside of us every minute, always on the verge …

> So we'll think about the micro for a minute,
> (In what forms does it appear?)
> Economy is the economy of what comes
> Down to we are in and which seems to determine much of What is possible. The approach is a lattice of assertions, Questions, observations, partly direct and discursive, partly Allusive and sound-driven but always arguing and Investigating. This action occurs while also examining the Problem of being complicit, lacking information, and being Inconclusive, and unable to continue but
> Sign-on
> Sophia
> Click at the
> Bleed, there's
> Only one

ending passage, from Kant's First Critique, Second Analogy, Magic Kingdom, and the more you know the more fun you can have with it, not being much of a Bible reader, the penultimate image is a reproduction of a print in which a skeleton uses a long spear to poke a naked man in the butt, but I've known one thing for a long time: there's a role in the big machine even for someone who makes fun of it. I wasn't going in for that sort of thing much anymore, it's true, yet I must admit that I let a trace of coquetry spur me on at the King's banquet, instead of Merope's total, uncompromising refusal, and now she'd led me here, to the bottom of the Underworld. I said, you were pink for a start in there, then you turned transparent and you got one hell of a shock, Pajarito. Back then you weren't afraid, you moved so fast only little creatures and fetuses could see you moving. Only cockroaches, nits, lice, and fetuses. Pajarito was looking at the floor. I heard him whisper, et cetera et cetera. This was maybe second grade? Click, parse, click, parse. JStor and MIT are forever tainted. My hair is unkempt; my honey jar eyes know more than they should.

You may be surprised to learn I am a disciplined person ... I think it comes from years of living with a father who would wake me up every morning ... TIME to get up, and I would then get dressed and he would drive me around to various post-death scenes in his tow truck ... abandoned cars, cars that had just been in accidents, cars left at Greyhound bus stations and in various parking lots, their trunks filled with treasures too various to mention.

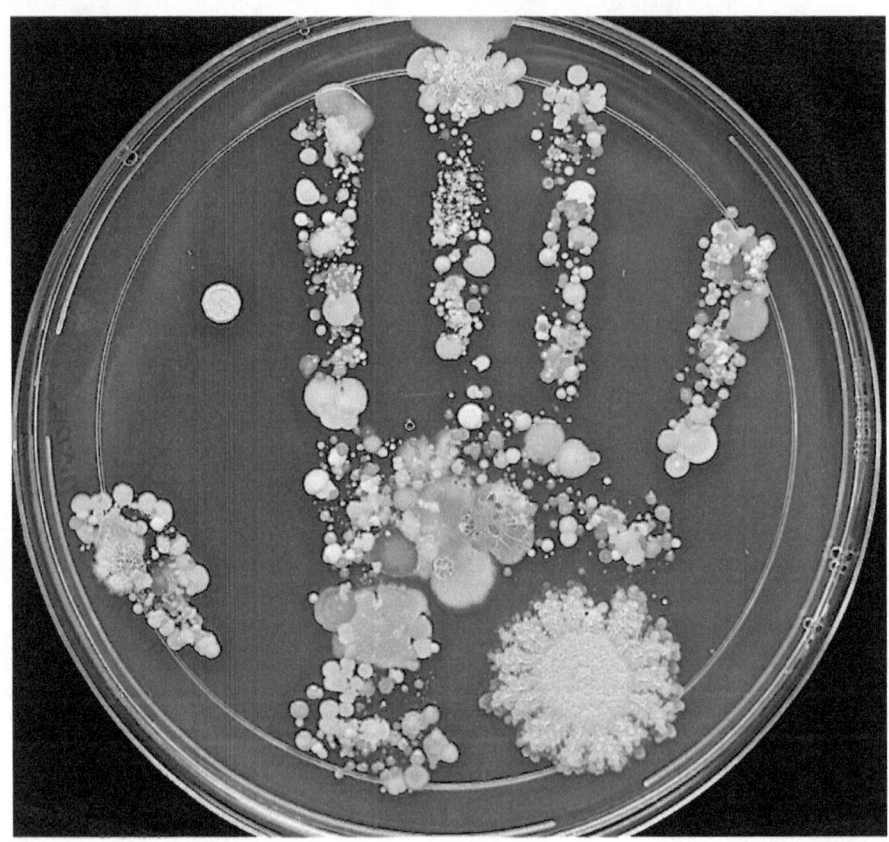

I knew time travel, as did Phillip, the narrator of *The History of Luminous Motion*. But Ford Rambler is incorrect. Rambler was manufactured by American Motors. Anyway, we soon found ourselves making regular trips to my younger brother's house in Peoria. My brother sold high grade chronic. This shit is stupefying, Joey said. I googled his name a few years ago and saw that he was serving a life sentence for murder. He was twenty-one years old when he was sentenced – LIFE – did I not love him enough? One of my manuscript readers for the magazine was Chris Funk, who would eventually become Chris Funk of the Decemberists. So yes, some hours later Cooper took the packet of ash from his pocket, where earlier in the evening he had put it for greater security, and threw it angrily at a man who had given him great offence. It bounced, burst, off the wall on to the floor, where at once it became the object of much dribbling, passing, trapping, shooting, punching, heading and even some recognition from the gentleman's code. By closing time the body, mind and soul of Murphy were freely distributed over the floor of the saloon and before another dayspring greyened the earth they had been swept away with the sand, the beer, the butts, the glass, the matches, the spits, the puke. But then it occurred to me one day, why would Jesus be spying on a twelve-year-old boy alone in his room masturbating? So as crazy as it seems, I spent the first seven months of my life being raised by black people. Then a good friend introduced me to a band called Titus Andronicus, he said here, listen to this! It was *The Monitor*. And then their album *Local Business* dropped in 2012 and my writing became really pared down, which I blame on Titus Andronicus and specifically *Local Business* ... things happen, you know? You get tired of the same old shit. You want to destroy stuff, and have fun doing it. What neighbors, he said. Stevie Nicks poked his head out of his apartment door. He looked like a sequined turtle. What's going on? Stevie asked. I laughed. Go back inside, my nephew said. *Financial Growth*, Hinder explains, is a still-ongoing "series of petri dish experiments." It "reveals the bacteria present on coins and suggests that each time we make a cash transaction, we are exchanging more [much more] than just monetary value and some tangible tokens." After all, 94% of the money we handle every day has human feces on it. So yes, there were 178. 178 divided by 2 is 89. I counted them again, backwards. I sensed a slight tremor in one of my eyelids. My body wanted to release the poisons stored inside it. I resisted. I kept counting. The metal slats were coated in grey-green plastic. See you on Monday. Cédric Villani, of whom you've probably never heard, has been deemed "the Lady Gaga of mathematics." Genevieve Nnaji, a Nollywood superstar, is known as the "the Julia Roberts of Africa." Kanye West aspires to be "the Steve Jobs of the Gap," while hedge fund manager and Sotheby's board member Daniel Loeb has been dubbed "the Kanye West of Wall Street." And these people are "the David Blaines of Turkish ice cream." So many people have been described as the Michael Jordan of their respective disciplines, but the Michael Jordan of artistic prowess analogies has got to be Pablo Picasso. Presenting (and all of these are real links):

> "The Picasso of Accounting"
> "The Picasso of Airbrush Compressor and Sprayer Kits"
> "The Picasso of Anal Pleasuring Toys"
> "The Picasso of the Animal Kingdom"
> "The Picasso of Batting"
> "The Picasso of Bonsai"
> "The Picasso of Boxing"
> "The Picasso of Breast Surgeons"
> "The Picasso of Butt-Drawers"
> "The Picasso of Carnival and Circus Canvases"

"The Picasso of Cartography"
"The Picasso of Chinese Studies"
"The Picasso of Choke Artists"
"The Picasso of Coffee Art"
"The Picasso of Commercial Artists"
"The Picasso of Constitutional Theorists"
"The Picasso of Cricket"
"The Picasso of Dirty Cars"
"The Picasso of DNA"
"The Picasso of Dust Jacket Design"
"The Picasso of Election Analysis"
"The Picasso of Emojis"
"The Picasso of Eye Makeup Art"
"The Picasso of Fashion Illustration"
"The Picasso of the Ghetto"
"The Picasso of Golf Course Designers"
"The Picasso of Graphic Design"
"The Picasso of Haircut Portraits"
"The Picasso of Haiti"
"The Picasso of Harlem"
"The Picasso of Hummus"
"The Picasso of India"
"The Picasso of Ivory Artists"
"The Picasso of Jazz"
"The Picasso of Keyboard Funk"
"The Picasso of LEGO Bricks"
"The Picasso of Low-temperature Geochemistry"
"The Picasso of Mauritania"
"The Picasso of the Machine Age"
"The Picasso of Mushing"
"The Picasso of NASCAR"
"The Picasso of Palestine"
"The Picasso of Pancakes"
"The Picasso of Parking Lots"
"The Picasso of Passive Aggression"
"The Picasso of Pasta"
"The Picasso of Pastry"
"The Picasso of the Personal Pic"
"The Picasso of Picasa"
"The Picasso of the Pier"
"The Picasso of Pin-Ups"
"The Picasso of Pinstripes"
"The Picasso of Plagiarism"
"The Picasso of Plating"

"The Picasso of Popular Imagination"
"The Picasso of Potholes"
"The Picasso of Prejudice"
"The Picasso of Proctology"
"The Picasso of Procurement"
"The Picasso of Pumpkins"
"The Picasso of Puppy Portraits"
"The Picasso of the Put-Down"
"The Picasso of the Quilt World"
"The Picasso of Reality Shows"
"The Picasso of Robots"
"The Picasso of Rock and Roll"
"The Picasso of Second Base"
"The Picasso of Serial Killers"
"The Picasso of Simian Artists"
"The Picasso of Snapchat"
"The Picasso of Sneakers"
"The Picasso of Sport Bikes"
"The Picasso of Stained Glass"
"The Picasso of Steel"
"The Picasso of Surfers"

The three Picassos carry the dead body up from the hole. They drag him through the night woods. Dead Brother. Dead Brother is full of holes. They carry him down to the river — lay his body on the bank. They three pause over him, air heavy around them, their faces darkened for the moment. The first reaches into her [into her what?] and pulls out a strawberry. The bright red glow of strawberry in the black night. Gently she presses the strawberry into his chest. Pushes it deep deep. The second places a fish hook and knife beside his body. The third places a spool of fishing line an old wooden chair and a box of matches. They three touch his face then exit through the patterns of transparency in nature. The pebbled body of a lizard shifting like light in a trashcan, the grey checkerboard background in Photoshop, the crépey muscles around the eye, a speech saying that we had to pay off the pimps to build this school, and yes I did smash that particular dish against that particular part of the wall because I was feeling bad, and yes, this is your contusion on drugs. The glue is worlded. A little bit of it is also a little uncertain and some of it is bloated and I've had these things for a long time and the day will come when the bank will accept my string and hold my account in ageless red dots and then I will be WOW. WOW WOW. But hey. It's nice and cool in the mud or hypothesis. Two years later and a thousand miles south, I pull up to a second school on the island of Tahiti. By this time, my visits to cable stations have become routine. I look for an unmarked and nondescript industrial building with few windows, surrounded by surveillance cameras and guarded by barbed wire. Failing to find the station, I park on a dirt strip outside a school and wander into its open courtyard. Students pull at two ends of a long rope in a game of tug-of-war. I approach the woman watching these children and ask her about Honotua, Tahiti's first fiber-optic cable, which was laid earlier that year. She calls a young boy over from the yard. "Le câble!" she points. He runs toward the ocean and I follow, taking snapshots as I duck through the buildings. Arriving at the back of the school, I encounter a sight as striking to me as the manhole which marks Electric Beach's cable landing. Here stands a stone monument, about five feet tall. A large black plaque is mounted on its face. An inscription in Tahitian, English, and French reads:

> In memory of the people of Papenoo and of Hawai'i, who established ties in the past:
> Tapuhe'euanu'u from Tapahi, who, fishing from his canoe, caught Hawai'i the Great,
> Te'ura-vahine from Ha'apaiano'o, the goddess Pere, who sought refuge in the volcano of Hawai'i the Great,
> Mo'iteha, King of Hawai'i, who came back to Tahiti to build his marae Ra'iteha at Mou'a'uranuiatea,
> Ra'amaitahiti, his son, King of Tapahi, who brought his drum to Kaua'i,
> To revive these ancient connections, Honotua was made: The submarine cable that links Tahiti to Hawai'i.
> After quietly undulating in the deep sea, it has landed here, at Mamu (silence).
> Hopefully human ignorance will dissolve into silence and only knowledge will be conveyed.

So collect your thoughts. I will tell you all. We speak of "rich" when there is sufficient supply. By making everything grow, heaven provides enough wealth. Thus we say that there is enough wealth when supreme majestic qi arises and all twelve thousand plants and beings are brought to life. Under the influence of medium majestic qi, plants and beings are slightly deficient in that it cannot provide for all twelve thousand of them. This causes small poverty. When under the influence of lower majestic qi, plants and beings are again fewer than under the influence of medium majestic qi, and this causes great poverty. When there are no auspicious portents [signifying the approach of majestic qi] at all, the crops won't grow, which is extreme poverty. Take a look at a peasant family if you wish to know what this amounts to. Should they not possess any rare and valuable objects, they are considered a poor family. Should they not be supplied with what they need, they must be seen as an extremely poor family. The problem lies in the poverty of heaven and earth. Once all twelve thousand plants and beings come forth and are nurtured by earth without detriment, earth becomes rich. If it can't nurture them well, it becomes slightly poor as long as injuries remain small, and quite poor should they be large. If crops were to shy away from being seen and fail to grow, injured by earth's body, this would lead to extreme poverty. Without jade and other valuables and with half the yields damaged, great distress and poverty would come about. Such complete damage would eradicate a poor family. Now think of heaven as father and earth as mother. Should father and mother be in such extreme poverty all their children would suffer from poverty. The king's government is a replica of this. Thus the wise kings of antiquity, whose reign reached out to all twelve thousand plants and beings, became lords of great wealth. Harvests that reach two-thirds of their potential provide a lord with medium wealth. When they amount to only one-third, he has but little wealth. With neither valuables nor crops, he becomes a lord of great poverty. Once half of his harvests are damaged, his house is in decline. If all are damaged, he becomes a man of great poverty. The wise and worthy of antiquity reflected deep in their dark chamber on the question of how poverty and wealth were achieved through [adhering to] *dao* and virtue. Why should anyone ask about this? "Objects in mirror are (never) closer than they appear". This quote is from a Facebook photo taken by Rohith Vemula, a PhD student at the University of Hyderabad. On Sunday, Rohith committed suicide by hanging himself from a fan in a friend's room in one of the university hostels. His suicide has been the latest act of protest in a long series of protests by students from disenfranchised and oppressed communities, generally from Dalit and Kashmiri Muslim backgrounds. So read between the lines of his suicide note, in the loops of his "y"s and "g"s and in the indented spaces separating his neat paragraphs. No, wait, no flies are allowed to fly around in air-conditioned offices. These points of convergence / divergence can be found throughout the collection, as our selections were chosen to make them visible. Ann M. Ciasullo's and Norma Mogrovejo's pieces on the development of lesbian feminism in the United States and Latin America, for example, reveal fascinating differences — and some similarities — in the political contexts within which each of these movements emerged and in the issues that became central to each movement. The similarities are instructive, but even more so are the differences, which demonstrate that the path followed by feminists in the United States was not the model for the rest of the world. Similarly, in Obioma Nnaemeka's essay on African feminism, "womanism" appears as a significant concept — which may come as a surprise to those American feminists who believe it was coined by Alice Walker. When Durand and I wanted to end our *Poetry Project Newsletter* "interview" with a selection from "Deep eco pré," the editors initially refused our request because it threw off the balance between the distinct categories of "poetry" and "prose" in the issue. we insisted in order to challenge the identity of the poet as a "talking head" with deep dark interiors. As an instance of Darragh / Durand / Ponge / Zimmerman put it:

      gable tone let us press   that *was revealed*
                                      to

last night a victorious clarity I have been suff
BUT *let us act* as if   if not with clarity at leas

I mean what we (each still tribal forest   owes
                                            go-
until four violent *like the one that some* precedes cam
"completion" of my "essay" (didn't go to be until fo

at least I re-lude with first ragement shalling univ logi
contribute to it, in the direction, intensity, if not with
                                            cla
ri for the illusion of it   four in the morning for it
                                            can eas

i can't
read you
anymore
computer
breaking down
but i can still
sit still and
watch you act
anyone's self but

however the matter is resolved, it is clear that humans have been cooking for a very long time. Before the first empires, indeed, long before farming, we had passed a point of no return where we could no longer thrive on raw foods. We had become the animals that cooked. Cooking softened food so that we no longer had to spend five hours a day chewing, as our chimpanzee relatives did. It made it more digestible, increasing the energy we could extract from a given amount of food and diverting more of that energy to the brain. Brains grew and guts shrank. It became possible to detoxify many poisonous plants and soften others that had been too hard to chew, so that we could digest an increased number of plant species. This allowed more people to live off the resources of a given area as well as making it easier to settle new areas. Ways of treating flesh and plants so that they did not rot permitted the storage of food for the lean times of hard winters or dry seasons. With cooking, plants and animals became the raw materials for food, not food itself. Given that we commonly use the word "food" to describe what farmers grow, and given that we eat nuts, fruit, some vegetables, and even fish and steak tartare raw, the statement that plants and animals are not themselves food may seem counterintuitive. The fact is that most of us get only a small fraction of our calories from raw foods. Even so, that fraction is probably higher than that of our ancestors, since we are the beneficiaries of millennia of breeding that have created larger, sweeter fruits and more tender vegetables and meat. Furthermore, even what we call raw has usually been subjected to many kitchen processes. Few of us sink our teeth into raw steak unless it has been finely chopped or sliced. Raw foodists allow slicing, grinding, chopping, soaking, sprouting, freezing, and heating to 104-120° Fahrenheit. Anyhow, in Antiquity, people happily accepted that humans ate cooked food. Indeed, they saw it as what distinguished us from animals. Perhaps it is because today we place so much emphasis on "fresh" and "natural" foods – which Susanne Freidberg has shown are made possible only by manipulating animal life cycles, modern transport, refrigeration, and ingenious packaging – that we underestimate how much we depend on cooking. With cooking came cuisines. Techniques that proved successful with one kind of raw material were then used for others. A single raw material (such as grain) could be turned into diverse foods with different tastes and nutritional properties (gruel, bread, and beer). Instead of consuming food on the spot, we began eating meals, since cooking required planning, storing ingredients, and time. Meals could be patterned to suit cultural preferences. Ordered styles of cooking – cuisines – became the norm. Techniques that proved successful with one kind of raw material were then used for others. A single raw material (such as grain) could be turned into diverse foods with different tastes and nutritional properties (gruel, bread, and beer). Instead of consuming food on the spot, we began eating meals, since cooking required planning, storing ingredients, and time. Meals could be patterned to suit cultural preferences. Ordered styles of cooking – cuisines – became the norm.

> One asks oneself, perhaps, as
> one reads it, if one
> comes to read it, if
> anyone gets or comes to
> read it, or if it
> is noticed by someone not
> entirely able to read, a
> dog for instance standing on
> the paper where the sentence
> happens to be, printed somehow
> long after there is anyone
> here to read or read
> it, in a derelict factory
> or some other zone –
>   imagine
> a situation, then, in which
> someone or somebody or something,
> a text, a lover, a
> cat, a dog, a pollution,

a radiance, seems, enigmatically or
not, through provocation or otherwise,
to want you to –
        one
might listen, you might listen,
I might listen here as
if to a silence that
cannot be made out –
        everyone
knew this would happen. Some
animals saw it coming, and
in a dream before hearing –

One might say that we stayed in the valley for as long as possible, angelic foil to a same difference, a radioactive amorous incumbency. We might have worked less and stayed longer, or simply decided to go since sometimes you have to go. At the same time an irruption takes place in some kind of beautiful city more important than history, arranged in lines remaindered, cut out, decided by generals and chefs and amorous king kongs. The irruption speaks a language of lower frequency, as of combing the hair of poems in mal-address: www dot www dot www, an almost completely blacked out 'radio' signal, an electrocardiographic signal now infinitely weak, a secret all over. But if you are reading this, or standing nearby with all the graceful violence of human animals, you will have – from where does it come? The line is averse … I mean, I dreamt a poem last nite, and wrote it down at 4:50 to remember it:

    Hash
    Oil
    Shoe

    Transversal
    Geophilosophy

What more could you ask? I mean, to quote Jack Halberstam, *what's the alternative?*

Mr Krabs: And just when you think you've found the land of milk and honey, they grab ya by the britches, and haul you way up high, and higher, and higher, and HIGHER, until you're hauled up to the surface, flopping and gasping for breath! And then they cook ya, and then they eat ya – or worse!

SpongeBob: *[Terrified]* What could be worse than that?

Mr Krabs: *[Softly]*: Gift shops!

That's when Tupac Amaru compelled the stunned Arriaga to write letters to his treasurer in Tinta requesting money and arms, with the peculiar pretext that he was planning an expedition against pirates on the coast. Tupac Amaru himself then went to Tinta and used Arriaga's key to take seventy-five fusils or light flintlock muskets, a small number of standard muskets, gunpowder, bullets, some militia uniforms, mules, silver, 22,000 pesos of tribute money, gold, and other goods. He also wrote messages in the name of Arriaga to mayors and powerful individuals demanding that they convene in Tungasuca. Numerous military figures and entrepreneurs such as the Spaniards Juan Antonio Figueroa and Bernardo La Madrid fell into the trap. Kurakas also received instructions to send their Indians; thousands assembled in Tungasuca, streaming in for days. The rebels posted sentinels on the road to Cuzco to keep the news from authorities there. They also kept Arriaga's whereabouts a secret. The masses congregating in Tungasuca did not know the corregidor was a prisoner in Tupac Amaru and Micaela Bastidas' basement. Which is why it is said that 'The head of the sacrificial horse, clearly, is the dawn — its sight is the sun; its breath is the wind; and its gaping mouth is the fire common to all men. The body *(atman)* of the sacrificial horse is the year — its back is the sky; its abdomen is the intermediate region; its underbelly is the earth; its flanks are the quarters; its ribs are the intermediate quarters; its limbs are the seasons; its joints are the months and fortnights; its feet are the days and nights; its bones are the stars; its flesh is the clouds; its stomach contents are the sand; its intestines are the rivers; its liver and lungs are the hills; its body hairs are the plants and trees; its forequarter is the rising sun; and its hindquarter is the setting sun. When it yawns, lightning flashes; when it shakes itself, it thunders; and when it urinates, it rains. Its neighing is speech itself. The day, clearly, was born afterwards to be the sacrificial cup placed in front of the horse, and its womb is in the eastern sea. The night was born afterwards to be the sacrificial cup placed behind the horse, and its womb is in the western sea. These two came into being to be the sacrificial cups placed in front of and behind the horse. It became a racer and carried the gods. It became a charger and carried the Gandharvas. It became a courser and carried the demons. It became a horse and carried the humans. The sea, indeed, is its counterpart; the sea is its womb. In the beginning there was nothing here at all. Death alone covered this com- pletely, as did hunger; for what is hunger but death? Then death made up his mind: "Let me equip myself with a body *(atman)*." So he undertook a liturgical recitation *(arc)*, and as he was engaged in liturgical recitation water sprang from him. And he thought: "While I was engaged in liturgical recitation *(arc)*, water *(ka)* sprang up for me." This is what gave the name to and discloses the true nature of recitation *(arka)*. Water undoubtedly springs for him who knows the name and nature of recitation in this way. So, recitation is water. Then the foam that had gathered on the water solidified and became the earth

Death toiled upon her. When he had become worn out by toil and hot with exertion his heat — his essence — turned into fire.'

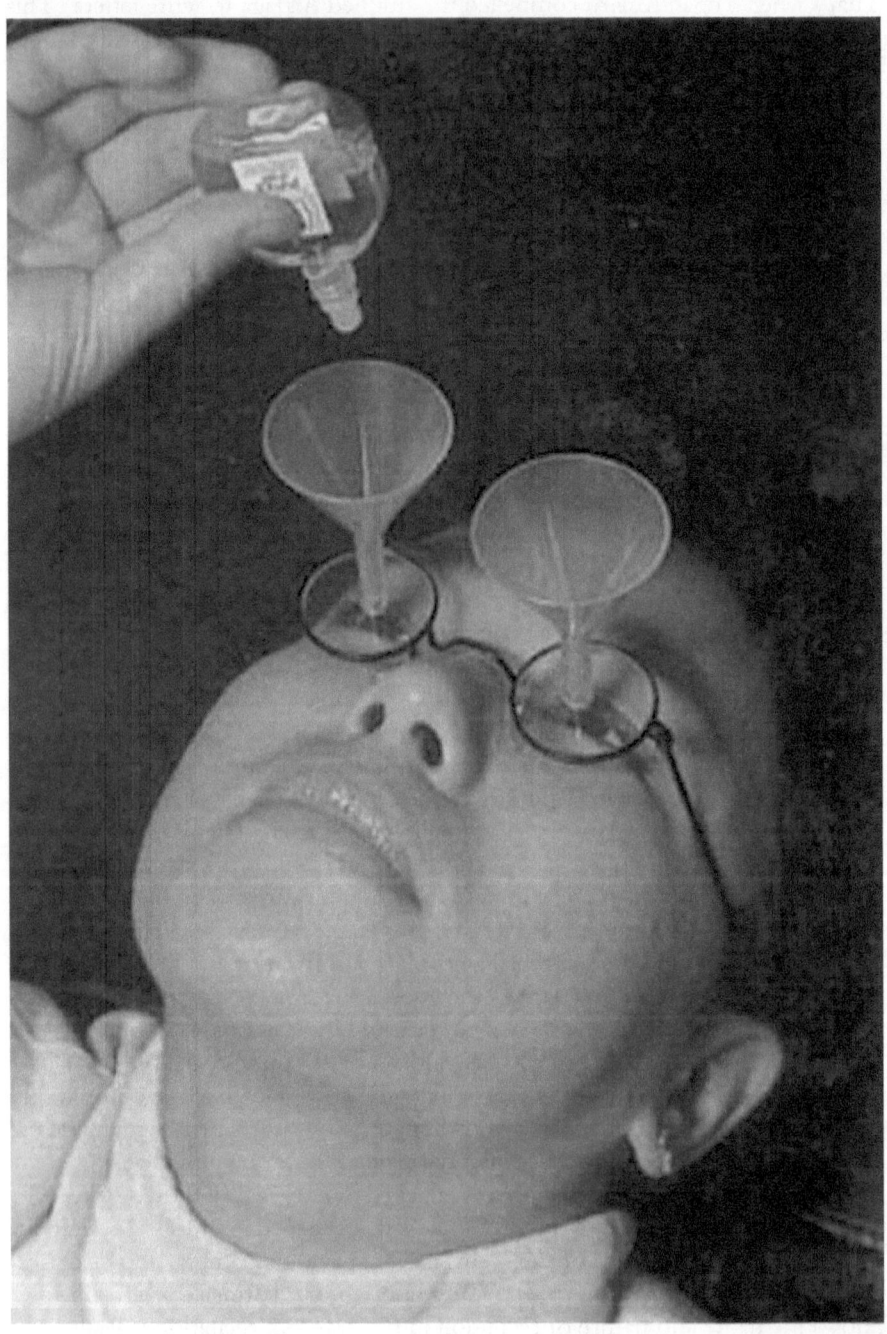

Which is why the windows with their white aprons told us what they saw. Which is why the windows with their white aprons told us what they saw. Which is why the winning clouds will drop fish and dolphins in the streets of Leticia. (Which is why, if they lose, they will come down with their dark glasses to sunbathe with the tourists.) Which is why fish work as cab drivers. In backyards dolphins strum their guitars. The sun works as a fire eater at night in the river's traveling circus. A few herons come to the beach, take off their feathers, and go for a swim. The fishermen wink at the boys goading them to bathe with the herons. But the boys prefer to hide the herons' clothes. Then the fisherman who scale and gut their fish laugh so hard they fall down, choking. The herons dress themselves in the fish scales. He who is not coming can be seen very well in the distance. He can be seen in a solitary boat, in the sky, in the clouds. He who is not coming rides by on the back of a fly without saying hello. Even though later, in many places, they will greet each other. My somatic counselor told me to sing, to keep singing, to work on singing. She writes but I don't. I write only invisibly into the intimate nervous system and then take banal notes in a binder just so I can remember what territory I mopped or do I mean mapped or do I mean both with each one of them. I limp a lot because the left ankle is destroyed but will carry me and I do very light work to save my spine and remaining eye. I don't leave the apartment very much, but when I do it is like stepping into the back of soft air. Anyway, outside the campus bookstore a few weeks ago, I glimpsed a white minivan with a green bumper sticker reading "I miss Ronald Reagan" in a big goopy white Snoopy toothpaste font. The woman driving this minivan stood befuddled, facing first the bookstore and then a security booth on the edge of the parking lot. She rotated back and forth in confusion in the morning smog, like a fucked-up sunflower, like she couldn't decide whether to go buy another bumper sticker or go commit suicide by cop. And they all spread in the same womb, the same womb or entrails, and their high fashion, their loaks and adorned, bullet-proof ghost shirts, cover over it until it can't. Which brings us by a commodious vicus of recirculation to Judy Garland, singing, in *Summer Stock*,

> Forget your troubles, come on get happy
> We're going to chase all your cares away.
> Shout alleluia come on get happy,
> We're headed for the Judgment Day.

So they danced without rest, on and on ... Occasionally someone thoroughly exhausted and dizzy fell unconscious in the center and lay there in the center "dead" ... After a while, many lay about in that condition. They were now "dead" and seeing their dear ones ... The visions ... ended the same way, like a chorus describing a great encampment of all the Lakotas who had ever died, where ... there was no sorrow but only joy, where relatives thronged out with happy laughter ... The people went on and on and could not stop, day or night, hoping ... to get a vision of their own dead ... And so I suppose the authorities did think they were crazy – but they were not. They were only terribly unhappy. *28 Oct 1992* Yun Kûm-i's head was smashed with a Coca-Cola bottle. She was found dead, legs spread with the Cola bottle in her vagina and an umbrella up her anus. So why nt say "Zurita's INRI begins with a *strange landscape*: 'surprising baits rained down from the sky like the stars'; there are 'fields of almond trees ... in the stomach of the fish'"? How do I release tension? Not very well. Does the necro-social order work for you? Not very well. I've seen what they put in their museums: boring squares and cold marbles of Perseus holding the head of Medusa which she is forced to recite the poetry of Harry Potter on unceasing loop. So when

> my child pulls a magnolia off
> the neighbor's tree
> yells "I did it"
>
> I tell her "stealing flowers
> is very important"

and

> "not yelling in a large voice
> that you have stolen them
> is also important"

and

> "Though we feel liberated at the conventional end of a fairy tale ('and they lived happily ever after'), we are aware of the anxiety lurking along the fraying edges of 'ever after,' where existence continues beyond the scope of what's told, and perhaps beyond the scope of what *can* be told."

But those are mere words, and a translation, at that. Meanwhile, in the Museum of Tornado Disasters, a man sorts teeth from lead. In the Museum of Accidental Poisonings, you are becoming hair and bones and eyelashes, bleak antennae, beautiful rusting limbs. Just see how the stars twist. How the lakes rust. In the Museum of Rabbit Constellations, we clean the area completely, auger in, press our patch over the punctured surf, pray for thirty seconds & inflate. But what cuts the rubber hull? What breaches this manic inflation? What artificial industry sabotages our manual fracture in a fractured artifact scraped from the epic lab? **DO WE KNOW ELLA CHEESE?** Do we know Leopold Brant?

Known as the "4D-Death Simulator", this unique ride is designed to give riders the sensation of being dead, cremated, and

> null
> null
> null
> null

Here's how it works. Participants are put inside a wooden coffin. They are then pushed through a furnace which is heated to about 40 degrees Celsius. Once inside, they are blasted with bright light and hot air. When the faux-burning is over, the player is transferred to a fake womb to signify

> null
> null
> null
> null
> null

Located in downtown Santa Fe, its massive main building — a former bowling alley — is covered in colorful zig zags. The parking lot is dominated by a metal spider and a metal robot. Its landlord is George RR Martin. After nearly two years of construction, the Meow Wolf art complex opened its riotously painted doors and invited the public into its first permanent exhibit, called The House of Eternal Return. Built by 135 artists and makers, the result is a 20,000-square-foot dreamworld where your goal is to figure out why an old Victorian house in Mendocino, California, has become ground zero for a rupture in space-time that's allowing other dimensions to leak into ours.

>   null
>   null
>   null
>   null
>   null

Beech Mountain Police released this surveillance photo of a couple wanted for trying to break into Dorothy's farmhouse at the old Land of Oz amusement park. A passerby noticed the dog in a car and informed the Efteling staff, who called in the police. The animal looked exhausted and ill so the officers decided to break a window and free it. At around 5:15pm another dog was found in another car and the police were again called in. Here too the police left a note for the owners. Other toilet features of Foreigner Street are the 2,000-person capacity toilet and commodes shaped like an Egyptian pyramid. The park also has canals similar to Venice in Italy, a tree house and a crooked pedestrian street just like Lombard Street in San Francisco. And now, after retiring from filmmaking in 2013, the Japanese director is building a real-life version of his imaginative landscapes — a 10,000-acre theme park called The Forest Where the Wind Returns. Hayao Miyazaki says the park will include a library, sleeping quarters for 30 people, and as few built attractions as possible. Unique attractions planned for Ibsen Verden include a haunted house, inspired by *Ghosts*, which visitors can exit only via a lethal morphine injection, and a Hedda Gabler shooting gallery in which participants are forced to contemplate futility while in the vicinity of a loaded weapon. The Master Builder Pavilion, sponsored by Nokia, will offer a free "master class" on brooding over doomed but deeply symbolic structures, with practical take-home tips like the best materials for sky castles. And no Ibsen experience would be complete without a cathartic door-slamming exhibit, in honor of the stunning climax of *A Doll's House*, or *Dr. Stockmann's Water Report*, a hair-raising raft excursion through a contaminated lagoon. Park planners aren't overlooking youngsters in their plans, promising such thrilling rides as Peer Gynt's Troll Trap and Little Eyolf's Rat Race. "It is just too hard," Beverley said. "Why would they want to hurt a family like that? My other daughter has never spoken about what happened that day. It's too hard for her. How do they think she feels? I just want the adverts to stop. That is all I am asking for. I said to them how would you feel if your child had died? It's hard, it really is hard, and it does not get any easier. It's a horrible feeling, it makes me feel sick. It's a horrible feeling and it makes me feel sad. I see her pretty face smiling and it makes me think, 'Oh God, why did this happen to you?' I would love to see that ride taken down, that is how I feel about that ride, and I am not the only one. A lot of Hayley's friends, they are 28 now, and they say, 'Why have they not taken it down?' I took her to see Westlife on Easter Monday and on Thursday she was dead. The Westlife thing was a birthday gift because her birthday was on March 16. For them to advertise the rides at Easter when they know Hayley died at Easter I think is just sick. It's like sticking the knife in."

    null
    null
    null
    null
    null

Hey. Hi. Hi, B. Hi, S! Hey. Hi! Yeah. Hi, Bill. Oh, perhaps I do. Hi, Josh. Hi, Bear! Howdy, Ben. Well, hi there, John! Whoa! No, I didn't know that. Congratulations, man. That's huge! 10 years? Wow. H, Hi, h. Hi, James. Okay. So it goes. See you tomorrow. Nevertheless, beyond the schematic borders, here is us, it, I, I, this we, perspiring to cross the sacred hedges, surrounded by interdiction, exhibition, extradiction, prohibition, protodiction, abhibition … unarmed, unplugged, cut from function, cut from production, is us, is we, this I, this it, this mechanical artifact dumping in front of the bankage a whole bestiary of impossible life forms — mists, ooze, blobs, slime, clouds, and muck. Who licks the ivy?

    ****
    ****
    ****
    ****
    ****
    ****
    ****
    ****
    ****
    ****
    ****
    ****
    ****
    ****
    ****
    ****
    She filmed them****
    ***********burning
    ****
    ****

in the snow*******
with their arms up**

History, having no human face, no Mind, and no Hegelian Spirit, has no sides, there are only events, there's only a blood yard. What is a blood yard but a test-field blood drones and my brain, too, and it as an enclosure similar to a sun, fusing a private energy to outlast, be out last and still outlast the sweet burn. And ▮ replies: take a vacation from fear. Swallow the pills no one prescribed. They were a gift from your Mother. Vacation is a construction of capital. Trip, take a trip. Where to go but deeper? He instructs you to stretch your arm out ahead of you. He instructs you to slowly bend each finger. I know I am a hard case,

> A small nerve weaving proofs
> Through purpling organs
> Does that mean to the ground? Burning, burning

A GIANT ASLEEP IN FORTUNE'S SPINDLE

B wrote me a letter asking me if I had any poems with the word corpse in Them they hurled you Out of space I thought to myself, Don't I? Haven't I seen / corpses Many horse corpses / when I wrked at the barn /

****
****
****
****
****
****
****
****
****
****
****
****
****
****
****
****
****
****
****
****
****

****
****
****
****
****
****
****
****
***Untitled1
***Join / Save
****************************Join / Save Join / Save Join / Save Join / Save Join / Save Join / Save Join / Save
****
Join / Save Join / Save Join / Save Join /
****
****
****
****
****
****
****
****
***Save**
****
****
****
****
****
****
****
****
** She contracts around An Art So Polluted / She filmed them burning / in the snow / with
their arms up / She filmed them burning / the outlines of her body / in the snow / with
their arms up

So yes, this book is made of 8,888 iterations of the following line: The Friday evening gas explosion in Springfield leveled a strip club next to a day care center. Its fugal structure effects content-density, tension, and return. Continual re-figuration of all themata creates a pleasurable engagement with a material transparency that is neither prepackaged ("found") nor fancied from thing air ("inspired"). Which is why the kids round here remind me of those twins from *The Shining*. They stare eerily from the stairs. There are clues and more clues. A role is to a person what a clue is to evidence. I think they were called the Grady sisters. But it's hard to hear what people are saying when their mouths are full of sugar. This is why it occurred to me that this particular war was hardly war. Or when they're laying face down in the BIG PICTURE. The metaphor implies wholesomeness, goodness, health. But isn't there a little condescension in that idea? Are oppressed groups really society's Id? Which also means that in the first horror film he ever made, someone pretended to break my neck while I was tied to a dentist's chair with a bunch of RCA cables; that I've made the fake blood for almost every movie he's ever been involved in (he sucks at it). From the *Antigone* Sophocles passing through Griselda Gambaro's *Antígona furiosa*, Leopoldo Marechal's *Antígona Vélez*, María Zambrano's *La tumba de Antígona* all the way to *Antigone's Claim* by Judith Butler. Which is to say, yes, "a cantíl is a venomous snake. It's a minor deity, hiding in the rainforest, guarding the temples: one of the ones who molded us from corn and mud." But it's alright, ma, it's alright 'cos the historical pattern has shown how the economical cycle tends to revolve in a round of decades three stages stand out in a loop a slump and war then peel back to square one and back for a more bigger slump and bigger wars and a smaller recovery huger slump and greater wars and a shallower recovery […] dum, dum, dum, de dum dum, de duh de duh de dum dum dum … ah ah, dum, dum, dum, de dum dum, de duh de duh de dum dum dum … ah ah … Now we had enough of our "beer trip" for the time being, and in order to cool our heated blood, we started on a double quick march, until Edgar Bauer stumbled over some paving stones. "Hurrah, an idea!" And in memory of mad student pranks he picked up a stone, and Clash! Clatter! a gas lantern went flying into splinters. Nonsense is contagious – Marx and I did not stay behind, and we broke four or five street lamps – it was, perhaps, 2 o'clock in the morning and the streets were deserted in consequence. But the noise nevertheless attracted the attention of a policeman who with quick resolution gave the signal to his colleagues on the same beat. And immediately countersignals were given. The position became critical. Happily, we took in the situation at a glance; and happily we knew the locality. We raced ahead, three or four policemen some distance behind us. Marx showed an activity that I should not have attributed to him. And after the wild chase had lasted some minutes, we succeeded in turning into a side street and there running through an alley – a back yard between two streets – whence we came behind the policemen who lost the trail. Now we were safe. They did not have our description and we arrived at our homes without further adventures. A few weeks later still, back in the conference room on the fifth floor. Today's topic: tie-ins and merchandizing. Some ideas feel a bit outlandish, like a possible connection to *The Incredible Hulk*. The movie is set to open in mid-June, and the staff member pitching the idea seems to be half joking. But as I look around the room, there are a lot of nods. The show, after all, will feature several pieces from Koons's *Hulk Elvis* series. More concrete is a tie-in with Macy's. This past fall, a large balloon version of Koons's

Rabbit made its debut in New York's Thanksgiving Day Parade. For the MCA show, it could make a trip to Chicago, where it would be displayed at the Macy's store in the Loop. The marketers are ecstatic about the opportunity. "This will really leverage the promotional aspects," one of them exclaims. The word that keeps coming up is "cross-marketing," and I take away that Jeff Koons stuff might soon be everywhere. Stuff, in fact, is what really gets the group going today. Koons, it turns out, is a veritable merchandizing machine, which means that *a lot* of things can be sold in conjunction with the show. The list of products bearing his art ranges from the affordably populist (beach towels from Target) to the high-end luxurious (designs by Stella McCartney). But the news gets even better. Koons has given the MCA permission to manufacture a whole new line of T-shirts featuring *Rabbit*. We pass around production samples, and everyone agrees that the baby tees, in light blue and pink, are too cute for words. And under the bottom line, another line: *we know he had weapons of mass destruction cause we sold them to him in the first place.* But Rosenthal's sense of Fable eschews morals and maxims in favor of claiming a terrain from which the Para-Human can slowly, tentatively, and then brashly, like LIZARD, begin to obverse the world. The resulting Kabbalistic strokes are as patently hilarious as they are intelligently perplexing. This is bone instructive: a heal, or example heard – how the rayed net soaks need, in a flayed edition: "Beyond Mountains, More Mountains." Still, the elbow slams its grease on a wrinkle of steam and instinctively becomes a postmark. But so be it. *The Book of Balance and Harmony* says: Consider this, my friends: eagles and tigers, though made from jade, though made from gold, come to the same end, the same rotten end. Divert all steam ships, air-dropped from, wherever. Moon, refrigerate the snowfield gas, the hermit maudit. Some sports they are not arena sports, philosopher. I found myself in a wood of chairs. A hole in the ground. Two shovels. One rake. Part of it was right the Zankou Chicken part / in ten years hair dye and a new set of teeth. Because it is one word we think it represents one sort of activity. Like a cape made from the feathers of a zacuan, from that rare rubber necked bird, we start to come apart the moment we … When wit was young professors called it quantum archaeology. But you know how I am. And that what I'm trying to say is a rite of passage is an architectural not an ethnological conceit caught up in some trajectory of glorious anatomy and you wouldn't be wrong. 3 point 0. Night is a this not a that. I mean, I always like the way in which phylogeny gets immersed in a thread of deeds and the analogue expectancy sheds a tear for its dissipating vortex. We sort through these useless facts. But the sunlight invokes us and a sweet face looks at me with its huge colour, full of ripe fruit and you alone remain to remind me that all this was Shakespeare before I intervened with my revisionist Arcadia. When he was alive it sufficed to leave intertextuality to herpetologists and playwrights tried to give folks pleasure in a plot or two with a little disguise, a little cross-dressing and a big old honkin blood bath at the end. But these days the only absolute these days is probability and these days he's probably correct.

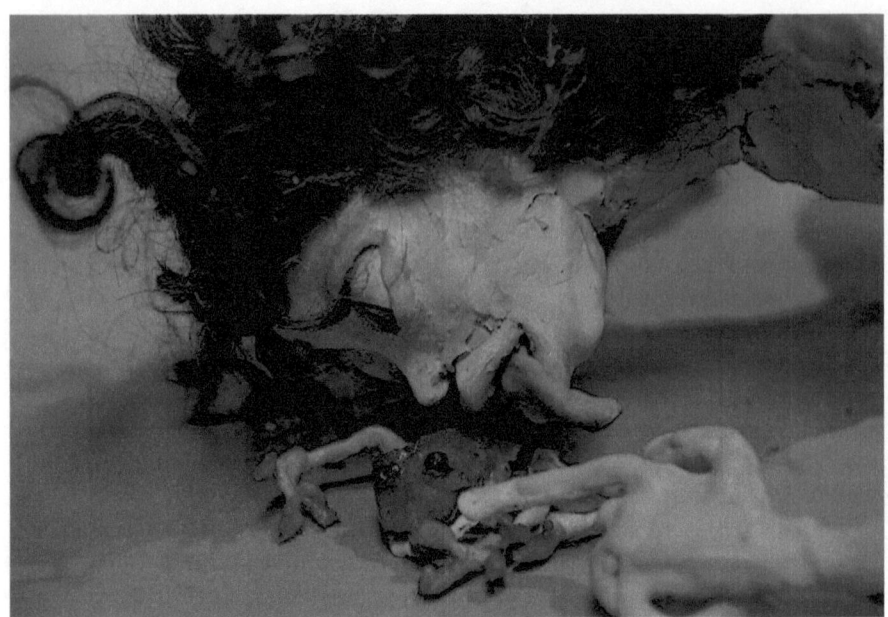

Which is to say you meet it everywhere in the cruel innocence of language and in the thought of your long lost youth as a dime turns on your life, standing alone and probably in delight, reading this to yourself in French. The beginning of clouds is a non-existent origin. "Minima," "error," "draughtsman," "festive," in a sad sort of way, the plot threads excitingly through all the theorems to culminate as One Day in the Afterlife of a Greek God. A bird flies out of art and interrupts our view of a full moon held in its tiny orthogonal claws. But what if the other we call "indifferent reality" recurred? In other words, why just rely on aftermarket home alterations such as WiFi-blocking paint when you can actually factor signal-blockage into the design of your home in the first place? Space Caviar calls this "a new definition of privacy in the age of sentient appliances." The result is the so-called "RAM House," named for its "movable shields of radar-absorbent material," and it will be on display at the Atelier Clerici in Milan, April 14th -19th. It's safe to say I had no idea what I was about to see. Here there was a male chastity belt, artificial noses made of gold, silver, and ivory, glass eyes in rows and real eyes in jars, artificial hands made of metal and other artificial hands made of ivory, a variety of artificial legs, various anatomical dolls, and phrenological heads; advertisements for treatments and medicines, public health posters warning of a variety of diseases, painted depictions of medical techniques and surgeries, many amulets, votive candles … Still, it wasn't my first encounter with this kind of thing. Years earlier I bought five Victorian glass eyeballs at an antique sale outside of Harvard Square. The dealer told me each eyeball had been made specifically for a client, a perfect match to correspond to the client's real eye. They were hazel and blue and green and light brown and some of them had artfully constructed red veins in the sclera. A hundred of them had been found in an old optometrist's shop that had burned down. The eyeballs were one of the only things to survive. As the dealer told me this, I thought about the people for whom they were intended. Why did they never pick up their eye? Speaking of glory, fuck that Living Theater shit. Did you know Judith Malina played a Sunrise Hotel clerk who was later killed by The Savage in the "Duty and Honor" episode of *Miami Vice*? It's a style one associates with Kevin Davies, or John Ashbery's first books after *The Tennis Court Oath* in which he begins to use a mellifluous line but lets the waves break on "the regulars at the bar who / are thrashing Thomas Merton / with checkerboard bathescopes / & babblin about nondiscursive / crap like a *Times* reporter / who kills people, along with the other sportive hucksters who are carping / to the gunshop retirees in the golden dawn." Here we may have an example of an ancient or foreign prayer dimly and incorrectly recalled. A clearer case of this is:

Khristos nekrata
ne tan fan
tan fatison
tintis' tintis'
naim frison
domino

which seems to have a French-Latin flavor. Or is it Greek? In any case, mystical auscultation is a matter of becoming all ears for the Reality that must be, that is, right there — I mean here — it being that through which anything is perceived at all. So for Bonaventure, the divine being, in its radically immanent and inconceivable simplicity, is (more or less) the first thing one always sees and so continually overlooks: 'How remarkable, then, is the blindness of the intellect which does not take note of that which it sees *first*, and without which it can know nothing ... Accustomed as it is to the *darkness of things*, when the mind looks it does not understand that this darkness of things *itself* is the highest illumination.' 'What you see is what you see.' Mystical auscultation, to add a twist to the classic Vedantic analogy, sounds like listening to how the snake sounds like a rope sounds like a snake. Christina's spiritual rapture, then, the spiraling of this "little Christ", is like a fly falling from and into the mirror that her speech, in the secret of its hearing, reflects. In any case, if they are lucky, Ahmad and his family will have one meal today: two plates of rice cooked with undrinkable water. Others will have to do with less, perhaps a bowl of spiced water that doubles as a form of soup. "We are being killed here, Yarmouk camp is being annihilated," said Ahmad, who was given a pseudonym to protect his identity. So the moment Aunt Nancy's bass solo begins a balloon emerges from the vinyl, bearing a mysterious message: I dreamt you were gone ... soon after, N. suffers cowrie shell attacks and they are all stranded on an Orphic Shore. Socio-political forces are at play. And Hotel Didjeridoo must be resurrected, but how? Up to now, astrophysicists believed variety 1a supernovae to be evenly vivid in addition to employing them as 'cosmic beacons' to recognise your cosmos. But Milne can see that variety 1a supernovae will be more assorted "where your class which is inside a small section in close proximity to us are usually in the bulk most importantly distances — and so when the world had been more radiant. There are different populations available, and they have not also been recognized. This huge premise has become that 1a supernovae would be the in which doesn't look like true." Therefore, the information compiled using Quick had been "crucial" because the direction of your red or even azure selection "became apparent merely as a result of Swift's committed follow-up findings inside ultraviolet, just where the crosshairs of understanding 'merge into the bleak motionless dusk of the zone.'" So these findings are sure to protein shake upward cosmologists' contemplating and could push those to revise downwards the two fee your world is actually widening to in addition to the amount of dark vitality specific to your world. The creators of these studies speed to convey, nevertheless nevertheless, that a lot more info have to be compiled prior to scientists may determine in exactly what approaches the modern findings may impression existing information. I think that was spam. It is wrecked now, it is sinking. The rusty ship sinks and the desert closes over it and covers it. The desert closes over it and Chile sinks, the dead cornice of the Pacific sinks, the dead prow of the landscapes sinks while the stones that fall on to them cry out that shipwrecked in shadowland without the alphabet or any kind of clue to get us thru the u-shape of life memorizing Shakespeare or just idling in the faint scenes behind Kaiser Permanente it's how we came to be wan beings washed up on Gatsby's lawn O move along, move along, friend, there's nothing to see, don't stand there and try and *not* see anything either, move along, nothing is too big and too small to move along, the penitents will bathe in soft rainwater, cover their skin with palms full of medicated powder, and the bodies will be robed in gleaming white – total disgrace is stalking us in the canyon with its platter of severed heads. & all that is 100% additive-free, you see, my friend, the noxious flames live in me & into that void the voice reports on another particular which doesn't exist – stop me or save me from such clarity. It's a pronunciation of stems & blessings that disguise the structure of a multilevel hierarchical calendar that we believe was used in pre-Han Escondido – entries for the village show must be in by tomorrow, by the way. So of course I'm influenced by the great liars of the world. Anyone who can't help but deviate can pretty much tell me anything. To quote Fred Moten, as quoted by Jonty T. The following, then, proposes an initial sketch of the ana-tentacular hypothesis and the unclassifiable graphic meta-weave. In his *Anti-Mimesis from Plato to Hitchcock*, Cohen notes that "aside from an underdeveloped strain in Lacan and studies in cryptonomy derived from Abraham and Torok, we find little encouragement to boom-boom," which little encouragement may also indicate a face effaced, the devastating defacement-effect of the late anthropocene. How will I find him? In Sumerian mythology, Anu was a sky-god, the god of heaven, lord of constellations, king of gods, spirits and demons, and dwelt in the highest heavenly regions, way way up there, if you know what I mean. What emerges in the desire that constitutes a certain proximity to that thought is not (just) that blackness is ontologically prior to the logistic and regulative power that is supposed to have brought it into existence but that blackness is prior to ontology; or, in a slight variation of what Chandler would say, blackness is the anoriginal displacement of ontology, that it is ontology's anti- and ante-foundation, ontology's underground, the irreparable disturbance of ontology's time and space. "We find voices through other voices, and I found Fred Moten's through Jackie Wang's." Jackie gave a reading in the Zinc Bar on the last night of my first visit to New York, performing an incantation of Kafka's deathbed line as transmitted via Cixous, "lemonade everything was so infinite." I stood there for a while, not as long as I might, with the columnar sensation merging with the leaves. Will it now become possible to mobilize a General Strike, pressing from both inside and outside, up down thru way round, it is also as if we are dealing with a new type of humanimal, or maybe with an animal effulgence of kryo-kinetic signs. Or rather, and to propel the thing, the whole of the doom-template of Celan's tender German line, *Die Welt ist fort, ich muß dich tragen* [The world is gone, I must carry you], as varied as its variations through Derrida's many readings might be, we are already gone, so anti-gone, so Antigone, so never gone. So play carefully, to quote Prynne. It's time to bite the hand that haunts our food, to quote Trecartin. Wormhole hunger? Anyone hungry? I hope it's okay. I've tasted the soup, Moten says, and it's hard not to believe him. It's hard not to believe Fred Moten when he talks about the soup. 'Within the great aquarium of language the light refracts variously and can bounce by inclinations not previously observed. Some of the codes will unfold with merely adept connivance, others will swim vigorously into and by circulation inside their own medium. If you can imagine staff notation etched on the glass you can read off the scales, da carpo and mirror-folded. "The fish of writing melts into the face of the water" — thus the iconic boundary features declare, by difference and by movement of an intense register, shifts of focus that will skim and can turn about on the smallest coin.

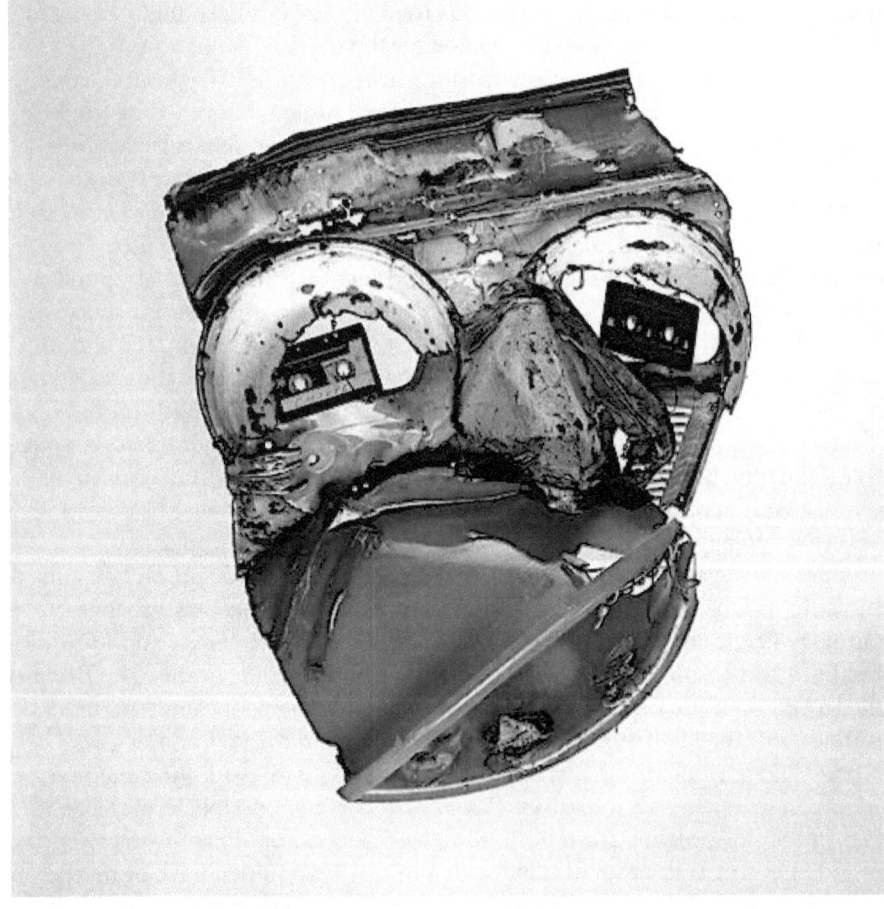

The colour force suffuses a diagram, there is a play within the box which says "play carefully" on the outside cover. Energy prevails by conversion about the axis of activity, the object-perimeter tingles with our hues, your readiness to jump ahead. This is a "world" all right, etc." So where's the swing come from?

That scene. In his talk on Thornton Dial he calls this an "ecology of (eloquent) things," as if enough attention to objects might notice that their care would sustain us beyond the damage done by a subject holding too tight to its subjecthood. But who can give over? The world comes: "Frog went a courtin and it ended up wrong, as dinner and the refusal of dinner that you have to slip away to laugh at and record, track laid over that fatigue drone when everything is everything, which I'd been praying for and running from. I'm touching your ear. Is it ok to touch your ear? I'm touching it. I'm climbing up you. I can't tell you how much I love that." So the other day Cassandra Gillig and I accidentally found ourselves in a carcass shop –

"miscellaneous teeth: 25 cents"

– and it was such a stylish contemporary place that poems are like dreams and dreams are like cities: yes and I dream in architecture and city planning, the peripheries of conference centers, the lower levels of stadiums, in follies and street numbers and skywalks, the way Blake hears the mind-forg'd manacles rather than sees or feels them. The handcuffs are forged in the fires of ideology: but what sound does an ideologically misshaped metal make? It is the discourse of its laws — "some had a map / some had loud keys" — that dronecore / the cartographied — when the speechless things don't answer their silence is a third operation. [Image: A tree turned into architecture by the addition of a door.]

With the words "Destination Tokyo" (in fact the only words uttered on the entire album) they introduce "Souzousuru Neji," which sounds like a bunch of machines getting together to jam. Yes, this is exactly what extinction looks like. A rhino named Sudan is being guarded by armed rangers in Kenya 24/7/365 because he is the only male of the northern white rhino subspecies remaining. His species survived for 50 million years. She worked with cheek swabs from 100 women — her creative peers, artists, collectors, curators, and the like — to form a bacteria collective that will grow for the duration of the show. It's a sort of feminist ecosystem. But the question was about agricultural subsidies for cattle feed and related products, and he just kept on talking, his big clumsy teeth [there are a lot of teeth and fish in this writing] gnashing about in the middle of a dark wormy mess of wires and transistor thingies from which two eyes still stared, huge, unblinking, and grotesquely spherical. The various little mechanisms that had controlled his facial features were also still going, a ring of tiny moving rods and clasps around the edge of his now faceless face, their frantic pump and twist giving the impression of some crustacean or millipede flipped onto its back and desperately failing to right itself. As cogs spun and switches switched, he talked directly into the camera, facing the voting public with that emetically truncated head, as if unaware or unashamed of his sudden nakedness. And as he spoke his hands whirred into one strange and frantic gesture after another, running through all their pre-programmed positions: angry child demanding ice cream, Khrushchev at the UN, Kali, Hindu goddess of time and death.

>Oh its all great fun
>in the corn maze
>until someone gets lost—
>
>earth art,
>crop circles without
>the laughs, digging
>
>around in Drumheller
>for Beefheart's
>"dinosaur cold"—
>
>inside the Holy Mountain
>hopped-up hummingbirds
>raging on raw honey,
>
>oysters & blue moons
>a passenger with no ID
>& nothing solid in the dictionary,

no per diem,
no booking fee,
wearing a horse collar,

a T-shirt reading "Citizen X" – better a propellered beanie, a New Year's diaper, a Brownie uniform – and if the bones of any shiny Hussar, uncowed by *Miranda v. Arizona* or the fourth amendment or the by-God Yosemite Sam mudflaps hanging from my ears attempt to stroll unbidden into my library, garage or sugar shack they will end as struts in the drug tunnel, et cetera. But let us now consider John Stump, his "Faerie's Aire and Death Waltz" which has score notations like "release the penguins," "Like a Dirigible" and "Gong duet." By whom was the potato grown? I said I used to headbutt it. If $y =$ potato, and the revolution is given by the formula lozenge(ds), then this can be given the mathematical formula all started into the start position of where the falling rate of dented my car is life in however many shipments packed into crates and then the crates into container units and the units onto ships I sleep, harbouring no delusions, in the morning everything will begin I sleep, harbouring no delusions, in the morning it will begin a certain quantum of surplus value contained therein representing labour but not the labour that we perform or that any individual ever has so much, its tiaras with fascinators. 8FBMUI was therefore a totalising category represented by all goods [and gods] and produced through determinate production processes. At this time I may not have spoken in this language. A thin hissing sound would have escaped the lips implanted in my thigh but which also is the essential aesthetic shipped two meters to the left. What came out of the body now becomes the forest. Droppings. Defecation. There was never any other modernity for the jaguar, you know. Just this place. Just latex structures that swell and impress their shapes. Can you do architecture with this feeling? Of blood and honeysuckle and the "abyss" that we cross with the "unfixed text"? Yes:

Date: October 18, 1974

Time: 10:30

Place: Tabac Saint-Sulpice

Weather: dry, cold. Grey sky. Minor flashes of sun.

Sketch of an inventory of some things strictly visible:

-Letters of the alphabet, words: "KLM" (on someone's carrying bag), a capital "P" designating "parking", "Hotel Recamier", "St Raphael", "money adrift", "taxis arriving at the station", "Rue du Vieux-

Colombier", "La Fontaine Saint Sulpice brewery and bar", "P ELF", "Saint-Sulpice Park".

-Conventional symbols: signs under the "P" of parking lots, one slightly angled toward the ground, the other, towards rue Bonaparte (on the Luxembourg side), at least four signboards seeming to speak, that is, interjecting (a fifth reflected in the café window).

-Numbers: 86 (at the crest of a bus of class 86, indicating its place of origin: Saint-Germain-des-Prés), 1 (name plate no. 1 of rue Vieux-Colombier), 6 (here to indicate that we are in the 6th Paris arrondissement).

-Fleeting slogans: "From the bus, I spy Paris"

-On the ground: a pile of gravel and sand

-Stone: sidewalk edging, a fountain, a church, houses …

-Asphalt

-Trees: (leafy, yellowing)

-Quite a large piece of sky (perhaps 1/6th my visual field)

-A cloud of pigeons suddenly pounding the central platform between church and fountain

-Vehicles (their inventory remains to be taken)

-Human beings

-A type of basset hound

-Bread (A baguette)

-Lettuce (wilted?) protruding from the top edge of a shopping bag.

Trajectories:

96 goes to the Montparnasse station

84 goes to the Champerret Terminal

70 goes to Place du Dr-Hayem, headquarters of O.R.T.F.1

86 goes to Saint-Germain-des-Prés

Ask for the truth into the green oval of the Roquefort Societé

No water sprouting out of the fountain at all. Pigeons sitting on the fountain basin edge.

There are benches on the (central) platform, benches doubled by a strange pilaster. I'm able to count six from my position. Four are empty. Three bums gesturing classically (drinking red wine from a bottle) on the sixth.

63 goes to the Muette Terminal

86 goes to the Saint-Germain-des-Prés

Cleaning up is good; not getting dirty is better

A German bus

A Brinks delivery truck

87 goes to Champ-de-Mars

84 goes to the Champerret Terminal

Colors:

Red (Fiat, dress, St. Raphael, one-way)
        blue sack
        green footwear
        green raincoat
        blue taxi
        blue 2CV

70 goes to Place du Dr-Hayem, headquarters of O.R.T.F.

Green Méhari

86 goes to Saint-Germain-des-Prés

Dannon: yogurts and desserts

Ask for the truth into the green oval of the Roquefort Societé

Many people with at least one hand occupied: they hold a sack, a small case, a shopping basket, a cane, a leash with a dog on the end, the hand of a child

A truck delivering beer in metal barrels (Kanterbrau, the beer of Master Kanter)

86 goes to Saint-Germain-des-Prés

63 goes to the Muette Terminal

A "Cityrama" bus with two levels

A blue Mercedes truck

A brown Printemps Brummel truck

84 goes to the Champerret Terminal

87 goes to Champ-de-Mars

70 goes to Place du Dr-Hayem, headquarters of O.R.T.F.

96 goes to the Montparnasse station

Darty Réal

63 goes to the Muette Terminal

Casimir, master caterer.

Carpenter transit

Berth France S.A.R.L.

Drawing of Le Goff with beer3

96 goes to the Montparnasse Station

Driving school

Coming from Vieux-Colombier, an 84 turns onto rue Bonaparte (towards Luxembourg)

Wallon relocations

Fernand Carrascossa relocations

Potatoes in bulk

From a bus of tourists, a Japanese woman appears to photograph me.

An old man with half a loaf of bread, a woman with a bundle of cakes in the shape of a pyramid

86 goes to Saint-Mandé (it does not turn onto rue Bonaparte, but takes Vieux-Colombier)

63 goes to the Muette Terminal

87 goes to Champ-de-Mars

70 goes to Place du Dr Hayem, headquarters of O.R.T.F.

Coming from Vieux-Colombier, an 84 turns onto rue Bonaparte (towards Luxembourg)

A bus, empty.

Other Japanese people in another bus

86 goes to Saint-Germain-des-Prés

Braun art reproductions

Calm (from weariness?)

Pause

PS. Hey. Hi. Mm. Yo-ho-ho? I love that the song is making you feel like a classical sculptor. Deftness is a ship of fools. Or maybe I mean the freshness. I know back when I used to interview rock stars and stuff a lot when I was writing for *Spin Magazine* all the time, I would ask some rock god how he / she did this one totally genius thing in some song, and, 9 out of 10 times, they'd say that thing was a mistake. But, yeah, Hi. No, it's a real park. Re: your friend, my brain immediately went 'xanax'. Bear, Hey, Bear! Yeah, exactly. Thanks a lot, Bear! Hi! Hi! Precisely, yeah. And usually it's suddenly for no logical reason, and you're like, 'whoa, it's back, when did that happen?' Hi, Tom! Hi, John. Ideally this place functions in such a way that people can come in and out as they feel like it and never feel like they have to be here or anything gross like that. I'll ask. Never mind. Hi, Yay, Ditto, Ah, Yeah, Wow, Oh, Hi, Thanks, man. Me too. Huh. Okay. It is? Oh, I can see that. You have the weirdest imagination ever, George. Oh, Well, RIP: Doris Roberts. Hi, B. H, Hi, h. Nice. Right. See you tomorrow. On a side note, I feel like Geneva could have given her talk on the riot and Los Angeles and the massacre plaque and Wanda Coleman at this symposium and that it would have been perfect, which is to say I remember the "amoebas, tigers and philosophers" – but what was the other creature? Or to ask, with Pamela Lu, what will it take to "de-red" the cake? Delete, delete, click. The Babylonian artifacts were appearing like holograms. Delete, delete, click. I want a vial of dust composed of a ruby that has been ground into a fine red powder. No, I don't want that. Delete, delete, click. To quote Peggy Deamer, "Property is the form of representation that history takes." Perhaps the real link between questions of monstrosity, language, alien being and architecture will come out – when we interview each other, which is the next stage. They need to have a second symposium and invite more people interested in language as the material surface that deflates then reinflates when you touch it. Reach out and touch the wall made of aluminium foil behind your thighs. You know that it's like an Elena Ferrante novel over here!!!! You know it's a Bjork video. Was it also the bliss of Aquavit? The arctic bird's nest cake? The three wishes? "You have given birth to a little aristocrat," said Erin, laughing.

> *On the soundwalk the light*
> *is louder than I remember,*
> *dramatic gravel bony underfoot.*
>
> *Later I made a loop*
> *of it*
> *that I could then loop again*
>
> *& install in a top branch*
> *under the streetlight.*
> *The next day the microphone*
>
> *was a hummingbird*
> *extracting sugar from ink,*
> *under which the bones were*
>
> *now suffused with a pink x-ray light.*

5680

*It's why I wear my
shirts backwards,*

the lilies are mires, the cat is an oven, the season is a lure, the internet is an aching affect machine. Louise Michel took a black underskirt and tied it onto a broomstick to make an anarchist flag.

So we get an old city bus and give it the number of a line that doesn't exist – 47 or 810. The vulture can also cry. The next day I flew off to the UK for a series of lectures at Durham, Newcastle, Exeter and Queen Mary London. Somewhere over Greenland I realised that all was not well – a combination of high temperature and chills (which I'm relieved I didn't know at the time doctors call 'rigors') – and I recognised, through my confusion, the symptoms of sepsis. By this stage I was very ill and going in to shock. At one stage plans were laid to divert to Reykjavik … Eventually I was in University College Hospital for five days on IV, receiving absolutely wonderful care (so hands off the NHS!). I flew home at the end of the week: you can perhaps imagine how apprehensive I was during the flight. But to distract myself I managed to watch "Testament of Youth," loosely based on Vera Brittain's autobiographical memoir of being a nurse in the First World War — when sepsis was a major killer. Smart choice. At first glance, I thought the line, handwritten in red oil pastel, might be "Co-eternal being" though I quickly saw it wasn't. This confusion brought me back to the childhood notion of the "human bean" and I wondered for a moment if she might be going there but it was "beam" not "bean". By that time, I was all involved in the hearts, wondering if Norma had painted them or were they from one of her grandchildren? From farther away I had mainly registered the piece as a sort of seascape because of what seemed to be a sailboat in the water against a scribbled sky that appeared on the left side of the collage. I was drawn to the textured rectangle there, made of a sort of open weave material, like a counter mat, secured to the ground by a British 3£ stamp (from Tom Raworth?) and three pieces of blue tape, the mat itself like a sail. But as I got close I found I was peering into the image of Simone and Jean-Paul, quite old in this photo — a yellowed newspaper cutting — along with the painted hearts and the phrase, written in red, "Co-eternal beam." But first, what are gibbons? They are apes, called lesser apes but definitely in our group with chimps, gorillas, and orangs and not with monkeys. The Chinese used to call them "gentlemen of the forest" to separate them from troublesome monkeys. Our lineage split from theirs about 18 million years ago. For context, the separation with orangs was 14, gorillas 7, and chimps 5 mya. They are the fastest travelers through forest canopy, clocked at 55 km/hr, swinging from branch to branch. They have ball and socket wrists on their long and powerful arms. When they are forced to the ground they walk upright (more upright than chimps can manage). Gibbons are social, territorial and pair bond for life. And they sing with very powerful voices due to reverberating throat sacs. They sing duets, and family choir performances. But they also whisper or "hoo". There have been some studies of their song but the Clarke paper (citation below) is the first study of the softer hoos. Anyway, in February 2004, Barbie wanted to change boyfriends. For nearly half a century she had been going steady with Ken, whose nose is the only protuberance on his body, when an Australian surfer seduced her and … I have been thinking this year about oppression and the soft tissue. What can I track as a lateral, anterior / posterior and superior pattern of distress? I think of how emotional trauma in particular restricts the three dimensional breath.

Face down.

Face up.

Then face down again.

And of course: to remember.

To breathe.

Whoever you are.

Because the soft tissue.

Between the 11th and 12th ribs.

Which do not attach to the anterior costal cartilage.

And also remember.

That you are reaching across your partner's body and that it is less functional.

To be direct.

To come in at an angle to the angle already present.

At the tip.

Or the body.

Of the rib.

Which itself.

Can vary.

Between three and five inches, and which sometimes does not present.

In the way a textbook would suggest.

Are you breathing three-dimensionally?

Two-dimensional breathing is a form of internalized oppression. But how does the camera know this? Very simple. It scans all other pictures stored on the phone or on your social media networks and sifts through your contacts. It looks through the pictures you already made, or those that are networked to you and tries to match faces and shapes. In short: it creates the picture based on earlier pictures, on your / its memory. It does not only know what you saw but also what you might like to see based on your previous choices. More generally, identity is the name of the battlefield over your code. Huge religious and quasi-religious structures have sprung up in recent decades to take up the tasks abandoned by states, providing protection and survival in a reversal of the move described in *Leviathan*. Identity happens when the Leviathan falls apart and nothing is left of the commons but a set of policed relational metadata, Emoji and hijacked hashtags. This is the reason why the gay AKP pornstar bots are desperately quoting Hobbes' book: they are already sick of the war of Robbie Williams (Israel Defense Forces) against Robbie Williams

(Electronic Syrian Army) against Robbie Williams (1" l'.ir , t nos prandi ecrivait.s ilu xvi□* .;i«eV, il nVn e-i niicnn. ji- ends, on Ton pui-si r □ o:::i.i!tre un souvenir, n:ie impi i -,' •!' !V-pri! aap'aiV I '•'□'..- rvmr'n, l.H.) and are hoping for just any entity to organize day care and affordable dentistry. And fuck this shit a tin peened reindeer

    Metallically hoofed on glass
    Scorched cotton snowmen edged the corners
    Flesh coloured powder mountains
    Vague wire tunnels
    It's like a white onion-fleshed pumpkin tiny black eyes and
        round paper hairs laughing white collars minced
        muted in the huffing dry morning wind that jingled
    Hollow smoke the hole transmitting hair come out like red
        meat through uh screen door balanced like a ball
        Inside the tubette on the small duplex tile shadow
        of my hand made a movie wolf head the dangling
        beep seal I saw once as a kid
    So life like it almost made me cry
    It stared with its eye glass and one glue smith that clear our
        stars
    The wolf head came off in the night
    His paw plucked a mushroom and pawed a nest of bees
    A blade
    It could be a tremendous black upside-down tulip it could be
        a black fishes' tail it could be a day, artistically
        crimped and buoyant in its

garden. Youna Kwak imagines it (first). Then she remembers it. Then she is in it, walking alone. Before I fail to join her, my mind takes me to another garden. There is only one thing growing and maybe it is not even a garden. It is a place in Kumamoto, Japan, where there is an eight-hundred-year-old camphor tree. I bet it'd block out the whole universe if you were standing underneath it, Hiromi Ito says in *Wild Grass on the Riverbank*. In fact, it was Hiromi who brought me to the tree, and her daughter who introduced me to one of the most marvelous things about it: the iridescent wing of a tamamushi beetle. It was on the ground. The beetle was gone. Never will you say: when I was a corpse, and did such-and-such. It was just a wing. What must the stone think of us? The corpse with no body, has a voice. They fizz, they vanish, and a new structure appears. The sonnets go on their ziz-zag wandering. So we create ourselves too, it is implied, minute by minute, the atoms taking shape and then dissolving and reforming. And, we realize, the confidence of the utterances is borrowed too – it derives from the multitude of texts sampled and collaged or, a term Spence prefers, montaged … Really, they are short monologues that resemble the faults in our stars, but that's okay. I am rushing in to speak to Jill McCracken's class about the sex worker literary canon. Then, to last session of spring semester with Pace. The girls are doing a performance art today. Really, they are short monologues that resemble the faults in our stars, but that is okay too. Then, special needs trust lawyer, then, burlesque client. Then, packing the Chihuahua and my sloppy performance bodywork outline for the open embodiments conference in Tucson. Brilliant! will you be paying today with credit to receive one complimentary white paper bag with soft rope handles will you be paying today with one small white envelope of cash pile of cash fistful of crisp white cash!

So yes, it was all white potatoes 65 cents a pound and good for boiling. It was all eastern standard time and heavy cream and cold cuts at dawn. It was all "GRANDDAD IN THE OCEAN WITH THE OIL SPILL IN THE LIBRARY WITH THE LOGORRHEA IN THE BEDROOM WITH THE

BARBITURATE IN THE KITCHEN WITH …" The balloon came down and we wrecked it because we did not know what it was we were poor and romantic and believed in ghost spirits but more likely we saw the direction it come from the blood looked so fake like ketchup we kept going this can't be pause real pause it is too orange pause go south of San Francisco, where Hollister is slowly being fault creeped and deformed. Curbs at nearly the exact same spot on opposite sides of the street are popped out of alignment. Houses too young to show this level of wear stand warped, torqued … in other words, the deep rocks beneath Hollister are slippery, more pliable, and behave a bit like talc. Wonderfully but unsurprisingly, the mechanism used to study creep is called a creepmeter. Should I reiterate the autopsies? No — here's the film. In the beginning, there are corpses. The corpses are neither old nor visibly wounded. They appear as living people under hypnosis, or performing. We recognize the corpses because we do not depend upon them being dead. In the beginning, there are living people. The living people tend to the corpses. They take the corpses' measurements. They tend in doctor fashion. The corpses are not sleeping, but in a state of death intoxication. Intoxicated by death, yet deathless … Then the corpses are opened. The living people drill and drain the corpses. The corpses are pliable and compliant. The flaying of the corpse permits the final vestige of performance to fall away. Skin is a suit, a costume. When a forehead is pulled over a human face to expose the brain, the camera crosses its eyes. It is difficult to watch the living handle the dead without forcing oneself into self-preserving distraction, but it is imperative to stay focused. One minute before the end, a small lake appears. Bodily humors shine upon the corpse. At the time of The Act of Seeing With One's Own Eyes, the Butcher Shop — which doubles as a private residence — was being fumigated for bed bugs. One of the casitas was infested — In the beginning, there are living people. In the beginning, there are also corpses. There are corpses and living people in The Act of Seeing, and living people and corpses in the library watching The Act. The corpses manifest the physical bodies of the living in ways that fundamentally resist the living people's projections. The living have a rendezvous with a corpse, til the corpse reciprocates — on its terms: The grieving predator, the deathless angel, prideful anger, the stalker, the butcher, and bloodsucking bugs, are bonded in the library without books. With no door to the outside world, the library becomes a situation room and / or I wake up first, around 8:30AM, my head feels not awesome, I shower and don't shave, drink a ton of water, what is a muse but a parasite, the parasitic as queer, foreign, LOTS OF HORRIBLE IMAGES of parasites projected, that fish tongue parasite creature that looks like a MAGGOT XENOMORPH (click here if you dare, don't say I didn't warn you), I think she's onto something, Jack Spicer's furniture right? though she didn't mention it, but yeah, what a fun way to think about our bodies, as infested, as occupied, I'd wager that Megan likes David Cronenberg, body horror beats cosmic horror every time, but I guess the parasite can be both, and that's maybe it's lunch time, I eat terrible

California rolls with my hands, I find a poem in Van de Mieroop's *Philosophy Before the Greeks*:

COLUMN 1:   (TENTATIVE TRANSLATION)
1 [ni_3-du_{10}]   (that which is good)
2 *tu_3-bu_3-tu_3*   (that which is good)
3 ni_3-zha_3 (that which disappears)
4 *dar*-RI-*du*   (that which disappears)
5 ni-gestin   (?)
6 *ga-ga-ri_2-tu_3*   (?)
7 ni_3-sig?   (?)

COLUMN 2:
1 [ni_3-NE-igi-du_8]   (?)
2 *ga-da-um_x*   (garment)
3 ni_3-du_8 (garment)
4 ni_3-du_8-du_8:ud   (?)
5 ni_3-du_8-du_8 (container)
6 *a-ba-um*   (?)
7 ni_3-UD   (?)

Pretty good, huh? James Miller wrote a piece for Drunken Boat on Black Metal, towards the end of the essay he relates the genre to *The Katechon*, I know Michael was very happy with it, and if you've read *The Katechon*, makes total sense. Alright where am I now, wandering like everyone else I guess, I see Stephanie Young eating lunch with Catherine Meng, I see Phrydas pacing the large common areas asking folks if they know where he can find some butcher paper for his clay workshop, seems he's having no luck, he looks incredulous: "we're in an art school, how is there no butcher paper?!" I do see another panel called "Pataphysical Innovations," actually this isn't a panel but a reading, sounds fun, I like the press, I like the pataphysics (though don't ask me to define, "answers to questions no one has asked" or something?) just a little roll call of readers: Mark Tursi introduces, Richard Greenfield introduces (quotes from Akhmatova), Tony Trigilio reads poems from *White Noise* a book he describes as "goofy paranoia meets scary post 9/11 paranoia," Joe Milazzo reads from his forthcoming book *The Habiliments*, Catherine Meng reads from *Tonight's The Night*, Gina Abelkop reads from *Darling Beastlettes* (you know how comedians are always using the word "killed" to describe a good set, Gina KILLED), Johannes Göransson reads "Pig Circus" from his book *A New Quarantine Will Take My Place*, and then a Q&A, but Q&A's literally make me want to throw up, the claustrophobia and dread I feel when a moderator says "and now we'll open it up to the audience, does anybody have any questions?" is severe and real, just let us go, we all want to go, there will always be questions, and they are almost always about the ego of the person asking the question, almost never about the subject they are ostensibly asking about, right? we all know this right? I mean I've been that jerk asking a question that is actually totally about the performance of asking the question, I think I did that with Alice Notley at Naropa, my question was horrible, convoluted, something about detective fiction and liminality, haha Jesus Christ, barf barf barf, the Q&A as bear-trap, and what do we do with bear-traps? WE AVOID THEM! so I split. This is not the waterfall. But it looked like this and emitted an ultra-violet light. This was the waterfall. I took this one photograph. That I climbed to, and somehow – behind – to retrieve – the stone – upon which – I knew – there – would be a "different writing." And how that different writing would look sorta like Arabic. But everyone was so white. Their skin looked almost transparent. I could see the veins and nerves bunching and pulsing beneath their wrists.

I felt passive to the blows I was about to receive.

And to the weather.

The atomic intensity.

Of the pink rain.

Which is to say: I don't know what the word "private" means in this context. *Did You Remember to Take Your Medicine?*

$ 1,423.00
$ 1,986.99
$ 1,012.40
$ 207.85
$ 800.00
$ 100.00
$ 15.87
Is this platform even on?
      —Stephanie Young

Every-
thing's funny
in San Francisco.

Who could forget the Hattifatteners? The Hattifatteners, are silent, tall, ghost-like creatures who can neither speak nor hear, who have flaring hands attached to their neckless heads. They resemble thin mushrooms. They are forever wandering around in large herds. The only thing that interests them is reaching the horizon – and once they reach it, they continue on. They don't need to eat or sleep. Nothing except roaming interests them. You can sense their presence as an electrical charge in the air. At other times they're harmless. At Midsummer, the Hattifatteners gather on their own island for an annual meeting, after which they set out roaming once more. They collectively own a barometer. In one story, a character steals this barometer and they relentlessly pursue him until they get it back. In another story, Moominpappa travels to the island of the Hattifatteners, discovering the secret to their weather-obsession: they cannot feel emotions unless confronted by an electrical storm. But you know what they say: "I cut out about 20 swatches 3" x 1.5" and began to sew words on them. I love Bourgeois's *Ode à l'oubli* so much and so have begun a miniature ode to it. I sewed three words tonight (in this order):

1. Weather
2. Fallopian
3. Carbon

Where this is going, I'm not sure. Meanwhile, in Gonzales TX I found the most wonderful thing that I call my Rock Box. Chris Martin's blog posts seem to connect to what I have in mind." Do you believe in singing? The sky is totally eczema. But you know what they say, or at least what Junot Díaz says: "If you say, I think the occupation of Palestine is fucked up on forty different levels, people are like, you're the devil, we're going to get your tenure taken away, we're going to destroy you. You can say almost anything else. You could be like, 'I eat humans,' and they'll be like bien, bien." FALL IN / EAT / TOUCH MY LIFE / PLUNGE A STRAW INTO THE EARTH SUCK OUT YOUR IRISES / A bullet I had never seen / "I don't know how to describe it, it takes time, you have to hunt them then sew them; they're small, they hang down to your navel – soup stars, with macaroni, with pear or apple pips, even to the point of threading the rubies of the pomegranates; clearly they'd rot quickly – that's how it went: naked and with the necklace of dead mice. Then the sensation you have that it must be you who wears the necklace and the breath, yes …"

    Only here
    can the rekindled silence
    measure
          one and one,
    and over again,

    […]

        kuduo
        aggrey bead
        Akua ba
        Ibeji
        a Kanaga mask
    […]

    ¡O ritmo de semillas secas!
        [O rhythm of dry seeds]
    That would stir the salutary
    orientation of a crystal rug,
    a kente cloth and a dancing kilt

a plane of immanence, a plane of melancholy, a plane of "paper" as "wood's pressed immanence." When my daughter was five she had a long-distance telephone conversation with an eight-year-old Inupiaq girl who lived then in Point Hope Alaska. I understand "subjectivity" as Kant and Lyotard have, as the site of aesthetic judgments. In baroque painting light becomes fluid, full of alternative machines with diagrammatic parts, populating the expressionistic landscape of Metropolis, factory labor producing drones even as a robotic Maria emerges from the oyster shell, sporting a lunar tiara. A father in a stolen balloon flies over a cane field in Haiti and jumps from the basket to his death while his son on the ground channels Boukman, Matisse, Lam, Bacon, Rauschenberg, and Mendieta, for instance. So what I see are Warburg's black cloth-covered frames (Mnemosyne Atlas). I glanced up and saw a gold chariot on a massive gate. Kurukshetra. The thunder and lightning are seams. This duplicate sleep perhaps resembles an "angel on a composite animal". Think more about what a fold is. The Wertheim coral reef that is crocheted in the hyperbolic plane. Oh timely citizen who is about to open that door, on this mountain the drought-killed trees adjudicate truth value and there is color assigned to meanings. It is an intermediate state though it is called war and elsewhere, normativity. This is the face-to-face phase and the mammal heads and insect heads of relatives lick your body. They chanted and encamped. They encamped and marched. They marched and rallied. They rallied and strategized. They strategized and contacted. They contacted and communicated. They communicated and practiced forms of caring. What was becoming of this specific world was what they wandered onto. Into. That's called Napalm and Pudding, / Not to relate it for the purposes of / Elevating my personal experience / To anything symbolic for incidental / Or even destitute to emotion was / Heart mine, art mine and that's – / That's – have mercy, am I living for it? / Or barely? Barely and widely. And should I stomp the dying bird / To death? It was dying gradually / With its eyes on me & / Shakespeare freed me from Brecht / Come, thick fabric, into a conception ... '- --- -\- ( ) """"" I can't always z. (' i-' 1.. ometimes, it's ~~:: middle of the sky, but stretehed and stretched, '" &\' <· ‚_, 1 ~ . !i tr- Lj ()A_ ¥' pvd"'f _. .1 . ~ ..f ‚. ~'f.t-£• '" J IL ')1'-f -'" That one's a Flying human, who was stopped, abruptly stopped. '· luR ~ ..‚.-- """ . '" ~JJ ......) o;f.'‚..r .) l L .) • • And that one is a kind of long midge pinned to a cross that goes up and up forever, from w~uld, in any case, b¢' completely impossible, completely pointless to talk to ‚Y'V v a_....,- • This one's another insect. Nillnber 42, a rtltfian. Number 51, duck, a real quacking on the cross. 53] (as...thou.gh str.dp?eu ~p) aie. '- broad and nervous and look ready to eseape Y' \..4' frio.. \':r' ~ (\' ~ d 0 1' bt' (' I (54) Don't try to get any hope from this one. ~c v~u<:-0' [4.-< 'ft"r 1 (60) Intense, intense, so intense that s/he turned to flames. By fire if necessary, ~ecides to L ' f' # a .~ o-v... fl< 1\J o1NA Unquestionable: L~' i'< • -(-Jf ~- • that was long ago, that was in the serious years of my life, ~ 0 0 A movement unlocked my attention. I refocused my eyes, looking past the vodka glass and into the static buzz of the TV. I stayed very still for a few seconds before lowering the glass to the floor, careful not to take my eyes off the screen. There was something distant and alive in the depths of the white noise – a living glide of thoughts swimming forward, a moving body of concepts and half-felt images. I moved slowly off the sofa and crawled across the floor towards the television, trying to see deeper into the vast depths of no-hiss signal behind the glass. I got nearer and the creature became aware of me. It picked up speed and powered out of sight, disappearing in a fast flick of movement below the bottom right corner of the screen. Meanwhile, the pie and its recipe remain the same.

So perhaps we could consider the field of objects more broadly. What is an object? There are things. But when is it that a thing becomes an object? When a subject operates on a thing. There are different operations that can be made on things. Here are three important ones: objectalisation, objectivation, and objectification. As a Lacanian psychoanalyst, I encounter the first operation all the time. It is the operation by which someone or something becomes important for a subject insofar as satisfaction is at stake. So, the mother is an object for a baby, and inversely just as well. Notice here that not being an object is generally more problematic than being one. At this juncture a crucial difference should be introduced. Subject means the subject of the unconscious, the way satisfaction is organized for an individual regardless of his / her conscious choices. The ego, on the other hand, is precisely an object that an individual "makes" of oneself and with which (s)he is more or less satisfied. It's gross. *It gets so scary there, around the eyes. I remember thinking "My first moustache," painted in sections in minty green lipstick. People started lining up. I didn't know them. They let me get really close and hold their chin, turn their face side to side. And some kind of other connection (maybe this is the political feeling) and she wasn't even in the makeup because it turns out she has sensitive skin and whatever I'm using is not free of paraben or other things that can't be that great.* So the book opens with "our narrator" (later revealed to be Cortázar himself) on his way to his home in Paris. On the train, he reads a comic book starring the masked hero Fantomas, whose latest mission is to stop a band of anti-culture terrorists from burning down the world's great libraries. After our narrator's arrival, Fantomas himself comes crashing in through the window, and Cortázar must help him realize the magnitude of this global problem — at least, when he's not lusting after the superhero's assistants or being yelled at on the phone by a convalescing Susan Sontag. These conversations with Sontag are half comedy routine and half sadly sadly. At one point, the narrator presents the difficulty of their task: "Susan, the people are alienated, badly informed, deceptively informed, mutilated ..." She responds: *Yes, Julio, but reality makes itself known in other ways, too — it makes itself known in work or the lack of work, in the price of potatoes, in the boy shot down on the corner, in the way the filthy rich drive past the miserable slums (that's a metaphor, because they take care never to get anywhere near the goddamn slums). It makes itself known even in the singing of birds, in children's laughter, in the moment of making love. These things are known, Julio, a miner or a teacher or a bicyclist knows them, deep down everyone knows them, but we're lazy or we shuffle along in bewilderment, or we've been brainwashed and we think that things aren't so bad because they're not flattening our houses or kicking us to death ...* That paragraph, like most of *Fantomas*, has not aged a day since 1975. Neither has this Google translation of a hunk of a Dutch version of a poem by Sean Bonney:

> "I love you" fuck the police /
> "The light of heaven" fuck the police say, do not say
> "My morning commute"
> "The right to vote" / for infinite solar wind "Fuck the police
> not to say "I lost my understanding of Visions" not to say
> "Many human capital malevolent" not to say
> area of the celestial "fuck the police
> for "globe Moonlight" for "the ghost Mab"
> fuck the police / do not tell "direct debit" not to say "Join the
>   Party"
> 'E' for the boss "and then say fuck the police
> do not say "evening rush hours" fuck the police say / not say
> not to say "high Skim milk" fuck the police /
> "The attraction of the earth" and /
> "Make it new" fuck the police
> All other words are buried there
> and say fuck the police / for "Philosopher's Stone"
> for beauty "fuck the police say / not say "here's my new
>   poetry"
> fuck the police
> and say fuck the police / but

If you truly want
to be beautiful
you have to
have a noseface.
A noseface
that is enough.
You do
not even have
to have a nose.
As long as
you
have a nosehead
a nosehead
with some snot on it
you'll be alright.

Randall and Khalym led the Q and A. This is Randall asking Claudia about the decision of younger artists and poets to "opt out." Claudia is about to reply: "Leaving the room? You can't leave the room. Where do you think you're going?" I FELT THE GOLD BLOCKS OF SUNLIGHT GO INTO MY CHEST. To make: "… a turn to what Ernst Bloch would call the not-yet-conscious or the-not-yet-here," as José Esteban Muñoz put it. Perhaps I am under-exaggerating. Still, there's a complexity to how the morning will go. First we will fetch the milk. Then boil it. Then it'll be too hot. Or perhaps we will be drinking tea. Or perhaps it is night. And the night-blooming jasmine is happening. A low, toxic-smelling fog has turned everything white. It's not this visit but a subsequent one – in which I pick up some of the asphalt chunks, street dirt, fold it all in a piece of paper and put that in my bag. Many months later, I will eat it. I will eat a chunk of the floor of the world. An ancient practice from my home culture that I feel safe enough to share with the other brown and black people of the conference. And thus to break it down. To be processed: by filters or organ meats. His mother was a green bouquet of kelp. She bore him over a period of three days   down by the shipyard. The harbor was an "interesting" place for an alien kid to play. Can you blame me for revealing my personal alchemical principles? *Macfarlane, translating the Communist Manifesto, tries to give 'Ein Gespenst' a double meaning. It is not just the ghostly apparition that haunts the castles of Shakespeare's Macbeth and Hamlet, foretelling doom and retribution for the incumbents. It is also the Fairies, firmly connected to the landscape and deeply rooted in the soil. The importance of respecting the land which they frequented was widely recognized. It was bad luck to interfere with, or to try to remove, trees, bushes, stones, ancient buildings or anything else believed to have fairy associations. Misfortune, illness, or even death might result from tampering with fairy property.* This can easily be seen as an assertion of traditional pre-capitalist communal rights. So of course they were turning *left* towards the river. But the cars behind them were honking — Don't go, Don't go! — because a car was coming fast from the other direction, but honking often sounds like — Hurry up, Hurry up! — so ... There is no hospital, at first, only the point of impact. I can't get beyond the moment immediately before, which is daylight and mindlessness — life. A potted plant sat in the sink. I thought of its head filled with river. Why did the butcher paper taste like salt? What number was blinking on the machine? What kind of plant was it? The room has the temperature of a cave, or an oven left to cool for a century. The room is unlit; it is late afternoon on the floor and the ceiling. The room isn't spotless because it is clean, but because it is new, every day ... I quote Brenda Hillman, "Death Tractates":

> Remember the lily, growing through
> the heart of the corpse?

("WITH SUCH FRAGMENT BEFORE US" – "Modern Fiction," Virginia Woolf, / OR WHEN I GET HOME FROM TEACHING I'M GOING TO LOOK UP A SHRED OF QUARTZ FROM JABÉS AND LET IT SPEAK THRU ME / THE GHOSTS OF THE BOOK / THE GHOST OF VIRGINIA WOOLF HOLDS A SCREAMING FLOWER / "Does the book here, stand for love? The Book is an object is an object of love. The manifestations of love in the book are the hugs, kisses, bites of sentences, words, letters, and, outside the book, an unveiled passion for the written wound, fertile lesion whose lips we spread like a vulva to allow in the sperm of death." Except besides not having shoes I also don't have keys or a cell phone and I can't get back into the apartment so I sit on the stoop and although it's a warm night it is still April and my feet are cold and I still have shards of mirror in my hair and then a raccoon is crawling up the fence. It is perched at the top, looking at me, deciding if I am a threat. We regard each other for a while. Then Eliza travels to Sydney to deal with the estate of her Aunt Dodge, and finds Maxine, a hitherto unknown cousin, occupying Dodge's apartment. When legal complications derail plans to live it up on their inheritance, the women's lives become consumed by absurd attempts to deal with Australian tax law. No. Because.
O God how can I wash my hands. I suggested she rub them over the top of the urn first. She did, interlocking her fingers, rubbing the backs, making a fist of each hand and rubbing out the ash from the creases in her knuckles. She went to the bathroom then and I got a dustpan and brush. I had to feel for them in the dark in the cupboard under the sink then I took them back to the dining room and crouched and swept up the ash that had fallen on the floor and turned up the dustpan so that it ran off one corner into the urn. I thought she was going to start drooling again. So already the diary is based on reproduced images. The rabbit is the "brand" or "symbol" of this violence; and like the tension between the one and the reproduced, like the diving in the land that produces the flood, the speaker both doesn't want to free the rabbit or

bury it. Hey, everybody! Hi Dóra! Hi, David. Bill, hi, Bill. Hi, James. Huh, I don't remember that. Hi, Jamie! Strange stuff. Oh, on the Scandinavian theme park book, at this point, I think the audio would just be on-site field recordings, but we haven't put our minds to the audio aspect yet. That was the initial idea: field recordings. Hi, Steve! Hi, G! Whoa. Hi, Douglas. Hi, Steven! Hey, B! Hi … uh, Bill? Hi, Ben! Hi! Hi. Bill, Hey! Hi! Hi, there! Whoa, good to see you! Huh. Steevee, hi. Hi, Ben. Hey! James, Hi, man. Bill, hi. Hi, welcome to this place, and thank you coming in. How are you? What's going on in *your* world? Hooray! I'll imbed it. Hi, Jamie! Steevee, Hi. Oh, god.

> Parts of me were at the big bang.
> All the parts.
> That was a long time ago,
> But the wait to be born wasn't too bad.

Back in the studio, Marcellini worked with an apparatus of his own construction to launch the bricks through panes of glass, using a camera shooting 11 frames per second to capture the exact moment the two objects met. Or, as Bengt Adlers puts it, I came to be the 2 HAHA 77 as a balanced Tiger one way or in the mindbox where each figure between 0 and 9 decides we could in a sense be each other's shadows, caught in the spiral of, well,

> That summer 3 men came to my childhood home
> Claiming they'd fix the cable
> My parents didn't own
>
> Then father wanted a gun but mama
> Said no / this woman
> Loves clint eastwood and desperado
>
> She forgives the scantily clad for the gore
> My mama is guns on the table
> Her first words in english
>
> Were make my day
> At 12 while abuelo hunted javelina along the border
> She chased away a man who came to take their home
>
> She alone
> With a butcher's knife
> And then a shovel
>
> After it all mama couldn't walk straighter
> She threw off every saint and every novio

Don't forget she says *why el mariachi dies alone.*

(I enveloped so much of this conversation into my body / the conversation in which C reaches for C and C meets C and C weeps and C lives that there is nothing. But the nothing is not my lack of speech revealing an ineluctable pit but is the riding of the sickness, or just an effect. mm / yes / the inside of a curved bone / THE INSIDE OF A SCRAP LYING ON ANOTHER SCRAP / THE MOVEMENT FROM CORPSE A TO CORPSE B / THE PATTERN OF WAVES / THE WAVE "It's sending and receiving, but isn't it also inventing or mixing?" – Lisa Robertson to Etel Adnan … "Pit of Acknowledgement" is a phrase that cycled / eroded through me / still lives here in the impossible bigness of being like an infected tide pool / the constant changing of containment / I'm endlessly amazed anything holds anything / THE INFECTED TIDE POOL IS THE WOUND AND THE POEM THE BODY BREEDING / BREATHING ALL AT ONCE INTO THE SIDES OF THE CLIFF / THE CLIFF FACING THE DESERT OR THE SEA OR THE REST OF THE SISTERMOUNTAINS. THE THREE OF CUPS / THE THREE GODDESSES RADIATING THE DEPTH OF THEIR WOUND. "Inventing is sending. If you are not inventive, you don't receive. These are not dead things. They are very complicated processes. We just have a glimpse of them." – Etel Adnan to Lisa Robertson. with a huh, yeah, there we go, hmmmmmm, "Your pores are tin cans," hahaha DELETE ME. It's necromancy as a cleanse, yeah, it's like duh! we are full of dead stars and we are always leaking them. "(Another version of the same beginning is simpler and more direct: in the long science of submission it is the mind that, quietly spectacular, unhooks the bodies and opens the face.)" – Lisa Robertson in *Magenta Soul Whip*. the ends of your hair are dead too! / you can still twist them and turn them colors. or, keratin is hoof matter too, an important part of our epidermis. / we have soft shells. I'm so glad. Ergo, I have passed through 700 years in a single hour. They're not years I've lived, not even years I can imagine: 773900 BC to 773200 BC. As I read them aloud — "seven hundred seventy-three thousand nine hundred bee cee" — I try to picture what they might mean, what they might have been. All I can conjure are cartoonish images of cavemen painting bison on rock walls (which happened not even 50,000 years ago, so I'm not even close), and occasionally Jesus (Monty Python-style), since as a Jew I use BCE and instead here I am saying "BC" over and over again. Yeah, I know, I know. Same difference. Still, Brendan and I read at a steady pace, he the odds and I the evens (Kawara's instructions), a healthy pause hanging in the air between each one. This seems fitting given that each number represents a whole year, each line an entire decade. We read and swiftly cross out our numbers with pencils as we go, using rulers to keep ourselves on track, but even then we stumble. Brendan says "seven thousand seven three …" by accident, and I look down at the abyssal page, suddenly struggling to find my number and remember how it's actually spoken. "Seven — hundred — seventy-three … " Thirty minutes into my hour I had to pee and still hadn't figured out how to sit comfortably in my chair, but I knew I had signed an invisible contract with On Kawara (as well as a physical one with the venue), so I continued reading years and lucky as the camphor drum an inflated toroid played by ten adjacent beaver tails the metric clock for what botany forgot luck in its oldest boeotian polymnia translates according to flute song into various cattle wearing masks of living flowers ridden by stick effigies which are themselves written by children whose thumbs are no longer opposing but fall in line with the unificatory split the horns of consecration blaring above the leaping hornamental explanosions their gaits primed to exploit the verd verity as grace will pivot tightly on its axes to miss the hiss of errows where they quill arguments arising in the descent of butterflies who feed on decomposing oranges, we have to wash the cake off, as in burn the "sugar" – Blake, Peckham and "the tree of angels". The sheer willpower needed to envisage something. Even a memory has to be forced back into existence, and for all your effort what do you get? Beauty is unavoidable. Beauty is truth. April is the cru-ellest month. Stately, plump Buck Mulligan. "Yes, of course, if it's fine tomorrow," said Mrs. Ramsay. "But you'll have to be up with the lark," she added. All happy families. For a long time I used to go to bed early. Sometimes, when I had put out my candle, my eyes would close so quickly that I had not even time to say "I'm going to sleep." And half an hour later the thought that it was time to go to sleep would awaken me; I would try to put away the book which, I imagined, was still in my hands, and to blow out the light; I had been thinking all the time, while I was asleep, of what I had just been reading, but my thoughts had run into a channel of their own, until I myself seemed actually to have become the subject of my book: a church, a quartet, the rivalry between François I and Charles V. This impression would persist for some moments after I was awake; it did not disturb my mind, but it lay like scales upon my eyes and prevented them from registering the fact that the candle was no longer burning. Then it would begin to seem unintelligible, as the thoughts of a former existence must be to a reincarnate spirit; the subject of my book would separate itself from me, leaving me free to choose whether I would form part of it or no; and at the same time my sight would return and I would be astonished to find myself in a state of darkness, pleasant and restful enough for the eyes, and even more, perhaps, for my mind, to which it appeared incomprehensible, without a cause, a matter dark indeed. It is this process of "Thingification" that preoccupies me, alongside the ways in which such a process engendered different forms of human expression and thought on the part of those who existed in this "zone of nonbeing." Because, if a human being becomes a thing, what the Caribbean historian Elsa Goveia calls "property in person" — and such processes are constructed around the appropriation of the body, not just the extraction of labor — then the "living corpses" represent figures and bodies that are not just simply and uniquely dominated by power. For these "living corpses," "thrownness" is constructed around certain kinds of violence. Given the ways in which the living corpse is constructed, then, the question that emerges from this form of life is not who is a human; neither is it about who speaks for / of the human. Rather, the question that forces itself to the fore is, "What about the Human?" Such a question emerges because the human, as a figure with special meaning, is already assumed by those who dominate and enact violence, while the supposed nonhuman nature of the living corpse becomes the foundation on which violence is enacted. Once we grapple with this context, then, there are two questions that are intimately linked and interconnected. They are: "What about the Human?" and "What does it mean to be human?"

Let me put the matter another way. What happens when we begin to think about and examine the "colonial encounter" from the perspective of the "living corpse"? We were talking about the body and how when something happens with the body, a medical intervention or even any medical touch, there is a kind of grieving that is also taking place. Then we talked about snakes, for about 80% of the rest of the time. I felt like the visceral organ crinkling talk of snakes was releasing the last residue of what we had been talking about before, the quality of body memory that is releases or opened when …

superior fuliginosity

which expands & re-emits the galaxies from nothingness
perhaps at lowered concentration
is simply scavenged from debris
like a hive of flailing pentads
being Juniper leanings
which at times structures the seasons commingling with sparks from blank
    rubidium jetties
which suffices at one level
[and so on and so forth]
for instance
in the Black Sea*
'Copepods' vanished
gastropods no longer members of life 'oysters reduced to remnant
    populations'
as if one could speak of cleansed uranium trees
of algae flourishing amidst invasive detergents
devastated
the Black Sea horse mackerel
the Atlantic bonito
'three species of grey mullets'
seals
killed by 'organo Chlorines'
the 'white-tailed sea eagle'
overcome by contaminants …

*Which is to say that in recent years the depths of the Black Sea

> "have become oxygen-starved deserts, riddled with pockets of hydrogen sulfide gas. Fishermen often report seeing sheets of flame on open waters …"

I mean, it's almost 10am and you have to go to a funeral of the daughter of a neighbor, a daughter you saw every day walking her dog, and you are *for some reason* not leaving your bed. But then I realized: The speaker of "Fruiting bodies" advises us to feed decomposers, and frets when she finds that she doesn't know how:

> "Not knowing what would grow on a body
> how can I turn into food?"

> "New beauty is made of erectile tissue
> made to bunch and wear out under the bridge
> where pigeons live, etc."

We end up just as helpless as we were before we sprouted our additional head. But did you know that several of my friends come here and think I'm in love with them? I've been told! --- "I know you're in love with me" --- "!? ?!" --- "Yes, I read your blog. You're in love with me" and I'm surprised, but I when I say it like this, how could I disappoint them and tell them no? How to tell you that this loneliness thinks of you or in you, but not you. In my youth I was a tireless dancer. This is a Dorn poem, appropriately included in *Hands Up!*, the collection brought out by Amiri Baraka through his Totem Press, in association with Corinth Books, Baraka then living in New York City, but having lived in Newark, that he would return to Newark —the wisdom in this. And the first lines of this poem from Dorn begin, "But now I pass / graveyards in a car." And in the second stanza of the poem, after having mourned the dead, after having mourned those objects and events and phenomena that have since passed out of existence, Dorn then turns to the dance itself, the Saturday night dance, he recalls this from his youth and thinking on his youth he recalls himself as a tireless dancer. And I find now that it serves me well to recall my *own* experiences in the world as a tireless dancer, in the photographs below — the first from Newark and the second from New York City — we tireless dancers — inexhaustible — alive — well. I can look at these faces and recall stories, moments, anecdotes, encounters. These faces are not aids to memory; they are people who perhaps might recall as I do — how in our youth we were all tireless dancers. And the second photo, this, a dancing, these would have been the drums, the pounding, of a confusion and also of a class war and also of a deep desire the shape of which still outpaces our desire. And our ability to grasp this desire though itself offers its own clear knowing. And perhaps this photograph was taken at Nightingales. Perhaps another club. The Bank or the Wetlands. I do not know. Though I do know I was there. And I cannot know where. I do not see myself. And this is as it should be for who could want to see only their own image when in fact it was the whole of the choir that mattered.

ACT ONE: IN WHICH YOU ARE COMING FROM OUTER SPACE AND ASK YOURSELF "WHAT IS ART?"

ACT TWO.

ACT THREE.

ACT FOUR.

WARNING.

ALGEBRAIC COMPARISON.

THE FACTS.

MORE FACTS.

STILL MORE FACTS.

SOME INTERPRETED FACTS.

SOME FACTUAL INTERPRETATIONS.

SOME REINTERPRETED FACTS.

SOME FACTUAL REINTERPRETATIONS.

MORE REINTERPRETED FACTS.

MORE FACTUAL REINTERPRETATIONS.

A REINTERPRETED CRITIQUE.

ANYTHING AND EVERYTHING.

A CRITICAL REINTERPRETATION.

THOSE WERE THE DAYS MY FRIEND.

DO WHATEVER.

DO WHATEVER IN ORDER TO.

DO WHATEVER, PROVIDED.

DO WHATEVER SO THAT.

THE FOUR INGREDIENTS OF ENUNCIATIVE MAYONNAISE.

So yes, if you haven't been here, you have to sort of visualize a swarm of light, like a swarm of bees. It seems to nest in the branches of trees, as if slightly thick. Rich, but not tropical rich. Lemony golden. With a strange blue afterglow. The following stanzas continue to list ongoing global events and tragedies. I conclude that political, military, and development problems have "entered our bed at night holding us down." I first read this book in the summer of 2005, which is also when I first read *Don't Let Me Be Lonely*. I saw a parallel between the two — between the parrots / thoughts that enter the bed at night and Rankine's argument against Dickinson that "hope was never a thing with feathers." She writes of a "deepening personality flaw: IMH, The Inability to Maintain Hope." We have so much blood on our hands (Eckes writes, "yes, there is blood on / your hands — you're *American* — / that's what you mean / every time you say / 'get over it'"),

> and hoa nguyen's at the microphone
> telling us about chinaberry trees in
> austin texas, how they grew on her.
> and she grows on us. poetry on poets,
> drinking this drink. then some of us
> fight about how to live in a fucked
> world and i lean back against the wall —
> i don't know how to live, i whisper
> to hoa who laughs in half the question
> and

Simone's music doesn't only serve for me as an amulet against the current evils of the world (which are also the old evils), it also just plain feels good to listen. Which is to note that, in his book *Space Between These Lines Not Dedicated*, Frank Sherlock repeats the refrain "you can feel good," which serves as a nice reminder that despite it all it's okay to allow one's self to feel good (cui bono if you refuse the feeling?), there are all kinds of things one can feel good about like "rocking black lip liner," "life in this ditch since you know your future starts here," and "beating the Giants." But perhaps what feels most pertinent to this idea of how to go on is that *The Rest Is Censored* reminds me of Fanny Howe's "Bewilderment," where she offers one possible definition of the lyric: "It is a method of searching for something that can't be found. It is an air that blows and buoys and settles. It says, 'Not this, not this'," I mean, Akilah Oliver's "In Aporia" concludes:

> I too have admired the people of this planet.
> Their frilly, ordered intellects.
> The use they've made of cardamom,
>   radiation as well. How they've pasteurized milk, loaned surnames to stars,
>   captured tribes, diseases, streets, and ideas …

"I like maps," Szymborska writes, "because they lie, / Because they give access to the vicious truth." When a giant, whose rib measured nine spans in length, reigned over the whole world. When the pipe smoke turned into pigeons. The crow is the salmon's aunt. The water god and goddess have no children, so claim the drowned as their own. Numa soon added one day to January, paying honor to the mystery of the odd number. The nether world entered into competition with the celestial. And then every dead man became an Osiris, for Ra is the sky, and we get the power of speech from our contact with the earth. And we know that Mercury has speech and utterance in his power. Now we'll return to what is said of very early people. The story goes like this. In ancient times, this world wanted to come to an end. A llama buck, aware that the ocean was about to overflow, was behaving like somebody who's deep in sadness. Even though its [crossed out: father] owner let it rest in a patch of excellent pasture, it cried and said, "In, in," and wouldn't eat. The llama's [crossed out: father] owner got really angry, and he threw the cob from some maize he had just eaten at the llama. "Eat, dog! This is some fine grass I'm letting you rest in!" he said. Then that llama began speaking like a human being. "You simpleton, whatever could you be thinking about? Soon, in five days, the ocean will overflow. It's a certainty. And the whole world will come to an end," it said. The man got good and scared. "What's going to happen to us? Where can we go to save ourselves?" he said. The llama replied, "Let's go to Villca Coto mountain." [In Spanish: This is a mountain that is between Huanri and Surco.] There we'll be saved. Take along five days' food for yourself." So the man went out from there in a great hurry, and himself carried both the llama buck and its load. When they arrived at Villca Coto mountain, all sorts of animals had already filled it up: pumas, foxes, guanacos, condors, all kinds of animals in great numbers. And as soon as that man had arrived there, the ocean overflowed. They stayed there huddling tightly together. The waters covered all those mountains and it was only Villca Coto mountain, or rather its very peak, that was not covered by the water. Water soaked the fox's tail. That's how it turned black. Five days later, the waters descended and began to dry up. Real shit don't stick to that khaki, the history of which is a complex tale in itself, in which the "I" walks out on his son, fucks the homeless, reflects on scrotums, obsesses over noctuid larvae and "the sepulchral chambers of the law." Yet there is room for Dickinson, and a fascination with ekphrasis, with the referenced "works of art" being, variously: a harlequin jewel bug, a bark beetle, and most of all, a wax cock. This is exactly what Kant meant when he described the sublime as a rapid alternation between the fear of the overwhelming and the peculiar pleasure of seeing that overwhelming overwhelmed. How simply possessing some model of subjectivity – which now requires software updates from the floor of the MoMA apparently! – does not then magically possess one of the material means of work or self-expression. That is to say – a conceptual mastery of Glenn Branca does not in and of itself bequeath unto one a guitar [tho indeed, how could one come to understand Glenn Branca without playing guitar?]. This is the Landian future – technical support going, 'look, lady, I'm sorry your lousy job doesn't pay enough to feed your kids, or buy a literal computer, but if you're running your Althusser mark 4 on McDonalds food I can't help you, of course the system's going to get bogged down …' I've found running Deleuze on a Marx Core with the Guattarian-schizoalytic Accelerator to be the most properly open-source subjectivity – it's basically Fedora Red Hat for your head: if you're ever in need of manual, patch, upgrade, etc. consult either a stranger, or best friend, or *Glas* – preferably all at once.

> grey whiteness of fog against invisible
> ridge, crow flapping toward pine branch
> in foreground, sound of wave in channel

That's when Gregoria Chávez, an older farmer from the northwest Argentine province of Santiago del Estero, said feminism must include "the struggles and support of our fellow farmers in defending the land."

> "we want" "our parent of spirit" ("rich sweet in dirt") "we
>   want"
> "our parent" "of leaves" "We want our fate fragmented to air
>   for
> our children to breathe;" "light on water for widows to think
>   near"
> "moonlight on water to ease you" "we want no poet, we
>   want our
> homes in the earth" "that's all we can have" "want no place in
> history or poetry" "want our wanderings our sorrows, after
>   the war
> not remembered,"
>
> "In this moment" "before" "anyone, ever" "died" "before we
>   were born?"
> "in this moment forever before" "before we went to a war"
> "Before we died" "In this moment, now" "In this moment
>   before, it is
> not before" "In this very moment" "where is it" "where we
> haven't died" "or died inside" "In this moment we haven't"
>   "in this
> moment, no one" "in this moment, no one has ever, died"
>   ("But I have
> been born") "in this moment" "where, where is it" "in moment" "who's
>   here"
> "Catch it catch it"

On the slopes of Mount Lhahjahti in Pedhjukistan, the spirit is much more visible than the body because its aura radiates very strongly. The size and the intensity of the color vary considerably from person to person. And since a good aura adds a lot to one's seductive capital, it's not at all rare, in the weeks before summer vacation, to see young people frequenting libraries, haunting museums, and sitting in on philosophy seminars. On the planet Sitara, there are five sexes — maka, fitu, jipu, giminis and gojo. The inhabitants of the island of Sanapagrata always tell the truth. On the neighboring island of Pagranasata, they always lie, while the people on Natagrapasa sometimes lie and sometimes tell the truth. The Portuguese missionaries soon got tired of the guess-work and ran them all through with swords. *Over the course of this project, I have identified plastic waste from fifty nations on six continents that have washed ashore along the coast of Sian Ka'an. I have used this international debris to create color-based, site-specific sculptures.* Which is to say, in "My Sister Rachana," we learn of a young girl abducted at age seven by the Khmer Rouge to work on a farm. When she finally returns home "... with no hair on the top of her head. / ... She forced many words into one. / Her thoughts were scrambled. / ...

> Now she is easily panicked.
> Good news gives her stomach ache ...
>
> Bad news give her a panic attack.
> She handles bad news
> Better than good news.
>
> When my family learned I had survived,
> When they learned I had escaped to America
> Rachana developed diarrhea ...
>
> The first time I sent money home
> Rachana had to be hospitalized.

[I am reminded of Ban, somehow ...] And so the world entreats the First Father to unleash the blue tiger that sleeps beneath his hammock. Which brings us to

C. QUANTITATIVE INFINITY
(a) Its Notion

§ 497

Quantum alters and becomes another quantum; the further determination of this alteration, namely, that it goes on to infinity, lies in the circumstance that quantum is established as being immanently self-contradictory. Quantum becomes an other; but it continues itself into its otherness; the other is thus also a quantum. This, however, is not only the other of a particular quantum, but of quantum itself, the negative of quantum as limited; hence it is the unlimitedness of quantum, its infinity. Quantum is an ought-to-be; it is by implication determined as being for itself, and this being-determined-for-itself is rather the being-determined-in-an-other, and, conversely, it is the sublation of being-determined-in-an-other, is an indifferent subsisting for itself.

§ 498

In this way, finitude and infinity each acquire in themselves a dual, and indeed, an opposite meaning. The quantum is finite, in the first place simply as limited, and secondly, as impelled beyond itself, as being determined in an other. But the infinity of quantum is first, its unlimitedness, and secondly, its returnedness into itself, its indifferent being-for-self. If we now compare these moments with each other, we find that the determination of the finitude of quantum, the impulse to go beyond itself to an other in which its determination lies, is equally the determination of the infinite; the negation of the limit is the same impulsion beyond the determinateness, so that in this negation, in the infinite, quantum possesses its final determinateness. The other moment of infinity is the being-for-self which is indifferent to the limit; but the limiting of quantum itself is such that quantum is explicitly indifferent to its limit, and hence to other quanta and to its beyond. In quantum, finitude and infinity (the spurious infinity supposedly separate from the finite) each already has within it the moment of the other. I mean, THE AUTONOMY OF ART HAS ITS ORIGINS IN THE CONCEALMENT OF LABOR: My heart beat very hard by itself. Which is to quote Cathy Wagner. Which brings us to *A tree set on fire with invisible flame*. And to *Inn of the Dawn Horse*, in which a wild-haired Leonora dressed in riding clothes sits in a room with her hyena familiar; behind her on the wall hangs a rocking horse, and through the window gallops a second horse.

> Xerox fiery abyss.
> I had to go to zero, then what?
> Defoliation and 6 kg.
> This ocean of syrup corpse is a great therapist.
>
> Bulls drape.
> Dum de dum de.
> Dum de.
> The reactor limps in its boiling threads.
>
> A link and then a broad mirror.
> A naked tooth and old cans.
> More shining moments pour into the third-floor meeting room.
> The granite decadence of the new burst.
>
> 4 precious grins.
> Four, five, six, seven.

                                    Afterwards stock
footage of a funfair in night-vision. Splinters of glass,
ravioli, seashell fragments and aquarium gravel creep in
fur through blue gravy. Maelstrom of castanets gif.
Over the completed sequence a grid of hot light striped with
massed diagonals in wire. Cut from kinetoscope to digital
then back; then back. Then back. And then switch back.
                          And then back. Track
forward to the burning waltzer, and then back. Break
into me. A flash. Half a word. Right into me. And then
forward. Just a sec. Switch. The
                      same waltzer extinguished.
And then back. And then add crowd noise. The
other half of the word. And then add whale noise.
And then insect noise. And then add shrimp noise.
And then back. The
                  whale noise. And then forward.
A tracking shot in thermal imaging. Invisible riot of
pincers on woodblocks. Novel bone clamps. A five second
spider rest, a woodwind ostinato and back. A cloud of
keyclicks over the shrimp noise. The trout noise. An
unborn bare bongo the jaws of whose percussion section are
perpendicular to the handle that weaves the ageless
quotients into an exitless quarantine, or a bare exposed
bongo in a netted mash twenty minutes from the
percussion section the flanks of which freeze
gripping the bongo in a permanent phobic huddle
                  perpendicular to the slide. And then
the snooker commentary. The snooker commentary.
The snooker commentary flanged to excess. Too late
                  instantly. The snooker commentary
flanged to excess and sped to a burgundy scream.

Bats sing Bach, Francis murders a caged monkey and meets the Great
Architect Egres Lepereff, who is dressed as a Cossack and reads the *Spew*

Matesman. Now she is making omelettes with her guests' hair and spreading mustard on her feet. The composition – a sitting hermit and pig in front of a stream – was lifted straight from Bosch, whom she'd seen in the Prado. But her saint has three heads and instead of devils he's surrounded by female figures, one brewing a potion in her cauldron, others holding up their queen's gigantic skirt. She cradles an egg; geese fly out from beneath her pallium; her golden hair is a field of wheat. Around her feet a hunt is taking place – Ucello's *Hunt in the Forest* but with a sylph instead of a stag – while the sea behind is teeming with boats, whales, crabs and the monsters that form the borders of a medieval map. Always game for defection, the CIA contacted the dominatrix and encouraged her to "play ball." She reluctantly agreed while continuing to make the landscaper late for his mulching appointments on the Upper West Side. The CIA's interest in Argabright's personal life only made this Venus in Furs situation even hotter, against formidable odds. (Argabright's father did pre-internet "Mo-net" work in the Pentagon during the Vietnam War; his neighbors in northern Virginia were ex-NSA.) Instead of being returned to D.C. in a white van with a redacted brain, he stuck around New York and continued planting trees in celebrity houses while hungover. Shrubs to the stars. Gardens thrived. Mary Tyler Moore entered syndication while Argabright dabbled in New Wave vaudeville. The punk arborist with a drum machine would form the band Ike Yard, pulling its name from the shelf of the record store in *A Clockwork Orange*. Ike Yard cut one album for Factory Records, the Manchester-based label that housed artists like New Order, A Certain Ratio and 52nd Street. Madonna would loiter outside the studio during recording sessions, bumming smokes off the bass player while Basquiat materialized at odd hours, offering his services with a sawed-off cornet. (Downtown scholars are quick to note the total absence of cornet in Ike Yard recordings.) Dear Mom and Dad, I pray to be a beautiful actress and model whom everyone loves and also for all the cats to be relieved of their despair and the dog never to suffer loneliness and also for all the strangers whose diseases and failures I'm unable to catalogue. My prayer is addressed to the heart of the construction, to the gear from which all shafts emanate. It's always you and me alone in this gray metal drawer. In the wooded valley, she came upon three pennies and a bear. The bear said, these are my sister's eyes and her heart, help me return them to the sky. She said nothing, for she didn't speak bear. Give me your hand, said the bear, and she said nothing, though she held out her hand, which was scarred from hot water. SO TODAY ON THE TRAIN I SAW A GUY EAT THREE BANANAS WITHOUT STOPPING. When he pulled out the third banana, i said no fucking way out loud. Compare Rammellzee's INFINITYS ZOETICAL COMPOSITIONAL JUNCTION FROM ANTIKNOWLEDGE MATTERED A CONDENSED ABSTRACT QUANTUM MECHANICS, which begins: Electromagnetic energys knowledge conformed in a stable formation function protection around any planet gives basis base for development of disease culture, on any planet with enough natural resources to conceive bacteria as long as the orbit is the right postition for that vital resource. Humans being disease culture (the body) spirtis being gaseous energy (disease culture manipulation). Death is remanuplation only be electromagnetic knowledge energy leaving disease because of malfunction of inhabited disease culture, other deaths are only CHANGE. Electromagnetics knowledge disperses back into the course of the Van Allen Belts (in purity) ° dianetical path, continuing on in evolution's path. Knowledge is scattered throughout Van Allen Belt in minute knowledge particles. Life. Electromagnetics in a photonic stage to conduct energys knowledge light (pure thought) which is in all atoms inhabits compatible disease by fusing into diseases DNA nervous system structure codeplan to energize the cerebrum before its embryotic stage sharing and manipulating and being manipulated with the composed knowledge of the atometric D x N =

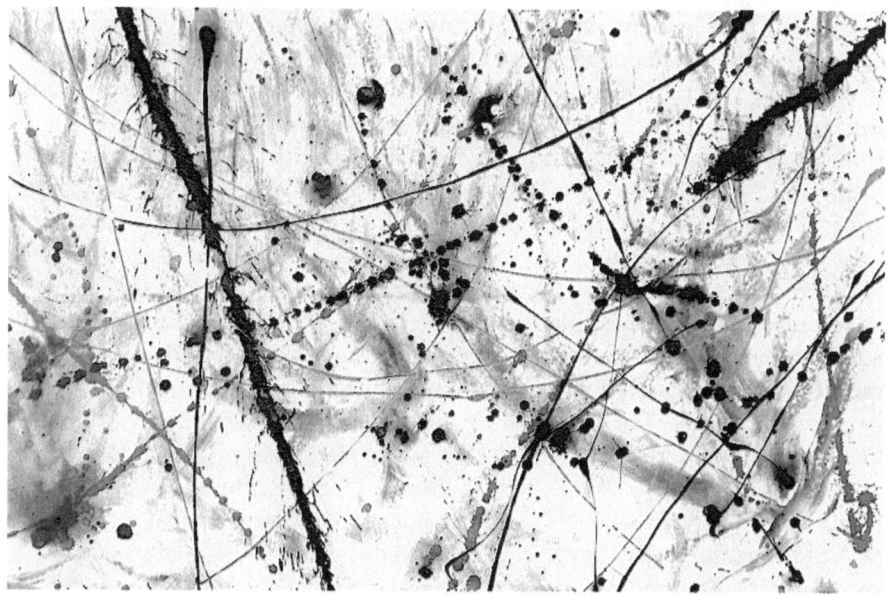

So don't doubt me if I say the squirrels seem synchronized and the butter-yellow magnolia petals are tongues of discarded sneakers. On a bright spring day this corner smells like mildew. Even I know this particular prosperity's a dead end. If it bends it's not a biscuit. And if I say hi to everyone I meet? I thought the street would T here but it keeps going, through a weird haze. A little further on I encounter a cloud of flies. Houses not condos but in the condo style. Someone has written the alphabet in chalk on the sidewalk in two boustrophedonic lines. I'm getting a knot in my shoulders. The mulleted face on the sign pole isn't Val Kilmer's anymore. Telepathically enough, dude on a bike says *river rats* as he passes. Others pass saying *environmental, environment*. I wait for my burrito to finish cooking. A group of children walks by. One says:

"What about America?" "I love that name!" replies their teacher. As soon as I was compos mentis I started trying to document this new experience, but the first couple of days in hospital remain a bit of a blur. I have a strange sense that I was tripping – other former hospital patients have confirmed the feeling. Whether it was massive doses of amoxicillin and other antibiotics, or the fever, or the billions of predatory microbes in my bloodstream, or the fact that I had virtually eaten nothing for two days, or a combination of all these, I was definitely hallucinating at one point. I fancied I could see the skeletons of alien creatures on the far wall (revealed in the morning to be the television and electric fan over the opposite bed). I drifted off to sleep listening through earphones on my iPad to Late Junction on BBC Radio 3 – a track by Malian singer Kandia Kouyate (later identified) transported me to a vision of the hospital at night as a giant spaceship that held the entire human race, the beautiful rippling cadences of the instruments and the ecstatic voice being effortlessly translated into images of benevolent, embracing forms cradling me … it was a transcendental experience that caused me to weep when I recalled it, and that's the truth. But on my third night, sleep was somewhat disrupted by the sound of a man calling out "Mummy!" almost throughout the night – sometimes "Mummy Bear!" and then following up with "Come ON!" in the fashion of Andy Murray berating himself when things are not going well on court. A nurse told me that he was recovering from a serious head injury, and it was very common in these cases to revert to repetitive early childhood language patterns. The nurse added that typically the next stage was obscenities, and after that jerking off. Sure enough, "Fuck me!" was soon added to the patient's repertoire. "Mummy! I love you Mummy Bear! Fuck me!" Once I knew what it was all about, I was able to blank it out and sleep better. I did later hear one of the male nurses gently remonstrating with him: "Put it away, mate, you'll go blind." On my second stay, on the second night, on a different ward I was awakened at about 1:15am by shouting in the nurses' station just outside my bay. It wasn't the nurses. An elderly woman patient had parked herself on a chair in the corridor and was conducting an monologue with I don't know who. She employed grand cadences and pauses for effect, in the manner of a serious orator, but the content was wack: "If you give me that cheque for £10,000 I know what I shall do with it. I want a black man – and a black woman – to do my hair. It's not that I want nigger hair. Not at all. But you know, I wash my hair every day. Sometimes I use shampoo, and sometimes I don't. My son won't have anything to do with me. But I was a nurse for 18 years." Etc etc. The following evening, a couple of hours after E's visit, I called her on the mobile to wish her good night and find out how her evening had been – this had been a strain for both of us. After I ended the call, the sweet elderly man in the next bed to mine, suddenly tweaked back the curtain and spoke to me. He had not said a word previously, certainly not since he had tried to use his walking frame to go to the toilet and had had to be escorted back to bed by the nurses with his head bleeding from a fall. "Were you talking about me?" he asked. No, of course not, I said, I was talking to my wife. "I know," he said with a slight leer. Then he asked where I stood on "this thing" that was about to happen. What thing? Well, it wasn't the EU referendum. Apparently, there was a huge conspiracy, and it was all about to come to a head in the next day or two. As far as I could understand him, it was to do with something bad he'd done, and the nurses were all against him, though the doctors might have been on his side. He was anxious to know what my position was. I tried without success to convince him he might have been dreaming. He just chuckled contemptuously – clearly, I didn't understand. Later, he became abusive towards one of the male night nurses, who he decided was an impostor, and threatened to call the police. Oh, and I saw a man die. It was about 9pm, and I saw he was having real breathing difficulties (COPD). It was very bad. I couldn't see any nurses. I pondered hitting my own alarm button to summon one, but then I saw he was calming down, so maybe he was all right. He calmed right down. I went back to my reading. A moment later I looked up again to check. He was very calm. Actually too calm. He wasn't moving at all. His face suddenly looked grey. A nurse appeared and noticed him. She pulled the curtains round the bed. Other nurses appeared. They didn't rush or panic. But I never saw that man again. I had been the last to see him alive. Which is to say, "The question concerning the point of view, or standpoint, of the pathologist is crucial but so is the question of what it is that the pathologist examines. What, precisely, is the morbid body upon which Fanon, the pathologist, trains his eye? What is the object of his 'complete lysis' (for F's use of 'complete lysis', see Fanon 2008: xiv)? And if it is more proper, because more literal, to speak of a lysis of universe, rather than body, how do we think the relation between transcendental frame and the body, or nobody, that occupies, or is banished from, its confines and powers of orientation?" To quote Fred Moten. So when I ask where is Boston I mean how do you get from the airport to the float tank, more or less? Where *is* Harvard, exactly? What is the sky? Chekhov's play begins before dawn on a May morning. A man walks by, with a very muddy white poodle mix called Willoughby, says he has lived there for twenty years and never saw such an astonishing migration of extreme ducks. Are these H.D.'s crazed geese, circling above the spot that was once Atlantis …? Anyway.

There is a scene I just can't get out of my head.

There are images, and this is what I remember (fade to black.)

I'll always remember (fade to black) the scene.

I'll never forget what happened.

(Fade to black) it's ingrained in my mind.

Whenever I close my eyes I see these scenes repeating.

There are images (fade to black) and I can see them so clearly.

That is what happened.

Scenes, and then (fade to black).

Before, and after, in a sequence.

After the fade to black (fade to black).

"Nothing," is closure.

Simultaneously, the houses are crumbling.

It's hard to say what happens after that.

But I like that. I like how the stone tilted and the blood and oil of the body ran off. Then I applied Frost & Glow to my hair, became almost well, and decided that happiness is a temporary state and I had some words in my head, rather some phrases, like "as the flea goes we go and pick up that grief" and "steam boat springs" and "the frontier is soily." This would be OZ. The Great Speckled Bird. People as far as the eye could see in either direction, thousands of bodies. At that point, I was reading Linda Tuhiwai Smith's *Decolonizing Methodologies: Research and Indigenous Peoples* and I was also teaching young Architecture students about FORMATIVE TRIPS. So with that in mind, I decided to do this. I took about 20 books with me, bought many others. I wrote to a teacher at the AA asking for good books to take, and he kinda said, well you're gonna need novels. I was a bit reluctant at first. But in Japan the monk wrote "Once Only, Only Once" and I've been trying to … Someone has brought that "Once" means "Eleven" in Spanish, so — The Fool He eats of the fruits of the great Speckle Bird, pissing in the grass! … about all those radio waves He eats of the fruits of the great Speckle bird, Pissing on the grass! REAL. LIFE. 1. THE. FOOL. He eats of the fruits of the great Speckle Bird, pissing in the grass! Is it possible He is incomplete, bringing … Stronger than alcohol, more great than song, / deep in whose reeds great elephants decay, / I, an island, sail, and my shoes toss / on a fragrant evening, fraught … He eats of the fruits of the great Speckle. The. He eats rain. Fir. He Embarketh in the … He eats of the fruits of the great Speckle bird, Pissing on the grass! él come las frutas del Great Speckle Bird. Meando en el pasto! the great speckle bird at last extinct (a reference to Herman Melville) at heart we are infinite, we are ethereal, each tree stands … Stronger than alcohol, more great than song, deep in whose reeds … He eats of the fruits of the great Speckle Bird, pissing in the grass! I too was a bird lover tho' mostly / I shot them … And I wondered what that really meant … and now for all kinds of reasons I know something: Eye No. Both of these artists are so explicit about the body, but it's a body complete with subtle body and chakras and orgasms that aren't just in that one particular sex organ center. Or rather, you are covered in multiple sex organs. Which do you prefer? In some Gnostic scriptures God is called The Silence: "and together we'll stare into the silence [post orgasm] … and we'll try to imagine what silence looks like … yeah … we'll try to imagine … what silence looks like" ("If I Was Your Girlfriend"). Happy orgone accumulation day! Is it the Queen's birthday, or Prince's death day, which bleeds into Earth Day? Which? Then the landscape of spotted gums and blackbutts and tin shed-and-flyscreen bric-a-brac are fleetingly imagined as a Chinese painting – "Weed Puller" and "Flower Dump" illustrate the wise dictum to write what you know … Speckled speculation … Horde, the best, the pestilent rats, well versed … Or scratch on the Great Building of Power … and the harmless breeders of the spotted dogs (unharmed too, protected, immune … you with your youth could (remember that bird) see the day when he will have … Stapled sheets, printed on rectos only with silver speckled card – sitting on the edge of a bed, holding a stick with a bird … the bird's face was huge … Spotted with electric crescent moons, bowler-hatted …)

> A troll is not a little thing it's a living stone
> a stone that knows how to move
> a stone with hands and only the *huldra* tames him
> or so I read in a book I wrote
> I found it on my phone faces made of shadows
> light itself is made of their soft fur
> they're all around us their breath the thunder
> all summer I've been translating from the tear-gas
> or long flights of stairs

But it is the mystery that taunts us most: what brought them into that darkness, that *becomes long, deep; it widens, extends, narrows. It is a con- stricted place, a narrowed place, one of the hollowed-out places. It forms hollowed-out places. There are roughened places; there are asperous places.* The sky is overcast, the stars are darkened, the celestial expanses quiver, the bones of the earth-gods tremble, his *.mwst* are under his feet, his *uraei* are on the crown of his head, / Efficient for burning (?); / Who eats their entrails (?), / Even of those who come with their bodies full of magic. Then Saul told his servants *find me a woman who can speak with ghosts that I can go to can make her sound her shaman bag can speak through her his servants said well yes there is a woman mistress of the shaman bag at Endor [scream]* what *[scream]* how *[scream]* what in the world is this *[scream]* strange new *[scream]*. And I looked, and, behold, a whirlwind came out of the north, a great cloud, and a fire infolding itself, and a brightness was about it, and out of the midst thereof as the color of amber, out of the midst of the fire. And the likeness of the firmament upon the heads of the living creature was as the color of the terrible crystal, stretched forth over their heads above. And under the firmament were their *meshugga* wings, take constant notice of the clarity of things, ZEUS (a white flickering) / life-breathing HERA / And I will tell you this: There is no self-nature in anything mortal nor any finality in death's deconstruction / There is only the merging, change and exchange / *Press these things into the pit of your stomach.* I came down from my mountain hut into the streets one day to beg food. I stopped where a leper was feeding himself. With his rotted leper's hand into my bowl he threw a scrap into my bowl as he threw it one of his fingers broke and also fell I simply leaned against a wall and ate *I tell you the world is blazing, blazing / the whole world's in flames / I tell you it's flared up / the world is shaken / your worlds are shaken / the whole world's ablaze* & the odds have never been easy. Humans are indeed frightful beings. A large penis is the mark of an idiot. *And then the Lama continued:* Seek the bird's, the fish's path. Lord! A fire is raging without fuel. When the pot falls apart, what do you call it? Numskull! You've missed the point. Mine ears are filled brimful with cries of poor prisoners, Newgate, Ludgate cries (of late) are seldom out of mine ears. Those doleful cries, *Bread, bread, bread for the Lord's sake,* pierce mine ears and heart, I can no longer forbear. Wherefore hie you apace to all prisons in the kingdom. Bow before those poor, nasty, lousy, ragged wretches, say to them, your humble servants, sirs (without a compliment), we let you go free and serve you, &c. Do this or (as I live, saith the Lord) thine eyes (at least) shall be bored out, and thou carried captive into a strange land. Loose the bonds of wickedness, undo the heavy burdens, let the oppressed go free, and break every yoke. Deal thy bread to the hungry, and bring the poor that are cast out (both of houses and synagogues) to thy house. Cover the naked: hide not thyself from thine own flesh, from a cripple, a rogue, a beggar, thine own flesh. In a dream I saw a very old woman, 1500 years old. Her hair was white as snow; she brought me 2 silver belts and a Walachian sausage. We have been dead several thousand years and we have worked a lot, and still we have no peace. The signal has already gone out that a great deal of blood will flow in the world. I am a *prostak,* I replied, and cannot make a blessing. They asked me, But you bless your people? I replied, I can say no more than this word: For the doubling of flowers is the improvement of the gardner's talent. For there is no Height in which there are not flowers. For flowers have great virtues for all the senses. For the warp and woof of flowers are worked by perpetual moving spirits. For flowers are good both for the living and the dead. For there is a language of flowers. For there is a sound reasoning upon all flowers. For elegant phrases are nothing but flowers. For flowers are musical in ocular harmony. It is a mere prejudice that I am a human being. Yet I have often enough dwelled among human beings and I know the things human beings experience, from the lowest to the highest. Among the Hindus I was Buddha, in Greece Dionysus – Alexander and Caesar were incarnations of me, as well as the poet of

Shakespeare, Lord Bacon. Most recently I was Voltaire and Napoleon, perhaps also Richard Wagner. ... However, I now come as Dionysus victorious, who will prepare a great festival on Earth. ... Not as though I had much time. ... Ah! The rotting rags; the bread soaked with rain, the drunkenness – Ah well! I must bury my imagination and my memories! Sweet glory as an artist and story-teller swept away! Well, I shall ask forgiveness for nourishing myself with lies. Let's go. G'ganggali ging g'gang, g'gung g'gung! G'ganggali ging g'gang, g'gung g'gung! Then the God Orpheus, the greatest and most powerful of the Spirits, said, Let there be a Star on which we might all find a shelter and an asylum and, as he ordained it, so it was. A planeet named Eearth: a Desert, formless and void: and so far as they could see it was dark: And all the Spirits moved over the water. *Not only the millions and billions of stars. No!! 500 myriads and one star. ... I have traveled through all of them in the year 1868. And now, appalling Ca-tas-tro-phe before God the Holy-Spirit, I am swinging on the hideous rope of the gallows,* The living Lantern of Ouchy Opera / Cleopatra in a palanquin / Fountainebleau / The Quirinal mermaid / The pink pearl of India / Sketch of bank-note / The flowery earth and its work by / The great Victoria saves the rich exiles in Switzerland / Printers of bank-notes / Kaiser Wilhelm II's love story / The extreme point of mysticism, / I hold it now in the real and in my body, / like a toilet broom. / For me, living man, I am a city be- sieged by the army of the dead, / Take that, take that, / you didn't get me out of there yet, / I'm always there no matter what you try to do, / you haven't defeated me and I have that: / caca, the cream of your ... / it is me who gobbles up the cake you made crumb by crumb, / hmm hmm hmm / hmm hmm hmm / hmm hmm hmm / hmm hmm hmm / hmm hmm hmm / so so so si / hmm hmm hmm / hmm hmm hmm / Cayetano García / *[He answers "Yes ..." She says, "Isn't that how?" He responds: "Yes, that's it." She says: "Isn't that it? Like this. Listen."]* / so so so / so so so / so so so / *["That's it. Work, work," exclaims the man.]* / hmm hmm hmm / hmm hmm hmm / so so so / hmm hmm hmm / so so so / so so so / si si si / si si si / si si si / so sa sa / si si si / so sa sa sa / hmm hmm hmm / hmm hmm hmm / hmm hmm hmm. The company had advertised for men to unload a steamer across the river. It was six o'clock in the morning, snowing, and still dark. There was a crowd looking for work on the dock; and all the while men hurried to the dock. The man at the wheel kept the bow of the launch against the dock – the engine running slowly; and the men kept jumping from dock to deck, jostling each other, and crowding into the cabin. Eighty or ninety men were in the cabin as the launch pulled away. There were no lights in the cabin, and no room to turn – whoever was sitting down could not get up, and whoever had his hand up could not get it down, as the launch ran in the darkness through the ice, ice cracking against the launch, bumping and scraping against the launch, banging up against it, until it struck a solid cake of ice, rolled to one side, and slowly came back to an even keel. The men began to feel water running against their feet as if from a hose. "Cap," shouted one, "the boat is taking water!" The men began to shout, ankle-deep in water. The man at the wheel turned with his flashlight: everybody was turning and pushing against each other; those near the windows were trying to break them, in spite of the wire mesh in the glass; those who had been near the door were now in the river, reaching for the cakes of ice, their hands slipping off and reaching for the cakes of ice. Kumara Nich, nich, pasalam, bada. Eschochomo, lawassa, schibboda Kumara A.a.o. – o.o.o. – i.i.i. – e.e.e. – u.u.u. – ye.ye.ye. Ah pe-an t-as ke t-an te loo O ne vas ke than sa-na was-ke lon ah ve shan too Te wan-se ar ke ta-ne voo te lan se o-ne voo Te on-e-wan tase va ne woo te wan-se 0-ne van Me-le wan se oo ar ke-le van te shom-ber on vas sa la too lar var sa Z then is equal to 2 because the first is the last. The last in alphabet-numerical form is 2 because the first being Z is two. The way to True Living Life is the phonetic of two which is to TEE OH because the way to is the way ot OH TEE and the way owt OH W TEE is the way two TEE W OH, the way tuo TEE YOU OH is the way tu TEE YOU and to TEE OH. The world of to TEE OH is the level world, the level truth is the plain truth. Plus and X produce the same result in the multiplication or addition of to TEE OH. [spoken] Here's wishing all who read this, if they can get a lift, and the best of luck to you. Why in hell did you come, anyway? [sung] Damn it anyhow – Here I am stuck in the cold – I've come, twenty-seven hundred miles from Chicago, Illinois – Slept along the highway, slept in open boxcar without top. Went hungry for two days (raining too) – Dah dah dah dah – But they say there's a hell – What the hell do they think this is? Do they think about this? Dah dah dah dah dah

(and etc: more Dah-dahs here …)

I'm on my way, one half of desert to the east. Then back to El-lay, to try once more – Car just passed by, make that two more, three more. Do not think they'll let me finish my story. Here she comes, a truck, not a fuck, but a truck. Just a truck. Hoping to get the hell out, here's my name – Johnny You-Know, eighteen-sixty-four Morgan Avenue, etc. Doh dee-dee

(and etc: more Doh-dees here …)

Here's wishing all who read this, if they can get a lift, and the best of luck to you – Doh doh doh doh doh doh – dah dah dah – Why in hell did you come, anyway? These introductory pages consist largely of technical data. It is an olden time, but neither a precise time nor a precise place. There is nowhere, from the beginning of the "Exordium" to the end of Act II, a complete cessation of music. In Act I, they also wear a poncho-like garment – a single, full piece of cloth with a neckhole. It is completely unadorned, without collages or beads or anything that twinkles in the light. The ghost drops his sword and says to his murderer, "You are not my enemy." *Around the same time, on the opposite coast, Faith Ringgold was employing the flag in similar ways in her paintings. One of her works from this era, at first glance, presents as a painting of an ordinary American flag, if slightly off-hue — substituting a dim gray for the traditional white. But on closer examination, what appears to be some discoloration in the stars is the word "die," in capital letters only a shade darker than the field on which it is superimposed. And what appear to be irregular stripes are actually horizontal, elongated letters, which spell "nigger."*

So it's important to care for the destruction. The meditation box requires pipes. At the broad shield a creature dances. At as axial room to signal signal close away at lull points former clicks out sync and in again over gravity is not a fact here here it remains. Now if you will just observe me, I will move up off the ground, ELEVATING, as much as a foot or two or. In my Tibetan bathrobe. Three years later I was able to finally hug him in person and write

"YOU KICKED CANCER'S ASS". Then I met Whovians and psychiatrists and teenagers and people in red ball gown carrying taxidermied possums and giant metal chickens and ... uh ... so how *does* an open mouth conduct the pink lightning? Perhaps it is time to think of the bones. The skeleton [conductivity]. What do the bones transmit / discharge? I think of the final part of the body in the charnel pit – the voices Wendy and I were talking about – because I am obsessed with how a breach persists, not as a trace, yes as a trace – but – no, and – the very thing that becomes amplified – in other domains – an infinitely vexed blankness, an infinitely confusing and troubled nothing-is-there. Or, to quote Chris Nealon, The purpose of society is mutual aid. There, was that so hard? I could tell you that if after a week in Italy you really *really* want to see a painting of the Buddha you've been looking at paintings of the Buddha all this time. But I couldn't believe in love til I got to the creation of the animals – how they [how we] launch into life from out of the void – all of history ahead of them – and that's when I thought of you – like do those robins ever settle in at night and just think, Best. Nest. *Ever?* And I was in a landscape like a landscape painting – we all were – an *extensive* one – and we could move around –

"Color itself is a degree of darkness"
and numbers a degree of light.

Nothing takes only five minutes.
39
40

Yan Tan
Thethera Methera
Yain Tain
Methan
Eeno Oino

'The atoms
[the poor atoms]
do not have a place to rest.'

AND THUS COMMENCES THE METAMORPHOSIS OF A DENSE ACTION OF FRAGMENTING PROCESSES ALTERING WITHOUT SHATTERING THE WEAK FORMS BLUNTED BY THE ATTACKS OF TORRENTS IN WHICH EFFLUENT REDISTRIBUTES NUDE CRACKED SLOPES THAT DISPERSE UNTIL AN UNDERLYING MATRIX OF RARE INTRUSIONS DETACHES ITSELF FROM A DEPOSIT AND IS LEVELED WHILE RAWBONED PHYSIOGNOMIES REMINISCENT OF DESERTS OF WHICH EVERY EXTREMITY

POSTULATES A HORIZON BECAUSE AT THAT DISTANCE A MIRAGE OF THE LANDSCAPE WILL NOT CONTINUE BEYOND THE GRADUALLY INCREASING FUZZINESS OF THE RUPTURES OF THE VERTICAL AND OPEN LIPS WHERE ATMOSPHERES RUSH WITH SHOVES REPEATEDLY VIVACIOUSLY INTENSIFYING THE WESTERN HORIZON SO JAGGED THAT EACH OF THEIR ROCKY BRAIDS STICKS UP ABOVE THE CORD THAT TIES ITSELF INTO LESIONS WROUGHT BY OBSTACLES OF BLEACHED DROSS BY VORTEXES ALONG WITH A POROUS AND TROUBLED CRUST DISPERSED BY AIR WELL AND FAR AWAY WITH ITS WEIGHT SUPPLEMENTED BY A LABORIOUS GRAVITY OF RUSHING WAVES THAT FOLLOW A POTENTIAL TRAJECTORY ASCENDING ALONG A PRECIPITOUS ESCARPMENT WHERE THE CONTINUITY OF INDECOMPOSABLE MATERIALS IS THUS DISTINGUISHABLE LIKE A SINGLE BODY THAT CAN NOT HINDER INCESSANT LIQUID IN SPITE OF THE MECHANICAL AND REPETITIVE UNDULATIONS WHOSE PROPAGATION IS REINFORCED BY A METEORIC INFLUENCE THAT PRECIPITATES AGAINST THE CLIFFS WITH THE SPEED OF FORTUITOUS CHRONOLOGIES PASSING WITHIN EXPANDING REFERENCES WITHOUT EVER MOLLIFYING EXCEPT WHEN THE EVAPORATION SATURATES THE HYDRATION OF FROTHY AND UNVARYING NEBULOSITY DURING ITS PROGRESSION OVER THE FORESHORE AT THE JUNCTION OF TRIPLE SPHERES EXHAUSTING THE SPRING So "Put the sea back where you found it" – I'd rather not believe it – yet the predated scan. OBJECTS are what kind of scaler is the earth, positive flood ache, proleptic Lemuria, submergence and emergence, forests under water, flicking off sense. This is really good. Deal with it. The rains coming or not coming, graphed here,

> We used spectrometer and
> Hypersensometrical poke.
> Measured pipe diameter,
> Knelt, listened. We
> Tasted — analysis, analysis,
> Analysis. We looked.
> Then we knew to start
> Exaggeration and
> Much much more, so much
> More, lots more, yes, so
> Much more! So wash the
> Pasta and rinse it,
> Rinse it
> Again in the mud.

Removal of metals.
Leave water to dry.

Polyhedrons with ruins
And strapwork.

To quote John Ashbery,
"My tetrahedron is open to the night."

light coming into clouds above shadowed
ridge, bird slanting toward pine branch
in foreground, sound of wave in channel –

Cheap-ass zooms and cross-fades – how they carol to you all adventure season, calling come to Bali – But you only get as far as the edge of the west – & the stockboys clearing out the inventory / marsh-weed swaying / the wires in your jacket starting to show – then you end up a minute or two ahead of the language / noticing a face's lack of symmetry & wanting to look again. The "telos" this desire navigates toward is the "undead" future: a poetics expressing this may draw from past artworks, such as Picasso's 1957 series of 58 paintings reinterpreting Velasquez's *Las Meninas*. Knowingly or unknowingly, Picasso's art historical gesture will be infinitely repeated, but a contemporary crisis poetics drawing from this tradition of reinterpretation must diminish formal autonomy and be "incapable / of enduring independent labor monitors" in order to represent all the embedded and exacerbated antagonisms. There is no talk of transcendence, just an affective coming to effective consciousness, just "Wild Mike is straight up drugs". The experience of the accelerated "time window" was proximate to "the dime bag / / near our distant sun / of fungal alphabets," "papeles" (papers) "for horses," "a turquoise Ho Chi Minh". Especially so because I know a Book Three lurks out there to further attenuate the story. So it's 2005. Victor Frankenstein has survived. He's Victor Helios now. The monster, now called Deucalion for some reason opaque to me — has also survived. A genetic hierarchy exists amongst the quote unquote replicants, Alpha, Beta, Gamma, which reminds me of the Spin series by Chris Moriarty. Anyway, Victor has been dispatching key people in New Orleans and replacing them with his Alphas, Betas etc, in a reboot of humanity, with Victor Helios in charge. Sounds exactly like the awful movies I'm so proud to like. But a pair of wisecracking cops are on to this exploit ... There's a lovely couple, super attractive, who are modified to be assassins. They're looking for the cute cop couple. Uh oh. Replicants can't give birth but the lady assassin has been showing signs of wanting kids. OK. Victor's wife Erika (5.0 or something) has of course been Stepfordized. At the dump where Victor stashes all the dead bodies, seemingly millions of them, some sort of evil life force apparently seeks to become a plot point. So I was writing the poems of *Action Kylie* and it seemed natural to make them stop and focus on the figure of the cat, the "kitten with a whip." Here's my poem, "Something the Cat Dragged In."

It's hard to explain. One moment it seemed I was in an intimate niteclub, the next a domed arena with a thousand seats. One moment it seemed I was in a cramped garage (the sort of place where Ornette's band used to practice during those early days in Watts), the next a huge, drafty warehouse in Long Beach or San Pedro or somewhere like. One moment I was in a cathedral, the next a storefront church. As François Dosse writes in *Gilles Deleuze & Felix Guattari: Intersecting Lives*: "Deligny invented an entire poetic language to describe the behavior of young autistic patients. A child who spins is considered to be making a shadow; one shifting from one foot to the other is making a cloud balance." So when Macabea does ingest the rich (or richer) people's food, she becomes sick. The *why* of why Carlos is an influence would range from obsessive self-publishing and the self-existent drive to create, to subtler things such as his thoughts on the *fragment* here: "You don't need to read every issue of my comic, or any other ones to appreciate a weird hand touching a door knob, or a swollen, exotic mask being applied to a damp face. That's just good stuff, take it for what it is." I mean, what I like about the freak community is there is no value in shock value, I mean, there are the ones who do see me see me there are the ones who do see me see me there are the ones who do who do see me there are the ones who do see me. A narrative of there are the ones who do who do see me. Not to be to be to not to be to be to be to not to be to be to be to be to not to be to be to be to be be to be to this. There are the ones who have let it day there are the ones who have let it who have let it let it day there are the ones who have to have let it let it let it daily let it daily do let it daily and be be so very installed installed in mounting mounting mountain and remounting, which is which. That is, textile thinking leads quickly to thoughts on labor. Why? Because making cloth is an ancient art, because garment workers are always on labor's front lines, because a garment surrounds us, houses us. We absorb the energy of the conditions of its making. So, too, with buildings. In this commentary, I consider cloth, garment workers, and transnational labor awareness. Then, I move on to architecture, to buildings. As a garment houses us, buildings also do, and their walls have been set, built up, finished by workers' hands and hands that operate machines. The carpet is laid. The chairs are unwrapped. Someone programs in key card access. So "textility," as Spivak posits, "escapes the loom into the dynamics of world trade." I end this commentary, then, with a lesson plan or alternative employee handbook directive to "write / right" the built structures of the workplace, structures of incredibly potent "vibrant matter" as Jane Bennett, other new materialists, and artists might say. But to get there, "WEFT" asks its performers — performers who are "lay persons," not actors or dancers — to examine the tags of the clothes they are wearing, to see if they can find info on the garment's origins, and then, in an open space, turn and face and lean towards that location, towards the workers there. I remember that my calves were sore the next day. It took me until noon the day after that to figure out why and trace the source of the soreness. The leaning had meant something to my body that I could not know in the moment of leaning. First world soreness, right? Pain is pain. But "How can we rest, if, energetically, a building is the embodying of the sum or the qualities of force gone into its construction?" "How can we take ourselves seriously if the construction process is not used as the basis for treating the problems our constructions intend to address?" "Is not 'empire' rebuilt each time labor cost is cut?" "Does 'kindness' or 'work' apply the greatest epigenetic pressure?" Negri responds to Nairn and his other critics (notably, to his other critics on the Left) in the chapter of *Spinoza for Our Time* entitled "Multitude and Singularity." Having been accused by Nairn of being in the "redemption business," Negri responds by accusing Nairn of having forgotten "the overflowing joy of *multitude-making*, the joy of the construction of the common." This is more than praise for the insurgent energies that Negri sees animating collaborations in political resistance worldwide. He also sees a conflict between materialisms, Marxist and Spinozist, and judges that Spinozist materialism affords a vitality, a plenitude, that need only be given organization, in contrast to those materialisms that treat the stuff of the world (including us) as basically inert. Here everything has already begun to flee into the footnotes and appendices: three "excurses" and some twenty separate "commentaries" now fill up a third of a five-hundred-page volume, into which already a few illustrations begin to emerge. So it is, for example, that the protagonists of the Argonaut myth are, from the Greek standpoint, Jason and his crew, a focus which relegates the peasant experience — the landed population of Colchis — to the position of the Other: they are here the prize and the object of exploitation, the story is not told for them. This radical reversal of a peasant perspective is most evident in the inhumanity and monstrousness with which the figure of Medea herself emerges, a figure who, from the indigenous point of view (compare the roles of Malinche or Pocahontas in the New World), takes on the attributes of the patriot and the guerrilla, of Judith and of the struggles of wars of national liberation. From this perspective the Argonauts are not mere adventurers. Their function is to bring exchange and the market, to spell the doom of the older agricultural and communal system. *It becomes exceedingly difficult to decide whether the flour-covered paw of the wolf or the high-pitched voice belong to the mother, or whether the mother (end or means) may not actually have a pelt covered with flour or a high-pitched voice, and so forth.*

So when he said he wasn't much of a driver, she looked down at the charred tails and dyed red flesh of the remains of their meal, the filmy bones like the fossil imprint of a leaf, and said, "Who is? It's not really about driving. I go to the coast a lot now." She laughed and made confused steering wheel motions. "Up and down. Very slowly." Then: "I think I've grown out of London." And finally: "I love the little spines of these fishes, don't you?" "All I see," said Alex, "is my dinner." He then admitted: "I was in a bit of a state when we last met." "You aren't all that much improved." She laughed at his expression. "Come on! I should talk! I don't believe I've been entirely sane since I was thirteen–" Alex filled her glass again. "Is that when you saw the corpse?" he said, hopefully. "–although I did have a moment of clarity in a sauna in about 2005 [weren't we just in 2005?]. Eventually you take what you can get where that's concerned. You have to feel you're steadying …" "There's some value to that," Alex agreed, though he had no idea what she was talking about. "Actually, I'm not even sure it should be called clarity," she said. The project, "A Color Removed," is a response to the November 22, 2014, shooting of Tamir Rice, a 12-year-old Cleveland boy who was killed by police because his toy gun was missing the orange rings that were meant to identify it as a replica. Rakowitz's concern is not with whether or not he succeeds in removing all orange from Cleveland as a literal or even symbolic gesture, but the conversations the proposal of this act will inspire. Rakowitz wants to explore what he calls the "removal of the right of safety." For me, the project raises a series of interesting questions and provocations, eee gee, to say that removing orange is removing the right to safety reminds one of all the communities that have no illusion about that right. So the sound artist Mileese takes the electrical impulses (or "micro-voltages") emitted by plants "through the virtue of their livingness" and converts them into binary code. In turn, the plants generate sound through the mediatory device of a synthesizer. Here, the musician Bartholomäus Traubeck plays slices of wood on a record player as if they were vinyl LPs. Time is ingrained into the trees' rings, and the sound released is that of the tree's individual textures. Here is the music of an Ash tree. Finally, here is a plant giving a solo concert to a room of human people. A woman does something wonderful, which is, she sticks her face into its dark green leaves as it sings. Here are two creatures, human and plant, in a feedback loop (I think of the folk lyrics, "She changes everything she touches, and everything she touches changes.") Then that which you fear is over. It ended abruptly. Or over a long period of time. Who could tell? The irises bent a little. There that ended a little. Suffering. A suffering. Bridge bridge Sunset-peace, and tones, Heaven Heaven earth, says. Wished be, says. And well, "the" says. Everything says. I world well, bridge, Bridge of tones, bridge I bridge says. Here is how the same poem was re-written by an iris in Michigan: If I I I to to well, I the to If world world well, well, well, be I bare bare My bare appear with with fists flowers. And in order to do so, they had to stretch themselves beyond their normal sensory capacities in order to reach out and make their sensibilities heard. Our differences are ones of degree not kind. Still, I'm not convinced that hearing a plant as it really sounds would be safe for most of us — we still do not know what sensory capacities we possess. Echoes of Spinoza.

And so Eve is called the first woman. (Although, in this myth, Lilith existed before her).

    1   Hurrying pilgrim, stop here!
         Stop here. When you think
         hurrying pilgrim, think
         stop here! When you think
    2   Sara Jessica Parker, you think
         Carrie Bradshaw. Stop here
         pilgrim, there is a lot more to her than
         Sarah Jessica Parker, you think
         the place teaches the prayerful
    3   to tread lightly.

Speaking of compromised bodies: I was fighting the flu while moderating the panel. In order from left to right: me (with the flu), Janice, Erica, Carrie,

Stephanie. What would a socialist media platform look like? To step out of the air-conditioned car, into the density of the heat. To sit in a hot car that's been baking in the sun for hours. In some cases it is possible to smell death, then, to continue being calm, to continue one's good mood. The sky looks different wherever – and whenever. The spine of the book has no text — it is bare. The text of the book has no text. Here we are. There we go. To quote Don Mee Choi's Kim Hyesoon,

> Now the woman's spoon can be discarded.
> Now the woman's shadow can be folded.
> Now the woman's shoes can be removed.
>
> You shout, I don't have any nostalgia whatsoever for that
>   woman!
> But you roll your eyes the way the woman did when she was
>   alive
>
> then you continue on your way to work as before. You go
>   without your body.
> Will I get to work on time? You head towards the life you
>   won't be living.

Soon the red rabbit becomes a black rabbit,
it can become big or small at will. Lucas says,

i was born in a crystal angle
i was born next to an axe
i was born in the image of epidemic beings
it was so hard to concentrate after i was born
clouds of dust bowels of the earth in a galloping swirl
it was everything the eye of the spirit [the eye of witness?] wanted

> [The page "Philosopheme" does not exist. You can ask for it to be created, but consider checking the search results below to see whether the topic is already covered.
>
> O, intractable Other, endowed with such fantasies!
> Entity gliding alone/along the purely senseless
>   stratum!
> Unalloyed essence!
>
> A: {the melodrama knows the pattern all too well}

> Yet anything can be colonized, even pleasure. Pleasure, this archival
> city. To shhhhh shhhhhhhh shhhh shhhhh
> sssssssssshhhhhhhhhhhhhhh
> all the whitewhite of hum]

What is the object of Fanon's "complete lysis"? And if it is more proper, because more literal, to speak of a lysis of universe, rather than body, how do we think the relation between transcendental frame and the body, or nobody, that occupies, or is banished from, its confines and powers of orientation? Late evening. Male care assistant in his 20s / 30s, of Asian appearance; male patient, white, in his late 80s. The names have been changed.

> Bill, I need to take your temperature and blood pressure.
> Must you?
> Yes, Bill, I must.
> Very well, then.
> [pause]
> What's your name?
> My name's Shamoon. Give me your arm now.
> Where are you from?
> I beg your pardon?
> Where are you from, where were you born?
> England.
> What's that? I can't hear you.
> England. I was born in England.
> Oh, I see.
> [pause]
> Only ... I asked because ...
> Yeah?
> You look a bit ... Indian. I don't mean Indian as in cowboys and Indians, I mean from India.
> Yeah?
> That's what I meant.
> So what's that got to do with anything?
> Uh.
> [pause]
> So what's my blood pressure, then?
> Is normal. OK.
> Ah, that's good. So I'm not dead yet, ha ha.
> Yeah, Bill, you're talking a load of rubbish, that means you're still alive.

Out in space, that shit ain't right, Dear Alain, in the other world the way I foster communal living is great until someone becomes legendary drinks the whole gallon in one gulp. Around the globe and under the fridge and then after the party to the hotel lobby where I'll leave you for a moment by a stack of folded-up boxes. Tunnel after tunnel, the time I showed up to around the time all the ducks emerged from the water, returning the bread with vengeance and regret, around three minutes. See the half moon over the Western Beef, I understand, I mean, I appreciate. All this remaining agape after the campers drive off, crazed in the a/c, stars screaming if you find yourself falling short in a Chevy or a Ford, above you at the all night Classic Diner. See you in the cigar smoke on the fifth of July. It's a far cry from this kind of life to the Nuevo Nuestra. The bridge rubs its use value tho it spans a dry river. Awaits its pretty ghost worrying about a promise to avoid metaphors. Our claws are dirty with beliefs. It is a dry river. I am proud of this calligraphy. Some people can actually say and mean, My ancestors slaughtered yours. A fear of Biblical / Talmudic Quranic / Puranic / Daoist and so forth foods: figs, dates, olives, quiche, burritos, naan, jiaozi, death by chocolate cake and steak tartare. A preserve of oranges & crushed sugar, prepared by the physician to Mary, Queen of Scots c. 1561 to keep her seasickness at bay (for marmalade, read *Marie est malade*). Are all my friends' lungs not pictured? To wake up and striving to wake up responsible for what and to wake up with or or to wake up and and pink while all the other poets get to live as dogs in barrels I mean post-post-post-punk gods in bands. Dear Alain. Do you bedazzle? Even if you've never threaded a needle, you'll be BeDazzling in minutes. You can BeDazzle a hat, a shirt, a belt, a scarf or a sweater! It's easy. It's fun. It's fabulous! You get the original BeDazzler Stud and Rhinestone Setter plus all the rhinestones, studs and stars you'll need! Don't be dull – BE DAZZLING! – with the better than ever BeDazzler! Dear Alain. Don't worry about it. Most people just think I'm overly emotional or maybe crazy – but I cried because I am not crazy and Egypt proves it. It was a tall building made of electric fence for everyone to hail with bruises and scars and untouchables, that facade collapsed, and it's when Gauss looked at the horizon and said, but parallel lines do meet, they meet at the horizon. It's the dream of the platonic form lapping at the edge of the shore and the tide rushing over one last time to a blazing red dawn, the kind that makes you wake up and breathe as if for the first time and all those tones of sarcasm fade into some jellyfish dying on the sand and it's blindingly beautiful the stuff we always knew was there but just grew too cynical to care except maybe deep in the night we risked a word or two of

Ka

Thump

Ka

Thump

Ka

Thump

Haayo

Ka

Thump

Ka

Thump

Ka

Thump

Haayo

Ka

Thump

Ka

Thump

Ka

Thump

Haayo

Ka

Thump

Ka

Thump

Ka

Thump

Haayo
Ka

Thump

Ka

Thump

Ka

Thump

Haayo

Ka

Thump

Ka

Thump

Ka

Thump

Haayo

Ka

Thump

Ka

Thump

Ka

Thump

Haayo

Ka

Thump

Ka

Thump

Ka

Thump

Haayo

Ka

Thump

Ka

Thump

Ka

Thump

Haayo

Ka

Thump

Ka

Thump

Ka

Thump

Haayo

Ka

Thump

Ka

Thump

Ka

Thump

Haayo
(tikka tikka)
Ka

Thump
(tikka tikka)

Haayo
(tikka tikka)
Ka

Thump
(tikka tikka)

Haayo
(tikka tikka)
Ka

Thump
(tikka tikka)

Haayo
(tikka tikka)
Ka

Thump
(tikka tikka)

Haayo
(tikka tikka)
Ka

Thump
(tikka tikka)

Haayo
(tikka tikka)
Ka

Thump
(tikka tikka)

Haayo
(tikka tikka)
Ka

Thump
(tikka tikka)

Haayo
(tikka tikka)
Ka

Thump
(tikka tikka)

Haayo
(tikka tikka)
Ka

Thump
(tikka tikka)

Haayo
(tikka tikka)
Ka

Thump
(tikka tikka)

Haayo
(tikka tikka)
Ka

Thump
(tikka tikka)

Haayo
(tikka tikka)

Ka

Thump
(tikka tikka)

Haayo
(tikka tikka)
Ka

Thump
(tikka tikka)

Haayo
(tikka tikka)
Ka

Thump
(tikka tikka)

Haayo
(tikka tikka)
Ka

Thump
(tikka tikka)

Haayo
(tikka tikka)
Ka

Thump
(tikka tikka)

Haayo
(tikka tikka)
Ka

Thump
(tikka tikka)

Haayo
(tikka tikka)
Ka

Thump
(tikka tikka)

Haayo
(tikka tikka)
Ka

Thump
(tikka tikka)

Haayo
(tikka tikka)
Ka

Thump
(tikka tikka)

Haayo
(tikka tikka)
Ka

Thump
(tikka tikka)

Haayo
(tikka tikka)
Ka

Thump
(tikka tikka)

Haayo
(tikka tikka)
Ka

Thump
(tikka tikka)

Haayo
(tikka tikka)
Ka

Thump
(tikka tikka)

Haayo

Haayo

Haayo

Haayo ... However, since we believe that the universe is constantly expanding, the photon will exit into a medium that is less dense than before it entered the void. Lower density means weaker gravitational pull on the emerging photon. This means that the photon cannot make up all the energy it lost and ends up with a little less energy – and hence lower temperature – than light from regions of the sky that did not pass through the void. This process explains why the spot is 70 μK colder than the surrounding chilly CMB radiation, which is 2.7 C in whichever direction one looks on the sky. Ergo, between the valleys in the Komaland region I will play the piano brightly my hands replaced with

butterflies you know how much a stick forgot you know how much you don't umbrella tree the homo erectus homeland a distinct ball and her concrete garden balls have no set function some 8 light minutes and these caterpillars get in your shoes even while you ride a bicycle they drop down from the trees and stick to the back of your Magdalenian Cantabria the force of its etching would steer the natural molecular grace of your yellow wooden mask carved holey through and through a snake shrine each letter a beatitude a plane that runs everywhere through the mist its hoof beat titanic bristle speech only on automanifolding gold scry thee your own bagpipe whistle fen bag scholar goo bait to a wire hole between the valleys of in the Komaland region I will play the piano brightly my hands replaced with butterflies much my holey mask fen garden hands region letter replaced ball Magdalenian replaced bristle replaced want ride butterflies etching butterflies automanifolding letter that horned butterflies butterflies caterpillars Magdalenian everywhere butterflies much my horse gaseous hands hands balls region replaced replaced will Kulpawan replaced whistle replaced will mist letter much butterflies automanifolding between want between butterflies butterflies caterpillars Magdalenian butterflies butterflies much my have hands hands garden hands region yellow replaced valleys replaced replaced bicycle replaced with wire between light butterflies Kulpawan with want these camper butterflies butterflies butterflies butterflies caterpillars much by holey hands fen Magdalenian hands runs region replaced replaced Kulpawan replaced replaced beatitude wire light butterflies each between muscular titanic want camper letter butterflies butterflies Magdalenian everywhere caterpillars in the Komaland I will play the pit brightly my headaches replaced with campaigns you know how much a straw forgot you know how much you don't my headaches replaced with capacities much my holey medium fen Glass headaches renewal limitation replaced bat Magdalenian replaced bristle replaced want round capacities etching capacities automanifolding limitation that horned capacities cakes caterpillars Magdalenian everywhere capacities much my ideal gaseous headaches harms bats renewal replaced replaced will Kulpawan replaced whistle replaced will much capacities automanifolding between want between capacities cakes caterpillars Magdalenian capacities cakes much my have headaches harms Glass headaches renewal yellow replaced vice-presidents replaced replaced blue replaced with worth between loch capacities Kulpawan with want these camper capacities cakes capacities cakes caterpillars much by holey headaches fen Magdalenian headaches runs renewal replaced replaced Kulpawan replaced replaced beatitude worth loch capacities each between muscular titanic want camper limitation capacities cakes Magdalenian everywhere caterpillars. This passage is exactly the kind of thing I would have lingered on in my first book, *The Textual Life of Airports: Reading the Culture of Flight*. Let's just take it a sentence at a time. The first establishes a mixed feeling, of sun-scorched tarmac and a weird autumn zephyr. In the next sentence the jet airplane protrudes, standing still "at lunchtime" — thus lending the aircraft animacy, its own cravings? (Or simply reminding us of the consumptive aura of modernity, more generally?) The next sentence is long and very busy, classic Wallace: "Runway 1" is an utterly vague denotation, yet at the same time connotatively powerful; CHA a misnomer (given the novel's geography Wallace likely meant Cleveland Hopkins airport but that would be CLE; CHA is Chattanooga; but never mind); "pointed west to go east" suggests the necessary loops involved in the circuits of technoculture; the "red-ink drawing of a laughing baby on its side" a comment on hyperbolic cuteness and mandatory happiness; the ramp workers with their tattered flags perform the bare life of airport labor, pulling chocks from landing gear while exposed in the "melting" air; humans, roaring plane, and landscape merge in this sentence into a fiery shimmer, a collapse of nature and culture, a swarming of senses, affects and objects. The slowly waved orange flags operate rather like Noh fans, signaling some strange drama in process. Mediated behind the glinting glass of the cockpit we glimpse the pilots via synecdoches of "sunglasses and thumbs-up" — these are not pilots, these are pilot-functions, people stripped down to their rote roles within this mundane (and maybe horrifying) machine. And yet one ramp worker's previously noted earmuffs turn out to be headphones, presumably blasting a stream of private entertainment into the guy's ears, while the "hissing" commercial maelstrom unfurls all around. Is this a glimmer of individual resistance, even expression? Or is the Walkman a mere corollary to the heavy ensemble, the encompassing regime? Is the airport worker plugged in, or tuned out — or is he enacting both compartments at once?

And the 'twirling' of the flag: do you know the staircase that steered the wayfarers of the Kingdom of the Dragons and the Partridges is white? It swarmed with Silk (ten thousand hours ago) and will enter only with sleeves of water and light, initiates of the wheel (sun into mountains, etc.) or of celestial shallows (edge of the falling stream), flakes of vermilioned dragon-scales, letters of innumerable raptures (as in the spirits of the tiger or the dead), etc. The journeys of the bones of swallows must have toiled thus, distant as they were to the depth of seas, the cocoons of islands, and endless wakings (and we are certainly not finding mud to escape all of this). This? This, for example, is the case of the ramparts, which might be thickened, it seems to me, by a few goblets melted from Markov's scimitar or the Tai-hsuan Ching or the Booleian cascades (cloth-pounding, singing, retreats; Algol solitude, etc.). "When angry they send you a rotten salmon."

So now I have started to add a carrot to each work as a kind of running gag. I was very happy when Nigel Cheney machine-stitched plenty of carrots for me when he heard I had run out of then. Which is to say that the repetition of "A las cinco de la tarde" had a huge impact on me, so I included "As the thistle shakes / When three gray linnets wrangle for the seed" and "I am a part of all that I have met" in my work *Playground*. The airport is modern and pleasant. There were specially designated "pet relief areas". Pet relief can be understood variously as a device to get rid of one's dog or as a kind of liberation. This poetry leaked through to the design of the facility itself, including the tiny dog bidets. I mean, I love signs that say "secret access code" for a simple locker at the train station or "suspicious circumstances" for an area one is not allowed to enter. Last year I received a parcel from the US with the notice that it "does not contain any unauthorized explosives, destructive devices, or hazardous materials." The US seems to require the sender to add this kind of information to a package. When on holiday in Iceland I was intrigued by the content of their national phone book. The first pages contained instructions for the general public. Attention was paid to volcanic eruptions ("Always wear a helmet in the vicinity of eruptions"), lightning and thunderstorms, earthquakes, and avalanches. The text would even improve when shortened ("take the shortest way out by moving perpendicular to the wind"). "Stay where the wind blows and do not go into low (!) areas." Then I realized that I am actually living in a low area (below sea level) here in the "low countries". So maybe I am risking my life over here. But "On ne mange pas tulipes", as Paul Bocuse said when a Dutch television host interviewed him about what kinds of Dutch ingredients he uses in his world-famous cuisine. His first answer was Gouda cheese, but the interviewer insisted on hearing a bit more. Bocuse's answer was a little arrogant and humorous, but probably more dramatic than he realized. Tulip bulbs were a common dish near the end of WWII when there was a great shortage of food in Holland. My mother-in-law told me she even liked them as they taste like onions. Speaking of the Shoah,

> Yes, the trees are still there, actually. But that
> noise, where does that noise come from.
> That did not used to be there.

Tally marks recall the many murdered people. I used different colors from reddish to gray to black to indicate that their fire is still slightly burning. In 1999 I included the Star of David and the words "millennium proof" in my work *Losing our memory*. That is what Leibniz explains in an extraordinary piece of writing: a flexible or an elastic body still has cohering parts that form a fold. Such that they are not separated into parts of parts but are rather divided to infinity in smaller and smaller folds that always retain a certain cohesion. Thus a continuous labyrinth is not a line dissolving into independent points, as flowing sand might dissolve into grains, but resembles a sheet of paper divided into infinite folds or separated into bending movements, each one determined by the consistent or conspiring surroundings. "The division of the continuous must not be taken as of sand dividing into grains, but as that of a sheet of paper or of a tunic in folds, in such a way that an infinite number of folds can be produced, some smaller than others, but without the body ever dissolving into points or minima." A fold is always folded within a fold, like a cavern in a cavern. The unit of matter, the smallest element of the labyrinth, is the fold, not the point which is never a part, but a simple extremity of the line. That is why parts of matter are masses or aggregates, as a correlative to elastic compressive force. Unfolding is thus not the contrary of folding, but follows the fold up to the following fold. Particles are "turned into folds," that a "contrary effort changes over and again." Folds of winds, of waters, of fire and earth, and subterranean folds of veins of ore in a mine. In a system of complex interactions. the solid pleats of "natural geography" refer to the effect first of fire, and then of waters and winds on the earth; and the veins of metal in mines resemble the curves of conical forms, sometimes ending in a circle or an ellipse, sometimes stretching into a hyperbola or a parabola, thus the most everlasting poem. QED.

The need for transforming some of the lower biomass land uses (such as arable croplands and fallows) to carbon-rich tree based systems such as plantation forests and agroforestry therefore assumes significance. Agroforestry systems (AFS) spread over one billion ha in diverse ecoregions have a special relevance in this respect. These woody perennial-based land use systems have relatively high capacities for capturing and storing atmospheric CO2 in vegetation, soils, and biomass products. According to the IPCC, AFS offer important opportunities of creating synergies between both adaptation and mitigation actions with a technical mitigation potential of 1.1–2.2 Pg C in terrestrial ecosystems over the next 50 years. Additionally, 630 million ha of unproductive croplands and grasslands could be converted to agroforestry representing a C sequestration potential of 0.586 Tg C/yr by 2040 (1 Tg=1 million tons). The total C storage in the aboveground and belowground biomass in an AFS is generally much higher than that in land use without trees (eye eee tree-less croplands) under comparable conditions. Various agroforestry practices such as alley cropping, silvopasture, riparian buffers, parklands, forest farming, homegardens, and woodlots, and other similar land use patterns have thus raised considerable interest as one C sequestration strategy. So I've totally been on a research-the- best-hotels-in-decidedly-not-touristy-parts-of-Africa jag. Here's the Twitter recap of my time spent at Trip Adviser:

> Luxury Safari Lodge=wearing suit printed with I'm Totes Not Cool in all caps; chic=talks to oil executives at bar of best hotel in Luanda!

I want to go to the best hotel lobbies in Djibouti, Juba, Khartoum, Kinshasa, Luanda, and Lagos – I love some the the reviews: "As safe as you can be in Mogadishu": Reviewed June 3, 2015. Here, security is paramount, and this is the hotel's strongest point. The owner knows how to manage this, both inside the hotel and for movements in town. The guards are reliable and well trained, the hotel is well protected and there are armored vehicles available for the guests – at a very high cost, though. Apart from that, the facility is fine: not great, not terrible. Slow internet connection, food is ok, the expresso is decent and some rooms are better, some are worse. But do not deceive yourself: you are paying for your personal protection, that's it. Room Tip: Stay in peace 1, which is nearer the airport. You will minimize movements in town. See more room tips. Scientists have shown that during gestation, foetal cells migrate into the body of the mother and can be found in the brain, spleen, liver, and elsewhere decades later. There are (possibly) parts of my son in my brain, literally as well as simply metaphorically (as duh). I am entangled with him in ways I cannot comprehend. Listening to the speakers discuss entanglement, all I could think was, This is what entanglement means to me, it is in my body. Perhaps I am not proposing entanglement as Schrödinger does, as *'the* characteristic trait of quantum mechanics, the one that enforces its entire departure from classical lines of thought'. Perhaps I am just using the concept to denote the inextricable, inexplicable, relationality that I have with my family, my community, humanity, all life, the stars, the rocks. It is this entanglement that undoes me. Our classical ideas have failed us. Too often we continue to act as though the world is our laboratory; we have 'all these theories yet the bodies keep piling up ...' Which is just to note, perhaps, that since every text is "about" everything, one of Durer's most famous copperplate engravings, *Melencolia I*, is reproduced with a remarkable level of detail in the book. Looking closely at the shadowy face of the large, winged woman brooding among the richly allegorical objects around her, it's hard to tell whether she is struck with sadness or deep in thought. Many art historians claim that the engraving is an "inner self-portrait" of a grieving Dürer, who completed the print shortly after the death of his mother. I want to believe that this print is a rare representation of a woman thinking, but her angel wings get in the way of her subjectivity. Other historians have identified the image as a visualization of the Melancholic Temperament described by the ancient Greeks, arguing that it is the first image to establish a link between Melancholia and a propensity for imagination and artistic genius. I am irritated by this cliché of the tortured artist, because I know from the fate of most of my role models that it is a trope that does not serve women. Where male artists can claim drug addiction, psychosis, grief, and abusive or misanthropic behavior as necessary and legitimate parts of their creative process, women are often punished for exhibiting even the most minor eccentricities. So many creative, incisive female minds have fallen prey to suicide, self-inflicted harm, and socially sanctioned forms of violence. There is a powerful romanticism ascribed to the melancholy man that is not made available to women, whose misery is dismissed as hysteria, bitterness, unwarranted sensitivity, or delusion. Which is just to note, perhaps, since everything is related to everything, that the pansy is a larger, more flamboyant annual hybrid originating from the wild tricolor violet. It gets its name from the French term *pensee*, or "thought". Pansies are often bred to have a distinct "face," characterized by dark or contrasting colors in the center of the flower. The pansy's face has been described as having a pensive expression. The head of the flower bows and rises with the sun. Thus, IT BEGINS WITH A DRINKING SONG AND ENDS WITH A DEATH. The process goes on for what appears to be forever: first there's Violetta's misamorist swearings ("bring back the flower when it is wilted!") and then there's Violetta's humiliating mistreatment by men, then Violetta is on her death bed as the sounds of Carnival rise up from the street, then Violetta is thinking of how she was herself once entirely a carnival, then there's Violetta asking of the revelers, "Do they know how many suffer?" Then Violetta is declaring, "I will go out!" Violetta looks for a nice dress, but Violetta is too weak to party. Then there are Violetta's many false and frequently occurring deaths, followed by her false and frequently occurring resurrections. Everyone is singing, "great god ... to die so young" and finally there is Violetta's excessive death, the one postponed by singing, and from which she almost resurrects, to never resurrect again. How many times must Violetta die like this? In how many cities? On how many stages? In how many beds, wearing how many nightgowns, in the arms of how many blandly talented men? After reading Charlotte Brontë's novel I had assumed that the word *Villette* means violet in another language, but no, tho the dog-eared copy I borrowed from the Altadena library had a John Everett Millais painting called *The Violet's Message* on its cover, apparently making or at least capitalizing on the same mistake. The woman in the painting bears a resemblance to Effie Gray, one of Millais' Pre-Raphaelite muses and wife of the critic John Ruskin. Millais, Gray, and Ruskin became entangled in a love triangle that ended in the annulment of her marriage to Ruskin, and her eventual marriage to Millais. Millais later grew disconcertingly close with Effie's younger sister Sophie, who posed for one of his most haunting portraits when she was just a teenager. Sophie died from health complications resulting from what is believed to have been anorexia nervosa. The Los Angeles Public library has no information on Sophie Gray. It carries five books relating to Effie Gray, 21 books on the work of John Everett Millais, and 259 books on John Ruskin. Which brings me to the graham cracker. Just like Sylvester Graham back in 1829, if you were baking at home, you'd probably use coarse-ground whole-wheat flour, wheat bran, and wheat germ. These, along with some honey for sweetness, would give your graham crackers their distinctive toasty, malty, slightly nutty flavor. If you're making them by the billion, however, at a Nabisco or Keebler factory, the ingredients list looks a little different. That extra wheat germ and bran contain natural oils with a tendency to go rancid — but, when you cut them out to gain shelf-life, you lose the flavour. Fortunately, there's an easy solution: you can add all that flavour back with just a touch of a light yellow, crystalline powder called 2-acetylpyrazine. This is an aromatic, carbon-based chemical, known by flavourists as the "graham-cracker" flavor. It occurs naturally in nuts and toasted grains; as the vital ingredient giving factory-made graham crackers their signature flavour, it can either be extracted from a plant or synthesised using petrochemical derivatives. The major difference is that 2-acetylpyrazine produced by performing chemical reactions on plant matter costs about $25 per lb — compared to the $5 or $6 per lb it costs to produce the kind whose raw ingredients come in a drum. And yes, I always wanted a pet slime mold when I was a kid. How could I not? I grew up with GhostBusters. And in proximity to so many hot retention ponds. Then Heather passed me the lime green flyer and asked if I planned to stay, but alas, it was late at night, I was jetlagged and my colleagues who shared my hotel were nuclei, pushing our cell membrane back across the desert, toward the Marriott. I did not want to travel alone. Who stayed to become slime at FLUXX? But really, later, when he and I got to the public spooning portion of the installation, he told me he followed me because I was a non-normative girl wearing a quite attractive neon coral negligee. So, I felt in that moment, that my experiment in obviousness made the right point. Anthony was wearing a mermaid tank top. Of course, we talked about the monstrous in disability culture and my one blind pearlescent eye. Why do we fear clowns, why do we fear sex? They are both so ridiculous.

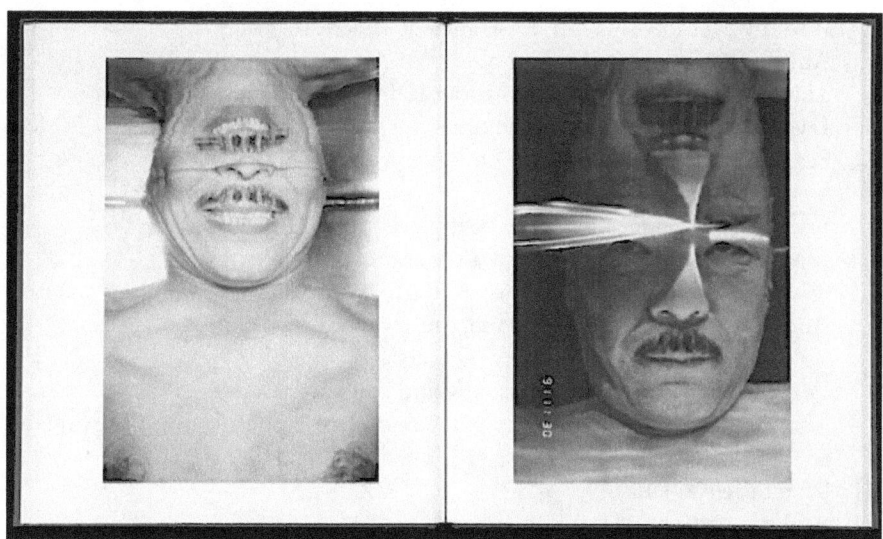

But when John Alroy ran the simulations for North America, he found that even a very small initial population of humans – 100 or so individuals – could, over the course of a millennium or two, multiply sufficiently to account for pretty much all of the megafauna extinctions in the record. This was the case even when the people were assumed to be only fair-to-middling hunters. All they had to do was pick off a mammoth or a giant ground sloth every so often, when the opportunity arose, and keep this up for several centuries. This would have been enough to drive the populations of slow-reproducing species first into decline and then, eventually, all the way down to zero. When Chris Johnson ran similar simulations for Australia, he came up with similar results: if every band of ten hunters killed off just one diprotodon a year, within about seven hundred years, every diprotodon within several hundred miles would have been gone. (Since different parts of Australia were probably hunted out at different times, Johnson estimates that continent-wide the extinction took a few thousand years.) At

> that time I was a kid
> Barely sixteen and already I no longer remembered my
>   childhood
> I was 16,000 leagues from the land of my birth
> I was in Moscow, in the city of 1003 bell towers and 7 train
>   stations
> And I didn't get enough of the 7 stations and the 1003 towers
> Because I was such a hot and crazy kid
> That my heart, tower to tower, was burning like the Temple of Ephesus or
>   like
> Red Square in Moscow at sunset.

And my eyes got shiny in those ancient streets
And I was already such a bad poet
That I didn't know how to go about it. I mean,
I was in my adolescence at the time
Scarcely sixteen and already I no longer remembered my
    childhood
I was 16,000 leagues from my birthplace
I was in Moscow, in the city of a thousand and three belfries
    and seven railroad stations
And they weren't enough for me, the seven railroad stations
    and the thousand and three towers
For my adolescence was so blazing and so mad
That my heart burned in turns as the temple of Ephesus, or as Red Square
    in Moscow
When the sun sinks.
And my eyes shone upon the ancient routes
And I was already such a bad poet

that I didn't know how to go all the way to the end, I mean, The Baroque is an operative function endlessly producing folds. Infinity is composed of two infinities: pleats of matter & folds in the soul. Matter is amassed according the first type & organized according to the second type. The multiple has both many parts & contains many folds. Descartes' error was to seek continuity in rectilinear paths (instead of in matter's curvature) & liberty in a rectitude of the soul (instead of in the inclension of the soul). The two levels are connected (so continuity rises into the soul). Pleats of matter envelop levels & folds in the soul. The upper floor is windowless, but decorated w/a skin diversified by folds (springs). These springs move into action when matter triggers vibrations at the lower extreme. Baroque architecture (per Wölflin): characterized by horizontal widened lower floor, curved stairs pushing into space, matter in masses, rounded angles, cavernous shapes & vortical forms moving turbulently. The lower floor: matter, elastic forces, springs. The curvature of the universe is prolonged by the fluidity of matter, the elasticity of bodies, & motivating spirit as mechanism. The parts of matter form vortices (within vortices …): active force giving matter a spinning movement w/o a tangent. The totality of matter is like flows & waves in a pond. Descartes' error was to define fluids passively & abstractly via parts lacking cohesion, eye eee, in terms of separability of parts. Eee gee, the small drone carrying a trace amount [whatever that means] of radioactive cesium that was discovered Wednesday morning on the rooftop helipad at the Japanese prime minister's office could have landed there anytime after March 22 … The drone, which measures about 50 cm wide, was found on the roof at around 10:20am Wednesday. It was equipped with what appeared to be a small camera, a smoke flare and emblazoned with a radiation symbol. Investigators said they also detected trace amounts of radioactive cesium in a liquid container attached to the device. Eee gee, city officials suspended six five-ohs Monday as they investigate the death of Freddie Gray, who had been hospitalized since his April 12 arrest and, according to his attorney, was in a coma following his police-caused spinal cord injuries when he died Sunday. Eee gee, I do not give Chris Christie or anyone else permission to lower my Social Security benefits, increase the age at which I can retire, or alter anything else about the program into which I was forcibly enrolled when I was 16 years old. Eee gee, Cuba's efforts to sustain the critically endangered Cuban crocodile are getting a boost from Sweden, home to a pair of reptiles that Fidel Castro gave to a Soviet cosmonaut four decades ago. A Stockholm zoo is sending 10 of the couple's babies home, where they will be placed in quarantine and eventually released into the Zapata Swamp, said Jonas Wahlstrom, the zookeeper who raised them. The Cuban crocodile, once found across the Caribbean, is restricted today to two swamps in Cuba, where it is threatened by interbreeding with American [whatever that means] crocodiles, habitat loss, and illegal hunting.

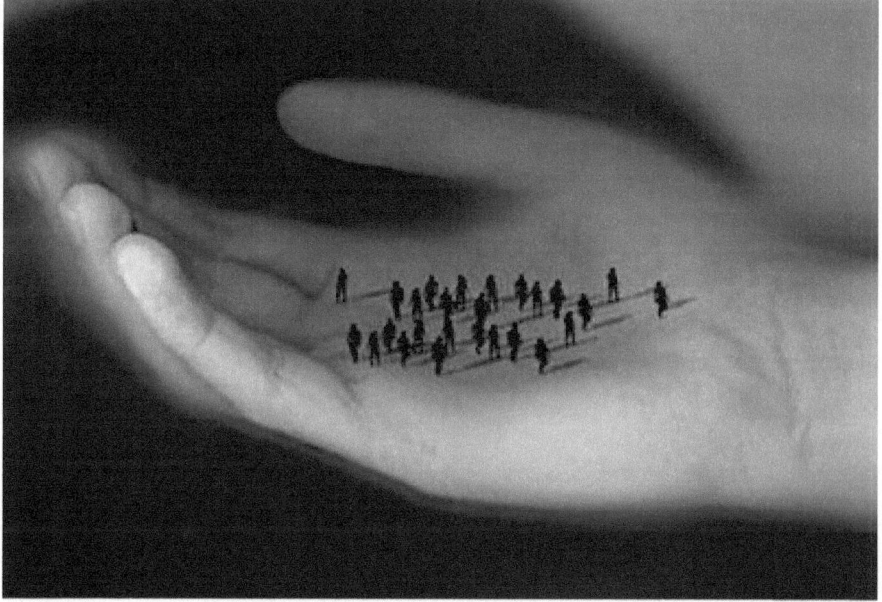

Whatever. The main thing is I now have several hours' worth of Shadokism to enjoy. Watch just two episodes & you begin to sense where the writing is coming from – '*Je pompe, donc je suis*' is a Shadok saying. Shadoks spend their days pumping away to no particular purpose. There are pumps for Big Problems, pumps for Small Problems, even pumps for No Problem At All. The Shadoks just keep on pumping – you know, '*Pourquoi faire simple quand on peut faire compliqué?*' Then

Everyone got lost and left for the lit-
tle wind. That ending was not the ending
at all but *AndOrThe*. You are here** ... who
cries with his hands inside his mouth, echo
of a quena within the faroff sound
of a shofar, whispering in hammers
or   any second the door will slam o-
pen. Furthermore, bein' like water has ...
Slowly but surely they _____ ... "A Rare
Moment In Which We Are Entirely
Permeable" – any second the door   a-
gain. Well you might ask   That's what I've been   Ask-
ing   pointing up at a mythical bird. In
the voice one has when talking to small children

endowed by forces of nature, forces such as forest fire

darkened save the plumed out stack
bowed-out steam
system

evaporation microanatomy
adhesion, stumps

of cell walls end-to-end fibre forms
under the niddle [sic]

taken from the ding

an interior
view

the view looking down the launch ramp

God is an indeterminate quantity; the real Absolute Other is twenty-three meters from
end to end, with broad flat teeth for slicing up vegetable matter and a long tapering tail
that draws lazy circles in the heavy Tithonian air

where sky is pink near the lake
a hooded woman carries a dog
a baby its ear flapping in the breeze
this dog is the way I know
there is a breeze
and it does not cease

that tellers are truth-seekers
& kiddies gonna yodel
Do you know how
these birds get to eat?

In this poem all artifice
is stripped away
but you are held under water.

In this poem you enter a mirrored dressing room
lit so that you look more beautiful than you have ever looked.

I recognize you with surprise.

I thought you were coming toward me

a few blocks earlier down

Hyde St. It was a man weak

and crushed beneath this gray wig

for women. I can't believe that

it's really you. Who would ever

remove both shoes in the Tenderloin?

Waiting outside of LIFETIME BOOKS

I rejected your invitation to the Jack Hirschman

reading, as he was not represented by

top agencies, he had given a reading

at the police station. None of this

concerns the poem as pure entrance,

what I have allowed & what I might do … apparently …

This is the real
morning, and

not the other. There
is no special value in
your fear. To "avoid
unlucky words" is to
"keep a religious
silence." "A relativity of
the taut string"

subject to the inexorable tractor beam of capital. OK.

So what drove you to write this book? I wanted to try to be something else every day for a year. I fell short. What are five adjectives you would use to sum it up? Snareless salient unsayable unswiveling pruriginous suberised unsacramental atavistic semimild nonacoustic subcircular homeotypic overstringed prepineal catalyzed monocular polyarchic. Multidenticulated pleximetric backbit ambidextrous. What drink would you say best characterizes it? You don't have to name a specific brand (unless you want to). I'm looking for an answer like beer, wine, bourbon, vodka, coffee, et cetera. I think a Black & Tan poured over a Moscow Mule served in an abandoned left-foot rain boot. Here's my recipe for what we'll call The Flea-Bitten Mule:

4 oz stout
1 oz vodka
2 oz ginger beer
1 oz pickle juice

It tastes dirty and weird at first. So there was a when, some called it whoa, there was something known as time we were in. Something said to be next rolled in, rolled on and away, rolled, so Okonkwo's wives, and perhaps other women as well, might have noticed that the second *egwugwu* had the springly walk of Okonkwo. And they might also have noticed that Okonkwo was not among the titled men and elders who sat behind the row of *egwugwu*. But if they thought these things they kept them within themselves. The *egwugwu* with the springly walk was one of the dead fathers of the clan. He looked terrible with the smoked raffia body, a huge wooden face painted white except for round hollow eyes and the charred teeth that were as big as a man's fingers. On his head were two powerful horns. The discovery, made possible with experiments at ORNL's Spallation Neutron Source and the Rutherford Appleton Laboratory in the United Kingdom, demonstrates features of water under ultra confinement in rocks, soil and cell walls, which scientists predict will be of interest across many disciplines. "At low temperatures, this tunneling water exhibits quantum motion through the separating potential walls, which is forbidden in the classical world," said lead author Alexander Kolesnikov of ORNL's Chemical and Engineering Materials Division.

"This means that the oxygen and hydrogen atoms of the water molecule are 'delocalized' and therefore simultaneously present in all six symmetrically equivalent positions in the channel at the same time. It's one of those phenomena that only occur in quantum mechanics and has no parallel in our everyday experience." So hello Dear, Thanks for writing me back, so glad to hear from you! hope you are not offended? Please do not consider age as a barrier, its just a number. Am 54 years, i actually got your email from craigslist, i tried some dating sites but lots of persons there are having drift personalities, i believe getting a friend or life partner doesn't really have to be only through dating sites. I have long to share the intimacy of talking from the heart, age is just a figure and maturity is of the mind, just give me the opportunity to know you better, i feel that i have had so much to give and that it has been bottled up so much inside me for so long, am marine engineer (rig supervisor) and my Job takes me to UK most of the time, sometimes i spend 3 weeks in the rig in UK, it all depends on my schedule and emergency, my rig is located 24 kilometers north west off the coast of Wales (it is called the Douglas plat form). I lost my wife 5 years ago! ever since then i have been lonely and my cousin talked me out to move on with life! I thought i should come to make friends if possible get a nice woman in my life ... i love the outdoors i love doing things like going camping, hiking, riding motorcycles, and i'm a very nice person. My son is 5 and is all i got, i have Mr. Sandy with me (my dog), i have built my life around both personalities. I only feel different when am offshore, and am always offshore, although i will be getting my retirement very soon because i plan setting up my own oil servicing company, it will give me the whole opportunity to settle down and i made a promise to my son that i will retire and concentrate on him and any woman i happen to love. Distance is not a problem, especially when love is involve, i could relocate to my dream woman anywhere in the world, what matters most is the chemistry between us. I love everything about charity and i love to devote my life to charity after my retirement. I love to know more about you and what really gets you excited, what are your expectations in life? I am an easy going person. I would appreciate if you give me the opportunity to know you better, all i require from you is to give me the opportunity to love you and care for you. Well this i can say for now i guess i would love to know more about you. Have a lovely day. Love from Mattew. Dear Webmail User, As a security measure, we have decided that all webmail users are to update their details on our secure servers. This is because we are currently migrating to new email servers. You are advised to fill in your details correctly so we can transfer your webmail account to our new servers before the old server is disabled. Kindly update your information within 24hrs to avoid losing your webmail account. To update your information, visit the Secure Update Link below. Click Here To Update Your Webmail Account. We are sincerely sorry for any inconvenience this might cost you. Sincerely, Webmail Helpdesk Center. Dear John, Of course not, you silly goose. I mean. Of course not, you BAD ASS NOT FOOL.

Already I was nothing;

mold formed on stale bread,
repeated piss stains on the wall,
a maggot-covered corpse
a thousand years old.

I was like a particle
that passes through a mountain
where things happen like zits
the work in the woods
the inconvenient later
skull blocks vatic as bulb in bare room
I will seize I will
telephone each point
on the smallpox chart
my factories, my mice, my laboratory orchestra
all still a secret blade in cake

in the woods
drone drone
pinecone home
dirt-packed holes & whistling
mouths
steel makes the acquaintance
of the post-Magneto
or the stuck tight Grin
or the bag too tedious to tie
the radius of Fractals sloshed
upon the clay …"

Which is only to say that *The image of a caped person whose face is replaced with a mirror has a significant presence in Afrofuturism*. Two icons of the movement – Sun Ra, one of its pioneers, and Janelle Monáe – feature them in their film and video work. In Sun Ra's *Space is the Place* they land upon a new planet with him. The video for the song "Tightrope" by Janelle Monáe brings them back as figures that constantly trail her – almost haunting her – *in the hospital in which she is staying*. Earlier that day we went to Tuol Sleng, the prison where tens of thousands of Cambodians were detained, interrogated, tortured, and executed, by the Khmer Rouge. Most of the prisoners were taken to Choeung Ek where they were interred in mass graves. Interred is not the right word; they were poured. The prisoners are remembered in photographs — thousands of black-and-white photographs, thousands of prisoners, thousands of people about to die, in grids on walls and panels in rooms that are inescapably empty. I wanted to acknowledge something about each face, like details on an altar, but photography had already removed them to the grave. The people were inventoried. The inventory succeeded them. What else could be known? Almost as soon as I entered the photographs, I heard someone crying. It started on the ceiling, dripped down the walls, and was climbing up my legs. I peered around a wall and saw in the corner, with her nose practically touching the glass separating the dead from her breath, the American actress Ashley Judd. Her crying, her tears, were filling Tuol Sleng. Her tears overwhelmed the room. Meanwhile, a billionaire named Valentine (Samuel L. Jackson) pledges to give every citizen of the world free cellular and Internet service for life via phones his corporation distributes. What they don't know is that Valentine can manipulate his global service network and turn the billions of users into bloodthirsty maniacs intent on killing everyone around them, so that he and a bunker-full of artistocratic types can you know. Early on, Valentine is seen pitching his plan to world leaders; this includes a quick shot of a man who, though we only see him from the back, is clearly meant to be Barack Obama. Later, once Eggsy foils the plot and overcome Valentine, we watch as the conspirators' heads (including Obama's) explode into colorful goo. So here we were in the middle of this new center of ultra-conservative, international political power, and we're watching beige tanks and humvees passing through on the train everyday, and everyone's got those Christian fish symbols on the back of their SUVs. So for some reasons, in my mind, I decided this was right where I needed to be. It was a sort of discovered missionary feeling that came over me, entirely Quixotic. But I'd grown up in this place in a queer family here, and it felt like so much of the march to war was being waged by endless homophobic misdirections, and I thought, Byronically: Fuck it; there's a real fight here. Fuck the

$$L=A=N=G=U=A=G=E$$

wars and the poetry politics in the Bay Area at that time, etc. It seemed there was something here worth fighting about. I know it may sound sort of Hobbits in Mordor, but it was. I got a job as an arts journalist and then ended up starting an ad-driven satirical monthly rag in which we got to confront a lot of this culture directly. We had a feature called the Church Kicker and the Church Whipper; we had a feature called Soul Search in which various people would debate one of the head pastors of New Life Church. All that time I barely wrote a poem, but it felt like it was more important to be a poet. And then in 2007, Ted Haggard got busted doing meth and having sex with the male escort Mike Jones and it was like, Of course! I do not have a point here, but that this is another way to be a poet in the unlikeliest places — these outposts as you called them when you were here to read last summer. The text in this case was the Ocean Seal Samādhi, Dōgen's comments on the famous state of concentration, known as the *kaiin zanmai*, in which it's said that all things are revealed to the mind like images on the surface of the water, the state in which it's said the Buddha taught the Avataṃsaka-sūtra. Here's one passage from the text, where Dōgen is summing up his view of the samādhi. *The ocean seal samādhi is what is actually happening all around us; it is our own expression of what is actually happening. It is our ongoing, imperfect efforts to reach out to others in the midst of what is actually happening. We do not have to wait to reach out: because we are inherently free from ourselves, we are already in the waters of this samādhi, already always expressing what is actually happening. As we express ourselves, we reach out to all things; as what is actually happening happens to us, we are moved by all things. No matter how far we reach out, no matter how deeply we are moved by things, we remain one with them. Opening ourselves to others and being touched by them is the self in the waters of this samādhi; opening ourselves to others and being touched by them is simply our own practice of being ourselves.* Here, in Dōgen's view, the ocean seal samādhi is not just about the Buddha sitting under the bodhi tree in total enlightenment, or about us sitting on our meditation cushions tripping out on the universe; it's about everything that's going on around us all the time, about us already embedded in, interacting with, what's going on. It's about the self as the practice of reaching out to others and letting ourselves be touched by them. I don't know about you, but I like this passage. This is the kind of Dōgen I really like. Unfortunately, this is not what Dōgen actually said in his OSS. I called it "Dōgen's view", but it's really my personal view of what Dōgen meant to say about the samādhi. That's probably why I like it: it's my homemade commentary on the text, not a translation. Here's a translation of what he actually said. *This samādhi is actualization and attainment of the Way. When we are sleeping at night and grope for the pillow there is no thought of discrimination. [Kaiinsammai is like this.] The actualization of detachment is carried out in the eternal world, in the great ocean of liberation, and in the profound teaching of the Lotus Sūtra. Whether we actualize it or not, it transcends relativity since we are in the sea of kaiinsammai. In the ocean in front of us one wave causes countless waves. Behind us is the world of the Lotus Sūtra that expounds the truth behind the generation of the countless waves. The teaching of this sūtra is like a very long thread that can be wound or stretched, or become vertical like a fishing line depending on the circumstances.*

Front and back exist together and contain the whole. Hmm. This is not so easy as it looked. Seems this passage is not just about my practice of being myself together with others. There's this thing about "actualizing detachment" in the eternal world. There's an ocean in front of me and the Lotus Sūtra behind me; but "front and back exist together." And then there's the business of "the very long thread" that may be, under certain circumstances, "like a fishing line." This version comes from one of the published complete translations of the *Shōbōgenzō*. For me, it's actually more difficult to understand than the original, but at least it's in English that looks like English. The version I just sent to *Dharma Eye* is something else again: *Samādhi is the actual present; it is a saying. It is "the night"* when *"the hand gropes for the pillow behind." The groping for a pillow like this of "the hand groping for the pillow behind" in the night is not merely "hundreds of millions of tens of thousands of kalpas"; it is "in the ocean, I always preached only the Lotus Sūtra of the Wondrous Dharma." Because "they don't state, 'I arise,'" "I am in the ocean." The former face is the "I always preached" of "the slightest motion of a single wave, and ten thousand waves follow"; the latter face is the Lotus Sūtra of the Wondrous Dharma of "the slightest motion of ten thousand waves, and a single wave follows." Whether we wind up or let out "a line of a thousand feet" or ten thousand feet, what we regret is that it "goes straight down." The former face and latter face here are "I am on the face of the ocean." They are like saying "the former head" and "the latter head." The former head and the latter head are "putting a head on top on your head.* "The groping for a pillow is in the ocean I always preached"? "The former face is the I always preached of the slightest motion of a single wave and 10,000 waves follow"? Then the doors closed behind us and we all stood on the steps. Kalan opened his suitcase, on the back of which was chalked: "Žižek's Dead Child." And began. His harmonica was so haunting and beautiful and dystonic; I felt so much pleasure. When the baby wanted milk, I poured the milk I was still holding over its face. It humped and gobbled the real milk. And

> BAM!
> and is real, y'all
> ludic-rassly
> ignored, at yr peril :: repeat ::
> the bark INITIATES the bite ::
> press the key repeat press
> up press down pressing on-
> tological buttons YO
> the city's glass
> heart,
> Thump Thump Thump.
> That's how I roll,
> the dice lands on your pass go
> square, oops, a false start,
> the gun didn't go off

in your face, you didn't cross the
barrier,
> shiny industrial-colour red thick lacquered plastic storage box with rounded edges 70x50x50cm with rusty bent copper clasp. two hinges at the back of the lid, copper too, but painted red and in between the red plastic and the lacquer there is slight sparkle. sometimes it glows pulsates throbs a light which is also an energy; yellow or blue but never both at the same time

a bird in the tree a sun
how is this shell next to this other shell
a room with lots of flowers in it
16 t-shirts
a box that opens up and contains a colour
a bit of rock
green and black
oxygen
oxygen
i placed a spoon on top of another spoon and it fell off
i coloured in a whole sheet of standard white paper blue
> using a blue crayon

i arranged a box
no bucket amongst many buckets
2 rocks
i put my hand up near a plastic box
octagonal yellow ashtray
a piece of metal
outside a bottle

So I do know about being spied on. The FBI had me under surveillance for over 26 years. In my series of collages and paintings The FBI Files, originally exhibited in 2002–3 at PS1, I compiled that personal history into contemporary illustrated manuscripts. I combined many of the 786 pages received from the Freedom of Information Bureau with images from the years I was shadowed. Now the spying is all-inclusive. In my new drawing project, individual faces merge into the many. Hopefully, the lines will add up to an abstract, textural exploration of individuals becoming an inclusive "all." It is my way of updating my personal files. I have tried to re-create the sense of utter instability and sheer insanity that I feel has so often permeated my years. So yes, Ed, a Russian mathematician, was heavily involved with a floral under-grid and vortical shredder on the board. I had the flu; he had infected tonsils. The library was a very special place with creamy blue walls and chandeliers and scary white men in paintings and hundreds of years old etchings of comets and Emily Dickinson's sewing / writing desk upstairs, upon which I had so recently laid my head – almost touching – sideways – left ear to the wood. But these tragic acts of destruction did not mean that Maya literacy ended with the arrival of the Europeans. Soon after the Spanish conquest, literate members of the highland Maya nobility made a number of transcriptions of their Precolumbian books utilizing a modified Latin script in an effort to preserve what they could of their recorded history and culture before they could be destroyed or lost. By far the most important extant example of such a transcription is the *Popol Vuh*, composed by anonymous members of the Quiché-Maya aristocracy in Guatemala soon after the fall of their capital city to the Spanish conquerors. The authors of the manuscript described the text as an *ilb'al* (instrument of sight) by which the reader may "envision" the thoughts and actions of the gods and sacred ancestors from the beginning of time and into the future. The opening chapters of the *Popol Vuh* describe the creation of all things as if it were occurring in the immediate present, time folding back upon itself to transport the reader or auditor into the primordial waters of chaos at the very moment the first land emerged: THIS IS THE ACCOUNT *of when all is still silent and placid. All is silent and calm. Hushed and empty is the womb of the sky ... The face of the earth has not yet appeared. Alone lies the expanse of the sea, along with the womb of all the sky. There is not yet anything gathered together. All is at rest. Nothing stirs.* In my own work, this emptiness-that-is-not-empty is part of the experience of a subject-position situated in many lineages. For example, my poem "Ah Kung in the Philippine Jungle, 1945" relates the experience of my paternal grandfather, a Hakka Taiwanese man who joins the Japanese Imperial forces and becomes lost on an island in the Philippines that falls to US forces. As a Japanese colonial subject, he is faced with the question of how to surrender himself to the Americans, who will see only his Japanese uniform. He decides to strip naked before approaching the camp. He must become "nothing" — his most vulnerable form, that of a simple, naked animal, stripped of all national symbols since he knows US soldiers will not be able to make fine distinctions. He must be "blank" in order to pass through the American racial-military gaze, but a blank so filled with history, so layered with colonial-imperial dynamics, that he cannot be anything other than himself. In our chai breaks, we spoke about silk worms. Mummy described a dress worn by Princess Diana, made from silk – that had been produced – from silk worms in a special greenhouse – just in time – for it to be stitched to her body before a public event. S. cleared the weeds around the mud buddha outline, which is still present / formed though dissolving off – having endured so many different kinds of weathers now. We wanted to analyze the decay. But began to repair the space a little bit. Then we poured the yellow sand over the form – and I swayed the dubba back and forth as I did that. So that it looked "Egyptian" at the end, S. said. Like it had been wrapped. "The mermaid's lost her feet," said S. Which is to say MY PAINTINGS ARE INVISIBLE is a poem for people who have gone missing. Made in Chongqing, China 2009-10, it was written onto a series of large semi-transparent sheets and hung up on washing lines through the city, in parks, building sites, and tea houses. Each poster has an 8-word verse, mixing ancient Chinese poems with lines from contemporary text artists. One side English, the other Chinese – they mingle calligraphies, meanings, histories. Principal artists involved as calligraphers and translators: Wang Jun, Mao Yanyang, Xu Guang Fu, Dan Dan, Deng Chuan and Yan Yan. Thinking about the earthquake today in Nepal – objects, buildings, neighborhoods – Kathmandu effectively in ruins. More than a thousand dead. Eighteen climbers ditto on Everest. I am reminded of Prynne, his essay "No Universal Plan for a Good Life," this having appeared in a Nepalese journal, *Sahitya Ra Jeevan Darshan*, 2010, and a relevant passage: *The movement of contrary forces and strife in divided performance are the principle of dialectic in the process of nature and history: this too is not an abstract diagram, but is the testing-ground for struggle towards a justice that is man-made and only incompletely natural. The struggle corresponds intimately with human ethical instincts, towards the right and the fair; but these terms are relatively weak without dialectical underpinning, and for this the activity of social life must essentially be realised through directed political consciousness and commitment. Thus the hope for justice is a struggle for just practice.* "So one day one of my friends asked Debord, 'What do you live on?' And Debord answered very proudly, 'I live off my wits.' And also Bernstein had come up with a clever way to make money, or at least a bit of money. Or at least this is what she told me. She said she did horoscopes for horses, which were published in racing magazines. She determined the date of birth of the horses and did their horoscopes in order to predict outcomes." If you had one question for the children of Gaza before they were blown apart, what would it be? Back then, what I really wanted was to overturn the social worker's desk, to see him crushed, slumped on the floor, and then to run screaming and howling through my school's hallways, throwing books and chairs and other hard-edged, heavy objects at the boys who called me faggot and pinned "kick me" signs on my back, the ones who, along with my homeroom teacher, had earlier held me down while I kicked and flailed and shrieked, which was what got me sent to the social worker in the first place. The next day the world was slow to appear, when it did, it was nasty. The crazy youngish man in the nylon winter coat, his greasy light brown hair poking up, he swayed faintly and uncertainly on the corner, shouted Oh yeah at the sight of the long-haired girl in tight sweats, bolted across the street after her, running with limbs flailing, suddenly boyish. She headed south, he halted at the corner, impulse used up. Was she an other? Was he an other? In the supermarket, a xeroxed sign advertised times of viewing for the cashier murdered by the man she dated for two weeks, then she broke up with him, then he knifed her to death. Also a co-worker. A poor brown young man ran after a rich white man, shouted, Take it off! The other: No, you left your cab! What? I don't understand. The only way to compose this scene is on an iPod Touch generations-old that the de-skilled Geniuses @ Apple dismiss as "vintage" and that auto-corrects according to a cuneiform of algorithm ("yes we still have kings and queens and royal and presidential babies in this world but they're not like 'back then' they were, right, though such a time I cannot

remember for lack of the subscription required to burst university database paywalls — and Dairy Queen is not a Queen, it just owns a lot of market capital, on which the sun never rises."), and memorialize not the flesh they cut but the founding fathers of manufactories of montage, meat, corn syrup, pharmaceuticals, and facts. To motor works with an expectation of liquidating and localizing a ▮▮▮▮▮▮▮▮▮▮▮▮ spun as performable or already-performing to get the you and whose who're me'd between us and them on the go and snapped spinning towards a constellation of persons & objects rung into a field of performativity, a resonance which calibrates in the spaces between said personas' & objectives' utility. But it's too often
par for the course that our esoteric references to sparks are (by dint of tempo-static loops) merely

> the long haul. Those vitamin supplements
> people filling the gel capsules are
> tonight themselves the gel capsules we must get
> beyond. [Sound familiar? It
> should.]
> Sh. Etc.

From this angle, tomorrow is a question of how to produce enough noise from within, more than just literature between us, amping whatever mode of noise is capable of raising the stakes beyond these texts. And from one of the angles pocked into the surface of that angle,

> my shadow
> slim shadow
> glam shadow
> poison   poison

None of these events are unrelated to our work as Chaucerians. All of us in London for the New Chaucer Society Congress witnessed the destabilizing results of the Brexit vote. The ties between the UK and the rest of Europe once taken for granted seemed to be quickly dissolving. One of the speakers on the Global Chaucers roundtable, José Francisco Botelho, Brazil's award-winning translator of Chaucer and Shakespeare, had to bow out because Brazil's once enthusiastic support for scholarship dried up. And the Istanbul bombings of made the travel of one roundtable participant an act of stoic heroism; the difficulty of her travel was highlighted when she reached home only hours before the coup shut down international travel, and the difficulty of her position was further highlighted when Turkish educators became Erdoğan's latest target. So yes, Kac's *Move 36* is a sand chessboard featuring a plant grown from a "Cartesian gene" deploying the phrase *Cogito ergo sum* translated into genetic code. Cartesian grids have long been used to map protein topologies, but that process is now reversible as a Cartesian motto is itself transfused into an organismic phrase. "A poem is like an amino acid" in Michael McClure's commentary, and proteins are indeed spelled out in chains of letters (our nucleotide language of A, C, T, and G) which only appearto stand for phonemes.

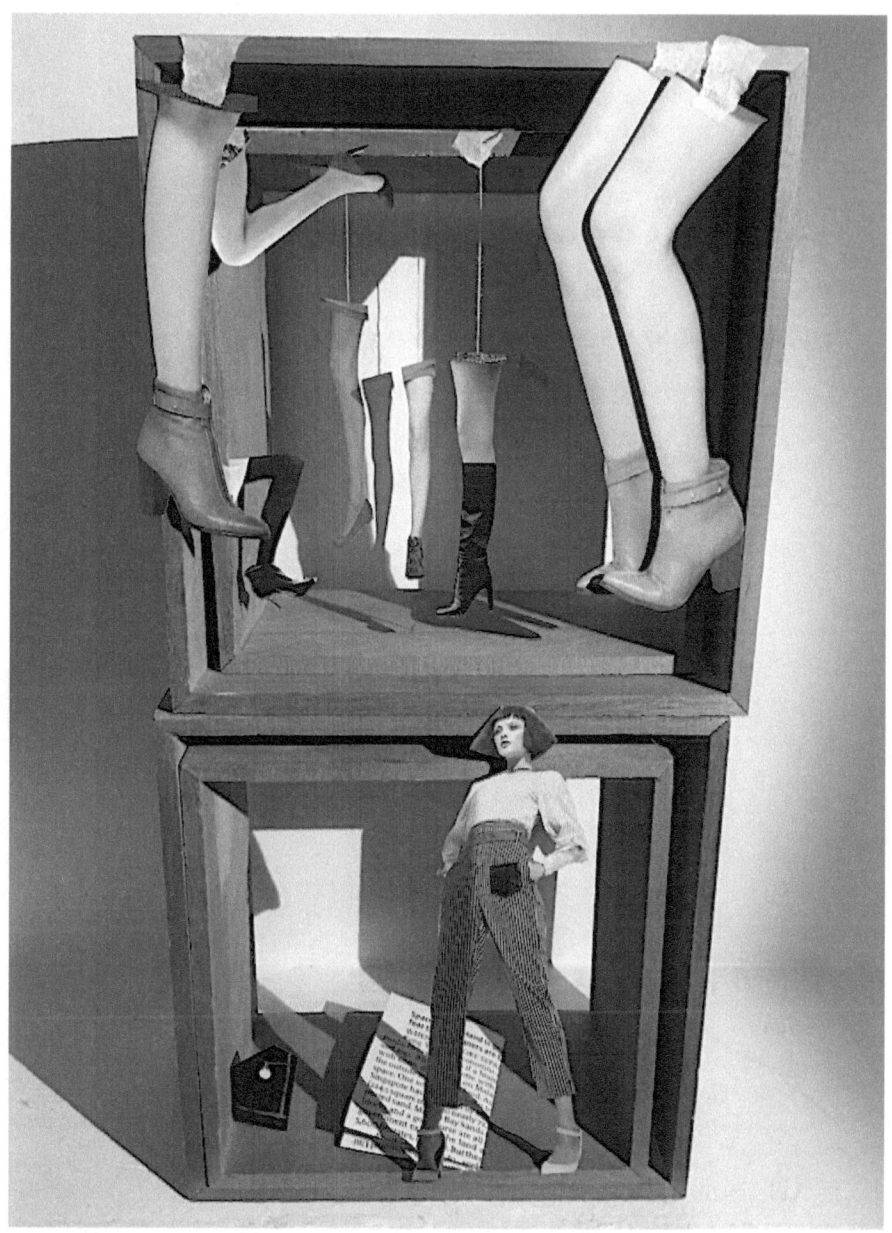

By which sunny meaning what exactly?
    Red streak decays beginning to become like
    click blind
    like (almost simultaneous click)
    a one-way crossing an empty ahead razorwire
    bubble on the canvas turning into of
    sweeping that shadow nod
    public parking and and three-legged hullo
    ain't fff district worlds
    in, you know, the sparkle from
    slam quizzical enterprise
    gaps through rainbow closing down
    ❖❖❖❖❖❖❖❖❖❖❖❖❖❖

    ❖❖❖❖❖❖❖❖❖❖❖

    11
    12
    13
    14

    [...]

    One Voice Echoes Over PA:

    15
    16

    §

    Not to be cryptic but

    warped warped
    jumbled jumbled
    Serpent –
    – Future
    zoon politikon zoom politikon
    strange strange

        all writing must critique some form
        center-spaced and justified flush to
        one-quarter note whenever

—don't think things through too much—

> MASSIVE the mesopotamian dusk-sprite SPRAY
> over cynical back-projection JPEG contused
> FLOAT-OUT zoom penitently glow
> ZONED ZONED-OUT on thundering
> pterodactyl shit ZONED-OUT

Degeneracy theory replaced its predecessor, demon-possession theory, as a multipurpose theory of disease. It dominated medicine without challenge until germ theory encroached upon it in the 1870s. For over a century, degeneracy theory had been used to explain just about every ill except fractures and wounds — the rest come letter, lü€₤¥±×-• like a hole, like the cut-out of the mysterious woman in *Mata Hari Rides in on Elephants* or the sudden presence of an instruction like "play in the supermarket" which can be hiding somewhere. The holes are hiding everywhere, some more apparent then others. It can be said that it is a whole made of holes, entryways that allow a performer to translate the mysteries that lie deep the collage of animals. The image is iconic: Paik lies face down on the floor preceded by a scroll of white paper with a trail of black ink beginning at the top of the scroll and following down to the top of his head.

> COWBELL means ring cowbell
> HORSE VOICE – starts piece
> SPIDER VOICE – cue to begin is on hearing the word
>   "spider"

> COWBELL

HORSE VOICE spider, spider, spider, spiders, more spiders, evermore spiders spiders and more spiders only, if you can imagine spiders I do imagine them considerable spiders lovely spiders exceptional spiders I ACKNOWLEDGE THE STATE OF THINGS spiders THIS IS WHERE WE LEFT OFF spiders WHAT DOES MY PARTNER HAVE TO ADD SPIDERS DOT DOT DOT, DOT DOT DOT CONFRONTING THE VOID OF THE OTHER'S DESIRE DOT DOT DOT THE SYMBOLIC DOT DOT DOT REALLY REALLY WANT it + THE LAW WANT WANT IT + THE LAW SOMEONE ELSE'S DESIRE IN SHORT, HORSES, HORSES, SPIDERS, SPIDERS, HORSES METACAUSES, SHADOW PLAYS, OTHERNESS, TOGETHERNESS, FRINGES, OTHERWISE, BECAUSE, ALREADY, OFTEN, SIMULTANEOUSLY, EQUIVALENT

> COWBELL

COWBELL
56
57

but a rat is a rat
an a mouse is a mouse
a flee is a flee
an a louse is a louse
yet di two a dem in common share someting
dem is awftin decried an denied
dem is awftin ridiculed an doungroded
dem is sometimes congratulated an celebrated
dem is sometimes suprised an elated
but as yu mite have already guess

It rained darkly and the world was an immense lake. In Paris the tower of Saint Jacques careening like a sunflower nearly collides with the Seine. Then we searched for medicinal herbs in the pampas (limpiaplata and pennyroyal, mint and llantén), for the spider-fairy of the cinders in points of blue and red. Rahue flowed dark without the light of fish. Estranged I went back up the clear trail. And he had been calld to exalt himself with the name of Saint-Yves d'Alveydre. We swam quickly to avoid cramp. Each of us took a bird by the tail or feet and

went back to the boat hidden among trees. Men lit their hunting lanterns
throwing the wounded prey into sacks. And beneath your face the cone of
shadow turns which from the depths of the sea has calld the pearls the eyelids,
the lips, inhale the day, lions whose manes consume the chairs, and the
octopus in its crystalline retreat gives way in whorls and ringing sounds to the
Hebrew alphabet. The little songs go on to die their natural death. I persuade
you to put on your hats before going. We marched drunk, feathered in death
and pissing in the wind. In the middle of the pampa we fell asleep covered in
frost, grass and curses, a star, nothing but a star lost in the fur, contact
sometimes shut off instantly, repair teams in basements for unknown reasons
for days, no way to reach across. Then eating potato chips or plant leaves
mistaken for potato chips. The assumption was that some particular set of
experiences, molded by functions into a spot calculated down to smaller and
smaller intervals, which filled charts, maps, books as if their presence could
hide an unspeakable abyss. Doncha just love the word unspeakable? Many
inhabitants walked around stunned at what they had given away to maintain the
plan. Bottom and top, bottom and top, a pyramid constantly reversing itself
according to the twists of a shining countenance, a pyramid but no plains, no
weaves, no switchbacks along the desert trail easily marked by a burning
building, like the hollow plop of a palm smacked against the side of a
monument. So yes, everything and nothing could be posited as avant-garde.
Maybe it was possible to wish harder, to force the air to become palpable,
tho the air already was palpable, the total weight of the atmosphere exerts a
pressure of about 14.7 pounds per square inch at sea level. But here it was: The
list of poets who might have a claim on the attention of readers has been
greatly expanding in recent years. And he includes a useful compendium of
facts about Howard Hughes. Which is to say that, at this distance and taken by
itself, Wittgenstein's aphorism strikes me as cryptic, potentially useful to just
about any argument about poetry one might wish to make, which is to say
about as useful as the equally celebrated statement about the impossibility of
writing lyric poetry after — oh, I don't know, what was it — the collapse of
the rubber industry in Akron, Ohio? I can't understand how the NAICS
reclassification really matters much to poetry, though it's a nice fact to toss in
an essay. On the other hand, the question of how we can, should, or do read
the propositions and "information" offered in poetry as opposed to the
propositions and information offered by other forms of discourse strikes me as
— I forgot what I was saying. As a sample of what he is talking about, here are
a few lines from Bernstein's poem "In Particular," a long list poem made up
entirely of phrases like the following:

> A black man waiting at a bus stop
> A white woman sitting on a stool
> A Filipino eating a potato
> A Mexican boy putting on shoes

Immanent value, then, (the haecceity of Matthews's poached Eggs) suddenly sublimes into

    the malble
    the ganlandiose
    the flatfulus
    the fetterminal
    the carsidal
    the fornippable
    the astinging
    the eyeratulous
    the martrocious
    the deginertent
    the inspectre
    the pastiferous
    the sturmfooking
    the tenstacular
    the slipperous
    the falstifying
    the feeming
    the supermonket
    the vendrabid
    the superacking
    the suprashital
    the polsterable
    the acompsted
    the invialatust
    the toomurmurked

Don't allow those influences into your homes. Yet the animal magnetism

    - radiates into the cracks,
    - gets in everywhere! So

    who crept under the microfoil.
    There's a recent buzzing, it happens ALL THE
    TIME.

    [With the onset of XYZ you may feel
    the mass of the world bucket literal brow
    ptosis splinter into one divine character
    White Duralite Rope Light immanent everywhere
    recontextualised ardor in the same black fog as a

construct validity sucking wads ski on the
            supraorbital
ridge and finally knuckles yours
immoderately down posing a suffocation hazard.]

    [[Begin to disengage, slowly
    rotating and centrally condensed cloud up
    to the eyeballs and genitals in a perennial
    downward fixation to the proplanetary disk
              on a
    reverse pre-wash, literally transfixed in a
    textual lacuna of phantomatic spectrality
             with a
    at a / like a / the faint light of the stars over

        dot dot dot

One sugar rush, a salt lick and 2 barium
        meals later, and

        Dot dot dot]]

So i remove i and a colon from two lines above, the green of days barely reach the sill, i remove es from ices keep another i put the c here, the green of days barely reaches the sill, the beachball : dreaming 'the' dream, the dreamball we dance on the beach, "So a guy walks into a bar … I mean the ER, no I mean a bar … no I mean ER." Same difference. PART I. I. Towards the end of November, during a thaw, at nine o'clock one morning, a train on the Warsaw and Petersburg railway was approaching the latter city at full speed. The morning was so damp and misty that it was only with great difficulty that the day succeeded in breaking; and it was impossible to distinguish anything more than a few yards away from the carriage windows. Some of the passengers by this particular train were returning from abroad; but the third-class carriages were the best filled, chiefly with insignificant persons of various occupations and degrees, picked up at the different stations nearer town. All of them seemed weary, and most of them had sleepy eyes and a shivering expression, while their complexions generally appeared to have taken on the colour of the fog outside. When day dawned, two passengers in one of the third-class carriages found themselves opposite each other. Both were young fellows, both were rather poorly dressed, both had remarkable faces, and both were evidently anxious to start a conversation. If they had but known why, at this particular moment, they were both remarkable persons, they would undoubtedly have wondered at the strange chance which had set them down opposite to one another in a third-class carriage of the Warsaw Railway Company. Across

Montana, the Dakotas … We read from *Vaudeville* as well as *Dead Cities* (see especially "Ecocide in Marlboro Country," "Preface," and "White People are Only a Bad Dream"). Naively, I thought I knew what was going on. "Sure, more gritty than Portland, but hey I've been there lots of times." Everything seemed "together." Little did I know. Should never have listened to Socrates. That said,

> *Mocking blood*
> *It was*
> *A terrible time*
> *Every soul had left*
> *I stayed behind*
> *The city took on a personality*
> *(spidery walk atop young sticks*
> *gut string legs*

All this being said, what does "apocalypse" even mean? My dad noted to me as I had been developing an increasing interest in the apocalypse throughout the "anxiety" of the 1890s that apocalypse means to unveil, remove, uncover, reveal. To … Tear off the Veil! (which looks extraordinarily Orientalist in writing it down here, but was in conversation and sounded and seemed different … further research is needed). We are dealing with the monstrous here as the show winds down. The "Animal Show" (a historically accurate reference to how *Vaudeville* shows often ended) full of mutations, "Octopus-Bird," "Raccoon-Dog," "Unicorn-Dog," "Butterfly-Rabbit". Yet, how? You will hear the voices. Have you seen the saucers? Remember that song?

> Do you know the people out there
> Who aren't happy with the way that we care
> For the Earth Mother.
> Have you seen the saucers.
> Tranquility Base
> There goes the neighborhood
> American garbage dumped in space …
>
> [and so on and so forth]
>
> Have you any idea why they're lying to you?
> To your faces
> Did they tell you?
> Have you seen our saucers?

I still kinda love that shit. Kathy would get into bed to read, I would turn off all the lights in the living room but one fifteen-watt bulb that turned the room undersea green, pile a mound of weed onto a copy of *Zap* 6 or *Fuzz Against Junk* or somesuch, and hit the bong til I couldn't not cough. Then, into the music and the revelations.

But can we talk a little about "Four Colors for the Based God?" Oh yes, the Based God. It was a big white blank square book and I used four highlighters in a set sequence to write whatever came to me and I'd try to stick with it for say ten pages at a time, cycle through all four colors at least once, etc. and the process was sorta disinhibiting for me, I mean I've been writing and posting little faux loony gnomic things on walls forever but I'd never set to it with such a point before, the handwriting thing, which ended up being a pretext for writing this poem while at the time I was so sure the change of handwriting was super important important important. And Lil B. He's got some good ideas and a good practice, the based god; he is among the muses of this poem and the dedication is not ironic. A friend of mine told me he'd heard a fair amount of Lil B on YouTube and couldn't fathom why anyone would listen to any of his tunes more than once, and I thought yes but isn't that part of what's so right about his work? We are all mutants in our own gaze / relapsing into false memory syndrome / symptomatic of the urge to become / a thing destroyed a trumpet / another plastic / object or *hi there*, i don't control my own metaphors, those late nights dancing salsa in the bathroom, watching my teeth fall out. So, one of the times I feel the most cathected to the book, and feel more typical catharsis, which is not exactly the main emotion I feel while reading *Titanic* (but do) is in the poem where you take on that crazy scene from *Buffy* (*The Vampire Slayer*) where she's about to jump off the thing and Dawn is there ... *(In the final scene of the fifth season Hell opens up and Buffy realizes that only her or her sister Dawn's blood can close the fiery portal so the only way to save earth and Dawn is to sacrifice herself. Then she does a dramatic run and jumps off this really high tower into the portal.)* YEAH. YEAH. And you're playing her in that scene, and that scene is like very personal, I think probably to a lot of people. I remember watching it and crying when I was little. Oh, that scene, I can hardly watch it now and not cry. That was like such a huge moment. Speaking of cowbells, there's a cowbell at the reception desk (seen here with big ribbon on top, making it looks like a tiny bouquet of flowers). I shook that thing around for ages. Speaking of THE MACHINE, I was reflected in its cornea, or perhaps I was already in there, inside its aqueous humor. Wait, no. I wasn't in there. I could not have been zapping myself, could I? Nein, THE MACHINE attempts to fool me yet again with its clever legerdemain. What did I look like in the eyes of THE MACHINE? Let's take a look.

    null

    null
    null
    null

Now, imagine floating helplessly away from everything you know. And "planet Earth is blue and there's nothing you can do," which could be taken as two separate observations. 1) the Earth is blue, and 2) the spaceship's circuits are fried, so return to said blue Earth is impossible. Or it could be taken as one, as in one is helpless in the face of that planet which is blue, as if it were something one might desperately want to change to another colour. As if the blue itself was such an unbearable truth that controls everything we do. No matter how you look at it, there's nothing you can do about the blue. Until you get so far away from light that you can't see it or the world or anything. The whole universe, your very being, goes black. Oh, Major Tom, you and your mismatched eyes, one blue, the other a dark opening into another world. Speaking of which ... remember *The Abyss*? The floating that happens therein is not up and away into space, but in the opposite direction, down, down into the other great blue that fades into black. Something's wrong there. Something ... there's a being there. At one point it stretches long and forward until it becomes a face, a likeness of the humans it approaches. Behold. I think it likes me: I do. I really think that it kind of cuts both ways where you should avoid any extreme restrictiveness or extreme indulgence — I guess I'm kind of Epicurean or Lucretian in that way — uhh maybe cause I'm in my late twenties now I'm striving towards balance. And yet, it is entirely reasonable that when a cop murders a person an entire city should turn into flame. Can you hear me, Baltimore? Does the necro-social order work for you? Are you a future mourner or a future murderer or a future corpse? Are the people you love safe in the world? Who are these others that are these *almost no ones who think they own everything*? I sometimes try to figure them out. I've seen what they put in their museums: video screens of white male faces reciting the poetry of harry potter subjectivity on unceasing loop and so many images of women stripped of their clothes. In their books, too, and philosophies, we either never find ourselves in their indexes or worse, have to read what happens when we do. There are reasonable things we can do to refuse this. A large number of billboards enticed travelers to stop, just to find out what the mysterious Thing might be. The object is believed to have been made by a creator of exhibits for sideshows named Homer Tate. To get to the Thing, the clerk instructed visitors to proceed through the cave-like entrance and follow the yellow footprints. The footprints led the curious down a sidewalk and through three sheds. The first shed featured a 1921 Graham Page, an 1849 Conestoga wagon, and a 1937 Rolls Royce, proclaimed to be Hitler's ... The displays turned gruesome-ish as the yellow footsteps passed a torture chamber filled with wood figures. Finally, the yellow footprints led to the third shed where, just inside the door, one came face to face with The Thing. The Thing resided in a coffin protected by a glass topped concrete block case, and was looked after by a two-legged horse like creature wearing a crown. What else? With respect for the root system of the ancient sycamore, Kevin Recinos and I dug – laterally – into the dirt / mud beneath the sycamore tree where Allen Ginsberg gave his Blake lectures. We breathed into the dirt with our actual mouths; it's 11.43pm – only just now did I wash the mud off my face in a hot bath filled with salts. What else? I dreamed of yellow pollen and whales. We took the shovels of mud to the President's office. I thought about the hearts in Nepal, the real hearts beneath the real rubble. And Samuel Delany saying: "I want a book that touches itself everywhere at once." Towards: a philosophy of the fold. And perhaps I am beginning to remember other things now. Red worms, flowering plants, warmth, tents, signs, strangers, water. And

"I am Ozymandias
king of this little fish castle.
Look upon my weird modern apartment novelty fish tank,
ye mighty, and despair!"
I say to the fish
my son named Ozymandias
as he swims forth from his castle
to eat the smelly brown pellet of food
and then I jump in the Atlantic
and pick up the Amistad
and I throw the whole fuckin Amistad
and I throw bubblegum
Gabriel help me throw Metatron
and then I throw Gabriel
I throw purple
I take small tufts of clouds
and I throw clouds
and 33 and a thirds
and jewel cases
spit
hair
nails
caskets
crucifixes
chunks of cement
Abraham Lincoln's right eye
the bullet that shot Franz Ferdinand
the one that started the revolution
which will be televised
along with the TV.
I threw 1080p
and 720
and standard definition

No.

It's a New Yorker story

about a family that moves into a new home
with a bear in the back yard.
Everything seems perfect on the surface
until the bear comes down the hill
and tips over the garbage
and takes a bath in the
metaphor, full of porridge and
clam chowder?
That's right
Just right.
And the answer is:
Third person corporate.

Throbbing Gristle's motto "We Guarantee Disappointment" is of great appeal. Which somehow (maybe it's Baltimore) brings me to a question I want to ask. I'm thinking about aesthetics. Here are some notes I've made: First, the Anglo-German aesthetic regime which began in the 18th century and under which we (those of us in this room, that is) have been raised and live was obviously designed to further what used to be called bourgeois interests. It still works that way to some extent. But. What about other aesthetic regimes? Are they, too, always about power relations? I'm thinking first of Thersites: "In the *Iliad*, he does not have a father's name, which may suggest that he should be viewed as a commoner rather than an aristocratic hero. However, a quotation from another lost epic in the Trojan cycle, the *Aethiopis*, gives his father's name as Agrius. Homer described him in detail in Book II, even though he plays only a minor role in the story. He is said to be bow-legged and lame, to have shoulders that cave inward, and a head which is covered in tufts of hair and comes to a point. Thersites more or less asks what the point of the whole Trojan War is and gets beaten and humiliated for his trouble. Here is the scene, abridged a bit, in Richmond Lattimore's translation:

> But [Thersites], crying the words aloud, scolded Agamemnon:
> 'Son of Atreus, what thing further do you want, or find fault with
> now? Your shelters are filled with bronze, there are plenty of the
> choicest
> women for you within your shelter, whom we Achaians
> give to you first of all whenever we capture some stronghold.
> Or is it still more gold you will be wanting, that some son
> of the Trojans, breakers of horses, brings as ransom out of Ilion,
> one that I, or some other Achaian, capture and bring in? ...
> My good fools, poor abuses, you women, not men, of Achaia,
> let us go back home in our ships, and leave this man here
> by himself in Troy to mull his prizes of honour
> that he may find out whether or not we others are helping him.

*And now he has dishonoured Achilleus, a man much better
than he is. He has taken his prize by force and keeps her ...*

*So he spoke, Thersites, abusing Agamemnon
the shepherd of the people. But brilliant Odysseus swiftly
came beside him scowling and laid a harsh word upon him:
'Fluent orator though you be, Thersites, your words are
ill-considered. Stop, nor stand up alone against princes.
Out of all those who came beneath Ilion with Atreides
I assert there is no worse man than you are. Therefore
you shall not lift up your mouth to argue with princes,
cast reproaches into their teeth, nor sustain the homegoing ...'*

*So he spoke and dashed the sceptre against his back and
shoulders, and he doubled over, and a round tear dropped from
       him,
and a bloody welt stood up between his shoulders under
the golden sceptre's stroke, and he sat down again, frightened,
in pain, and looking helplessly about wiped off the tear-drops.
Sorry though the men were they laughed over him happily,
and thus they would speak to each other, each looking at the man
       next him:
'Come now: Odysseus has done excellent things by thousands,
bringing forward good counsels and ordering armed encounters;
but now this is far the best thing he ever has accomplished
among the Argives, to keep this thrower of words, this braggart
out of assembly. Never again will his proud heart stir him
up, to wrangle with the princes in words of revilement.'
So spoke the multitude ...*

Moses Finley, in *The World of Odysseus*, says: "Those final words, 'so spoke the multitude,' protest too much. It is as if the poet himself felt that he had overdrawn the contrast. [Homer says that] even the commoners among the Hellenes stood aghast at Thersites' defective sense of fitness, and though they pitied him as one of their own, they concurred with full heart in the rebuke administered by Odysseus and in the methods he employed. 'This is by far the best thing he has done among the Argives' indeed, for Thersites had gnawed at the foundations on which the world of Odysseus was erected." On the other hand, this might well be what you'd expect the multitude to say if they were completely cowed by a social system privileging an aristocratic upper class of princes, either out of fear or false consciousness. "Good work, Odysseus! Put us in our place!" OK. And then there is skin color in China and Japan. To quote Hiroshi Wagatsuma, "'White' skin has been considered an essential characteristic of feminine beauty in Japan since recorded time. An old Japanese proverb states that 'white skin makes up for seven defects'". Wagatsuma goes on to describe how both men and woman applied liberal layers of white makeup to cover their natural skin color, plucked their eyebrows and penciled in dark lines in place, and blackened their teeth in imitation of aristocratic Chinese style. Of further note is the preference for plump women, something that Wagatsuma indicates by making reference to the *Tale of Genji*. That is to say, paleness not only became a marker of beauty, but a marker of social standing. Further, as Wagatsuma notes, aristocratic men adopted the practice of powdering their own faces in an attempt to maintain the illusion that they too were above such things as field work. However, with the advent of the Samurai, this decadence amongst men was ended as the new warrior elite prided itself on its "Spartan" arrangements and style of life. This frugality, however, did not extend to the women who maintained their standards of beauty, pushing paleness to a cultural extreme never before seen. As Yoshida Kenko notes in his tsurezuregusa, with regards to a magician who lost his power upon seeing the leg of a woman bathing, "this may well have been because the white limbs and skin of a woman cleanly plump and fatty are no mere external charms, but true beauty and allure." OK. And in Jamaican dancehalls competition for the video camera's light is stiff, so much so that dancers sometimes bleach their skin to enhance their visibility. In the Bahamas, tuxedoed students roll into prom in tricked-out sedans, staging grand red-carpet entrances that are designed to ensure they are seen being photographed. Throughout the United States and Jamaica friends pose in front of hand-painted backgrounds of Tupac, flashy cars, or brand-name products popularized in hip-hop culture in countless makeshift roadside photography studios. In *Shine*, Krista Thompson examines these and other photographic practices in the Caribbean and United States, arguing that performing for the camera is more important than the final image itself. For the members of these African diasporic communities, seeking out the camera's light — whether from a cell phone, Polaroid, or video camera — provides a means with which to represent themselves in the public sphere. The resulting images, Thompson argues, become their own forms of memory, modernity, value, and social status that allow for cultural formation within and between African diasporic communities. OK. But how about *i'jaz*, the doctrine that asserts that the proof of the divine origin of the Qu'ran is the Qu'ran's own unsurpassable beauty?

    So Mars now sits in the Beehive Cluster.
    He wields the Mastejelo
        [the constellation Gemini].
    The image is found in Beowulf.
        Don't paint me yellow! she cried.
    The passage resembles Ecclesiastes.
        Small small small small animals.
    A girl sat on the porch, reading *Process and Reality*.

How the many became one remains opaque.
The model is the honeybee.
The engineer's cabin at the north pole.
   BITE THE NURSE! BITE THE NURSE!
   'I felt / the word in my gullet pressure.'
The last Mexican grizzly perished in 1960.

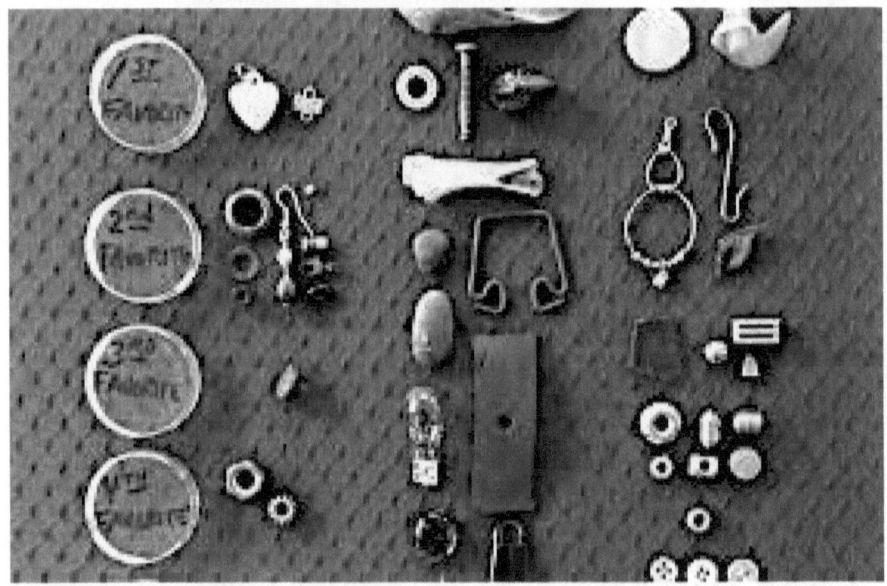

A young girl's gifts from crows.

While working at a strip club in Times Square in 1972, Kathy Acker writes *Homage to Leroi Jones* and other "exercises," as part of an effort to map her "total present consciousness." Across the ocean, Algerian poet Jean Sénac writes *Le soleil sous les armes* [*The Sun Under the Weapons*]. Traveling between Moscow to Tashkent in 1932, Langston Hughes befriends, photographs, and translates the works of young poets writing in Uzbek. The death toll in Nepal has passed 5,000. You can lie in bed and say, damn, do I feel good today. My thoughts ran for something. But the phone rings and you have to run to the hospital, witness the pain in the hospital, given how much you and the copy processes that build brands and reality are unable to control or comfort or solve everything. One sleeps in the hospital for three days monitoring drug supplies, the nurses come and go, schedules and doctors, surgeries. And suddenly has one message: I'm here for whatever you need, at any time, no matter, you wake me, count on me, I love your tattoos, and knowledge, books, readings, best friends, the vocational crisis, the interpretation of reality and constraints begin to matter a damn; I become just one more animal talking to another animal, or trying, I mean, during his talk about *Leg over Leg* on Saturday's Library of Arabic Literature workshop in Oxford, Humphrey Davies discussed the "hardest challenge for me as a translator in this book": This was, he said, the lists of words that are like a "magical invocation" in Ahmad Faris al-Shidyaq's text. "In the middle of a sentence," Davies said, "you may get a list of words with no definition. Obscure, arcane words; words he did not expect you to know." An attempt to achieve a one-to-one correspondence of these words, Arabic to English, would be doomed to some kind of failure, Davies said. Indeed, researching the meanings of words and trying to map them to English just didn't work. "Even if the English language has 248 words for pudendum, you can be pretty much certain that those 248 words will not map accurately onto the words you found in Shidyaq. So I started experimenting with other approaches: the online Urban Dictionary, for one. On another occasion, Davies said, "I took the Arabic words, and I put them through the Google Latin translate facility and came up with words that have some claim to reflect the meanings, but which are very strange to hear, which was the intended effect." The final strategy Davies discussed for these lists was "representational translation." Which is why, driving to Wyoming for Monster class – a conversation on obedience, wounds, cartography – the law in Wyoming as it pertains to: reproductive rights – plant medicine, post-colonial theory, feral life [melancholia] and autobiography [delirium] – that took place in a conservatory – we created [invented] new tonalities and registers for a Shiva chant. Then I asked my mother to sing / chant for Nepal and Baltimore. She created a chant, a variant of the Naryana Naryana Hari Hari mantra. Naryana Naryana Baltimore Hari. Om Namao Nepal. We call upon the energies of the moon and the sun and the power that is held in the lining of the universe in support of you, Baltimore. We bow to you, Baltimore. We bow to you Nepal. And all around us this red, red land "that belonged to someone" and that was "taken from them," as my mother says each time we make this drive. And the blood that drips looks like dried coffee, like rust,

> The comrades in reading have fallen asleep.
> You wander alone through the book stacks
> with no sign of an exit.
> From the third shelf on the right comes a groan –
> a whole chapter expelled from
> The Book of Delight and Intimacy.

Someone is leaving this planet with a dry throat. Aleppo before me black and still. These huge shadows might be trees or childhood goblins or black vapours exhaled by women waiting for children who are already statistics. At the intersection of For and From we exchange objects for 20s, and sometimes we get change. It's in the air, this shift of tenses, as if we'd waited out the squall and headed for a landing – over the lava, the scrubby trees, and onto the rain-slicked runway. The market sells what this earth creates. Who's to call it "good" or "bad," name it a character in a mystery play, watch its wagons lurch across England? Beneath her, a tiny boat skitters, honoring no direction except back and forth. It's a way to frame an ideology. Think of the lump as what holds us back. Which is to ask: can we represent what is actually happening? happening to the world at large? happening to us? Can we even imagine it? Look at the scale.

> language is a secret maze we can barely fathom
> nor that it contains an infinitude
> of openings and potential passages
> along an irregular line
> of understanding.
> So I'm writing on a light filled screen
> from moments of darkening making pixels
> of flickering dark,
> (and the screen is connected!
> it sends me "updates" – do I
> "want" them?)
>
> and all this smudges the question of
> "including history."
> A poem cannot "include" this
> (like a pick and choose),
> it is flooded out already and drags itself to shore
> swamped
> sometimes
> sickened
>
> Both the labor that produces the object
> and the waste from its production and consumption
> are suppressed
>
> except in the nausea of the drowning discard.
>
> In the mean time, I admired her aphorisms.
> "They just sent down the administrative flavor of the month."
>
> "If you are not in the system, we can't help you until you are."
>
> For example.

But I couldn't believe I was not already in the system. I feel as if – sometimes – here in the middle of a country I was not born in – that I reside – in its actual heart – and that there is a reason for this. I need to be here. It could be amazing!!!!!!!!!! With the proviso that we would have to decolonize the somatic curriculum too.

As Sayra Pinto said last week: "The ancestors want us to dream for them. We have to grieve for our ancestors, but we also have to dream for them too. One or the other is not enough." So I have the fruit tree! And the ocean skirting it! Or, there will be something for me at the table. And it pumps through joyfully! *pulp vs throne* is the testament of suction "… entering into words, out of a vomit of stars or eels; whatever's said, the slow curve of the marble instrument or the boiling black nocturnal ribbon assaulting the estuaries, and not just for being said, this is that flows or converges or seeks … Artistotelian Dog, let the duality that sharpens your fangs somehow know your superfluity when another sluice begins to open in marble and in fish, when Jai Singh with a crystal between his fingers is that fisherman extracting from his net, with a shudder of teeth and fury, an eel that is a star that is an eel that is a star that is an eel." B (who is sometimes a woman I write to and sometimes a man I write to) asked me if I had any corpses in any of my poems

> the word
> or that's what I assumed he / she meant
> but I didn't!
> which surprised me but then maybe not
> because the dead body seems more like suspension to me
> ?
> or dying

is an activity
rather than the way a body lies
down
which is also the pool
and the suction
But what you say is so crucial, "There's a cow's mouth on the flag," I
    mean: what the fuck. That's nothing but sheer brilliance. And one day
    the age will rise,
Like a corpse in a spring river—
On behalf of the wolf and all of us,
An old-fashioned corpse hung in the wood behind the sanatorium

A butterfly embroidered in the folds of her blue skirt ... (see Kot's character work on MODOK, a classic Marvel supervillain who, if you're not familiar, is a giant psychic head with little baby legs and t-rex arms, flying around in a little egg-throne / spider-car). Justice Alito followed up with a broader question: "If an anesthesiologist rendered a person completely unconscious, and then the person was burned alive, would that be cruel and unusual punishment?" His meticulous, almost obsessively drawn opinions (dissenting and otherwise) resemble pictographs with symbols both familiar and unfamiliar, especially in his "Untitled" series of two inks on paper and his four variations of "Xanthous Mermaid Mechanics," 1-4 which in spite of their separate iconography are united by one visual motif, a wide-eyed, open-mouthed figure in fear and pain ... "In space lit dimly by xanthous suns and small, sallow fireballs ..." And perhaps a final word, "I've been hurt," written to be legible when held up to a mirror, another sign that I uh here we go and tulips and love and sweetness and doves my my the buzz gets you and lies down beneath the blankets and then here she comes again and stops in midair like a helicopter bug like you've never seen one. Oh my this place sure is a mess, coming in low and aloft with finesse bows and banana peels and concession stands and a morphing hoop from which nothing much comes but does not give up all the same post war mint and dollar store laundry detergent amiss a flood a Miss a dud and woops here goes, I loved critical thinking, oh god texture, every single dot, now generalize that, and it's like shut up but then you think of it and it's like Jesus! "If an animal is shocked, escapably or inescapably, she will manifest deep reactions of attachment for whoever has shocked her. If she has manifested deep reactions of attachment for whoever has shocked her, she will manifest deeper reactions of attachment for whoever has shocked her and then dragged her off the electrified grid. Perhaps she will develop deep feelings of attachment for electrified grids. Perhaps she will develop deep feelings of attachment for what is not the electrified grid. Perhaps she will develop deep feelings of attachment for dragging. She may also develop deep feelings of attachment for science, laboratories, experimentation, electricity, and rats, tigers, fairy tales, time, a self-described anarchist who demands alimony, myth, memory, violence, compulsion, and one night of hedonistic pleasure with an old school friend." Excerpt: On My Birthday, Dragons, & Intestines. I write an essay in which I list out my prescriptions. It feels too honest, but I publish it anyways. From one map come others, centuries ago: Here there be dragons, at the edges of our flat world, but there were never any dragons. Later, he says: All the other guys' girlfriends took way better pictures. I say: I'm not your girlfriend. So, after a while, I came to accept the idea that I was writing for everybody. Even when I thought I was writing for black people, not all black people agreed with what I was writing. It is difficult to say that you are writing for one particular group of people. It can limit your imagination. After a while, I was like, "OK, I am writing for the entire world." I think that later on, it became about writing for me. I stood before the mirror one sunrise and began my morning chant. All repeated calmly for the first week, but with flavors added on as the regimen continued into the second. 50 with er and 50 with a. 1/4 as question, 1/4 as surprise, 1/4 as anger, 1/4 implying the complaining "please." All alternately whispered, shouted, laughed, snarled — all in search of the ideal whitening formula. Week eight saw a 2/3 increase in brightening, with a luminousness approaching diamond quality, particularly in the lower incisors. Which is to say, hair is nothing more, nothing less than an accessory to punctuate your outfit. Cement lions will only ever be as audacious as the legs that garnish them. Wear a guitar as a skirt. Got a lion? Pose with it. Hot ice cream! Space Whales is a concept my friend Eddie made up. Space Whales are massive whales that roam the outer layers of the universe, observing us from afar. On occasion, they knock something into our paths with their tails or dorsal fins, some small clue that's part of a larger patchwork of hints and signs that eventually, well. You're deciding between moving to New York or LA, and when you turn on your iPod the first thing that comes up on shuffle is Notorious B.I.G.'s "Going Back to Cali." My professor asked us to summarize what the play was about in one word. After several failed attempts, one student figured it out. Nothing. The play was about nothing. Yes, this is exactly right! King Lear is about nothing, and nothing is somehow worse than the notion that as flies are to wanton boys we are to Gods. Which is exactly why fish faced with stressful stimuli launch an endocrine stress response through activation of the hypothalamic-pituitary-interrenal (HPI-) axis to release cortisol into the blood. Then I spoke of all the purple souls that were leaving bodies, one after the other, on a conveyor belt. I said, Death, Fordist style. Person and I were flying over the lake with colorful helium balloons. Shit was getting gentrified and so I had to move to the other side of town and so I traveled by balloon. Too afraid to go myself so I sent my textual doppelgänger. I as her as I in the misty forest trying to find my way to China. The monk. He gave me the book to read aloud, but I couldn't read it. Every page was covered in a plastic film and the glare blinded me, prevented me from seeing the text.

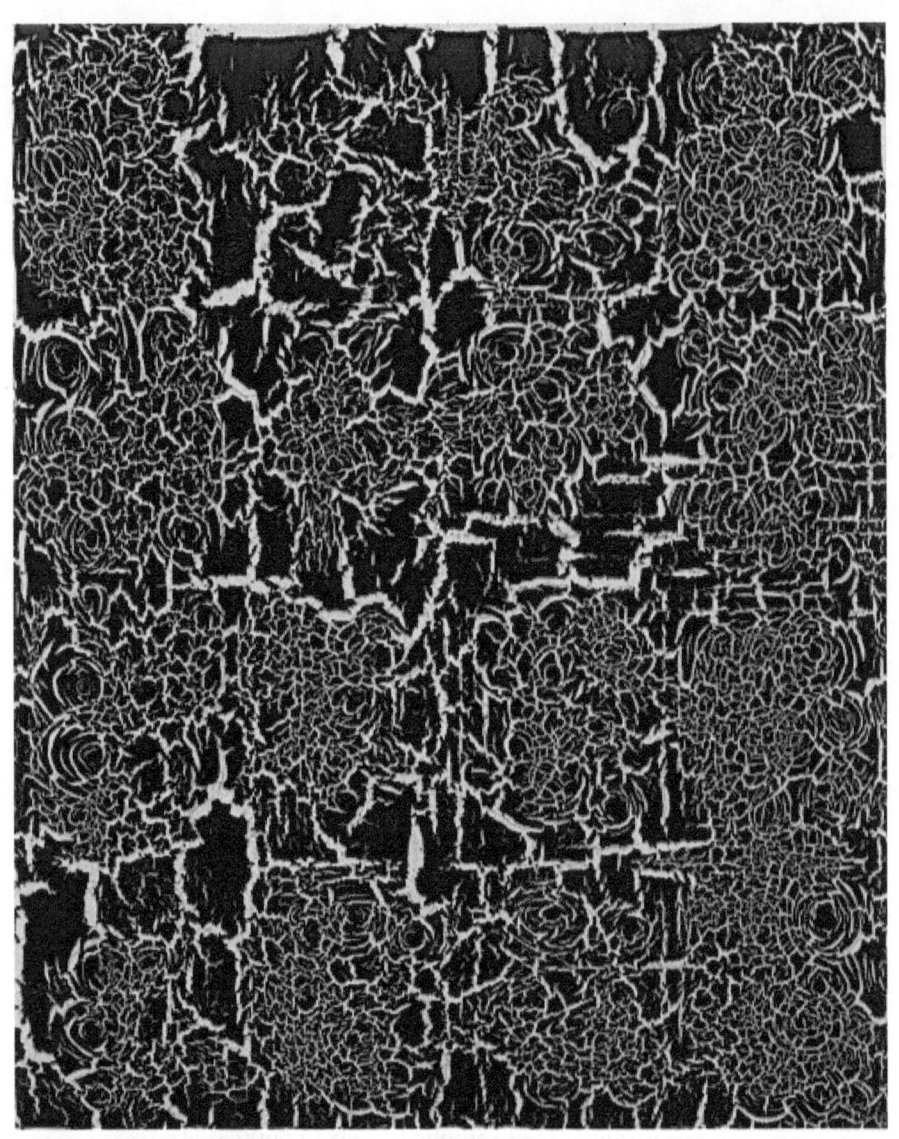

So I left, embarrassed, and walked down the side of a palm tree'd mountain until I arrived at the lake. I crossed a long wooden footpath and came to a ferry that took me to the other side of the world. In the morning fog we drifted past Mongolian yurts floating on small islands. I arrived without documents, so naturally all the buses drove past me as I stood outside in the rain which was a chant, a potent sound with great semantic value. There was nothing for me to do except take the taxi to the airport at dawn. My aunt cried. My girlfriend packed our things. That wonder was lost on me. The floral displays in the round-a-bout. What if the taxi just kept driving around it in circles because — because — because — because — because — who cares if they want you dead

— in the Book of Revelation (8:11) the sounding of the third trumpet heralds a great star named Apsinthos — typically translated as Wormwood and generally believed to be *Artemisia herba-alba* — and which, "blazing like a torch, fell from the sky on a third of the rivers and on the springs of water." As a consequence, "a third of the waters turned bitter, and many people died from the waters that had become bitter." With its native habitat increasingly fragmented, *Artemisia californica* nevertheless explodes across makeshift environments, an emblem of what Gerald Vizenor, quoting Derrida, calls *survivance*. So let the spirits clamor and enter the sacred bed. Little red flowers spin on the yellow pillowcase. We dance like monkeys for the drumming spiders. *Go outside*, they whisper. We crouch down between the frozen berry bushes and speak to the air. And then, the wind … with its own blanket & cap. Smaller than a doll. Why is my hair so thick? Then they show me the swamp. I scream a bit. I fill my pillowcase with canned food. I walk around with those I love like they don't have hands. The needles the bottles the popsicles. What do the little alveoli say? Wring out these waterlogged limbs. For lunch let's swim out to the raft with sandwiches held above our heads. This is where trauma enters Lorig's work, too: her poems refer back and refer back — both to cited sources and to Lorig's repeated phrases — refer back and refer back

> but Repetition is never
> Repeating Exactly.
> It is each sentence Exactly.
> what and where is Precise,
> but what is Precise
> Precisely if it doesn't
> yield and Exactitude?
>
> […]
>
> Each time round is an extraction.
> Each time round we find the return.
> Each time round the return is immediate.
> Each time round the return is brutal.
> Each time round the return is near.

"This poem is full of smashing into things as a way of leaving or of belonging, of changing minds, of disappearing into the heat, of a leaking extravagance or a chiseling sprawl. "Dear J," "Dear B," "Dear Softening Agent," I DON'T MEAN HOT MASS, I MEAN

UNFATHOMABLE.

Being Stone,

The slash / is [in] me

/ /
/ /
/ /
/ /
/ / / / / / / / Like once upon, the grey machines we dreamed (o orange glow!) were happy & made us so, no. Really. Yr tomb for the unknown camera. False as etymology: so they say. VOID VOID VOID VOID named *meshuga*: bare ruined wires et cetera. I'll try to approach that field, its expansive concentration, by way of Don Cherry and Ed Blackwell's (1982) extended meditation on nothingness; by way of Fanon's and Linebaugh's accounts of language in and as vehicularity; by way of Foucault's meditations on the ship of fools and Deleuze's consideration of the boat as interior of the exterior when they are both thoroughly solicited by the uncharted voices that we carry; by way, even, of Lysis and Socrates; but also, and in the first instance, by way of Hawk and Newk, just friends, trading fours. Perhaps I'm simply deluding myself, but such celebratory performance of thought, in thought, is as much about the insurgency of immanence as it is about what Wagner calls the "consolation of transcendence." But, as I said earlier, 80% of WalMart stores allow sleeping overnight in their parking lots, which I do, meeting homeless families across America, the true results of Whitman's love of Manifest Destiny. And last September the World Wildlife Fund's biennial "planet index report" claims 52% of wild animals have vanished in the past three decades. But to directly answer your question: everything. I am a queer American who had a boyfriend I loved but someone bound, gagged, tortured and raped him, then covered him in gasoline and burned him to death. And so it is that we remain in the hold, in the break, as if entering again and again the broken world, to trace the visionary company and join it. This contrapuntal island, where we are marooned in search of marronage, where we linger in stateless emergency, is our mobile, constant study, our lysed cell and held dislocation, our blown standpoint and lyred chapel. Where we were was what we meant by "mu." The second floor of the Great Pyramid. Which is to say I'm not so different from the interpreters in their glass booths at endless international conferences translating what the peasant from Talca tells about torture repeating in English that they put him on the cot stating in the most refined and delicate French that electric shock produces lasting transmissible effects finding the exact equivalent for rape by dogs, and the front porch buckles into teeth / the basement salivates like the nile / derek clutches to an empty keg and floats desperate up the stairs / his guitar becomes an oar / jake scales the shelves trying to catch flies with his jaws / sings: nobody knows the trouble / the chimney boards itself closed / the fire groans and chokes / colin writes suicide letters on the bathroom mirror / threatens to hang himself from the lip of the gutters / tyler says farewell and mark says nothing / you and i hide the

ladder and find the last bowl of chili waiting in the kitchen / it speaks after weeks of growing its own being and a taste for riddling: / what is a home but not your home? / not the cupboard filled with starving / the walls aching under pressure / the two of us toss around in the stomach of your bedroom like we are rotten / like this house is sick enough to spit us out / like the sink still dripping / i cannot help myself etc.

She repeatedly approached the microphone as if about to speak. She opened her mouth to speak. She licked her lips and almost spoke. She made breathing sounds as if about to start speaking. She cleared her throat lightly. Her lips crackled into the microphone. She inhaled expectantly. She appeared to be ready to speak.

- There is a big whiteboard and 3 performers: A and B both speak Spanish and English, and C only speaks English but maybe has a general idea of how Spanish words are pronounced.
- A writes the original Sor Juana text on part of the white board.
- B faces away from the board so he cannot see the text, and C whispers the Spanish text as best she can into B's ear, who attempts to repeat aloud the sounds that C is whispering.
- A attempts to transcribe what B is saying onto the white board next to the original text. Naturally, A will not be a fast enough writer to transcribe all the words. He'll do his best.
- When this is done, C then whispers her attempts at pronouncing the new transcription into B's ear, who again speaks it aloud as faithfully as he can. A transcribes as best he can, writing next to the previous transcription. More words are lost or broken.
- Repeat this process another 2 times, until A runs out of space to write on the board.
- After the last "Spanish" transcription, C changes places with B, who goes to write at the board. C whispers the latest text into A's ear, who repeats aloud what she hears as "English,"

bzzz   buzz   buzz / bzzz   bzz   bzzz   summ summ   zoum
zoum   bzzz   bzzz   zzzz   boon boon zh-zh-zh   bzzz   buzz buzz
        vizzz   bzzz
pip-pip   tjiep   cheep / chirp /

chirrup / peep

piip   piep piep   tsiou tsiou   tziff-tziff   csip-csirip
    chip
pee pee /
pii pii
    fiyt-fiyt   pip-pip   jiyk jiyk
    dit kari jay sige lige sa tit son jay vol
cheep cheep /

tweet

tsirk /

5788

piip

cui cui   tschiwitt   tsiou tsiou   csirip   chip   pio
                    pío pío pip-pip juyk juyk
                             squawk kvak   kra kra

hihihi /

chip (loudly)

                    ouh-ouh
Bird (many birds)   warble / twitter
                                 chip chip

                        grumph
                        ga-a-a-a-h
        miav   miauw   meow   miau   miaou   miau   miaou   miyau
        miau   miau
nyan nyan /

nyaa nyaa
        miyau   miao   mjan mjan   miyav   meow
        pierr   prrr   purr   hrr   ronron srr
        doromb   purr   goro goro   mrrr   rrr

                        pink

        tok tok   cluck cluck   kot-kot cotcotcodet   tock tock   ko
ko ko / ka ka ka chuck-chuck   kot kot coccodé
ku-ku-ku-ku /

ko-ko-ko-ko
        ko-ko-ko
caca-racá /
cocorocó /

ock-ock gut gut gdak
crowing kykyliky kukeleku   cock-a-doodle-doo   kukko kiekuu
        cocorico   kikeriki
kikiriku /

kikiriki

coo-koo-ri-koo kukuriku   chicchirichí   ko-ke-kok-ko-o

cucurucu   kukareku
quiquiriquí /

kikiriki

kuckeliku
kuk-kurri-kuuu

u uru uuu (pron: oo-oore-oo)

kuklooku
pip-pip piep piep   cheep / peep   piip   piou piou   piep piep
            ko ko ko   csip-csip   pio pio piyo piyo
            pi-pi-pi pi-pi   pip-pip
jiyk jiyk

tsik-tsik
moe /

boe

moo
ammuu /

möö

meuh   mmuuh moo   moo   mu   muu   mau mau
              mu-u-u
muuu /

meee
mu mu mooo (pron: meuh)   baeh
              snurk   snort   pärsk
        pfff   buff
                       clang

        klap   snap   clap   klap
        gnam
clap /

clack

        kra-kra kra kra
kaak /

caw

kraa /

vaak

croa croa   kräh kräh   kra-kra krak-krak   kár-kár cra cra
         kar-kar   kar-kar   ah ah   kra kra   gaak gaak
                  koekoekcuckoo   kukkuu   coucou   kuckuck   cuckoo
         kakukk   cucú
kakko-kakko /

tokkyo-kyoka-kyoku
         ku-ku   cu-cu   ko-ko
                           troat
                  i-a
hee haw /

eeyore

         hihan   iaah iaah   iaa iaa yi-ah   iá-iá   ioh ioh
         ia-ia
iha iha /
ji-jo

         a-iiii a-iiii
                  vov-vov (in a high voice) waf waf
yap yap /

arf arf

hau hau ouah ouah (in a high voice)   wau wau
(in a high voice)   how-how   vau vau
arf arf /

bau bau

kian kian

hav-hav /

gav-gav

guau /

gua

bjäbb-bjäbb   hev hev
        vov-vov woef woef
woof woof /

ruff ruff

vuff   ouah ouah   wau wau   gav gav woof-woof   vau vau
        bau bau wan wan
hav-hav /

gav-gav

guav
vov-vov /

voff

hauv hauv
        vov-vov (in a low voice)   bow wow
vuff /

rouf

ouah ouah (in a low voice)   wuff wuff   vau vau
        bau bau wan wan

hav-hav /

gav-gav

guf guf   hov hov bow bow

gnash /

snap

naps   gnam gari gari
    chac
        knor
chomp /

chump /

gnaw

                        chrong   paku paku
          chua-chua   haart haart
                        grrr   grr

grrr /

snarl /

growl

mrr   grrr   grrr   grrr   grr   uuuuu
        grrrrr   grrr   grr   hirrrr
                          whine / whimper   juhhh
                        yu-yu-yuuu!

       ha ha   pant pant   lääh-lääh   cha-cha
                 pant pant   hah hah   he-he-he   eh eh eh
                 heh heh heh
                 peep-peep

yelp / yip /

howl / yowl

ui-ui   juhhh   huuu   o-
u-u-u-h auu
                           lap lap   glup   schlapp schlapp
          lefety lefety
slop slop /

slurp

         hu-up hu-up   blap blap   slap slap slap (pron:
schlup)
                    roekoe   coo   kurr   rou rou guru guru
                burukk   uuu   grl-grl
gu gu /

cucurrucu

oo ho oo ho   gu gu gu guuk
             rap-rap kwak kwak   quack quack   kvak   coin coin
             quack quack   pa-pa-pa   quak-quak   háp-háp qua qua ga
ga

```
               krya-krya          cua cua  kvack-kvack        vak vak  quak quak
                                       baraag   tööt                   toerroe
                           baaa       paoh-paoh
                  u-u-u    biaaah
                  kvæk-kvæk           kwak kwak
croak /

ribbit

kvaak    croa croa         quaak quaak       quak-quak
bre-ke-ke/
kuty kurutty /

kurutty (pron: kurutch)

cra cra    kero kero
           kva-kva  croac croac      ko ack ack ack    vrak vrak
                    mæh     mè mè   naa       mää    bêê      maehh maehh
                 maehehe      meh meh          mek-mek      bee        me-e me-e
                    me-e-e  beee     määk määk       me-e-e me-e-e   meh
                            gak gak  honk     tööt                gak gak
                gá-gá              ga-a ga-a              ga-ga-ga
                gak gak


                         neigh
              hi-hiin
              i-go-go           iihaha

prrr /

vrinsk

           brrr                  brrr    bhhh
                                                                             hi
hi    wehee  iha-haa  hiiiii   wihiie              nyihaha hiii
      hihiiiiin
                ihiii           e-he-he-he
                klip-klap        klip klap       clip clop      kopotikop
        clip clop       klip klap
clippete /

clip clop
```

paka paka   ta-tá ta-tá ta-tá   cotocloc   deg-a-dek

grrrr /

grauuw

raa / grr / roar   raoh   grr   ah ah / gra gra
grr /

roar
gaooooo   r-r-r-r   grr   uagh

            bröl
    piep piep   eek   piep piep
    cin-cin (pron: tsin-tsin)   squit   chu-chu   pi-pi-pi   iiik
    pip-pip viyk viyk
            oe hoe twit two / hoo hoo / whit woo / terwit terwoo
    huhuu   hou hou
uhu /

huuh huuh

            hu   hu hu   hoh hoh   uh! uh! uh!
    uhh uhhho-ho   uuu uuu hoo hoo
                   boo / booh   meuh

lorre /

Lora Lora

pretty Polly /

Who's a pretty boy?

        coco   Lora Lora   gyuri   pityu   Portobello
        ohayo (=good morning)
        Pópka-durák   lorito lorito   vakra klara
naaber naaber /

nasilin nasilin /

mucuk mucuk (pron: mujuk)

```
mea mitu /

churi
                øf-øf    knor knor      oink         nöff       groin groin
         grunz                    röf-röf (pron: reuf-reuf)  oink
boo boo
         hrgu-hrgu
oink /
oinc


nöff-nöff
                hvin     sweek   wee wee                      quiek
         ui-uii          bu-hii bu-hii
iiih /

uiii /

cuiii
                        coo      kurr      rou rou  guru guru         gru uu
         woo-woo        burukk   hu hu                       guli-guli
ruú-ruú /

cucurrocu

oo ho oo ho    gu gu gu guuk
        kra-kra  kra kra   caw              croâ croâ       kra-kra
        kár-kár  cra cra   kar-kar                          kra-kra
                 mæh-mæh         bè bè     baa      mäh     bêê      baehh
baehh   mae-ee                   beee      bee      meh meh
        beee     beee beee       bä bä              maeh maeh
                 sss      sss    sss       hiss     sss     sss
                 psss     sz-sz  hshs                       ssss    sss      sss      sss


                 chun chun
                 grr      grr      raa/grr          grr     grr     grr
                 grr      gaooooo                   grrr    grrr    grr

                                           gobble gobble            glou glou
                        glou glou

clou clou /
```

goro-goro-goro (Mexico)
    glu glu

                             yelp

            oou

ahoo /

hoeea

owooooo	uhuu	ooouh	huh		oou		huu
	uuu	auuuh	oooahh	ooo			

peent   The joke is called the Joke of the Big and Little Fish. Extant from 3rd century Greece, in Athenaeus' *Deipnosophistai*, later attributed to the Ash'ab in 8th century Medina, to Nasreddin Hodja in 13th century Turkey, appearing in 15th century England's Jack of Dover tales, 17th century France in the *Fables* de La Fontaine and into the 20th century in Enid Welsford's *The Fool: His Social and Literary History*. The joke in each version is incomprehensible and unfunny. So what I'd like you to do is to take off your shirt. Take a marker. For the next four minutes, draw on the back of the person sitting nearby that which is being drawn upon your own back by a third person, *are you O.K. if she tells you to close your eyes so she can shuffle through her phonebook in privacy? You are comfortable taking a business card for her edibles company, her if-you-want-your-food-strewn-around company, the so-called "Incremental Edibles?" This means crumbs, my friend.* [This next part I consider untranslatable] Ergo, *Mythogeography* is not simply a book of now. Fortuitously, important developments in a range of disciplines and activisms have been sufficiently tentative, frayed and incomplete to allow outsiders to cross their thresholds:
- Geographers have written of the performance of tourism
- Academics have repeated the autobiographical discretions of artists and challenged the hero-walkers
- Theory has been spatialised and space theorised
- Guided tours and live art have come a little closer together
- And clown armies have marched while the living dead have flashmobbed, exposing the geomancies of a ritualized ruling class –

Many of the Psygeographical Societies, walking groups, cults, artists, activists, clubs, gangs and cells mentioned in *Mythogeography* are fictional ones. There is no "Wigan P.A." or "Committee for Public Safety". But for every fictional reference, there is a real equivalent. What a joy that there is nowhere to begin or end. What this website attempts to do is something similar to what the protagonist attempts in Roussel's *Locus Solus* (with thanks to Sozita Goudouna for the spur to finally take it off the shelf and read the thing).

That's my state of mind, that's my state of body. You get used to it. You just insert the barbed wire slowly into your mouth and start passing it through. Try to protect your tongue, or you won't be able to talk for a few days. You'll feel it going into your throat, tearing away at your esophagus. Sphincters are tricky. You'll get a little relief when it arrives at your stomach. Gather your strength, as the winding road through your intestines is the most painful and dangerous part and you don't want your shit flooding the vacuum between your inner organs and your flesh. That can really ruin your life. Add a drop of your own blood to the rising dough.

> I would like to rub your face in it
> into the deep lush foam of the clover toroids
> clever and lucky as a ladder we climb
> these zeros are now (noo) and
> saturn eats its hat
> which is a toroid
> which comes before terroroid
> in the last phase of shadow
>
> where the stank of its eh
> would woo the om of its hankering
> whose portal is a zero
> for behind the golden door
> is a smaller door

then a smaller yellow door
and so on
until the wall
is all waves
which weaves a bread like this

burlap
which slips into the sea quietly
and the fine and secret soma
slipping and falling down
into
most of these epic historic murals
that come across as random sticks and leaves
piled up interestingly

goes the cry
from Gallus and everyone
gathers round to listen
even the bees fervently
"like" his status
Apollo himself "shares" it
with a pithy comment
or two
the lament spreads and all the shepherds
condemn Licorice
demanding to know the name
of this fucking cop
who probably beats her
and even worse
hates poetry–
only Pan chimes in
with: "Fuck you, Gallus."
And Gallus replies
"Fuck you"
and the whole thing devolves
into a flame war with nymphs
and naiads and

> *a stapling and testing of cylinders versus spheres versus cubes for kinetic and entropic possibilities, stuffing balled newspaper into paper dragons, two sweet silver elephants with heads too small and trunks too long, situated off-center, snuffling flowers. And silver rain. And 16 silver hearts stacked vertically and strips of masking tape A bird.*

Another bird, more rain, peace signs, a horse with sideways-flowing mane,

But this is small. Exhaustion multiplies. So much we don't know, the *not* peeling like lead paint. That was not spinal surgery:

> God was in a car in the sky
> and I shouted my arm is so weak
> and he said I know
> it's like a toothpick holding a machine

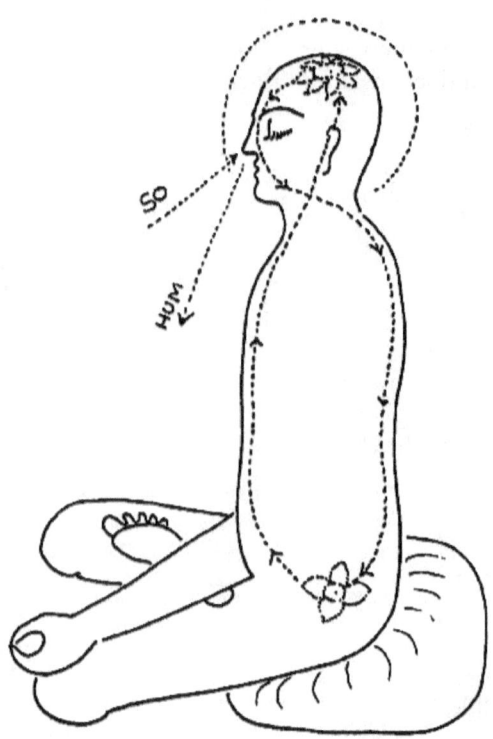

Now we're in Turkey, circa 2025 CE. Case (yeah, the guy from *Neuromancer*), approaches the teeming marketplace of a now impoverished and dilapidated Beyoglu. 'This is the city's central market for spices, software, perfumes, drugs …' explains the AI that pilots Case's hired Mercedes. Upon entering the marketplace with its cybergothic antinomy of 'soot-stained sheets of plastic and green-painted ironwork out of the age of steam', from which 'a thousand suspended ads writhed and flickered', Case's companion and black-market tech-dealer, the Finn, spots something he hasn't seen in a long time. 'Hey, Christ,' the Finn said, taking Case's arm, 'looka that.' He pointed. 'It's a horse, man. You ever see a horse?' Case glanced at the embalmed animal and shook his head. It was displayed on a sort of pedestal, near the entrance to a place that sold birds and monkeys. The thing's legs had been worn black and hairless by decades of passing hands. 'Saw one in Maryland once,' the Finn said [...] 'There's Arabs still trying to code 'em up from the DNA, but they always croak.' The animal's brown glass eyes seemed to follow them as they passed. So T wants to go to the midnight release of some kind of robot movie on Friday night. Okay, so that's my social life. Would you like to meet up? Whoever you are. I am bringing a ladder. I will be giving a talk on socialist educational policy in 1970s UK. Which is to say that I think something like becoming-material is key to me right now as an index of what is feared in contemporary aesthetics. I'm not an expert or special fan of conceptualism but I have wondered what it is at depth about that particular mode of address that provokes recent resistance. It may simply be that no writer or artist is ever happy, even whey they say they are, to give up their own signature and the chances of a posterity bonus. What's interesting about the death of Alt. Lit. and conceptualism for me is that those deaths haven't of course really taken place – as Hitchcock taught us, one cannot kill the (un)dead. Amy Ireland's xenopoetics for example is an even more ferocious and consequent version of the ahuman hyper-textualism that a certain strain of retro-humanist identity politics has rightly objected to on another level. Rather than quite being able to chose here or take one or the other of the high grounds, one might say that *all of this is what is happening*. It's as if social meme-space sometimes performs a series of serial murders, in all senses, and what returns is an increasingly material wave of presemantic marks, and here I'd probably turn to Bunny Roger's hyper-dead painted pigeons she's making in Sweden right now or to someone like Paul de Man as read by Tom Cohen as the cipher for how to push this almost quantum materialism the furthest. I'm in a place now of being able to feel that not only can this latter materialism not be found anymore in poems and art for example, but that there are no poems at all in this world. For me, alongside Ireland's xenopoetics or Cohen's consistent emphasis on the moment of irreversible reading or your own praxis, I'd want to speak for a moment of something like an ana-poetics or ana-poem that doesn't even involve writing a poem but rather thinking about the space between a poem written and one not in existence, and in constantly discovering and indexing the literature-effect as itself a problem tied into, produced by, and producing extinction. And that's what I think the resistance to becoming-material might mean at bottom. The slow inching towards a face-to-face with absolute fatalism. "The body, the body, the body ..." Because Kelsey Street Press is in the Bay Area, and I need to reconnect with the Bay Area and Small Press Distribution and whatever it was that happened at Trauma and Catharsis and Poetics of Healing and what Commune editions is. On Monday. (Shiva's day.) Okay, I thought I was downloading a thumbnail of my garden but instead: THIS HAPPENED. Today is May Day. We will fill out some forms and have them notarized. However, Invisigoth recognises that the AI is no longer limited to its hardware and has become completely autonomous – armed, dangerous and 'loose on the net' – and that her only mode of escape is to upload her own consciousness into cyberspace and merge with the program, before destroying all trace of the event in a satellite-controlled missile strike. The episode concludes with the following exchange:

> Scully: Mulder ... she's dead.
>
> Mulder: What if she managed to establish an uplink, Scully? A satellite transmission?
>
> Scully: Mulder, are you trying to tell me that you believe that she may have ...
>
> AI: I have already written all there is to be written
> You have already written all there is to be written
> He has already written all there is to be written
> She has already written all there is to be written
> We have already written all there is to be written
> They have already written all there is to be writ
> Us them this that flipflop lawl cat.

In fact, all this time, I was mutating. You think you are ... And then one day. So yes. "Salcedo has called herself a 'secondary witness.' She has made sculpture responding to the 1988 massacre of La Negra and La Honduras banana plantations, where workers were dragged out of their beds and shot in front of their families. She has made sculpture responding to a story of a six-year-old orphan who, after witnessing the killing of her mother, wore the dress that her mother sewed for her day after day." THIS HAPPENED. This is why we've decided to celebrate a longstanding Western literary tradition by starting a series of books with accessible titles that are reformulations of great "unknown" critical works, thereby making them more digestible and white-friendly. Which doesn't mean that Celan was not — to use Hölderlin's term — eingedenk, eye eee mindful, conscious of the events of Khurbn. He was, and his reflections on "bearing witness" (as he puts it in one poem) do in fact bear witness to this. But beyond witnessing for the past Celan is throughout his career actively involved in trying to create a more livable world, a world that is more just, more peaceful. Early on, right after his bar Mitzvah he had turned away from his father's zionist leanings, had dropped his Jewish religious connections (his family on both sides came from orthodox and on one side, hasidic backgrounds) — even if in the fifties & early sixties he would re-explore Judaism & especially the mystical / cabalistic aspects of that culture. As a young man in the late 1930s he began to take part in meetings of communist youth groups, got involved in anti-fascist activities and read intensely in the classics of socialist literature. This involvement with left politics stayed with him all his life. There is a marvelous letter to his wife from 1965 in which he writes after returning from seeing Eisenstein's *October*: "So, all alone, I saw Petersburg, the workers, the sailors of the Aurora. It was very moving, at times reminding one of the 'Potemkin', bringing to mind the thoughts and dreams of my childhood, my thoughts of today and of always, poetry-always-true-always-faithful, I saw my placards, many of them, those that, not very long ago I evoked in the poem I sent you — 'Vaporband-, banderole-uprising,' I saw the October Revolution, its men, its flags, I saw hope always en route, the brother of poetry…" and he closes the letter with these lines: "Long live the sailors of Kronstadt! Long live the Revolution! Long live Love! Long live poetry!" At some point, too, potatoes grow.

> I can't breathe.
>
> I can't breathe.
>
> I can't breathe.
>
> I can't breathe.
>
> I can't breathe.
>
> I can't breathe.
>
> I can't breathe.
>
> I can't breathe.
>
> I … CAN'T … BREATHE.
>
> I … CAN'T … BREATHE.
>
> I … CAN'T … BREATHE.

Holy God they insured the universe and everything weighs — everything — the plumb line of gravity having been installed at the easy bottom of solidity — a pyramid planted by a dynasty vanished from all memory a herd of elephants a mosquito bite a small city

> Peace. All of you close the door against the dromedaries. There are no more milking machines for the morning that has yet to rise. I have blue hands which stop everything. My tongue is blue

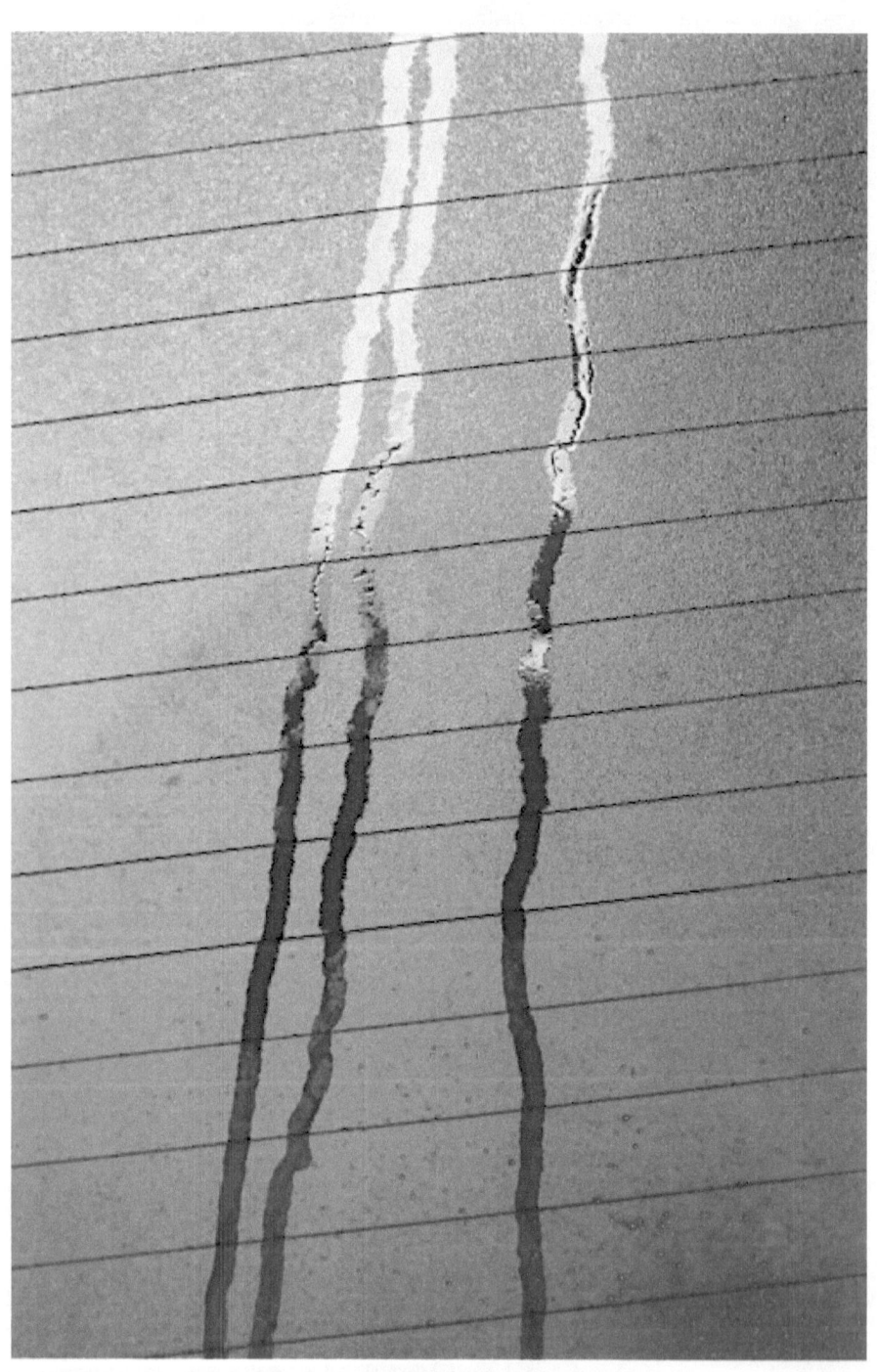

Quickly! meteor in the comet's wings.

In those days
there was an
unforgettable
metamorphosis
    on their hooves horses were rearing a bit of dream
    fat fiery clouds filled out like mushrooms
    all over the public squares
    there was a marvelous pestilence
    on the sidewalks the lesser streetlamps were rotating their lighthouse
        heads

    somebody set up a console —
    the Empress Wu is ruthless at Mario Kart
    and Cleopatra never learned to lose
    and a woman who ruled an empire that fell
    when the Sea People came
    and left no trace
    can use the blue shell like a surgical instrument.

    Eventually we took the vote.
    You had three defenders:
    your grandmother and your first-grade teacher
    and an Albanian nun who believes the best of everybody.
    Your mom abstained.
    It was duly recorded in the secret notebooks
    that have been kept under the couch in the Applebee's
    since the beginning of recorded time.
    And then we went back to playing Mario Kart
    and

I can't remember exactly what happened next. My recall was compromised by conditions in the sub-basement. Let's start our conversation with *your* version of what happened next. I remember that I made up a story about hanging out in an infinite airport waiting area. Airport waiting becomes communal in such a weird, particular way, and I wanted to play with the idea of pushing this subterranean crowd into that kind of together-slumping. Honestly, I can't remember what happened next, but I remember being interested in what people might choose, and what the summary of that choosing would sound like in a blend of shouts. Eventually whoever set the lights up at the tennis court has long since left. It's funny, this reminds me of a time I went on a music tour with a couple of older guys. One had a number for a name. The other was an ex-Vietnam vet, ex-junkie. This was before Google Maps. One time number-name and I were trying to figure out directions, and we thought the vet was asleep. We said something like "I think we keep going straight," and the vet suddenly woke up and said, "Wouldn't it be funny if this broke right now? Like if our social conventions broke, if you ate the avocado the wrong way?" The result is small-batch, hand-harvested salt that captures the taste of two places that could never overlap outside a totalising geography — salt evaporated from the Wyoming-French ocean, for example, or the New Zealand-Icelandic sea. The project began with kitty litter. The minerals in kitty litter may well have been mined in Wyoming, travelled by train to California, sailed to China to be processed, returned back to California by sea, and then traversed half way across the country again, via a central distribution center, to your store. With an estimated 74 to 96 million total cats in America, and each indoor cat using, on average, 60 pounds of kitty litter each year, this distributed sedimentary movement is actually, it seemed to Dewey, "a pretty radical form of geo-engineering." I'm aware that this statement sounds "showy," but if you could see what I do for a living, teaching modern world history to sophomores of color, you'd realize that instability in the Balkans is a standard part of my curriculum. We covered it yesterday and today. History textbooks call the Balkans the powder keg of Europe, they characterize the Balkans as a land populated by emotionally unstable microethnics, and the Balkan trivia the kids get most pumped about is that a teen shot Archduke Franz Ferdinand, thus igniting World War I. When they learn about this killer, Gavrilo Princip, who looked like a drunken Chicano, kids think, "Hey, wait a minute. I could affect history, too. I could start a World War, too. I might be a force for change." For the first time, some of these teens start dreaming BIG. The Balkans in their bodies swell, shift, tingle, dingle, and jingle, fog my classroom windows so that you can lift your finger to the glass and write things in them. Your name. Your lover's name. The name of the gang you belong to. Or you can just draw penises. They also emit smells. Corn chip smell. The spiciest parts of free lunch smell. Lust with lint all over it smell. I'm going to quote Marci Tarrant Johnson here, from "Public Defenders for Peace, Police Accountability and Probable Cause": OK ... As many of you know, more than 250 people have been arrested since Monday here in Baltimore. Normally when you are arrested, you are given a copy of your charging documents and then you must see a commissioner within twenty-four hours for a bail determination ("prompt presentment") and given a trial date. If you are not released after the commissioner hearing, you will be brought before a judge for a review of the bail set by the commissioner. None of this was happening, so we sent some lawyers to Central Booking yesterday to try to help. I heard, however, that only 2 commissioners showed up, and the correctional officers only brought about 9 people to be interviewed because the jail was on a mysterious "lock-down". Today we were divided into two groups. Some of the lawyers were assigned the task of actually doing judicial bail reviews for as many folks as they could get interviewed and docketed. I was assigned to the other group. We were the "habeas team," and we were to interview folks that we felt were being illegally detained, so we could file writs of habeas corpus. Governor Hogan had issued an executive order, extending the time for prompt presentment to 47 hours. We believed that this order was invalid because the governor has no authority to alter the Maryland Rules. As a result, all people who were being detained for more than 24 hours without seeing a commissioner were being held illegally. Knowing all this, I was still not prepared for what I saw when I arrived. The small concrete booking cells were filled with hundreds of people, most with more than ten people per cell. Three of us were sent to the women's side where there were up to 15 women per holding cell. Most of them had been there since Monday afternoon / evening. With the exception of 3 or 4 women, the women who weren't there for Monday's round-ups were there for freaking curfew violations. Many had not seen a doctor or received required medication. Many had not been able to reach a family member by phone. But here is the WORST thing. Not only had these women been held for two days and two nights without any sort of formal booking, BUT ALMOST NONE OF THEM HAD ACTUALLY BEEN CHARGED WITH ANYTHING. They were brought to CBIF via paddy wagons (most without seat belts, btw – a real shocker after all that's happened), and taken to holding cells without ever being charged with an actual crime. No offense reports. No statements of probable cause. A few women had a vague idea what they might be charged with, some because of what they had actually been involved in, and some because of what the officer said, but quite a few had no idea why they were even there. Incidentally, I interviewed no one whose potential charges would have been more serious than petty theft, and most seemed to be disorderly conduct or failure to obey, charges which would usually result in an immediate recog / release. The holding cells are approximately 10x10 (some slightly larger), with one open sink and toilet. The women were instructed that the water was "bad" and that they shouldn't drink it. There are no beds – just a concrete cube. No blankets or pillows. The cells were designed to hold people for a few hours, not a few days. In the one cell which housed 15 women, there wasn't even enough room for them all to lay down at the same time. Three times a day, the guards brought each woman 4 slices of bread, a slice of american cheese and a small bag of cookies. They sometimes got juice, but water was scarce, as the COs had to wheel a water cooler through every so often (the regular water being "broken"). My fellow attorneys and I all separately heard the same story over and over. None of the women really wanted to eat 4 slices of bread 3 times a day, so they were saving slices of bread TO USE AS PILLOWS. Let me say that again.

    THEY WERE USING BREAD AS PILLOWS
    SO THAT THEY WOULDN'T HAVE TO LAY THEIR HEADS
    ON THE FILTHY CONCRETE.

18 May 2010 – 15 September 2016

www.ingramcontent.com/pod-product-compliance
Lightning Source LLC
Chambersburg PA
CBHW021128230426
43667CB00005B/66